OXFORD STUDIES ON THE ROMAN ECONOMY

General Editors
ALAN BOWMAN ANDREW WILSON

In this volume, Philip Kay examines economic change in Rome and Italy between the Second Punic War and the middle of the first century BC. He argues that increased inflows of bullion, in particular silver, combined with an expansion of the availability of credit to produce significant growth in monetary liquidity. This, in turn, stimulated market developments, such as investment farming, trade, construction, and manufacturing and radically changed the composition and scale of the Roman economy.

Using a wide range of evidence and scholarly investigation, Kay demonstrates how Rome, in the second and first centuries BC, became a coherent economic entity experiencing real per capita economic growth. Without an understanding of this economic revolution, the contemporaneous political and cultural changes in Roman society cannot be fully comprehended or explained.

OXFORD STUDIES ON THE ROMAN ECONOMY

This innovative monograph series reflects a vigorous revival of interest in the ancient economy, focusing on the Mediterranean world under Roman rule (*c.*100 BC to AD 350). Carefully quantified archaeological and documentary data will be integrated to help ancient historians, economic historians, and archaeologists think about economic behaviour collectively rather than from separate perspectives. The volumes will include a substantial comparative element and thus be of interest to historians of other periods and places.

Rome's Economic Revolution

PHILIP KAY

OXFORD
UNIVERSITY PRESS

OXFORD
UNIVERSITY PRESS

Great Clarendon Street, Oxford, OX2 6DP,
United Kingdom

Oxford University Press is a department of the University of Oxford.
It furthers the University's objective of excellence in research, scholarship,
and education by publishing worldwide. Oxford is a registered trade mark of
Oxford University Press in the UK and in certain other countries

First published 2014
First published in paperback 2016

Published in the United States of America by Oxford University Press
198 Madison Avenue, New York, NY 10016, United States of America

British Library Cataloguing in Publication Data
Data available

Library of Congress Cataloging in Publication Data
Data available

ISBN 978–0–19–968154–9 (Hbk.)
ISBN 978–0–19–878854–6 (Pbk.)

For Alexandra, Matilda, Arthur, Benedict, and Daisy

Acknowledgements

Were it not for the support and encouragement of my friend and inspirational former Ancient History tutor, Peter Derow, late of Wadham College, I might never have embarked on the course of study that resulted in this book. His continued enthusiasm over the intervening years for subjects that we had first addressed together when I was an undergraduate in the 1970s stimulated me to delve further into the history of Republican Rome during the second and first centuries BC. Peter was joint supervisor, with Professor Chris Howgego, both of my M.Phil. and, until his untimely death, of my D.Phil. thesis from which this volume emerged. I hope that it does some justice to his precise and insightful historical approach.

To Chris, who subsequently shouldered the full burden of supervising my D.Phil. thesis and reading drafts of the additional chapters that went to make up this book, I owe an enormous debt of gratitude. He has provided unstinting help and advice. His comments have always been acute and to the point, and I was hugely fortunate to be helped by a friend who has not only an enormous knowledge of Roman history and numismatics, but also an excellent understanding of economics, finance, and commerce.

My wife, Alexandra, my children, Matilda, Arthur, Benedict, and Daisy, my late father, Louis, and my mother, Trudy, provided me with more support than I deserved when writing this book, particularly as I was simultaneously running an investment management business. Without their indulgence, I would have been unable either to start or to continue with this project, and to them I am extremely grateful.

Numerous friends have helped me with suggestions and support, and to them I extend my heartfelt thanks. They include Jonathan Allum, Matthew Bladen, Ed Bragg, Annelies Cazemier, Mary Gaudin, James Holt, Georgy Kantor, Peter Knox, Georgina Longley, Julian Phillips, Chris Taylor, Ryan Wei, Mantha Zarmakoupi, and, in particular, Julian Bloomfield, with whom, in the best 'Derow-ian' tradition, I have enjoyed many stimulating discussions over too many bottles of wine.

Professor David Llewellyn, Professor Nick Mayhew, Pamela Nightingale, Jo Quinn, Professor Dominic Rathbone, Professor Peter Temin, and Professor Andy Wilson have been generous with their time and extremely helpful in their comments when discussing particular points with me. Professor Alan Bowman and Professor Michael Crawford (the examiners of my D.Phil. thesis) have generously read successive drafts of various chapters of this book and I am grateful to them, as I am to OUP's anonymous reviewer, for their enormously helpful comments, guidance, and advice. I am of course solely responsible for all remaining errors of fact or opinion.

Lastly, I would like to thank Alan Bowman and Andy Wilson for encouraging me to publish this monograph in their *Oxford Studies on the Roman Economy* series.

Contents

List of Figures xi
List of Tables xiii
Abbreviations xv

Introduction 1

1. Rome and its Economy at the Time of the Second Punic War 9

PART I: SOURCES OF REVENUE

2. Indemnities and Booty 21
3. Mining Revenues 43
4. State Finance and the *lex Sempronia de provincia Asia* 59

PART II: THE ROMAN MONEY SUPPLY

5. Cashing in the Plunder 87
6. Credit and Financial Intermediation 107

PART III: THE APPLICATION OF FUNDS

7. Investment Farming and Agricultural Exploitation 131
8. Trade, Capital, and Interconnected Markets 189
9. The Creation of 'Material Complexity' 215
10. After the Credit Crunch 235

PART IV: QUANTIFICATION

11. Forecasting the Past 269

Summary and Conclusions 327

Bibliography 335
Index of Sources 359
General Index 373

List of Figures

3.1. Lead records for the period from 2000 BC to AD 2000. From I. Renberg, R. Bindler, and M.-L. Brännvall (2001), 'Using the Historic Atmospheric Lead-Deposition Record as a Chronological Marker in Sediment Deposits in Europe', *The Holocene* 11: 511–16. Reprinted by permission of SAGE. 48

5.1. Roman silver coins in circulation 157–50 BC (in millions of denarii, by 3-year periods). From K. Hopkins (1980), 'Taxes and Trade in the Roman Empire (200 BC–AD 400)', *JRS* 70: 109. Reprinted by permission of Cambridge University Press. 90

7.1. Mediterranean shipwrecks by half century, using probability per annum. From A. I. Wilson (2009), 'Approaches to Quantifying Roman Trade', in A. K. Bowman and A. Wilson (eds.), *Quantifying the Roman Economy: Methods and Problems*. Oxford Studies on the Roman Economy 1, fig. 9.4. By permission of Oxford University Press. Data from Parker (1992). 144

List of Tables

2.1. Indemnities received by the Romans during the 3rd century BC 38
2.2. Indemnities received by the Romans 201–152 BC (in talents of silver) 39
6.1. Bank balance sheet 1 111
6.2. Bank balance sheet 2 111
6.3. Bank balance sheet 3 111
7.1. Census Figures 265 BC–AD 14 174
7.2. Selected Roman censuses (% change) 177
7.3. Italian free population (estimated) 178
7.4. Italian slave population (estimated) 182
7.5. Italian total population (estimated) 182
7.6. Italian population breakdown (estimated) 183
10.1. Bank balance sheet 1 253
10.2. Bank balance sheet 2 253
10.3. Bank balance sheet 3 254
11.1. Mediterranean seaborne trade by volume (estimated) 281
11.2. Inflation and the GDP deflator (estimated) 284
11.3. Power-law distribution of households by income: 150 BC 291
11.4. Power-law distribution of households by income: 100 BC 294
11.5. Power-law distribution of households by income: 50 BC 295
11.6. State income in millions of denarii (estimated) 298
11.7. Cost of army stipends in millions of denarii (estimated) 299
11.8. Total military costs in millions of denarii (estimated) 300
11.9. Expenditure: state consumption in millions of denarii (estimated) 301
11.10. Expenditure: state investment in millions of denarii (estimated) 301
11.11. State expenditure in HS m. (estimated) 303
11.12. Expenditure GDP in HS m. (estimated) 305
11.13. Other private consumption and investment in HS m. (estimated) 306
11.14. Breakdown of other private consumption and investment in real terms (HS m., estimated) 309
11.15. Denarii (m.) in circulation (estimated) 312
11.16. Total bank deposits in mainland Italy in millions of denarii (estimated) 314
11.17. Level of monetization in mainland Italy: non-agrarian expenditure and urban personal consumption (HS m., estimated) 315
11.18. Level of monetization in mainland Italy: agrarian expenditure: small independent farms (HS m., estimated) 316
11.19. Level of monetization in mainland Italy: agrarian expenditure: large estates (HS m., estimated) 317

11.20. Level of monetization in mainland Italy: total nominal value of monetized expenditure in HS m. as percentage of nominal income GDP (estimated) 317
11.21. Velocity of circulation of money in mainland Italy (estimated) 319
11.22. 'Mayhew' *V* 320
11.23. Mainland Italian *MV* and GDP (estimated) 322
11.24. National disposable income, in HS m., of mainland Italy (estimated) 323

Abbreviations

Abbreviations of Latin and Greek authors and academic journals are taken from S. Hornblower and A. Spawforth, *The Oxford Classical Dictionary* (3rd edn., Oxford, 2003)

CAH	*The Cambridge Ancient History* (14 vols., 2nd edn., Cambridge, 1970–2001)
CGL	G. Goetz, *Corpus Glossariorum Latinorum* (7 vols., Amsterdam, 1823–1901; repr. Amsterdam, 1965)
CIG	A. Böckh, *Corpus Inscriptionum Graecarum* (3 vols., Berlin, 1828–77)
CIL	Th. Mommsen *et al.*, *Corpus Inscriptionum Latinarum* (17 vols, Berlin, 1863–)
FGrH	F. Jacoby, *Die Fragmente der griechischen Historiker* (4 parts, Leiden, 1923–63)
IDélos	F. Durrbach, P. Roussel, M. Launey *et al.*, *Inscriptions de Délos* (7 vols., Paris, 1926–72)
IEph.	R. Merkelbach *et al.*, *Die Inschriften von Ephesos* (8 vols., Bonn, 1979–84)
IG	A. Kirchhoff *et al.*, *Inscriptiones Graecae* (51 parts, Berlin, 1873–)
IGCH	M. Thompson, O. Mørkholm, C. M. Kraay, *An Inventory of Greek Coin Hoards* (New York, 1973)
IGRom	R. Cagnat *et al.*, *Inscriptiones Graecae ad res Romanas pertinentes* (vols. 1, 3, 4, Paris, 1906–27; repr. Chicago, 1975)
ILLRP	A. Degrassi, *Inscriptiones Latinae Liberae Rei Publicae* (2 vols., 2nd edn., Florence, 1963–5)
ILS	H. Dessau, *Inscriptiones Latinae Selectae* (3 vols., Berlin, 1892–1916; repr. 1954–5)
IMagn.	O. Kern, *Die Inschriften von Magnesia am Maeander* (Berlin 1900)
IPerg.	M. Frankel, *Die Inschriften von Pergamon* (Berlin, 1890–95)
IPriene	F. Hiller von Gaertringen, *Die Inschriften von Priene* (Berlin, 1906)
Lex agr.	*Lex Agraria*; *CIL* I^2 585; M. H. Crawford, ed., *Roman Statutes* (London, 1996), no. 2
Lex rep.	*Lex Sempronia Repetundarum*; *CIL* I^2 583; M. H. Crawford, ed., *Roman Statutes* (London, 1996), no. 1
MRR	T. R. S. Broughton, *Magistrates of the Roman Republic, Amer. Phil. Assoc. Monogr.* 15 (3 vols., New York and Atlanta, 1951–85)
OGIS	W. Dittenberger, *Orientis Graecae Inscriptiones Selectae* (2 vols., Leipzig, 1903–5; repr. Hildesheim, 1960)
ORF^4	H. Malcovati, *Oratorum Romanorum Fragmenta* (2 vols., 4th edn., Turin, 1976–9)
POxy	B. P. Grenfell, A. S. Hunt *et al.*, *The Oxyrhynchus Papyri* (London, 1898–)
RC	C. B. Welles, *Royal Correspondence in the Hellenistic Period: A Study in Greek Epigraphy* (New Haven, 1934)
RDGE	R. K. Sherk, *Roman Documents from the Greek East: Senatus Consulta and Epistulae to the Age of Augustus* (Baltimore, 1969)
RRC	M. H. Crawford, *Roman Republican Coinage* (2 vols., London, 1974)
RRCH	M. H. Crawford, *Roman Republican Coin Hoards* (London, 1969)
Sammelb.	E. Preisigke *et al.*, *Sammelbuch griechischer Urkunden aus Ägypten* (Strasburg, 1913–)
SEG	J. J. E. Hondius *et al.*, *Supplementum Epigraphicum Graecum* (vols. 1–25: Leiden, 1923–71; vols. 26-: Amsterdam, 1979–)
Syll.^{3}	W. Dittenberger *et al.*, *Sylloge Inscriptionum Graecarum* (4 vols, 3rd edn., Leipzig, 1915–24; repr. Hildesheim, 1960)
TPSulp.	G. Camodeca, *Tabulae Pompeianae Sulpiciorum. TPSulp: edizione critica dell'archivio puteolano dei Sulpicii* (2 vols, Rome, 1999)

Introduction
The Creation of Complexity

This book examines economic change in Republican Rome between the Second Punic War and the middle of the first century BC.[1] To date, little attempt has been made to explain why, or indeed even whether, the Roman economy of the first century BC was significantly different, in qualitative or quantitative terms, from that of the late third century. But how, for example, did the Romans move from a position in 214 BC, when their treasury was virtually empty, to one in 88 BC when their economic interests in Asia were so significant that the invasion of that province by Mithradates VI of Pontus caused a credit crisis at Rome?[2]

We know from our ancient sources that Rome's military conquests during the second century brought in significant wealth in the form of booty, slaves, and indemnities. Mining revenues followed and, in time, an additional and more stable source of wealth presented itself in the form of provincial taxation. Furthermore, Rome acquired control over developed trade and communication networks throughout the Mediterranean. The establishment of Rome's empire produced an extraordinary return on investment, as the accumulated surpluses of the Mediterranean and adjacent lands were appropriated by the conquerors.

One result of this accumulation of capital was that Rome's military victories during this period became nearly costless, in an economic sense, as conquered nations footed the bill for further expansion. A second was a profound impact on Rome's social and economic structure as it adapted to its newly found wealth. Although the treasury had been nearly bankrupted during the Second Punic War, its financial position by 167 was such that Rome no longer needed to tax her own citizens directly. The recycling of this wealth through the system changed economic behaviour patterns in both the public and private sectors of the Italian economy. At a state level, it resulted in increased construction activities on public works. It led to the monumentalization of Italy, growth in the population of the city of Rome, and an increased role for the *publicani*, since no public sector bureaucracy existed to deal with the expansion of the state's economic activities.[3]

[1] All dates are BC, unless otherwise indicated.

[2] 214 BC: 'inopia aerarii' (Livy, 24. 18. 2: the emptiness of the treasury); 88 BC: 'Romae solutione impedita fidem concidisse... haec fides et haec ratio pecuniarum, quae Romae, quae in foro versatur, implicata est cum illis pecuniis Asiaticis et cohaeret' (Cic. *De imp. Cn. Pomp.* 19: there was a collapse of credit at Rome, because repayments were interrupted... this credit and this system of moneys, which operates at Rome in the Forum, is bound up in, and is linked with, those Asian moneys).

[3] *Publicani* were private sector businessmen who acted as contractors to the Roman state.

Importantly Rome's appropriation of precious metal, particularly silver, from the Mediterranean world in the second century resulted in an increase in the production of Roman denarii and a significant expansion in monetary liquidity in Italy. At a private level, the impact of this influx of capital was even more profound, with certain families becoming very rich indeed. The wealthier elements of society were then faced with decisions on how to spend and invest their money. This in turn resulted in increased material sophistication and the creation of what Ward-Perkins has termed 'economic complexity':[4] as the second century progresses, we see increases in both the geographic spread and intensity of commercial and trading networks, and a marked shift in the direction of agricultural investment towards specialization, as well as the development of financial intermediation and an increased availability of credit. We also see cultural changes as diverse as the use of concrete in construction and the dietary revolution of bread-eating (instead of the eating of porridge, *puls*).[5] A number of these economic developments represent the continuation of processes that had begun in the third century or before; but the economy of the first century was not just that of the third century increased in scale. It was a much more sophisticated entity. There was a remarkable qualitative change in the structure of the Roman economy between the end of the third century and the middle of the first century BC.

The evidence of this change is scattered amongst limited sources. Those ancient historians who wrote about the second and first centuries BC, and whose work survives, were concerned with military and political history, and any references to what might broadly be termed economic subjects are included only because they help illustrate the main narrative. As Purcell puts it: 'The nature of our evidence about economic production in the ancient world is such that we usually know far more about the cultural and intellectual repercussions of changes than we do about the changes themselves.'[6] Epigraphical and papyrological evidence bearing on Republican Rome and her economic expansion is also not plentiful. Unlike, say, in the late medieval world, where there is significant archival material to inform our view of economic activity, very little has survived from the second and first centuries BC. For an economic historian of the late Roman Republic, books such as Spufford's *Power and Profit: The Merchant in Medieval Europe* or Origo's *The Merchant of Prato* are eye-openers—not because the business structures they portray are necessarily so different from what one might imagine to have existed in Rome by the first century BC, but because they are in large part based on substantial archival material.[7] Even documents from other periods of Rome's history, for example the Vindolanda tablets and documentary papyri from areas under Roman rule, such as Egypt, represent significantly more archival material than anything that has survived from the Republic. The period between the Second Punic War and the 130s BC is one of the few times during the history of Roman numismatics when the iconography of imperial coins issued in Italy is

[4] Ward-Perkins 2005: 104, 150; he uses 'economic complexity' as a generic term to refer to the industrial, commercial, and trading networks that had existed in the northern provinces of the empire under Roman rule and which he believes suddenly disappeared around AD 400.

[5] Tchernia 1986: 58–60. According to Pliny the Elder (*HN* 18. 107) there were no bakers in Rome until the time of the Third Macedonian War; before that it was the job of the Roman woman to bake bread at home.

[6] Purcell 1985: 1.

[7] Spufford 2002; Origo 1957.

relatively standardized, restricting the use that may be made of coin types as evidence for socio-economic change and developments. Furthermore, archaeological evidence is by no means plentiful. Many urban remains from the Republican period lie uninvestigated beneath their imperial successors. In the case of rural sites many remain undiscovered in the Italian countryside and, although survey work can shed some light on such topics as the density of rural occupation, precise chronologies and the details of settlement patterns are frequently frustrated, not least by the difficulties of interpreting sherd data from black-slip fineware. On the other hand, evidence for certain types of trade is more accessible because of the quantities of ceramic finds in both marine and terrestrial contexts, and chronologies are somewhat easier to establish because of variations in the design of transport amphorae.

The scarcity of numerical evidence in particular is problematic. Modern economic analysis makes extensive use of data, mainly produced by governments, industry associations, and corporations, that are collected and subjected to statistical analysis. In Rome of the second and first centuries, there is no evidence to suggest that anyone collected data of this kind. There are piecemeal survivals of some figures, mainly cash items such as the amounts of bullion in the Roman state treasury, the *aerarium Saturni*, and war indemnities and booty from defeated enemies. There are occasional references to amounts of expenditure. The problem is well summarized by Peter Temin in his discussion of Roman GDP:

> A large *caveat* is in order before we begin. All of these estimates [of Roman GDP], mine included, rest on an exceedingly narrow evidentiary base. They are at best conjectural estimates based on a few observations, some about the early Roman Empire and some about modern economies. Not only are the assumptions needed to build on these observations open to question . . . but the observations themselves are subject to unknown errors.[8]

Such paucity of data has two consequences. The first is that it is difficult to test for economic growth numerically, since quantification based on a series of empiric data points is mostly impossible. This means, for example, that questions such as 'did the Roman pillaging that took place between 250 and 100 result in increased per capita growth?' cannot be answered with any degree of precision. We know neither the population of Rome (let alone Italy) nor its GDP for any moment of its history. As we shall see, some scholars have sought to circumvent such problems of quantification by constructing models of the Roman economy. The second consequence is a tendency amongst many modern scholars, when analysing the third and second centuries BC, to slip in as supposed evidence the much more plentiful testimony of the first century (especially from Cicero) or even later. The danger is always that anachronistic evidence from subsequent, better-documented periods is casually retrojected.

Perhaps because of these limitations, modern analysis of the structure of the economy of Rome and Italy in the second and first centuries BC has been patchy.

[8] Temin 2006: 32; cf. Saller 2002. Even for such financial data as do exist, Scheidel (1996) has issued a salutary warning about the tendency of ancient authors to stylize monetary valuations into conventional figures.

Most work has tended to focus on the Principate, where we have a greater corpus of relevant evidence;[9] and even *The Cambridge Economic History of the Greco-Roman World* devotes little space to economic developments in Republican Rome.[10] That said, there is of course a considerable modern scholarship, produced by historians, archaeologists, and numismatists, on a whole range of individual aspects of the Republican economy, of which extensive use is made in what follows. Thus Tenney Frank's and M. Rostovtzeff's discussions of a variety of features of the Republican economy remain fundamental to any analysis.[11] Peter Brunt built on the work of K. J. Beloch in the area of Italian demography, while, more recently, Walter Scheidel and Luuk de Ligt have been in the forefront of a major re-evaluation of some of the fundamental issues underpinning the subject.[12] Dominic Rathbone and Sakia Roselaar have both produced original and important work on public land (*ager publicus*) and have helped to alter perceptions of the second-century agrarian crisis.[13] C. Domergue's work on Roman mining in Spain is indispensable, as is Ernst Badian's on the growth of the *publicani*.[14] John Richardson has written persuasively about the start of Roman provincial taxation and exploitation, and A. N. Sherwin-White, Fergus Millar, and David Stockton are essential reading on Gaius Gracchus's reforms.[15] Our knowledge of the early fiscal development of the Roman province of Asia has been revolutionized by the discovery, and the publication in an excellent edition, of the *Customs Law of Asia*.[16] I. Shatzman has contributed a study of senatorial wealth, compiling evidence on the financial interests of nearly three hundred senators from 200 BC to the end of the Republic.[17] Numismatic evidence for the Republican period has been thoroughly documented by Michael Crawford, and fruitfully commented upon by Andrew Burnett and Christopher Howgego, amongst others.[18] C. Barlow, Jean Andreau, David Hollander, and William Harris have worked on Roman banking and credit provision, and have shown that financial intermediation was considerably more sophisticated in the Roman Republic than had previously been thought.[19] Archaeological research has also paid dividends. J. Oleson and Andrew Wilson have demonstrated how the technological development of a range of devices, aimed at maximizing economic returns, led to increased capital investment in Italy during the second century BC.[20] The boom in Italian exports of wine and olive oil during the same period would be unknown, were it not for the work produced on amphora types by such scholars as D. Peacock and D. Williams, and for the collation of ancient shipwreck data by A. Parker.[21] Recent research into some of the Hellenistic economies, such as Vincent Gabrielsen's on Rhodes and Makis Aperghis's on the Seleucids, has helped

[9] e.g. Duncan-Jones 1974, 1990, 1994.
[10] Scheidel, Morris, and Saller 2007.
[11] Frank 1933; Rostovtzeff 1957.
[12] Beloch 1886; Brunt 1971*a*; Scheidel 2004, 2005, 2006, 2008; Scheidel and Friesen 2009; De Ligt 2004, 2012.
[13] Rathbone 2003; Roselaar 2010.
[14] Domergue 1990; Badian 1972.
[15] Richardson 1976; Sherwin-White 1982; Millar 1986; Stockton 1979.
[16] Cottier et al. 2008.
[17] Shatzman 1975.
[18] Crawford 1969*a*, 1974, 1985; Burnett 1987*a*; Howgego 1992, 1995.
[19] Barlow 1978; Andreau 1987, 1999; Harris 2006; Hollander 2007.
[20] Oleson 1984, 2008; Thomas and Wilson 1994; A. I. Wilson 2002*b*.
[21] Peacock and Williams 1986; Parker 1992.

to highlight the linkages between the Romano-Italian economy and the eastern Mediterranean. In particular, Nicholas Rauh has pulled together epigraphical, literary, and archaeological evidence to demonstrate the emergence of Delos, during the second half of the second century, as the centre of a massive trade in slaves and luxury goods between the eastern Mediterranean and Italy.[22] To these and to other scholars, whose detailed work on particular subject areas is acknowledged in the main body of the book, we owe an enormous debt of gratitude for illuminating previously obscure aspects of the developing Roman economy.

But, in general, little attempt has been made to explain why, or indeed even whether, the Roman economy of the mid-first century BC was different from that of the late third century BC. There are a few exceptions to this. In the 1930s, Frank assembled and commented on most of the literary evidence relating to the Republican economy.[23] Erich Gruen gave a relatively brief 'helicopter view' of the subject in *The Hellenistic World and the Coming of Rome*, but he was mainly concerned to prove his proposition that 'no single decision on eastern affairs [by the Romans] exhibits an economic component demonstrable as central or primary'.[24] William Harris, in *War and Imperialism in Republican Rome 327–70 BC*, has argued that the most important factors that brought about the wars of the second century were the Romans' desire for the glory and the economic benefits that warfare brought.[25] In particular, the first chapter of Keith Hopkins's book, *Conquerors and Slaves*, sets out the general proposition that the second century BC was a time of profound economic change.[26] He pointed to a strong link between 'imperial profits, the increased wealth of the elite and the formation of large landholdings'; and to 'a sequence of conquest and plunder, the import of booty and slaves into Italy, the impoverishment of Italian peasants and their extrusion from their farms, their recruitment to the army (or their migration to the city of Rome) and their subsequent demands for Italian farms of their own'.[27] But Hopkins was principally concerned to prove his main proposition that 'underemployed smallholders were expelled from their plots by the rich who replaced them with a smaller number of slaves'; and he placed less emphasis on other economic influences, stating simply that 'manufacturing, trade and urban rents were of minor importance in comparison with agriculture'.[28] More recently, a growing appreciation, if not a consensus, can be sensed amongst some scholars that the major period of growth in the Roman economy was in the second to first centuries BC, with only limited growth during the Principate. As P. Bang says: 'It is thought-provoking that the phase of most explosive commercial development is not the peaceful Principate but the war-ridden late Republic.'[29] Morley, commenting on the lack of evidence for year-on-year expansion of economic activity

[22] Gabrielsen 1993, 1997, 2001; Aperghis 2004; Rauh 1993. [23] Frank 1933.

[24] Gruen 1984: 288–315; cf. Badian 1968: 20: 'the whole myth of economic motives in Rome's foreign policy at this time [the second century] is a figment of modern anachronism'.

[25] Harris 1979. [26] Hopkins 1978. [27] Hopkins 1978: 48, 95.

[28] Although he does allow that 'in Italy at the end of the period of imperial expansion, the proportion of the population engaged in urban occupations may have risen towards thirty per cent' (Hopkins 1978: 2, 6).

[29] Bang 2009: 202; cf. 204-5.

under the early Principate, observes that 'the great expansion had already taken place under the Republic'.[30]

There is, however, no comprehensive study that has tackled economic development in the Roman world between 200 and 50 BC in any detail, nor one that charts the flows of money and the impact of increased monetary liquidity on economic growth during this period and attempts to quantify that growth.

Our argument is that, during the second century, increased inflows of bullion, in particular silver, combined with the contemporaneous expansion of the availability of credit to produce significant growth in monetary liquidity. This increase in the supply and availability of money in turn resulted in real per capita economic growth in the Italian peninsula during the second and first centuries BC, which radically changed the composition, scale, and complexity of the Roman economy. In large part, no doubt, because of the dead weight of 'Finleyan primitivism', monetarist explanations of economic developments in the ancient world have been rare.[31] Moreover, finance in general seems to be viewed by some modern Roman historians more as an arcane offshoot of the Eleusinian Mysteries than as a dynamic service industry that can increase the prospects for wealth creation by helping economic agents, such as merchants and farmers, to obtain resources that will allow them to implement ideas for increased production. However, monetarist accounts of economic behaviour are not uncommon in analyses of the medieval and early modern periods, in which the supply of money is regarded as being the crucial determinant of economic performance. Thus the arrival of vast amounts of bullion from the New World is the standard explanation for sixteenth-century AD Europe's rapid steps towards a more specialized, urban, market economy. From AD 1500 to 1640, the population of England, for example, more than doubled, and the population living in substantial towns quintupled, driven by the flow of people from the countryside to the growing economic prospects of the urban centres. In addition, changes in agricultural practices led to significant increases in output, while the growth of trade networks and the redistribution of the relative sizes of landed holdings led to major changes in the specialization and commercialization of agriculture.[32] As we shall see, some of these changes were not dissimilar to ones we can observe in late second-century BC Rome.

But this book is not a diachronic economic history of late Republican Rome; rather, it seeks to identify important points of economic change and to explain why they occurred. The intention is to fill a major gap by explaining how the economic world of Cicero came into being. Sir Ronald Syme, in *The Roman Revolution*, analysed the political struggles that took place in Rome during the late Republic.[33] More recently, Andrew Wallace-Hadrill, in *Rome's Cultural Revolution*, has examined the equally significant cultural and social developments

[30] Morley 2007: 589; cf. Morley 2010: 76; Bowman and Wilson 2009*b*: 47.

[31] Even Harris in a recent article on Roman money (2006: 24) appears to fight shy of such an explanation, saying: 'The purpose of this article has not been to demonstrate that per capita growth occurred in the late Republic or under the Principate, but rather that shortage of money was not to any important extent a brake on growth.' The views of Sir Moses Finley, Professor of Ancient History at Cambridge University in the 1970s, who believed in the primitive nature of the ancient economy, exercised considerable influence up until the 1990s.

[32] Goldstone 1984: 1124–6.

[33] Syme 1939.

in Rome and Italy during the same period.[34] The present work compliments these types of account by detailing and offering an explanation of the fundamental economic changes that occurred in the Roman world of the second and early first centuries BC. Without an understanding of this economic revolution, the contemporaneous political and cultural changes in Roman society cannot be fully comprehended or explained. At the same time, the plausibility of a 'non-Finleyan' Roman world is greatly enhanced by an understanding of these developments.

We shall, then, be using evidence, mostly qualitative and circumstantial, necessarily very little of it quantitative because of the nature of our sources, to identify instances where the signs of economic growth are significant. The importance of economic growth lies in its contribution to the prosperity of a community or groups within a community and the focus here will be on the Roman state and on the Roman (and, to some extent, the Italian) elite, rather than on the huge majority of the population of the nascent Roman Empire—the peasantry and the urban poor. This is because it was principally the economic behaviour patterns, business structures, and institutions of the elite that changed the Roman economy during the second and early first centuries BC. We begin in the first chapter by contextualizing Rome and its economy at the time of the Second Punic War. Thereafter the book is divided into four main sections. In the first, we consider the sources and the scale of revenue that the Roman state and its elite derived during the second century from booty, slaves, war indemnities, and the silver mines of Spain and Macedonia. We go on to examine how the Romans moved from a tradition of plunder to a stable system of taxation, as they took control of well-established agricultural economies that already had institutionalized methods of taxation. The second section looks at the monetary impact of these revenues, which was a significant increase in the minting of Roman silver denarii and a contemporaneous expansion in the availability of credit provided by bankers. The third part considers the effects of increasing monetary liquidity on the economy. At a state level, this principally comprised a high level of expenditure on the military and increased spending on Rome's physical infrastructure. In the private sector, the liquidity boom led to increasing prosperity, particularly amongst the Italian elite. It led to the creation of an enormous material culture that was to reach its apogee under the Principate; and it stimulated a more complex system of production and distribution, exemplified by developments in agriculture, trade, construction, and manufacturing. But there were also negative side effects, with the credit crisis of 88 BC and the monetary problems of the 80s producing a change in the institutional structure of credit provision and so restricting the growth potential of the Roman economy. In the final section, a probabilistic quantification is presented of the performance of the Italian economy during the period 150 to 50 BC. This model suggests that it is highly likely that real per capita economic growth occurred and tentative numbers are attached to that growth.

[34] Wallace-Hadrill 2008.

1

Rome and its Economy at the Time of the Second Punic War

... ut veteres dixere[1]

In order to set Rome's economy at the time of the Second Punic War in context, it is necessary briefly to go back further into the third century.

In 295, Rome still controlled an area equivalent to only about one quarter of modern Belgium. That year a combined army of Samnites and Gauls was defeated by the Romans at Sentinum in Umbria. They were part of a wider, if unlikely, coalition that included Etruscans and Umbrians, these having been diverted elsewhere at the time of the engagement.[2] This great victory, probably the largest battle that had occurred in Italy, was followed in 293 by a crushing defeat of the Samnites at Aquilonia. Livy's complete text breaks at this date and, with Diodorus finishing at 302 and no *Fasti Capitolini* surviving for the period 290–283, some of the details of the final stages of Rome's conquest of Italy are unclear. However, by 290, it seems that the Romans had completely subdued the Samnites, Sabines, and Praetuttii. As a result of these victories, the Romans annexed a wide strip of territory stretching across Italy from the Tyrrhenian Sea to the Adriatic, the purpose no doubt being to prevent the possibility of their southern enemies ever again joining forces with their northern ones. The Gauls continued to cause problems, especially during Pyrrhus' invasion of Italy, but were finally heavily defeated at Lake Vadimon in 283. This allowed the Romans to annex territory along the northern Adriatic which was occupied by the Senones and to secure control of this district (the *Ager Gallicus*) by founding a *colonia maritima* at Sena Gallica (160 km to the north of Hatria), in 283. This was followed by foundations of Latin colonies at Ariminum (70 km north-west of Sena), in 268, and at Firmum Picenum (roughly midway between Hatria and Sena), in 264. By the outbreak of the First Punic War, Rome was in control of peninsular Italy and, by 225, she also controlled Corsica, Sardinia, and part of Sicily. She was capable of mobilizing more than 700,000 foot soldiers and 70,000 cavalry from her own and her allies' resources.[3]

The increasing hold of Rome on Italy is perhaps most obvious in the system of roads that developed in the late fourth and third centuries. The first was the Via Appia, built in 312 into Campanian territory and extended to Brundisium some

[1] Plin. *HN* 3. 60: 'as old writers have said'.

[2] Livy, 10. 27.

[3] Polyb. 2. 24. 16; cf. Scheidel 2004: 3–4.

time in the mid-third century.[4] This was probably followed by the Via Clodia (inland to the north-west) in the 280s, the Via Aurelia in 241 along the Tyrrhenian coast, the Via Amerina to Falerii Novi at about the same time, and the Via Flaminia (also to the north) in 220.[5] Along with the roads came colonies, whose town planning took their model from Rome itself. Latin colonies founded during this century, for example Cosa and Paestum, had *fora* containing temples of Jupiter, circular *comitia* and *tabernae*.[6]

The city of Rome itself was probably by this stage one of the largest conurbations in the Mediterranean. The most persuasive argument in favour of rapid growth in the size of the city, at the end of the fourth and beginning of the third centuries, is the building of the first two aqueducts into Rome: the Aqua Appia in 312 with an estimated capacity of 73,000 m^3 per day and the Aqua Anio Vetus in 272. The latter had an extraordinarily high capacity estimated at 176,000 m^3 per day and seemingly obviated the need to build another aqueduct for another 128 years.[7] Population size is as uncertain as the capacities of the aqueducts. The range for population estimates at Rome, in 270, is between 90,000[8] and 150,000,[9] or even 190,000.[10] The consensus view would probably be that, by 200 BC, the city had a population of at least 200,000;[11] but all these estimates are based on flimsy evidence. We know comparatively little about the physical appearance of Rome's urban area at the end of the third century, although there are a few literary anecdotes. On the one hand, as late as 182, the enemies of the pro-Roman Macedonian prince, Demetrius, poked fun at 'the appearance of the city itself which had not yet been adorned in either its public or its private spaces' (speciem ipsius urbis nondum exornatae neque publicis neque privatis locis).[12] On the other, Livy recounts a prodigy, in 218, in which a cow climbs up to the third floor of a building in the Forum Boarium, indicating a degree of high-rise development.[13]

Large civil construction projects were possible, as is shown by the building, between 378 and about 353, of the 11 km Republican city wall from tufa, and of the roads and aqueducts just mentioned.[14] But marble continued to be totally unknown in the architecture of central Italy, with the earliest marble temples appearing only after the sack of Corinth. Construction was in a variety of more or less local and traditional methods, such as a structure of dry stone at Bolsena, or the *opus craticium* at Aufidena, which consisted of a clay structure supported by

[4] The Via Appia was probably extended to Brundisium some time after 267, when the Romans captured the seaport (Zonar. 8. 7).

[5] Wiseman 1970*b*. The dating of some of these roads is notoriously difficult. Harris (1971: 163–8), for example, tentatively dates the Clodia to 183 and the Aurelia to 144 (with 200 as an alternative possibility).

[6] Morel 1989: 488.

[7] Frontinus, in his *De aquae ductu urbis Romae*, gives figures for the volume of water delivered by each of the aqueducts, but the problem is that scholars cannot agree on how much water this actually represented. The modern estimates for each aqueduct are however in the same proportions as Frontinus' figures (Dodge 2000: 184–5, with figs. 8.5 and 8.11).

[8] Starr 1980: 11–26. [9] Cornell 2000: 46–7. [10] Brunt 1971*a*: 384.

[11] Morley 1996: 39; Cornell 2000: 47; Scheidel 2007: 344 n. 88. To put this in some sort of context, Venice in AD 1600 is estimated to have had a population of 140,000 and London 200,000 (De Ligt 2012: 338).

[12] Livy, 40. 5. 7. [13] Livy, 21. 62. 3. [14] Livy, 6. 32. 1, 7. 20. 9.

an armature of wood, on a stone base. The Circus Flaminius, built by the censor Gaius Flaminius in 221–220, was quite probably constructed of wood.[15]

The great majority of Republican temples are known only from literary sources and then mainly because their construction had been vowed on the battlefield. Most were probably small isolated shrines in the 'Etrusco-Italic' style, built of wood and tufa, with 'the terracotta decorations of the Roman gods' (antefixa fictilia deorum Romanorum), which Livy represents M. Porcius Cato as contrasting with the 'baubles' (*ornamenta*) of Corinth and Athens.[16] As far as elite domestic architecture is concerned, we have little idea of what it looked like. In the past, Pompeii has been used as a comparator;[17] but recent archaeological evidence suggests that the house type with Tuscan *atrium*, *alae*, and *tablinum* in line with the entrance did not appear in Pompeii until the second century. Before that there only existed housing of a more elementary character.[18] Physically, therefore, Rome probably had a rather unsophisticated, haphazard appearance; it had no marble and no basilicas (the first, the *Basilica Porcia*, was built in 184). But it already had a sizeable population, and had already begun to embark on the construction of some significant infrastructure. As Dionysius of Halicarnassus, writing at the end of the first century BC, put it:

> ἔγωγ' οὖν ἐν τρισὶ τοῖς μεγαλοπρεπεστάτοις κατασκευάσμασι τῆς Ῥώμης, ἐξ ὧν μάλιστα τὸ τῆς ἡγεμονίας ἐμφαίνεται μέγεθος, τάς τε τῶν ὑδάτων ἀγωγὰς τίθεμαι καὶ τὰς τῶν ὁδῶν στρώσεις καὶ τάς τῶν ὑπονόμων ἐργασίας.[19]
>
> (Indeed, in my opinion the three most magnificent works of Rome, in which the greatness of her empire is best seen, are the aqueducts, the paved roads, and the construction of the sewers.[20])

The third century also witnessed the growth in the usage, from very small beginnings, of minted silver and bronze coins. These were initially struck in tiny quantities at the end of the fourth century, but issuance gradually increased during the third century, a growth generally understood to be connected with army and naval expenditure. By the time of the Second Punic War, the Romans had established their own individual system and standard for coinage, although it would probably be wrong to suggest that the economy had been anything more than partially monetized by this time. The *aerarium Saturni*, the Roman state treasury, was the central repository of the state cash and 'near-cash' assets of the Roman people. It was managed by two urban quaestors, or rather by a body of *scribae quaestorii* under their nominal direction.[21] Polybius tells us that no payment might be made out of the *aerarium*, except by the authority of a *senatus consultum*.[22]

The staffing of the treasury should remind us of how small the executive machinery of Rome was at this time, with the exception of the army. There was no permanent bureaucracy that would have depended on, and therefore indicated, the delivery of a large economic surplus. The only senior magistrates (with a tiny staff under them) were two consuls, four praetors, four aediles, and—once in a quinquennium—two censors. The junior magistrates were ten tribunes, eight

15 Zevi 1976: 1048–9; Morel 1989: 491.
16 Livy, 34. 4. 4; Cornell 2000: 48.
17 Cornell 2000: 47.
18 Carafa 1997: 28.
19 Dion. Hal. *Ant. Rom.* 3. 67. 5.
20 Trans. Loeb II p. 241.
21 Plut. *Cat. Min.* 16; A. H. M. Jones 1960 : 101–4.
22 Polyb. 6. 13.

quaestors, and a few other minor figures. Given the size of the city of Rome itself, the size of its armies and navies, and the size of the territories it already controlled, it is therefore unsurprising that the *publicani* begin to enter our sources on a more regular basis as suppliers of goods and services to the Roman state as the empire expands. But what is remarkable is the scale of their operations, for which we begin to find evidence at the time of the Second Punic War. As Badian has shown, the capital value of a contract to supply clothing to the legions in Spain could have come to at least 800,000 denarii (133 talents). We know that the contract was won by a syndicate of nineteen *publicani* and that therefore the capital contribution of each of them was just over 40,000 denarii (6.7 talents), an amount equivalent to 40 per cent of the property qualification for equestrian status in the late Republic.[23] Now, this of course happened at a time of extreme crisis, when the Romans were fighting for their very survival. But it nonetheless implies that groups of wealthy men could raise huge sums of cash more easily than the Roman state itself, even if their action was ultimately for the benefit of the state.

The archaeological evidence for the expansion of Roman trade in the third century is present in the form of pottery. The black-slip vessels from the *atelier des petites estampilles* had a wide distribution in the early third century, not only throughout Italy but also overseas to Corsica, and throughout the coastal region extending from Liguria to Catalonia, and the territories dominated by Carthage (Africa, western Sicily, and Sardinia).[24] More importantly, in the second half of the third century, Graeco-Italic transport amphorae provide evidence for the first export trade in agricultural produce (in this case, wine) from Italy of which there is tangible proof since the Etruscan wine amphorae of the seventh and sixth centuries.[25] The kilns that manufactured these amphorae seem largely to have been located in Etruria, Latium, and Campania, and the products themselves are found both in shipwrecks and in terrestrial archaeological contexts.[26] The trade represented by these amphorae is discussed in more detail in a later chapter, but its chronology has now been shown to be longer and more complex than previously imagined. For example, sherds from Graeco-Italic amphorae have been found on 223 different sites in central and Mediterranean France. Detailed analysis of the Republican amphorae from the department of Puy-de-Dôme, in central France, has revealed fifteen find-spots of the Graeco-Italic form, including several whose morphology is compatible with early vessels of the late third and early second centuries.[27]

[23] Badian 1972: 21–2. Every Roman citizen was assessed by the censors according to the extent of his possessions. At some point, five *classes* had been created (attributed to Servius, but probably much more recent); however; it is clear that, by the second century, the only important demarcation was that between the first class and the rest. It is not known what the property qualification for equestrian status was at the end of the second century. Wiseman (1971: 66) speculates that it was about HS 40,000 or HS 50,000. By the late Republic, the qualification was 100,000 denarii, and although it is not known for certain when this change was introduced, it was probably under the *lex Roscia* of 67 (Brunt 1988: 146). As Wiseman (1971: 67) puts it, 'the distinction between senators and *equites*, though intermittently of great political importance, tends to disguise the essential homogeneity of the moneyed class', and we agree with Nicolet that at this time a senator was an *eques* who had held a senior magistracy. Therefore, from a financial perspective, an individual merely had to satisfy the qualification of being an *eques* in order to be a candidate for such a magistracy (Nicolet 1976: 20–30, 2000*b*: 26).

[24] Morel 1989: 480. [25] Morel 1989: 487.

[26] Loughton 2003: 179. [27] Loughton 2003: 194.

An interesting third-century BC parallel to this long-distance trading network comes from Euesperides, the most westerly Greek settlement in Cyrenaica, which is located in the suburbs of modern Benghazi, in Libya.[28] Numismatic finds show that Euesperides was abandoned between about 258 and 250 and never reoccupied. As a result there is a *terminus ante quem* for all stratified material at the site. Evidence of long-distance trade comes from ceramic survivals. Imports account for 90 per cent of the finewares found, with 80 per cent of the total coming from Attica. Transport amphorae originating in the Aegean, southern Italy, Sicily, and Punic north Africa, as far west as the Straits of Gibraltar, are found in quantity. A surprisingly high proportion (35%) of the coarseware for cooking was imported, mainly from Corinth, the Cycladic arc, and the Punic world. All this shows that the volume of maritime trade between Euesperides and the wider Mediterranean must have been sufficient to guarantee the arrival of relatively cheap pottery in considerable quantities, even though this pottery must have represented 'only a small fraction of the total imports, much of which must have been in perishable goods that must have arrived on the same ships'.[29] In return, the city probably exported silphium, grown on the steppe to the south of the city and attested on the coinage, and purple dye, since large amounts of murex shells were discovered in the lower city.[30]

Archaeology, then, provides fascinating evidence of expanding trade links in both the southern and the northern Mediterranean during the third century, in the wake of Alexander's capture of the Persian Empire and its treasuries.[31] But there is also literary evidence that attests to the growing importance of long-distance trade. Shortly after the end of the First Punic War, we hear of an embassy to Carthage on behalf of some five hundred traders, imprisoned there after 'sailing from Italy' and supplying rebels in the Mercenary War.[32] This showed not only that the senate was prepared to go to some lengths to protect Romans (or perhaps Italians) who engaged in foreign trade; but also, given that they swapped a much larger number of Carthaginian prisoners for the traders, the importance that they attached to them. Secondly, in Polybius' account of the causes of the First Illyrian War, he states that there had been a number of complaints to the Roman senate in the past from 'Italian merchants' (Ἰταλικοὶ ἔμποροι), which the senate had overlooked, but that the senate decided to send ambassadors to Illyria when the number of these complaints increased.[33] It was perhaps in relation to incidents such as these that, in the late 70s BC, Cicero posed the rhetorical question,

> Quot bella maiores nostros et quanta suscepisse arbitramini, quod cives Romani iniuria affecti, quod navicularii retenti, quod mercatores spoliati dicerentur?[34]
>
> (How many great wars, do you think, were waged by our forefathers, because Rome's citizens were alleged to have been wronged, her sailors arrested, her merchants robbed?[35])

Then there is the *plebiscitum Claudianum* of 218, introduced by the tribune Q. Claudius and passed against senatorial opposition. Indeed, supposedly only one senator, C. Flaminius, supported it (after all, turkeys do not vote for Christmas).

[28] A. I. Wilson et al. 2002, 2003, 2004, 2005, 2006; all usefully summarized in A. I. Wilson 2006*a*.
[29] A. I. Wilson 2006*a*: 149. [30] For silphium, see Horden and Purcell 2000: 65.
[31] See p. 190. [32] Polyb. 1. 83. 7–8. [33] Polyb. 2. 8. 3.
[34] Cic. *II Verr*. 5. 149. [35] Trans. Loeb VIII 631, revised.

The law forbade any senator or son of a senator from owning a seagoing vessel that could carry more than 300 amphorae.[36] Livy adds that this size of vessel would suffice to transport produce from their own farms and that 'every form of profit-seeking was seen as unseemly for senators' (quaestus omnis patribus indecorus visus).

There are several points arising here. First, Livy's explanation of the reason for the passing of the *plebiscitum Claudianum* is misleading, as we have the near contemporary funeral eulogy of L. Caecilius Metellus in 221, quoted by Pliny the Elder, which cites as one of a list of Metellus' praiseworthy aims 'to obtain a great amount of money in a good way' (pecuniam magnam bono modo invenire).[37] Secondly, as D'Arms says, 'if some Roman senators were not deeply and directly involved in commercial shipping by 219, there would clearly have been neither need for restrictive legislation nor senatorial opposition to its precise terms'.[38] Indeed, the explanation for the introduction of tribunician legislation of this kind, against massive senatorial opposition, can only be that senators were engaged in maritime trade on such a significant scale that it was feared by certain people at Rome that this commerce was, or could be, damaging to the Republic. Perhaps, for example, senatorial trade was perceived to have begun to affect Roman decisions on foreign policy. At any rate, by 70 BC, the law was categorized by Cicero as being amongst 'those ancient . . . and dead laws' (antiquae . . . istae leges et mortuae) still on the statute books but unenforced, even though it was subsequently re-enacted by a *lex Iulia repetundarum*, probably in 59 BC.[39] No doubt one of the reasons for the redundancy of the *plebiscitum Claudianum* was that within a generation of its enactment, a simple way of evading its provisions had been dicovered. By lending money to a *societas* in which he himself might also have a minority stake, a senator was still able to benefit from the large profits available in the maritime trade; and we shall see an example of this in Ch. 7.[40]

The expansion of Roman trade in the Mediterranean during the third century shows that the Roman economy did not exist in a vacuum and that its contacts with foreign territories were not limited only to diplomacy and warfare. In particular, its economic relationships with the Hellenistic world seem to have pre-dated the Second Punic War by several decades. Rome's first silver coinage was minted at the end of the fourth century on a Greek model that is generally believed to have derived from contact with the Greeks of Campania.[41] Bankers, *argentarii*, probably first appeared at Rome during the last two decades of the fourth century and it is likely that their banking techniques were inspired by or inherited from those of the Greek *trapezitai*.[42] By the middle of the third century, the first Italians begin to appear in Greek territories, with epigraphical references

[36] Livy, 21. 63. 3.

[37] Plin. *HN* 7. 140; Polyb. 6. 56. 1–3 echoes this sentiment.

[38] D'Arms 1981: 33.

[39] Cic. *II Verr.* 5. 45; Scaevola *ap. Dig.* 50. 5. 3; the re-enactment is confirmed by the Leiden fragment of the jurist Paulus' *Sententiae* (Archi et al. 1956: 5, para. 3): 'Senatores parentesve eorum, in quorum potestate sunt, vectigalia conducere, navem in quaestum habere, equosve curules praebendos suscipere prohibentur: idque factum repetundarum lege vindicatur.' The exclusion of senators from most public contracts probably continued until the end of the Republic (Ascon. 93C; Dio. Cass. 55. 10. 5), on which see Badian 1972: 50, 120 n.16; Harris 1979: 80 n. 2; D'Arms 1981: 36.

[40] Plut. *Cat. Mai.* 21. 5–6, quoted on p. 145.

[41] Crawford 1985: 28.

[42] Livy, 9. 40. 16; Andreau 1987: 337–40.

and anecdotal contacts becoming more amply attested.[43] As we shall see in Ch. 7, the 'villa system' of farming, described by Cato the Elder in his *De Agricultura*, was probably modelled on Greek farms in Magna Graecia and Sicily and on Carthaginian plantation estates and introduced into the Roman world in the second half of the third century. The influence of the Greek world, particularly of the more economically developed Hellenistic kingdoms, seems to have intensified during and following the Second Punic War. New technologies, such as mechanical water-lifting devices, which had probably been developed at Alexandria, began to reach Italy;[44] and Rome's approach to provincial exploitation was perhaps influenced by contact, first in Sicily, with Hellenistic methods of taxation.[45] As we shall see later, these links with the economies of the eastern Mediterranean grew exponentially in the second century.

We are at the point now where we must consider the level of wealth in Rome at the time of the Second Punic War. At a state level, it is clear that following Cannae in the autumn of 216, Rome was in serious trouble financially as well as militarily. The commanders of forces in Sicily and Sardinia reported that they could neither pay nor feed their troops. Livy talks of *penuria argenti* (paucity of silver), in the context of Rome obtaining a loan as well as a supply of corn for six months from Hieron II of Syracuse.[46] In the spring of 215, when the six months were up and the Romans could not repay the loan, Hieron extended the credit still further by sending more supplies of grain.[47] Also a *tributum duplex* (double tribute) was introduced.[48] In the same year, Rome could not afford to pay the army in Spain and contracts for supplies on indefinite credit were agreed with three groups of *publicani*.[49] In 214, crews for the fleet were paid directly by wealthy individuals, not by the state;[50] and *publicani* promised to continue to work on state building contracts let by the censors, even though they would not be paid. The trust funds of orphans and widows were borrowed by the state, and many of the *equites* and centurions in the army waived their pay.[51] In 210, Rome borrowed from her citizens—the only time in her history that she did so.[52] In the same year Livy refers to a shortage of slaves.[53]

But it is not only Livy who provides evidence of the problems being faced by Rome at this time. During this same period, the coinage also shows the impact of the *inopia aerarii* (the emptiness of the treasury).[54] The bronze coinage falls in weight dramatically. At the outbreak of war, the bronze *as* had still in theory weighed ten Roman ounces. The following year after Trasimene it was reduced to a semilibral level (thus becoming a fiduciary currency), with an *as* in theory of six ounces, then to a triental, and finally to a quadrantal level. The final stage in the collapse of the didrachm coinage system, with which Rome had begun the Second Punic War, was the debasement of silver from about 97 per cent fine down to

[43] See Ch. 8. [44] See pp. 157–8. [45] See Ch. 4.

[46] Livy, 23. 21. 4–5. [47] Livy, 23. 38. 12–13.

[48] Livy, 23. 31. 1–2; the *tributum* was an annual contribution that citizens imposed on themselves to cover war expenditures.

[49] Livy, 23. 48. 9–49. 4. [50] Livy, 24. 11. 7–9.

[51] Livy, 24. 18. 10–15. [52] Livy, 26. 36.

[53] Livy, 26. 35. 5; Livy, 28. 11. 9 again refers to a similar shortage (*inopia servitiorum*) in 206.

[54] Livy, 24. 18. 2.

about 89 per cent, probably in 213.[55] In these circumstances, the Romans began to look overseas for help. Polybius mentions that an embassy was sent to Ptolemy Philopator in Egypt, at some point between 215 and 210, in order to obtain a supply of corn;[56] and we are inclined to follow Meadows's arguments that, instead of corn, Ptolemy did in fact, in 213 or thereabouts, provide the Romans with the bullion that was used to mint the unusual Mars/Eagle and thunderbolt gold coin issues that appear at about this time (the eagle on the thunderbolt being a clear iconographic reference to the coinage of the Ptolemies).[57] In fact, in 212, an entirely new denarius coinage system was created, based on a sextantal standard for the bronze: on an *as* of two ounces, and with the types Head of Roma/ Dioscuri.[58] Finally, in 209/8, the gold that was kept in the *aerarium sanctius* 'to meet extreme emergencies' was withdrawn for use by the Roman state.[59]

Apart from the fact that the Roman state was very nearly bankrupt during the Second Punic War, the main feature to emerge from Rome's fiscal problems is the degree of support that her own citizens were able to provide. The Roman economy in the third century BC may, as Hopkins suggested, have been 'dominated by a wide central band of self-sufficient yeomen, that is by peasants who owned and cultivated their own farms'.[60] But behind Livy's (no doubt embellished) patriotic tale of senatorial altruism, with the matrons of Rome contributing their jewellery to the war effort, lies the impression that, at the end of the third century, the senatorial and equestrian classes were in fact relatively prosperous. We have already seen the size of the contribution of a group of *publicani* for the contract to supply the army in Spain. No statistics exist for the wealth of senatorial families, so our evidence here is also anecdotal. But it neverthelesss gives a clear picture of the wealth and property holdings of some of the men who achieved the consulship in the last decade of the third century and the first decade of the second. This reveals that certain senators of consular rank had plentiful funds available during and just after the Hannibalic War. For example, P. Cornelius Scipio Africanus (*cos.* 205, 194) staged games, as aedile in 213, which were 'magnifice facti'.[61] L. Valerius Flaccus (*cos.* 195) staged games in 201, as did M. Claudius Marcellus (*cos.* 196) in 200. Q. Minucius Rufus (*cos.* 197), as aedile, gave feasts as well as games in 201.[62] Finally, C. Cornelius Cethegus (*cos.* 197) put on splendid games as aedile in 199.[63] We also know something of the land holdings of the senatorial class. Claudius Marcellus' father, the conqueror of Syracuse, had a house, gardens, and a suburban estate at Rome, according to a tradition reported by Cicero.[64] Flaccus, the consul of 195, had estates in Sabinum, near M. Porcius Cato.[65]

55 Howgego 1995: 112. 56 Polyb. 9. 11a.

57 Coins: *RRC* 44/2–4 and 72/2; Meadows 1998.

58 Crawford 1985: 56; Buttrey et al. 1989: 215–26.

59 Livy, 27. 10. 11: 'aurum vicesimarium quod in sanctiore aerario ad ultimos casus servabatur'. The *aerarium sanctius* was a special reserve into which was paid the 5% manumission tax on the emancipation of slaves.

60 Hopkins 1978: 22. 61 Livy, 25. 2. 6–8.

62 Livy, 31. 4. 7. 63 Livy, 32. 7. 13–14.

64 Cicero, at *II Verr.* 4. 121, is speaking of his own time, but makes it clear that these properties had been inherited from generation to generation in the family of the Marcelli, and that they were known to have belonged to the conqueror of Syracuse.

65 Plut. *Cat. Mai.* 3. 1; Val. Max. 2. 4. 5.

Although Cato stressed the frugality, austerity, and hard work of his youth, it is clear that, to some extent, this was just a posture.[66] He inherited several estates in Sabinum from his father, and Cicero relates a tradition that he had a comfortable house in Tusculum, which he had probably also inherited from his father, as he had been born there. He already had some slaves and employed hired workers.[67] Finally, Scipio Africanus had a house near the *Forum* (described by Seneca as very modest[68]) and probably gardens near the city.[69] The Scipionic family had an estate near Rome, outside the *Porta Capena*, where their sepulchral monument is situated.[70] Africanus also owned an estate at Liternum, described by Pliny the Elder as a prosperous farm, although this may have been acquired in 205, when the state sold lands in Campania.[71] He married Aemilia, the daughter of the L. Aemilius Paullus who died at Cannae, and she probably inherited some property from her father.

Towards the end of the war, in 205, Livy mentions that 'because of a shortage of money for the war' (quia pecunia ad bellum deerat), part of the Campanian territory was sold off.[72] The significant point here is not that the Roman state was short of money; rather that there were Roman citizens with the resources available to buy this land at this late stage in the war. At a time, then, when the Roman state had a serious fiscal shortage, there is evidence suggesting that levels of private wealth were relatively unaffected.

There is also a possible hint of even greater wealth in the background. In 210, Scipio took with him to Spain 400 talents, probably a year's pay for the four legions there.[73] Where did the money for this come from? Certainly not from the treasury. Perhaps it was contributed by the Scipios themselves, but more probably it represented the result of Rome's borrowing from her citizens, which, as we have seen, occurred in that year. If so, it provides a further indication of the relatively high level of private wealth that already existed at Rome at the end of the third century.

In this context it is worth considering how much identity there was between Rome's aristocratic plutocracy and the state. Legally, of course, there was a complete separation. The impression conveyed from the pages of Polybius and Livy is that the quaestors responsible for the *aerarium* and the censors responsible for letting state contracts always behaved with the utmost probity and with due regard to the distinction between private and state expenditure. Any departure from this was treated as both shocking and noteworthy. Thus, in 179, there was a public outcry when the censor, M. Aemilius Lepidus, constructed a pier near his estate at Tarracina: 'Lepidus molem ad Tarracinam, ingratum opus, quod praedia habebat ibi privatamque publicae rei impensam inseruerat'[74] (Lepidus built a mole at Tarracina, a work that brought him censure, because he owned property there and had included some private expenses with the expenditure chargeable to the state). But, aside from the legal aspects, what also emerges from Livy is that

66 Festus 350L. 67 Cic. *Rep.* 1. 1; 3. 40; Nep. *Cat.* 1. 1; Plut. *Cat. Mai.* 1. 1; 2. 2; 3. 2.
68 Sen. *Ep.* 86. 69 Livy, 44. 16. 10; cf. 28. 38. 8.
70 Shatzman 1975: 246; *ILLRP* 309–17; Cic. *Tusc.* 1. 13; Livy, 38. 56. 4.
71 Plin. *HN* 14. 47–9; Sen. *Ep.* 86. 4; Val. Max. 2. 10. 2. Sale of land: Livy, 28. 46. 4–5.
72 Livy, 28. 46. 4–6. 73 Polyb. 10. 19. 2; Livy, 27. 36. 12. 74 Livy, 40. 51. 2.

when the going got tough, the Roman population at all levels was prepared to contribute funds to the Roman state.[75] The senatorial class may have had an identity of interest with the *aerarium*, but then so did the whole of Roman society in the dark days of the war. As we have seen, shortage of funds in the state sector was not necessarily mirrored in the private sector.

[75] Livy, 26. 36. 11–12, 24. 18. 10–15.

Part I
Sources of Revenue

2

Indemnities and Booty

ποίαις δυνάμεσι καὶ χορηγίαις χρησάμενοι Ῥωμαῖοι πρὸς ταύτας ὥρμησαν τὰς ἐπιβολάς, δι᾽ ὧν καὶ τῆς γῆς καὶ τῆς θαλάττης τῆς καθ᾽ ἡμᾶς ἐγένοντο πάσης ἐγκρατεῖς.[1]

INTRODUCTION

During the half century that followed the end of the Second Punic War, war booty, war indemnities, and eventually mining revenues began to arrive in Rome on a scale that dwarfed anything that had ever occurred previously. These inflows meant that within thirty-five years of the end of the war, in 167, the state treasury's financial position was such that Rome was able to suspend direct taxes on her own citizens. The value of the war indemnities alone, which were received between 201 and 152, totalled a massive 27,280 talents (see Table 2.2). These inflows resulted in profound and radical changes that transformed not only the physical appearance of the city of Rome (and of a number of the provincial cities in Italy) but also its economy and the level of individual wealth. We shall chart these effects later, but in the next three chapters we shall focus on the actual inflows of bullion, starting with war booty and war indemnities.

The Latin term for war booty, *praeda*, covers a multitude of possible items from coins and gold and silver plate to armour, weapons, and slaves, the last of which could be sold off for cash. As the jurist Gaius put it in the second century AD, but looking back to the Romans of the Republic, 'maxime ea sua esse credebant, quae ex hostibus cepissent' (they believed that property to which there was the strongest claim of lawful ownership was that which they had captured from their enemies).[2] In addition to grabbing plunder, the Romans had historically charged a defeated enemy for what they claimed were the costs of the war that had just been waged. In modern scholarship, this type of payment, by a defeated state to its conqueror, is commonly referred to as a 'war indemnity'. But the Latin term, *stipendium*, was wider in meaning, as Cicero makes clear:

[1] Polyb. 1. 3. 9: 'with what powers and resources the Romans embarked on that enterprise which has made them masters of land and sea in our part of the world'.

[2] Gai. *Inst.* 4. 16; cf. Gai. *Inst.* 2. 69: 'ea quoque quae ex hostibus capiuntur naturali ratione nostra fiunt' (those things also that are captured from enemies become ours by natural reason).

Inter Siciliam ceterasque provincias, iudices, in agrorum vectigalium ratione hoc interest, quod ceteris aut impositum vectigal est certum, quod stipendiarium dicitur, ut Hispanis et plerisque Poenorum quasi victoriae praemium ac poena belli, aut censoria locatio constituta est, ut Asiae lege Sempronia.[3]

(Between Sicily and the other provinces, judges, there is an important difference in the system of land taxation. In the others, either a fixed tax, called a stipendiary tax, has been imposed, as it has been on the Spaniards and most of the Carthaginians, as if it was a reward for victory and a penalty of defeat, or it is let out by the censors, as it is under the Sempronian law concerning Asia.)

Stipendium was a term derived from the words *pendere* (to weigh out) and *stips* (a gift, payment, or donation). Its original meaning was the regular monetary emoluments paid to serving soldiers.[4] Over time, and by extension, the word *stipendium* appears to have developed from meaning just 'money to pay for the army' into a term for a monetary tax or a war indemnity. As we shall see, when we look at the whole pattern of the evidence, the differences between war indemnities and tax revenues (or 'tribute') are not always clear.[5]

In our sources, the amounts for war indemnities and booty are sometimes given in Roman denominations, but more often in Greek talents or by physical weight. Thus, Pliny the Elder mentions that the *aerarium Saturni*, the Roman state treasury, at an unspecified point in 157 contained 6,135,400 sesterces in coin (that is, 1,533,850 denarii), 17,410 pounds of gold, and 22,070 pounds of silver.[6] Since we know the weight of Roman silver coins (roughly 84 denarii to a pound of silver) and the ratio between gold and silver (1:10), it is possible to say that the treasury at this time contained gold worth 14,624,400 denarii and silver worth 1,853,880 denarii, giving total holdings, including the coin, of 18,012,130 denarii.[7]

It has generally been assumed that Polybius equated the Greek drachma with the Roman denarius. This seems to be what is implied by a passage which gives us our first evidence for the rate of *stipendium* in the Roman army:[8] according to Polybius, the legionaries received two obols daily (equivalent to one-third of a drachma), centurions four obols, and cavalrymen a whole drachma; and it has been generally accepted that, in the mid-second century, the legionary was paid at the daily rate of one-third of a denarius, or 120 denarii for a full (360-day) year.[9] Polybius was writing for a Greek audience, for the majority of whom the standard Greek currency would have been the drachma of an Attic standard (weighing

[3] Cic. *II Verr.* 3. 12.

[4] Varro, *Ling.* 5. 182: 'Hoc ipsum stipendium a stipe dictum, quod aes quoque stipem dicebant... Militis stipendia ideo, quod eam stipem pendebant'; cf. Plin. *HN* 33. 43; Festus, 379L; Ulp. *Dig.* 50. 16. 27; Isid. *Etym.* 16. 18. 8.

[5] H. Müller (2009) claims that the Romans of the Republic had a system for calculating reparations; but Crawford (forthcoming) argues that a comparative reading of the evidence shows that, in so far as such a notion existed in antiquity, it is a retrospective rationalization by Appian.

[6] Plin. *HN* 33. 55.

[7] Crawford 1974: 595, 626 n. 1, and 635. In quoting these numbers so precisely (with none of the conventional stylization noted by Scheidel (1996)—see Introduction n. 8), Pliny was presumably using a treasury record (see p. 27). Polyb. 31. 32. 8 gives a ratio of 1:10 for gold to silver in connection with the Aetolian indemnity.

[8] Polyb. 6. 39. 12.

[9] Brunt 1988: 262 n. 94.

roughly 4.3 g), which approximates to the Roman denarius (weighing around 3.86 g).[10] We may therefore understand a talent of silver, the amount in which the indemnities are expressed, as approximating to a figure of 6,000 denarii (or, in weight, 23.16 kg[11]). The amount of 18 million denarii in the treasury in 157 would therefore have been equivalent to 3,002 talents.

Over 80 per cent of this figure by value, however, was accounted for by holdings of gold bullion and this raises the important question of why the Romans struck no gold coins between the end of the Second Punic War and the time of Sulla, with the exception of a small issue of gold staters, which carry the legend T.QUINCTI and which were probably minted in Greece in the mid-190s by T. Quinctius Flamininus, or produced in his honour.[12] It is clear, first of all, that there was no shortage of gold during our period, since, apart from these treasury holdings, we know that gold was mined by the Romans;[13] that large amounts of gold were captured by them as booty;[14] and that some gold might even have been received through the payment of war indemnities.[15] Various more or less speculative hypotheses have been advanced to explain both the absence of a gold coinage and the possible uses of the large amounts of gold that did come into Roman hands. The ancient evidence is limited and ambiguous. A few notices reveal that gold was used for the gilding of temples and their accoutrements, suggesting an association of gold with divinity, reinforced by the fact that the *aerarium sanctius* contained only gold.[16] But evidence for gold bullion as a means of payment, though assumed by various scholars, is virtually absent from our sources before gold coins start to be minted in the 40s BC.[17] The gold from the *aerarium sanctius* was, it is true, used to make payments in 209 (for government contracts), but this was at a time of crisis.[18] Cicero mentions prohibitions on the export of gold and silver from Italy, but that is in the 60s.[19] In the late second century, Lucilius refers jokingly to a quaestor paying him gold from the *aerarium*, but we do not know the context;[20] and the killer of Gaius Gracchus was rewarded in gold.[21] The fact, though, is that virtually no other evidence exists for the use of gold as a means of payment and, significantly perhaps, only two of the 412 Republican hoards, catalogued by Crawford for the years 211 to 27 BC, contained gold bars, and these were both from the first century.[22] There can be no settled conclusion on the issue, but the safest interpretation would be that gold

[10] Brunt 1950: 51. [11] 6,000 × (say) 3.86 g (see Crawford 1974: 594) = 23.16 kg.

[12] *RRC* 548; Radnoti-Alföldi 1984; Leu Numismatics 2005: 16–17; in fact no substantial issues of gold coins were minted until the mid-40s. Howgego 1992: 8–12 and Hollander 2007: 20–4, 31–9 have useful discussions of gold use.

[13] Strabo, 4. 6. 7; Plin. *HN* 33. 78; Polyb. 34. 10. 10–15; I Macc. 8. 3.

[14] See p. 30.

[15] e.g. the Aetolians were offered the option of paying part of their indemnity in gold (Polyb. 31. 32. 8); Pliny (*HN* 33. 5) was nevertheless amazed that his forebears generally preferred silver: 'equidem miror populum Romanum victis gentibus in tributo semper argentum imperasse'.

[16] e.g. gilded shields were installed on the pediment of the Temple of Jupiter in 193 (Livy, 35. 10. 12); ornamental ceilings on the Capitoline were gilded (Plin. *HN* 33. 51).

[17] Harl 1996: 50; Hollander 2007: 37. [18] Livy, 27. 10. 11; see p. 16.

[19] Cic. *Vatin.* 12; Cic. *Flac.* 67. [20] Lucil. 456–7.

[21] Vell. Pat. 2. 6. 5; Plin. *HN* 33. 48.

[22] *RRCH* 259 from Spain in the 80s and *RRCH* 357 from Italy in the 40s; gold bars were also discovered on the Antikythera 'A' wreck, dating from 80 or just after, which could have been carrying

was used by the Romans principally as a store of value, that it was in some way associated with the gods, that it was not normally used as a way of making payments, and that the reason why the Romans did not mint gold coins was simply for the banal reason that, as Hollander puts it, 'they rarely needed them'.[23] As we shall see in Chs. 5 and 6, a silver and bronze coinage, combined with the availability of credit, did the job.

Our sources, then, give the figures for indemnities and sometimes for booty in talents of silver. But these amounts are largely meaningless unless we can give some idea of what they could actually buy. The following examples give some indication of the cost of major undertakings during the middle and late Republic. They range over time as well as geography, but that is because we have very few reports of the costs of major projects in the second century. So these examples are given purely in order to illustrate the magnitude of the figures we are about to consider.

From the corpus of subscription lists that survive from the Hellenistic world, a group of inscriptions, probably from a single contribution towards the building or repair of a temple in Smyrna, in the second or first centuries, suggests that the cost was something of the order of between 4 and 5 talents.[24] A subscription list from Colophon, dating from between 311 and 306, indicates that the cost of building fortifications totalled about 50 talents.[25] As we have seen, in 210, Scipio took with him to Spain 400 talents, probably a year's pay for the four legions there, and we can therefore assume that, roughly, 100 talents paid for the cost of one Roman legion for a year.[26] Dionysius quotes C. Acilius (who was writing in about 150 BC) as saying that an overhaul of the sewage system at Rome (probably at some point in the first half of the second century) cost 1,000 talents.[27] The customs duties levied at Rhodes in the early 160s amounted to 167 talents per annum on a through-put of goods valued at 4,166 talents per annum.[28] Finally, the cost of building the Aqua Marcia aqueduct is given by Frontinus (quoting the late first-century antiquarian annalist Fenestella) as 180 million sesterces (7,500 talents).[29] The aqueduct, which was 91 km long, was constructed in the years 144 to 140 and was the first to be built since the Anio Vetus, 128 years previously. It probably brought somewhere in the region of 188,000 m^3 of water into Rome every day and increased the city's water supply by 80 per cent.[30] It was the single most expensive building project undertaken during the Republic.

an instalment of the reparations exacted from Pergamum after the Mithradatic War (Parker 1992: 55–6).

23 Hollander 2007: 24.

24 Petzl 1987: nos. 687–92.

25 Migeotte 1992: no. 69.

26 Polyb. 10. 19. 2; Livy, 27. 36.12; see n. 40.

27 Dion. Hal. *Ant. Rom.* 3. 67. 5; the reference to the censors 'letting out' the cleaning and repairing contract (to *publicani*) and the amount of the contract (which happens to be the same as one of the annual instalments of Antiochus' indemnity) combine to suggest this dating.

28 Polyb. 30. 31. 2; Walbank 1979: 459–60; see p. 199.

29 Frontin. *Aq.* 1. 7; the *sestertius* was adopted by the Roman state as the official unit of reckoning in place of the *as* in or shortly before 141 (Crawford 1974: 621–5).

30 Dodge 2000: 187.

SELF-PERPETUATING WARS

The intensity of Roman militarism should not be underestimated. During our period, Rome is best seen as a warrior state. She was at war in every year from 218 to 157 and at peace for only four years in the whole of the second century.[31] No political candidate could run for even the lowest public office without having served ten campaigns in the army.[32] According to Hopkins, 'during the second and first centuries, a higher proportion of Roman citizens was under arms for longer than in any other pre-industrial state'.[33]

During the first half of the second century, there were only two major items of state expenditure, the military and the construction of utilitarian infrastructure (such as roads and commercial facilities), of which the former was probably by far the more significant.[34] Expenditure on state administration was not a meaningful factor during the Republic, as there was virtually no state bureaucracy, apart from the tiny staffs supporting the senior magistrates, the law courts, and the treasury. Nor was there any systematic provision of what might be termed 'social services' by the state, before the introduction of a grain subsidy by Gaius Gracchus in 123 BC.

The cost of Rome's military commitment was enormous. Indeed Frank estimated that military costs accounted for 77 per cent of total revenue during the first half of the second century.[35] Given the inevitable lack of precision surrounding any figures for the aggregate income and the aggregate expenditure of the Roman state, we should probably take Frank's number as a metaphor for 'a very high percentage of revenue' rather than as a fact or statistic, but it may not be too far from the truth. A significant proportion of citizens were liable to serve in the army during the second century for anything between six and sixteen years.[36] Over the two centuries from 225 to 23, the median size of the army amounted to perhaps 13 per cent of adult male citizens.[37] And this affected the Italian population in general. During the period 200 to 168, the Italian allies contributed a majority of the total Roman armed forces and the average size of the Roman/Italian armies was about 110,000 men. The average number of legions in the field between the end of the Second Punic War and the end of the Third Macedonian War was 8.7, and it was 6.48 between 167 and 91.[38] The number of active legions then ballooned during the Social and Civil Wars. In addition, occasional

31 Harris 1979: 10. 32 Polyb. 6. 19. 5. 33 Hopkins 1978: 11.

34 See Ch. 11. 35 Frank 1933: 146.

36 The manuscripts of Polyb. 6. 19. 2 give six years as the period of military service that a foot soldier must complete, but the text is corrupt and is usually emended to sixteen (Walbank 1957: 698). This latter figure is probably a maximum, as it is for the ten years of cavalry service that Polybius mentions, although he goes on to say that twenty years' service could be demanded of a foot soldier in an emergency. Brunt (1971*a*: 399–401), however, claimed that this period of service was anachronistic in the second century and refers to an earlier period when wars were short; he argues that the normal length of military service was six years and points to Appian (*Hisp.* 78), who states that six campaigns became the norm in 140. Harris (1979: 45), while accepting that sixteen years was the maximum, suggests that twelve years was usual. Rosenstein (2004: 189–90, 286 n. 12) sees no reason why the normal length of service could not have been the full sixteen years.

37 Hopkins 1978: 31; Scheidel (2006: 222 fig. 8) estimates the proportion at about 15% during the second century.

38 Brunt 1971*a*: 422–34.

fleets had to be manned with anything between 8,000 and 30,000 men.[39] It is possible to produce a very rough estimate of the total cost of Rome's military commitment. If we follow Tenney Frank's calculation that, at the end of the third century, approximately 620,000 denarii paid for the stipend of one Roman legion for a year,[40] and use Peter Brunt's figures for the number of legions each year,[41] we can calculate that, between 200 and 168, the Romans had, on average, to find about 5.4 million denarii or 900 talents per annum to cover the cost of the army's pay alone. In addition to being paid, Roman troops needed to be supplied.[42] Continuous warfare required the procurement of vast amounts of weapons, tents, and logistical equipment, such as pack mules, wagons, and transport ships.[43] There were other elements of military expenditure too, with fleets of up to 150 quinqueremes being commissioned.[44] Frank conjectured that the cost of these additional items of military expenditure was equivalent to roughly 50 per cent of the military stipend.[45] If this estimate is even remotely correct, it suggests that the total cost of Rome's military effort during this period was, on average, of the order of 8.1 million denarii per annum (1,350 talents).

At the same time, the financial infrastructure of the Roman state was undeveloped. The *aerarium Saturni*, the Roman state treasury, was simply where the bullion, cash, and documents were stored. Two annually elected quaestors were in charge but they could only make payments when required to do so by law or by *senatus consultum*. Oversight of the state's finances and decisions on the level of coin production were in the hands of the senate.[46] Private sector banks existed, as we shall discuss in Ch. 6, but there was no state central bank. The Roman state only ever borrowed once, and that was from its own citizens, in 210 BC, in the dark days of the Second Punic War.[47] There was certainly no concept of the regular issuance of government debt and there was no bond market. Unlike, say, the British government, which financed its way through the Napoleonic Wars by issuing large amounts of bonds through the Bank of England, the only way that the Roman state could continue to fight its wars was by having enough precious metal coming into the treasury with which to pay its troops. One may dispute the presence of economic motives in Rome's foreign policy in the second century BC, but the simple fact is that Rome's involvement in warfare, during this period,

39 Brunt 1971*a*: 424–5.

40 Basing his estimates on Polyb. 6. 39. 12, Frank (1933: 76) calculated the annual cost of the stipend of a legion to have been 619,200 denarii (just over 100 talents). Support for this analysis comes from Polybius' statement (at 10. 19. 2) that, in 210 BC, Scipio took with him to Spain 400 talents, which was probably a year's pay for the four legions there; cf. Brunt 1950: 51.

41 Brunt 1971*a*: 424.

42 Morley 2010: 78.

43 Polybius states (6. 21. 6–7 and 6. 39. 15) that weapons were supplied by the state, but that deductions were made from military pay for food, clothing, and replacement arms. It was not until C. Gracchus' *lex militaris* that the terms of military service were altered so that clothing was also supplied at the expense of the state (Plut. *C. Gracch.* 5; Diod. Sic. 35. 25).

44 After the Hannibalic War, the Roman navy had been allowed to decay. For the war against Antiochus, fifty new quinqueremes were built (Livy, 35. 20. 12, 35. 21. 1, 35. 24. 8, 36. 2. 15). Only twenty ships were built, as far as we know, in the ten years following Apamea; Livy (40. 18. 7–8) says they were constructed in 181 and assigned to guard the coasts of Italy. For the war against Perseus, another fleet of one hundred ships had to be built and fifty old quinqueremes recommissioned (Livy, 42. 27. 1; 43. 12. 9).

45 Frank 1933: 142–4.

46 Williams 1998: 174.

47 Livy, 26. 36.

would not have occurred on the same scale or to the same extent if the money had not been available to pay for its armed forces. Furthermore, the only way that the high rate of expenditure on Rome's military could be financed quickly was by the proceeds of warfare itself: from the bullion obtained by plunder, and by charging a defeated enemy for what the Romans claimed were the costs of the war that had just been waged. In this sense, warfare became economically self-perpetuating. Continuous wars of imperial conquest led to the plundering of conquered territories, which led to the import into Italy of booty, war indemnities, and chattel slaves, which in turn led to the financing of further wars. In other words, the prevailing fiscal model for the Romans, before about 180 BC, was to grab as much precious metal as possible through warfare rather than through the regular monetary taxation of annexed territory. Polybius realized this:

> τὸ μὲν οὖν τὸν χρυσὸν καὶ τὸν ἄργυρον ἀθροίζειν πρὸς αὑτοὺς ἴσως ἔχει τινὰ λόγον· οὐ γὰρ οἷόν τε τῶν καθόλου πραγμάτων ἀντιποιήσασθαι μὴ οὐ τοῖς μὲν ἄλλοις ἀδυναμίαν ἐνεργασαμένους, σφίσι δὲ τὴν τοιαύτην δύναμιν ἑτοιμάσαντας.[48]
>
> (There was, therefore, perhaps a certain logic in appropriating all the gold and silver for themselves; for it was impossible for them to aim at world domination unless they deprived other peoples of such resources and acquired them for themselves.[49])

Some indication of the importance of bullion in Roman fiscal thinking comes from Livy's precise descriptions of the amounts of booty carried in various triumphs, and from the detailed accounts of war indemnities that are preserved in our ancient sources, which imply that public records of these items were maintained and survived. We know from Plutarch that the treasury's financial records certainly went back as far as Sulla.[50] We also learn, from a passage in Cicero's *Verrines*, that lists of the types and quantities of booty that were carried in the triumphs were themselves deposited in the treasury:

> P. Servilius, quae signa atque ornamenta ex urbe hostium, vi et virtute capta . . . populo Romano apportavit, per triumphum vexit, in tabulas publicas ad aerarium perscribenda curavit.[51]
>
> (Publius Servilius brought to the Roman people, from the city of his enemies, the statues and art objects which had been captured by his strength and courage . . . carried them in triumph, and had them recorded in detail on public tablets at the treasury.)

Unlike the general tendency of ancient authors to stylize monetary valuations into conventional figures (about which Scheidel has issued a salutary warning), the figures for booty and indemnities, which we can find in Polybius, Livy, and other authors, appear to be of a different order of accuracy.[52] They suggest that these authors were working from treasury records that went back at least to the third century.

Badian believed that 'the whole myth of economic motives in Rome's foreign policy at this time is a figment of modern anachronism'.[53] Gruen argues that 'no single decision on eastern affairs exhibits an economic component demonstrable as central or primary . . . The demands of international politics predominated in

[48] Polyb. 9. 10. 11. [49] Trans. Loeb IV 27. [50] Plut. *Cat. Min.* 18. 5.
[51] Cic. *II Verr.* 1. 57. [52] Scheidel 1996. [53] Badian 1968: 20.

actions and decisions on the East. Material advantage was a welcome adjunct rather than a central ingredient.'[54] But as Harris has elegantly put it, 'The presence of economic motives is not excluded by the fact that the stated reasons of war were of a quite different kind.'[55] The assumed absence of economic motives is no doubt in part due to the nature of our sources who did not have direct access to the transcripts of senatorial debates. A modern parallel would be the public pronouncements of the US administration over the war in Iraq in the first decade of the twenty-first century. These emphasized America's support for democracy, although there has always been a widely held suspicion that its intervention was to a greater or lesser extent prompted by a wish to secure oil supplies. One might compare T. Quinctius Flamininus' letter to Chyretiai, which disclaims economic motives.[56] In fact, to Roman senators, economic gain both public and private was a normal outcome of successful warfare and of the expansion of power. Thus, Livy describes how Ti. Gracchus' successes in Sardinia were commemorated by an inscription in 174: 'vectigalibus restitutis exercitum salvum atque incolumem plenissimum praeda domum reportavit'[57] (With the taxes having been restored, he brought home his army, safe, unharmed, and laden with booty.) The text of the inscription, with the ablative absolute clause '*vectigalibus restitutis*' placed first, emphasizes the purpose of the mission; Gracchus' economic achievements are reflected both in that clause and in the statement that the army returned laden with booty.

The evidence suggests that pillaging was a normal activity of the Roman state. Indeed several of the actions during the First Punic War seem to be plundering raids: Polybius mentions that, in 253, a Roman fleet made a number of landings on African soil before being grounded off the island of Jerba, while 20,000 people were enslaved in the expedition of Regulus.[58]

There are other examples too. The attitude of certain senators is clear from some individual incidents. In a speech dating from 167 and handed down to us by Aulus Gellius, Cato defended the Rhodians, 'quorum opibus diripiendis possidendisque non pauci ex summatibus viris intenti infensique erant'[59] (towards whom not a few of the most distinguished men were bent on hostility through a desire to plunder and possess their wealth).

In 151, the consul L. Licinius Lucullus, 'being greedy of fame and in need of money, because he was in straitened circumstances' (δόξης τε ἐπιθυμῶν καὶ ἐκ πενίας χρῄζων χρηματισμοῦ), attacked a Celtiberian tribe and extracted 100 talents of silver.[60] The senate passed a decree at some point before 129, under which it banned the planting of olives and vines by *transalpinae gentes*.[61]

At a more sophisticated level, the examples of the *plebiscitum Claudianum* and the Antiochus III indemnity, as well as the closure and reopening of the

[54] Gruen 1984: 342–5.

[55] Harris 1979: 92. He argues against the doctrine of 'defensive imperialism', expounded *inter alios* by Badian and Gruen, believing that the most important factors that brought about the wars of the second century were the Romans' desire for the glory and economic benefits that warfare brought. Rich (1993), on the other hand, argues that the pattern of Roman warfare and expansion was 'a good deal patchier' than Harris's model implies and that 'the levels of Roman belligerence fluctuated greatly'.

[56] *RDGE* 33. 12. [57] Livy, 41. 28. 8–9.

[58] Polyb. 1. 39. 1–2, 1. 29. 7; cf. Zonar. 8. 16 (Hippo, 247 BC); Zonar. 8. 18 (Gauls, 237 BC).

[59] Gell. *NA* 6. 3. 7. [60] App. *Hisp.* 51–2. [61] Cic. *Rep.* 3. 16.

Macedonian mines (which we shall discuss in Ch. 3), show that the senate had an awareness of the economic consequences of its actions. One could also point to the fact that the Romans understood the effect that creating Delos as a free port would have—an 85 per cent loss of customs duties for Rhodes.[62]

The majority of senators must have had a clear notion of the size and main sources of Rome's revenues. Most of them had been quaestors and each year, at least, the senate probably received a computation of the treasury's contents and a motion concerning the coming year's expenditure.[63] There is a high level of financial awareness revealed by Cato's *De Agricultura* in, for example, the detailed monetary calculations over the acquisition of an olive crusher;[64] or in his advice that the *paterfamilias* should review the cash accounts on his arrival at his farm.[65] It might be objected that these are fairly trivial subjects. The sums at the state level may indeed have been larger, but (*si licet parva componere magnis*) the former British Prime Minister Margaret Thatcher would have identified with the 'good-housekeeping' principles in both cases. The senate was composed of 300 individuals who had at least a passing understanding of how to run an estate, and it did not require a higher degree of financial sophistication to run the Roman state at this time.

BOOTY

Captured booty benefited the individual as well as the state; and it is clear from the comedies of Plautus, who was writing at the beginning of the second century, that war was believed to bring enrichment.[66] It can be inferred from a passage of Polybius that soldiers were as keen to sign up for the army at the time of the First Punic War, because of the prospect of plunder, as Livy says they were at the time of the Third Macedonian War.[67] An inscription survives from the base of a triumphal column listing the booty which C. Duillius (*cos.* 260) captured from the Carthaginians;[68] and, tellingly, the Roman–Aetolian treaty of 211 specifically gave the Romans the right to 'anything apart from the city and the land', in other words moveable property: [ὃ] δέ κα παρὲξ τᾶς πόλιος καὶ τᾶς χώρας.[69]

Quantifying the amount of plunder that came into Rome is problematic. Reliable data on the value of booty captured during the third century are very limited and that makes comparisons with the second century difficult.[70] However, for the period from the Second Punic War until the loss of the full text of his history in the 160s, Livy gives us numerous detailed descriptions of the amounts of

62 Polyb. 30. 31. 12; see p. 199.
63 Crawford 1974: 617 esp. n. 2.
64 Cato, *Agr.* 22. 3.
65 Cato, *Agr.* 2. 5.
66 References in Gruen 1984: 290 n. 7.
67 Polyb. 1. 11. 2; Livy, 42. 32. 6; cf. Plut. *Caes.* 12. 2 for the first century BC.
68 *ILLRP* 319.
69 *IG* IX 1^2 2. 241. 9; Gruen (1984: 289) argues that 'the Aetolians held the upper hand in that alliance' and that they left 'to Rome what (for the Aetolians) was of secondary interest'. It is more likely that the Romans were motivated by a desire for booty and slaves, because of the very severe financial problems that followed the disaster of Cannae in 216 (see pp. 15–16).
70 Cf. the comment of Frank (1933: 43 n. 3) on the untrustworthiness of some of Livy's figures for the Samnite wars.

booty that successful Roman generals carried in their triumphs.[71] His notice on Scipio Africanus' triumph in 201 is typical: 'argenti tulit in aerarium pondo centum viginti tria milia.'[72] (He brought into the treasury one hundred and twenty-three thousand pounds of silver.) Frank estimated the value of the booty that came in during the period 200 to 157 at 109.5 million denarii (18,250 talents). As he himself admits, this valuation is highly hypothetical, but it nonetheless gives some indication of the scale of the income from this source.[73] His figure, in any case, seems to be an underestimate, particularly if one considers the value of the captives taken by Aemilus Paullus in Epirus in 167, which is discussed below.

Some of the triumphs during this period were exceptionally large. T. Quinctius Flamininus' triumph lasted three days.[74] But even the more modest ones brought in massive amounts of riches. In his triumph over Hither Spain in 194, for example, Cato carried 25,000 pounds of silver, 123,000 denarii, 540,000 pieces of 'Oscan silver', and 1,400 pounds of gold, which makes a total of possibly 4 million denarii, or nearly 670 talents—enough to cover the pay of nearly seven legions for a year. And this was after Q. Minucius Thermus had triumphed over the same *provincia* in the previous year and had already brought in 34,800 pounds of silver, 73,000 denarii, and 278,000 pieces of 'Oscan silver' (a total of approximately 550 talents).[75]

As the Romans overran more and more of the areas surrounding the Mediterranean, slaves became an increasingly important part of the take. In 197, Flamininus captured 5,000 prisoners in Greece, some of whom were immediately sold off, with the rest being given as booty to his soldiers.[76] In 177, there was an auction of 5,632 Istrian prisoners;[77] and then, on a rather different scale, 150,000 Epirotes were enslaved by Aemilius Paullus in 167 as he marched back from Greece.[78] If we are conservative and give a value per slave of 400 denarii, it would mean that Flamininus' captives were worth 2 million denarii or 333 talents, the Istrians 2.25 million denarii or 375 talents, and the Epirotes 60 million denarii or 10,000 talents. Even if one assumes a rock-bottom price of 67 denarii a head for the Epirotes, this would still have produced revenues of 10 million denarii or 1,700 talents.[79]

Although booty was a major source of revenue during this period, it is less evident who actually received it. Of course, much of the booty went into the

[71] Frank 1933: 127–38 quotes the main instances; see too Beard 2007.

[72] Livy, 30. 45. 3; cf. 31. 20. 7, 31. 49. 2, 32. 7. 4, etc. and Frank 1933: 127–37.

[73] Frank 1933: 141.

[74] Livy, 34. 52. 4–11.

[75] Livy, 34. 46. 2–3, 34. 10. 7; cf. 34. 10. 4, where, also in 195, M. Helvius carries 119,439 pieces of 'Oscan silver' in triumph and 40. 43. 6, where, in 180, Q. Fulvius Flaccus carries 173,200. Livy's term 'argentum oscense' is still a mystery. The whole issue is discussed in Ch. 5 pp. 95–6. For simplicity's sake we have assumed, in calculating the value of the booty from Spain, that a piece of Oscan silver is equivalent to a denarius.

[76] Livy, 33. 10 .7; 33. 11. 2.

[77] Livy, 41. 11. 8.

[78] Polyb. 30. 15; Livy, 45. 34. 1–6; Plut. *Aem.* 29. 4.

[79] Frank 1933: 101 for the value of slaves, although the author of II Macc. 8. 10–11 talks about Nicanor of Syria in 165 offering 90 slaves for a talent in order to raise 2,000 talents, which was due to the Romans (see Table 2.2n.). That implies a price per slave of 67 drachmas. Livy (45. 40. 1, cf. Diod. Sic. 31. 8. 11 and Plut. *Aem.* 32. 4–9) quotes Valerius Antias as saying that the value of the 'captured' silver and gold in Aemilius Paullus' triumph was HS 120 m., which probably did not include the revenue from the sale of the enslaved Epirotes. Plin. *HN* 33. 56, on the other hand, gives a figure of HS 300 m., which is either a mistake, or does include this additional revenue. Polybius (18. 35. 4) reports that Perseus had stored up a treasure of 6,000 talents, which would equate to HS 144 m.

treasury, but we have little idea about the proportions in which *praeda* was divided between the treasury, the commander, the officers, and the men. That booty was divided up in some way by the quaestors is known from the description which Polybius gives of the procedure which he says was used to do just that on the battlefield.[80] What is also clear is that (probably additional) payments were made, out of the booty, to the *equites*, centurions, and foot soldiers at the time of a triumph. Thus we have, in our sources, sixteen occasions between 210 and 167 when distributions of money were made to soldiers in this way.[81] These range in amount from the sum of 7 denarii to foot soldiers, 14 denarii to centurions, and 21 denarii to *equites* in 197,[82] to the distribution of Aemilius Paullus thirty years later, when the figures were 100, 200, and 300 denarii respectively.[83]

The Roman general had the exclusive right to distribute the booty.[84] There does not appear to have been any fixed formula for the proportions in which the booty was divided up. It is only rarely that we get hints of certain conventions that had to be followed, usually through reports of accusations and prosecutions which were brought against Roman generals. Thus the consul of 219, M. Livius Salinator, was fined on a charge of unequal division of booty.[85] Thirty years later, Livy says that M'. Acilius Glabrio, commander of the Roman army in Greece against Antiochus III in 191, was prosecuted by two tribunes: 'quod pecuniae regiae praedaeque aliquantum captae in Antiochi castris neque in triumpho tulisset neque in aerarium retulisset'[86] (because some of the royal money and booty which had been captured in Antiochus' camp had neither been carried in the triumph nor brought into the treasury). On the other hand, Q. Fulvius Flaccus (*cos.* 179) gave nothing to the treasury, but distributed money to his soldiers at his triumph, and was not prosecuted;[87] nor was L. Aemilius Paullus, who gave his soldiers smaller amounts than they had expected, but who then went on to give a small amount of silver plate from the booty to his son-in-law and the library of Perseus to his sons.[88] In 150, Ser. Sulpicius Galba (*cos.* 144) gave part of his booty to his friends; and we can see that generals gave money to their officers from references in Livy and from an inscription recording a dedication in Tusculum by a military tribune, M. Furius, who was using the booty he had received.[89] This seeming lack of any fixed procedure is, in a sense, not that surprising. The main reason for the distribution of the booty was to reward those who had helped to win the battle; Aemilius Paullus' son-in-law, for example, had been a legate in the army.

[80] Polyb. 10. 16. 2–9; Ziolkowski (1993) probably correctly calls this an idealized description; but cf. the character Chrysalus, at Plaut. *Bacch.* 1075, who says 'nunc hanc praedam omnem iam ad quaestorem deferam' (now I'll bring all this booty to the quaestor).

[81] References in Brunt 1971*a*: 394.

[82] Livy, 33. 23. 7–9.

[83] Livy, 45. 40. 5; Plut. *Aem.* 29. 5 says that in Epirus his soldiers received only 11 drachmas each.

[84] Shatzman 1972: 202 n. 113 cites ten examples where Livy explicitly says that 'a certain general distributed (or gave) a sum of... asses (sesterces, denarii) to every soldier'.

[85] Frontin. *Str.* 4. 1. 45.

[86] Livy, 37. 57. 12. Shatzman (1972) believes that the prosecution was politically inspired, had no hope of success, and was intended to damage Glabrio's reputation.

[87] Livy, 40. 59. 1–2.

[88] Livy, 45. 36. 6; Val. Max. 4. 4. 1; Plut. *Aem.* 28. 11.

[89] App. *Hisp.* 60; Livy, 26. 48. 14; *ILLRP* 100, 221.

But what did the generals pay themselves? There has been much scholarly debate concerning the authority of the Roman commander over booty.[90] Our sources do not provide sufficient information for us to decide what part of the booty the commander kept for himself, nor indeed whether there were any stated criteria for determining his share. Indeed the ancient evidence is confusing and contradictory.

The academic debate has centred around the meaning of the term *manubiae*, since, in our sources, there seems to be a distinction between *manubiae* and *praeda*. Thus, according to Livy, the praetor of 171, C. Lucretius Gallus, used his *manubiae* to build a water channel near Antium, but used *praeda* to decorate the temple of Aesculapius:

> . . . is eo tempore in agro suo Antiati esset, aquamque ex manubiis Antium ex flumine Loracinae duceret. Id opus centum triginta milibus aeris locasse dicitur; tabulis quoque pictis ex praeda fanum Aeculapi exornavit.[91]
>
> (. . . he was at that time on his estate at Antium and was building a water channel from the River Loracina using his *manubiae*. It is said that he had let the contract for this work for one hundred and thirty thousand asses.[92] He also decorated the temple of Aesculapius with painted tablets from the *praeda*.)

Most of the ancient evidence points to *manubiae* being anything reserved for the general's use. A *scholion* to Cicero states this and adds that *manubiae* are booty received from an enemy who has surrendered (as its supposed etymology, *manu habere*, would imply): 'Spolia quaesita de vivo hoste nobili per deditionem manubias veteres dicebant; et erat imperatorum haec praeda, ex qua quod vellent facerent'[93] (our ancestors called spoils sought from a living noble enemy through surrender *manubiae*; and this was the booty of the generals, from which they did what they chose). So too the grammarian Placidus: '"Manubiae" dicuntur spolia hostium quae a rege aut duce eius de manibus deportantur, ut exuviae et induviae dicuntur'[94] (the spoils of enemies that are carried off from a king or a commander, from his hands, are called *manubiae*, as are called *exuviae* and *induviae*). Tacitus seems to confirm this: 'Expugnatae urbis praedam ad militem, deditae ad duces pertinere'[95] (the booty of a city that has been stormed belongs to the troops; of one that has surrendered, to the commanders).

If, in its strictest sense, the term *manubiae* had originally meant booty received from an enemy who had surrendered, it would certainly be logical for the general to receive this booty for his own use, since it was presumably down to his strategy or to his negotiating skills that the surrender had occurred, so obviating the need for any fighting or casualties. On the other hand, it would also be logical that all the troops should share in any booty (*praeda*) that had been captured by force of arms, as they would have helped to win the battle. It is also reasonable to assume that, by extension and over time, the term *manubiae* came to mean the portion of any booty, however obtained, that the general retained for his own use.

[90] Shatzman 1972 and most recently Churchill 1999; references to earlier debate in Shatzman 1972: 177–9.

[91] Livy, 43. 4. 6–7.

[92] i.e. 13,000 denarii, just over 2 talents.

[93] Ps.-Asc. schol. *ad* Cic. *II Verr.* 1. 157.

[94] *CGL* 5. 32. 1.

[95] Tac. *Hist.* 3. 19.

Therefore, the generally accepted view would now be that of Shatzman: that the commander had complete authority to divide booty between soldiers and officers, that he could retain a portion of it for himself (termed *manubiae*), and that he could set aside part of the booty for other purposes such as the erection of public buildings, the holding of games, or donations to temples. Finally, he could decide what part, if any, of the booty should be handed over to the treasury. But he was not bound by law to submit an account of how the booty had been divided.[96]

There have, however, been two objections to this view. Mommsen believed that the term *manubiae* referred to money obtained from the sale of *praeda*, because this was the definition given by the *rhetor* Favorinus in a passage from Aulus Gellius:[97] 'Nam "praeda" dicitur corpora ipsa rerum quae capta sunt, "manubiae" vero appellatae sunt pecunia a quaestore ex venditione praedae redacta'[98] (for *praeda* is used of the actual objects making up the booty, but *manubiae* designates the money collected by the quaestor from the sale of the booty). But Shatzman confirmed that this definition was impossible, given references to the sale of *manubiae*, which could not therefore already have been monetized.[99] More recently, Churchill has argued that, although a general would have been entitled to custody of the *manubiae*, this was not the same as owning them outright.[100] Rather, the *manubiae* would have stayed in public ownership and could have been used (only) 'for future expenses on behalf of the public'. Now, it is perfectly possible that the meaning of *manubiae* changed over time, as the legality of a general's retention of a portion of the booty for himself diminished. Indeed, much of the contradictory evidence comes from later authors. Thus, Dionysius of Halicarnassus (writing at the end of the first century BC, but in a reference back to the fifth century) states that '*λάφυρα . . . δημόσια εἶναι κελεύει ὁ νόμος, καὶ τούτων οὐχ ὅπως τις ἰδιώτης γίνεται κύριος, ἀλλ' οὐδ' αὐτὸς ὁ τῆς δυνάμεως ἡγεμών*'[101] (the law ordains that booty is public property and that not only no private citizen, but not even the commander of the forces himself, can have control of it). Similarly, Livy, writing 170 years or so after the event, states that the senate's advice to P. Cornelius Scipio Nasica was to use his *manubiae* to pay for games that he had previously vowed, when he was fighting in Spain in 193 BC, suggesting that there was a distinction between *manubiae* and the personal financial resources of the general:

> Novum atque iniquum postulare est visus; censuerunt ergo, quos ludos inconsulto senatu ex sua unius sententia vovisset, eos vel de manubiis, si quam pecuniam ad id reservasset, vel sua ipse impensa faceret.[102]
>
> (It was seen as a new and unfair demand; the senate therefore decided that, as regards the games which he had vowed on his own initiative and without consulting them, he should stage them either out of the *manubiae*, if he had reserved any money for this purpose, or at his own expense.)

[96] Shatzman 1972; 1975: 63. [97] Mommsen 1879: 443 n. 62.
[98] Gell. *NA* 13. 25. 26–7. [99] Shatzman 1972: 179–80. [100] Churchill 1999.
[101] Dion. Hal. *Ant. Rom.* 7. 63. 2; a passage in fact mentioned neither by Shatzman nor Churchill.
[102] Livy, 36. 36. 2.

Frontinus reports that the huge Aqua Anio Vetus was constructed, in 272, out of the *manubiae* that had been captured from Pyrrhus, which suggests that at the time he was writing, at the end of the first century AD, the word had come to signify booty in a more general sense.[103]

There are, however, a number of incidents mentioned in our sources, in which generals did not retain booty for their own use, and it seems that these incidents were considered noteworthy precisely because they were unusual. One of these (and the only contemporary second-century reference to *manubiae*) is to be found in a fragment of one of Cato's speeches, and it implies that *manubiae* could just as easily be distributed to friends as the *praeda* could. This would clearly have been impossible if the *manubiae* had stayed in public ownership, and if the *manubiae* could only have been used for future expenses on behalf of the public: 'numquam ego praedam neque quod de hostibus captum esset neque manubias inter pauculos amicos meos divisi, ut illis eriperem qui cepissent'[104] (never have I divided booty, neither that which has been captured from enemies nor *manubiae*, amongst a little group of my friends, so as to grab it from those who had captured it). Since the tone of Cato's statement suggests that he is adopting a high moral position rather than advancing a legalistic argument, we should probably infer from it that there were, at the time Cato was writing, no fixed rules relating to the use of *manubiae*, but that the behaviour of generals, in respect of how they used their retained portions of the booty, was coming under increasing scrutiny.

Shatzman has collected the data available on men of senatorial rank, during the period from the end of the Second Punic War to the end of the Republic, about whose economic status we have at least two items of information. On this basis, he can provide 'economic prosopographies', as he terms them, on thirty-six senators for the period between the Second Punic War and the Gracchi.[105] There are some interesting aspects to these prosopographies. First, all except three of the senators are recorded in our sources as having obtained booty in some way. Secondly, the majority of the references in our sources to the economic activities (in the broadest sense) of these senators are to dedications made from captured booty after a campaign. So M'. Acilius Glabrio, the commander in Greece against Antiochus III, captured many prisoners of war and took booty from the city of Lamia, as well as after the battle of Thermopylae.[106] He vowed a temple before that battle and this was completed in 181.[107] He also gave gifts to the temple of Apollo at Delphi.[108] Significantly too, when Glabrio was a candidate for the censorship of 189, he gained favour by giving 'much largesse' (*multa congiaria*) to the people, and was subsequently (unsuccessfully) prosecuted.[109] Again, and from the same war, the praetor for 190, L. Aemilius Regillus, defeated Antiochus' fleet and brought booty to Rome, where he was granted a naval triumph. He used

[103] Frontin. *Aq.* 1. 6.

[104] *ORF*[4] 82, probably from his speech *De Sumptu Suo* before 164; cf. Polyb. 18. 35. 4–12, who praises L. Aemilius Paullus (wrongly) and P. Cornelius Scipio Africanus Aemilianus for not taking any booty themselves after the defeats of Macedon and Carthage respectively; cf. too Gaius Gracchus' self-defence at *ORF*[4] 182, quoted on p. 77; and Sall. *Iug.* 41. 7: 'praedas bellicas imperatores cum paucis diripiebant' (the commanders split the booty of war with a few).

[105] Shatzman 1975: 241–61.

[106] Zonar. 9. 19; Livy, 37. 5. 3; 37. 46. 3–4.

[107] Livy, 40. 34. 5; Val. Max. 2. 5. 1.

[108] *Syll.*[3] 609, 610.

[109] Livy, 37. 57. 11.

the booty for, amongst other things, the construction of a temple for the *Lares permarini*, which he had vowed in the battle. He also gave a crown to the temple of Apollo on Delos.[110]

A CASE STUDY OF SENATORIAL FINANCES: SCIPIO AFRICANUS

There is in fact only one family on whose financial standing we have any meaningful data for the first half of the second century, and that is the Scipios.

As we have already seen, at the time of the Second Punic War, Scipio Africanus owned property in or near Rome.[111] After the war, there are indications that the level of his expenditure began to increase. He had already given games as aedile in 213, but he went on to hold them twice more: in 205, after he returned from Spain, when it is specifically stated that the senate agreed that the cost would come 'from the money which he himself had brought into the treasury' (ex ea pecunia quam ipse in aerarium detulisset);[112] and again, when he came back from Africa.[113] No mention is made of any senatorial allocation for these latter games; rather, Polybius states that the the cost of these games was provided for by Scipio's 'generosity' (*μεγαλοψυχία*). There can be no doubt that he paid for these games himself and he probably did so out of the booty which he brought back from the war in Africa. In addition, in 205, he sent a golden wreath weighing two hundred pounds and 'representations of the spoils' (simulacra spoliorum), made of silver weighing a thousand pounds, to the temple of Apollo in Delphi, 'from the booty of Hasdrubal' (ex praeda Hasdrubalis);[114] in 194, he despatched a golden crown to the temple of Apollo in Delos;[115] and so received honours from the Delians in return.[116] Finally, in 190, he built an arch and erected seven gilded statues on the *Capitolium*.[117]

When Africanus' widow, Aemilia, died in 163/2, her heir was P. Cornelius Scipio Africanus Aemilianus (*cos.* 147, 134), who had been adopted by Africanus' son.[118] We know that when Scipio Aemilianus' natural father, L. Aemilus Paullus (*cos.* 182, 168), died in 161/0, Scipio Aemilianus already had assets of at least 60 talents. This is because he surrendered to his brother, Q. Fabius Maximus Aemilianus (*cos.* 145), the rights to his share of the assets which they had jointly inherited from Aemilius Paullus, on the grounds that his brother was not well off and he wanted Fabius to posssess a fortune equal to his own.[119] The inheritance from Paullus coincidentally totalled 60 talents. Since one can reasonably safely assume that Fabius and Aemilianus would otherwise have had similar assets, the only reason for Aemilianus having 60 talents more than his brother, as is implied

110 Livy, 40. 52. 4; *SIG*^{2} 588. 104. 111 See p. 17. 112 Livy, 28. 38. 14.
113 Polyb. 16. 23. 7. 114 Livy, 28. 45. 12. 115 *Syll.*^{3} 588. 102.
116 *Syll.*^{3} 617. 6. 117 Livy, 37. 3. 7.
118 She was therefore both his aunt and his adoptive grandmother. Walbank (1979: 503) discusses the alternative ways in which it was possible for Aemilianus to have inherited.
119 Polyb. 31. 28. 3.

by this account, can have been that he had inherited it from Aemilia and so ultimately from Africanus.[120]

In addition to this sum, Polybius states that Africanus had agreed to give dowries of 50 talents to each of his two daughters. After his death, Aemilia paid half these amounts to the husbands of her daughters, at the time of their marriages. Scipio Aemilianus, Aemilia's successor, then paid off the balance (a total of 50 talents) within ten months of her death and so over a year before the death of Aemilius Paullus.[121] These 100 talents are therefore in addition to the 60 talents that Scipio Aemilianus inherited from Aemilia and that he still had at the time of Aemilius Paullus' death. Shatzman rightly makes the further point that Africanus had two sons (L. and P. Cornelius Scipio) and that it was unlikely that they would receive assets worth less than the dowries that went to his sons-in-law.[122] We should therefore assume that each of them received 50 talents too, so that it is perfectly conceivable that, in his last years, Africanus had accumulated assets of at least 260 talents.[123]

If we assume that towards the end of the Second Punic War, Africanus' assets consisted mainly, if not entirely, of his property in or near Rome, and that the value of these was, say, roughly equivalent to the amount that Scipio Aemilianus inherited from Aemilia (60 talents), it is probable that Africanus increased the value of his *patrimonium* (patrimony) by at least 200 talents as a result of his campaigns in Spain (where he captured Carthago Nova) and Africa, and against Antiochus in Asia Minor. Livy states that upon Africanus' return to Rome after Zama, he brought into the treasury 123,000 pounds of silver (equivalent to 10.3 million denarii or 1,720 talents) and gave 400 asses (i.e. 40 denarii) apiece to his soldiers.[124] There were probably of the order of 29,000 infantry and 6,000 cavalry at Zama. Even without assuming that the centurions and cavalry received larger amounts than the foot soldiers (as happened in all subsequent donations), the cost of this donative would have been approximately 1.4 million denarii or 230 talents (and was additional to the amount given to the treasury). Let us then hypothesize that the value of the total booty captured in Africa had been just over 2,000 talents; if Africanus had, for example, given 85 per cent to the treasury (1,720 approximately), 10 per cent to his troops (200 talents), and kept 5 per cent for himself (100 talents), he would have more than doubled his patrimony at the time and probably not been regarded as being too greedy by his peers. It is, of course, likely that Scipio increased his *patrimonium* by means other than simply through warfare (for example through agricultural investment), but there is no

[120] Aemilianus had been born in 185/4 and was therefore probably 17 years old when he fought at Pydna and 24 when Paullus died in 161/0. It is unlikely therefore that he would have had enough time to increase his net worth so much more significantly than his brother. The only other way in which Aemilianus might conceivably have acquired this amount of assets would have been if he had received it for fighting at Pydna. But both brothers fought in that battle and it is unlikely that a 17-year-old would have been rewarded more generously than his older brother. In any case, the tradition (Plut. *Aem*. 28. 11) was that the sole reward they received was the library of Perseus.

[121] Polyb. 31. 27. [122] Shatzman 1975: 248.

[123] By comparison, Polybius (21. 26. 9–14) states that, in 189, Alexander the Isian was the richest man in Greece, with a fortune of 'more than 200 talents'.

[124] Livy, 30. 45. 3.

doubt that Scipio became very rich and that booty is an obvious way in which he did so.

If we are correct in assuming that Africanus kept 5 per cent (at a minimum) of the booty for himself, how typical was his behaviour compared to that of other Roman commanders in the second century? We can point to a group of senators who were sufficiently wealthy to engage in holding games, making donations to Delphi and Delos, building temples and public buildings, and erecting statues. They all had the opportunity to retain part of the captured booty for themselves and they even had a word for it: *manubiae*. Even if the amount retained was only 5 per cent of the booty, that could still be a very large sum. It is the (very small number of) commanders who did not take booty for themselves upon whom our sources remark; and that is because they are the unusual ones. Aristocratic enrichment is after all what we might have expected to result from the expansion of Rome's empire. P. Cornelius Rufinus was alleged to have been expelled from the senate, in 275 BC, because he possessed 10 pounds by weight of silver tableware; whereas a *senatus consultum* of 161 attempted to limit the amount to be used at any one banquet to one hundred pounds by weight.[125]

WAR INDEMNITIES

Like booty, the importance of war indemnities is reflected in the detailed accounts of them that were preserved. One of the earliest records of these reparations is in 293 when the consul, Sp. Carvilius Maximus, granted a year's truce to the Faliscans in return for 100,000 of *aes grave* and a year's *stipendium* for his troops (Table 2.1).[126] Under the treaty with Hieron II of Syracuse thirty years later, a payment of 100 talents was demanded.[127] The first sizeable indemnity comes at the end of the First Punic War, when the Romans imposed on the Carthaginians one of 3,200 talents, with 1,000 talents to be paid immediately and 2,200 to be paid in annual instalments over ten years.[128] Four years later in 238, they demanded and received an extra 1,200 talents, when they took over Sardinia.[129] That indemnities were becoming a regular part of Roman policy towards its defeated enemies is further indicated by the unquantified '*phoros*' (Polybius) or '*stipendium*' (Livy) imposed on Teuta under the settlement at the end of the First Illyrian War in

[125] References to Rufinus at *MRR* I. 196; *senatus consultum* of 161: Gell. *NA* 2. 24. 2.

[126] Livy, 10. 46. 12. What is *aes grave*? It is not clear that Livy would have known. The term is commonly used nowadays to refer to the round bronze coins, weighing 1lb, which were circulating at this time (cf. Thomsen 1957), but Livy could be using an archaizing term for a reference in his sources that he did not understand.

[127] Polyb. 1. 16. 9; Eutr. 2. 19. 1 and Oros. 4. 7. 3 record 200 talents and Diod. Sic. 23. 4. 1 gives the equivalent of 25 talents. None of these sources, all later, seem preferable to Polybius. The indemnity, presumably paid in annual instalments, was cancelled in 248 when Rome entered into φιλία ('friendship') with Hieron (Zonar. 8. 16); Harris (1979: 64) believes that we have here an indemnity *and* an annual tax.

[128] Polyb. 1. 62. 8–9, 1. 63. 3, 3. 27. 5. The Roman general Lutatius initially negotiated an indemnity of 2,200 talents over 20 years, but the Roman People did not accept this and appointed ten commissioners who imposed these stricter terms.

[129] Polyb. 1. 88. 12; 3. 27. 8.

Table 2.1. Indemnities received by the Romans during the 3rd century BC

			Talents
Faliscans	293 BC	100,000 *aes grave* + 1 yr's *stipendium*	= (?)50
Hieron of Syracuse	263 BC	100 talents over (?)20 yrs (remitted)	75
Carthage	242 BC	1,000 immediately and 2,200 talents over 10 yrs	3,200
Carthage	238 BC	1,200 talents (?immediately)	1,200
Teuta of Illyria	228 BC	Unknown	(?)100
TOTAL			4,675

228.[130] But, in the third century, we find only five references or partial references to indemnities, probably totalling somewhere between 4,500 and 5,000 talents.

The reparations demanded from Carthage at the end of the Second Punic War, however, are the first in a succession of indemnities that cumulatively meant that, by 167 (when they suspended the *tributum* on their own citizens), the Romans had received 24,280 talents from this source alone. Carthage had to contribute a total of 10,000 talents, payable in annual instalments of 200 talents over fifty years.[131] Then, under a *senatus consultum* of 196, Philip V of Macedon had to pay 1,000 talents, half immediately and the balance in ten annual instalments of 50 talents.[132] In the same year, the Boeotians were ordered to pay 30 talents.[133] Shortly after, in 195, Nabis of Sparta had to pay 500 talents: 100 talents immediately and 50 talents per annum for the eight years thereafter.[134] The indemnity imposed on Aetolia (which had allied with Antiochus III), in 189, also totalled 500 talents, with 200 payable up front and 50 talents per annum for the next six years.[135] In addition, the 'crown' of 150 talents presented to the Roman commander by the Ambraciots, on their surrender in the same year, looks suspiciously like an indemnity.[136]

But then in 188 something changes. The sum demanded from Antiochus III was a massive 15,000 talents: enough to build two aqueducts the size of the Aqua Marcia and three times the amount that our surviving sources suggest was paid in indemnities in the whole of the third century.[137] Moreover, the details of payment

[130] Polyb. 2. 12. 3; Livy, 22. 33. 5. Larsen (1938: 314) suggests that the Livian passage (from the year 217 and referring to the *stipendium* as overdue) indicates a second indemnity at the end of the Second Illyrian War; Harris (1979: 64) believes that this indicates that tribute was imposed.

[131] Polyb. 15. 18. 7–8; Livy, 30. 37. 5; Plin. *HN* 33. 51 gives 16,000 lb of silver p. a. (equivalent to 224 talents p.a.); see Table 2.2.

[132] Polyb. 18. 39. 5–6, 18. 44. 7; Livy, 33. 13. 14–15, 33. 30. 7; Plut. *Flam.* 9. 5; App. *Mac.* 9. 3; Livy (33. 30. 8) mentions that Valerius Antias and Claudius Quadrigarius gave different numbers. It is not clear whether the 200 talents demanded up front at the preliminary peace negotiations (Polyb. 18. 39. 5–6) was included in the final settlement of 1,000 talents or was in addition to it. Larsen (1938: 314) assumes the former, but most modern commentators (whom we have followed) believe the latter. The indemnity was cancelled by the Romans, in 190, when Philip proved his goodwill to them (Polyb. 21. 3. 3, 21. 11. 9). By this time, Philip had probably paid six annual instalments totalling 300 talents in addition to the initial 500 talents.

[133] Livy, 33. 29. 12. [134] Livy, 34. 35. 11.

[135] Polyb. 21. 30. 2, 21. 32. 8–9; Livy, 38. 9. 9. The Romans had originally demanded 1,000 talents.

[136] Polyb. 21. 30. 10; Livy, 38. 9. 13; cf. Walbank 1979: 89 and 130.

[137] Of course, an enormous sum but only equivalent, in nominal terms, to the annual tribute that Darius the Great received from his satrapies in the early fifth century, according to Hdt. 3. 90–6 (cf. Burn 1962: 123–6).

Table 2.2. Indemnities received by the Romans 201–152 BC (in talents of silver)

BC	Carthage	Macedonia	Boeotia	Sparta	Aetolia	Ambracia	Syria	Cappadocia	Total
201	200								200
200	200								200
199	200								200
198	200								200
197	200								200
196	200	500	30						730
195	200	50		100					350
194	200	50		50					300
193	200	50		50					300
192	200	50		50					300
191	200	50		50					300
190	200	50		50					300
189	200			50	200	150			600
188	200			50	50		3,000	300	3,600
187	200			50	50		1,000		1,300
186	200				50		1,000		1,250
185	200				50		1,000		1,250
184	200				50		1,000		1,250
183	200				50		1,000		1,250
182	200						1,000		1,200
181	200						1,000		1,200
180	200						1,000		1,200
179	200						1,000		1,200
178	200						1,000		1,200
177	200						1,000		1,200
176	200								200
175	200								200
174	200								200
173	200						1,000[a]		1,200
172	200								200
171	200								200
170	200								200
169	200								200
168	200								200
167–152	200 (p.a.)								3,200
TOTAL	10,000	800	30	500	500	150	15,000	300	27,280

[a] Part of the Syrian indemnity was paid late in 173. Livy (42. 6. 6–7) makes clear that the whole debt was paid off on that occasion (we assume one instalment but it may have been more). Therefore II Macc. 8. 10, which refers to a *phoros* of 2,000 talents owing to the Romans in 165, is probably wrong (so Habicht 1979: 239 n. 10b).

no longer envisioned a lengthy term. Five hundred talents were to be paid immediately, 2,500 more upon the ratification of the peace by the senate and the Roman People, and twelve annual payments of 1,000 talents each.[138] Only three years earlier, in 191, the Carthaginians had proposed to pay off the balance of their entire indemnity and the Romans had rejected their approach, saying

[138] Polyb. 21. 17. 4–5, 21. 42. 19; Livy, 37. 45. 14, 38. 37. 9, 38. 38. 13; App. *Syr.* 38; Diod. Sic. 29. 10. There was also an additional payment of 540,000 *modii* of corn.

that they would not accept the money before it was due.[139] That meant that the payments under the Carthaginian indemnity still had thirty-nine years to run. Why did the Romans demand such a large amount from Antiochus, and why a much shorter payment schedule than the one that they had imposed on Carthage?

Rome's intentions in insisting that Carthage must continue with its long-term payment schedule can only have been to emphasize the latter's subservience and to provide a repeated reminder of her defeat.[140] In the case of Antiochus, however, we appear to be dealing with an entirely different circumstance. An obvious explanation here is that the Romans were simply aware that they were dealing with a much wealthier enemy than had been the case hitherto, and that they therefore demanded a higher sum because they believed that they would be paid it by Antiochus. When Antiochus offered to pay half the cost of the war, they had no hesitation in demanding that he pay the full amount, on the rather spurious grounds that he had started it: 'ἀλλὰ πᾶσαν δίκαιον ἐστιν Ἀντίοχον ἀποδοῦναι· φῦναι γὰρ τὸν πόλεμον ἐξ ἀρχῆς οὐ δι' αὐτούς'[141] (but it was fair for Antiochus to pay the whole cost, because the war was originally due to him and not to them). The fiction of course in all this was that these indemnity payments were somehow related to the cost of the war (δαπάνη); but, if that was the case, why did the Romans charge the Carthaginians, against whom they had fought a much longer and more devastating war, only two-thirds of what they demanded from Antiochus?

There are indications that the size and term of the payments represent a change in certain senators' attitudes towards indemnities. These come from political events at Rome after Apamea, and specifically from the accusations and prosecutions that were aimed against the brothers L. Cornelius Scipio Asiaticus (*cos.* 190) and Scipio Africanus.[142] It seems that the attack against the Scipios went through three stages: the first in the senate probably in 187, the second a prosecution of Asiaticus, and the third a prosecution of Africanus. While these proceedings are reasonably difficult to chart, the attack in the senate can nevertheless be identified relatively clearly. Polybius says that someone in the senate (according to Gellius, the demand came from the tribunes Petillii) demanded an account 'of the moneys that Africanus had received from Antiochus, before the peace, for the pay of his army' (τῶν χρημάτων ὧν ἔλαβε παρ' Ἀντιόχου πρὸ τῶν συνθηκῶν <εἰς> τὴν τοῦ στρατοπέδου μισθοδοσίαν).[143] Africanus said that he was not obliged to render an account to anyone, but asked his brother to fetch the book of account. When it was brought, he proceeded to rip it up in front of the senate. He then

> asked why the senators wanted an account of how and by whom (πῶς καὶ διὰ τίνων) the 3,000 talents had been spent, but not of how and by whom the whole (καθόλου) 15,000 talents had been brought in, nor how the Romans had become masters of Asia, Libya, and Iberia.

139 Livy, 36. 4. 5–9.
140 So Gruen 1984: 293. Indemnities penalized as well as reimbursed.
141 Polyb. 21. 14. 7.
142 Polyb. 23. 14; Livy, 38. 50–60; Gell. *NA* 4. 18, 6. 19.
143 Polyb. 23. 14. 7.

(τοὺς δ' ἄλλους ἤρετο πῶς τῶν μὲν τρισχιλίων ταλάντων τὸν λόγον ἐπιζητοῦσι πῶς ἐδαπανήθη καὶ διὰ τίνων, τῶν δὲ μυρίων καθόλου καὶ πεντακισχιλίων ὧν παρ' Ἀντιόχου λαμβάνουσιν, οὐκέτι ζητοῦσι πῶς εἰσπορεύεται καὶ διὰ τίνων, οὐδὲ πῶς τῆς Ἀσίας καὶ τῆς Λιβύης, ἔτι δὲ τῆς Ἰβηρίας κεκυριεύκασιν.)[144]

As we have seen, it would appear that a commander had complete authority to divide booty as he saw fit between soldiers, officers, and himself (*manubiae*) and that he could decide what part, if any, of the booty should be handed over to the treasury. But he was not bound by law to submit an account of how the booty had been so divided.[145] Also, as far as we know, the issue of how to deal with an indemnity had not arisen prior to this episode involving the Scipios, since previously no general had collected part of an indemnity and used it for his own purposes.[146] Under the terms of the *senatus consultum* that concluded the war against Aetolia, the first instalment of 200 talents was to be paid to the 'consul then in Greece', but there is no hint that the consul who did collect the moneys did anything other than hand them over to the treasury.[147]

No doubt political infighting lay behind the tribunes' demand for an account of the money from the Scipios (and their subsequent prosecution), but the real issue here seems to have been whether the 500 talents, paid as a preliminary instalment by Antiochus to Asiaticus, counted as public money or as booty. If it counted as public money, it would all have to go to the treasury. If it counted as booty, then he could distribute it amongst his troops and keep a portion for himself.

As mentioned earlier, Polybius reports that under the terms finally agreed with Antiochus III, 500 talents had to be paid immediately and 2,500 more upon the ratification of the peace at Rome. Therefore, the amount of 3,000 talents mentioned by Africanus in Polybius' account of the episode in the senate was presumably the sum of 500 talents paid to Asiaticus (before the ratification of the peace) and the 2,500 talents collected by Cn. Manlius Vulso (*cos.* 189) after the ratification.[148] As Walbank says, unless Polybius (or his source) had made a mistake, there must have been some discussion of the use of Manlius' money too.[149] The issue therefore does not appear to have involved any charge of *misuse of funds*, but was rather one of *definitions and procedures*. And this debate reflects the same growing awareness of the importance of these indemnities to the state, as do the increased amount, and the shortened period for payment, of the indemnity from Antiochus. Certainly the terms of the indemnity of Antiochus represent a more aggressive stance by the Romans towards raising funds. The debate over the categorization of the funds received by Scipio and Manlius indicates an awareness

[144] Polyb. 23. 14. 7–11; it was an iconic incident and was retold by a number of later writers: Livy, 38. 55. 10–12; Gell. *NA* 4. 18. 7–12; Diod. Sic. 29. 21; Val. Max. 3. 7. 1.

[145] Cic. *II Verr.* 1. 77, however, suggests that by the 70s a governor was expected at least to hand his *rationes* into the *aerarium*.

[146] It is possible that part of the indemnity of Philip V had been used by T. Quinctius Flamininus to mint the gold staters that carry the legend T.QUINCTI; but these coins could well have been used to pay for military supplies for Flamininus' army.

[147] Polyb. 21. 32. 8.

[148] Scipio: Polyb. 21. 17. 5; Manlius: Polyb. 21. 40. 8.

[149] Walbank 1979: 245; cf. Livy, 39. 6. 4–5, where the lateness of Manlius' triumph is ascribed to his fear of becoming entangled in the Scipionic disaster.

for the first time on the part of the Roman senate and people that they could raise significant state finance from defeated enemies.

At any rate, by the time the final indemnity of this period had been demanded (a lump sum, or so it appears, of 300 talents, paid in 188 by Ariarathes IV of Cappadocia, who had collaborated with Antiochus[150]), the Romans had extracted, over the fourteen years from the end of the Second Punic War to 188, promises of a total of 27,280 talents in indemnities from defeated enemies, and had actually received cash payments during that period of 7,780 talents.[151] Or to put it another way, over those fourteen years, Rome had received, in bullion, nearly twice the amount of the indemnities that she had probably received during the whole of the third century.

CONCLUSION

Rome was a highly militarized society. Its success in war meant that during the second century vast quantities of bullion came to Rome in the form of war booty and indemnities from most of its defeated enemies, notably Carthage, Macedonia, and Syria. We have precise figures from literary sources for war indemnities, which totalled 27,280 talents between 201 and 152—possibly as much as five times the amount that Rome received in the whole of the third century. This figure was equivalent to 630 tonnes of silver, and the indemnities were mostly paid in that metal.

Booty is more difficult to quantify. Livy gives us some very detailed descriptions of the amounts of booty borne in various triumphs, which implies that detailed public records of the amounts captured were maintained, but the record is incomplete. Frank offered a 'highly hypothetical' estimate of the value of the booty that came in during the period 200 to 157 of about 18,250 talents, which gives some indication of the scale of the income from this source. When this amount is added to the value of the indemnities, Rome received, over a fifty-year period, nearly 46,000 talents from warfare alone. Although the booty in particular came in various forms, this total is equivalent to 1,050 tonnes of silver.

The immediate beneficiaries of this inflow of capital were the military in general (because of the high proportion of revenue that was spent on this area) and, as shown by the example of Scipio Africanus, military commanders in particular (because of the *manubiae* which they were able to cream off). But, as we shall see in later chapters, the impact of these inflows on the Roman economy eventually proved to be much wider and more profound.

[150] Livy, 38. 39. 6.

[151] By 188 BC, Rome had received these cash payments: from Carthage: 2,800 talents; Macedonia: 800; Boeotia: 30; Sparta: 450; Aetolia: 250; Ambracia: 150; Syria: 3,000; Cappadocia: 300.

3

Mining Revenues

Publicani autem sunt, qui publico fruuntur (nam inde nomen habent), sive fisco vectigal pendant vel tributum consequantur.[1]

INTRODUCTION

The development of the Spanish gold, silver, lead, copper, and iron mines resulted in a massive flow of mineral wealth, particularly bullion, into the hands of the Romans over at least four centuries. During the second century BC, the Romans exploited the silver mines and, although some scholars probably exaggerate the sums received by the Roman state from this source before the 160s, these revenues did grow to be very significant thereafter.[2] In Spain, for the first time, the Romans had to evolve methods whereby the substantial mineral deposits of an overseas province might be exploited and we consider their procedures for doing this. Then, with the defeat of Perseus in 167, the Romans acquired additional sources of bullion in the form of the Macedonian gold and silver mines. We examine the reasons behind the Roman decision not to exploit these new acquisitions for a period of nine years, and how that decision is connected with the state of Rome's finances at the time.

SCALE

Italy has limited exploitable mineral resources. The island of Ilva (Elba) and the hills of Etruria and Liguria were mined for their base metals by the Etruscans, and the island of Pithecusae (Ischia) by the Greeks. Certainly at Elba, these activities continued under the Romans.[3] It is probable that mines in Italy were being worked during the third century and the first half of the second century.[4] Polybius says that through the whole of Italy a vast number of contracts were let by the

[1] Ulp. *ad Dig.* 39. 4. 1: 'And the *publicani* are those who handle the public funds (for it is from there that they take their name), whether they pay tax revenue to the treasury or collect tribute.'

[2] Harl (1996: 41–2) provides a conjectural and perhaps overly optimistic table of revenues from the Spanish mines for the period 201–151.

[3] Diod. Sic. 5. 13.

[4] Walbank 1957: 675.

censors and this included mines (*μετάλλα*).[5] However, Pliny the Elder states that at some point they were closed by what he terms 'an old *senatus consultum*'.[6] The Romans appear to have had access to only limited supplies of precious metals, if we can judge by the small quantities of silver coin produced during the third century (and Rome's dependency on a crude bronze coinage before that), especially compared to the coinages of Carthage and the cities of Magna Graecia during the same period. For example, the amount of precious metal minted by Carthage during the First Punic War was possibly as much as seventy times greater than that minted at Rome.[7] Indeed the size of Roman silver coin issues appears to increase only following inflows of booty and war indemnities. Thus, for example, the value of the spoils captured by C. Duillius, at the battle of Mylae in 260, was about the same as the probable value of an issue of didrachms, depicting a she-wolf suckling twins (*RRC* 20), which dates from the same period.[8]

The silver mines of Spain, on the other hand, were recognized by ancient writers as being the most important in the Mediterranean.[9] The Carthaginians exploited the area: Diodorus reports that the Carthaginians used the silver to pay their mercenaries;[10] and Pliny the Elder claims that Hannibal derived 300 pounds of silver per day (equivalent to about 1,500 talents per annum) from a single mine, probably located near Carthago Nova, and called Baebelo after the person who discovered it: 'ex quis Baebelo appellatur hodie, qui CCC pondo Hannibali subministravit in dies'[11] (one of these mines, now called Baebelo, provided Hannibal with 300 pounds of silver per day).

It is not entirely clear what areas were actually mined by the Romans in the second century. Strabo reports silver at Castulo, over one hundred miles to the west of Carthago Nova, but the development of the mines there probably took place only at the very end of the second century.[12] On the basis of pottery evidence, it is believed that the vast silver mines at Rio Tinto in southern Spain date back to the late second century.[13] But it is for the region around Carthago Nova itself, which probably saw the initial focus of Roman mining activity, that Polybius provides the only surviving contemporary description of mining operations. He visited the area in person, probably in 151 or possibly in 146, and Strabo reports the following:

> *Πολύβιος δὲ τῶν περὶ Καρχηδόνα Νέαν ἀργυρείων μνησθεὶς μέγιστα μὲν εἶναι φησι, διέχειν δὲ τῆς πόλεως ὅσον εἴκοσι σταδίους, περιειληφότα κύκλον τετρακοσίων σταδίων, ὅπου τέτταρας μυριάδας ἀνθρώπων μένειν τῶν ἐργαζομένων, ἀναφέροντας τότε τῷ δήμῳ τών Ῥωμαίων καθ' ἑκάστην ἡμέραν δισμυρίας καὶ πεντακισχιλίας δραχμάς.*[14]

[5] Polyb. 6. 17. 2; Walbank (1957: 692) correctly believes that Polybius retrojects conditions in 150 into his account of the Roman state at the time of Cannae; cf. Ch. 9 n. 66.

[6] Plin. *HN* 3. 138, 33. 78, 37. 202.

[7] Burnett 1989: 45.

[8] Burnett 1987*a*: 13.

[9] Strabo, 3. 2. 8; Diod. Sic. 5. 35. 1.

[10] Diod. Sic. 5. 38. 2; cf. App. *Hisp.* 19.

[11] Plin. *HN* 33. 97.

[12] Strabo, 3. 2. 10; Domergue 1990: 182–9; Keay 2003: 162 n. 123.

[13] G. D. B. Jones 1980: 156–7.

[14] Strabo, 3. 2. 10 = Polyb. 34. 9. 8–9; for Polybius' autopsy see p. 102; the similarities in the yields (1,500 talents per annum) of one mine, the Baebelo mine under Hannibal, and of the whole Carthago Nova region in the mid-second century, are probably to be explained by the fact that the most productive and easiest period of extraction from a mine (the 'bonanza') normally occurs at the start of its exploitation.

> (Polybius, in speaking of the silver mines near Carthago Nova, says that they were very extensive and were about twenty *stades* distant from the town, extending in a circle for four hundred *stades*. Here 40,000 miners lived who, at that period, produced for the Roman *demos* a daily sum of 25,000 drachmas.)

Polybius, then, tells us that 40,000 workers were producing, in an area of around one hundred square miles, 25,000 drachmas per day for the Roman People. That daily amount is equivalent to about 9 million denariii, or 1,500 talents, per annum. In volume terms it is equivalent to about 35 tonnes of silver per annum.[15]

It is clear that Polybius is describing an enormous undertaking and, while it is easy to treat his account with scepticism, it would probably be wrong to do so. The extraction and refining of silver was a hard and complicated business and therefore required a large amount of manpower. About 16 kilogrammes of ore had to be extracted and processed to produce each silver denarius, weighing about 4 grammes.[16] For the area around Carthago Nova, therefore, 35 tonnes per annum of refined silver implies the extraction and processing of 140,000 tonnes of ore per annum. Now it is perfectly possible that Polybius' figure of 40,000 workers is a formulaic or conventional representation of a large number;[17] but in fact the figure does not seem excessive. First, these numbers would equate to 3.5 tonnes of ore extracted and processed by one man in a year; which, if anything, implies an underestimation; and, secondly, modern estimates of the size of the workforce in the Athenian mines at Laurium in the fifth century vary from 11,000 upwards.[18]

In fact, other literary and archeological evidence also supports Polybius' account of the scale of mining operations. Pliny the Elder is a particularly valuable authority on mining in Spain, as he actually saw it in action in AD 72–4, while he held an official post. His account of gold mining stresses the scale of the operations and the enormous expense involved.[19] The same author also mentions an old law limiting to 5,000 the number of men that the *publicani* could use to work the gold mines at Victumulae in Gallia Cisalpina (probably in the foothills of the Alps to the west of Milan and north of Turin): 'extat lex censoria Victumularum aurifodinae in Vercellensi agro, qua cavebatur ne plus quinque milia hominum in opere publicani haberent'[20] (a censorial law has survived, concerning the gold mines of Victumulae in the territory of Vercellae, under which it was prohibited for the *publicani* to have more than five thousand men employed in the work). From archaeological remains, we can gain an impression of the huge levels of production that eventually occurred in Spain. For example, by the first century AD, the high-altitude hard-rock gold mine at Puerto del Palo in north-west Spain contained a vast opencast which is over 200 m deep. At the Las Medulas mine, where the opencast workings are 2 km across, there were seven aqueducts, one up

[15] 3.86 g. × 25,000 per day × 360 days = 34.8 tonnes p.a. (cf. Ch. 2 n. 11).

[16] Rihll 2001: 115.

[17] Scheidel (2006: 224) points to decupled multiples of 400 as a pattern of stylization in ancient writers. He also points to a category of stylization made up of powers of ten, which might be taken to cast doubt on Polybius' number of 25,000 drachmas per day, since 1 drachma = 4 sestertii and therefore 4 × 25,000 = 100,000 sestertii (see Introduction n. 8).

[18] Rihll 2001: 134; cf. Potosí in Peru where, in the sixteenth century AD, there were 30,000 people involved directly or indirectly in mining (J. S. Richardson 1976: 153).

[19] Plin. *HN* 33. 72–7, 33. 97.

[20] Plin. *HN* 33. 78.

to 50 km in length, bringing in water for the hydraulic excavation processes.[21] The silver and copper mines of Rio Tinto were possibly the most important source of bullion in the early Principate, on the basis of an estimated 6 or 7 million tonnes of visible silver slag and 1 million tonnes of copper slag.[22] Andrew Wilson has demonstrated that the degree of technological development and the scale of capital investment that these undertakings represented were colossal. The technique used, hydraulic mining, effectively accelerates natural weathering processes by artificial means, using the erosive power of water to do the bulk of the work and enabling operation on a huge scale. Wilson believes that Roman mining, particularly in the gold and silver mines of the Iberian peninsula during the first two centuries AD, 'saw some of the most advanced and large-scale applications of technology to economically critical work ever practised before the European industrial revolution, and some of the most impressive investment in infrastructural engineering works'.[23]

But this is principally evidence from the early Principate. What of the second century BC? Already by this period, we hear of technological applications that entailed significant capital investment. Both Diodorus and Strabo mention the use of the Archimedes screw for pumping out water;[24] and Polybius also shows that we are dealing with something more than a cottage industry when, as quoted by Strabo, he describes the use of water for the crushing of ore.[25] Most importantly, Polybius' report of the extent of silver production around Carthago Nova is now corroborated by scientific evidence of large-scale, man-made, atmospheric lead pollution, related to silver extraction in the second century, which has left its 'signature' in European peat bogs and lake sediments and in the ice sheet of Greenland.

The study of the problem of 'acid rain', from the 1970s onwards, drew attention to the existence of a strong south-to-north atmospheric transport that carries acid emissions from industrial centres in continental Europe and Great Britain to Scandinavia, northern Russia, and Greenland. It is now clear that there is a similar strong south-to-north transport of lead and other pollutants.[26] In the early 1990s, lead concentration analyses of sediment cores, from nineteen forest lakes in Sweden, confirmed that atmospheric lead pollution started at least 2,600 years ago.[27] Although the evidence for physical mine workings in Spain mainly comes from the first two centuries AD, these sediment cores showed that the concentration of lead fallout from the atmosphere rose rapidly during the second century BC, reaching a clearly detectable peak at the end of the first century BC. These findings imply high mineral extraction rates during our period because, in ancient times, silver was produced by smelting lead-silver alloys from lead sulphide ores (galena) and cupelling silver from the alloys. Shortly after the Swedish study, an analysis was published that showed a synchronous lead deposition pattern in the ice sheet of central Greenland at a high elevation of 3,228 m.[28] Snow, as it descends to earth, collects and traps atmospheric pollution and, in the Arctic,

21 A. I. Wilson 2002*b*: 19.
22 G. D. B. Jones 1980: 165; A. I. Wilson 2002*b*: 28.
23 A. I. Wilson 2002*b*: 17, 26.
24 Diod. Sic. 5. 37. 3–4; Strabo, 3. 2. 9.
25 Strabo, 3. 2. 10 = Polyb. 34. 9. 10–11.
26 Renberg et al. 2000: 152.
27 Renberg et al. 1994.
28 Hong et al. 1994; A. I. Wilson 2002*b*: 25–6; de Callataÿ 2005; Kehoe 2007*a*: 547.

then forms a distinct annual layer distinguishable from that of other years by a partial thaw in the summer and a subsequent refreezing. By coring into the ice cap and analysing samples, it is therefore possible to reconstruct the history of atmospheric pollution through the ages. Isotopic analysis of the lead found in these ice cores suggests that around 70 per cent of this anthropogenically produced lead pollution may be related to smelting operations in southern Spain.[29] Subsequent studies, based on detailed reconstructions of the lead accumulation records preserved in radiocarbon-dated cores from ombrotrophic peat bogs in Spain and Switzerland, and from additional investigations of Swedish lakes, have also demonstrated the ubiquitous nature of the Roman lead peak.[30] This peak is also visible in the sediment of a lake on the Kola peninsula in Russia.[31] The size of these peaks is sometimes less pronounced than in the Greenland ice cores, which indicate a level of activity not seen paralleled again until the European industrial revolution. Thus, the Roman pollution peak, in the northern Swedish lake Kassjön, is lower than the twelfth-century AD peak caused by medieval silver extraction in Germany. Conversely, the analysis of a peat bog in north-west Spain showed a much larger increase in lead deposition during the second and first centuries BC, presumably because of its relative proximity to the mine workings in southern Spain.[32] But the trends in all these investigations are very similar, with all of them showing synchronous increases in lead deposition during the second and first centuries BC. This can be seen in Fig. 3.1.

This evidence, then, shows that, at the time of which Polybius was writing, smelting activities from silver and lead mining in Spain were creating rising levels of atmospheric pollution over Greenland and Europe. It also provides a striking confirmation of Strabo's description of atmospheric pollution from silver mining in southern Spain: '*τὰς δὲ τοῦ ἀργύρου καμίνους ποιοῦσιν ὑψηλάς, ὥστε τὴν ἐκ τῶν βώλων λιγνὺν μετέωρον ἐξαίρεσθαι· βαρεῖα γάρ ἐστι καὶ ὀλέθριος*'[33] (they build their silver-smelting furnaces tall, so that the thick smoke from the ore is carried high into the air; for it is heavy and deadly). It is important to emphasize that the nature of silver extraction, during the second century, was probably very different from the large-scale opencast operations in the goldfields of north-west Spain under the early Principate. The guiding principle in the collection of ores for smelting is, naturally, the expenditure of the minimum effort. Underground mining in the Roman period was, therefore, a last resort, reserved for precious metals. Only when opencast mining became impractical did any tunnelling take place, for example at the gold mines of Dolaucothi in south-west Wales.[34] But argentiferous ore normally runs in veins deep underground and tunnelling, often to a great depth, is usually unavoidable. Archaeological and literary evidence suggests that, although large opencast pits did occur, tunnelling was the usual

[29] Rosman et al. 1997. Friedman (forthcoming) gives a less optimistic view of the credibility of the data for atmospheric pollution.

[30] Spain: Martínez-Cortizas et al. 1997, 2000; Switzerland: Shotyk et al. 1998, 2001; Sweden: Renberg et al. 2000, Brännvall et al. 1997, 1999. A good overview is provided by Renberg et al. (2001). 'Ombrotrophic' refers to soil that receives all its water and nutrients from precipitation rather than from streams or springs. Ombrotrophic peat bogs therefore only record *atmospheric* lead deposition.

[31] Renberg et al. 2000: 151. [32] Renberg et al. 2001: 515.

[33] Strabo, 3. 2. 8. [34] Greene 1986: 144–5; Stewart 2002: 71, 78–80.

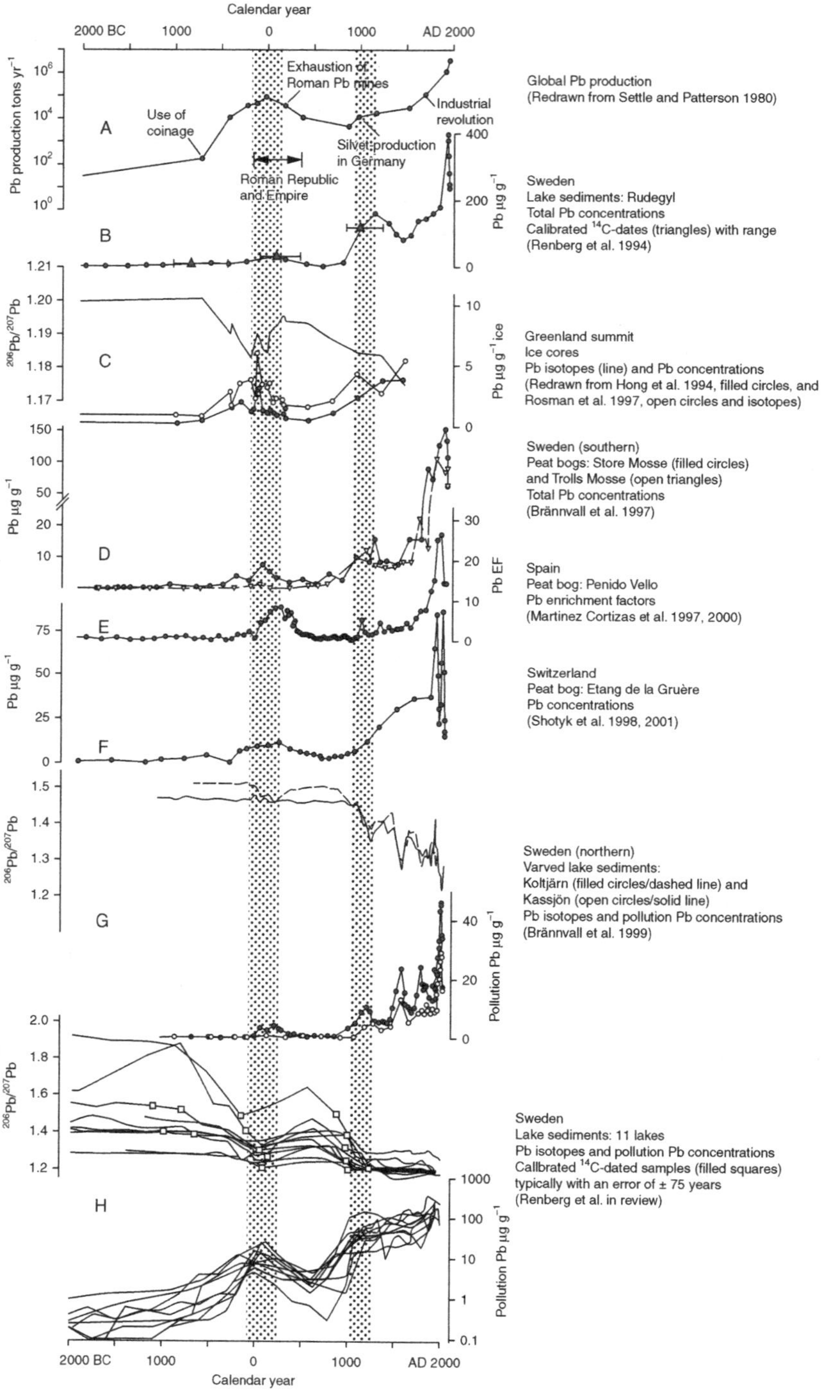

Fig. 3.1. Lead records for the period from 2000 BC to AD 2000 showing the historical production of lead (A), together with published data from studies on the long-term development of atmospheric lead pollution (B–H). The two vertical shaded bars indicate the peak in Roman lead production (100 BC to AD 200) and the Medieval increase in lead pollution (AD 1000–1200).

method employed in the mines near Carthago Nova, with a network of narrow veins being mined and deep shafts being sunk.[35] Richardson interpreted the narrow galleries, which appeared to allow access only to restricted numbers of workers at a time, to indicate small-scale operations which employed limited numbers of men in each mine and which, in general, did not correspond with a large-scale enterprise.[36] The data from the above analyses of Roman lead pollution would tend to disprove his conclusion, but his comments have implications for the methods, institutions, and organizational structures the Romans used in the process of metal extraction from the silver mines of Spain.

PUBLICANI

The Spanish mines must have fallen into the hands of the Romans in 209, when Scipio captured Carthago Nova. But it is not clear whether they were exploited immediately. According to the author of I Maccabees, Judas Maccabaeus had heard in the 160s of how the Romans had seized the gold and silver mines in Spain and so, if this tradition was accurate, the Spanish mines were presumably operating in Roman hands by then.[37] Scholarly opinion has, however, been divided, first, as to whether this exploitation began immediately after the capture of Carthago Nova or at some other date during the early part of the second century and, secondly, as to the role of the *publicani* in the process.

The date at which the Romans started to exploit the mines is unknown. Since there is no mention of any form of mining by the Romans in our sources until 195, Domergue believes that there was no mineral extraction between 209 and 195, because the necessities of war would have had priority over mining works. In addition, he believes that the Punic system of exploitation, whatever it was, had probably disappeared, which made for an inevitable delay before the introduction of another procedure.[38] He recognizes that Rome was in desperate need of great quantities of precious metal, but believes that these were provided by booty, beginning with that captured by Scipio at Carthago Nova.[39] Frank, on the other hand, believes that Scipio would have continued to exploit the mines, after presumably taking them over in 209, and would have immediately placed the slaves in the Carthaginian mines under the direction of the Roman engineers. Scipio, he argues, would hardly have closed them, since, at the time, Rome was in great need of money.[40]

The first mention we have of Roman exploitation comes in Livy, who says that in 195, Cato, 'having pacified the province [of Hispania Citerior], imposed great taxes on the iron and silver mines, from which point the province daily became

[35] Diod. Sic. 5. 36. 4–37. 2; Davies 1935: 109–10: 'the workings descend to a depth of 300 metres, with no ordered system of levels'; J. S. Richardson 1976: 145.

[36] J. S. Richardson 1976: 145–6.

[37] I Macc. 8.3: *καὶ ὅσα ἐποίησαν ἐν χώρᾳ Σπανίας τοῦ κατακρατησâι τῶν μετάλλων τοῦ ἀργυρίου καὶ τοῦ χρυσίου τοῦ ἐκεî.*

[38] Domergue 1990: 249.

[39] Livy, 26. 47. 7–8; Domergue 1990: 250.

[40] Frank 1933: 154–5.

richer' (pacata provincia, vectigalia magna instituit ex ferrariis argentariisque quibus tum institutis locupletior in dies provincia fuit).[41] This seems to be a reasonably straightforward statement, suggesting that Cato took measures to extract revenue for the Roman state from the iron and silver mines.[42] Indeed, Cato's enthusiasm for the mineral resources of southern Spain is made clear in a sentence from his lost work, the *Origines*, which is quoted by Aulus Gellius: 'Nam cum de Hispanis scriberet qui citra Hiberum colunt, verba haec posuit: 'Set in his regionibus ferrariae, argentifodinae pulcherrimae'[43] (For writing about the Spaniards who live on this side of the Ebro, he set down these words: 'But in these districts are the finest iron and silver mines').[44] It seems likely that Livy would have made reference to the reopening of the mines, if that is what Cato had done; but instead, the Livian passage suggests that *vectigalia* are being imposed on something that is already operational. It is possible, therefore, that the Romans had already begun to work the mines in a limited way before 195 BC. A passage of Polybius suggests that the Roman army was capable of improvization when it came to maintaining 'business as usual'. He says that Scipio, after the fall of Carthago Nova, said of two thousand captured *χειροτέχναι* (craftsmen) that for the time being they would become the public property of Rome (*διότι δημόσιοι τῆς Ῥώμης εἰσί*) and appointed a Roman overseer over every group of thirty.[45] Perhaps similar arrangements were instituted in some of the mines.

It is even possible that the *publicani* themselves were immediately involved in the Spanish mines after their capture by Scipio, since they were already active in Rome in 214, arming the fleet and supplying the Spanish army.[46] But it seems more likely that it was indeed in 195 that Cato handed over responsibility for exploiting the mines to them. There are three arguments in favour of this. The first is that Livy, as we have just seen, states that Cato instituted *vectigalia magna*, and some kind of process for collecting them must have been introduced at the same time. Secondly, the sheer scale of the mining operations themselves would have required a high degree of professional management.[47] Thirdly, when we do come across mention of mines being worked in other parts of Rome's embryonic empire, *publicani* are always involved in the process. Thus, Livy defines the doctrine of the state in regard to state-owned mines, when discussing the closure of the Macedonian ones in 167, as follows: 'nam neque sine publicano exerceri posse'[48] (for [the leases] could not be operated without a *publicanus*). Strabo mentions the involvement of *publicani* in the exploitation of mines in the territory of the Salassi in the Alps near Eporedia;[49] as we have seen, Pliny the Elder cites an old law restricting the number of men that the *publicani* could use to work the gold mines at Victumulae in Gallia Cisalpina;[50] and, of course, Polybius talks about the letting of contracts to the *publicani* in connection with the Italian mines.[51]

[41] Livy, 34. 21. 7.

[42] Cato probably took these measures in the name of, and on the order of, the senate, as did Aemilius Paullus in 167, when the senate set out the general outline of the proposed settlement with Macedonia, and the detail was left to Paullus (Livy, 45. 18. 8, 45. 29. 11).

[43] Gell. *NA* 2. 22. 29. [44] Ed. Loeb I 191, slightly revised. [45] Polyb. 10. 17. 9–10.

[46] Livy, 23. 49. 1; see p. 12. [47] Cf. Greene 1986: 147.

[48] Livy, 45. 18. 4; see pp. 54–5. [49] Strabo, 4. 6. 7.

[50] Plin. *HN* 33. 78 (quoted on p. 45). [51] Polyb. 6. 17. 2.

Texts such as these have led a number of modern scholars to the conclusion that the *publicani* had responsibility for the Spanish silver mines from 195.[52] After all, if recourse to the *publicani* was the normal solution elsewhere, then why not in Spain?

But Frank believed that the *publicani* started to exploit the mines only from 179, when the censors M. Aemilius Lepidus and M. Fulvius Nobilior instituted new customs dues and taxes: 'portoria quoque et vectigalia iidem multa instituerunt'[53] (the same censors also instituted many customs duties and taxes). His argument is, first, that in 195 Cato would not have reorganized the mines so as to give a role to the *publicani*, because he was not on friendly terms with the *equites*; and would not therefore have surrendered (assumed) state supervision in favour of 'equestrian control'.[54] Secondly, the largest body of evidence on Roman withdrawal of precious metal from Spain is Livy's record of the amounts of silver, gold, and minted coin brought back to Rome by various governors.[55] Frank believed that, prior to 178, this booty included mining revenues, since after that date the amounts of booty declined.

Frank's hypothesis, however, appears unlikely for a number of reasons. To begin with, Cato's hostility to the *publicani* did not manifest itself until later, in 184, during his and Valerius Flaccus' censorship.[56] Secondly, although none of the amounts is described by Livy as *praeda*, it is significant that all but one of the eighteen reports of Spanish bullion is in the context of claims for a triumph or *ovatio* (the exception is M. Marcellus in 168[57]). It seems highly improbable that the senate would have allowed a returning general either to have included mined bullion in their triumphs or to have made a personal claim (i.e. taken *manubiae*) on spoils of this kind.[58] Thirdly, the booty, before 178, contained large quantities of gold, and the gold mines of Spain are situated in the north-west and were not exploited by the Romans until the time of Augustus. The only source of gold nearer to the Mediterranean, at Bilbilis, is not mentioned until the Imperial period.[59] Finally, there are other explanations for the decline in the amounts of booty that Livy records as having been brought to Rome: the level of fighting going on in Spain between 179 and 154 fell dramatically and, in any case, of course, Livy's history breaks off in 167. Only in the case of L. Manlius Acidinus, returning from Hispania Citerior in 185, is there any suggestion of money that was not part of accumulated booty. In addition to the booty he claimed to have brought back, Acidinus reported that his quaestor was about to deposit 80 pounds of gold and 10,000 pounds of silver.[60] This was probably the surplus on the money collected during the two years he was in his *provincia*, and the fact that he mentioned it at all suggests that the sum was unusually high.

Richardson, on the other hand, takes a more extreme view, emphasizing that nothing is actually said by Livy about the nature of the taxes introduced by Cato in

52 Listed at Domergue 1990: 244 n. 25; most influential are Brunt 1988: 150 and Badian 1972: 31.

53 Livy, 40. 51. 8; Frank 1933: 154–5.

54 Livy, 39. 44. 8; Plut. *Cat. Mai.* 19.

55 Collected in Van Norstrand 1937: 129, and more accurately in Etienne 1958: 94.

56 Livy, 39. 44. 7–9.

57 Livy, 45. 4. 1.

58 Badian (1972: 125 n. 21) highlights the randomness of the amounts of booty.

59 Although, as we have seen (n. 37), the author of I Maccabees does mention gold mines.

60 Livy, 39. 29. 6–7.

195: 'The probability is that the administrative machinery developed *ad hoc*, and that it was not, at least in the early days, the heavily centralized method of five-year contracts assigned to the *societates publicanorum* by the censors in Rome. The evidence indicates a series of much smaller-scale operations.'[61] He argues that the exploitation, on behalf of the Roman state, of the silver mines in Spain was simply one facet of the exploitation of the newly acquired province as a whole;[62] and that the methods of revenue collection probably developed in response to the conditions on the spot, rather than being imposed from the centre.[63] In particular, he points to Posidonius (quoted by Strabo), who seems to indicate small-scale, private enterprise, when he says that: 'individuals (τίνες ἰδιωτῶν) can make a Euboeic talent in three days'.[64] There is also Diodorus' statement that 'later on, after the Romans had conquered Iberia, a large number of Italians flocked to the mines and made great fortunes, on account of their greed. For they buy a large number of slaves and hand them over to those overseeing the mining operations' (ὕστερον δὲ τῶν Ῥωμαίων κρατησάντων τῆς Ἰβηρίας, πλῆθος Ἰταλῶν ἐπεπόλασε τοῖς μετάλλοις, καὶ μεγάλους ἀνεφέροντο πλούτους διὰ τὴν φιλοκερδίαν. ὠνούμενοι γὰρ πλῆθος ἀνδραπόδων παραδιδοῦσι τοῖς ἐφεστηκόσι ταῖς μεταλλικαῖς ἐργασίαις).[65]

'This report of individual effort and individual profits', says Richardson, 'sounds much more like a nineteenth century gold-rush than the operations of the great financiers of the republic.'[66] Individual enterprise is, he believes, also suggested by the results of underwater archaeology, which has furnished a large number of ingots of lead (as much as a 300:1 by-product of the silver extraction process), stamped with the names of their producers, of which several come from the mines of Carthago Nova. The oldest come from the end of the second century BC, and carry the names of individuals. Only a handful of examples of inscriptions on lead ingots have survived that explicitly mention *societates publicanorum* in connection with silver.[67]

As Domergue says, Richardson's work was useful in that it showed that there may not have been a single administrative model. 'If, as seems reasonable, it was the tax farming of the silver and iron mines of Spain which Cato instituted, the possibility of tendering was theoretically open to all the categories of *publicani*, the great societies as well as the small enterprises.'[68] After all, Polybius does not say that the 40,000 workers all belonged to one enterprise and it could well have been a mixture of large and small *societates*, as well as individual enterpreneurs who leased the right to exploit the mines.

[61] J. S. Richardson 1976: 147, criticized by Brunt (1988: 150).

[62] For the other types of taxation in Spain, see pp. 55–6.

[63] J. S. Richardson 1976: 151; cf. Ñaco 2006, 2007.

[64] Strabo, 3. 2. 9 = Posidonius *FGrH* IIA 87 F. 47; cf. Diod. Sic. 5. 36. 2; J. S. Richardson 1976: 141–2.

[65] Diod. Sic. 5. 36. 3–4.

[66] J. S. Richardson 1976: 142. But cf. Polyb. 6. 17. 3, where πλῆθος seems to designate *publicani*; see Ch. 9 n. 66.

[67] Domergue 1990: Tableau X, pp. 256–7, nos. 1045 (*AE* 1907: 135), 1040 (unedited), 1044 (*CIL* XV 7916): SOCIET.ARGENT.FOD.MONT.ILUCR.GALENA, 1041 (Parker 1992: 45), 1042 (Parker 1992: 252); Liou and Pomey 1986: 564. For *galena*, see Plin. *HN* 33. 95, 34. 173 and this chapter p. 46.

[68] Domergue 1990: 251.

In fact, it does appear that the majority, at least, of the Spanish mines were in state ownership during most of the second century, and probably also during the early first century. Polybius, as we have seen, states that the Roman *demos* received 25,000 drachmas every day from the mines near Carthago Nova, while Strabo (who was writing early in the first century AD) says that, by his time, the silver mines of Carthago Nova and elsewhere were no longer δημόσια, but had become private property, implying that they had been in public ownership at some unspecified point in the past.[69] Having said that, we have no evidence as to the precise legal status of this state ownership, nor do we know when or why the change from state to private ownership happened. In 63 BC, Cicero mentions *agri publici* near to Carthago Nova and it is possible that these included the silver mines.[70] But, if this was the case, then it is difficult to explain away the assertion of Plutarch that Crassus personally owned numerous silver mines.[71] On the other hand, Crassus' mines might, for example, have been in Greece rather than in Spain. The evidence is therefore ambiguous and the issue is at present incapable of resolution. Our tentative conclusion would be that the upheaval and confiscations of the Sullan period probably gave the opportunity for the surviving rich to accumulate investments in silver mines, in which case the Spanish mines would not have been part of the *agri publici* mentioned by Cicero in the *De lege agraria*.

But Richardson raises one final potential problem.[72] If the mines were in state ownership, it may still be considered strange that Polybius' description of the income from the Carthago Nova mines as 25,000 drachmas *per day* does not correspond with the standard modalities of the censorial *locatio*. The usual method of contracting to the *publicani* at Rome was through the censors, with the *publicani* paying lump sums for the right of exploitation during the five-year period of the censors' *lustrum*.[73] As Richardson says: 'If this was the system employed in the New Carthage mines, then the amount of silver produced daily was strictly speaking irrelevant to the amount of cash accruing to the Roman people.' But do we really need to be so pedantic about Polybius' formulation? Polybius was no doubt impressed by the amount of revenue produced for the Roman state by the Spanish mines and was looking to make an impact on his readers. Rather than giving a large but meaningless figure for the value of a five-year contract, he would have looked for a striking characterization, and it would have been natural for him to translate this into a daily amount, having more relevance for his Greek readership. After all, Posidonius does the same, when he talks of individuals making a Euboeic talent in three days.[74]

We should follow Polybius' testimony, which does not contradict the framework we have assumed for Cato's measures, and conclude that, in the second century, the Spanish silver mines did belong to the state, since it was to the *demos* that the revenues went; that the *publicani* were responsible for exploiting them; and that they were given this privilege in 195 by Cato. As to the revenue that accrued to the Roman state, the only evidence is Polybius' assertion that the amount was 25,000 drachmas per day, at a time that was probably in the late 150s. Any attempts to quantify the

[69] Strabo, 3. 2. 10. [70] Cic. *Leg. agr.* 1. 5; 2. 51.
[71] Plut. *Crass.* 5: ὄντων δ' αὐτῷ παμπόλλων ἀργυρείων. [72] J. S. Richardson 1976: 142.
[73] See pp. 80–2. [74] Strabo, 3. 2. 9 = Posidonius *FGrH* IIA 87 F. 47.

revenues from the Spanish mines for the earlier part of the century are unfortunately pure guesswork, although one would probably not be too far off the mark to suppose that there was a gradual build-up in revenue from the late 190s onwards.

MACEDONIA

Following Rome's victory in the Third Macedonian War over Perseus in 167, and in the same year in which it suspended the collection of *tributum* from its own citizens, Aemilius Paullus, acting on instructions from the senate, closed the Macedonian gold and silver mines. But he permitted the iron and copper mines to continue in operation at half the *vectigal* that had previously been paid to the Macedonian king:[75] 'Metalla quoque auri atque argenti non exerceri, ferri et aeris permitti. Vectigal exercentibus dimidium eius impositum quod pependissent regi'[76] (furthermore, the mines of gold and silver were not to be worked, but those of iron and copper were permitted. The tax on those who worked the mines was set at half what they had paid the king).[77]

Two ancient authors, Livy and Diodorus Siculus, give the reasons for the decision of the senate to close the bullion mines. Livy's account states:

> Metalli quoque Macedonici, quod ingens vectigal erat, locationes praediorumque rusticorum tolli placebat; nam neque sine publicano exerceri posse et, ubi publicanus esset, ibi aut ius publicum vanum aut libertatem sociis nullam esse. Ne ipsos quidem Macedonas id exercere posse; ubi in medio praeda administrantibus esset, ibi numquam causas seditionum et certaminis defore.[78]
>
> (It was also decided not to lease out the Macedonian mines, a source of immense revenue, or the crown lands. For the leases could not be operated without a *publicanus* and, where there was a *publicanus*, either the state was deprived of its right, or there was no freedom for the allies. Nor could the Macedonians themselves operate the leases, for where booty was available to those overseeing the process, there would never be a lack of reasons for conspiracies and strife.)

Livy, then, attributes the decision partly to distrust of the *publicani* and partly to the senate's fear of a Macedonian insurrection funded by the revenues from the mines, if the Macedonians themselves were allowed to exploit them.

Diodorus' account basically agrees with that of Livy. The senate, he says,

> did away with the income from the gold and silver mines, in order to avoid injury to the local inhabitants [sc. from the *publicani*] and to avoid anyone being able, with the support of the money acquired from the mines, to rebel in the hope of seizing the kingdom of Macedonia.
>
> (*κατέλυσαν δὲ καὶ τὰς ἐκ τῶν μετάλλων ἀργύρου καὶ χρυσοῦ προσόδους διά τε τὸ τῶν ἐνοικούντων ἀνεπηρέαστον καὶ ὅπως μή τινες μετὰ ταῦτα νεωτερίζοιεν διὰ τῶν χρημάτων ἀνακτώμενοι τὴν Μακεδόνων ἀρχήν.*)[79]

[75] The new rate was 100 talents p.a., according to Plut. *Aem.* 28. 6. In addition, royal land was taken over as Roman *ager publicus* (Cic. *Leg. agr.* 1. 5; 2. 50).

[76] Livy, 45. 29. 11.

[77] Trans. Loeb XIII p. 349.

[78] Livy, 45. 18. 3–5.

[79] Diod. Sic. 31. 8. 7.

And indeed, according to Livy, Perseus had relied heavily on money from the mines and, in his preparations for war with Rome, had reopened abandoned workings and started new ones.[80]

But Richardson argues that the first of the two reasons that Livy attributes to the senate for the closure of the mines, distrust of the *publicani*, looks odd.[81] As we saw earlier, Livy's comment, 'nam neque sine publicano exercere posse', suggests that the *publicani* were considered to be the normal solution to the problem of how to exploit the mines. But Livy then goes on to give what Richardson regards as an unlikely reason for not involving them in the process. He argues that the concept of the absence of *ius publicum*, 'the right of the state', is anachronistic, and the reference to lack of 'freedom' (*libertas*) for Rome's allies even more so. Richardson believes that Livy's pejorative reference to the *publicani* is more applicable to the first century than to the second. However, on balance, Brunt's interpretation is probably to be preferred. He suggests that 'the agreement between Diodorus Siculus 31. 8. 7 and Livy 41. 18. 3–5 shows that Livy's specific reference to the *publicani* is not his own interpretation anachronistically imported from the later influence of the publicans, which already in 169 had all but ruined a censor (Livy, 43. 16), but surely drew on a fuller statement in [sc. a lost passage of] Polybius'.[82]

But the more important question for us is a financial one: why did the Romans, whatever their reasons for closing the Macedonian mines in 167, feel able to forgo the revenues from them for the period 167 to 158? The fact remains that if they had been desperate for money, they would presumably have found some way to exploit them, and part of the reason for their disinclination to do so may have been that the Romans did not have an immediate fiscal need for the output of the mines. In fact, the indications are that their state finances in the aftermath of the Third Macedonian War were very healthy.

After defeating Perseus in 167, Aemilius Paullus brought back to Rome a sum of HS 120 million (5,000 talents) as well as the revenues from the sale of 150,000 Epirote slaves, which, as we have seen, were probably worth somewhere between 1,700 and 10,000 talents.[83] The combined value of the indemnities and booty which Rome had received over the course of the previous thirty-four years had been something of the order of 42,000 talents, and Pliny the Elder explicitly states that it was after receiving the booty of Paullus that Rome ceased to tax its citizens.[84] In addition, the Romans imposed a *stipendium* of 100 talents per annum on the Macedonians and they still had 200 talents per annum coming in from Carthage. These amounts were bolstered by the revenues that they were receiving from Spain, both in the form of mined bullion (1,500 talents per annum in the late 150s, but probably less in the 160s) and taxation on the local population. The date at which the Romans began to tax Spain is unknown, but Cicero

[80] Livy, 39. 24. 2; 45. 40. 2.

[81] J. S. Richardson 1976: 144.

[82] Brunt 1988.

[83] See p. 30.

[84] Plin. *HN* 33. 56: 'a quo tempore populus Romanus tributum pendere desiit' (from which time the Roman people ceased to pay tribute); cf. Cic. *Off.* 2. 76; Plut. *Aem.* 38. We do not know the value of the *tributum simplex*. De Sanctis (1916: ii. 626) estimated it at 900,000 denarii (150 talents) p. a. during the Second Punic War. Frank (1932: 139) thought it might be 2 million denarii (330 talents) p.a. at the time of its abolition.

makes clear that the main tax was a fixed monetary payment (*vectigal certum stipendiarium*) as distinct from the *decumae* of the Sicilian system.[85] Harris believes that the start of taxation in Spain can be dated back to the beginning of Roman rule there, but there is no concrete evidence for this.[86] Richardson argues that in Spain before 180, *stipendium* had not developed beyond its original meaning of 'money to pay the army', and that it was levied ad hoc and at the instance of the governor.[87] The date at which this ad hoc collection was replaced in Spain by the *vectigal certum* cannot be established with certainty, but the most likely time is during the reorganization carried out in the governorship of Ti. Sempronius Gracchus in Hither Spain in 179. As mentioned earlier, Appian talks of taxes being imposed on the defeated Celtiberians.[88] These taxes would also suit the context of the 'carefully defined treaties' (συνθήκας ἀκριβεῖς) that Gracchus is said by Appian to have instituted.[89] The *stipendium* may have amounted to 600 talents, if we are correct to identify the *phoros* of 600 talents, which, according to Posidonius, was exacted by M. Claudius Marcellus from Celtiberia in 152, with the regular assessment.[90] In the 160s, therefore, the Romans could have been receiving anywhere between 900 talents' and 2,400 talents' worth of silver bullion annually, depending on when the Spanish mines started to contribute revenue and what the amounts were.

How much expertise in financial management can we attribute to the Roman senate? Surely enough for us to suggest that a senate which could decide that it had sufficient holdings of bullion to suspend a tax on its own citizens could also decide that it had sufficient resources not to need to exploit the Macedonian gold and silver mines for the time being. And there was a precedent: we have already seen how Pliny the Elder states that, at some point, the mines in Italy were closed by what he terms 'an old *senatus consultum*'.[91]

However, Cassiodorus, writing in the sixth century AD, says that, in 158 BC, the Romans did start to exploit the Macedonian mines: 'M. Aemilius et C. Popillius . . . His conss. metalla in Macedonia instituta'[92] (M. Aemilius and C. Popillius . . . When they were consuls, the mines in Macedonia were set in operation). This reference to

[85] Cic. *II Verr.* 3. 12 (quoted on p. 22) makes an explicit contrast between the 'vectigal certum' and the 'censoria locatio . . . ut Asiae lege Sempronia' (referring to C. Gracchus' *lex de provincia Asia*).

[86] Harris 1989: 129–30.

[87] J. S. Richardson 1976: 147–9; see p. 22.

[88] App. *Hisp.* 44: *φόρους τοὺς ὁρισθέντας ἐπὶ Γράκχου.*

[89] App. *Hisp.* 43.

[90] Strabo, 3. 4. 13 (= Posidonius *FGrH* IIA 87 F. 51). In addition to the *vectigal certum*, it is virtually certain that, at some date before 171, a 5 per cent levy (*vicensima*) had been imposed on at least some of Rome's Spanish allies. A passage in Livy (43. 2. 12) describing regulations laid down by the senate in 171 implies that there was already a system in place: 'in futurum tamen consultum ab senatu Hispanis, quod impetrarunt, ne frumenti aestimationem magistratus Romanus haberet neve cogeret vicensimas vendere Hispanos quanti ipse vellet' (for the future, however, a decree of the senate gave the Spaniards what they had requested: that no Roman magistrate should determine the value of corn, or compel the Spaniards to sell the *vicensimae* at any price he wished). J. S. Richardson (1976: 149) connects it with the governorships of Gracchus and Albinus in 180–178 and assumes it to be a corn levy. Lintott (1993: 73) believes it may have been a *portorium*.

[91] Plin. *HN* 3. 138, 33. 78, 37. 202. Harris (1979: 62 n. 1) believes that this was probably a short-lived provision immediately following the conquest of Italy.

[92] Cassiod. *Chron. sub anno* 158 BC; Crawford (1974: 74 n. 3) gives the verb as *reperta*, but Mommsen (1861: 616), on the basis of his readings of the manuscripts, gives *instituta*. The mines already existed, so *instituta* has the sense of 'set in operation': cf. Livy, 39. 24. 2.

the reopening of the mines is one of the very few events mentioned in Cassiodorus' *Chronicon*, which is otherwise a list of Roman kings, consuls, and emperors (Polybius' and Livy's accounts of this period survive only in summarized or fragmentary form, if at all). Clearly, for Cassiodorus or his sources, the reopening of the Macedonian bullion mines was a very significant occurrence. Assuming, therefore, that Cassiodorus is representing an accurate tradition in allocating the reopening to 158, we would be inclined to the view that the *publicani*, rather than the Macedonians, were involved in working the mines, on the basis of Livy's statement that it was impossible for a mine to be exploited without the involvement of the *publicani*.[93] But why did the senate decide to reopen them at this point?

We know from Pliny the Elder that, at an unspecified point in 157, the year after the Macedonian mines had reopened, the *aerarium* contained the equivalent of 3,000 talents.[94] This was not a negligible amount; it was enough to pay the cost of six legions, the average military deployment at this time, for three years. Nevertheless a lot of money had left the *aerarium* in the intervening ten years, and Rome had not secured any further war indemnities or any significant booty during that period. Although the Spanish mines must, by this stage, have been generating close to the 1,500 talents per annum in revenues for the state which Polybius suggests they were producing by the late 150s, the reopening of the Macedonian mines in politically more stable conditions would have been an obvious way to increase revenues.[95]

One final point is worth making. Polybius reports that in his time (ἐφ' ἑαυτοῦ) a gold mine was discovered not far from Aquileia which was very easy to work and which produced very pure gold. He goes on to say that 'within two months, the price of gold in the whole of Italy fell by a third' (ἐν διμήνῳ, παραχρῆμα τὸ χρυσίον εὐωνότερον γενέσθαι τῷ τρίτῳ μέρει καθ' ὅλην τὴν Ἰταλίαν).[96] We do not know the precise date at which this happened and Gruen is right to dismiss Perelli's conjecture that the Macedonian mines were closed because an oversupply of metal 'depressed its value and fed inflation'.[97] Nevertheless, the behaviour of the price of gold after the discovery of the Aquileia mine must at least have taught the senate some home truths about supply and demand. When we put the closure of the Macedonian mines beside the events surrounding the indemnity of Antiochus

93 Livy, 45. 18. 4; so Badian (1972: 44), contra Gruen (1984: 306).

94 Plin. *HN* 33. 55–6; see p. 22 for the details of the holdings. The manuscripts inadequately preserve the figures that Pliny gave for the holdings of the *aerarium* in the years 157, 91, and 49 BC, and the only record that appears to be complete is that for 157. So we do not know the value of the treasury's holdings in 49. It is not, therefore, clear whether the sentence, 'nec fuit aliis temporibus res publica locupletior' (nor was the Republic richer at any other times), which comes at the end of the corrupt list of the holdings in 49, refers just to the value of the holdings in that year, or, in addition, to the values of the holdings in 157 and 91, which immediately precede it.

95 There was a small amount of booty from Illyria, after the defeat of Perseus in 167 (Livy, 45. 43. 4). After that Livy is lost, but other sources report only four further small-scale triumphs before 146.

96 Polyb. 34. 10. 10–15 = Strabo, 4. 6. 12. The location is possibly Carinthia in modern south-west Austria, but no certain identification is possible: Walbank 1979: 612.

97 Perelli 1975; Gruen 1984: 427 n. 159. Implicit in Perelli's view is the assumption that the senate had an understanding of the linkage between a growing money supply and 'inflation'; this must be anachronistic; cf. Howgego 1995: 121ff.

III (discussed on pp. 38–42), we can begin to see evidence of the senate's intuitive and growing (if still dim) awareness of the ways in which state finances might be managed.

CONCLUSION

Our principal thesis in this book is that, in second-century Rome, increased inflows of bullion combined with an expansion in the availability of credit to produce a large increase in monetary liquidity, which in turn resulted in a major inflection in Roman economic activity and complexity. Both Polybius and the archaeological record suggest that, by the mid-second century, significant quantities of bullion were being mined in Spain. The region around Carthago Nova probably saw the initial focus of Roman mining activity and Polybius provides the only surviving contemporary description of these operations. He tells us that 40,000 workers were producing 25,000 drachmas per day (about 1,500 talents per annum) for the Roman *demos*. That is equivalent to approximately 35 tonnes of silver per annum. Polybius' evidence is supported by the extraction rates implied by the investigations that have been conducted on the ice cap of Greenland, and on lakes and peat bogs in Spain, Switzerland, Sweden, and Russia. The data from these studies show that, during the period of which Poybius was writing, smelting activities from silver and lead mining in Spain created levels of atmospheric pollution high enough to be measurable over Greenland and Europe.

Polybius does not give details of the organizational structure by which the Roman *demos* obtained its silver bullion. But we do have evidence from a variety of ancient authors for Roman mining activities in other parts of the Mediterranean at this period. This suggests that the exploitation of the mines in Spain, which were in public ownership during the second and early first centuries, was chiefly handled by the *societates publicanorum*, who were given this privilege by Cato in 195 BC.

The Romans acquired the gold and silver mines of Macedonia in 167, but immediately closed them. Livy and Diodorus attribute this decision partly to distrust of the *publicani* and partly to the senate's fear of a Macedonian insurrection, funded by the revenues from the mines, if the Macedonians themselves were allowed to exploit them. But the senate was only able to make this decision to close the mines because, in 167, the Roman state, flush with Aemilius Paullus' booty, did not need the revenues. However, by 158, with no further indemnities or booty arriving in the *aerarium*, there was a requirement for new sources of revenue. Both the closure and the reopening of the Macedonian mines can therefore be attributed in large part to the varying financial requirements of the Roman state.

4

State Finance and the *lex Sempronia de provincia Asia*

vectigalia opulentissimarum provinciarum.[1]

INTRODUCTION

In examining the economic history of Rome during the first half of the second century, we have charted an emerging awareness of basic financial management at a state level on the part of the senate. The *plebiscitum Claudianum*, the Antiochus indemnity, the closure of the Macedonian mines—all combine to indicate that senators were becoming more financially aware.

With Gaius Gracchus, however, we have the first clearly identifiable attempt by an individual Roman magistrate to produce a systematic state budget in support of a massive programme of public expenditure. The economic programme on which he embarked during his tribunates in 123 and 122 covered grain subsidies, military and agrarian reform, colonial foundations, and infrastructure spending. The cost, although now incalculable, must have been enormous and a new source of income was needed in order to finance it. C. Gracchus' solution was to come up with a new, robust method of provincial exploitation through his *lex Sempronia de provincia Asia*. In this chapter we shall examine the background to this law and consider the chronology of the introduction of Roman taxation in Asia, the system of revenue collection which C. Gracchus introduced, and his economic motives for doing so.

THE *LEX SEMPRONIA DE PROVINCIA ASIA*

The *lex Sempronia de provincia Asia* is not mentioned explicitly by Plutarch or Appian in their accounts of the 120s. But in a speech before the assembled representatives of the Greeks and 'other peoples' in the province of Asia in 41, Marcus Antonius is quoted by Appian as saying that the Romans had freed them

[1] 'The taxes of the wealthiest provinces' (Tac. *Hist.* 3. 8, referring to the eastern provinces).

from paying taxes to Attalus and that it was only with the appearance of demagogues (*δημοκόπων ἀνδρῶν*) that the Romans imposed taxes. Clearly the two things to which Marcus Antonius is referring are the acquistion of the kingdom of Pergamum by the Romans after the death of Attalus III and the *lex Sempronia de provincia Asia* of C. Gracchus:

> *Ὑμᾶς ἡμῖν, ὦ ἄνδρες Ἕλληνες, Ἄτταλος ὁ βασιλεὺς ὑμῶν ἐν διαθήκαις ἀπέλιπε, καὶ εὐθὺς ἀμείνονες ὑμῖν ἦμεν Ἀττάλου· οὓς γὰρ ἐτελεῖτε φόρους Ἀττάλῳ, μεθήκαμεν ὑμῖν, μεχρί, δημοκόπων ἀνδρῶν καὶ παρ᾽ἡμῖν γενομένων, ἐδέησε φόρων. ἐπεὶ δὲ ἐδέησεν, οὐ πρὸς τὰ τιμήματα ὑμῖν ἐπεθήκαμεν, ὡς ἂν ἡμεῖς ἀκίνδυνον φόρον ἐκλέγοιμεν, ἀλλὰ μέρη φέρειν τῶν ἑκάστοτε καρπῶν ἐπετάξαμεν, ἵνα καὶ τῶν ἐναντίων κοινωνῶμεν ὑμῖν. τῶν δὲ ταῦτα παρὰ τῆς βουλῆς μισθουμένων ἐνυβριζόντων ὑμῖν καὶ πολὺ πλείονα αἰτούντων, Γάιος Καῖσαρ τῶν μὲν χρημάτων τὰ τρίτα ὑμῖν ἀνῆκεν ὧν ἐκείνοις ἐφέρετε, τὰς δ᾽ὕβρεις ἔπαυσεν· ὑμῖν γὰρ τοὺς φόρους ἐπέτρεψεν ἀγείρειν παρὰ τῶν γεωργούντων.*[2]
>
> (Greeks! Attalus, your king, left you to us in his will and immediately we were better to you than Attalus. For we released you from the taxes that you had been paying to him until the action of the demagogues who arose amongst us made taxes necessary. But when they became necessary, we did not impose them upon you according to a fixed valuation, so that we could collect an absolutely certain sum. We required you to contribute a portion of your yearly harvest so that we might also share with you the difficult times. When those who collected these taxes on the authority of the senate abused you by demanding much more, Gaius Caesar remitted to you one-third of the amount you were giving the collectors and stopped the abuses; for he turned over to you the collection of the taxes from those who farm the land.)

Until the discovery of the inscription of the *Senatus Consultum de Agro Pergameno* (*RDGE* 12) in the late nineteenth century, the general view was that Appian was right and that no revenues were collected by the Romans in Asia until the *lex* of C. Gracchus was enacted in 123/122.[3] Support for this view was provided by a text from Diodorus which referred to C. Gracchus having given the right to collect revenue to the *publicani*: '*τῇ μὲν τῶν δημοσιωνῶν τόλμῃ καὶ πλεονεξίᾳ τὰς ἐπαρχίας ἀπορρίψας ἐπεσπάσατο παρὰ τῶν ὑποτεταγμένων δίκαιον μῖσος κατὰ τῆς ἡγεμονίας*'[4] (he tossed away the provinces to the recklessness and greed of the *publicani* and provoked the subject peoples to a just hatred of Rome's rule). Additional evidence came from Cicero, who makes reference to the *censoria locatio* having been instituted by this law:

> Inter Siciliam ceterasque provincias, iudices, in agrorum vectigalium ratione hoc interest, quod ceteris aut impositum vectigal est certum, quod stipendiarium dicitur, ut Hispanis et plerisque Poenorum quasi victoriae praemium ac poena belli, aut censoria locatio constituta est, ut Asiae lege Sempronia.[5]
>
> (Between Sicily and the other provinces, judges, there is an important difference in the system of land taxation. In the others, either a fixed tax, called a stipendiary tax, has been imposed, as it has been on the Spaniards and most of the Carthaginians, as if it was a reward for victory and a penalty of defeat, or it is let out by the censors, as it is under the Sempronian law concerning Asia.)

[2] App. *B. Civ.* 5. 4. [3] Marquardt 1892: 242. [4] Diod. Sic. 34/35. 25. 1.

[5] Cic. *II Verr.* 3. 12; cf. Fronto, *Ep. ad Ver. Imp.* 2. 1. 13: 'iam Gracchus locabat Asiam et Karthaginem viritim dividebat' (now Gracchus farmed out Asia and divided the territory of Carthage into individual plots).

However, the new inscription suggested that revenue was in fact being collected by the Romans before this date and most scholars since have tended to disbelieve Appian's account.[6] This is because the inscription concerns the resolution by a Roman magistrate of a dispute between the Pergamenes and the *publicani* concerning the boundaries of the Pergamenes. The decree is commonly dated to 129 because it appears to be possible to restore the names of the consuls of that year, C. Sempronius and Manius Aquillius. At line 17 we find: '[*Μάνιος Ἀκ*]*ύλλιος ὕπατος, ν ἐὰν αὐτῶι φαίνηται, ΘΙ* [. . .]' ([Manius Aqu]illius, the consul, [*vacat*] if it seems best to him, THI[. . .]), and, at line 9, '[*καὶ Μάνιος Ἀκύλλιος Γαίος Σεμπρώ*]*νιος ὕπατοι*' ([and Manius Aquillius, Gaius Sempro]nius consuls). It was therefore taken as evidence that the province of Asia continued to be taxed after the death of Attalus, that the *publicani* were already responsible for collecting these taxes (farmed out in the province under the control of the governor), and that the legislation of C. Gracchus merely instituted a change (for example, that the collection of the tithes be let out in Rome by the censors) in a system that was already functioning. In other words, C. Gracchus was merely trying to improve the efficiency of revenue collection. There are variations on this theme. Lintott, for example, believes that it is likely, in view of their general practice, that from 129 the Romans at least drew revenues from *portoria* in Asia and imposed an indemnity or tribute on the cities that had sided with Aristonicus, in addition to the rents on public land.[7] On any of these views, the words put into the mouth of Marcus Antonius by Appian would be regarded as wrong or, more charitably, as severely compressed.

As a result, the questions raised by Rostovtzeff as long ago as 1941 are still relevant: Are we justified in accepting Marcus Antonius' statement in full? When speaking of the temporary immunity of Asia, does Marcus Antonius refer to the period directly after the death of Attalus III or to the reorganization of the province after 129? May we infer from Marcus Antonius and from the above passage of Cicero that before C. Gracchus no *publicani* were active in the province? Rostovtzeff himself believed that the province of Asia was never immune from taxation.[8]

CHRONOLOGY

Badian states that 'after the land of King Attalus became Roman, *publicani* were sent out—no doubt after the next census (131/0)—to collect its revenues'.[9] In fact, there is absolutely no evidence for this assertion.

In late 134 or in the spring of 133, Attalus III Philometor of Pergamum died and bequeathed his kingdom to the Roman people. A variety of ancient authors refer to this act with fascination.[10] It seems that, under the terms of Attalus' will, Pergamum was given its freedom and control of the land around it.[11] Except for

6 Sherk 1969: 71–2 lists the scholars who by that time had supported or rejected the date of 129.

7 Lintott 1994*b*: 35. 8 Rostovtzeff 1941: 813. 9 Badian 1972: 63.

10 Cf. Strabo, 13. 4. 2; Plut. *Ti. Gracch.* 14; Just. *Epit.* 36. 4. 5; App. *Mith.* 62; Livy, *Per.* 59; Flor. 2. 3; Ampel. 33. 3; Eutr. 4. 18; Oros. 5. 8. 4; Euseb. *Chron.* 2. 130–1; Vell. Pat. 2. 4. 1; Val. Max. 5. 2.

11 *OGIS* 338; now confirmed by *SEG* 50. 1211. 11—see p. 63. Presumably the freedom of Pergamum was ratified by the *Senatus Consultum Popillianum de Pergamenis* (*RDGE* no. 11) and put into effect by

a hint in Plutarch that the Romans were to settle the status of the cities included in the kingdom, we have no evidence regarding them.[12] So far as we know, Attalus left everything else to the Romans. This would have included not only the royal treasury and the king's personal belongings, but the royal slaves, workshops, crown lands, private estates, and claims to tribute and service.[13]

Early in the summer of 133, Eudemus of Pergamum brought the will to Rome for ratification, arriving shortly after the passing of an agrarian law by the tribune Tiberius Gracchus. The latter would appear to have heard of the testament first because of his hereditary connections with the Attalids. Both Plutarch and Livy's epitomator suggest that Tiberius, needing money for his ambitious domestic schemes, then proceeded to pass a law to auction the king's personal property and to divide the proceeds amongst the recipients of land under his agrarian law, with Plutarch adding that it was to be used for 'stocking' their farms.[14]

Following the death of Ti. Gracchus and in the following year (132), the senate, once again the undisputed arbiter of foreign affairs, passed the *Senatus Consultum Popillianum de Pergamenis*, ratifying the will of Attalus and guaranteeing his acts and those of his predecessors up to one day before his death.[15] It refused the commissioners, who were to be sent to Asia, the right to change these arrangements.

But in any case, it would appear that the five commissioners who did then go to Asia, under the leadership of the Pontifex Maximus, P. Cornelius Scipio Nasica (*cos.* 138), were prevented from getting far with the organization of the new province by the revolt of Aristonicus, which had probably started in the autumn of the previous year (133).[16] On their return to Rome (without Scipio Nasica, who died after his arrival in Asia), they no doubt communicated the seriousness of the situation in their new province, with the result that the consul of 131, P. Licinius Crassus, was despatched to Asia with a well-equipped army.[17]

The following two years were taken up with the attempts of the Romans to put down the revolt. In the process Licinius Crassus was killed, despite having a large army and the support of Mithradates V, Nicomedes II of Bithynia, Ariarathes V of Cappadocia, and Pylaemenes of Paphlagonia.[18] In the end it was the consul of 130, M. Perperna, who finally defeated Aristonicus himself, but the rebellion seems to have continued well into 129.[19]

the five commissioners who accompanied Scipio Nasica; otherwise *OGIS* 338 would not have been recorded.

[12] Plut. *Ti. Gracch.* 14.

[13] Flor. 1.35: 'populus Romanus bonorum meorum heres esto'; cf. Sen. *Controv.* 2.; the *agri Attalici* of the Thracian Chersonese formed part of the Roman public land (Cic. *Agr.* 2. 50); Hansen 1971: 149.

[14] Livy, *Per.* 58; Plut. *Ti. Gracch.* 14.

[15] *RDGE* no. 11; a secure date has now been established since in lines 3 and 11 the name of the proposer can now be read as Publius Popillius, *cos.* 132 (*SEG* 50. 1212; Wörrle 2000: 566–8).

[16] Plut. *Ti. Gracch.* 21; Val. Max. 5. 3. 2; *ILLRP* 333; Strabo, 14. 1. 38. It is clear, from *OGIS* 339 and *IGRom.* 4. 134, that this commission also met envoys from neighbouring states.

[17] Oros. 5. 10. 1–3; C. P. Jones (2004) believes that *RDGE* no. 11 is a decree passed late in 132 (after the return of the four surviving commissioners), which sent Crassus to Asia.

[18] Strabo, 14. 1. 38; Val. Max. 3. 2. 12; Eutr. 4. 20; Oros. 5. 10. 1–4.

[19] Strabo, 14. 1. 38; Holleaux 1938 : 179–98 ('Le décret de Bargylia en l'honneur de Poseidonios'); Hansen 1971 : 159 n. 150; Lintott 1994*b* : 34 n. 31; C. P. Jones 2004: 485.

As far as we can tell, therefore, from 133 until well into 129, Asia was engulfed in war. It is highly unlikely that during this period '*publicani* were sent out... to collect its revenues'. Indeed it was not until late in 130 (or even early 129) that Perperna, just before he died (of disease) in Asia, was finally able to send the king's personal possessions to Rome for auction, presumably a somewhat simpler task than trying to establish a machinery to collect tax from a large area engulfed in rebellion:[20] 'Perperna... Attalicasque gazas hereditarias populi Romani navibus impositas Romam deportavit'[21] (and Perperna... sent off to Rome by ship the treasures of Attalus, which had been bequeathed to the Roman people). A second group of ten commissioners then accompanied the consul of 129, Manius Aquillius, for the purpose of arranging the affairs of the new province under the terms of the *Senatus Consultum Popillianum de Pergamenis*. Strabo says that 'he organized the province into the scheme which it retained in his own day' (the early first century AD): '*Μάνιος δ' Ἀκύλλιος, ἐπελθὼν ὕπατος μετὰ δέκα πρεσβευτῶν, διέταξε τὴν ἐπαρχίαν εἰς τὸ νῦν ἔτι συμμένον τῆς πολιτείας σχῆμα*'.[22] Strabo's comment cannot be a reference to the overall territorial extent of Asia, which had altered by the Augustan period, nor to any financial arrangements (which had also changed by then). It is also an unnatural way to refer to any road-building activity. It most likely refers to the establishment of the *conventus* or *διοικήσεις* (assize districts) into which Asia was divided and which remained a key element of provincial organization.[23]

An interesting development in our knowledge of the history of this period has been the discovery of an honorary decree for a certain Menodoros, son of Metrodoros, which probably dates from after 125.[24] The relevant part of the inscription is well preserved and clarifies a number of points. First, it makes clear, in line 11, that Pergamum did receive its freedom 'with the establishment of a democracy' after the death of Attalus: '*μεταπεσόντων τε τῶν πραγμάτων εἰς δημοκρατίαν*'. It then goes on to state, at lines 13–14, that at some point 'after this' Menodoros served on the *bouleuterion* associated with the 'Roman law-giving';[25] and finally, at lines 18–20, the document refers to a time 'when the consul Manius Aquillius and the ten commissioners were in Asia'.[26]

The establishment of the *bouleuterion* associated with the Roman *nomothesia* seems to occur some time before the arrival of Aquillius and his legates, and is therefore likely to refer to the initial attempts of Scipio Nasica and his commission of 132 to establish a legal framework in accordance with the *Senatus Consultum Popillianum de Pergamenis*, an attempt which, as we have seen, was interrupted by the revolt of Aristonicus (although the document contains no reference to this event). At any rate the *nomothesia* must have been the fundamental Roman system of laws for the Pergamene community, analogous to the 'constitution

20 Cf. Ñaco 2006, 2007.

21 Just. *Epit.* 36. 4. 9; cf. Varro, fr. 68 ; Plin. *HN* 8. 196, 33. 148–9; Eutr. 4. 20; Oros. 5. 10; Prop. 2. 32. 12; *IPriene* 108. 223f.

22 Strabo, 14. 1. 38.

23 Mitchell 1999: 22.

24 *SEG* 50. 1211; Wörrle 2000; Canali de Rossi 2002: 244–8.

25 *καὶ μετὰ ταῦτα ἐν τῶι κατὰ τὴν Ῥωμαικὴν νομοθεσίαν βουλευ- / τηρίωι γενόμενος.*

26 *ὄντος ἐν τῆι Ἀσίαι Μανίου τε Ἀκυλλίου στρατ[η]- / [γοῦ] ὑπάτου Ῥωμαίων καὶ τῶν δέκα πρεσβευτῶν.*

and laws' (πολιτεία καὶ οἱ νόμοι) and 'the laws on the subject of common jurisdiction' (τοὺς περὶ τῆς κοινῆς δικαιοδοσίας νόμους) which had been devised for the newly annexed areas of Greece in 146.[27] The reference to the commission that accompanied Aquillius in 129 is less enlightening. It does not make any mention of the specific purpose of the commission, but given that Menodoros is praised for his negotiations with the legates, one can reasonably assume that the commission of 129 was in Asia to complete the unfinished business of the one that had visited in 132, that is the Roman *nomothesia*, now that the revolt was dying down. Again though, there is no specific mention of any process of revenue collection by the Romans and certainly there is no reason to infer the presence of *publicani* in the province at this stage.

With the rebellion rumbling on, Aquillius faced an enormous task just in terms of the geopolitical organization of the area that had been bequeathed to the Romans. The lack of official Roman contact with Asia Minor before the death of Attalus III is striking. This is important because the lack of contact suggests also a lack of information. The Romans had no permanent representatives in the Pergamene kingdom before the bequest. Of course Roman mercantile trade was already active in the Aegean and traders would visit Asia Minor.[28] But this would merely have meant that irregular and sometimes no doubt unreliable reports about the situation in Asia would have been fed back to the senate. Prior to the bequest there is no sign of them wanting to be involved in the area either militarily or diplomatically. Ineffectual embassies are dispatched at times of crisis but that is the only commitment. No ships, no troops, no time is dedicated to Asian affairs. The corollary is that little information is coming back in the opposite direction. The new province covered a vast area and included a great diversity of character, civilization, categories of land, and city life.

Under Aquillius' settlement, the possessions of the Attalids outside Asia Minor were joined to the province of Macedonia. These included the Chersonese and the other districts of Thrace, as well as Aegina and probably also Andros.[29] In Asia too the kingdom was dismembered, for the Asian kings who had assisted the Romans against Aristonicus had to be rewarded. Lycaonia and part of Cilicia were assigned to the sons of Ariarathes V, since the king had himself died in the war.[30] Most of Greater Phrygia was granted to Mithradates V.[31] Nicomedes of Bithynia and Pylaemenes of Paphlagonia may have been given portions of Phrygia Epictetus;[32] but the basin of the Maeander and the Lycus must, on the evidence of milestones, have been included in the Roman province. Telmessus was restored to the Lycian League, which had obtained its independence from Rhodes by a senatorial decree of 167. Rhodes had lost Caria at the same time and this district also was now added to the Roman province.[33]

[27] Polyb. 39. 5; cf. *RDGE* no. 43 from Dyme, probably dating from 144 or 143, which talks of rebels proposing laws 'in defiance of the *politeia* given by Rome to the Achaeans'; Mitchell 1999: 24 n. 28. It is important to distinguish between laws for a province, for which there is no evidence before the first century BC, and laws for communities, which go back to Flamininus at least.

[28] See Ch. 8. [29] *IG* IV 1. 2. [30] Just. *Epit.* 37. 1. 2; Strabo, 12. 1. 4.

[31] Just. *Epit.* 37. 1. 2; 38. 5. 3; Gell. *NA* 11. 10; App. *Mith.* 12. 57.

[32] Strabo, 12. 4. 1; 12. 8. 1; 12. 3. 7. [33] Strabo, 14. 3. 2–4.

At the time of its formation, therefore, the province of Asia comprised the western littoral of Asia Minor: Hellespontine Phrygia, Mysia, Lydia, south-western Phrygia, and Caria, exclusive of the Rhodian *peraia*.[34] The status of the Greek cities under the new order is attested in only a few cases. Those that had supported Aristonicus probably lost their autonomy, and Phocaea, which had opposed Roman control, both at that time and in the war against Antiochus III, was saved from destruction only by the intervention of her daughter city, Massilia.[35]

Aquillius and the Roman commissioners needed three years to lay the foundations of the new Roman province. Aquillius was unable to celebrate his triumph until late in 126 and was presumably prosecuted in connection with the Asian political settlement some time after that. The final settlement was probably ratified only in 125 or 124 and it may be considered to be extremely unlikely, in circumstances in which the physical extent of the territory was probably still under negotiation, that a comprehensive taxation system would have been imposed.

In any case, a long delay before the commencement of revenue collection should not surprise us. As we have seen, the Romans closed the Macedonian mines between 167 and 158, seemingly for the simple reason that they did not need the money. Another example comes from Cyrene at the beginning of the first century. In 96 Ptolemy Apion died and bequeathed his kingdom to Rome. The senate made no effort to do anything about it. They did not annexe it or take over administrative responsibility. For a long time after, we do not hear of the *publicani* being there, even though the country was undoubtedly, under a Ptolemy, a well-organized, lucrative field of exploitation. It was not until 75–74 that an arrangement (possibly a temporary one only) was at last made to collect the revenues of Cyrene, since money was urgently needed in a grain shortage.[36] Another bequest followed in 88, when Ptolemy Alexander I left the kingdom of Egypt to Rome. It was undoubtedly the richest bequest ever received but the senate did not bother to take up their inheritance.[37] So was there any reason for the Romans to speed up the economic exploitation of their new province of Asia in the early 120s? Badian believed that the attempts at land reform by Ti. Gracchus showed that by the late 130s Rome was in 'economic recession'.[38] But in fact there is no indication that the Roman state was unable to finance its regular expenditure.[39]

There are a number of indications that spending on construction continued into the 120s (examined in Ch. 9), and there is no evidence from the coinage to suggest that the Roman economy was in decline during this period. Many of the issues from 138 onwards are on a scale hitherto unprecedented and, in these circumstances, it is difficult to believe that the treasury had any serious

[34] Hansen 1971: 160. [35] Just. *Epit.* 37. 1. 1; Broughton 1938: 507–12.

[36] Sall. *Hist.* 2. 43; on the whole subject of Rome's slowness to annex territory, see Mommsen 1920: i. 683–782; Badian 1968: 22–3 and 30–1; Harris 1979: 133, 154; Kay (2013).

[37] The Romans appear to have struck coins from money bequeathed to them by Ptolemy Alexander (Crawford 1974: 605), if that is the correct interpretation of three issues from 86–85 BC bearing the legend A[rgentum] P[ublicum], but the point here is that the Romans chose not to annex Egypt as a province.

[38] Badian 1972: 53–4.

[39] For the agrarian issues raised by Ti. Gracchus, see pp. 160–85 and Ch. 11.

problems.[40] Of course, major incremental expenditure across a number of projects, carried out simultaneously, was a different matter, as we shall see when we come to consider C. Gracchus' economic measures.

SENATUS CONSULTUM DE AGRO PERGAMENO

There are a number of possible objections to the proposition that no *publicani* were active in the province of Asia before C. Gracchus.[41]

A Pergamene decree, dating from the 120s, honours a certain Diodorus Pasparus for obtaining, during the war with Aristonicus, a number of exemptions from the Romans with the exception of 'the *phoroi*'. Most scholars accept that this refers not to a regular tribute but to a 'contribution' usually given to the Romans by allies in time of war.[42]

There is also a passage of Lucilius which some have taken to indicate that, from the beginning of the province, there were *publicani* in Asia:

> Publicanus vero ut Asiae fiam, ut scripturarius
> pro Lucilio, id ego nolo et uno hoc non muto omnia.[43]

(I have no desire to become a *publicanus* in Asia, as a collector of pasture-taxes instead of Lucilius, and I am not changing everything for this one thing.)

Although this text comes from an early book of Lucilius, thought to date from before 123, we know that the satirist's work was republished at least once using a different arrangement of books before his death in about 106 and these verses could be a later addition.

There is also an interesting example of the priority given to tax collection in a newly conquered province in the *lex de provinciis praetoriis*, which dates from early 100 and probably assigned all the praetorian provinces overseas.[44] The relevant section of the law states that T. Didius has added eastern Thrace to the Roman province of Macedonia and the first thing it enjoins the governor to do is to arrange for taxes to be raised.[45] The decree goes on to say that before he leaves the province, the governor should establish 'the boundaries of the *vectigal* of the Chersonese' (ὅρια τῆς Χερσονήσου τῆς προσόδο[υ]), 'as he shall deem it proper, as quickly as possible' (ὡς τάχιστα).[46]

But the biggest problem for our analysis is the *Senatus Consultum de Agro Pergameno*. This document was found in three fragmentary Greek copies, the first not far from the site of ancient Adramyttium, the second in the *agora* of Smyrna,

[40] Crawford 1974: 636; see Ch. 5.

[41] Brunt (1971*b*: 86) misleadingly quotes Vell. Pat. 2. 38. 5 (a passage that refers to Pompey's settlement of the East) in support of his statement that Asia became liable to tribute in 129.

[42] *IGRom.* 4. 292; cf. Magie 1950: 1045 n. 34.

[43] Lucil. 650–1; Warmington 1938: pp. xx–xxiv.

[44] Crawford 1996 no. 12; it has sometimes been known as the 'Piracy law' or the *lex de piratis persequendis* or the *lex Cnidia de piratis*.

[45] Crawford 1996 no. 12, Cnidos Copy, column IV, 8–17.

[46] Crawford 1996 no. 12, Cnidos Copy, column IV, 24–30.

and the third at Ephesus.[47] These places were probably chosen to have copies of the document inscribed, because they were three of the nine assize centres that operated in the province of Asia during the late second and early part of the first centuries and because the content of the document had an exemplary character that was of interest to other Greek cities.[48]

The document concerns a dispute that has arisen between the Pergamenes and the *publicani* over land (line 22):

[...] περὶ χώρας ἥτις ἐν ἀντιλογίαι ἐστὶν δημοσ[ιώναις...]

([...] concerning the land that is in dispute between the *public[ani* and the Pergamenes])

A Roman magistrate is to conduct an investigation in order to determine the boundaries of the Pergamenes (lines 5–7):

[... περὶ δὲ τῆς χώρας, ἥτις ἐ]ν ἀντιλογίαι ἐστὶν κα[ὶ...]
[...] τῶν πραγμ[άτ]ων, περὶ ὧν λόγους ἐπ[οιήσαντο...]
[... ἐ]πιγνῶι τίνες ὅρο[ι] Περγαμηνῶν εἰσιν[...]

([concerning the land that] is in dispute and [...] | the matters about which they spoke [...] | is to determine what the boundaries of the Pergamenes are.)

'Those who farm out the taxes of Asia' are mentioned, although it is not entirely clear in what connection (line 15):

[...] τῆς Ἀσίας τὰς προσόδους μι[σθῶσιν...]

A consul, [...] υλλιος ὕπατος (line 17), is to provide accommodation for the magistrate and his *consilium*. The members of this *consilium* and the (unreconstructable) fragments of their decision follow.

Since the inscription refers to a dispute over the taxability of the land mentioned at line 22, it seems reasonable to infer that this land had been assigned to the city of Pergamum by the will of Attalus III and that, in spite of the senate's ratification of the arrangements made by the king, who had declared Pergamum and its territory free and non-contributory, the *publicani* had tried to tax it. Furthermore, the inscription could also be interpreted as indicating that the *publicani* were already collecting taxes in Asia before the *lex Sempronia*. As we saw earlier, the consul mentioned in line 17, whose name ends in -υλλιος(*-illius*), could be Manius Aquillius, the consul of 129. The phrase in line 17, ἐὰν αὐτῶι φαίνηται (if it seems best to him), shows that this consul is actually in office and so it appears to confirm the dating of the document to 129 and its reference to contemporary events. Additional reinforcement for this view seems to be provided by the fact that the name of one of the consuls mentioned in line 9 ends in -νιος(*-nius*); and Aquillius' partner in the consulship of 129, C. Sempronius, supplies the appropriate name ending.[49] Rostovtzeff was persuaded by these considerations

[47] *RDGE* no. 12; for the even more fragmentary Ephesian copy, see Petzl 1985 *EA* 6: 70–1.

[48] Mitchell 1999: 27; likewise the edict of Paullus Fabius Maximus (*RDGE* no. 65), proconsul of Asia in 9 BC, included instructions that it was to be published ἐν ταῖς ἀφηγουμέναις τῶν διοικήσεων πόλεσιν (in the leading cities of the assize districts [i.e. *conventus*]).

[49] *RDGE* p. 68.

and believed that the decree provided evidence for the imposition of taxes on Asia at that time.[50] He, therefore, understandably doubted the accuracy of the words that Appian puts in the mouth of Marcus Antonius and believed that Gracchus merely instituted a reform in a system that was already functioning.

However, David Magie and, subsequently, Harold Mattingly, have persuasively argued that the document should be dated much later.[51] Their suggestion is that the consul mentioned in line 17 who is being recommended by the senate to take certain actions is a *younger* Manius Aquillius, the consul of 101, and that the document was inscribed in that year. The dating of the decree to 101 appears to be convincingly supported, in the first place, by the usage in the decree of certain phrases. For example, we have just enough senatorial decrees to be able to trace changes in formulation over the years. The phrase that appears in line 17, *ἐὰν αὐτῶι φαίνηται* (if it seems best to him), in the context of the provision of gifts for the embassy, is a translation of a Latin one, *sei ei videretur*, and is regularly added to decrees of the Sullan period and later, on occasions when the senate recommends specific action by consuls or other officials. It is not, however, found in any *senatus consulta* down to and including the *Senatus Consultum et Foedus cum Astypalaeensibus* of 105.[52] On the other hand, the document is unlikely to date from much later than 101, as the form of the lettering on the version of the inscription found at Adramyttium suggests that it was inscribed in the late second century. Secondly, the prosopographical evidence for the *consilium* at the end of the inscription fits 101 much better than it does 129. The *consilium* was composed of at least fifty-five members. The first thirty-three are certainly senators, but many of the later names look to be *equites*, as Mommsen noted many years ago.[53] As Mattingly says, a mixed *consilium* of senators and *equites* in 101 would be less surprising than it would be in 129 as, by the later date, *equites* 'were playing a prominent part in public affairs through the extortion and treason courts'. Moreover, Mattingly can provide eight convincing identifications for members of the *consilium*, as well as two plausible pairs of alternative choices, on the assumption that it is dated to 101, compared to the three or four only that proponents of the 129 dating are able to offer. Thus, the phraseology of the decree and the prosopographical evidence that it contains appear to tie the document down to 101, where Magie wanted to put it.

On this interpretation, then, the mention of the consuls in line 9 would be part of an allusion to previous consular arbitration, as is common in decrees of this kind. In other words, these consuls are not those of the current year (101), but those who were in office during an earlier attempt to resolve the problem of the taxability of the disputed land. Mattingly, therefore, proposes that the consuls mentioned at line 9 were the pair of 122—Cn. Domitius Ahenobarbus and C. Fannius, the latter supplying the ending, *-νιος* (*-nius*), required to fit the name of one of the consuls in line 9. If he is correct, as seems probable, this would mean not only that the argument of Rostovtzeff (for the collection of revenues near Pergamum before C. Gracchus) collapses, but that reference is being made in the

[50] Rostovtzeff 1941: 811–13. [51] Magie 1950: 1005–6; H. B. Mattingly 1972.
[52] *RDGE* no. 16. [53] See *RDGE* p. 72.

decree to events precisely at the time of the introduction of the new system of taxation under C. Gracchus.

EXPENDITURE

On becoming tribune, C. Gracchus embarked on a series of economic measures that not only must cumulatively have been enormously expensive but also followed a period of exceptional expenditure on the construction both of roads and of Rome's fourth aqueduct, the Aqua Tepula.[54]

There is evidence to show that the problem of feeding the city was considerable, despite the fact that tax grain from overseas provinces, which had been diverted to supply Roman armies during the first half of the second century, was reaching Italy.[55] An inscription from Thessaly dated to 129 shows an aedile, Q. Metellus, requesting the shipment of grain to Rome. The quantity was about 450,000 *modii* of wheat, which would perhaps have been about two and a half months' supply for the plebs of Rome in the late Republic, but at this time would possibly have sufficed for nearly double that time.[56] It has the hallmarks of a crisis measure to deal with a sudden scarcity, since the purchase seems to have been made in the period of spring to midsummer before the new harvests in the west, when the price of wheat would have been at its height. The *lex frumentaria*, which C. Gracchus promulgated, provided grain to the plebs at a fixed, subsidized price; and this was presumably at a much lower price than that prevailing in the market, although we have no price data at all for this period: 'Leges tulit, inter quas frumentariam, ut senis et triente frumentum plebi daretur'[57] (he carried laws, amongst which was the one relating to grain, which provided that grain should be given to the *plebs* for six and one-third asses). For storing grain for later distribution he built public granaries: '"Sempronia horrea" qui locus dicitur in eo fuerunt lege Gracchi ad custodiam frumenti publici'[58] (the 'Sempronian Granaries' were in the district of that name and were where public grain was stored in accordance with a law of Gracchus). He passed a law that probably gave back full judicial powers to the agrarian commission so that it could operate effectively again: 'Tulit . . . legem agrariam quam et frater eius tulerat'[59] (he carried . . . an agrarian law which his brother had also carried). Linked with his agrarian law, and perhaps incorporated in it, were plans for colonies in Italy at Capua, Tarentum, and Scolacium Minervum.[60] Through a fellow tribune named Rubrius he also enacted

[54] See pp. 220–1. There is no agreement about the order in which all of Gaius Gracchus' measures were passed. Brunt's view (1971*b*: 84) is that they all belong to 123.

[55] Erdkamp 2005: 212.

[56] Garnsey, Gallant, and Rathbone (1984); Garnsey and Rathbone (1985).

[57] Livy, *Per.* 60; cf. *Schol. Bob.* p. 135 St; Oros. 5. 12; Cic. *Off.* 2. 21. 72 and Cic. *Tusc.* 3. 48 call it a *largitio*; App. *B. Civ.* 1. 21, Plut. *C. Gracch.* 5, and Vell. Pat. 2. 6. 3 describe it, probably wrongly, as a free gift of grain at public expense.

[58] Fest. 370L; cf. Plut. *C. Gracch.* 6. 3.

[59] Livy, *Per.* 60; Plut. *C. Gracch.* 5; Cic. *Leg. agr.* 1. 21; *De vir. ill.* 65; Vell. Pat. 2. 6. 3; *lex agraria* 6.

[60] *De vir. ill.* 65 names C. Gracchus' colonies as Capua and Tarentum; to these, Vell. Pat. 1. 15. 4 adds Scolacium Minervum.

that a new colony should be founded on the territory of Carthage, to be called Junonia, with generous allotments of up to 200 *iugera* in the hinterland:

> Continuato in alterum annum tribunatu legibus agrariis latis effecit, ut complures coloniae in Italia deducerentur, et una in solo dirutae Carthaginis; quo ipse triumvir creatus coloniam deduxit.[61]
>
> (Having been re-elected to the tribunate for a second year, he passed land laws so that several colonies could be founded in Italy, as well as one on the site of Carthage, which had been destroyed. He himself was elected as a triumvir and led out the colony.)

Six thousand men were eventually enrolled, although Appian says that the colony was a failure.[62]

According to Plutarch and Appian, C. Gracchus embarked on a large road-building programme.[63]

Under a *lex militaris* terms of military service were also altered. No soldier of less than 17 years old could be conscripted and, from a fiscal perspective, there were to be no deductions from pay for clothing, which henceforth would be supplied at the expense of the state.[64]

C. Gracchus' enemies held that the *lex frumentaria* in particular drained the treasury dry.[65] But there is no sign whatsoever that this happened and in fact C. Gracchus' approach to the problem was entirely prudent and pragmatic. As Stockton has said: 'The money had to be found from somewhere, either by more efficient management of existing resources or by the provision of new sources of income.'[66] In his speeches, C. Gracchus was entirely clear about his objective of raising taxes to facilitate the provision of benefits to the Roman People and to improve the administration of Rome:

> Ego ipse, qui aput vos verba facio, ut vectigalia vestra augeatis, quo facilius vestra commoda et rem publicam administrare possitis, non gratis prodeo; verum peto a vobis non pecuniam sed bonam existimationem atque honorem.[67]
>
> (I myself, who am now recommending to you to increase your taxes in order that you may the more easily serve your own advantage and administer the Republic, do not come here for nothing; but I ask of you not money, but honour and your good opinion.[68])

ASIA

In setting up these revenue arrangements, C. Gracchus was following in a family tradition. His own father, Ti. Sempronius Gracchus, had a history of imposing taxes. Appian talks of 'the taxes defined under Gracchus' (*φόρους τους ὁρισθέντας ἐπὶ Γράκχου*), referring to the senior Ti. Gracchus' governorship of Hither Spain in 179 and in the context of the treaty arrangements he made with the defeated

61 Livy, *Per.* 60; cf. Vell. Pat. 1. 15, 2. 6, 2. 7; Plut. *C. Gracch.* 6, 8, 10; *lex rep.* 22; *lex agraria* 22, 59; Oros. 5. 12; Eutr. 4. 21.

62 App. *B. Civ.* 1. 24; cf. pp. 137–8.

63 Plut. *C. Gracch.* 6; App. *B. Civ.* 1. 23; *ILLRP* 458.

64 Plut. *C. Gracch.* 5; Diod. Sic. 35. 25.

65 Diod. Sic. 35. 25.

66 Stockton 1979: 156.

67 Gell. *NA* 11. 10. 3 = *ORF*[4] 187.

68 Trans. Loeb II 323, slightly revised.

Celtiberians.[69] Indeed it can almost be said that C. Gracchus' father stands at the transition point from booty to taxation. Livy quotes an inscription which the senior Ti. Gracchus set up in the temple of Mater Matuta in 174, to record his subjugation of Sardinia. The inscription states that 'vectigalibus restitutis exercitum salvum atque incolumem plenissimum praeda domum reportavit'[70] (with the taxes having been restored, he brought home his army, safe, unharmed, and laden with booty). The younger Tiberius, as we have seen, intended to raise money for his agrarian reforms by auctioning the personal possessions of Attalus III; and it was to the *vectigalia* of Asia that C. Gracchus now turned.

The wealth of the Attalids was proverbial. Philetaerus had laid the foundation of the dynasty with a treasure of 9,000 talents;[71] and, more than a century after the death of the last member, the poet Horace used the term 'Attalid' as indicative of unlimited means.[72] Following the bequest in 133, Tiberius Gracchus proposed that τὰ βασιλικὰ χρήματα, Attalus' 'royal moneys', should be used to stock the farms of the recipients of public land.[73] According to the elder Pliny, when the Attalid royal treasures were eventually auctioned off in Rome three or four years later, they provoked a major boom in consumerism: 'Romae in auctionibus regiis verecundia exempta est'[74] (all modesty entirely disappeared at the auctions of the king's effects at Rome).

But it was Eumenes II Soter who really built up the kingdom territorially, militarily, and economically. He inherited from his father, Attalus I Soter, a relationship with the Romans that had begun during the First Macedonian War. He also inherited a kingdom that Polybius describes as confined to 'a few wretched towns'.[75] Pergamum gave loyal service to Rome during the war against Antiochus III of Syria and was rewarded well. A *senatus consultum* was promulgated which provided the framework for the treaty concluded at Apamea in 188.[76] Eumenes obtained the bulk of cis-Tauric Asia Minor together with Antiochus' holdings in Europe, effectively increasing the land area under his control by as much as ten times.[77] Cities that formerly paid tribute to Antiochus now had to make payment to Pergamum. He also received indemnities from Antiochus totalling just over 527 talents. During the years 188 to 173, Eumenes skilfully created a web of alliances with a number of the larger local rulers and succeeded in establishing what McShane has termed an 'Asian Panhellenic entente'.[78] The economic effect of this was of course considerable; Eumenes became, in Hansen's phrase, 'the master builder of Pergamon'.[79] He launched his own currency, the cistophorus, which seems to have been a closed currency, similar to the Egyptian coinage, in that it had its own standards and seems to have circulated only within the territory of

[69] App. *Hisp.* 43–4. [70] Livy, 41. 28. 8–9. [71] Strabo, 13. 4. 1.

[72] Hor. *Carm.* 1. 1. 11–14: 'Gaudentem patrios findere sarculo | agros Attalicis condicionibus | numquam demoveas, ut trabe Cypria | Myrtoum pavidus nauta secet mare.' Hor. *Carm.* 2. 18. 1–6: 'Non ebur neque aureum | mea renidet in domo lacunar; | non trabes Hymettiae premunt columnas ultima recisas | Africa, neque Attali | ignotus heres regiam occupavi.'

[73] Plut. *Ti. Gracch.* 14.

[74] Plin. *HN* 33. 149: cf. Varro, fr. 68: 'ex hereditate Attalica aulaea, clamides, pallae, plagae, vasa aurea' (from the Attalid legacy came tapestries, cloaks, robes, coverlets, golden vases).

[75] Polyb. 32. 8. 3. [76] Polyb. 21. 24. 6–8, 21. 45. 2–3; Livy, 37. 55. 5–6; 37. 56. 1–4.

[77] Polyb. 21. 22. 15; see Thonemann (2013*b*). [78] McShane 1964: 172.

[79] Hansen 1947: 106.

Pergamum. In short, Eumenes II turned the few wretched towns that he had inherited from his father into a kingdom that, according to Polybius, 'rivalled the greatest contemporary powers'.[80]

The Attalids' chief sources of income were the tribute from the subject cities and the taxes on the indigenous communities. It is unlikely that the Attalids fixed an arbitrary sum as the tribute of individual cities; rather, the tribute was reckoned on the basis of the size and fertility of the city territory, a tenth of the produce of some year probably serving as the usual norm.[81] Appian's report of the speech of Marcus Antonius supports the view that tribute paid by the Greek cities was a fixed sum (*τὰ τιμήματα*) rather than one that varied from year to year according to the income of the community (*μέρη τῶν ἑκάστοτε καρπῶν*). Thus, the Pisidian city of Amlada paid an annual *phoros* of 2 talents, the revenue for which was derived largely from the production of wine.[82] We do not know the total amount of revenue that the Romans or the Attalids obtained from this land tax, but Herodotus tells us that, in the fifth century BC, the Achaemenids were already collecting a total of 1,260 (Babylonian) talents from their three nomes in western Asia Minor.[83] Of course, this was a considerably greater area than the enlarged kingdom of Pergamum, but it does give some indication of the scale of the revenues that were possible—perhaps about 700 talents per annum from the area controlled by Eumenes would be a reasonable guess. In addition to the *phoros*, the citizens of the various towns had to pay some municipal taxes, including a poll tax.[84] A Pergamene document mentions the exemption granted to one of its citizens 'from all taxes of which the city was in control' and a decree of Teos also concerns some land offered to the association of Dionysiac artists which was 'free from the taxes imposed by the city'.[85]

Under the Romans, the taxes from Asia consisted of *portoria, decumae*, and *scripturae*.[86] Some idea of the scale of the revenues that Rome was eventually extracting from the province comes from Cicero's time. Before Pompey's conquests, the regular public revenues were said by Pompey himself (who perhaps had an interest in depreciating them) to be 50 million denarii per annum from up to twelve provinces:

> *ἔφραζε διὰ τῶν γραμμάτων ὅτι πεντακισχίλιαι μὲν μυριάδες ἐκ τῶν τελῶν ὑπῆρχον, ἐκ δὲ ὧν αὐτος προσεκτήσατο τῇ πόλει μυριάδας ὀκτακισχιλίας πεντακοσίας λαμβάνουσιν.*[87]

[80] Polyb. 32. 8. 3: *ταῖς μεγίσταις τῶν καθ' αὑτὸν δυναστειῶν ἐφάμιλλον ἐποίησε τὴν ἰδίαν ἀρχήν.*

[81] As Ma points out (2000: 133), some forms of Attalid taxation must have been a legacy from the Seleucid administration of Antiochus III.

[82] App. *B. Civ.* 5. 4. Strabo, 12. 7. 2; *OGIS* 751 = *RC* 54, lines 7–8: *ἀπὸ τῶν δύο ταλάντων ἃ τελεῖτε κατ' ἐνιαυτὸν [κου]-/ φίσαι ὑμᾶς*. Hansen (1971: 204) argues that the Attalids' annual income from Aegina was 10 or 12 talents.

[83] Hdt. 3. 90. 1–2. It is clear from Hdt. 6. 42. 2 that this was a land tax.

[84] An inscription from 181 contains a letter from Eumenes in response to a petition from the village of the Cardaces. It mentions a poll tax (*συντάξις*) of four Rhodian drachmas and an obol, payable by each adult citizen (Segre 1938: 190, lines 10–11). On Attalid taxation, see further the correspondence of Eumenes II with Apollonioucharax in Lydia (Herrmann and Malay 2007: 49–58, no. 32) with the corrections of Thonemann 2011. See too Thonemann (2013*b*).

[85] *Syll*³.1007. 20–1; *SEG*.2. 580.

[86] Cic. *De imp. Cn. Pomp.* 15.

[87] Plut. *Pomp.* 45. This is a much disputed passage. Frank (1933: 322–4) believed that Pompey had increased the overall revenues from 50 m. to 85 m. He was followed in this view by Broughton (1938: 562), Hopkins (1978: 37 n.49), Harris (1979: 70 n. 3), and Duncan-Jones (1994: 253). However, the preferable interpretation, which makes better sense of the Greek, is that of Mommsen (1894: 361), who

(He said on the placards that there were already 50 million drachmas from the taxes, but that, from those places that he had added to the city, they were taking 85 million drachmas.)

That is equivalent to 8,300 talents per annum, or more than five times the 1,500 talents per annum that, according to Polybius, the Roman *demos* received from the mines of Spain in the 150s.[88] In 66, in the *De Imperio Cn. Pompeii*, Cicero emphasized that Asia provided a large part of the sum:

Nam ceterarum provinciarum vectigalia, Quirites, tanta sunt ut eis ad ipsas provincias tuendas vix contenti esse possimus, Asia vero tam opima est ac fertilis ut et ubertate agrorum et varietate fructuum et magnitudine pastionis et multitudine earum rerum quae exportentur facile omnibus terris antecellat.[89]

(For while the revenues of our other provinces, citizens, are barely sufficient to make it worth our while to defend them, Asia is so rich and fertile as easily to surpass all other countries in the productivity of her soil, the variety of her crops, the extent of her pastures, and the volume of her exports.[90])

Later on in the same work Cicero describes the Asian taxes as being the 'the sinews of the Republic':

Nam et publicani, homines honestissimi atque ornatissimi, suas rationes et copias in illam provinciam contulerunt, quorum ipsorum per se res et fortunae vobis curae esse debent. Etenim si vectigalia nervos esse rei publicae semper duximus, eum certe ordinem, qui exercet illa, firmamentum ceterorum ordinum recte esse dicemus.[91]

(For the *publicani*, those most honourable and accomplished men, have transferred their businesses and their wealth to Asia; and their property and fortunes ought, in their own right, to be your concern. In truth, if we have always considered our revenues to be the sinews of the Republic, then we shall certainly be right to call the order of men that collects them the mainstay of all the other orders.)

Of course, such statements are rhetorical, but sixty years earlier, with about half the number of provinces, the relative importance of Asia must have been much greater. The decision that C. Gracchus had to make in the late 120s was how best, given his expenditure plans, to exploit the new province.

TAXES

The main issue for any government or administration facing a large programme of public expenditure is how to raise the income to cover its cost. One way is to develop supplementary methods of raising taxes, and at some point the Romans,

believed that Pompey acquired an additional 85 m. in revenues over and above the 50 m. already received, so bringing the total incoming taxation revenues of the Roman state to 135 m. Other scholars who have agreed with Mommsen include Badian (1968: 78–9), Brunt (1971: 39), and Crawford (1974: 695).

[88] Polyb. 34. 9. 8–9.

[89] Cic. *De imp. Cn. Pomp* 14. The financial sagacity of those running the Roman state should not be underestimated. Strabo (4. 5. 3), writing in the reign of Augustus, states that the customs duties on trade with pre-conquest Britain exceeded the likely revenues of imposing a tribute and the costs of collecting it.

[90] Trans. Loeb IX 27, slightly revised.

[91] Cic. *De imp. Cn. Pomp.* 17.

perhaps following Hellenistic precedents, began to introduce *portoria*, customs dues, which are, of course, a tax on trade. Indeed the very fact of their imposition in the early second century suggests that there was, at that time, an increasing level of trade that could be so taxed.

The first mention in our sources of censors letting contracts for *portoria* is in 199 at Capua and Puteoli.[92] In 179 additional *portoria* and *vectigalia* were instituted.[93] After that, perhaps because of our loss of Livy's account beyond 167, we hear no mention of any new ones until the late 120s.[94] Then, according to Velleius Paterculus, C. Gracchus introduced new customs duties ('nova constituebat portoria').[95]

Cicero makes it clear that the Asian customs dues went on to become one of the principal sources of Rome's revenue: 'Quid nos portus Asiae... quid omnia transmarina vectigalia iuvabunt tenuissima suspicione praedonum aut hostium iniecta?'[96] (What help will the ports of Asia bring us... or all our overseas taxes, if there is the slightest suspicion of pirates or enemies?) But, in discussing the legislative programme of C. Gracchus, Stockton, as recently as 1979, was able to say only that 'we have no way of knowing... whether these new *portoria* were in Italy and connected with his colonization programme, or in Asia'.[97] Now we do.

'The Customs Law of Asia', an inscription of which 154 lines survive, was found at Ephesus in 1976 and first published in full in 1989.[98] This document sets out the law for the collection of customs dues on imports and exports to and from the province of Asia by land and sea. The document is dated to the reign of Nero, when, on 9 July AD 62, records in the office of the curators of the public records in the Basilica Julia at Rome were copied so that they might be translated and eventually inscribed on a stone set up in the city of Ephesus, the leading port of the province of Asia. It appears to consist of successive modifications of earlier laws for the collection of customs dues. Thus, the early part of the law (lines 7–72) seems to be an example of Roman economic imperialism dating from the last third of the second century BC. The first positive dating in the inscription is at lines 73 and 75, where the *locatio* of the consuls for 75 BC, L. Octavius and C. Aurelius Cotta, is mentioned; and the first magistrates whose additions appear in the text (at line 84) are the consuls of 72, and censors of 70, L. Gellius and Cn. Lentulus. No more modifications are described until 17 (lines 88–103), when a number are listed. These are followed by futher additions in 12 BC (103–9), 7 BC (109–12), and 2 BC (113–15). The names of the consuls of AD 37 can be restored and then there are two more modifications before those of the Neronian curators (lines 138–43).

For our purposes it is the early part of the document (lines 7–72) that is most interesting. The belief of the original editors was that the main body of the law

92 Livy, 34. 45. 1. 93 Livy, 40. 51. 8.

94 It is possible, however, that the original *lex Hieronica* provided for individual *portoria* in Sicily; cf. Cic. *II Verr.* 3.167; Badian 1972: 133n.55; De Laet 1949: 68.

95 Vell. Pat. 2. 6. 3. 96 Cic. *Leg. agr.* 2. 80. 97 Stockton 1979: 156.

98 First published in full in Engelmann and Knibbe 1989, following a preliminary notice in Engelmann and Knibbe 1986. A new text, translation, and commentary on the Law has been published recently: Cottier et al. 2008. Lintott (1993: 70–96) has some useful comments. The inscription has been variously entitled the Customs Law of Asia, the 'Monumentum Ephesenum', the *lex portus Asiae*, and the *lex portorii Asiae*.

dates to 75 BC, although it contains elements that must already have been present in earlier regulations for customs collection in Asia.[99] This was because of the mention of the consuls of 75 BC, at lines 73–5, as being responsible for the leasing of public contracts during that year. Heil believed that the early section of the law (lines 7–84) would have been drafted in 74 BC in connection with the annexation of the province of Bithynia.[100] However, a major objection to Heil's thesis is that, if these consuls had been responsible for drawing up the earlier part of the law, they would more likely have been mentioned at the beginning of the text, rather than 73 lines into it. But the most significant argument in favour of dating the early part of the law to the 120s is that four sections of the text refer explicitly to arrangements that had existed under the Attalids. Line 27 mentions '[the land] formerly of (the) monarchy'; line 36 refers to pre-existing customs buildings; line 68 talks of 'buildings and royal [staging posts] which king Attalus the son of Eumenes had for the purposes of the exaction of the *telos*';[101] and line 69 refers to cities and tribes that were not subject to Attalus.

As Mitchell says,[102] all these clauses are most reasonably dated to the period immediately after the bequest to Rome of Attalus' kingdom, a period which should be taken as extending up to 123. If the law had been drafted in 74, it is unlikely that buildings would still have been connected with Attalus sixty years after his death. It is perhaps just about possible to date the original drafting to between 129 and 126, when M'. Aquillius was setting up the legal framework of the province and constructing its original road system. Roads and customs laws have a certain symmetry. But as we argued above, it is unlikely that any kind of revenue laws would have been introduced during a period in which the boundaries of the province were still unclear. The Customs Law is more likely to have been drafted as part of C. Gracchus' legislation, especially as literary sources credit the establishment of *portoria* to him. On this analysis, C. Gracchus set up a comprehensive customs system for taxing trade in an area extending from the Bosporus to Pamphylia, with the exception of a tax-free zone in Lycia. The Bosporus, the most lucrative source of tolls, was identified as the most important area for the collection of customs dues, generally at a rate of 2½ per cent. A system of *locatio* was used to let the taxes to *publicani*. All communities, including free cities, were liable to the *portorium* and no significant exemptions were allowed except for officials, soldiers, or *publicani* acting on Roman official business.

To turn now to the agricultural tithes, there were three models of tax collection available to C. Gracchus. According to Cicero, the Romans had inherited from Hieron of Syracuse a method of taxation which they referred to as the *lex Hieronica* and which, probably at the end of the third century, they imposed on most of the rest of Sicily, Sardinia, and possibly Corsica, with the 10 per cent grain tithe, the *decuma*, being sold by the praetorian governor himself rather than by the censors in Rome:

[99] Engelmann and Knibbe 1989: 160, 162. [100] Heil 1991: 9–11.

[101] *ἐποίκια / [καὶ σταθμοὺς βασ]ιλικοὺς οὓς βασιλεὺς Ἄτταλος Εὐμένους υἱὸς τελωνίας χάριν ἔσχ [εν].*

[102] Mitchell (2008: 126–34) also adduces several other powerful arguments based on geography to suggest that lines 7–72 were drafted much earlier. For example, four Pamphylian ports are included in the early part of the law, although Pamphylia became part of Cilicia after 102. Similarly the Bosporus is included, despite its transference to Bithynia in 74.

sed ne legem quidem venditionis decumarum neve vendundi aut tempus aut locum commutarent, ut certo tempore anni, ut ibidem in Sicilia, denique ut lege Hieronica venderent.[103]

(but [our forefathers] did not even change the law relating to the sale of the right to collect the *decumae* nor its time or place, so that it would take place at a fixed time of year, in the same place in Sicily, and in accordance with the *lex Hieronica.*)

Then there was a second form of taxation, a fixed monetary payment (*vectigal certum stipendiarium*), which had been imposed by the Romans on 'the Spaniards and most of the Carthaginians'.[104] Under the third system of tax collection, the *censoria locatio*, the contracts to collect the tax were auctioned in public at Rome to the *publicani* by the censors (or, when they were not in office, by other magistrates, usually the consuls), for a *lustrum* of five years at a time.[105] This was the system that *C. Gracchus* chose. From Appian, Cicero, and the Customs Law of Asia, it is clear that the principal tax on crops imposed in Asia was to be the *decuma*, one-tenth of the agricultural produce.[106]

GAIUS GRACCHUS' ECONOMIC THINKING AND THE *CENSORIA LOCATIO*

As we have already seen, the executive machinery of Rome during our period was tiny.[107] Minute staffs supported the senior magistrates. There was no civil service providing long-term employment to men of high status and, as a result, there was no effective alternative to tax-farming available. The Asian taxes had therefore to be collected by the only people with the necessary combination of ability, organization, and financial resources to do this—the *publicani.* The first appearance in our literary sources of the *publicani* collecting revenues under the system of *censoria locatio* is in 184, but as we have already argued, it is probable that they were involved in this type of activity at an earlier stage.[108] Since then the scope of their revenue collection had been increasing for half a century and they had presumably undertaken the 7,500-talent construction of the Aqua Marcia and were handling vast contracts in the Spanish mines.

The modalities of this form of revenue collection will be discussed in more detail later, but first a brief excursus is necessary on C. Gracchus' speeches and on the extortion law, the *lex Sempronia repetundarum*, which he introduced, in order to understand the economic thinking behind his selection of this method.[109]

[103] Cic. *II Verr.* 3.14; Cic. *II Verr.* 3.13 states that there were variations in Sicily which depended on the status of each community. For the grain tithe sold by Sicilian governor, see Cic. *II Verr.* 3.151. For taxation in Sardinia, see Livy, 36.2.13; 37.2.12; 37.50.10; 42.31.8.

[104] Cic. *II Verr.* 3. 12, quoted on p. 22. Spanish taxation is discussed on pp. 55–6.

[105] e.g. Customs Law of Asia, line 108. The best brief description of the *censoria locatio* system is Lintott 1993: 76–7, 86–91.

[106] App. *B. Civ.* 5.4; Cic. *De imp. Cn. Pomp.* 15; Customs Law of Asia, line 72; Cic. *Att.* 5. 13. 1.

[107] See pp. 11–12.

[108] Livy, 39. 44. 7; see pp. 49–54.

[109] The *lex Sempronia repetundarum* will be referred to in these notes as '*Lex rep.*' and the text is that of Crawford 1996: no. 1. References to the *lex agraria*, the law inscribed on the other side of the

The ideas that the funds of the Roman state belong to the Roman people and that taxes facilitated the provision of benefits to the Roman people are expressed most clearly in C. Gracchus' speech to the people (termed, by modern scholars, the *dissuasio legis Aufeiae*) against a law apparently intended to readjust royal territories in Asia Minor at some point during or after Aquillius' settlement of the new province. The rumour was that Mithradates had offered a larger bribe than Nicomedes of Bithynia to secure Greater Phrygia. As Millar says, the important points in this passage are the right of the people to the profits of empire and the suspicion that senators were lining their private pockets, by not pressing the public interests of Rome as against those of allied kings:[110]

> Ego ipse, qui aput vos verba facio, ut vectigalia vestra augeatis quo facilius vestra commoda et rem publicam administrare possitis, non gratis prodeo; verum peto a vobis non pecuniam sed bonam existimationem atque honorem. Qui prodeunt dissuasuri ne hanc legem accipiatis, petunt non honorem a vobis verum a Nicomede pecuniam. Qui suadent ut accipiatis, hi quoque petunt non a vobis existimationem verum a Mithridate rei familiari suae pretium et praemium.[111]
>
> (I myself, who am now recommending to you to increase your taxes in order that you may the more easily serve your own advantage and administer the Republic, do not come here for nothing; but I ask of you not money, but honour and your good opinion. Those who come forward to persuade you not to accept this law are not seeking honour from you but money from Nicomedes. Those who persuade you to accept are also not seeking a good opinion from you but money and profit from Mithradates for themselves.[112])

A further expression of C. Gracchus' views on the responsibilities of provincial magistrates comes in a speech he made when he returned to Rome from Sardinia in 124 and was charged with dereliction of duty for not having stayed on there with the governor, L. Aurelius Orestes, whose proconsular appointment had been prorogued. This passage was also no doubt an attempt to inflame resentment and suspicion against those senators whom he regarded as being guilty of extortion and peculation in the provinces:

> Itaque, Quirites, cum Romam profectus sum, zonas quas plenas argenti extuli eas ex provincia inanes retuli. Alii vini amphoras quas plenas tulerunt eas argento repletas domum reportaverunt.[113]
>
> (Therefore, citizens, when I set out for Rome, I brought back empty from the province the money-belts that I had brought out full of silver. Others have brought back the amphorae stuffed with silver that they had carried out full of wine.)

Tabula Bembina, are to Crawford 1996: no. 2. Although the *lex repetundarum* on the Tabula Bembina makes no mention of an author, the principal argument for regarding the text as Gracchan is the use of non-senatorial juries (cf. App. *B. Civ.* 1. 22) and their clearly innovatory nature.

110 Millar 1986: 9.

111 Gell. *NA* 11. 10. 3–4 = *ORF*^{4} 187–8. The gift of Greater Phrygia was eventually withdrawn after the death of Mithradates in 120, although further evidence for Roman administrative delay comes from a fragmentary inscription that suggests that the principles by which Rome would govern the territory were not laid down until perhaps 116 (*RDGE* no. 13).

112 Trans. Loeb II 323, slightly revised.

113 Gell. *NA* 15. 12. 4 = *ORF*^{4} 182; cf. Plut. *C. Gracch.* 2. 5. Both Gellius and Plutarch appear to quote the same passage, although the latter places it in a speech *apud censores* and the former in a speech *ad populum in contione.*

A theme in these two fragments is that the wealth that is due to the Roman people is in danger of being creamed off through the avarice of Roman magistrates; and this threat leads us to the dilemma faced by C. Gracchus. If the *lex de provincia Asia* was aimed at securing the revenues due to the Roman people, this could in part be achieved by ensuring that the allocation of the contracts to the *publicani* was done by the censors at Rome, before the people. Cicero himself emphasizes this point in arguing, against the Rullan agrarian bill of 63, that 'it is never permitted to farm out the taxes unless it is done in this city, in this place, in full view of you all'.[114] But the fact remained that corrupt magistrates could exploit their provinces. This prompted Gracchus to introduce his *lex Sempronia repetundarum*, a law about the recovery of property improperly seized by Romans in authority from provincials, because, at the time when C. Gracchus was first elected tribune, there was no legislation that was effective in securing the conviction of (and therefore acting as a deterrent to) such magistrates.

The first evidence we have of the exploitation of provincials by governors and their staffs is in 171, when Spanish envoys complained to the senate about the corrupt practices of three Roman governors from the two Spanish provinces.[115] The senate set up an enquiry but one governor was acquitted and the other two slunk off into exile at Tibur and Praeneste, during an adjournment of their trial. Clearly the senate was unwilling to exact severe punishments against governors who had overstepped the mark.[116] Over the next twenty years a number of scandalous events culminated, in 149, in a failed attempt by the tribune L. Scribonius Libo to set up a court (*quaestio*) to try Ser. Sulpicius Galba, who, as proconsul in Hispania Ulterior, had killed part of a group of Lusitani, whom he had persuaded to surrender to him, and sold the rest into slavery.[117]

In the same year, the tribune L. Calpurnius Piso Frugi did succeed in carrying a law, the *lex Calpurnia de rebus repetundis*, to set up a standing court of justice (*quaestio perpetua*). Our only references to the law are in Cicero and in the *lex Sempronia repetundarum*, which refers both to the *lex Calpurnia* and to an unknown *lex Iunia*.[118] Important though the *lex Calpurnia* was, it was only concerned with providing *Roman citizens* with a means for the recovery of money or property from a magistrate misusing his *imperium* for his own ends.[119] This should not surprise us, since the economic interests of Roman citizens, both in Italy and overseas, were expanding during this period. But the law was probably of little, if any, use to provincials. As far as we can tell, the procedure that was followed in 171, whereby non-citizens lodged a complaint with the senate, was still the only form of redress available in the mid-120s when, according to Appian, three men who were supposedly

[114] Cic. *Leg. agr.* 2. 55: 'vectigalia locare nusquam licet, nisi in hac urbe, hoc ex loco, hac vestrum frequentia'; cf. Millar 1986: 8.

[115] Livy, 43. 2.

[116] That said, they did change the rules for the Spaniards (Livy, 43. 2. 12 quoted at Ch. 3 n. 90).

[117] App. *Hisp.* 59; Livy, *Per.* 49.

[118] Cic. *Brut.* 27; Cic. *II Verr.* 3. 84, 3. 195, 4. 25; Cic. Off. 2. 75. The *lex Iunia* was proposed by an otherwise unknown tribune M. Iunius D.f. (*Lex rep.* 74).

[119] J. S. Richardson (1987) esp. 4–7.

guilty of extortion were acquitted: L. Aurelius Cotta, a mysterious Salinator, and M'. Aquillius.[120]

There can be little doubt that the acquittal of these three on charges of *repetundae* proved to C. Gracchus the need for a new law on this crime. Gracchus' *lex Sempronia repetundarum*, like the *lex Calpurnia de rebus repetundis*, still treated what we call extortion as essentially a civil action for recovery. As Sherwin-White pointed out in an excellent article published in 1982, the law was purely about material property and did not deal with other abuses of magisterial power, such as bribery or physical abuse, although Gracchus was clearly aware of them.[121] It forbade all methods of acquiring property and money: 'In annos singolos pequniae quod siet amp[lius sestertium nummum?] . . . ablatum captum coactum conciliatum aversumve siet'[122] (in any one year whatever money that is more than [?sesterces] . . . may have been taken, seized, extorted, procured, or diverted). Possible plaintiffs are defined as 'the citizens of the allied and Latin states of Italy, the citizens of external peoples of the Roman people' (quoi socium nominisve Latini exterarumque nationum, quoive in arbitratu dicione potestate amicitiave populi Romani)[123] and Cicero is clear that the law was introduced so that allies could bring a case in Rome; citizens, under the *lex Calpurnia*, already had a process in law:

> Quasi vero dubium sit quin tota lex de pecuniis repetundis sociorum causa constituta sit. Nam civibus cum sunt ereptae pecuniae, civili fere actione et privato iure repetuntur.[124]
>
> (There is absolutely no doubt that the *lex de pecuniis repetundis* was introduced for the benefit of our allies. For when money is stolen from Roman citizens, it is generally recovered in a civil action and under civil law.)

Fifty jurors were to be selected from a panel of 450 with no connection with the senate or magistrates.[125]

The text of the law reveals C. Gracchus' motivation in drafting it, and it is clear that it is similar to the motivation that lay behind his choice of the *censoria locatio* as the method for letting the contracts in Asia. The advantage to C. Gracchus of the *censoria locatio* system was that the auction for the Asian contracts would take place under the eyes of the Roman people and their officers, the tribunes, who might be expected to be quick to spot and to check flagrant corruption. This was completely different from the Sicilian system of the *lex Hieronica*, under which the revenues were auctioned away from Rome under the supervision of the governor of a province. Similarly, under his *lex repetundarum*, it would be easier for accusations of corruption against a Roman ex-magistrate in a province to be heard in Rome, now that non-citizens had the right to prosecute in that city, in front of jurors who were not the ex-magistrate's peers. The recent example of the acquittal of M'. Aquillius, qua former governor of Asia, served as a warning not

120 App. *B. Civ.* 1. 22; these and the other known cases between the late 140s and 120s, which appear to concern *repetundae*, are discussed in detail by J. S. Richardson (1987: 11–12).

121 e.g. Gell. *NA* 15. 12. 4 = *ORF*[4] 182 and Gell. *NA* 10. 3. 3 = *ORF*[4] 190–2; Sherwin-White 1982.

122 *Lex rep.* 2–3.

123 *Lex rep.* 1.

124 Cic. *Caecin.* 18; cf. Cic. *Caecin.* 65; Cic. *II Verr.* 3. 218.

125 *Lex rep.* 12–13, 16–17, 22–3.

only of the ineffectiveness of prosecuting Roman ex-magistrates under the *lex Calpurnia* or in a senatorial *quaestio*, but of the dangers of allowing financial matters to be dealt with in the provinces. As Cicero planned to say (with a flourish) at the trial of the Sicilan governor, Verres, in Rome:

> Grave crimen est hoc et vehemens et post hominum memoriam iudiciaque de pecuniis repetundis constituta gravissimum, praetorem socios habusisse decumanos.[126]
>
> (It is a fearful and terrible charge—it is the most terrible that any man can remember since our extortion courts were set up—this charge against a governor of being in league with the collectors of tithe.[127])

But given that the whole reason for choosing the *censoria locatio* system was so that the auction of the Asian tax contracts took place at Rome, how quickly did C. Gracchus imagine that he would be able to receive the money he needed for his economic programme? Would it be a fixed or variable stream of revenue? The specific arrangements and obligations of the *publicani* under the contracts to collect the Asian taxes are not known. It may be that the Romans adopted or adapted an Attalid system, but the precise modalities of any such arrangements are also lost. The supplement to the Customs Law of Asia by the consuls of 17 BC envisages yearly payments, as does the addition to the same document by the *curatores* appointed in AD 62.[128] Lintott believes that yearly payments may have been an innovation and thinks it likely that, under the Republic, the *publicani* became liable for the sums they owed only at the end of a *lustrum*.[129] On the other hand, the editors of the new text of the Customs Law of Asia rightly point out, in their commentary, that the reference to yearly payments in the supplement of 17 BC could just be 'because pre-existing practice had grown slack'.[130] In any case, it seems inherently improbable that C. Gracchus, in drafting his new law for the taxation of Asia, would have allowed a period of five years to pass before the Roman people received any revenue at all from the new province. That the revenue to be received was fixed and predetermined is suggested by the only example of a contract with a *societas publicanorum* surviving from the Republican period. It dates from 105 and is a tiny one for the building of a wall in front of the temple of Serapis at Puteoli.[131] Under the terms of the contract, payment was to be made in two instalments, half at the time of contracting and the balance upon the completion and approval of the work. Similar economics are suggested by the *decuma* in Sicily, which, although contracted by the governor in Sicily rather than the censors in Rome, was sold for a fixed amount of grain, which suggests that the successful bidder bound himself to deliver this amount of grain to the authorities and made his profit by collecting more than the amount he had bid.[132] Fixed-price contracts are also implied by the nature of the disputes between the *publicani* and Cato the censor in 184: 'et vectigalia summis pretiis, ultro tributa infimis

[126] Cic. *II Verr*. 3. 130. [127] Trans. Loeb IX 159.

[128] Customs Law of Asia, lines 99–101, 144–7. [129] Lintott 1993: 89.

[130] Cottier et al. 2008: 98.

[131] *ILLRP* 518, grandly named by modern scholars the *lex Puteolana de parieti faciundo*; Badian 1972: 68.

[132] Cic. *II Verr*. 3. 75; cf. 3. 113, 3. 116; the abuses arising from this system are described at Cic. *II Verr*. 3. 84ff.

locaverunt'[133] (and they farmed out the taxes at the highest price and public works contracts at the lowest). All these passages suggest that the *publicani* undertook these projects at a fixed rate, which gives a clue to the procedure for the contracts in Asia. There, although the percentage rates of tax were fixed (2½% for the *portorium* and 10% for the *decuma*), both the *portorium* and the *decuma* would have produced revenues that varied in amount, depending on the value of trade crossing the borders of Asia, in the first case, and on the level of crop production in the province in the second.[134] This variability is emphasized by Marcus Antonius in his speech to the Greeks of Asia when he says:

> *ἐπεὶ δὲ ἐδέησεν, οὐ πρὸς τὰ τιμήματα ὑμῖν ἐπεθήκαμεν, ὡς ἂν ἡμεῖς ἀκίνδυνον φόρον ἐκλέγοιμεν, ἀλλὰ μέρη φέρειν τῶν ἑκάστοτε καρπῶν ἐπετάξαμεν.*[135]
>
> (But when they became necessary, we did not impose them upon you according to a fixed valuation, so that we could collect an absolutely certain sum. We required you to contribute a portion of your yearly harvest.)

But the bids to collect these taxes made by the *publicani* at the auction in Rome must have been at fixed prices. The episode in 61–59 BC (described by the scholiast on Cicero's *Pro Plancio* 31, a speech delivered in 61), in which the *societas publicanorum* that had contracted for the Asian taxes requested a reduction in what it owed under the contract, makes no sense unless the *publicani* had bid a fixed price to collect a stream of variable revenue, which, in the event, resulted in significantly less income than the price bid for the contract:

> Cum princeps esset publicanorum Cn. Plancii pater, et societas eadem in exercendis vectigalibus gravissimo damno videretur adfecta, desideratum est in senatu nomine publicanorum, ut cum iis ratio putaretur lege Sempronia, et remissionis tantum fieret de summa pecunia, quantum aequitas postularet, pro quantitate damnorum quibus fuerant hostili incursione vexati.[136]
>
> (When the father of Gnaeus Plancius was the head of a group of *publicani* and the same society appeared to have been hit by a very serious loss on the collection of the taxes, he requested in the senate in the name of the *publicani* that the account with them under the *lex Sempronia* should be settled with an equitable deduction from the sum of money due, in view of the size of losses which they had incurred from the hostile incursions.)

In making their bids to collect a tax, the revenues from which would vary annually, the *publicani* would, therefore, have had to estimate how much revenue they thought it likely that the tax in question would produce over the forthcoming

133 Livy, 39. 44. 7.

134 From Cicero we learn that the profit margins of the publicani in Sicily also varied. We hear of 10% and 6% (Cic. *Rab. Post.* 30; Cic. *II Verr.* 3. 116).

135 App. *B. Civ.* 5. 4.

136 *Schol. Bob.* p. 157 St.; Cic. *Att.* 1. 17. 9 also refers to this demand for remission. Lintott (1993: 89) is probably correct to suggest that at issue in 61 was the contract due to end in March 60, probably let by the censors of 65, the excessive optimism of which became apparent as the term of the contract came nearer. But this does not necessarily indicate that the *publicani* were only liable for the sums that they owed at the end of the five-year period. If they had contracted at a fixed rate, with payment on an annual basis (as discussed earlier), they might have realized that they would make a loss during the first, say, three years of the contract, but gambled that they would make a large profit during the last, say, two years.

five-year period. They were going on risk: if the actual outcome was that the tax produced more revenue than the cost of their bid, they made a profit. If it generated less, all they could do to protect their position was either to extract more from the hapless Asian taxpayers to make up the shortfall (Marcus Antonius must be referring to this when Appian makes him say: 'when those who collected these taxes on the authority of the senate abused you by demanding much more'[137]) or to appeal for a reduction in what they owed under their contracts, as happened in 61–59 BC. Consciously or not, this was also an exercise in risk mitigation by the Roman state. By selling the right to tax, the Roman state transferred its risk to the *publicani* and so was sure, in the absence of unforeseen circumstances, to receive predetermined amounts of revenue, which thus made budgeting for expenditure easier to achieve.

How did the *publicani* decide at what level to pitch their bids? They had precedents from the days of Attalid rule that could be used as a guide. We know from the Customs Law of Asia that the Attalids had a system of customs dues, and Appian's report of Marcus Antonius' speech makes clear that the Attalids had used fixed assessments rather than a variable rate to collect the agricultural tax. Probably, therefore, the *publicani* had some information at least on which to base their first bids in the late 120s. Thereafter their experience over the course of the first five-year contract period would inform their bids for the succeeding period.[138]

So much for the *publicani*. But what of the censors? How did they know at the beginning of a *lustrum* whether the *publicani* were bidding realistic prices? The efficiency of this method of revenue collection depended in part upon the censors making a correct assessment of the likely revenues to be collected from the Asian province. For the first *lustrum* they, like the *publicani*, could presumably use the records of the Attalids. That the censors were keen to make a correct assessment of likely revenues can be seen from the disputes between the *publicani* and Cato the censor in 184, which were all about price.[139]

CONCLUSION

We have argued that Appian's account is correct and that no revenues were collected by the Romans in Asia until C. Gracchus introduced his *lex Sempronia de provincia Asia* in the late 120s. There are good reasons for this judgement. First, the delay in the settlement of the new Asian province, caused by the war with Aristonicus and the subsequent negotiations over the new province's boundaries, would have made the imposition of a tax regime extremely difficult if not impossible in practice, since the taxable area of the province was probably not conclusively defined until some time after 126. Secondly, the only individual during this period who is connected with the taxation of Asia in any of our sources is C. Gracchus. He is also said to have instituted *portoria*, and we now have evidence

[137] App. *B. Civ.* 5. 4.
[138] Cf. Bell (2007) 191–3, using Cic. *II Verr.* 3. 120, for a model of how this might have worked in Sicily.
[139] Livy, 39. 44. 7–8.

of the introduction of such dues in Asia with the discovery of the Customs Law of Asia, the earliest part of which seems to date back to the 120s. Furthermore, in none of our literary sources is there any specific mention of any process of revenue collection in Asia by the Romans before C. Gracchus. The principal witness for the opposing view is the *Senatus Consultum de Agro Pergameno*, which could just as easily refer to events of 122 as of 129.

Although C. Gracchus' enemies accused him of draining the treasury dry, his approach of trying to match revenues and expenditure was in fact financially very prudent. As he makes clear in his speeches, his concern is to ensure that the Roman people benefit from the profits of empire. The *lex Sempronia repetundarum* was intended to deter magistrates from abusing their position of authority through embezzling property and funds that were due to the Roman people. It was, in this sense, an economic measure, designed to ensure that the Roman people actually received the revenues from Asia. His introduction of the system of *censoria locatio* under the *lex Sempronia de provincia Asia* was a measure to ensure that these revenues would be maximized and available to cover the cost of his economic programme. As such, it was the first clearly identifiable attempt by an individual Roman magistrate to produce a systematic state budget in support of a massive programme of public expenditure.

But the wider significance of these laws is that they mark the beginning of a more controlled and thoroughgoing exploitation of the resources of the Mediterranean by the Romans. The *censoria locatio* was intrinsically forward-looking. The Roman people would know that, in the absence of any unusual circumstances, a predetermined stream of revenue would be coming into the *aerarium*. Given the size of these revenues, it allowed the Romans to budget for large projects for at least five years ahead and reduced their dependency on less certain forms of income such as booty and mining revenues.

Part II

The Roman Money Supply

5

Cashing in the Plunder

Pecunia . . . signata forma p(ublica) p(opulei) R(omanei).[1]

INTRODUCTION

In the last few chapters we have seen how, during the second century, vast quantities of bullion came to Rome in the form of war booty and indemnities from most of its defeated enemies, notably Carthage, Macedonia, and Syria. These sources of precious metal were in time replaced by tax revenues from Rome's expanding empire. At the same time, both Polybius and the archaeological record suggest that, by the mid-second century, significant quantities of bullion were being mined in Spain. These inflows were on a scale that dwarfed anything the Romans had received previously. From booty and indemnities alone Rome received, over the fifty-year period that followed the Second Punic War, the equivalent of 1,050 tonnes of silver or an average of 21 tonnes per annum.[2] The Spanish mines, by the 150s, were generating 35 tonnes of silver per annum; and the provinces (of which Asia was the most important) were producing, by the time of Pompey's conquests, the equivalent of perhaps 190 tonnes of silver per annum (although of course the actual bullion component of provincial taxation is unknown, since this source included payment in kind).[3]

In other societies, similarly transformative inflows to these have had significant impacts. For example, many economic historians believe that Spanish gold and silver imported from America, in the sixteenth century AD, accounted for the 'price revolution'—the century and a half of sustained inflation that accompanied and, in the view of many, caused early modern Europe's rapid steps towards a more specialized, urban, market economy.[4] From AD 1400 to 1500, and from AD 1650 to 1750, prices in Europe remained virtually unchanged. Yet, in the

[1] 'Money . . . struck with the public type of the Roman people': *lex de Gallia Cisalpina* (*CIL* 1^2 592, Ch. XXI.1; Crawford 1996: no. 28).

[2] See Ch. 2.

[3] Spanish mines: see Ch. 3; provinces: 8,300 talents p.a. × 23.16 kg = 192.28 tonnes p.a. (see pp. 72–3).

[4] The annual inflows of New World bullion are estimated to have been between 3m. and 6m. 'rix-dollars' in the mid-sixteenth century (equivalent to between 86 and 172 tonnes of silver p.a.), rising to between 10m. and 13m. 'rix-dollars' p.a. (equivalent to between 287 and 373 tonnes of silver p.a.) by the end of that century (D. Fisher 1989: 886).

intervening century and a half, the price level rose by 500 per cent, a persistent 1.2 per cent per annum rise in prices.[5]

The monetary base of Rome in the second century consisted of a silver- and copper-denominated metallic coinage. Economic agents, whether individuals or financial intermediaries (that is, early 'banks'), held their liquid reserves in this form.[6] We might, therefore, expect, in this hard-money world, that the vast inflows of precious metals that Rome received in the second century would also have had a significant impact, at the very least in monetary terms, when they were injected into the Roman economy as bullion for minting coin.

The bullion theory of the sixteenth-century AD price revolution received its modern form from the combination of Fisher's quantity equation of money and Hamilton's research into Spanish imports of bullion.[7] The quantity equation encapsulates the relation between money and prices: in any time interval, the money supply (M) multiplied by its velocity of circulation (V) must be sufficient to purchase the real output of an economy (y) at its sale price (P). Thus $MV=Py$ (money supply × velocity of circulation = price × real output). Clearly, if V and y are constant, increases in M will translate into similar increases in P, unless there is at the same time a fall in V, or a rise in y. One sign of a healthy economy is, therefore, a growing money supply accompanied by low or negligible inflation. This can indicate that the real output of the economy is growing and, therefore, that the overall economy itself is expanding.

In relation to second-century BC Rome, the question, therefore, becomes whether the massive inflows of bullion were minted into coins. If the answer to this is in the affirmative, then a number of other questions follow. Did the increased supply of coins result in an increase in economic activity (an increase in real output, y), or an increase in inflation, P, or both (as appears to have happened in sixteenth-century AD Europe)? Alternatively, did this increase in production merely result in a greater depth of penetration of Roman coins, as the countryside and perhaps the cities were monetized? Furthermore, was there an increased geographic range of circulation, as the denarius, on the one hand, replaced local silver civic coinages in the west that had existed prior to the arrival of Rome, such as at Carthage, and, on the other, reached relatively newly monetized areas, such as Spain?

Prior to the Carthaginian indemnity at the end of the First Punic War, Rome had issued silver coinage only on a very small scale. That indemnity appears to have coincided with a growth in coin production. It is also clear that another increase in the minting of silver coins began around the middle of the second century, but the problem is to quantify that increase. No mint records have survived from the Roman world, and there is no other direct evidence for the quantity of coin produced, and so it is necessary to use other methods to estimate the amount of coined money in circulation.

[5] Goldstone 1984: 1122–3 with table 1.

[6] In Rome, as in many other societies, silver possessed the characteristics requisite for commodity money: 'relative inelasticity of supply of a scarce good having inherent utilitarian value coupled with some possibility of expansion of stock through trade or production' (Cohen 1992: 10).

[7] I. Fisher 1911; Hamilton 1934.

In the sections that follow, we shall begin by considering the validity of the 'Hopkins Model' as a means for estimating the amount of coined silver money in circulation. We shall then move on to consider the extent to which more denarii may have been produced simply in order to monetize the rural economy or to replace previously existing coinages in the Mediterranean. Finally, we shall try to determine whether there is any evidence for price inflation in the Roman economy during this period. By doing this, we hope to be able to gain a clearer idea as to whether Rome's increased money supply went into monetizing the empire, into price inflation, or into real economic growth.

THE ROMAN DENARIUS AND THE 'HOPKINS MODEL'

Although Rome had experimented with a wide variety of coin types and standards during the third century, the introduction of the silver denarius, in approximately 212, brought about a shift to a standard format that produced a consistency of metrology and a strict denominational relationship with its subsidiary silver fractions and the bronze coinage.[8] For a period of seventy-five years there was also a consistency in the typography of the denarius. On the obverse, the helmeted head of the goddess Roma always appeared, while, on the reverse, were the Dioscuri (*RRC* no. 44). As an alternative, from the beginning of the second century, a variety of deities in a *biga* chariot (e.g. *RRC* no.141) were shown on the reverse. Gradually, too, the names of the moneyers or their symbols begin to appear on coins. A dramatic change in typography occurred, probably in 137, when the traditional designs began to be replaced with a variety of types that often refer to past events or historical precedents and frequently have a political relevance. The denarius was minted at Rome in increasingly large quantities throughout the Republican period after the end of the Third Macedonian War.

In his article 'Taxes and Trade in the Roman Empire (200 B.C.–A.D. 400)', Keith Hopkins set out a model for the Roman economy, arguing for a connection between the development of trade and the payment of taxes.[9] Hopkins advanced seven propositions, the fifth of which was that the supply of Roman silver denarii increased enormously, perhaps tenfold, between 157 and 50. The chart that accompanied the article, reproduced in Fig. 5.1, has, for a number of scholars, acted rather like a red rag to a bull.

[8] The bronze coinage was produced on a huge scale in the first half of the second century, and on a much lower scale in the second half, after a probable switch in the medium of military pay from bronze to silver.

[9] Hopkins 1980; in a later article (2002: 191–2), Hopkins provides this definition: 'A model is roughly speaking a simplification of a complex reality, designed to show up the logical relationships between its constituent parts . . . The model is a sort of master picture, as on the front of a jigsaw puzzle box; the fragments of surviving ancient sources provide only a few of the jigsaw pieces.' This appears to be derived, via Finley (1985*b*: 182) from Chorley and Haggett (1968: 22).

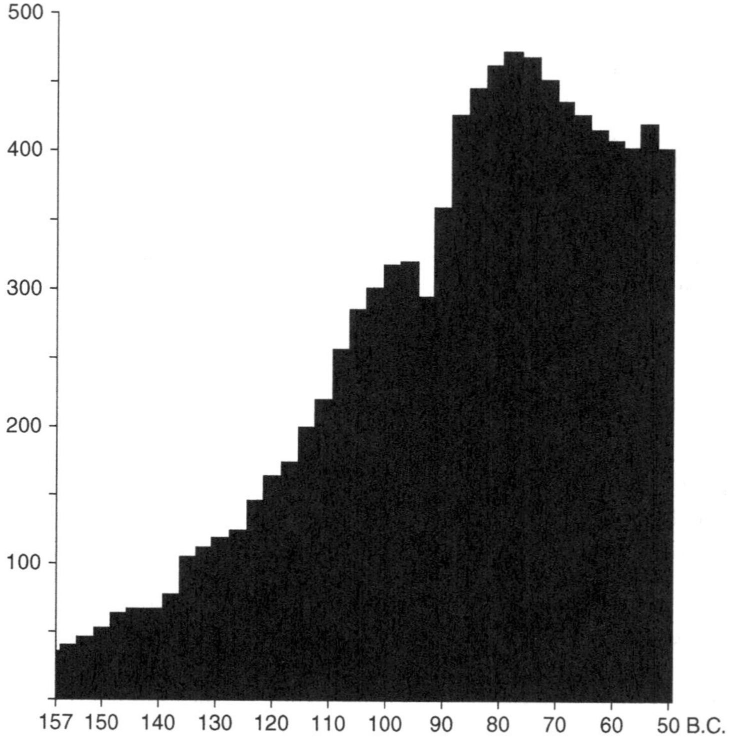

Fig. 5.1. Roman silver coins in circulation 157–50 BC (in millions of denarii, by 3-year periods)

Hopkins's fifth proposition and its accompanying chart were based on the work of Michael Crawford, who had attempted to determine the volume of coinage produced by the Roman mint from 157 to 50 by using this procedure:[10]

- 24 large Roman Republic denarius hoards were laid out chronologically by moneyer;
- These 24 hoards were aggregated by issue, (intuitively) adjusting some figures considered 'abnormal';
- Issues were selected where the dies had symbols on them and the number of obverse dies used was counted;
- This small number of issues (whose obverse dies had been counted) was then compared with the number of coins of each issue occurring in the aggregate sample. The ratios of coins to dies thus obtained were used for every issue as a multiplication factor to obtain an estimate of the number of dies used to strike that issue;
- The average coin production per die was calculated for the denarii of the general C. Annius (*RRC* 366, probably struck in 82 and 81), derived from Crawford's estimate of the requirements for legionary pay; and

[10] Crawford 1974: 633–707; this summary of the procedure is adapted from Buttrey 1993: 335–6.

- To quantify the annual production of denarii for all issues, the number of dies extrapolated for each was multiplied by the production figure calculated for Annius (30,000 coins per die).

In essence, therefore, what Crawford did was to extrapolate die estimates for the majority of issues from die studies of a few selected issues, using the relative frequency of issues in hoards as an index of their original relative sizes. His principle was that 'if an issue surviving in *x* specimens used *y* dies, and an issue surviving in *2x* specimens used *2y* dies', then it was likely that 'the first issue was half the size of the second'.[11]

Crawford's procedure ran into a barrage of criticism. Mattingly, Frier, and notably Buttrey attacked him for, *inter alia*, basing his die estimates on the combination of hoards of different dates, as well as for failing to establish that the coin finds and dies of any two issues fall into the same pattern.[12] De Callataÿ, however, sought to defend Crawford's approach of extrapolating from a relatively small sample size (a criticism that Buttrey had also directed against Walker's work on imperial coins found in Bath[13]). On Walker, de Callataÿ pointed out that, although his calculations were managed with a studied sample representing only 1/33,333rd of the theoretical total, this proportion was in line with sampling sizes in modern political polls. He went on to suggest, using his own work on early cistophoric coinage (for which there are both die studies and hoard evidence), that there is a 'generally valid' link between the number of dies used and the number of specimens discovered in hoards.

Crawford was also criticized in a number of ways for using an average figure of 30,000 coins minted per die. Mattingly argued that he erroneously deduced the cost of a legion, which is the calculation from which this figure of 30,000 is derived.[14] Burnett objected that comparative evidence on die output, available from the mints of London and Canterbury for the years AD 1279–1327, showed a considerable spread: at one extreme a year's average production of approximately 2,000 pieces per die and approximately 78,000 pieces per die at the other.[15] Ripollès, in a conventional study of the limited coinage of the mint of ancient Valentia, further demonstrated that there can be genuine disparities in coin production between dies.[16] On top of all this, there is absolutely no literary or epigraphic evidence to support Crawford's theory that soldiers were paid only in new coin.

But de Callataÿ argued that, however erroneously arrived at, the number of 30,000 coins per die, as an average, would appear to have some justification for silver of the medieval period in England. This is because, whereas the average *annual* productivity ranges from about 2,000 to about 78,000 coins per die, the average of the averages *over the whole period* tends towards 30,000 to 35,000 per die. There is also evidence to suggest that die productivity from a screw press in nineteenth-century Paris was in this area too. Finally, he developed his own work on the tetradrachms of Mithradates VI of Pontus to show that an average output of 30,000 coins per die can be very roughly deduced from a coinage where we have a very precise chronology.[17]

11 Crawford 1974: 641.

12 H. B. Mattingly 1977; Frier 1976, 1981; Buttrey 1989, 1993, 1994.

13 De Callataÿ 1995; Walker 1988.

14 H. B. Mattingly 1977: 206–8.

15 Burnett 1991: 46.

16 Ripollès 1987.

17 In a forthcoming article, Crawford argues that 'if one takes that figure [*c*.30,000] and multiplies it by the extrapolated number of dies for the so-called 'Legionary' issues of M. Antonius, the volume of coinage predicted is exactly the figure at which one arrives for one *stipendium* by multiplying one third of the probable total cost of a legion in 31 BC by the number of legions involved'.

But other difficulties remain. Any attempt to model from hoards found in different parts of the embryonic Roman Empire is problematic because there can be geographic variations in hoard patterns, due to the unequal distribution of coinage between, for example, Italy and Spain.[18] Also, Crawford's die estimates do not take account of the 'attrition rate' (the rate at which coins are lost and fall out of circulation). The absence of an attrition rate from Crawford's estimates might explain why Hopkins's graph of the money supply between 157 and 50 rises so spectacularly through time. It could be argued that the supposed rise occurs, not because successive issues of denarii were even larger, but only because the earlier the issue, the more was omitted in the original calculations. Even if (continues the criticism) one does assume an attrition rate, as Hopkins does (of 2%), such a rate cannot have been stable, first because of the varying numbers of hoards buried and not recovered by their owners in each year, and secondly because of the different reasons for hoards being buried in the first place. Even Volk does not suggest that the Lohe deposit, where we have both coins and mint records, can provide a general circulation model for the currency of eighteenth-century AD Sweden.[19]

Again de Callataÿ leapt to Crawford's defence, adducing studies done by Preston, Volk, and Depeyrot.[20] All have done work on the attrition rate of Republican coins and have come up with figures in the 2–3 per cent range: 'I have no problem in recognising that the 2% rate might be a poor approximation and that a rate of 3% changes the shape of the curve [of the Hopkins money supply graph]'.

Persuasive support for Crawford's estimates also comes from a simulation study by Lockyear and a study of hoard evidence by Backendorf.[21] Lockyear makes no attempt to defend the number of 30,000 coins per die in his study, assuming in his formula that this factor is 'any large number'. What he claims to show is that it is possible within a reasonably homogeneous series such as the Republican denarii to calculate the *relative size of issues* and to model the composition of the coinage pool. He believes that Crawford's die-count figures are an excellent approximation of the relative size of issues released into the coinage pool over the whole series; and that 2 per cent is a good average figure to use for the attrition rate, although a 1 per cent rate may be evident for second-century coins. He concludes that his results do not prove that Crawford's die estimates are accurate, but rather that it would seem that the inaccuracies balance themselves out over the whole period. In other words, Crawford's approach works because of the large number of hoards used in the sample. He rightly points out that Hopkins never claimed that the 30,000 figure was accurate, but that the average number of coins struck per die was roughly stable over a period of a century.[22] Lockyear, therefore, believes, on the basis of his simulations, that the increase in the total pool of denarii was between five- and tenfold. Backendorf has tried to reconstruct the relative quantities of coins produced between 150 and 25 BC, by using a totally different method. In essence, what he does is to analyse the impact of the minting of a new issue on the existing general population of

18 Volk 1995. 19 Volk 1987: 166.

20 De Callataÿ 1995; Preston 1983; Volk 1987: 180–1, 189; Depeyrot 1993: 77–81, 107–10.

21 Lockyear 1999; Backendorf 1998; cf. Hollander 2007: 137.

22 Hopkins 1980: 107: 'we can regard [the money supply graph] as being drawn on a ratio scale'.

coins. If a new issue represents a large proportion of the coins in a hoard, then the (coinage) money supply to which this issue was added must have been small (and vice versa). Backendorf also concludes that there was a huge increase in the minting of coins over the period surveyed.[23]

Crawford's critics have shown that some of his detailed arguments are based on a degree of subjective interpretation, which inevitably limits the accuracy of the whole procedure. But Lockyear's and Backendorf's studies have confirmed that the general trends in denarius production put forward by Crawford are correct, if approximate, and, crucially, that there was significant relative growth in the amount of denarii in circulation between 157 and 50.

MONETIZING THE EMPIRE AND THE COUNTRYSIDE?

What drove this huge expansion in Rome's production of denarii? Did the increased supply of denarii result from more coins being introduced to replace barter, especially in the countryside? For the Roman period in general it used to be argued by Burnett and Crawford that the countryside was not monetized;[24] but Howgego, using documentary and archaeological evidence, presents an overall picture suggesting that while agricultural produce, particularly corn, played a substantial role alongside money, in taxation, rents, wages, and credit, money was the dominant means of exchange for goods, not only in the cities, but also in the countryside.[25] The evidence for the Republican period is inevitably limited, and Howgego's analysis focuses on the Principate, but there are some anecdotal indications. First, the structure of the denarius coinage, introduced in 212, included denominations small enough to cope with everyday purchases, which suggests that monetization of the retail trade was largely well under way, at least in the cities.[26] As we shall see in Ch. 6, the plays of Plautus, which date from the late third and early second centuries, also reveal an urban environment that is highly monetized.[27] As far as the countryside is concerned, Polybius refers to the use of coin in country inns in Cisalpine Gaul (presumably in about 151);[28] and Cato the Elder reveals a world that is at least partly monetized. In his *De Agricultura*, the *paterfamilias* is advised to review the cash accounts on his arrival at his farm.[29] Finally, there is some archaeological evidence: a number of rural sites throughout Italy have yielded both silver and bronze denominations.[30]

23 Backendorf 1998: 202, 538–42.

24 Crawford 1970: 45; Burnett 1987*a*: 96.

25 Howgego 1992: 20–2; cf. Hollander 2007: 122–35.

26 Monetization may be simply defined as 'an increase in the use of money for more activities'.

27 The current consensus would be that, by 150, urban monetization was very advanced: Crawford 1970: 42; Howgego 1992: 29; Burnett 1987*a*: 95; Hollander 2007: 111–18.

28 Polyb. 2. 15; for the date see n. 91.

29 Cato, *Agr.* 2. 5; implied too by Cato, *Agr.* 145, 149, and 150, in the context of auctions of agricultural products.

30 Hollander 2007: 131, citing Small 1974; Small et al. 1992; Barker 1995: 207; Gazzetti 1995; and Visonà and Frey-Kupper 1996: 81.

So if the increasing depth of penetration of Roman coins does not fully account for the large increase in their supply, does an increased geographic range? To answer this we need to consider what civic and local coins continued to be struck and used in areas under Roman control, and examine the likely dates for the introduction of the denarius outside central Italy.

From the end of the Second Punic War the new denarius coinage in all its constituent parts was dominant in Italy. While a small number of cities (Paestum, Brundisium, and about ten others) did produce some low-denomination bronze coins at various points after this, these issues were far too small to represent any form of serious civic expenditure. In the vast majority of cases, Roman coins replaced the multiplicity of Italian silver and bronze coins in circulation there. This seems to represent a conscious Roman decision to demonetize the earlier Italian coinages and to denominate all monetary transactions in Roman coins.[31]

Outside Italy, however, the spread of the denarius was extremely slow. It is true that Roman coinage quickly became dominant in Sicily, with the Romans striking there during the Second Punic War (although some local bronze coins continued to circulate as late as the early Principate), and in Cisalpine Gaul in the early second century. But after that every situation was different. During the second and first centuries, there was a patchwork quilt of coinages in the areas controlled by the Romans. Even Augustus did not impose Roman denominations on all areas under Roman control. Indeed it was not until the reign of Diocletian, nearly five hundred years after the introduction of the denarius, that the end of the Ptolemies' closed coinage system finally occurred.

In fact, what is striking about the numismatic history of the areas under Roman control, in the second and first centuries BC, is how limited the adoption of the denarius actually was.

In Africa, the Carthaginian gold, silver, and bronze coinage is presumed to have disappeared after 146 to be replaced by Roman denarii.[32] It is probable that the Romans melted down and re-coined the Carthaginian coinage; but the hoard evidence is very thin, with only eleven hoards known to contain Republican denarii having been found.[33] The (presumed) earliest hoard, with a mixture of Republican denarii down to 146 and late Punic silver, is assumed by Burnett to be plunder taken from the destruction of Carthage (it also included silver ornaments) and so not typical of coinage in circulation.[34] For the remaining hoards, there are few reports of their contents so it is not possible to see if there is any pattern in their geographic or chronological distribution. It is perfectly possible that Roman coins did not begin to appear in Africa on any scale until about twenty-five years after the final destruction of Carthage, when the colony of Junonia was established by C. Gracchus.[35] The main evidence for the presence of Roman coin in Africa is provided by references in Sallust and Plutarch to coinage being shipped to Africa in 111 and 110, and then again in 82.[36] The earlier dates would of course coincide both with

[31] Burnett 1982: 126.

[32] Burnett 1987*b*: 175; Crawford 1985: 140; Burnett et al. 1992: 182; but cf. Buttrey 1989: 70.

[33] The hoards are listed in Crawford 1985: app. 42 and Burnett 1987*b*: 180–1.

[34] *RRCH* 132; Burnett 1987*b*: 176.

[35] See pp. 69–70 and 137–8.

[36] Sall. *Iug.* 27. 5; 36. 1; Plut. *Pomp.* 11.

the sale of *ager publicus* mentioned in the *lex agraria* of 111 and the presence of merchants in Utica, Vaga, and Cirta, at the time of the Jugurthine war.[37] But neither the hoard nor the literary evidence is sufficient to give any indication of the amount of denarii circulating in Africa at this time.

To turn to Spain, local coinages are present on the eastern coast during the Second Punic War, probably because both Roman and Carthaginian armies required their production to pay troops. In the second century, local production continues on this coast and along the Ebro and Guadalquivir valleys, with most of the coins being found close to towns, mining areas, and trading ports. Not all cities issued coins and, as an example (and rather surprisingly, given its proximity to the silver mines), Carthago Nova started to issue coins only from the middle of the first century. Roman types do not appear to have inspired the iconography of these coins, which seem to take their designs more from Hellenistic styles. The Iberian script is commonly used. From the late second or early first centuries, some signs of Roman cultural assimilation are visible in the iconography and legends on Iberian coins. But this happened only in a limited number of cities, where Latin started to be introduced for place or personal names, and designs were taken from Roman models.

The Roman denarius begins to appear in Spanish hoards from 125 onwards, and travels to Spain in large quantities from about 115 onwards. Bronze civic coinages continue to appear until they cease under Claudius. But the major development in the Spanish coinage during the second century was the production of what has been termed the 'Iberian denarius'. This consists of a silver coin of the weight of a Roman denarius, with silver and bronze fractional pieces. The usual type is a Male Head/Horseman, but these Iberian denarii are, apart from their iconography, clearly based on the Roman currency. They constitute a substantial element of the hoard stock lost during the last quarter of the second century.[38] Crawford believes that the coins were first minted in 155–154, at the time of the switch in the medium of payment for Roman soldiers from bronze to silver.[39] Frank, on the other hand, believed that the mysterious term *argentum oscense* (oscan silver), used by Livy in the context of a number of triumphs in the 190s, referred to the Iberian denarii.[40] This would push the date for the introduction of the Iberian denarius back by forty or more years. Knapp agrees with Frank and suggests that the origin of the term *argentum oscense* is to be found in the issues of the native Spanish town of Osca (modern Huesca).[41] They are the coins whose native legend reads BOLSCAN, later latinized on the coins to OSCA. He further believes that the cumulative evidence of literary references, hoards, coin types, and weights suggests that these Iberian denarii were introduced at the end of the third century. The issue of the date of their introduction is mainly relevant because of the possibility that they were struck to pay regular taxes to the Romans. But this must now be rejected. Important recent work using hoard evidence suggests that very few mints issued Iberian denarii during the first half of the second century and that their output was small in economic terms, with

[37] See Ch. 7 n. 49. [38] Volk 1995: 51. [39] Crawford 1985: 95.
[40] Frank 1933: 127; Livy, 34. 46. 2–3, 34. 10. 4, 34. 10. 7, 40. 43. 6; see p. 30.
[41] Knapp 1977, 1987.

significant quantities being found only from the last third of the second century.[42] This would appear to settle the argument for the time being, and we suspect that Livy did not know what he was referring to when he used the term, *argentum oscense*; it is perfectly possible that he was using an archaizing term for a reference in his sources that he did not understand.

All silver coinages of the Roman period were struck in the province of Hispania Citerior and no satisfactory explanation for their absence from Hispania Ulterior has yet been found. As Ripollès says, this surprising difference is one of the objections that must be addressed by those who believe that the creation and production of Iberian denarii were related to the payment of taxes.

Occasional examples of the denarius are found in Greek hoards from the middle of the second century, and the first appearance in a Delian inscription can be dated to 153;[43] but significant quantities are not found in hoards until the time of Sulla and, even then, the denarius does not seem to have been a major currency in the Greek world.[44] It is only with Marcus Antonius that it appears to have enjoyed wider use.[45] In the meantime, it competed against an array of local coinages, which continued to be struck by individual Greek *poleis* and which used iconographical types that made no reference to, or mention of, Rome (with the exception of some issues from Macedonia in the early 80s that have legends partly in Latin).[46]

After Rome's defeat of Macedonia, the 'New Style' or 'Wreath' Athenian tetradrachms ('stephanephori'), with the reverse type encircled by a wreath of oak, olive, laurel, or ivy, became by far the largest of these civic coinages. The only serious competitor was the federal coinage of the Achaean League, although, later in the first century, there were quite substantial issues of civic triobols in Sparta, Messene, Korone, Argos, Sikyon, and Megalopolis. The theory that, after Pydna in 168, the Romans ordered the withdrawal of all Macedonian regal coinage, including posthumous tetradrachms in the name of Alexander, and their replacement by the New Style coins has been discredited. First, the issue and circulation of the Alexanders continued well after 168 and, secondly, it now appears likely that the striking of the New Style coins began at some point around 180.[47] Nevertheless, what is striking about the New Style Athenian tetradrachms is the upsurge in their production in the early 160s, which resulted in 'a coinage with a regional significance, a quasi-provincial currency of large denomination', which continued to be struck in substantial quantities down to the 40s.[48]

[42] Ripollès 2005: 82–4; López-Sánchez (2005) hypothesizes that these issues might be related to the payment of native auxiliaries enrolled in the Roman armies.

[43] Thebes (*IGCH* 233) 1; Agrinion (*IGCH* 271) 39: this is now believed to date from about 130 (Warren 1999: 381) ; *IDélos* 1421; Price 1987: 99.

[44] Sullan hoards: *RRCH* 228, 242, *IGCH* 346.

[45] Delos: *RRCH* 465: 649 denarii; Euboea: *RRCH* 467: 97 denarii; Preveza (Actium): *RRCH* 473: 41 denarii.

[46] Warren 1999; De Callataÿ 1998; Crawford 1995: 197.

[47] Mørkholm 1980, 1984; Waggoner 1979; Touratsoglou 1987: 54; furthermore, the notion that a date in the 160s somehow fits in with a wave of economic prosperity at Athens, following the defeat of Macedonia, is contradicted by Pausanias' statement that Athens was in a state of direst poverty in the late 160s/early 150s as a result of the Third Macedonian War (Paus. 7. 11. 4–8).

[48] Price 1987: 96.

An important Amphictyonic decree from Delphi belongs some time around the fall of Corinth or later in the century.[49] It states that all the Greeks are to accept the Attic 'tetrachm' for four drachmas of silver and lays down various punishments for people who 'do not accept or do not give according to what has been written'. What exactly occasioned the decree is not known and it may merely acknowledge what was already a status quo. Unlike the Athenian decree on weights and measures from the second half of the fifth century, it does not prohibit other coinages from circulating. What it does do is to underline the importance of the Athenian tetradrachm or, as Crawford puts it, 'the fiscal acceptance in the Greek world of the silver coinage of Athens as a sort of international currency'.[50]

In Asia Minor, Eumenes II Soter of Pergamum had, at some point between the late 190s and the 160s BC, introduced a cistophoric coinage into his kingdom, recently enlarged by the settlement of Apamea. The cistophorus was named after its type, a sacred chest (*cista*), and the cistophoric tetradrachm was 25 per cent lighter than the Attic tetradrachm.[51] The reason for its introduction and the precise date at which this happened are still matters for debate. It seems that the cistophoric coinage was a very significant one. If François de Callataÿ and Andy Meadows are correct, then the annual value of minting under the Attalids, as represented by the output of cistophori, was higher than the output of both Seleucid tetradrachms and Athenian stephanephori.[52] This begs the question of why the cistophori were minted on such a grand scale, since this was in marked contrast to the level of minting before their introduction. In fact, the rate of production of cistophori appears to have been six or seven times greater than the minting of Attalid philetairi during the previous century. The most likely explanation of this is that the Attalids adopted a 'closed' monetary system, along Ptolemaic lines, with silver obtained from abroad, for example through customs duties, being re-minted, retained in the Attalid kingdom, and used to pay soldiers and state contractors (such as workers engaged in the monumentalization of Pergamum).[53] At the same time, a number of civic coinages of Attic weight were struck by certain of the Greek cities on the western littoral of Asia Minor. It seems that these were produced under Attalid supervision, more often than not using Attalid-supplied silver. Since these Attic weight coins have generally been found outside the kingdom, they perhaps represent a currency used by Pergamum in external transactions, from which the cistophori were excluded.[54]

Until recently, it had generally been believed that the cistophorus was introduced at some point between the late 190s and the 170s.[55] But Meadows has now argued, on the basis of hoard evidence, that the date of the introduction of the cistophoric coinage should be moved down to the middle of the 160s.[56] Arguably, too, the historical context of the 160s would fit the introduction of the coinage better, as this was a time when Eumenes' previously excellent relations with Rome went badly off the rails after he was suspected of having had secret dealings with Perseus during the Third Macedonian War.[57]

49 *Syll.*³ 729. 50 Crawford 1985: 127. 51 Howgego 1995: 54.
52 Meadows (2013); de Callataÿ (2013). 53 Ashton (2013).
54 Kinns 1987: 106. 55 Howgego 1995: 54. 56 Meadows (2013).
57 Kay (2013); Kleiner and Noe (1976: 16–17) also date the introduction of the cistophoric coinage to about 166 BC, on the grounds that it makes more sense to place it at a time when Eumenes was on bad terms with the Romans.

But whatever the date of its introduction, a desire to retain as much silver in his kingdom as possible may have prompted Eumenes' launch of a closed currency system. The Attalid kingdom does not appear to have had significant natural sources of silver;[58] and there are hints in our sources that the supply of bullion in the East was becoming tighter during this period. As we saw in Ch. 2, a huge war indemnity of 15,000 talents had been imposed on Antiochus III by the Romans, in 188, and part of the indemnity was paid late, in 173. Livy makes clear that the whole debt was paid off on that occasion and the assumption is that this was only one instalment, although for all we know it could have been more.[59] But there are also a couple of texts, in II Maccabees, that hint at the problems that the Seleucid kingdom had had in paying off the indemnity. One passage refers to a *phoros* of 2,000 talents owing to the Romans in 165.[60] It is highly probable that the dating is wrong,[61] but it is an intriguing reference to the monetary problems that the payment of the Syrian indemnity was perceived to have caused. According to the author, the Seleucids planned to raise funds for the *phoros* by selling captured Jews into slavery. The second passage also suggests that the Seleucids were short of money and attempted unsuccessfully to raise '400 talents of silver and 200 talents of gold' from the Temple treasury of Jerusalem.[62] Whatever was going on, the Seleucids were clearly having problems with their supplies of silver bullion. There is also numismatic evidence for a more general problem with the supply of silver, at the time of the Third Macedonian War, which is perhaps to be linked with the drain of bullion in the direction of Rome. The weight standard of the Macedonian coinage fell by between 7 and 8 per cent and, just before the war, the weight of Seleucid tetradrachms minted at Antioch was reduced by 2 per cent.[63] To compound the problems with the supply of silver, the Romans, as we have seen, acquired the gold and silver mines of Macedonia at the end of the war with Perseus. These mines were said to have been a source of enormous revenue (*ingens vectigal*) for the Macedonian kings, but the Romans immediately proceeded to close them;[64] and they remained shut for nine years, until reopened in 158.[65] Eumenes may have felt, because of this move and because of the problems that the Seleucids were facing, that supplies of silver in the eastern Mediterranean would contract even further, leading him to introduce a closed monetary system that would conserve his own kingdom's holdings of silver.

In 133, Attalus bequeathed his kingdom to Rome, but, despite this, some cities, including Pergamum itself and Ephesus, were given their freedom, so that their status was henceforth theoretically identical to that of places such as Smyrna. The pre-existing cistophoric mints continued to strike as before, and the creation of the province of Asia brought absolutely no change to either the silver or the bronze currency of the region. As in Greece, there is no sign of the suppression of any of the local coinages and there do not appear to have been any innovations,

[58] The only potential source of silver available to the Attalids would have been in the Troad, but 'the quantity of silver ores available could not vie with the richer deposits in the Taurus Mountains' (De Jesus 1978: 100). The Taurus Mountains were still under Seleucid control.

[59] Livy, 42. 6. 6–7. [60] II Macc. 8. 10. [61] Habicht 1979: 239 n. 10b.

[62] II Macc. 3. 11; cf. Dancy 1954: 43, Mørkholm 1966: 136.

[63] Howgego 1995: 114. [64] Livy, 45. 18. 3–5, 45. 29. 11.

[65] Cassiod. *Chron. sub anno* 158 BC.

apart from the very rare mention of denarii, for example in a section of the Customs Law of Asia, which probably dates from the 120s: '[ὑπὲρ σωμάτων ἀνδρείων ἢ θηλείων ἐκτὸς σωμάτων]παιδαρίων κορασίων μὴ τι πλεῖον τέλους ἑκάστης κεφαλῆς δηναρίων πέντε διδόναι ὀφειλέτω{ι}'[66] ([For male or female slaves except] male and female child [slaves] one is not obliged to pay as *telos* more than five denarii a head).[67] Indeed the period 133 to 88 may have seen an even greater proportion of silver being struck as cistophori, principally at Pergamum and Ephesus, than had been the case in the first fifty years of the coinage's existence.[68] The fact that Ephesus continued to strike cistophori, despite being one of the first cities to come out in support of Mithradates VI in 88, suggests that these coins were not regarded as a Roman coinage.

Production of the cistophoric coinage, certainly at Ephesus and probably at the other mints, ceased in 67. In the late 60s, bronze issues appear carrying the name of the proconsul and then, in the 50s, cistophori carrying the names of Roman governors are struck. While this represents a considerable contrast with the previous non-interventionist policy in Asia, it merely serves to underline the fact that Republican denarii played little, if any, role in Asia Minor before 50 and there is no hoard evidence of any significance before the 40s.[69] As Cicero implies in his letters, there was no ready convertibility between the cistophorus and the denarius, and so it looks as though the closed monetary zone continued under Roman administration. Cicero's profits of HS 2.2 million as governor of Cilicia remained on deposit in Asia for at least a year. The sum was in local cistophori, which may have been the reason for its not being repatriated at once. Getting use of the money involved a *permutatio* or currency-conversion;[70] and even Roman governors had to pay bankers' commission to change cistophori into denarii.[71] It is only during the civil wars that denarius production and circulation in Asia Minor start in earnest with issues from Lentulus, Brutus, Cassius, and Marcus Antonius.

One final point that is worth making, in this discussion of the geographic range of the denarius, is that the movement of coin to areas outside the emerging Roman Empire would not have been great at this period. In general, coins were used in the exchange process with less monetized areas only when it made economic sense (that is, when it was profitable) to do so. The massive trade in wine with Gaul, which will be discussed in Ch. 7, seems largely to have occurred without the denarius.[72] The finds of Roman coin beyond the German frontier, and even in Scandinavia, date only from later in the first century and the first significant leakage of coin (into Dacia) does not come until the 60s.[73] Furthermore the trade routes to India, which, according to Pliny the Elder, resulted in large outflows of coin to purchase luxury goods, were not fully developed until the first century AD.[74] It is true that Egypt's closed monetary system could have

66 Customs Law of Asia 12; see pp. 74–5 for dating.

67 Trans. M. H. Crawford in Cottier et al. 2008: 31.

68 Kinns 1987: 109. 69 Kinns 1987: 112.

70 Cic. *Att.* 11. 1–2 = Shackleton-Bailey: 1966: 211–12, with editor's comments; Cic. *Fam.* 5. 20.

71 Cic. *Att.* 12. 6. 1: 'sed certe in collybo est detrimenti satis'; cf. Cic. *Att.* 2. 6. 2, 2. 16. 4, 11. 1. 2.

72 See pp. 144–5. 73 Crawford 1985: 232; Harl 1996: 292, 464 nn.6–7.

74 Strabo, 2.98-99; Plin. *HN* 12.84.

meant that any incoming Roman coins were melted down to be restruck as local coins, but, overall, the amount of leakage of Roman coin to areas outside its area of control would probably have been small during the second and early first centuries.

Two different pictures emerge, therefore. In the Greek East, virtually no denarii circulate during the period under consideration. Conversely, a number of local currencies of the Greek world do not appear to have travelled to any noticeable extent outside the states to which they belonged, and they seem not to have been legal tender outside the borders of the state that minted them. Certainly it is clear that none of the other bullion currencies that existed within Rome's expanding empire ever circulated within Italy itself. Presumably foreign coins which were taken to Rome as part of a shipment of booty or in payment of an indemnity were melted down and reissued as denarii. But in the West, denarii form the currency in Italy, Sicily, and Cisalpine Gaul; and they appear to have been used in Africa (although the evidence is very limited). In Spain, however, hoard evidence suggests that the Roman denarius circulated only after 125 and that Iberian denarii constituted a substantial element of the coinage there.

Why did the denarius not spread eastwards? As we shall see in Ch. 8, there is considerable evidence for a very significant increase in trade through the Mediterranean in the last third of the second century. So would the denarius not have been driven eastwards by commercial factors? After all, the Customs Law of Asia, in a passage that probably dates from the 120s, does envisage the movement of coin across borders, when it states that: '*ὑπέρ τε χαλκοῦ καὶ ἀργύρου κεχαραγμένου, νομίσματος τε ἠριθμημένου . . . τέλος μὴ διδότω*'[75] (on struck bronze or silver or on coin that has been tallied . . . one is not to pay *telos*).[76] The absence of the denarius from the East is all the more surprising because the movement of central European silver, from the mining areas of Bohemia, Meissen, and Harz, through France and Italy to the eastern Mediterranean and ultimately to Cathay, was one of the reasons why Spufford was able to chart the commercial revolution of the thirteenth century AD.[77]

There are a number of possible answers to this conundrum.

First, the movement of coin did not always map trade. Where inter-regional trade took place, it did not necessarily generate money flows between regions on any scale commensurate with the volume of trade.[78] Maximizing the proceeds of maritime trade meant loading a ship with cargo on each leg of her journey, to be sold at a later port of call. The second-century AD trading contract which Scaevola cites shows a two-way traffic in cargo.[79] The shipper borrows money with which to buy a cargo in Berytos (Beirut). He does so on condition that he will buy other cargo at his destination in Italy and then repay the loan when he gets back to Berytos, after selling his second cargo. Money changes hand in Berytos, when the loan is made and the first cargo is bought. Money will change hands again in Brundisium, when the original cargo is sold and when the second cargo is

[75] Customs Law of Asia 61–2. [76] Trans. M. H. Crawford in Cottier et al. 2008: 51.

[77] Spufford 1988: 137, 154; it would also be at odds with Hopkins's 'Taxes and Trade' model, in which he argued that silver coinage was 'the most important element in financing long-distance trade', and that 'merchants and their customers needed money to buy what was traded' (Hopkins 1980: 106).

[78] Howgego 1995: 92. [79] Scaevola *ad Dig.* 45. 1. 122. 1.

purchased. But the coin itself appears not to travel, since the money used in Berytos stays in Berytos, and the money used in Brundisium stays in Brundisium.[80] That said, this 'natural' restriction on the movement of coin would have been as present in the thirteenth century AD as it was in the second century BC.

Secondly, there is no doubt that the risks involved militated against the transportation of large sums of coin by sea. According to Plutarch, the younger Cato shipped 7,000 talents from Cyprus to Rome, with cork marker buoys on board, in case the ship went down.[81] Few finds of large quantities of coin have been made on shipwrecks.[82] However, coin and bullion must have moved around the Mediterranean to some extent; otherwise Spanish silver and the indemnities and booty of the second century would not have reached Rome.[83] Indeed, in the treaty of Apamea, ships sailing with the *phoros* (in other words, the annual payments of the Syrian indemnity) are specifically envisioned.[84]

Thirdly, it is possible that there existed permanent prohibitions on the export of gold and silver, from Italy, of the type we find in the mid-first century. However, this too is unlikely. The way that these restrictions are mentioned by Cicero suggests that they were exceptional events.[85] Moreover, the expansion of trade with the East, which we shall discuss in Ch. 8, is unlikely to have occurred without some kind of expansion in monetary liquidity.

A more interesting line of enquiry is suggested by the consideration that, in the medieval period, there was only very limited silver coin in the eastern Mediterranean, while, in the Roman period, there already existed highly developed and plentiful coinages there. As we have already seen, the Athenian tetradrachm was the 'international' currency of choice. It is, therefore, entirely possible that Roman silver did move eastwards, but had to be exchanged with, or even melted down into, local coin on arrival. After all, as late as the middle of the first century, Cicero still had to exchange cistophori for denarii in Cilicia. Equally importantly, it seems probable that Roman traders were able to make payments at a distance, in other words without the direct use of coins, through the intermediation of bankers who afforded them credit.[86] The presence of bankers on Delos, in the later second century, provides support for this view, as will be discussed in Chs. 6 and 8.

[80] Duncan-Jones 1990: 42.

[81] Plut. *Cat. Min.* 38. 1; Plut. *C. Gracch.* 6; cf. Cic. *Fam.* 2. 17. 4. From time to time, large quantities of coin were shipped, but references to this in ancient authors are rare. In 130/129, the royal treasures of Pergamum were taken by ship to Rome (Just. *Epit.* 36. 4. 9). Plut. *Brut.* 24, 25 mentions treasure ships sailing from Asia to Greece which are encountered by Brutus. Caes. *B. Civ.* 3. 103 describes Pompey's preparations for his final voyage, when he took on board a large amount of bronze coin for army pay, which had been seized from the tax-farmers in Syria.

[82] Only small amounts of coin have in general been found on ancient wrecks (Parker 1992: 30), e.g. the wreck at La Madrague de Giens (Parker 1992: 250). A notable exception is the Antikythera 'A' wreck, which contained gold bars and coins (Ch. 2 n. 22).

[83] Lead and copper ingots have been found on shipwrecks from Spain, but there is no evidence for the shipment by sea of large quantities of mined silver from Spain to Rome. Perhaps one of the reasons for the construction of the *Via Domitia*, probably at some point between the late 150s and 118 BC (Polyb. 3. 39. 8), was to make the land transportation of silver more efficient.

[84] Polyb. 21. 42. 14. [85] Cic. *Vatin.* 12; Cic. *Flac.* 67. [86] Harris 2006: 11.

PRICES AND INFLATION

Inflation is a decline in the purchasing power of money. In virtually every other period in which there has been a rapid growth in the money supply, inflation has followed. This was as true of the years after Alexander the Great as it was of the sixteenth century AD and as it was of Germany in the 1920s. For each of these periods, sources are available for quantitative research. For the Hellenistic world, Tarn was able to analyse the dramatic increases in prices for various staples recorded in the temple accounts at Delos at the end of the fourth and beginning of the third centuries, following Alexander's capture of the Persian Empire's treasuries.[87] The history of prices in England begins in the thirteenth, or even the late twelfth century AD, from which time the data continue more or less unbroken to the present day.[88] No such luxuries are available to the economic historian of Republican Rome, since we have only a pitiful supply of data on prices from this period.

Our sources are completely silent about any inflationary problems affecting basic commodities, but a general drift upwards in prices can perhaps be inferred from the increases in the rate of military *stipendium* in the first century and in the levels of property qualifications in the second and first centuries BC.[89] Polybius does give prices for a range of foodstuffs from Cisalpine Gaul and Spain.[90] They probably come from his autopsy, since he visited both places, probably in 151, and we assume in the following discussion that these figures represent prices from that period.[91] Of these foodstuffs, the only one for which Polybius supplies prices and for which there is also a smattering of prices from the first century is wheat. For Cisalpine Gaul, Polybius gives a price of wheat of 4 obols per Sicilian medimnus and for Spain of 9 obols per Sicilian medimnus.[92] These numbers equate to HS 0.44 per modius and HS 1 per modius respectively. Then, in the *Verrines* (and, therefore, with reference to the late 70s BC), Cicero says that the official Roman compensation price for wheat in Sicily ranged from HS 3 to HS 4 per modius, but that the usual market price there was only HS 2, HS 2½, or, at the very most, HS 3 per modius.[93]

If we take the price of HS 0.44 per modius for wheat in Cisalpine Gaul in 151, provided by Polybius, and the highest market price of HS 3 per modius for wheat in Sicily in 70, given by Cicero, we can calculate an implied inflation rate of 2.43 per cent per annum over the eighty-year period; and, if we compare the (still noteworthy for Polybius) price of HS 1 in Spain, in 151, with the highest price, in 70, of HS 3 per modius, this produces an implied inflation rate of 1.38 per cent per

[87] Tarn 1923; see p. 190. [88] Mayhew 1995*a*: 238. [89] See Ch. 11.

[90] For Spain, (Polyb. 34. 8. 7–8), the range of prices is from 1 obol for a hare or a medium-sized kid to 10 drachmas for a ploughing ox. For Cisalpine Gaul (Polyb. 2. 15. 6), the range is from 2 obols for a metretes (39 litres) of wine to 4 obols for a Sicilian medimnus (51.5 litres) of wheat. It is worth noting in passing that, if these prices had been those obtaining in metropolitan Italy at this time, Roman coins in circulation at this period would have been adequate to meet the needs of everyday transactions.

[91] Polyb. 3. 59. 7; Walbank 1957: 4, 173; an alternative but less likely date for the visit is 146.

[92] As we saw in Ch. 2 (p. 22), Polybius equates the drachma with the denarius. On this basis, 1 obol would have been equivalent, approximately, to one-sixth of a denarius.

[93] Duncan-Jones 1976: 249; official compensation: Cic. *II Verr.* 3. 163, 3. 188; market prices: HS 2: Cic. *II Verr.* 3. 174, 3. 189; HS 2½: Cic. *II Verr.* 3. 84, 3. 90; 3. 173; 3. 175; HS 2–3: Cic. *II Verr.* 3. 189, 3. 194.

annum. A less extreme approach would perhaps be to compare Polybius' price of HS 1 in Spain in the late 150s with Cicero's price of HS 2 in the late 70s, which suggests an average inflation rate of 0.87 per cent per annum over the intervening period. At worst, therefore, these data suggest that the price of the main staple food for the Roman population was increasing at an annualized rate of 2.43 per cent per annum. This may not, at first sight, appear to be a dramatically high rate of inflation. Indeed, a modern central bank would be delighted with price increases of this order (at the time of writing, the Bank of England's inflation target is 2%). But not only is a rate of 2.43 per cent twice as high as the rate of inflation during the 'price revolution' of the sixteenth century AD, which we mentioned at the beginning of this chapter, but it also of course implies a doubling of prices roughly every twenty-nine years, because of the effects of compounding.

Burnett points to these figures as evidence that there was a general rise in the level of prices 'after the second century' and that this was due to the increase in the money supply suggested by Hopkins. He goes on to say that 'the increase in the level of monetary activity need not exclude a contemporary inflation of prices, and the evidence of prices, such as it is, suggests that this may have been so'.[94] But in fact these prices are not necessarily a reliable guide to the rate of inflation between 150 and 70 BC. Polybius mentions the prices of foodstuffs in Cisalpine Gaul and in Spain, precisely because they were notably low. So it is highly questionable whether the wheat prices from these two locations can be used as valid comparators, as we really have no idea of what a 'normal' price for wheat in Rome would have been in the 150s. The price of wheat was volatile. It varied year by year or from season to season (a fact which Cicero recognized[95]), as its price was heavily influenced by weather patterns over the short and the long term.

Arguably a more robust indicator of retail food price inflation is provided by the numismatic history of small-denomination Roman bronze coins. In the last years of the Second Punic War, the sextans (one-sixth of an as) was minted in large quantities, but a century later the coin had in effect ceased to be a functional coin and was only occasionally struck. Eventually it was no longer minted, which left the quadrans (one-quarter of an as) as the smallest bronze coin (Crawford dates this change to 91/90).[96] This development suggests that, between the middle of the second century and about 90 BC, prices of low-value goods had risen at a rate sufficient to make the sextans unusable in the marketplace. Crudely, if an item which in 150 was priced at a sextans (16.66% of an as) could only be purchased in 90 for a quadrans (25% of an as), the implication is that the price of that item had risen by 50 per cent during the intervening period of sixty years.

The shift from the sextans to the quadrans is probably to be connected with the retariffing, in about 141–140, of the denarius at 16 asses instead of at 10 asses and the subsequent expression in sestertii of assessments previously denominated in asses.[97] The impact of this change on the relationship between the silver coinage and the small-denomination bronze coinage would have been as follows. Before

[94] Burnett 1982: 133–4. [95] Cic. *II Verr.* 3. 216, 3. 227.

[96] Crawford 1985: 177: 'the numismatic evidence is borne out by the testimony of Cicero, *de Oratore* 2. 154, where the late second century Q. Granius is made to say of something that it was not worth a sextans; in the first century, the quadrans is used in similar phrases (Cic. *Cael.* 62; Hor. *Sat.* 1. 3. 137)'.

[97] Crawford 1985: 144–51.

the retariffing, when 1 denarius equalled 10 asses, 1 bronze sextans (one-sixth of a bronze as) was equivalent to one-sixtieth of a silver denarius. After the retariffing of the denarius at 16 asses, 1 bronze quadrans (one-quarter of a bronze as) was equivalent to one-sixty-fourth of a silver denarius.[98] This suggests that there was hardly any difference between the fraction of the silver denarius represented by the bronze sextans before the retariffing and the fraction represented by its successor, the bronze quadrans, after the retariffing. But to a holder of bronze coin, the retariffing was an inflationary increase, since the purchasing power of the bronze coinage relative to silver was sharply reduced. The official retariffing can perhaps be explained by assuming that it occurred following a period during which vendors of goods and services preferred to be paid in silver rather than in bronze and, in order to encourage this, offered lower prices in silver coin than in bronze coin for the same item. A modern analogy can be found in the tendency, in some Third World countries, for some prices to be expressed in US dollars and for these prices to be lower (when converted at the prevailing exchange rate) than the prices for the same items expressed in local currency. One of the reasons for this occurring might be, for example, because US dollars are regarded as more attractive to hold in a country experiencing a high rate of inflation. In Rome, this phenomenon presumably reflected a growing preference to hold silver rather than bronze coin as a store of value, a trend encouraged by the wider availability of silver coin resulting, in turn, from increased minting.[99]

There is also evidence that prices paid by the elite for luxury goods increased significantly during this period. For example, the censors of 89 set a maximum price for choice wines of HS 400 per amphora;[100] thirty years earlier the price had been HS 100 per amphora.[101] The same trend is implied by individual notices in our sources of the costs of such items as specialist slaves and tableware.[102] Finally, significant asset-price inflation can be deduced from the prices being paid for houses and estates in Italy in the mid-first century. For instance, Clodius' mansion in Rome was worth HS 14.8 million (616 talents), and the Tusculan villa of Scaurus HS 30 million (1,250 talents).[103] These prices can be compared with the entire fortune of Scipio Africanus, a little over 110 years earlier, which we estimated, in Ch. 2, at about 260 talents. It is precisely this rise in the prices of luxury goods and elite residential houses that underlies the moralizing of ancient commentators on this period.

[98] When 1 denarius = 10 asses, 1 sextans = 1/6 as = 1/60 denarius.
When 1 denarius = 16 asses, 1 quadrans = 1/4 as = 1/64 denarius.

[99] Different explanations have been offered for the retariffing. Burnett (1987*a*: 36) attributes it to the fact that 'the huge scale of minting [during the first half of the second century] made the bronze asses relatively common compared to the denarius'; Harl (1996: 8) puts it down to 'bronze coins becoming so worn that 16 passed as the equivalent of 10'.

[100] Diod. Sic. 37. 3; Plin. *HN* 14. 95.

[101] Plin. *HN* 14. 56.

[102] Specialist slaves: Polyb. 31. 5. 5; Diod. Sic. 31. 24. 1, 36. 2a. 1, 36. 2. 2, 37. 3. 5; tableware: Plin. *HN* 33. 147; the need for sumptuary legislation during the second century, especially the official restrictions on expenditure on meals (Gell. *NA* 2. 24. 2–7; Ath. 6. 274c), implies that socio-economic inequalities were widening.

[103] Plin. *HN* 36. 103; 36. 115.

CONCLUSION

It seems probable, therefore, that the silver coinage element of Rome's money supply expanded rapidly between the middle of the second century and the middle of the first century. War booty, indemnities, and silver from the Spanish mines meant that there was no shortage of metal for minting, and the leakage of coinage to areas outside those controlled by the Romans during this period was probably small. The evidence for the Italian countryside is limited, but such as there is indicates that, during the second century, it was already at least partially monetized. That said, although there is no evidence for denarii being used to any significant extent in Greece or Asia Minor until the 40s at the earliest, there can be no doubt that some part of the coinage element of the money supply was used to (re)monetize Africa and to a lesser extent Spain (although locally produced Iberian denarii appear to have formed the bulk of the currency there). It is of course impossible to quantify the proportion of denarii circulating outside Italy; but even if one assumes that a high and rising proportion of the output of denarii, between 157 and 50 BC, went to Sicily, Africa, Spain, and Gallia Narbonensis, the increase in the coinage element of the Italian money supply would still have been dramatic, as we shall see in Ch. 11.

The monetary impact of an increase in the money supply of a particular territory would normally be either to cause prices to rise or to increase the level of economic activity in that territory. But we have only a handful of data points for commodity prices in the Roman world during the second and first centuries BC; and we cannot tell whether the variations in the price of wheat which we find in Polybius and Cicero are due to temporary supply/demand influences or to more persistent ones. The limited numismatic evidence does, however, seem to confirm a trend of rising retail prices; and price inflation is even more pronounced for luxury goods and elite residential housing. We shall discuss inflation and the monetization of mainland Italy in greater detail in Ch. 11, where we shall attempt a hypothetical quantification of these factors.

But the workings of a monetary economy depend not only on how much money is 'in circulation', but also on how hard it works (in other words its velocity of circulation). As Howgego points out, any attempt to measure the velocity of circulation from coin wear (such as that of Duncan-Jones[104]) does not work, because it contains a basic flaw. From the economic point of view, the velocity of circulation of coin is concerned with the number of transactions that take place, rather than with the extent to which coin is carried around. If coin is carried around but is not used for exchange, then it does not circulate; by contrast, coin kept in a bank, but transferred from one party to another, does circulate.[105] One way forward is to examine factors that are likely to have affected the velocity of circulation, such as monetary credit and changes in financial structures. Monetary credit is relevant to the velocity of circulation because it enables one man's store of wealth to be used by another as a means of exchange. In the next chapter, we shall investigate the non-coinage element of Rome's money supply and, in Ch. 10, the changing financial structure of the economy during the first century.

[104] Duncan-Jones 1987. [105] Howgego 1992: 12–16.

6

Credit and Financial Intermediation

When the music stops, in terms of liquidity, things will be complicated. But as long as the music is playing, you've got to get up and dance. We're still dancing.

Charles 'Chuck' Prince III, Chief Executive of Citigroup (Quoted in the *Financial Times*, 10 July 2007—fired 4 November 2007)

INTRODUCTION

In this chapter we shall consider whether the activities of early Roman financial intermediaries such as bankers provided a mechanism for the creation of money beyond the available supply of precious metals. This is an important issue because the presence or absence of deposit banks would have had a direct bearing on the prospects of activity within the wider Roman economy. In any economy that has deposit banks or functionally similar institutions, the money supply is not limited to the volume of coinage issued by the central authorities. The reason for this is that the deposit and credit mechanisms of a deposit bank produce a 'money multiplier' effect, which will expand the money supply, and such expansion will usually influence the level of economic activity. Deposit banks are, therefore, normally part of a healthy market ecology. This statement may seem strange to some, since one modern view is that a banker is essentially somebody who stuffs his balance sheet with absurdly complex securities, ascribes ludicrous valuations to them, pays himself bonuses equivalent to the GDP of an Eastern European republic out of the (notional) profits, and goes running to his local government when it all goes wrong. But, as Peter Temin puts it, 'Good financial markets and institutions help people who have ideas for production to get resources to implement those ideas. Empirical investigations of recent economic growth have exposed a clear connection between financial institutions and economic growth; without these markets and institutions, the prospects for economic progress appear far more limited.'[1] The presence or absence of deposit banks could, therefore, indicate changes in the level of economic activity at a given time. If Rome's early bankers arranged for deposits to be lent out (rather than just providing safe deposit facilities, the equivalent of hoarding), such mechanisms

[1] Temin 2004: 705; for a fuller account, see Levine 1997.

would have served to expand Rome's money supply and, thereby, to encourage an increase in effective demand. In other words, a growth in bank lending would have led to an expansion in the volume of commercial transactions and activity.

We shall demonstrate that the money supply at Rome consisted not only of cash in circulation but also of bank liabilities ('deposits'). We shall show that financial institutions, which performed the function of mediating between borrowers and lenders, already existed in Rome by the early second century and that there is every reason to think that, by this time, the existence of a system of credit provision enabled the Romans to extend their money supply beyond the limits of their monetized metal.

THEORIES OLD AND NEW

Until very recently most ancient historians have tended to follow Finley, who simplistically asserted that the money supply in the ancient world was essentially inelastic because of its reliance on coin and the lack of 'machinery for credit beyond the lending of coins'.[2] On this view all Roman money (*pecunia*) consisted of official Roman coinage:

> The money supply in Republican Rome was constituted primarily by the amount of coinage in free circulation. There was, so far as we can tell, no other commonly acceptable way of making public or private payments, contracting debts or making loans other than through transactions involving Roman coin . . . It was, in essence, a hard money economy. The maintenance of the monetised economy thus depended on a sufficient supply of coinage, without which it could not function properly.[3]

Recently, however, a small number of scholars have begun to challenge this view by demonstrating that Roman banking was considerably more sophisticated than previously portrayed.[4] Temin, for example, has used a theoretical hierarchy of financing methods to evaluate the effectiveness of financial markets in the early Roman Empire.[5] He argues that, under the Principate, the Romans had a relatively sophisticated financial structure and that their economy was comparable in several ways to the most advanced agrarian societies that are known to us, for example eighteenth-century France.[6] The methodology of the approach in this chapter owes much to Temin's work and we shall apply a number of his principles to an earlier period, Rome of the second century BC.

Harris too has challenged the Finleyan dogma, in arguing that *pecunia* (money) included both coin and credit. As he points out, the formal definition of Hermogenianus in the *Digest* suggests this: '"Pecuniae" nomine non solum numerata pecunia sed omnes res tam soli quam mobiles et tam corpora quam iura continentur'[7] (in the definition of *pecunia* is included not only coinage but everything

[2] Finley 1985*b*: 196–7. [3] Williams 1998: 173; cf. Verboven 2002: 116.
[4] Barlow 1978; Andreau 1987, 1999; Temin 2004; Harris 2006; Rathbone and Temin 2008.
[5] Temin 2004: 707–13. [6] Temin 2004: 729.
[7] Hermogenianus *ad Dig.* 50. 16. 222, cited and translated by Harris 2006: 1, 7; cf. Ulp. *ad Dig.* 50. 16. 178.

else both immovable and movable, and whether it is an object or a claim). Harris goes on to argue that 'Cicero in the *Verrines* simply takes it for granted that *nomina* were a form of *pecunia*' when Verres' victim Apollonius protested that 'pecuniam sibi esse in nominibus, numeratum in praesentia non habere'[8] (his money was in *nomina* and he did not at the moment have minted coin).

Whilst we would agree with Harris's interpretation of this and other passages, that they provide strong evidence for the Romans having extended their money supply beyond coinage, his translation of the term *nomina* in this passage from the *Verrines* is problematic. Harris believes that *nomina* were 'outstanding loans'.[9] He argues that these loans (which he implies were principally made by wealthy individuals—those whom Andreau has termed 'aristocratic financiers'[10]) were negotiable and thus transferable, and that they were, by the second century BC, if not earlier, routinely used as a means of payment for other assets (so providing a fair amount of evidence for non-coinage payments).[11] He believes that in the absence of bonds, governmental or otherwise, the Roman well-to-do relied heavily on *nomina* as their 'standard cautious investment'. In other words, they were functionally similar to what we would term 'negotiable notes' or even 'securitized debt'. As we shall see in Ch. 10, Harris makes a very good case for the existence of such a system of negotiable notes in the mid-first century BC. However, in the second and early first centuries, the evidence is less clear-cut.

In classical Latin, an entry in an account was called a *nomen*, a term probably influenced by Greek usage.[12] Originally the word meant just that, a name with some numbers attached. By Cicero's day *nomen* was a very flexible term and only the context can guide us as to its meaning, since it could variously refer to an entry in an account book in respect of a sale, a fine, a debt, or a loan.[13] Sometimes, therefore, *nomen* does seem to have the meaning that Harris ascribes to it of 'outstanding loan'.[14] The trouble is that this is not always the case and, indeed, even some of the examples which Harris himself cites can be interpreted differently to mean an 'account entry [with a bank]'. Thus, in the passage from the *Verrines* just quoted, *nomina* can just as easily be understood to refer to deposit accounts with a bank or banks.[15] Again, when a Roman *eques* decides he wants to buy a property at Syracuse and *nomina facit, negotium conficit*, Harris translates this as 'he provides the credits [i.e. outstanding loans] <and so> completes the purchase'.[16] An alternative translation would be 'he makes the entries <and so> completes the purchase', a procedure which, as we shall see, would be similar to one in the late 160s described by Polybius. In coming to his alternative model of

[8] Cic. *II Verr.* 5. 17; Harris 2006: 7. [9] Harris 2006: 9.

[10] For 'aristocratic financiers', see pp. 235–6.

[11] Harris 2006: 4, 15; cf. Heichelheim 1938: 554–7; Barlow 1978: 155–68.

[12] Cf. Demosthenes 52. 4: *τοὔνομα γράφειν*. [13] Barlow 1978: 156–7.

[14] e.g. Cic. *II Verr.* 1. 28: 'nomina sua exegisse' (i.e. called in his debts) and Cic. *Att.* 16. 6. 3: 'nomina mea, per deos, expedi, exsolve' (by the gods, clear off my debts, pay the lot!); cf. Cic. *Q Rosc.* 4.

[15] Cf. Cic. *II Verr.* 1. 100: 'hinc ratio cum Q. et Cn.Postumis Curtiis, multis nominibus, quorum in tabulis iste [Verres] habet nullum' (hence the account Verres kept with Q. and Cn. Postumius Curtius with many entries, not one of which appears in Verres' books); Columella, *Rust.* 3. 3. 9: 'nomen si ut faenerator cum debitore . . . fecerit' (as a moneylender creates an account with a debtor).

[16] Cic. *Off.* 3. 59.

Roman financial behaviour, Harris inevitably relies to a great extent on the evidence of Cicero's letters for his interpretation. In fact the Ciceronian corpus mentions few *argentarii* and in this respect, as we shall see in Ch. 10, the financial behaviour that Cicero portrays differs markedly from that which appears to have existed in the second century.

A BANKING MODEL

As Temin explains, the problem of funding economic activity is that savers are not necessarily entrepreneurs. How do you get one group to lend to the other? In essence it is a question of risk. When a borrower is a member of his family, a friend, or from his local religious group, the lender is in a position to evaluate whether or not the borrower is likely to repay the loan (and, as Harris correctly highlights, the Ciceronian corpus shows that first-century capital markets certainly did depend much more on personal ties than modern ones do[17]). If, however, the potential borrower does not fall into one of these categories, it becomes significantly more difficult for the lender to assess his creditworthiness (that is, the risk of lending to him), assuming that the lender is operating in a pre-print culture in which economic information is scarce and unreliable.

There are two ways around this problem, which is in effect one of lack of information.[18] First, a broker, as an introducer, can bring the two parties together. The lender can get to know the borrower and become more comfortable, but he still takes the credit risk of the borrower directly himself. The alternative is to use a financial intermediary, such as a deposit bank. To quote Temin again:

> Financial intermediaries collect funds from people with resources they have saved, pool them together into a single fund, and then make loans from this pooled fund of resources. Individuals lend money to banks by depositing money in them, and the banks then lend their accumulated funds to other individuals. There is no direct connection between the final borrowers and the lenders; they communicate only with the financial intermediary. The presence of this intermediary... solves a lot of the former information problems... The bank solves the problem of finding borrowers and lenders because they each know to go to the bank to place their excess purchasing power or to borrow. It also assumes the risk of not being paid back by a borrower. The lender [depositor] need not worry, unless the bank operates with such bad judgement that it has so many failed loans that it fails itself.[19]

The essence of a deposit banker's expertise is the evaluation of the creditworthiness of potential borrowers. He makes his money by 'taking a margin'. The margin is the difference between the rate of interest the bank pays on the deposits that it accepts and the rate of interest it receives on the loans that it grants. This margin is the bank's return for the risk it is taking that it may not get its loan back from the borrower.

As we said at the beginning of this chapter, the operations of deposit banks produce a 'money multiplier' effect. This is because their deposits and loans serve to expand the money supply, bringing into existence assets that can be used for

[17] See Ch. 10. [18] 'Asymmetric knowledge' in the jargon. [19] Temin 2004: 710–11.

Table 6.1. Bank balance sheet 1

Assets	HS	Liabilities	HS
Silver coinage	66,000	Deposits of silver coinage	66,000

Table 6.2. Bank balance sheet 2

Assets	HS	Liabilities	HS
Silver coinage	48,000	Deposits of silver coinage	66,000
Loans receivable	18,000		
TOTAL ASSETS	66,000	TOTAL LIABILITIES	66,000

Table 6.3. Bank balance sheet 3

Assets	HS	Liabilities	HS
Silver coinage	57,000	Deposit (senator)	66,000
Loans receivable	18,000	Deposit (*negotiator*)	9,000
TOTAL ASSETS	75,000	TOTAL LIABILITIES	75,000

making payments and creating the substance with which it is possible to buy things without diminishing anyone's assets. Such expansion of the money supply through bank deposits can be simplistically demonstrated:[20]

A new bank starts operating in Rome.[21]

A wealthy senator, deposits HS 66,000 of silver coinage with the bank. The bank's balance sheet on its first day of business would therefore look like Table 6.1.

The bank owes the senator HS 66,000 (which is called a liability) but the bank actually has the senator's 66,000 silver coins, which is an asset.

An *eques* (knight) has great ideas for developing his vineyard and needs HS 18,000 to buy a wine press. He approaches the banker for a loan and the bank lends him this amount in silver coin.

The balance sheet of the bank now looks like Table 6.2.

The bank now has HS 48,000 of silver coins; it has a loan to the *eques* of HS 18,000 and it still owes HS 66,000 to the senator. And of course the *eques* has HS 18,000 in silver coin. So without any increase in the bank's liabilities, there has been an increase of HS 18,000 in money circulating outside the bank.

The *eques* then buys his wine press from a *negotiator* (businessman) at a cost of HS 18,000. So the *negotiator* now has HS 18,000 in silver coins. However, the *negotiator* has no immediate use for half of these coins, that is HS 9,000, so he decides to deposit them at the bank.

The balance sheet of the bank will now appear as in Table 6.3.

20 Harris (2006: 5, 11, 20) implies that such expansion can only happen in a 'partial reserve' or 'fractional reserve' banking system. But in fact a system of this kind, though prudent, is not a necessity for the money multiplier to operate (for a fuller account see Fischer, Dornbusch, and Schmalensee 1988: 173–5).

21 The following example is adapted from Cohen 1992: 12–13; cf. Havrilesky and Boorman 1982: 10–48.

The bank now has deposits of HS 75,000 compared to the HS 66,000 with which it started. However, the senator believes he still has HS 66,000, because he has a deposit with the bank. The *negotiator* thinks he has HS 18,000 because he too has a deposit of HS 9,000 with the bank and he also has HS 9,000 in silver coin at home. Meanwhile, there has been an increase in effective demand leading to a commercial transaction whereby the *eques* has purchased a wine press that he would not otherwise have been able to afford. But the *eques* does of course still have his loan outstanding from the bank in the amount of HS 18,000.

So, in economic terms, the Roman money supply has expanded by HS 9,000.

Clearly the total amount of bank deposits (that is, claims that on request can immediately or eventually be turned into silver) has been increased without a corresponding increase in the amount of silver. The Roman money supply will expand whenever any part of the proceeds of a bank loan is redeposited in a bank by the ultimate recipients of the funds advanced.[22] The corollary to this is that if banks only act as safe-deposit institutions, without lending on the money so deposited, this will take money out of the system and have a negative impact on the money supply.

Now if Rome's early bankers arranged for deposits to be lent out in this way, such mechanisms would have served to expand Rome's money. In turn, an expansion of the money supply will generally encourage an increase in effective demand. In other words, a growth in bank lending in Rome in the second century would, following the Fisher quantity equation of money and assuming no increase in inflation, have led to an expansion in the volume of commercial transactions and activity.[23]

The amount of increase in the bank portion of Rome's money supply would have depended on the volume and velocity of circulation of bank loans, that is the percentage of these loan funds immediately or ultimately redeposited in the banks. Monetary expansion through bank activity would have been substantial, if deposits represented a significant part of the total Roman money supply, if these deposits were in turn lent out, and if a reasonable portion of the new purchasing power generated by these loans was immediately or ultimately redeposited in the banks. Hoarding would have had the opposite effect. Any increase in the amount of hoarding, that is the extent to which coin is used as a store of wealth, would have had a direct negative effect on the velocity of circulation and would have resulted in monetary contraction as the coin was taken out of circulation. As

[22] We have deliberately simplified the above example for the sake of clarity. Normally a banker would hold a proportion (known as a 'reserve ratio' in modern banking parlance) of the coin deposited with him as a cash reserve, so that he could provide the necessary liquidity to depositors wanting their coin back. This in turn would restrict the amount a bank could lend to a certain proportion of the aggregate amount of its deposits. Although there is no evidence either way, there is every reason to believe that Roman bankers would have maintained reserve ratios for prudential reasons. See pp. 252–4 for more on this subject and a slightly more complex example. As we shall see below, it also appears that Roman bankers operated a system that allowed the transfer of money from one account to another within the same bank without the use of coin. The effect of this would have been that bankers would have needed to hold less coin to meet transfers of this kind and this would have enabled them to maintain lower reserve ratios and to lend out more of the coin deposited with them.

[23] For the Fisher equation see p. 88.

Howgego points out, this was understood in antiquity: Caesar sought to alleviate a shortage of coin in 49 by limiting hoarding by individuals to 60,000 HS.[24]

THE EVIDENCE FOR FINANCIAL INTERMEDIATION

One of the focuses of recent academic work on finance has been the function of financial instruments and institutions.[25] Under this 'functional' approach, the emphasis is not on the precise modalities of the arrangement or on who provides it (a bank, insurance company, fund manager, etc.), but on the finance function that it is designed to perform. Indeed there is a school of thought that argues that (abstracting from the detail) all forms of finance can ultimately be reduced to one of three basic types of financial contract (or, of course, a combination of more than one): debt, equity, and insurance.[26] With this approach, therefore, we can pose the question: did institutions functionally similar to modern deposit banks exist in Rome during the second century?

Bankers function largely in a world of hidden transactions and of confidential dealings, and so evidence would be limited even without the problem of the general scarcity of ancient source material, but we do in fact have sufficient material, principally literary, to show that Romans in the early second century had credit-providing mechanisms and businesses. We must emphasize at the outset that the purpose of this enquiry is economic rather than sociological. What we are interested in discovering is whether there were financial intermediaries that expanded Rome's money supply and, if so, what the economic consequences of that expansion were. Much of the work that has been carried out to date on the Roman banking system, in particular on the early period of its existence, has focused on the development of the occupations, business techniques, and social status of the professional 'money handlers' in the Latin-speaking world.[27] In addition, as Andreau admits, he has himself tended to present a non-chronological, static picture of the six centuries from 300 BC to AD 300, although it is highly likely that Roman banking institutions varied by time and place.[28] As we have mentioned, more recently Temin, Rathbone, and Harris in particular have demonstrated the pervasiveness of credit in the Roman world during the late Republic and early Principate. In his article, Harris cavalierly dismisses the earlier Republican part of the story, prior to 100, as 'quite speculative (although not difficult to construct in outline)'.[29] An outline follows.

Bankers, *argentarii*, probably first appeared at Rome during the period 318–310.[30] By the late third and early second centuries we begin to find evidence

[24] Dio Cass. 41. 38. 1–2; Howgego 1992: 12.

[25] Llewellyn 2009; Miller 1986; cf. Clayton 1971: 15.

[26] See the discussion of Cato's financial interests in Ch. 7.

[27] e.g. Andreau 1987, 1999; Barlow 1978; cf. De Ligt 1991: 490–1.

[28] Andreau 1999: 127. [29] Harris 2006: 2.

[30] Livy, 9. 40. 16; Andreau 1987: 340; Crawford 1985: 17 n. 2 says that the passage 'obviously refers to silversmiths' establishments and not to banks'.

that their activities have become sufficiently commonplace to crop up without comment in contemporary literary works. During this period, these *argentarii* seem to have fulfilled the same functions as the *trapezitai* of the Greek world. That is to say, they changed money, took deposits, and gave loans. Andreau believes, probably correctly, that the banking techniques of the Roman *argentarii* were inspired by or inherited from those of the Greek *trapezitai*;[31] and given that there is evidence of other kinds of financial and physical contact at the end of the third century with the Greeks in Campania, this would be logical.[32]

In the opening words to his *De Agricultura*, which was perhaps written around 160, Cato the Elder makes clear that lending money was sufficiently common amongst the Roman elite to be compared with commerce: 'Est interdum praestare mercaturis rem quaerere nisi tam periculosum sit, et item fenerari, si tam honestum sit[33] (it is true that to obtain money by trade is sometimes more profitable, were it not so hazardous; and likewise money-lending, if it were as honourable).[34] Two other points are noteworthy in this passage. First, it is clear that by this time the noun *fenerator* and the verb *fenerari* had taken on a specialized sense. Secondly, although Cato here adopts the posture that he despises usury (and indeed, as praetor in 198, expelled the professional moneylenders from the island of Sardinia and restricted the lending of money at interest[35]), we know from his biographer that he himself participated in syndicates that provided maritime loans.[36]

Howgego has pointed out that the importance of credit in the economy is seen first and foremost from the prominence of debt as a cause of political change under the Roman Republic.[37] The sources record no fewer than twenty-seven bills aimed at limiting the rate of interest (either by prohibiting loans altogether or permitting them only in special circumstances) or protecting debtors against unduly harsh treatment inflicted on them by their creditors.[38] As far back as the Twelve Tables (451–449), it seems that loans in kind or in money were seen as a threat to the social order and had to be controlled through legislation.[39] In a remarkable passage, Livy reports that in 193 prohibitions against higher interest rates were evaded by transferring the loans to *socii*, who were not subject to the same rate restrictions:

> Instabat enim cura alia, quod civitas faenore laborabat et quod, cum multis faenebribus legibus constricta avaritia esset, via fraudis inita erat, ut in socios, qui non tenerentur iis legibus, nomina transcriberent; ita libero faenore obruebantur debitores. Cuius coercendi cum ratio quaereretur, diem finiri placuit Feralia quae proxime fuissent, ut, qui post eam diem socii civibus Romanis credidissent pecunias profiterentur, et ex ea die pecuniae creditae, quibus debitor vellet legibus, ius creditori diceretur. Deinde postquam professionibus detecta est magnitudo aeris alieni per hanc fraudem contracti, M. Sempronius tribunus plebis ex auctoritate patrum plebem

[31] Andreau 1987: 342, 347; cf. Andreau 1968.

[32] e.g. the building of the Via Appia, the type of Rome's first silver coinage, which has clear Greek influences, and the presumed mint (Neapolis) for this coinage.

[33] Cato, *Agr. praef.* 1.

[34] Trans. Loeb 3.

[35] Livy, 32. 27. 3–4: 'asperior tamen in fenore coercendo'.

[36] Plut. *Cat. Mai.* 21. 5–6.

[37] Howgego 1992: 13.

[38] Rotondi 1912: 99–100.

[39] Aubert 2004: 165.

rogavit, plebesque scivit, ut cum sociis ac nomine Latino creditae pecuniae ius idem quod cum civibus Romanis esset.[40]

(For another anxiety had arisen—that the public was burdened by debt, and that, although greed was held in check by numerous usury laws, a way of evasion was opened up because accounts were transferred to allies, who were not subject to these laws; thus debtors were overwhelmed by unrestricted interest charges. When a method of curbing the practice was sought, it was determined that a day should be fixed, namely, the last occurrence of the festival of the Feralia; that whatever allies had, after that date, lent money to Roman citizens, should make a public statement to that effect and that proceedings regarding money so loaned after that date should be governed by the laws of whichever state the debtor should elect. Then, after the great size of the debt contracted by this evasion was revealed by these public declarations, Marcus Sempronius, tribune of the people, with the authorisation of the senate proposed to the assembly, and the assembly voted, that the allies of the Latin confederacy should have the same law regarding the lending of money that applied to Roman citizens.[41])

The denouement of this episode was the prosecution by the following year's curule aediles of a number of moneylenders and the probable introduction of a *lex Iunia de feneratione* the year after that;[42] but this denouement is less important to the current enquiry than the picture this episode gives of the nature of Roman moneylending in the 190s. This has, as Temin points out, a surprisingly modern ring to it, both because of the picture of financiers evading regulations by going 'offshore' and because it appears to have been easy to transfer the ownership of loans among interested parties.[43]

But what precisely does *nomina transcriberent* in the above passage from Livy mean?

The Latin term for the procedure by which the payer transferred a *nomen* (in the sense of an outstanding loan) which was owed to him to the seller was *delegatio*.[44] It is a practice reflected in Cicero's letters. For example, Cicero writes to Atticus that there are three possible methods of realizing a *nomen* which was in some way due to him from Caesar in 46: 'aut emptionem ab hasta . . . aut delegationem a mancipe annua die (quis erit cui credam. . . .) . . . aut Vettieni condicione semissem'[45] (either a purchase at an auction . . . or a transfer by the principal a year hence (whom could I trust? . . .) . . . or a half-payment on Vettienus' terms). In fact the earliest mention of this procedure is by Cato: 'donicum pecuniam solverit aut satisfecerit aut delegarit, pecus et familia, quae illic erit, pigneri sunto'[46] (until he pays, makes good, or transfers the money, let all the herds and slaves which are there be held in pledge). According to the second-century AD jurist, Gaius, *nomina transscripticia* are debt transfers recorded in written accounts:

40 Livy, 35.7.2-5. 41 Trans. Loeb X 19, slightly revised.

42 Livy, 35.41.9-10; *ORF*^{4} 26; Barlow 1978: 57–60.

43 Temin 2004: 721; rather surprisingly Harris 2006 does not mention this passage.

44 *Dig.* 46. 2. 11ff.; Berger 1953 s.v. *delegatio*.

45 Cic. *Att.* 12. 3. 2; cf. too Cic. *Att.* 12. 47. 1: Cicero contemplates a purchase but cannot do it without a particular *nomen*: 'Faberianum nomen explorandum est . . . emere nos velle nec posse sine isto nomine' (we must see what can be done about Faberius' *nomen* . . . I want to buy and cannot do so without that *nomen*); Harris 2006: 15.

46 Cato, *Agr.* 149. 2.

Litteris obligatio fit veluti in nominibus transscripticiis... A persona in personam transscriptio fit, veluti si id, quod mihi Titius debet, tibi id expensum tulero, id est si Titius te <pro> se delegaverit mihi.[47]

(An obligation in writing occurs for example in account entries evidencing a transfer... A transfer from one person to another occurs when, for example, I enter as paid out to you what Titius owes to me, that is to say, if Titius shall have delegated you to me as a substitute debtor in place of himself.[48])

This passage from Gaius, then, refers to the transfer of a debt obligation recorded in written accounts from one debtor to another that relies on *delegatio*. The episode in 193 which Livy describes presumably also refers to the same process of *delegatio*, even though it relates to the disposal of a loan by the original lender to another person, who becomes the new creditor (i.e. the substitution of a creditor rather than of a debtor as in the Gaius passage). In practical terms, the *via fraudis*, 'the way of evasion' to which Livy refers, was presumably that bankers or financiers were selling their loans to *socii* and making the relevant transfer entries in their account books.[49]

Livy states, at the beginning of the passage, that the allies of the Latin confederacy had not been subject to Roman usury laws before 193 and, at the end of the same passage, that, as a result of the evasions, a law was passed to correct this position. As the evasions were happening on a large scale (magnitudo aeris alieni per hanc fraudem contracti), it has interesting implications for the scale and closeness of business relations, before 193, between individual Romans and individual *socii*, who were presumably dealing with each other under the right of *commercium*, even though, in the case of a dispute, the injured party would not have been able to claim protection from a Roman law court.[50] Even more importantly, however, the passage indicates the level of financial sophistication and the scale of credit provision in Rome at the end of the first decade of the second century.

Compelling evidence for the existence of deposit banking at this period also comes from the plays of Plautus and, to a lesser extent and later in the second century, the plays of Terence.

Plautus' plays are, in the words of Erich Gruen, 'our chief document for the cultural convergence of Hellas and Rome'. All his plays are set ostensibly in the Greek world, and characters repeatedly call attention to the Greek locale. Yet the way in which characters emphasize their 'Greekness' often only serves to remind the spectators that they are not really Greek at all; and characters also make frequent allusions to Italy and Rome that are incongruous among Greeks.[51] A good analogy would be with those plays of Shakespeare that are set in Italy.

[47] Gai. *Inst.* 3. 128–30.

[48] Trans. Gordon and Robinson 1988: 339, revised.

[49] As we have emphasized, lending money involves the risk that the loan might not be repaid, so it would probably be correct to assume that these loans would have been sold at a discount.

[50] Jolowicz and Nicholas 1972: 59 for the right of *commercium*.

[51] Gruen 1990: 157. T. J. Moore 1998: 50. Plautus' self-conscious response to setting was not completely without precedent. Aristophanes' Olympus (*Peace*) and Cloudcuckooland (*Birds*) are decidedly theatrical locations. Naevius, Plautus' older Roman contemporary, had his Greek characters make allusions to cities near Rome (Ribbeck 1898: 21).

As important as the overall Hellenizing character contained in Plautus' plays is the selectivity of their engagement with Greek culture. Leigh points to 'the tendency of Plautus overtly to revel in the hybridity of the form and to play with the boundaries which divide Greece and Rome'.[52] So does their derivation from Greek 'New Comedy' prototypes create a significant barrier to historical interpretation? Is it possible to use them as documents for assessing contemporary Roman social and economic behaviour?

In placing his plays in Greece, critics have noted, Plautus protected himself from the charge that he ridiculed Romans, whilst providing his audience with the exoticism and prestige of Greek culture.[53] For example, the character Epidicus, in the play that bears his name, parodies Roman augury (l. 182) and refers to such things as the senate (l. 188) and a Roman-style colony (l. 343). A joke in the play's first scene calls attention to the *Epidicus*' status as both Greek and Roman:

THESPRIO: Iam tu autem nobis praeturam geris?
EPIDICUS: Quem dices digniorem esse hominem hodie Athenis alterum?
TH.: At unum a praetura tua,

Epidice, abest.
EP.: Quidnam?
TH.: Scies:

lictores duo, duo ulmei

fasces virgarum[54]

(TH: What, do you already hold the praetorship?
EP.: Who in all Athens today is better qualified to hold it, would you say?
TH.: Well, Epidicus, there's one thing missing from your praetorship.
EP.: So? What?
TH.: I'll tell you: two lictors and two bundles of elm rods.)[55]

In itself, Thesprio's reference to Epidicus' praetorship may not have seemed incongruous in a Greek setting, for Plautine characters refer to the praetor casually and frequently enough that the word may have been taken as a generic word for a magistrate.[56] The addition of lictors, however, would let the audience know that Thesprio means the Roman praetor, who was accompanied by lictors bearing *fasces*.

The *Curculio*, like most Plautine plays, has deception at its centre. Phaedromus is in love with Planesium, who belongs to the pimp Cappadox and has been promised to the braggart soldier, Therapontigonus. After several comic scenes between Phaedromus, Cappadox, and various other characters, Phaedromus' parasite Curculio enters. He has stolen Therapontigonus' seal ring; with it, he acquires Planesium for Phaedromus by deceiving Cappadox and Lyco, the banker who holds on deposit the money that Therapontigonus will pay for Planesium. When Therapontigonus tries to reclaim Planesium,

[52] Leigh 2004: 5. [53] T. J. Moore 1998: 51. [54] Plaut. *Epid.* 25–8.
[55] Ed. Loeb II 279, slightly revised.
[56] Cf. Plaut. *Aul.* 317; *Capt.* 505; *Merc.* 664; *Poen.* 727.

he discovers that she is his long-lost sister and he willingly gives her to Phaedromus.

A distinguishing feature of the *Curculio* is in fact its Roman allusions. The play has no prologue to establish its setting and Epidaurus, where the plot occurs, is not named until almost 350 lines into the play. The audience is thus discouraged from associating the action with a specific Greek locale. A number of conspicuous Roman allusions encourage them instead to connect the play's plot with Rome. These turn the play into sharp satire; for, through them, Plautus insists that the spectators acknowledge that the play offers not just a parcel of deceitful foreigners, but criticism of deception in their own Rome.[57]

A leitmotif of Roman topography runs through the *Curculio*, beginning with Cappadox's allusion to the Capitolium at line 269 and continuing with two mentions of the forum at lines 502 and 507. But crowning them is the play's longest monologue and the longest and most striking Roman allusion in all of Plautus. When Curculio goes off with Cappadox and Lyco to arrange the transfer of Planesium at line 461, the play's producer, the *choragus*, steps beyond the production and into the world of the audience, saying that he will show them where they can find anyone they are looking for (ll. 466–9). The first stop in the ensuing tour sets the tone for what is to follow: spectators can find a perjurer in the *Comitium* (l. 470); the lying and boastful can be found at the shrine of Venus Cloacina (l. 471); rich and profligate husbands can be found in the shadow of the basilica. At line 476 we find: 'in medio propter canalem, ibi ostentatores meri' (pure pretenders)—the *canalis* was an open drain that ran south from the shrine of Venus Cloacina through the middle of the forum.[58] The *Lacus Curtius* appears at line 477, the temple of Castor and Pollux at line 481, the *vicus Tuscus* at line 482, and the last stop is the Velabrum at 483. As Moore says:

> the effect of this tour of the Roman forum must have been stunning, for it is not merely a reference to things Roman, but the most blatant possible reminder that the production occurs in the city of Rome. All distinction between play, production and real life has been obliterated; and as the physical landscapes of 'Epidaurus' and Rome become one, the audience is forced to recognise the applicability of the Epidaurian social landscape to their own city, Rome.[59]

The play contains a number of references to banks and bankers. For example, in the *choragus*' speech just mentioned, money is borrowed and lent 'below the old shops': 'Sub veteribus, ibi sunt qui dant quique accipiunt faenore'[60] (There, below the old shops, are those who give and receive at interest). There is also the character of Lyco, the banker, who is presented as being cunning and crooked. Plautus elsewhere portrays greedy moneylenders on stage and offers harsh satire of *argentarii* as a class, but only in this play does a deceptive

[57] T. J. Moore 1998: 127.
[58] L. Richardson 1992: 68; Steinby 1993*a*: 226.
[59] T. J. Moore 1998: 137; Moore believes that the *Curculio* was first performed in the Roman forum on a temporary stage 'just south of the *Comitium* facing east' so that 'almost everything on the tour would be visible to the *choragus* and his audience'; cf. T. J. Moore 1991. But Goldberg 1998 argues that performances took place on the Palatine.
[60] Plaut. *Curc.* 479.

banker play a major role.[61] This is relevant because, a little further on in the play, the comparison is drawn by the character, Curculio, between bankers and pimps:

CURC.: Eodem hercle vos pono et paro; parissimi estis hibus.
Hi saltem in occultis locis prostant, vos in foro ipso.
Vos faenore homines, hi male suadendo et lustris lacerant.
Rogitationes plurimas propter vos populus scivit,
quas vos rogatas rumpitis; aliquam reperitis rimam.[62]

(CURC.: And, by heaven, I put you people [pimps and bankers] in the same category; you match them perfectly. They, at least, do business in private, you in the open forum. You mangle men with interest; they do it with solicitation and dens of vice. The people have passed bills without number against you, and once they pass them, you smash them; you always find some loophole.)[63]

This reference to laws against bankers and the flouting of those laws probably connects Lyco and his antics to contemporary controversies in Rome over moneylending. As we have already seen, in 193 new laws were passed to prevent moneylenders from avoiding earlier laws against usury by lending in the names of non-citizens.[64] The allusion to Roman laws and to the flouting of those laws makes clear what Plautus has implied throughout the play: Lyco is a satirical portrait not so much of a hypothetical Greek banker as of a Roman *argentarius*.[65]

As Andreau has pointed out, up to thirty-four passages from Plautus and five from Terence concern banking matters.[66] This suggests two things. The first is that bankers were part of everyday life. The second is that there is no reason to suppose that the plays are only reflecting a Greek banking reality.[67] If they were, then they would be incomprehensible to a Roman audience and Plautus would not constantly and subtly mix up Greek and Roman banking terminologies. It is true that these texts speak sometimes of *argentarii* or of *argentariae (tabernae)*, sometimes of *trapezitae* or *tarpessitae*, sometimes of *mensae*. In fact, in the plays of Plautus, the term *argentarius* is used ten times across five plays, while the term *trapezita* is used fourteen times across six plays.[68] Andreau's working hypothesis that Plautus principally

61 Moneylenders: Plaut. *Epid.* 620–47; *Mostell.* 532–54. Satirical portrayal of *argentarii*: Plaut. *Cas.* 25–8; *Pers.* 433–6, 442–3; *Pseud.* 296–8. Leigh 2004: 117 n. 82 lists a number of comic attacks on bankers and moneylenders in Greek plays.

62 Plaut. *Curc.* 506–11.

63 Trans. Loeb II 243, slightly revised.

64 Livy, 35. 7. 2–5.

65 A number of Plautus' denunciations of bankers come from the *Curculio*, which has led many to suggest that the play was written contemporaneously with the crisis of 193: Teuffel 1889: 325; Buck 1940: 64–6; Schutter 1952: 63–4; Barlow 1978: 88; T. J. Moore 1998: 131.

66 Andreau 1987: 333. Twenty-five passages of Plautus and 3 of Terence definitely concern banking matters; six passages of Plautus and two of Terence probably do; and three other passages of Plautus possibly do.

67 Contra Andreau (1968 : 526), who says : 'les œuvres de Plaute et de Térence semblent beaucoup plus utiles à la connaisance de la banque grecque qu'à celle de la banque romaine'.

68 Andreau 1968: 469–70.

chose the terms *argentarius* and *trapezita* on dramatic criteria is at least credible: '[*Trapezita*] désigne un banquier de la comédie, probablement hérité du modèle grec. [*Argentarius*] désigne un banquier extérieur à l'action, dont on parle pour faire allusion aux banquiers de Rome.'[69] Thus, in the case of the *Curculio*, although Lyco himself is generally called by the Greek name *trapezita*, he and other characters refer to his class by the Latin term *argentarii*, which suggests that his behaviour represents that of bankers in Rome.

Of the thirty-nine passages of Plautus and Terence that appear to refer to banking, only four do not give any information on specific banking operations. The rest mention activities that are relatively sophisticated and refer to them in such a way as to suggest that these activities are considered both by the playwright and by the audience to be commonplace, at least in an urban context.

First, it is clear that bankers conducted their business in the forum and that one could go to them to arrange payments:

> 'Sequere sis me ergo ad forum,
> ut solvam;'[70]

(Follow me to the forum, then, | so that I can settle up;)

and

> 'Sequere me, viaticum ut dem a trapezita tibi;'[71]

(Follow me so that I can give you some money for travelling expenses from the banker;)

and

> 'Ego quidem pro istac rem solvi ab trapezita meo;'[72]

(I myself settled for that girl through my banker;)

They would go to a banker to arrange payments, because it was with him that money was kept, as the next passage shows:

> 'Ibo intro atque intus subducam ratiunculam
> quantillum argenti mi apud trapezitam siet.'[73]

(I shall go in and reckon up my small account, | and see how little money I have with the banker.)

We also see that money is put on deposit with bankers:

> 'Mirum quin tibi ego crederem, ut idem mihi
> facere quod partim faciunt argentarii:
> ubi quid credideris, citius extemplo a foro
> fugiunt quam ex porta ludis cum emissust lepus.'[74]

[69] Andreau 1968: 477. [70] Plaut. *Pseud.* 1229–30. [71] Plaut. *Capt.* 449.
[72] Plaut. *Curc.* 618. [73] Plaut. *Capt.* 192–3. [74] Plaut. *Pers.* 433–6.

(Are you surprised that I wouldn't trust you | to do the same to me as some bankers do? | If you entrust them with anything, | they are out of the forum faster than a hare from its cage door at the games.)

Moreover, it appears that money deposited with a banker could be transferred by a written entry in the banker's records, without the movement of cash, by 'writing *nummi*': 'Nunc satagit: adducit [sc. trapezitam] domum etiam ultro et scribit nummos'[75] (now he settles up: furthermore, he brings [his banker] to the house and 'writes money').

We can compare not only Livy's use of the verb *transcribere* and Gaius' use of the noun *transcriptio* in the passages we discussed earlier, but also Polybius' account of how, in the late 160s, Scipio Aemilianus decided to pay off fifty talents, which was the balance of the dowries owed to his adoptive aunts and a very large amount of money. This money was on deposit with a banker (*τραπεζίτης*), who was instructed by Scipio to make what appears to have been a paper transfer of the money (*διαγραφή*, literally a 'writing through') into the accounts of each of the husbands of the aunts. The two husbands were Tiberius Sempronius Gracchus the Elder and Publius Scipio Nasica Corculum:

> *'ὁ Σκιπίων συνέταξε τῷ τραπεζίτῃ τῶν εἴκοσι καὶ πέντε ταλάντων ἑκατέρᾳ ποιήσασθαι τὴν ἀνταπόδοσιν ἐν τοῖς δέκα μησί . . . τοῦ δὲ Τεβερίου καὶ τοῦ Νασικᾶ Σκιπίωνος . . . προσπορευομένων πρὸς τὸν τραπεζίτην καὶ πυνθανομένων, εἴ τι συνετέτακτο Σκιπίων αὐτῷ περὶ τῶν χρημάτων, κἀκείνου κελεύοντος αὐτοὺς κομίζεσθαι καὶ ποιοῦντος τὴν διαγραφὴν ἑκατέρῳ τῶν εἴκοσι καὶ πέντε ταλάντων, ἀγνοεῖν αὐτὸν ἔφασαν·'*[76]
>
> (Scipio instructed the banker to make a payment of twenty-five talents to each lady in ten months time . . . Tiberius Gracchus and Scipio Nasica . . . approached the banker to ascertain if Scipio Aemilianus had arranged with him about the money; and, when the banker insisted that they should accept the money and made out a transfer (*διαγραφὴν*) of twenty-five talents for each of them, they said he was wrong.)

How did the banker pay this amount at a time when Rome had no gold coinage? As Harris says, it seems highly unlikely that the banker counted out and loaded 1.2 tonnes of silver coins and transported this cargo through the streets of Rome.[77] Nor is there any evidence to suggest that large payments at this time were made in gold bullion.[78] What the banker must have done for them, therefore, was to make them payments 'on paper' into their accounts.[79]

This story, then, is noteworthy for a number of reasons. It shows the transfer of money without the use of coin and it reveals how much a banker could have on deposit at this time.[80] The fact that Romans were willing to trust

[75] Plaut. *Asin.* 440; cf. Barlow 1978: 77; Harris 2006: 16. [76] Polyb. 31. 27. 6–7.

[77] $300{,}000 \times 3.86\ g = 1158\ kg$ (an adaptation of an example given by Harris 2006: 2–3); cf. Ch. 2 n. 11.

[78] See pp. 23–4. [79] Harris 2006: 12.

[80] At least 11 talents and possibly more were on deposit at the bank of Pasion in Athens in the fourth century. At the same time, that bank had at least 50 talents loaned out (Dem. 36. 5–6; Cohen 1992: 129–36).

deposit banks with such large sums, even if they sometimes withdrew them, testifies to the health of banks and to their loan-generating capacity.[81] But it also contradicts the orthodox view that Roman bankers did not have much to do with the Roman elite, since both Tiberius Gracchus and Scipio Nasica were senators;[82] and, in similar vein, there is the curious story related by the author of *De viris illustribus* that, in the last third of the second century, the future consul of 115, Aemilius Scaurus, considered becoming a banker.[83]

> 'Marcus Aemilius Scaurus nobilis, pauper: nam pater eius quamvis patricius ob paupertatem carbonarium negotium exercuit. Ipse primo dubitavit, honores peteret an argentariam faceret; sed eloquentiae consultus ex ea gloriam peperit.'[84]
>
> (Marcus Aurelius Scaurus was noble, but poor: for his father, though a patrician, on account of his poverty practised the business of a charcoal-burner. He himself at first hesitated as to whether he should seek honours or whether he should operate a bank; but because he was skilled in eloquence, he acquired glory from that.)

To return to Plautus, the characters in his comedies borrow money from bankers. In this passage from the *Epidicus*, Stratippocles is talking to Epidicus:

> STR.: Quid istic? Verba facimus. Huic homini opust quadraginta minis
> celeriter calidis, danistae quas resolvat, et cito.
> EP.: Dic modo unde auferre me vis. A quo trapezita peto?
> STR.: Unde libet. Nam ni ante solem occasum e loculis adferes,
> meam domum ne inbitas.[85]
>
> (STR.: So what? These are just words. I am a man that quickly needs forty piping hot *mina*, so I can pay a lender, and fast!
> EP.: Just tell me where you want me to bring them from. Which banker shall I ask?
> STR.: Wherever you like. Because if you don't bring them from their coffers before sunset, you needn't enter my house.)

In a passage already quoted from the *Curcilio*, the comparison drawn between bankers and pimps again shows that the former lend money: 'Vos faenore homines, hi male suadendo et lustris lacerant'[86] (you mangle men with loans, those pimps do it with solicitation and debauchery). There is even evidence of what, in modern parlance, would be called an 'interbank' market. In the same play, the pimp Cappadox is owed money by the banker Lyco, who pretends he does not have any. The latter goes round the other bankers to try and borrow the amount owed: 'Vel ille [sc. Lyco], decem

[81] Silver 2007: 208.

[82] As Rathbone and Temin 2008: 405 say: 'The only senators specifically said anywhere to use a bank are Scipio Aemilianus and the husbands of his aunts. But the state loans made available to senators in AD 33 were provided through banks (Tac. *Ann.* 6. 17), and slaves and freedmen of the emperor and of senatorial ladies appear in the Sulpicii documents'.

[83] On the other hand, M. Antonius mocked Octavian because of his low birth, saying that his great-grandfather had been a freedman and his grandfather a banker (Suet. *Aug.* 2. 3, 3. 1, 4. 2). Antonius' jibes suggest that, by his time, some circles still considered bankers disreputable.

[84] *De vir. ill.* 72. 2. [85] Plaut. *Epid.* 141–5. [86] Plaut. *Curc.* 508.

minas dum solvit, omnes mensas transit'[87] (that Lyco is going round all the banks so he can pay me ten *mina*).

We know that Greek bankers in the fourth century practised both deposit taking and lending;[88] and since it seems probable that banking practice at Rome developed under Greek influences, it is difficult to imagine that bankers did not fulfil both a deposit and a credit function. Indeed there is evidence for this in Plautus. In the last passage quoted, the fact that Lyco claims not to have any money seems to indicate that he has lent out the funds he has received on deposit. Lyco says at one point:

LYCO: Beatus videor. Subduxi ratiunculam,
quantum aeris mihi sit quantumque alieni siet.
Dives sum, si non reddo eis quibus debeo.
Si reddo illis quibus debeo, plus alieni est.
Verum hercle vero cum belle recogito,
si magis me instabunt, ad praetorem sufferam.
Habent hunc morem plerique argentarii,
ut alius alium poscant, reddant nemini,
pugnis rem solvent, si quis poscat clarius.[89]

LYCO: (I seem to be blessed. I've drawn up a little account to work out how much money would be for me and how much would be debt. I'm rich, as long as I don't repay those whom I owe. If I do repay my creditors, there's more around to borrow. Truly though, by Hercules, when I think about it calmly, if they pressurize me any more, I'll bring it up with the praetor. Most bankers have the habit of demanding their money back from everyone and repaying no one. They settle it with a fight, if anyone demands their money back too loudly.)

In this passage, the line 'quantum aeris mihi sit quantumque alieni siet' suggests that Lyco is considering his balance sheet of assets (loans) and liabilities (deposits).

In the prologue of the *Casina* we see the same balance sheet implied. While the games are on, bankers do not pursue their debtors, but neither do they, when the games are finished, return the deposits which they have taken:

Eicite ex animo curam atque alienum aes,
ne quis formidet flagitatorem suom.
Ludi sunt, ludus datus est argentariis;
tranquillum est, Alcedonia sunt circum forum.
Ratione utuntur, ludis poscunt neminem,
secundum ludos reddunt autem nemini.[90]

(Clear your mind of care and debt; let no man fear that someone will beat him up! The games are on and the bankers have a game too; all is peaceful and tranquillity surrounds the forum. The bankers are looking at their accounts: during the games they make no demands, but nor do they repay anyone after they're over.)

And in the *Pseudolus* we see a similar accusation that bankers chase up loans but do not return deposits:

PSEUD.: postquam hercle isti a mensa surgunt satis poti viri,
qui suom repetunt, alienum reddunt nato nemini,
postilla omnes cautiores sunt, ne credant alteri.[91]

[87] Plaut. *Curc.* 682. [88] Bogaert 1968: 331–62; cf. Cohen 1992: *passim.*
[89] Plaut. *Curc.* 371–9; cf. Ter. *Phorm.* 923–4. [90] Plaut. *Cas.* 23–8.
[91] Plaut. *Pseud.* 296–298.

PSEUD.: By Hercules, after those bankers rose, well bloated, from the bench—the ones that demand back their own money but never repay a deposit to a living soul—after that, everyone's more careful about lending to anyone else.

All of which implies that bankers are not just acting as custodians of deposits (that is offering a safe deposit facility) but that they are utilizing these deposits to provide loans.[92]

The clearest reference though to the giving of loans and receiving of deposits comes in the prologue of the *Truculentus*:

> Nam nusquam alibi si sunt, circum argentarias
> scorta et lenones qui sedent cottidie,
> ea nimia est ratio; quippe qui certo scio,
> ibi plus scortorum esse iam quam ponderum.
> Quos quidem quam ad rem dicam in argentariis
> referre habere, nisi pro tabulis, nescio,
> ubi aera perscribantur usuraria:
> accepta dico, expensa ne qui censeat.[93]

(Because, if they're nowhere else, the whores and pimps that sit round the banks every day make a fair old number. I know for certain that you'll find more whores there than weighing-scales. I've no idea what the point is of having whores and pimps in banks, unless they're being used as account books for recording interest bearing money—I mean deposits received, in case you thought I meant loans made.)

Here there is a clear reference to interest-bearing money (*aera usuraria*) being recorded in a banker's *tabulae* as both assets (*expensa*—loans) and liabilities (*accepta*—deposits).

Plautus, then, provides compelling evidence at the beginning of the second century for the activities of deposit bankers at Rome. He portrays them not as a strange new profession but as part of the fabric of everyday Roman society. It is clear not just from Plautus, but also from the Livy passage about the debt crisis of 193, that bankers must have been present in Rome in some numbers. That is important, because a certain minimum amount of monetary activity must have been required before a community could provide a livelihood for one professional banker, let alone a number.

THE GROWTH OF THE PROFESSION

Confirmation that the bankers that appear in the plays of Plautus and Terence are not merely a literary conceit is provided by epigraphic evidence from the Greek island of Delos, which, by the end of the second century, had developed into a major entrepôt between Italy and the eastern Mediterranean.[94] A number of Delian inscriptions from this period mention bankers from the Italian mainland

[92] Cf. Plaut. *Aul.* 530; Andreau 1987: 550–1, 583–8.
[93] Plaut. *Truc.* 66–73.
[94] Rauh 1993.

as being present on the island. The earliest known Italian τραπεζίτης (banker) on Delos is Marcus Minatius Sexti f. He gave the comparatively large sum of 7,000 drachmas to a *collegium* of merchants, the Poseidoniastai of Berytos, in about 152, and in return (and amongst other honours) had a statue and a crown dedicated to him.[95] After him came the Gerillani. Six Gerillani are attested on Delos, at least two of whom were bankers. In an inscription from about 100, the merchants of the island, in honouring Maraius Gerillanus in a dedication to Apollo, Artemis, and Leto, refer to him as a τραπεζίτης (banker).[96] The Gerillanus family continued to operate its bank into the 80s, with a Maraius Gerillanus—perhaps the son of the earlier Maraius, perhaps the earlier Maraius himself—being honoured with two dedications, one set up by all the inhabitants of the island, including the merchants and ship captains, the other by the businessmen alone: [οἱ ἐν Δήλωι πραγματε]υόμενοι.[97] Our knowledge of the financial affairs of the Aufidii derives principally from an inscription erected in honour of an Aufidius Bassus on Tenos in the 70s or 60s, which describes in detail the financial services of the Aufidii to the island's government.[98] Ten Aufidii are attested on Delos, two of them definitely bankers. L. Aufidius was honoured by two inscriptions erected in the 80s, one set up by his freedmen, the other by the merchants and ship captains of the island.[99]

Within Italy itself, evidence for the scale of lending by the 130s comes from Appian. He reports that moneylenders (*daneistai*) were opposed to Ti. Gracchus in 133, because their loans were guaranteed by mortgages on public land that he was planning to recover from their occupants.[100] The pervasiveness of debt in the 120s is suggested by a passage from Nonius. Quoting Book 4 of Varro's *de Vita Populi Romani*, he states, in a context that suggests that reference is being made to Gaius Gracchus, that 'in spem adducebat non plus soluturos quam vellent'[101] (he gave them hope that they would not have to pay back more than they wished). Moreover, scenarios involving the comic portrayal of bankers on the stage seem to have continued. We know that Lucius Afranius, a writer of *fabulae togatae* and active between about 160 and 120, produced a lost work, entitled *Depositum*.[102]

At the same time there are signs of progress in banking techniques, particularly the development of different types of specialization. The regular participation of bankers in giving credit to buyers at auctions and the appearance of bankers who specialized in this kind of lending (*coactores argentarii*) occur in the early first century, which confirms the progress made by financial businesses and the widening diffusion of monetary transactions and credit.[103]

Although it is tempting to connect the so-called *tesserae nummulariae*[104] with increasing financial sophistication, it is very much open to debate whether it is correct to do so. These enigmatic pieces of bone or ivory, usually inscribed with *s(ervus)* (slave) as the subject, the name of the slave's owner in the genitive, the verb *spectavit* (looked at, or inspected), and a date, begin to appear from the end of the second century. They were interpreted by Herzog to be tags from sacks full of

95 *IDélos* 1520; Bogaert 1968: 187–8.
96 *IDélos* 1725.
97 'Those doing business on Delos': *IDélos* 1726, 1727.
98 *IG* XII 5. 860.
99 *IDélos* 1728, 1729.
100 App. *B. Civ.* 1. 10.
101 Nonius 728.
102 Kenney 1982: 193.
103 Andreau 1999: 31, 133–4.
104 The Latin phrase disguises a modern term.

sound coins.[105] Herzog's theory was that slaves (*nummularii*) were trained to assay coins, that the sacks to which the tags were attached could contain large sums, and that the *tesserae* would guarantee the coins' value. For large transactions, the sacks could be counted and weighed. The problem with this theory is that there is no corroborating evidence. Even if Herzog is correct, the frequent assumption that these activities related to the activities of bankers is in any case dubious, since a *tessera* has been found that was issued in 94 by an agent of a mining firm.[106] This suggests that some at least of the assayers (if assayers they were) were owned by *societates publicanorum* and possibly too by other types of *negotiator*.[107] On the other hand, Wiseman has pointed to the high correlation of the names of moneyers with those of individuals recorded on *tesserae*.[108] That might be thought coincidental, were it not that the moneyer Lollius Palicanus seems actually to advertise his family's business with a bank-*tessera* design on his coins. In 45, he minted a sestertius carrying types that might represent a container for money and a *tessera nummularia*.[109] Furthermore, this moneyer has interesting antecedents. In the second century, there was a M. Lollius Q.f. Men. on Delos.[110] The *horrea Lolliana* in Rome was possibly established by M. Lollius Palicanus (*tr. pl.* 71; *pr.* ?69);[111] and the Lollius referred to in a *tessera nummularia* of 62 could conceivably be associated with the Palicani.[112] So the jury is still out on the whole issue.

There can be little doubt, however, that the financial transactions of the elite expanded between the beginning of the second century and the time of Caesar and the second triumvirate. The size of the Roman financial system and its geographic extent, by the first half of the first century, is confirmed by a passage from Cicero's *Pro Fonteio* which gives hints of conditions in Gaul in 74:

> Referta Gallia negotiatorum est, plena civium Romanorum. Nemo Gallorum sine cive Romano quicquam negotii gerit, nummus in Gallia nullus sine civium Romanorum tabulis commovetur.[113]
>
> (Gaul is stuffed with businessmen; it is full of Roman citizens. Not one of the Gauls can transact any business without a Roman citizen; no coin can move in Gaul without the account books of Roman citizens.)

Even if we allow for the obvious rhetorical exaggeration, this is a statement that confirms the existence of a reasonably advanced financial infrastructure in a western province. In any case it is clear that by the middle of the first century,

[105] Herzog 1919.

[106] *CIL* I^2 2663a: *Piloxen. Soc. Fer.* | *C.Coil.L.Dom* | *Spectavit* | *N. Apr.*

[107] Andreau 1999: 80–9; Harris 2006: 19. Barlow 1978: 109–10 assumes uncritically that all *nummularii* worked for *argentarii* and uses *tesserae nummulariae* as evidence for Roman banking and moneylending in the western provinces before 80.

[108] Wiseman 1971: 199–201: Appendix IV, List C: Pomponius, Cloilius, Malleolus, Dossenus, Axius, Lollius, Procilius, Petillius, and Brutus were all either moneyers themselves or related to moneyers; Wiseman 1971: 85.

[109] *RRC* 473/4.

[110] *ILLRP* 747; D'Arms 1981: 66; cf. Rauh 1993: 50 for the Lollii.

[111] Wiseman 1971: 237–8 no. 231.

[112] *ILLRP* 1025; Wiseman 1971: 85.

[113] Cic. *Font.* 11.

monetary debt was a systematic part of aristocratic political life.[114] Shatzman lists twenty-five senators attested as moneylenders in the last century of the Republic and Nicolet lists seventeen *equites*.[115] By the mid-first century, we can see a world in which the economic activity of Cicero and his correspondents is carried out in monetary terms.[116]

The quantity of credit available presumably varied, perhaps moving in step with the cash money supply, as it did in medieval Europe. Then, as coin became more plentiful, more credit became available; when coin became scarce, credit too was quickly shut down.[117] It was a question of liquidity and the repercussions of a shortage of liquidity can be seen from comments made during the turbulent years of the early 40s. Caesar mentions that in 49 *fides* was *angustior* and Cicero's letters of 49 and 48 return often to this theme of *nummorum caritas*.[118] As Frederiksen says: 'In times of insecurity, credit could collapse and a man's wealth reverted to the sums of money that literally supported the credit relationship'.[119]

CONCLUSION

If a bank is defined in its generally accepted sense—a business having an obligation to repay funds ('deposits') received from a multitude of sources, but with the interim right to make loans and investments for its own account—the *argentarii* of the second century functioned as bankers. Between the Roman bank and the modern bank, there are of course striking differences—in technology, legal position, and the scope of operations. Roman banks, as far as we can tell, were unincorporated businesses operated by individual proprietors or partners, almost entirely free of regulation by the state.[120] Yet the ancient evidence and modern banking codes fix on the same basic factors in finding the necessary essence of a bank in its generation of revenue through loans funded by outside deposits, *aes alieni*, 'other people's money', which the bank must return. For Demosthenes, the *trapeza* was 'a business operation producing risk-laden revenues from other people's money';[121] and that definition would have been recognized by the *argentarii* of second-century Rome, as it would be today by the Chief Executive of Citigroup.

In reality, far from the 'the absence of credit-creating instruments and institutions remaining as an unshaken foundation of the ancient economy', Roman *argentarii* did create credit and money, *pecunia*, beyond the available supply of precious metals.[122] As we shall see in Ch. 11, there is only limited evidence on

[114] See Ch. 10. [115] Shatzman 1975: 76; Nicolet 1966: 372–3.

[116] The scale could be impressive: see Ch. 10.

[117] Nightingale 1990, 1997, 2004. [118] See pp. 260–1.

[119] Caes. *B. Civ.* 3. 1. 2; Cic. *Att.* 7. 18. 4, 9. 9. 4, 10. 11. 2, 10. 15. 4, 11. 11. 2; Cic. *Fam.* 2. 16. 5; Frederiksen 1966: 132.

[120] Harris 2006: 11 believes that the orthodox view that 'Roman bankers seldom if ever had many partners, if any, probably needs to be modified, if not rejected, in every respect'. See pp. 243–4 for evidence that, from the early first century at least, *societates* were formed between bankers.

[121] Dem. 36. 11: *ἐργασία προσόδους ἔχουσ' ἐπικινδύνους ἀπὸ χρημάτων ἀλλοτρίων.*

[122] Quotation from Finley 1985*b*: 198.

which to base even a conjectural quantification of the size of the Roman deposit banking system, and so it is difficult accurately to trace changes in the level of monetary credit over time. But the qualitative history of the professional bankers of the Roman world in the second and early first centuries does provide a clear indication of the scale and diffusion of financial intermediation. As the number of bankers grew, and the scale of their lending increased, there would have been a profound impact both on the size and on the velocity of circulation of the Roman money supply, as coins which would otherwise have been hoarded were put to economic use. As Harris says, there are no data of any kind that should make us suppose that credit was relatively small in quantity: 'The argument is not that credit had the same role in the Roman economy as it did in, say, industrializing countries in the nineteenth century, but simply that it was pervasive and institutionalized and added enormously to the money supply.'[123]

[123] Harris 2006: 13, 22.

Part III

The Application of Funds

7

Investment Farming and Agricultural Exploitation

dives agris, dives positis in faenore nummis.[1]

INTRODUCTION

Our argument is that the accumulation of wealth at both the state and private level during the second century led to significant growth in economic activity. In this chapter we consider the evidence for increased agricultural exploitation by the Roman elite and its impact on the Roman peasantry. In the second century, the Roman state was a rapidly urbanizing society, but agriculture would still have represented by far the largest sector of the economy in terms of output, and food would have accounted for the largest proportion of private sector consumption demand.[2]

We shall begin by examining the growth of elite estates in Italy during the second century and what our evidence suggests about their size and location. We also look at the new overseas territories that Rome acquired during the second century. We have already discussed how, at the state level, Rome developed or inherited techniques for taxing these areas, but did individual members of the Roman elite mirror this exploitative behaviour by farming overseas?

We then move on to examine one indicator of increasing agricultural production on elite estates in the second half of the second century: a trade in wine from Italy to the western Mediterranean, in particular to Gaul. With the growth in the popularity of scuba-diving in the last fifty years or so, there have been a large number of discoveries of ancient Mediterranean shipwrecks. Many of these finds have subsequently been investigated by archaeologists and their analysis has revealed a steep increase in the number of wrecks, and, therefore, presumably in the volume of shipping and of cargoes carried, in the second half of the second century. An overwhelming majority of the shipwrecks dating from this period and found in the western Mediterranean were carrying wine amphorae, most of which were manufactured in central Italy.

This sharp growth in wine exports from central Italy and other contemporaneous developments (such as increasing urbanization and, therefore, growing

[1] Hor. *Ars P.* 421: 'rich in land, rich in coins put out on loan'.

[2] See Ch. 11.

demand for agricultural products from non-rural consumers, in particular in Rome) suggest that there was a significant inflection point in the level of agricultural exploitation by the Roman elite in the middle of the second century, at least in central-western Italy. Cato's *De Agricultura*, probably written in the 160s, is the first work in Latin to provide advice on agricultural specialization and the production of cash crops by absentee landlords. This treatise, together with subsequent ones in Latin by other agronomists, suggests a growing interest in the dissemination of the stock of knowledge about agricultural techniques, and it marks the start of a period of expansion in a particular form of investment farming by the Roman elite. The 'villa system' was primarily based on slave labour and there is considerable evidence for growth in the size of the rural slave population in the second century. In addition, there were a number of major technological advances, some mentioned by agronomists, such as Cato, some found in casual references by other ancient writers, and some discovered through archaeological investigation. Many of these new technologies were adopted in the second century by elite Roman landowners investing in plant and new forms of agricultural production to maximize returns.

An expansion in investment farming, if it occurred, is likely to have had a major impact on Italy's rural economy and we shall consider the relevance of the growth of elite estates to the agrarian crisis of 133 BC. How large a part did investment farming play in the supposed decline and impoverishment of the Roman peasantry presented by our two principal ancient sources, Plutarch and Appian?[3] What can the events of 133 tell us about the development of the Roman agricultural economy, about the availability of land, the status of land, and who was occupying it?

In answering these questions we have to be constantly aware of the limitations of our evidence. First, comparatively little is known about farming in ancient Italy, despite its enormous economic importance, and it is only relatively recently that scholars have begun systematically to collect relevant material, especially archaeological evidence. Secondly, we lack a Cicero for the second half of the second century and beginning of the first. For example, without Cicero's *Pro Quinctio* and *Pro Fonteio*, we would have little idea about the level of Roman commercial involvement in Gaul in the 80s and 70s and it may, therefore, be dangerous merely to assume that the activities there and elsewhere overseas of Roman farmers (*agricolae*) and ranchers (*pecuarii*) do not pre-date this period. Thirdly, the principal clue to the dating of villa sites, particularly in Italy, during the Republican period is the black-slip pottery that, from the fourth century, became the customary tableware for even the most modest families. There is a very clear *terminus ante quem* of about 30 BC when the red-glaze fabrics of Arezzo, Puteoli, and elsewhere completely took over the market for fine-quality tableware. But care is needed when interpreting the evidence of black-slip ware; as we shall see, the Tiber Valley Project was able to date only about 20 per cent of the

[3] All definitions of 'peasant' are very contentious. Woolf (2000) gives the following sensible suggestion: 'Free workers, primarily engaged in agricultural production on their own and/or others' land; living on, or close to, the land; and usually in families; *relatively* poor, yet paying rent and/or tax, and so *relatively* disempowered by richer farmers, landlords and the state; and especially vulnerable to external impositions, political crises, ecological change and the operations of the market.'

available material with any precision. The classification and interpretation of artefact scatters is also a problem. To divide them into 'villas' and 'peasant farms' is more or less to beg the question. In particular, the identification of large scatters, including building materials and mosaic *tesserae*, with the particular form of estate described by the Roman agronomists is at best arguable. Witcher has highlighted the danger of this approach:

> as site recognition is based on pottery, by extension, the assumption is that sites in different areas are equally visible... A final assumption is that the per capita consumption of pottery was constant... [and] that the quantity of pottery (on sites) is a direct proxy of the number of people. [On this assumption] any variation in the amount of pottery therefore reflects variation in population rather than pottery use or discard.[4]

ELITE INVESTMENT IN LAND IN THE SECOND CENTURY

'Omnium autem rerum, ex quibus aliquid acquiritur, nihil est agri cultura melius, nihil uberius, nihil dulcius, nihil homine libero dignius'[5] (but of all the occupations from which it is possible to make money, none is better than agriculture, none more productive, none sweeter, none more worthy of a free man). This comment from Cicero's *De Officiis* and Cato's similar remark in the Preface to his *De Agricultura* have led modern historians to be unanimous in accepting the importance of agriculture in the Roman Empire, to the extent of contending, in some cases, that it was so important that no other form of economic activity could possibly be considered as significant. Finley often emphasized the point that fortunes made in commercial activity were not reinvested 'productively' (i.e. in manufacturing), but were spent on land and other 'respectable' pursuits.[6] Hopkins talks of the massive investment by the rich of the profits derived from empire in Italian land. 'Land was their prime source of wealth,' he says.[7] Brunt concurs: 'In the economic life of ancient Italy agriculture was of dominant importance. Land was the safest investment and the chief basis of wealth.'[8] The general belief is that, as members of the Roman elite grew richer, they invested a considerable part of their wealth in agricultural land in Italy, since land was the only safe and prestigious large-scale investment available. It was the chief source of livelihood and the predominant form of distributable wealth.[9]

[4] Witcher 2006*a*: 46. [5] Cic. *Off.* 1. 151.

[6] e.g. Finley 1985*b*: 139; Greene 1986: 67. [7] Hopkins 1978: 4, 50.

[8] Brunt 1988: 241; cf. Shatzman 1975: 16: 'Agricultural possessions constituted the main part of the property of senators'; Lintott 1994*c*: 56: 'The bulk of private booty would have been used to buy land in Italy'; Astin 1978: 240: 'The opportunities of empire and the spoils of the major wars of the period produced a great influx of wealth, much of which passed directly into private hands and was spent on agricultural acquisitions and enterprises'; and even D'Arms 1981: 12: 'The fact that throughout most of antiquity, including the period in question, the foundation of economic life for all persons was not commerce and industry but agriculture...'

[9] See Harris 1979: 79–80, admitting, however, 'a large penumbra of uncertainty'; D'Arms 1981: 36; Hopkins 1978: 65.

Closely related to all this is Cicero's opinion that trade, *mercatura*, is *sordida* if it is on a small scale, but is not altogether to be disparaged if it is on a large scale, and becomes eminently praiseworthy if it produces a large fortune to be invested in land.[10] In this light, Aubert interprets the *plebiscitum Claudianum* of 218 (discussed in Ch.1) not as a sign of a conservative backlash against a growing involvement in trade by the Roman elite, but as a clarion call to invest more in land: 'Faced with the restriction on seaborne trade imposed by the *plebiscitum Claudianum* of 218, aristocrats were *expected to invest their increasing wealth in agricultural land* [my italics]. Many did so by channelling their money into large estates in desirable locations not too far from Rome (the Bay of Naples and South Etruria).'[11] On this view, 'the upper-class expressions of contempt for *mercatura* and *mercatores* and the legal sanctions against senatorial engagement in overseas trade imply the existence of another and related attitude: that the economic pursuits becoming to a man of *dignitas* were pre-eminently agricultural.'[12]

But all these modern scholars overstate their case. Plutarch says that in later life Cato gave up on agriculture and concentrated his business interests on the exploitation of natural resources and on finance.[13] We have seen, in Ch. 6 and earlier in this chapter, the importance of *faenus*, lending, as an asset class for investment by elite Romans. To these comments we may add the emphasis of Polybius, around 150, on the numerous public contracts let out by the censors for the building and repairing of Italian public works, rivers, harbours, parks, mines, and lands, and his assertion that 'almost, so to speak, everyone is involved either in the sale of these contracts or in the kinds of business (ἐργασία) to which they give rise'.[14]

In fact most of the evidence for the importance of large-scale investment in land comes from later periods, and we must beware of casual retrojections. From Cicero and later authors we gain an impression of the Roman upper class as deeply concerned with real property, sometimes on a grand scale.[15] Cicero tells us that 'agrum Praenestinum a paucis possideri' (the *Ager Praenestinus* is owned by a few men), and Horace refers to an imaginary villa stretching from Tusculum to Circeii, which is a huge exaggeration of course, but still indicative.[16] In the Augustan period, the freedman C. Caecilius Isidorus, after losing heavily in the civil wars, left large estates and ranches with some 4,000 slaves, 3,600 yoke of oxen, and more than 250,000 head of sheep.[17] Pliny the Younger invested most of his wealth in landed estates.[18] Finally, there is his uncle's statement about the deleterious effect of large land holdings: 'verumque confitentibus latifundia perdidere Italiam' (and if the

[10] Cic. *Off.* 1. 150–1.
[11] Aubert 2004: 169.
[12] D'Arms 1981: 5–6.
[13] Plut. *Cat. Mai.* 21. 5–6; see pp. 145 and 230.
[14] Polyb. 6. 17; Rosenstein (2008: 20, 24) is even more sceptical about the economic importance to members of the elite of income from land, arguing that a senator's urban properties and other non-agricultural commercial ventures provided a much greater share of his ordinary income than revenue for the sale of staple crops. 'Prestige more than profit is likely to have been the purpose of holding land, the accumulation of symbolic rather than economic capital... agriculture was not where [senators] expected to make their money'.
[15] Rawson 1976: 85, 100, 102; we even find the first evidence for estate agents: Cicero mentions a certain C. Sergius Orata, whose activities in Campania fall into the 90s.
[16] Cic. *Leg. agr.* 2. 78; Hor. *Ep.* 1. 129–30.
[17] Plin. *HN* 33. 135.
[18] Plin. *Ep.* 3. 19. 8: 'sum quidem prope totus in praediis' (I am almost completely in land).

truth be told, industrialized farms have destroyed Italy).[19] More commonly, however, there is evidence of a considerable class of absentee landlords, whose estates were not situated in a single neighbourhood, but scattered about in different regions.[20] Indeed Shatzman lists sixty-seven senators from the period between Sulla and Augustus who own more than one estate, a number of them ten or more.[21] This type of development is well illustrated from the holdings of Cicero himself, who owned a number of estates at different locations in Latium and in Campania.[22] Then there is Roscius of Ameria, an *eques*, who in the mid-first century owned thirteen separate *fundi* (farms) in the Tiber valley. Most of these properties had river frontages for easy transport of produce: 'nam fundos decem et tres reliquit qui Tiberim fere omnes tangunt'.[23] The importance of this type of location (also emphasized by Varro and Pliny the Younger[24]) probably stems from the fact that the *plebiscitum Claudianum* in effect allowed the senatorial landowner the use of boats only large enough to transport goods to market by river or along the coast. The value of Roscius' estates is given as HS 6 million (250 talents) which suggests that each estate comprised about 400–600 *iugera* and the total property 5,000–7,000 *iugera*.[25] The scattering of estates is unusual when compared to patterns of aristocratic landownership in, for example, eighteenth-century Europe, where estates tended to be concentrated in one area. Perhaps it reflected Roman dowry and partible inheritance patterns. It was, for instance, a legal obligation upon guardians not to leave any spare capital of their wards unproductive: they had to do with it one of two things—either to lend it out at interest (*faenus exercere*) or to purchase a farm (*fundos comparare*). The existence of these requirements presumably helped to increase the number of potential buyers for land and the dispersion of land holdings at any one time.[26] An alternative, and perhaps more attractive, explanation is that the fragmentation and dispersal of landholdings was deliberate, because it diversified risk. On this analysis, scattered and isolated estates evidenced a rational approach to agricultural investment, since, if land was owned in several different locations, the risk, for example of a poor harvest, could potentially be mitigated as a result of variations in local microclimates.[27]

Such literary evidence as does exist for landownership by the Roman elite during the second century suggests that land holdings were largely confined to a limited area in central-western Italy and points to the existence of more small and

[19] Plin. *HN* 18. 35. [20] White 1967: 74.

[21] Shatzman 1975: 27, 34. [22] Shatzman 1975: 403–9.

[23] Cic. *Rosc. Am.* 20: 'For he left thirteen farms almost all of which border the Tiber'; cf. Siculus Flaccus (Gr. P. 116 Th.): 'in multis regionibus comperimus quosdam possessores non continuas habere terras' (in many areas, we find that several landowners have estates that are not contiguous).

[24] Varro, *Rust.* 1. 16. 6; Plin. *Ep.* 5. 6.

[25] Cic. *Rosc. Am.* 21; Shatzman (1975) 20; 1 *iugerum* = 2,546 m^2; one football pitch = 10,800 m^2 or about 4 *iugera*.

[26] *Dig.* 26. 7; Crook 1976: 71.

[27] On the significance of microclimates, see Horden and Purcell 2000: 152. On the fragmentation of landholdings as a strategy to spread risk, see Erdkamp 2005: 73. This scattering of estates no doubt also reflected their piecemeal purchase by elite landowners from peasants. Cf. Hopkins 1978: 49, although he prefers to attribute the fragmentation of estates to 'expropriation' by elite landowners, following 'the expulsion of indigenous free peasants'.

medium-sized estates. According to our sources, senators' possessions were, during the second and early first centuries, to be found from Etruria in the north to Lucania in the south, but with a particular concentration in Latium and Campania. Even by the middle of the first century, Cicero's more prominent friends rarely owned estates farther north than Arretium or farther south than Pompeii, both incidentally places very easily accessible by major roads.[28] Shatzman is able to list fifty senators from the period between the Second Punic War and Sulla who have estates or landholdings outside Rome.[29] As in the first century, a senator's land was not necessarily consolidated in a single unit: it might be made up of several separate estates, perhaps in different regions.[30] In addition to a house in Rome and gardens near Rome, Scipio Aemilianus (*cos.* 147, whom Polybius describes as a man of moderate means compared with other Romans) had three estates: at Lavernum, Laurentum, and Caieta.[31] Cato's possessions were scattered over several regions. He inherited properties in Sabinum and Tusculum and the local knowledge he displays in his *De Agricultura* implies that he afterwards acquired estates in several places in Latium and Campania.[32] Individually, these estates are not large. The farms Cato discusses in the *De Agricultura* range in size from about 100 to 240 *iugera* (roughly 60 to 150 acres). Q. Aelius Tubero (*tr. pl.* 177, *leg.* 168) in the mid-second century had perhaps 150–200 *iugera* at Veii.[33] Pliny states that Scipio Africanus' estate at Liternum was a prosperous farm with a vineyard of perhaps 60 *iugera*; Seneca notes that Scipio's *villa urbana* in Rome included an olive plantation and a vineyard.[34] It is possible too that he had a small estate at Misenum, because Plutarch says that his daughter had one there which she might have inherited from her father.[35]

Although the evidence is limited, what it does appear to suggest is that estates of the second century were smaller than those of the mid-first century. The key point is whether the change was sudden or the result of a gradual development. Jaczynowska believes that the Sullan period opened a new stage in the growth of large-scale property ownership by the elite.[36] But while there is no doubt that a number of large fortunes were acquired by people closely connected with Sulla, who received the estates of proscribed *equites* and Italian *municipes* as gifts or bought them very cheaply, the archaeological evidence, which we shall examine later, suggests a more gradual transition.

[28] Nor do we hear of rich Romans anxious to own urban property anywhere else than at Puteoli and Rome in Cicero's time (Rawson 1976: 97).

[29] Shatzman 1975: tables I and II, 440–3.

[30] Shatzman 1975: 45; an interesting, though much later, parallel comes from a second-century AD inscription from near Viterbo (*ILS* 5771) which suggests a dense landholding pattern. It refers to an aqueduct running through eleven estates in less than six miles, with some of the landowners owning two or three estates along its course (discussed by A. I. Wilson 2008).

[31] Polyb. 18. 35. 9–10; Cic. *Rep.* 1. 14; Cic. *Nat. D.* 2. 11; Cic. *Amic.* 6: Cic. *De or.* 2. 22; Livy, *Per.* 59; Macrob. *Sat.* 3. 16. 3; Suet. *Vit. Terent.* 1; Shatzman 1975: 13, 248.

[32] Cic. *Rep.* 1. 1, 3. 40; Plut. *Cat. Mai.* 1. 1, 4. 4; *ORF*^{4} 51; Cato, *Agr.* 22, 135–6, 146.

[33] Val. Max. 4. 4. 8; Plut. *Aem.* 5. 4; estimate of size of estate by Shatzman 1975: 13, 241–2.

[34] Plin. *HN* 14. 47–9; Sen. *Ep.* 86. 14, 17–20; Shatzman 1975: 13, 246–7.

[35] Plut. *C. Gracch.* 19. 1; Shatzman 1975: 13, 247.

[36] Jaczynowska 1962: 487.

Outside Italy, the evidence is even less clear-cut. Of course, Rome's incorporation, during the second century, of much of the Mediterranean littoral within its *imperium* greatly increased the available land and resources. Survey evidence shows that ultimately large tracts of this newly acquired land in Africa, Gaul, Spain, Greece, and Sicily were subjected to centuriation and arable development on an unprecedented scale down to the third century AD. A significant part of this new territory was already under cultivation and thus immediately capable of generating income and revenue. As we saw in Ch. 4, the Roman state proceeded to tax agricultural production overseas. But evidence for agricultural exploitation overseas by individual members of the Roman elite in the second and early first centuries is largely lacking, with the exception of Sicily.

In Africa, following the defeat of Carthage in 146, Scipio Aemilianus annexed to Rome what survived of Punic territory, after Numidian claims had been satisfied. A ten-man commission, established by a *lex Livia* (according to the *lex agraria* of 111), or chosen by the senate (according to Appian), then arrived and drew up the tax regime for the territory. Appian states that the commission imposed both land and poll taxes, not only on all men but, unusually, also on all women who remained within Rome's new province, outside the free cities. The *lex agraria* mentions the collection of 'quae vectigalia in Africa publica populi Romani sunt' and 'scriptura'.[37] Seventy years later, Cicero mentions a 'certum stipendium' derived from Africa.[38]

Sallust's comment on Africa, that it was 'ager frugum fertilis, bonus pecori, arbori infecundus, caelo terraque penuria aquarum', should not be taken to imply the abandonment of Punic arboriculture, of which the treatise of Mago (discussed further on pp. 147–8) was the expression.[39] It is true that Pliny the Elder says that Proconsular Africa was, in the middle of the first century AD, first and foremost a supplier of wheat to Rome, with wine and oil being secondary.[40] But vines, formerly cultivated by the Carthaginians, were present along the coast and olive trees still grew there. Caesar's fine of 3 million pounds of olive oil on Leptis Magna could not have been paid if there was not already in existence a significant production base of that commodity.[41]

Unfortunately there is no firm indication as to whether any Roman actually farmed in Africa during the quarter century after the destruction of Carthage. Cicero mentions that Scipio Aemilianus assigned some territory to the Roman people (presumably in 146). But the first sign of any Roman agricultural activity comes only with the establishment on the site of Carthage of the citizen colony of Junonia, under a *lex Rubria* devised by C. Gracchus.[42] The allotments could reach a maximum of 200 *iugera*, which would have required more labour than the family of a single colonist could supply, suggesting that the settlement was not for subsistence farmers but for the reasonably well off.[43] The colony was a failure, according to Appian, but the provisions of the *lex agraria* of 111, which

37 App. *Pun.* 135; *lex agraria* 86: 'whatever public taxes of the Roman people there are in Africa'.

38 Cic. *II Verr.* 3. 12.

39 Sall. *Iug.* 17. 5: 'The land is fertile for crops, good for grazing, unproductive of trees, with a low rainfall and dry soil.'

40 Plin. *HN* 15. 8.

41 Caes. *B. Afr.* 97. 3; Plut. *Caes.* 55.

42 References at Ch. 4 nn. 61–2.

43 Brunt 1971*b*: 85.

consolidated land assignments in Africa into a permanent pattern, and which coincided with the beginning of military operations against Jugurtha, suggest a continuing Roman peasant presence. French aerial surveys have shown that there is an extensive system of centuriation in north-west Tunisia covering approximately 15,000 km^2. Attempts have been made to link this grid with the land distribution carried out under the *lex Rubria* or even with a possible assignment of land to citizens or allies in this area immediately after 146, either through sale or through lease by the censors, as is attested later in the *lex agraria* of 111.[44] There must have been some centuriation before 111, since it is mentioned in the *lex agraria*, but unfortunately there is absolutely no way of dating the large grid, and the bulk of the centuriation could just as easily date from the Augustan period or later.[45] A second settlement, but without colonial status, may have been founded at the end of the century, this time in Numidia. Saturninus, as tribune, presumably in 103, proposed that Marian veterans should each receive 100 *iugera* and violently overrode the veto of his colleague, Baebius.[46] Brunt, however, believes that the colony may not have been implemented because of the military and political turmoil of the following years.[47] Despite (or because of) these developments, there are absolutely no signs at all during the second or even the early part of the first century of the genesis of elite land occupation which culminated in Pliny's comment (exaggerated or not), in the first century AD, that: 'sex domini semissem Africae possidebant, cum interfecit eos Nero princeps'[48] (six landlords owned half of Africa, when Emperor Nero put them to death). We hear of Roman traders at Utica, Vaga, and Cirta during the Jugurthine War, but receive no indication of their status, elite or otherwise, nor of any agricultural interests.[49] Sallust mentions attacks on *villae* during the same war, but gives no indication as to whether their owners were Roman or African.[50] In fact, the earliest named individual of whom we hear owning land in Africa is the father of M. Caelius Rufus, an *eques*, who already has his holding by 61.[51] He is followed by L. Iulius Calidus, who was probably in Africa in 56 (Cicero writes a letter to the governor of Africa recommending him) and who thirteen years later, on the occasion of his proscription by the Triumvirs, is described by Nepos as having 'great estates in Africa'.[52] As always, the absence of any mention of elite investment in agriculture before this could just reflect a gap in our sources; but most of the notices of the involvement of the Roman elite in this activity seem to occur only after Julius Caesar won at Thapsus in 46 and commenced a further programme of colonization. Before that, it would appear from the sporadic notices we have that wealthy Romans resident in Africa could just as easily owe their fortunes to business as to agriculture. A group of Roman citizens, the 'Utican Three Hundred', who were fined the colossal amount of HS 200 million by Julius Caesar after Thapsus for

44 *lex agraria* 70–2, 82–3, 85–9; Chevallier 1958; Piganiol 1954: tab.I; App. *Pun.* 136; Lintott 1994*a*: 5, 1994*b*: 27–8; Crawford 1996: 173.

45 *lex agraria* 66; Crawley Quinn 2004: 1601.

46 *De vir. ill.* 73. 1; A. J. N. Wilson 1966: 45.

47 Brunt 1971*a*: 579–80.

48 Plin. *HN* 18. 35; the term *latifundia* is post-Augustan, as White (1967) has shown.

49 Utica: Sall. *Iug.* 64. 5; Vaga: 47. 1; Cirta: 26. 3.

50 Sall. *Iug.* 44. 5.

51 Cic. *Cael.* 73.

52 Cic. *Fam.* 13. 6. 3–4; Nep. *Att.* 12. 4.

their support of the Pompeian side, had not made their fortunes from farming but from trading and lending.[53]

In Spain the archaeological evidence for agricultural exploitation or attempts to increase yields is largely absent for the Republic.[54] The first evidence for viticulture dates to the end of the second century BC, as do the first villas, although more were erected during the course of the first century. At the villa of Tolegassos, 5 km to the south-west of Ampurias, the Roman building superseded an earlier native dwelling at the end of the second century. It stayed in use until the beginning of the first century AD, comprising a domestic building and an enclosure surrounding 75 *dolia*. This wine store is reminiscent of those in Campania and conceivably could indicate the presence of Campanian immigrants.[55] But most of the evidence for large-scale production dates from the Principate, in this case the manufacture of large quantities of wine amphorae along the coast of Catalonia. The first mention in a literary source of oleiculture in Hispania Ulterior comes only in the second half of the first century when, during the civil wars, the Pompeians make their camp in an olive grove.[56]

In the East, the Achaean League had revolted in 147 in reaction to Roman instructions that Sparta, Corinth, Argos, and Orchomenos should be separated from it. The settlement, imposed by L. Mummius after the rebellion had been crushed, was, in part, a reprisal. Tribute was demanded and oligarchic governments imposed.[57] The territory of Corinth became Roman *ager publicus* and, in 111, was being surveyed with a view to sale or settlement, according to our only source, the *lex agraria*.[58] Aside from that, a handful of stray references attest to Roman involvement in farming in Greece. For example, we know that the grandfather of C. Pandusinus managed an agricultural business, at Thisbe, that produced wheat and oil;[59] and an inscription from Delos, dating from 156/5, mentions two men with Latin names, Publius Aemilius and Gaius Annius, who are said to be living on Delos. It refers to them taking a lease on an area referred to as the 'sacred isthmus' on Mykonos.[60] We have no idea why two Romans were leasing land on the island at this time. It may have been to farm, but it could equally well have been for other purposes. The isthmus on Mykonos is mentioned in a number of earlier texts from Delos, dating from the period 219–179, and all refer to payments made to people for activities in relation to the isthmus. Pasturing is mentioned, but so too is ship-hauling and murex dye manufacturing.[61] As for Asia, the earliest notices of landownership by Roman citizens are only to be found in contemporary references in the Ciceronian corpus dating from

[53] Plut. *Cat. Min.* 59. 2, cf. 61. 2.

[54] Polyb. 34. 8. 8 and Strabo 3. 3. 1 do not suggest Roman involvement in farming.

[55] Brun 2004: 265.

[56] But we should bear in mind that an olive grove takes a number of years to establish; *BHisp.* 27. 1–3; Brun 2004: 279.

[57] Paus. 7. 16. 9–10.

[58] *lex agraria* 96ff.

[59] Hatzfeld 1919: 38.

[60] *IDélos* 1416. 5–8. I am grateful to Dr Annelies Cazemier for drawing my attention to this inscription.

[61] Previous texts from Delos: *IDélos* 353. 29–30, 33–4, cf. 35; 354. 29–30; 395. 12; 396. 2, cf. 356bis. 22; 359. A. 3; 368. 42; 399. 88, 90–1; 442. 154.

the second quarter of the first century.[62] In fact, therefore, there appears to be no surviving evidence of any significant agricultural exploitation by members of the Roman elite in either province during the late second or early first centuries.

Unlike elsewhere, Sicily was a province in which the Romans were already well established by the 130s, and in which they and wealthy Greek Sicilians had probably begun to run large arable and livestock estates. Cato's description of Sicily as the 'nutrix plebis Romanae' (the wet nurse of the Roman plebs), a supplier of hides, clothing, and corn, seems to suggest this, as does Florus' comment on the state of Sicily at the time of the first Slave War: 'terra frugum ferax et quodam modo suburbana provincia latifundiis civium Romanorum tenebatur'[63] (the land, rich in corn and almost a suburban province, was occupied by the large estates of Roman citizens). As we shall see below, we do have some specific names of Roman slave-owners at the time of the second revolt.[64] Also, the sheer numbers of slaves involved in the rebellions show that agricultural exploitation was taking place in Sicily on a significant scale in the second half of the second century. By the time we get to the 70s, the *Verrines* present a picture of large numbers of Romans involved in agriculture in the province.[65] These speeches do not suggest that these Roman farmers were recent arrivals; rather they were well established on the island by the time the *Verrines* were written.[66] In fact, the only possible mention of a member of the senatorial order with provincial investments before the end of the second century is the poet Lucilius, who not only had estates in south Italy, near Tarentum, but also in Sicily and Sardinia. According to Cichorius, Lucilius was a Roman citizen and a senator.[67] Indeed, it is only after Sulla that we begin to get notices of senatorial possessions in provinces outside Italy and only on a significant scale during the Principate.[68] By the time of Sulla, however, we do begin to find increasing evidence of *equites* farming provincial estates in areas other than Sicily. As we have seen, the *Pro Quinctio* deals with a partnership which had been formed in southern Gaul many years before 81 (the date of its composition) between two Romans, Quinctius and Naevius. The men engaged on an extensive scale in farming and grazing north of Narbo: 'pecuaria res ampla et rustica sane bene culta et fructuosa'.[69] In the *Pro Fonteio* of 74, the Romans in Gaul are designated in four groups: *publicani, agricolae, pecuarii, ceteri negotiatores.*[70]

In sum, therefore, there is very little evidence before the first century for agricultural exploitation in the provinces by the Roman elite outside Sicily. A possible explanation for this is simply the nature of our source material—in

[62] Landowners in Asia: Caerellia (Cic. *Fam.* 13. 7. 2); Maeculonius (Cic. *Flacc.* 46); P. Septimius (Cic. *Flacc.* 88); A. Trebonius (Cic. *Fam.* 1. 3. 1); L. Octavius Naso (Cic. *Q Fr.* 1. 2. 10); T. Annius Milo (Cic. *Att.* 6. 1. 19, 6. 5. 2); Broughton (1938) 551.

[63] Cic. *II Verr.* 2.5; Flor. 2. 7. 3.

[64] See p. 180.

[65] Cic. *II Verr.* 2. 5–7.

[66] For example, the Roman *eques*, Q. Lollius, nearly 90 years old in 70s, farming near Aetna (Cic. *II Verr.* 3. 69); cf. Cic. *II Verr.* 3. 93, 3. 97.

[67] Lucil. 287–8, 655; Cichorius, *ad Ulp.* 14–22; Shatzman 1975: 19, 277.

[68] Shatzman 1975: 30.

[69] Cic. *Quinct.* 12: 'a considerable rural ranch that was very well maintained and productive'.

[70] Cic. *Font.* 46: 'state contractors, farmers, ranchers, and other businessmen'; cf. Cic. *Font.* 12: 'negotiatores, coloni, publicani, aratores, pecuarii' (businessmen, farmers, state contractors, ploughmen, ranchers).

particular the lack of a Cicero for the second half of the second century and beginning of the first. There are, however, other considerations which suggest that, before the 120s at least, agricultural exploitation by elite Romans was limited mainly to Italy. In the first place, after 167, the collection of the *tributum* assessable on Italian land owned by Roman citizens was suspended, whereas provincial land continued to have tax levied on it. As Hopkins pointed out, this is one of the factors that accounts for the high price of Italian land in the late Republic, since, other things being equal, rent could equal rent plus tax on provincial land.[71] Secondly, as far as senators, specifically, are concerned, they were apparently restricted from travelling abroad privately and forbidden explicitly from owning land outside Italy. This may partly explain the concentration of senatorial estates in central-western Italy.[72] Thirdly, Frank long ago expressed the view that it was the activities of the Gracchan land commission in the Italian *ager publicus* that induced wealthy Romans to invest more overseas; and indeed one of the revolutionary elements of Ti. Gracchus' legislation was the seizure of excessive amounts of *ager publicus* from the rich and their redistribution to the poor.[73] This may be one possible reason, for example, for the Roman civilian presence in Africa being apparently so limited during the quarter century after the destruction of Carthage. But a final explanation for the apparent absence of large-scale elite agricultural exploitation in the provinces before the first century is also to be found in the booming trade in Italian wine and olive oil during the second half of the second century, which we discuss in the next section. Was there any need for a landowner to invest overseas if he could make a high return from growing wine or olive oil in Italy for the export market or from producing grain, fruit, vegetables, and meat for rapidly expanding urban populations?

A BOOM IN EXPORTS

The construction of new port and commercial infrastructure in Rome during the first half of the century suggests that, in general, overseas trade from central-western Italy was already expanding.[74] There are other indications too, such as the building of a pier at Terracina by M. Aemilius Lepidus in 179, which is explicitly connected by Livy with the proximity of his estates, and was presumably completed in order to facilitate the easier transport of commodities from those estates.[75] However, during the second half of the second century, the production

[71] Hopkins 1978: 38.

[72] Cic. *II Verr.* 5. 45: 'privatim autem nec proficisci quoqam nec arcessere res transmarinas ex iis locis in quibus te habere nihil licet' (privately, however, you are not permitted to make journeys at all, nor to send for your overseas resources from areas in which you are not in any case allowed to hold any). These restrictions are more likely to have stemmed from considerations of good governance than from any economic motive. We argued earlier (p. 14) that the *plebiscitum Claudianum* had been introduced because trade was perceived to have begun to affect senatorial decisions on foreign policy. The restrictions referred to by Cicero must have been born of a similar logic.

[73] Frank 1933: 388; App. *B. Civ.* 1. 10; cf. Cic. *Sest.* 48.

[74] See pp. 217–8.

[75] Livy, 40. 51. 2, quoted on p. 17; D'Arms 1981: 36; DeLaine 1995: 560.

and export to Gaul of Italian wine amphorae and their contents increased at a bewildering rate. The amphorae were, at first, Graeco-Italic and, then, of a type known as Dressel 1, which continued in use until the late first century BC. The regular and standardized shapes of these amphorae will have made them simple to stack and store.

Analysis of the fabrics of Graeco-Italic and Dressel 1 amphorae, from sites in southern France, suggests that the majority were manufactured in Etruria, Latium, and Campania.[76] The principal contents of Graeco-Italic amphorae are not known for certain but are assumed to be wine. The evidence of painted inscriptions (*tituli picti*) and the remains of residues found in amphorae from marine contexts make it clear that the principal contents of the Dressel 1 amphorae were wine, although other commodities have been found in containers from wrecks, such as olives, *spondylus* shells, resin, and hazelnuts. The Lamboglia 2 amphorae, dating from the second half of the second century to around the mid-first century, probably mainly carried wine, although olive oil has been suggested.[77] These latter amphorae seem to have been produced in south-east Italy and are the type most commonly discovered in the Adriatic.

An overwhelming majority of the wrecks found in the western Mediterranean, and dating to the second and first centuries, carried cargoes mainly consisting of wine amphorae.[78] For example, in 1952, the contents of two Roman freighters were recovered from the waters off the north-east point of the island of Grand Congloué, south of Marseilles, at the foot of a cliff some 32 m to 45 m in depth. A later ship had sunk onto a previous wreck. The upper wreck bore a cargo of between 1,200 and 1,500 Dressel 1A amphorae, stacked in at least three layers, suggesting that the ship carried between 31,000 and 39,000 litres of wine (at 26 litres per amphora[79]). But the evidence for this trade does not just come from shipwrecks. These amphorae are also found in terrestrial contexts in France, Spain, Sicily, Switzerland, Luxembourg, Germany, and Britain. In France alone, as of 2002, there were 1,975 terrestrial find-spots of Republican transport amphorae, with the biggest concentration, over half, being in southern and central France in a band running from the Rhône delta, across to the Tarn, and then up to the Massif Central, and across to the Loire and Saône rivers.[80] Amphorae with the Sestius stamp are found inland as far as the Rhône and the Loire. But there are also a surprising number of find-spots in northern and western France, perhaps indicating an Atlantic trade in Italian wine. Possible Graeco-Italic rims have been found at Hengistbury Head in Dorset, on the south coast of Britain.[81] Further south, recent analysis of amphora evidence from Sicily has shown that the Roman conquest of the western part of that island at the end of the third century opened the door to a massive trade in Campanian wine.[82]

Parker argued that Graeco-Italic amphorae, first produced in about 350, ceased to be exported in about 150 and were immediately supplanted by Dressel 1A, with

[76] See p. 231. [77] Peacock and Williams 1986: 39–43, 84–90, 99–100.

[78] Parker 1992: 552 fig. 8; Morley 1996: 112–13. The total of Mediterranean wrecks from the ancient world discovered by May 2010 stood at 1,800.

[79] A. I. Wilson 2009*a*: 227. [80] Loughton 2003: 188–92, esp. fig 7.

[81] Loughton 2003: 202. [82] Bechtold 2007.

the first Dressel 1B appearing in about 100. Peacock and Williams and Tchernia believe the transition date from Graeco-Italic to Dressel 1 to be 130. More recent discoveries have suggested that the latest types of Graeco-Italic overlapped with Dressel 1, as both types have been found at the Roman camps at Numantia in Spain, which were abandoned in 133. The Dressel 1 form has apparently been found at Carthage, providing a date of about 150 for its origin. This shows that any dating made by using these amphorae is not only inexact, but also subject to controversy and eventual change.[83] That said, the broad outline of the wine trade to Gaul is reasonably straightforward. Graeco-Italic amphorae first appeared in Mediterranean contexts from the third century onwards, but were rare outside this area. It was not until the Roman conquest of southern Gaul, in about 121, that the Dressel IA was exported in large numbers to non-Mediterranean Gaul, with the number of find-spots in northern France increasing. The start of the boom in the export of Italian wine also seems to coincide with a dramatic decline in the export of Rhodian wine (the previous 'market leader') to the western Mediterranean and the Adriatic.[84]

Italian wine amphorae also become even more frequent in the shipwrecks that date from the late second century. There are about two and a half times as many cargoes of Dressel 1 and Lamboglia 2 amphorae, in the period between about 150 and 1 BC, as cargoes of Graeco-Italic amphorae, in the equivalent preceding period (about 300 to 150 BC).[85] The vast majority of the Dressel 1 cargoes come from wrecks in the western Mediterranean, especially from the coast of southern France. Recently, Wilson has analysed Parker's data in more detail and has produced graphs that attempt to allocate shipwrecks within narrower chronological periods. His graph showing Parker's data in 50-year periods (reproduced in Fig. 7.1) reveals a steep increase in the number of shipwrecks (and, therefore, by extension, presumably in the volume of shipping and of cargoes carried in the Mediterranean), in the second half of the second century and the first half of the first century, before reaching a slightly higher peak in the first half of the first century AD.[86]

Furthermore, the late second and early first centuries show a significant increase in the size of vessels. Before the late second century, ships carried a maximum of 75 tonnes of cargo, equivalent to about 1,500 amphorae. From then on, larger vessels begin to appear, such as the vessel wrecked at La Madrague de Giens in the 70s, which was about 40 m in length and would have carried approximately 400 tonnes of cargo, composed mainly of between 6,000 and 7,000 amphorae. The Albenga wreck, which sank in around 100–90, and is estimated to have been about 450–500 tonnes, probably carried some 10,000 Dressel 1 wine amphorae. Since each amphora contained about 26 litres, the cargo of this vessel must have totalled some 260,000 litres of wine (347,000 modern wine bottles).[87] The building of larger ships, such as these, reflects not only increasing volumes of trade but also improving technologies: the earliest definite examples of the bilge pump come from wrecks dating from the late second century.[88]

[83] Parker 1992: 16–35; Peacock and Williams 1986; Tchernia 1986; Loughton 2003: 179–80.

[84] See pp. 208–9. [85] Parker 1992. [86] A. I. Wilson 2009*a*: 223 fig. 9.4.

[87] Parker 1992: 249; A. I. Wilson 2009*a*: 227.

[88] Parker 1992: 28; earlier ships may have relied on bailing, impossible in larger vessels.

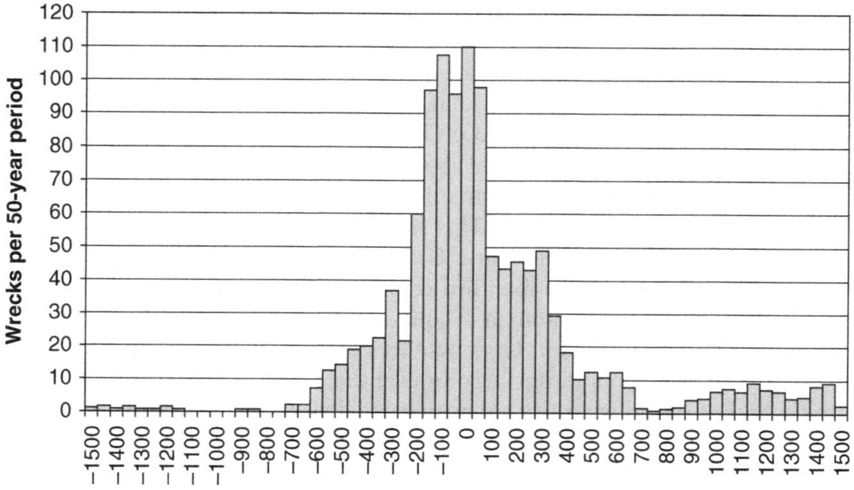

Fig. 7.1. Mediterranean shipwrecks by half century, using probability per annum

Finds of transport amphorae provide a better basis for establishing the beginning of market-oriented agricultural production than, say, villa sites. For example, the villa of Settefinestre near Cosa is as close as one could probably come to a model villa as described by the agronomists.[89] Its excavated remains imply the cultivation of grapes and olives for wine and olive oil production, grain growing, and milling, and, if the polygonal walled enclosure was an orchard, fruit (or, if it held animals, stock rearing). It had one olive press and three wine presses, which, together with the evidence of storage facilities, suggest that it was being used to support between 50 and 100 *iugera* of vines.[90] Cato's formula for viticulture deals with a vineyard size of 100 *iugera*.[91] Moreover, Settefinestre is located precisely in the region that has produced the most amphora evidence for the export of wine. But the villa was not built before the second quarter of the first century BC and flourished during the century 50 BC to AD 50.[92] Should this lead us to push the beginning of the boom in wine exports forward to the first century, or is it likely (as Morley has suggested) that intensified agricultural production may precede by decades the construction of the villa using the proceeds of successful viticulture?[93] On balance, the latter interpretation appears to be safer.

The archaeological record of amphorae, both in marine and terrestrial contexts, therefore, indicates a very significant trade in wine along the south coast and the main arterial rivers of Gaul. Tchernia tried to quantify Italian wine exports to Gaul by using the number of shipwrecks known in the early 1980s to produce an estimate of the average number of voyages per annum over the century in which Dressel 1 amphorae were in use. The total comes to around 6 million litres per annum, but the actual amount could well have been significantly more than this.

[89] The main difference is the lack of a distinction at Settefinestre between a *pars rustica* and a *pars urbana*.

[90] Carandini and Settis 1979; Rathbone 1981: 11–12; Greene 1986: 91.

[91] Cato, *Agr.* 11.

[92] Rathbone 1981: 20; Carandini and Ricci 1985.

[93] Morley 1996: 130–2.

Rosenstein estimates the size of the export trade in wine and olive oil to Gaul at between 6 and 15 million litres per year.[94]

Some historians have linked the increased Gallic demand for Italian wine, which seems to have stimulated the growth in this trade, with socio-economic change in Gaul, including the development of urban centres and archaic states. Others have connected it with the popularity of competitive feasting and drinking, and, for the second century, with the power of the Averni in central Gaul and the fabled wealth of their king.[95] Whatever the reasons, it is clear that the opening up of new markets by Roman traders in Gaul pre-dated Rome's imperial expansion there. Certainly there is no evidence to suggest that coins were involved in the exchange process, since the denarius is found only in small quantities, even in southern Gaul, before Caesar.[96] The evidence for the boom in Italian wine exports in the second century is archaeological rather than literary; but, by the time that Diodorus was writing in the second half of the first century, Roman traders were selling wine to Gallic tribes in exchange for slaves:

> *πολλοὶ τῶν Ἰταλικῶν ἐμπορῶν διὰ τὴν συνήθη φιλαργυρίαν ἕρμαιον ἡγοῦνται τὴν τῶν Γαλατῶν φιλοινίαν. οὗτοι γὰρ διὰ μὲν τῶν πλωτῶν ποταμῶν πλοίοις, διὰ δὲ τῆς πεδιάδος χώρας ἁμάξαις κομίζοντες τὸν οἶνον, ἀντιλαμβάνουσι τιμῆς πλῆθος ἄπιστον· διδόντες γὰρ οἴνου κεράμιον ἀντιλαμβάνουσι παῖδα, τοῦ πόματος διάκονον ἀμειβόμενοι.*[97]
>
> (Many of the Italian traders, induced by the love of money which characterises them, believe that the love of wine of the Gauls is a godsend. For they transport the wine on the navigable rivers in boats and through the level plains on wagons, and receive for it an incredible price; for in exchange for a jar of wine they receive a slave, getting a servant in return for the drink.[98])

Given the extensive finds of transport amphorae from the second century in areas that were not controlled by the Romans (their sherds are common at sites ranging from small farmsteads to large *oppida*), the barter described by Diodorus is a likely model for the kind of exchange that was already occurring in the second century.

It is surely no coincidence that Cato's interest in the financing of trade probably dates to the middle of the second century when the pickup in the wine trade begins. Plutarch gives a description of Cato's financial interests in shipping which is the earliest surviving example of the organization of a Roman business arrangement that does not involve the *publicani*:

> *ἐχρήσατο δὲ καὶ τῷ διαβεβλημένῳ μάλιστα τῶν δανεισμῶν ἐπὶ ναυτικοῖς τὸν τρόπον τοῦτον. ἐκέλευε τοὺς δανειζομένους ἐπὶ κοινωνίᾳ πολλοὺς παρακαλεῖν, γενομένων δὲ πεντήκοντα καὶ πλοίων τοσούτων αὐτὸς εἶχε μίαν μερίδα διὰ Κουϊντίωνος ἀπελευθέρου τοῖς δανειζομένοις συμπραγματευομένου καὶ συμπλέοντος. ἦν δ᾽ οὖν οὐκ εἰς ἅπαν ὁ κίνδυνος, ἀλλ᾽ εἰς μέρος μικρὸν ἐπὶ κέρδεσι μεγάλοις.*[99]

[94] Tchernia 1986; Rosenstein 2008: 17; see Ch. 11.

[95] Strabo, 4. 2. 3; Ath. 4. 152; Loughton 2003; Tchernia (2009) summarizes some fascinating (primarily archaeological) evidence for ritualistic feasting and the use of imported red wine from Italy in these ceremonies.

[96] Crawford 1985: 168; but compare and contrast, for southern Gaul, Cic. *Font.* 11 (quoted on p. 126).

[97] Diod. Sic. 5. 26. 3.

[98] Trans. Loeb III 167, slightly revised.

[99] Plut. *Cat. Mai.* 21. 5–6.

([Cato] also used to engage in shipping finance, the most discreditable form of lending, in the following way. He told his many borrowers to form a partnership. When there were fifty partners and as many ships, he himself held one share through a freedman, Quintio, who worked with and sailed with the borrowers. Cato did not therefore take the whole risk, but took only a small exposure in return for large gains.)

This commercial partnership was clearly very carefully structured. Cato lent the funds to finance the other partners, but he mitigated his own risk by himself only acquiring one share (μίαν μερίδα) in the partnership itself. A loan could no doubt have been guaranteed or secured in some way (perhaps against physical property) in order to reduce his credit risk, while a share would have functioned as an equity participation, exposing him directly to the risk of the enterprise. Even then he held this one share through a freedman, which perhaps indicates that here too he was trying to hedge his risk. Furthermore, the same freedman was present on the voyages to look after his interests. Finally and, in the present context, most importantly, it is clear that the partnership was both large and very profitable.[100]

As Woolf has highlighted, the geographic extent of the distribution of central Italian wine during this period was extremely unusual. Much more characteristic of the Mediterranean wine trade under the Principate were more localized regional distributions.[101] For our period, given the size of the wine trade with Gaul, one might have expected to find evidence for the shipment of large quantities of wine to Rome, but few amphorae dating to the Republican period have been found there and it is only with the development of Ostia under the Julio-Claudians that the origins of the city's imports can be studied by using amphorae.[102] So any attempt to estimate the size of the Roman market for wine, in the late second century, is necessarily speculative. However, Morley has attempted to quantify demand at Rome, using a population estimate for Rome in 100 of about 500,000 and an average level of consumption of about 250 litres per annum, which he modifies by giving half rations for women and children.[103] This gives a total for consumption of over 80 million litres per annum. If the level of consumption is halved, and the estimate for the population reduced to 300,000, the figure is 25 million litres per annum, still more than four times Tchernia's estimated level of exports to Gaul.[104]

But even transport amphorae have their limitations as evidence. Although the archaeological finds do not show olive oil production rising at nearly the rate of viticulture, an emerging market of some scale for olive products is implied in the attention accorded to all aspects of oleiculture in the agricultural treatises of Cato, Varro, Pliny, and Columella.[105] Furthermore, there are other commodities for which we have no evidence at all, because they were most probably transported overseas (if they were so transported) in containers that were themselves made of

[100] Cf. D'Arms 1981: 39–40.

[101] Woolf 1992: 287, 289.

[102] Tchernia 1986: 66–7.

[103] Morley 1996: 113; Purcell 1985: 13–15 suggests using the amount of 250 l p.a., the approximate amount that Cato allocated to his slaves.

[104] Although, as we shall see below, Jongman (2003*b*: 112–16) suggests that the size of the market for Roman agricultural goods was quite limited.

[105] Carandini 1989; Hitchner 2002: 73.

perishable materials, such as wicker baskets and sacks.[106] For example, cheese can be stored for long periods and transported easily. It provides an excellent means of converting milk surpluses into a marketable commodity, and we know that the growth of the northern Italian town of Luni was due to exports, not only of Carrara marble, timber, and wine, but also cheese.[107] Similarly, how would we find archaeological evidence for the export (or not) of a soft commodity, such as the fig?[108] It is possible that it was not just wine and olive oil that was being exported from Italy, but other agricultural commodities as well.

INVESTMENT FARMING

In any consideration of the export boom in wine (and perhaps other soft commodities too), Cato's *De Agricultura* looms large. Possibly written in the 160s, not only does it evidence aristocratic exploitation, but also it has greatly influenced the picture that has been drawn of farming in the time of the Gracchi. This is because the concentrated cultivation of the vine and olive as cash crops and the use of slave labour which it portrays appear to distinguish this type of investment farming, the 'villa system', from previous forms of agriculture in Roman Italy.

Cato's treatise is part of an extensive corpus of literature on Roman agriculture that survives from a range of authors who wrote between the second century BC and the fourth century AD. This corpus includes manuals of agricultural practice by Varro, Columella, and Palladius, as well as Vergil's *Georgics*. In addition, Pliny the Elder's *Natural History* also contains a considerable amount of information relevant to agriculture. We know too of other works that are now lost. The work attributed to the elder and younger Sasernae, probably dating from after 90, consisted of *libri* (books) in the plural and so was on a larger scale than Cato's single book.[109] All these authors drew on the knowledge of earlier Carthaginian and Greek writers. Indeed, the most widely read work on agriculture at the end of the second century was the Latin translation of the huge work in twenty-eight books in Punic of Mago the Carthaginian. We know very little about the organization of the work, one of the few details (from Columella) being that Mago wrote extensively on viticulture.[110] What we do know is that the senate decreed that a group of Romans 'experienced in the Punic language', of whom the most accomplished was Decimus Silanus, should undertake the translation.[111] This is enormously significant, since we know of no other occasion when the senate ordered

106 It should be noted that ancient shipwrecks are most often identified by the survival of (non-perishable) ceramic containers, marble columns, or metalwares, which form a silt-covered mound on the seabed.

107 Ward-Perkins et al. 1986: 107–9, 140–3; Greene 1986: 48, 80.

108 On the fig, see Horden and Purcell 2000: 210; cf. the famous story, at Plut. *Cat. Mai.* 27. 1, of how Cato contrived to drop a Carthaginian fig in the senate, telling the *patres* that the country where it grew was only three days' sail from Rome.

109 Varro, *Rust.* 1. 2. 22; Rawson 1985: 135–6; Greene 1986: 68.

110 Columella, *Rust.* 3. 12. 5, 12. 39. 1–2.

111 Plin. *HN* 18. 22; Varro, *Rust.* 1. 1. 10.

the translation of a book written in a foreign language. It highlights the interest of the Roman elite in the transfer of superior agricultural skills and techniques to Italy.

Cato concerned himself in his treatise only with certain types of farm and made no attempt to give advice on all the forms of agriculture actually practised in Italy at this time. As a result, his work cannot be considered typical of Italian agriculture in general, which varied considerably from one region to another. The three most important agricultural products traded in the Roman world were grain, wine, and olive oil, and their farming is known as 'polyculture'.[112] The cultivation of grapes and olives in the second century represented an intensive system of agriculture directed towards the large-scale commercialization of produce requiring complex processing. In complete contrast, there also existed in many regions of Italy (especially in Bruttium, the interior of Lucania, and a large part of Apulia) an economy founded on extensive stock rearing and on the development of forests yielding timber for construction and for heating, charcoal, and pitch.[113] Indeed stock rearing constituted one of the principal forms of elite investment for commercial purposes in Republican Italy, described in its most advanced form by Varro.[114] This type of farming is already attested in the second century, where there are notices concerning the punishment of ranchers (*pecuarii*) convicted of running more than the permitted maximum of stock on *ager publicus*.[115] According to Cicero, when Cato was asked what was most advantageous in the management of property, he replied, 'Good pasturing' (*bene pascere*). What second? 'Fairly good pasturing.' What third? 'Poor pasturing.' What fourth? 'Ploughing' [*arare*, which must mean 'arable farming', 'cultivating crops'].[116]

Market gardening (*pastio villatica*) was practised closer to towns and cities and must have been booming in the second century in the *suburbium* of Rome, as the population of that city grew. Varro even mentions a tiny estate in the *Ager Faliscus* of only one *iugerum*, the honey from which brought in HS 10,000 a year—clearly in the right area (in this case, within a day or two's journey of Rome) the most minute properties could be viable.[117] Such diversity was a product of the environment, the suitability of different crops for the locality, and the differing demands of urban markets in the vicinity. Indeed a completely accurate story of the Roman agricultural economy in the second century, if one were possible, would have to be based on the changing balance between the food demands of a growing urban

[112] Greene 1986: 72. On grain production, see Erdkamp 1998: 84–121.

[113] Morel 1989: 498.

[114] Varro, *Rust.* 2. *praef.* 6.

[115] Livy, 33. 42. 10 (196 BC); 35. 10. 11–12 (193 BC).

[116] Cic. *Off.* 2. 89; cf. Cato, *Agr.* 54. 5: 'nihil est quod magis expediat quam boves bene curare' (there is nothing more profitable than to care well for cattle). In good Catonian tradition this is, of course, completely at odds with the preferences he expresses at Cato, *Agr.* 1. 7: 'Praedium quod primum siet, si me rogabis, sic dicam: de omnibus agris optimoque loco iugera agri centum, vinea est prima . . .' (If you ask me what the best kind of farm is, I would say that it is one hundred *iugera* of land with all types of fields in a very good location, and that a vineyard is first . . .).

[117] Varro, *Rust.* 3. 16. 10–11; In general, there is no reason why smallholders could not have been productive and economically viable; in the early 1960s, vineyards in Piedmont had an average area of only around 3.75 hectares (Kron 2008: 106. n. 207). See A. I. Wilson 2008 for a discussion of suburban farming.

population in Rome and other Italian cities, an expanding export demand for certain commodities and products, and the available surplus of an agricultural sector seeing increasing productivity because of increasing specialization. In that context, it is worth noting that there is no evidence for the large-scale importation of agricultural products into Italy on a regular basis before the 120s. In particular, Erdkamp has demonstrated that, during the first half of the second century at least, tax grain from outside Italy was mainly shipped to Roman armies fighting overseas.[118]

The primary function of the estates that are discussed in the *De Agricultura* was to produce wine or olive oil for sale. That is not to say that these farms were by any means given over to monoculture. A variety of other crops were raised and animals were kept, probably in part to provide manure for fertilizer and only in an auxiliary role. Cato has in mind farms ranging in size from about 100 to 240 *iugera* (roughly 60 to 150 acres). In one passage he speaks of 100 *iugera* as being ideal, but there he is thinking primarily of a vineyard and that is indeed the size of the vineyard for which he later gives an inventory. The two olive-yards referred to in the text are both larger, one of them 120 and the other 240 *iugera*.[119] An exception to this emphasis on wine and oil is to be found in the brief digression on the 'suburban farm', *fundus suburbanus*, which is to be used to grow a considerable variety of produce marketable in the nearby town.[120]

The labour is primarily that of slaves, except for seasonal hired (free) labour, as will be discussed in more detail later. The slaves are controlled by a slave manager (*vilicus*) and his wife.[121] For most of the year these slaves are fed and supplied from the farm itself; a calendar of tasks is laid down, so that, in all seasons, they are kept occupied.[122] The names of places where particular items are to be purchased or marketed are confined to Latium, Campania, and the adjacent parts of Lucania. In these areas, at any rate, farming on the new intensive basis recommended by Cato could be made to pay. Equally clearly, and connected with the same areas, are the principal types of Republican wine amphora.[123]

Until comparatively recently, the standard view has been that Cato's *De Agricultura* gives us a glimpse of a major revolution in Italian agriculture in the second century. Purcell mockingly characterizes this orthodoxy thus: 'the Roman upper class seized huge tracts of land, avidly perused Hellenistic treatises on what Toynbee called "plantation agriculture" and were at once provided by a kindly fortune with the necessary colossal number of slaves to make it possible'.[124] Purcell believes that there are difficulties with this theory because Cato's treatise is about farms of modest extent and value and, in its Preface, it justifies agriculture as the producer of military manpower. More recently he has argued that Cato was no revolutionary, since the system of agriculture he described had probably been

118 Erdkamp 2005: 212.

119 Cato, *Agr.* 1. 7, 11. 1, 3. 5, 10. 1; Astin 1978: 243; we cannot, however, be certain that the *vinea* of 100 *iugera* represents a self-contained estate rather than what we should call a farm unit—a kind of module that could be used by the intending purchaser of an estate as a base for calculating the amount of stock and equipment, and the size of the workforce and supervising staff needed in an enterprise several times that size (White 1967: 63).

120 Cato, *Agr.* 7–8.

121 Cato, *Agr.* 5. 1–5, 10–11, 142–3.

122 Cato, *Agr.* 39ff.

123 See p. 231; Frederiksen 1970–1: 334; White 1967: 76; Purcell 1985: 6.

124 Toynbee 1965: i. 291ff.; for an example of this orthodoxy, see Astin 1978: 240.

in existence for several decades by the time he wrote his treatise.[125] This is because there is evidence that farming in the area of Capua had already, by the time of the Hannibalic War, developed on Hellenistic lines, a point on which Livy's description of the *Ager Falernus* in 217 seems reliable: 'arbusta vineaeque et consita omnia magis amoenis quam necessariis fructibus'[126] (orchards and vineyards and everything planted with agreeable rather than necessary fruit). Archaeological evidence demonstrates that a vigorous third-century Campanian wine trade preceded the acquisition of landholdings by Roman senators in Campania by some decades.[127] Also the prohibitions contained in the *plebiscitum Claudianum* of 218 suggest that, by that date, large-scale exportation to distant markets in Italy or overseas was starting to occur on a different scale from what had been happening previously.[128] Still in southern Italy, a prototype of the Catonian villa, probably dating from between the First and Second Punic Wars, has been discovered in non-Roman territory at S. Pietro di Tolve.[129]

It was natural that Campania in particular should have responded to such influences early, since there is little doubt that plantation agriculture originated in the Hellenistic world. A description of the Carthaginian countryside, in Diodorus' account of the Libyan campaign of Agathocles of Syracuse in 310, highlights this kind of landscape:

> *ἡ δ' ἀνὰ μέσον χώρα, δι' ἧς ἦν ἀναγκαῖον πορευθῆναι, διείληπτο κηπείαις καὶ παντοίαις φυτουργίαις, πολλῶν ὑδάτων διωχετευμένων καὶ πάντα τόπον ἀρδευόντων.*[130]
>
> (The intervening country, through which it was necessary for them to march, was divided into gardens and plantations of every kind, with much water being distributed in small channels and irrigating the whole area.[131])

Diodorus also gives us a vivid picture of the prosperity derived from heavy (but not exclusive) investment in oleiculture on the part of the Greek elite of Acragas (Agrigento) on the south coast of Sicily during the fifth century.[132] The trade was orientated towards the single market of Carthage. It seems very likely that a number of the other expansions of oleiculture and viticulture which are conspicuous in the ancient archaeological or literary evidence were also responses to the formation of particular markets of this kind, instances, essentially, of what Horden and Purcell call 'directed trade'.[133] There is also archaeological evidence, from Jerba in North Africa and Marsala in Sicily, suggesting that large courtyard villas were already in use there by the end of the third century.[134]

In rural Italy, there appear to have been two different types of establishment in the third and second centuries. There are a few grand residences, such as the auditorium site near Rome, whose origins stretch back to the fifth century

[125] Purcell 1985: 5; 2005*a*.

[126] Livy, 22. 15; cf. Polyb. 3. 91. 2–3; Plin. *HN* 3. 60; Frederiksen 1970–1: 338.

[127] See p. 12. [128] See pp. 13–14. [129] Di Giuseppe 1994.

[130] Diod. Sic. 20. 8. 3; cf. Varro's description of an Italian landscape, two and a half centuries later, so planted up with trees that 'it resembles one enormous garden' (Varro, *Rust.* 1. 2. 6).

[131] Trans. Loeb X 161, slightly revised.

[132] Diod. Sic. 13. 81. 4–5; cf. 11. 25. 5, 13. 83. 3.

[133] Horden and Purcell 2000: 212, 365–77; Gabba 1989: 236.

[134] Fentress 2001. This evidence, however, apparently comes from a geophysical survey, so it is not completely reliable as to date.

or earlier;[135] and a number of what are termed 'Hellenistic farmsteads'. The farmhouses of the latter tend to be much smaller, around 500 m^2, and most importantly show clear evidence of the production of an agricultural surplus for the market. So, for example, Site 11 on the Via Gabina in its earliest phase (1A) dates to the early third century. By the mid-third century, a pressing floor for olives or grapes is added. Likewise, the earliest phase of the Villa Sambuco in western Etruria, which dates from the first half of the second century (380 m^2), contained four large storerooms in which a large number of *dolia* had been set in the ground.[136]

Probably modelled, then, on Greek farms in Magna Graecia and Sicily and on Carthaginian plantations, this type of estate must have been introduced into the Roman world in the second half of the third century and have spread, in the first half of the second, as the most rational system of agricultural exploitation. Purcell, therefore, is probably correct to say that Cato was not a revolutionary. But what Cato's *De Agricultura* probably does represent is the start of a period of more *intensive* agricultural exploitation using techniques of plantation farming that had already existed in Italy for some time.

A key issue of debate in the last two decades has been the extent to which Roman landowners invested in improving their estates to maximize financial returns. For example, Rathbone has argued that a considerable degree of economic rationality was exhibited by landowners in Egypt, on the basis of the Heroninos archive relating to the management of parts of a large third-century AD estate in the Fayum. He sees one of the aims of the estate owner as the maximizing of profits from the estate.[137] By contrast, in a series of studies, Kehoe has argued that Roman landowners aimed to gain a steady income from their estates with minimal intervention, and that this was best done by leasing to tenants.[138] More recently, Rosenstein has attempted to tackle the question of how much income senators could actually have expected to receive from farming and has arrived at some very modest estimates, arguing that previous efforts have overestimated the size of demand from consumers. He is, therefore, sceptical about the economic importance to members of the elite of income from land, arguing that a senator's urban properties and other non-agricultural commercial ventures provided a much greater share of his ordinary income than revenue from the sale of staple crops.[139]

Be that as it may, there can be no doubt that the Preface of the *De Agricultura* shares with the rest of the work Cato's basic attitude that a book about agriculture will be concerned with farming carried on as a source of income for a wealthy absentee landlord.[140] Cato is insistent that the landowner whose property he

135 Terrenato 2001. 136 Rosenstein 2008: 7, with references. 137 Rathbone 1991.

138 Kehoe 1988, 1992, 1997; for a critique, see A. I. Wilson 2002*b*: 5. Cato does not mention tenancy as an option.

139 Rosenstein 2008: 2–3, 16, 20. The income numbers that he conjectures are considerably lower than Cicero's rich man's income of HS 100,000 from his estates in the mid-first century, to say nothing of his very rich man's HS 600,000 (Cic. *Parad.* 49). Cicero's shops in Puteoli brought in HS 100,000, the equivalent to his income from his estates (Cic. *Att.* 14. 11. 2, 14. 9. 1), as did two *insulae* on the Aventine and the Argiletum (Cic. *Att.* 12. 32. 2, 15. 17. 1, 16. 1. 1).

140 Contra Purcell 1985: 6, 8, who argues that 'it is to small-town landowners with an eye on their cousins in the harbour cities that Cato's treatise seems best suited, and not to the Roman senator who had benefited on a colossal scale from the Hannibalic War but whose interest in viticulture remains doubtful'. Purcell disregards the indications in the text that the owner is an absentee landlord and at best an occasional visitor to the farm; cf. Gabba 1989: 205.

describes must seek to sell his produce: he must be *vendax*, and we have seen in the previous section the archaeological evidence for the large-scale commercialization of wine and olive oil.[141] Cato emphasizes the importance of the estate's proximity to the market: there must be a sizeable town nearby; or it should be near the sea or on a navigable river, or on a good fast road.[142] Throughout the work there is an unmistakable concern with getting the best returns and spending as little as possible. The owner is encouraged to pay frequent visits, because, if he does so, 'the farm will be better, there will be less wrongdoing, and you will receive greater returns'.[143] In sum, it is clear that his attitude was dominated by a concern for profit and that his farm was viewed exclusively as a financial venture. The theme remained constant in later writers, too, and Varro, Vergil, and Columella all assume that the gaining of money is the main aim of the proprietor of such a farm.[144] As a result, what Romans would have learnt from agricultural writers was more concerned with the allocation of money and labour. Cato wishes to give us what Lintott terms 'an accountant's ideal, the simple arithmetic of a given labour force, and how expense can be cut, work increased, and profits made'.[145]

It is true that a few of the criteria that Cato applied to farm management were not exclusively financial. *Virtus* and *gloria* are mentioned as advantages, resulting from the possession of sound and ample farm buildings, and, in the Preface, lending is not *honestum* (respectable).[146] But these are rare instances. Cato automatically thought of agriculture in terms of a source of cash income for a largely absentee owner such as himself. In comparing alternative sources of income he readily thought of balancing greater security against the possibility of greater returns, preferring the former. Income from agriculture is 'especially secure' (*stabilissimus*).[147] This is an economic consideration.

Ignorance in the ancient world of double-entry bookkeeping (possibly not invented until the fourteenth century AD and not widely adopted for a few centuries more) has often been blamed for the restricted development of Roman agriculture, and cited as an example of the lack of sophistication of Roman economic thought, on the basis that the Romans lacked the essential key to accurate analytical accounting. In addition, there can be no doubt that other important accounting concepts, such as depreciation and the amortization of capital, which are often considered central to the calculation of the profitability of an investment in modern economic theory, were unknown. Nor were the

[141] Cato, *Agr.* 2. 7: 'patrem familias vendacem, non emacem esse oportet' (the head of the family should be eager to sell, not to buy); cf. Cato, *Agr.* 1. 6.

[142] Cato *Agr.* 1. 3: 'oppidum validum prope siet aut mare aut amnis, qua naves ambulant, aut via bona celerisque'.

[143] Cato, *Agr.* 4; cf. Cato, *Agr.* 39. 2: 'cogitato si nihil fiet nihilominus sumptum futurum' (bear in mind that, even if no work is taking place, expenses continue to accumulate none the less).

[144] e.g. Varro, *Rust.* 1. 2. 7–8.; cf. too Plin. *HN* 14. 48–52 and 18. 41–3, and the Neopythagorean author known as 'Bryson' (Swain 2013). Bryson (a pseudonym) wrote an 'Oikonomikos Logos', almost certainly in the first century AD, of which just two fragments survive in Greek. There is also testimony to the work in Greek authors, but for the most part we have an Arabic translation. This makes clear that Bryson's estate owner is expected to invest his money productively in farms and also in commercial ventures.

[145] Lintott 1994*c*: 56.

[146] Cato, *Agr.* 3. 2; Astin 1978: 260–1.

[147] Cato, *Agr. praef.* 4.

Romans habituated to thinking or expressing themselves in terms of economic abstractions:

> Lacking the techniques by which to calculate, and then to choose among the various options, for example the relative economic merits of growing or buying the barley for slaves and the stakes for vines; lacking the techniques by which to calculate the relative profitability, under given conditions, of one crop and another, or of agriculture and pasturage; relishing independence from the market as buyers, from reliance on others for their own necessities, the land-owners of antiquity operated by tradition, habit and rule-of-thumb.[148]

Finley, in making these remarks, is commenting on calculations made by Columella, writing in the first century AD, to demonstrate the profitability of viticulture. Duncan-Jones, in turn, criticizes Columella's calculations for failing to take account of depreciation and comments that 'they provide clear evidence that, at the high point of their agronomy, the Romans lacked both the conceptual tools and the technical ability to carry out such calculations'.[149]

A number of modern attempts to calculate the profitability of Roman estates have also been made. Using Columella's calculation as an examplar, Frank attempted to estimate the costs and profits of Cato's olive plantation of 240 *iugera* and concluded that the annual profit was (only) equivalent to a return of 6 per cent, after deducting depreciation at 2 per cent and 6 per cent interest on the basic investment (including the price of the land and the costs of buildings and implements).[150] Shatzman in turn followed Frank's calculations to suggest a rough estimate of costs and returns of a vineyard of 100 *iugera*.[151]

The results of these attempts are less interesting than the mistakes made by some modern commentators. First, in modern accounting practice, depreciation charges are not cash flow items and should not be included in a calculation that relates to a cash-based economy.[152] Secondly, Frank has misunderstood the 6 per cent interest on basic investment, which Columella included in his calculation. In the case of the estate represented in the *De Agricultura*, landowners of that period probably either inherited their tracts of land or acquired them by using the extraordinary gains they had made from their military exploits. There is no reason automatically to assume that they would have had to borrow money to finance the investment. It is much more likely they were, in effect, portfolio investors looking for the best return available on their capital and the interest figure of 6 per cent which Columella uses was the opportunity cost of the invested funds, whether borrowed or not.[153] Adding back the assumed depreciation of 2 per cent in Frank's calculation, we obtain a return of 8 per cent over an assumed bank deposit rate (in modern jargon, this would be the 'cost of capital') of 6%, a return that can be considered very satisfactory.

148 Finley 1985*a*: 117 on Columella, *Rust.* 3. 3. 8–10; cf. Astin 1978: 259: 'Cato's own approach shows no consideration of investing additional capital as a means of increasing productivity; rather his aim seems to be to reduce purchases to the minimum in order to widen the margin between cash receipts and cash expenditure'; Mickwitz 1937: 577ff.; De Ste. Croix 1956; Morley 1996: 73.

149 Duncan-Jones 1974: 33–59.

150 Columella, *Rust.* 3. 3. 8–10 suggests the use of a figure of 6% interest to gauge the return on a vineyard; Frank 1933: 170ff.

151 Shatzman 1975: 47–8.

152 Black et al. 1998: 147.

153 Temin 2004: 719.

Columella (and by implication Cato) has been defended in other ways too. Carandini has argued that certain inputs were simply not conceptualized in monetary terms. For example, it seems unlikely that the average farmer calculated the cost of his and his family's labour; Columella may have omitted the cost of maintaining the slaves in his vineyard because it was assumed that they would work to maintain themselves.[154] Furthermore, Macve's study has shown how unimportant double-entry bookkeeping was (and is) for business planning.[155] He argues that a farmer is capable of choosing between possible production strategies and does not need to employ double-entry bookkeeping to do so; medieval English estates were capable of organizing production quite adequately on the basis of single-entry account books.[156] Especially under the constraints of a pre-industrial economy, decisions on whether to increase production of certain crops depend on factors that would simply not appear in the accounts, such as the suitability of the land and the availability of labour. The documents of the Heroninos archive do include information that might be used to calculate the productivity of different crops, although this does not appear to have been their main purpose.[157] Even in modern farming, it is more or less impossible to locate the 'intensive margin'—the point at which increasing inputs cease to be productive—with any precision, especially as it varies with fluctuations in market prices. Instead, farmers operate within a 'zone of rational action', aiming for satisfactory results in the long run (just as conditions of uncertainty tend to favour longer-term strategies).[158] Reliance on rules of thumb, tradition, and experience, regarded by Finley as signs of economic primitivism, are instead valid tools in determining production strategies; Macve concludes that 'if the farmer is closely involved with day-to-day management, he may well get an adequate feel for how things are going without elaborate records'.[159] Knowledge of the soil and the climate, and a basic idea of likely prices may, therefore, be enough to allow him to develop a 'rational' strategy'.[160]

Whether or not Cato's *De Agricultura* makes sense to a modern accountant, it is in itself a sign of economic growth potential in that it indicates an interest in the dissemination of the stock of knowledge about farming. Its very existence, along with that of others now lost (especially the *magnum opus* of Mago, given the circumstances of that work's translation into Latin), underlines the size of the audience for advice on investment farming by absentee landlords.

The increased intensity of agricultural exploitation, exemplified by Cato and Mago, had been made possible by an influx of capital into private hands, and it in turn permitted the development of cash crops. As Kron says: 'Italian agriculture was booming in the second century with a flood of money from Rome's conquests, accelerating urban growth and the spread of Hellenistic standards of personal

154 Carandini 1983: 184–6. 155 De Ste. Croix 1956; Macve 1985.

156 Macve 1985: 240, 247–52; Pleket 1993: 341; Morley 1996: 74.

157 Rathbone 1991: 369–87: 'the main purpose of the accounting system was to provide a check on efficiency'.

158 De Neeve 1985: 88; Morley 1996: 74. 159 Macve 1985: 252.

160 Morley 1996: 75; as Harris 1993*b*: 25 says: 'Roman methods of calculating the profitability of an estate were as effective as those that were practiced by a progressive landowner in the seventeenth century AD.'

comfort leading to strong demand for agricultural produce including meat, wine, and olive oil.'[161]

INVESTMENT IN TECHNOLOGY

Roman agriculture in general, like other sectors of the ancient economy, has until recently been generally characterized as technologically underdeveloped, especially when compared to later periods.[162] The ancient world did not, of course, experience an industrial revolution. In agriculture, organic sources of power, such as human and animal muscle, were enormously important. There is much evidence for the use of basic techniques—plough and sickle, water and fire—in the agricultural development that occurred following Rome's conquest of Italy.[163] For example, the Etruria survey has shown that by the late first century dramatic changes had been effected in the area of Sutri. Matching Sutri's own internal growth, a belt of Ciminian Forest, which was still in existence in 310, had been cleared for as much as four kilometres to the north and south of the town.[164] Expansion and clearance at this stage are clearly reflected in the decline of woodland species present in samples of pollen from the area, and a 'drastic and sudden' increase in sedimentation in the lakes from which the pollen came, resulting from agricultural activity.[165] In 291, L. Postumius Magellus (*cos.* 305, 294, 291) was denounced for deploying two thousand of the soldiers under his command, not against the enemy, but in improving his estate through the clearance of woodland.[166] In the eyes of some scholars, the sophistication of agricultural intensification did not rise much further than these 'slash and burn' techniques.

Slaves are sometimes regarded as the most important technological breakthrough of antiquity and there is no doubt that the use of slaves led to significant increases in agricultural productivity and profitability.[167] As we have just discussed, a crucial element in the development of the Catonian estate was precisely its slave mode of production. We have only to look at Cato's list of *instrumenta*, or the similar lists in later writers, to see that most agricultural work was manual, and a number of Roman innovations (for example, plough coulters, large scythes, and sickles) reflect increased intensity of planting and harvesting by using human labour.[168]

But there were some radical technological advances, many of which were widely adopted, and Wilson attributes 'aggregate and per capita growth in the Roman Empire, especially in the latter centuries BC and the first two centuries AD, to

[161] Kron 2008: 88.

[162] e.g. Lintott 1994*c*: 56; cf. D'Arms (1980: 12) who talks of 'the negligible progress of technological innovation and improvements'.

[163] See Horden and Purcell 2000: 263–70 for a discussion of 'intensification and abatement'.

[164] Potter 1979: 96–7.

[165] Greene 1986: 103.

[166] Dion. Hal. 17. 4. 3; Livy, *Per.* 11 See Gabrielli (2003) for a discussion of a recently discovered fragment of parchment which refers to this episode and which has been identified as part of a historical work, probably Book 11 of Livy.

[167] Morley 1996: 115, 123.

[168] Greene 1986: 75.

significant technological progress . . . in agricultural technology to sustain a higher number of non-agricultural workers'. He argues that water-power and water-lifting devices (discussed on pp. 157–8) were used on a wide scale and in diversified forms to perform economically critical work.[169] Another example is the level of investment in *torcularia*, presses for olives or grapes. Their remains were found on twenty-five sites (dating from the first century and early Principate) by Quilici, in his survey of the Tor Sapienza quadrangle, an area of 95 km^2 around ancient Collatia, which is located only a few kilometres south-west of ancient Rome (and within its *suburbium*) on the north-west flanks of the Alban volcano, partly within the modern ring road.[170] An inscription on the remains of one of these presses even carries the name of one of the consuls of 55.[171] This combination of increased investment in slaves and machines should not surprise us. As Greene points out, on early nineteenth-century Caribbean sugar estates, steam engines were imported from Britain to fulfil specific roles in which they were more effective than human labour.[172]

Irrigation and the drainage of wet land were prime concerns of Italian agriculture from early times. Agriculture around much of the Mediterranean was and is heavily dependent on irrigation and, in many cases, the topography requires water to be diverted to cultivated areas or lifted out of wells or watercourses onto fields lying at a higher level. On the other hand, the Etruscans, because of the tufa landscape of south Etruria, were forced to dig extensive networks of *cuniculi* (tunnels), notably around Veii, to drain excess water from one valley into another, where the gradient of the higher valley was shallow and the ground, therefore, probably swamp.[173]

Thomas and Wilson have shown that, by the third and second centuries, Roman technology was able to provide an extensive hydraulic infrastructure to support intensive rural settlement. Farms and villas in Latium and southern Etruria show considerable evidence for investment in infrastructure (small aqueducts and large storage cisterns) for irrigated horticulture, doubtless to exploit the growing market for fruit and vegetables provided by Rome.[174] By the first century, according to Varro, the immediate surroundings of Rome were used mainly for *pastio villatica*, 'market gardening' or the large-scale production of perishable goods.[175] Examples of such infrastructure from the third and second centuries range from dams with associated channel aqueducts in the *Ager Faliscus* to field drainage works near Fidenae, which correspond closely to Cato's instructions for the drainage of olive trees.[176] In the Tor Sapienza quadrangle, rural settlement appears to have been intensive, especially in the region immediately around Rome. Indeed the settlement density appears to have been greater in some places

[169] A. I. Wilson 2002*b*: 1, 30.

[170] Quilici 1974: 33–45 for the dating of finds from the Republican period, and especially p. 38 with nn. 4–7, where he points to an increase in the sophistication of the remains from the second and first centuries, in terms of architectural decoration, paving, and the hydraulic infrastructure (the last discussed briefly below and at greater length by Thomas and Wilson 1994).

[171] Quilici 1974: 467–9.

[172] Greene 2000: 42.

[173] Thomas and Wilson 1994: 143.

[174] Thomas and Wilson 1994; A. I. Wilson 2002*b*: 6.

[175] Varro, *Rust.* 3. 2. 7, 3. 2. 14, 3. 2. 17, 3. 4. 3, 3. 5. 9, 3. 17. 5, 3. 17. 9.

[176] Cato, *Agr.* 43; A. I. Wilson 2008; Quilici and Quilici Gigli 1986: 403; Quilici Gigli 1987, 1989*a*, 1989*b*.

in the Roman period than it is today. The area includes villas, as well as larger settlements, dating from the late second and first centuries BC.[177] It is clear from Quilici's survey that numerous cisterns and water supply systems were built from the second century, or even earlier, to meet the water requirements of the area. Rainfall would have been sufficient for grains, olives, and vines most of the time. So the proximity of Rome, taken in conjunction with Cato's and, later, Varro's emphasis on market gardening as yielding a high return (despite its high labour intensity), suggests that the primary water requirement for which this enormous infrastructure was required was the irrigation of vegetables.[178]

This type of irrigated land (or 'hydraulic landscape'[179]) is reflected in a number of literary and epigraphic sources. Cato prefers watered meadows (*prata irrigua*) to dry meadows (*prata sicca*).[180] Quintus Cicero is told of the opportunity of creating fifty *iugera* of *prata irrigua*.[181] A *cippus* of Republican date bears a fragmentary inscription that appears to be an injunction against polluting an open watercourse;[182] and the importance of irrigation is underlined by the fact that the law on water rights had become an area of specialist study by the late Republic—Cicero refers to one M. Tugio as an expert in this field.[183] The evidence concerning L. Furius Purpurio (*cos.* 196) is equally suggestive. He captured booty in his campaign against the Gauls in 200 and built a temple that he had vowed.[184] Cato made a speech against an L. Furius, probably the same man, who bought cheap land after the Second Punic War and improved it by irrigation, using public water.[185]

As Wilson has emphasized, water-lifting is highly labour-intensive and, in the third century, probably at Alexandria, 'a new range of mechanical water-lifting devices was developed which revolutionised opportunities for irrigating land that could not be fed by gravity-flow irrigation systems'.[186] The aim of these devices was to increase the productivity both of labour and of the land. By the second half of the second century there is evidence to suggest that this new technology had begun to reach Italy: one of these devices, a bucket-chain (which could be powered by men on a treadmill or by animals turning a capstan), was in use in the baths near the forum at Cosa on the coast of Etruria, and was followed in the early first century by another beside the harbour, which was possibly installed to provide fresh water to a nearby amphora factory. Four bucket-chain devices from the Republican period have also been discovered in Pompeii, all of which date to the late second or early first centuries.[187] Although these examples come from urban contexts, there is

[177] Marzano (2007) catalogues villas in the *suburbium* of Rome and most date from the late second or early first centuries.

[178] Cato, *Agr.* 1. 7; Thomas and Wilson 1994: 158, 181–6, 189.

[179] So termed by Horden and Purcell 2000: 237–57, 279.

[180] Cato, *Agr.* 8–9.

[181] Cic. *Q Fr.* 3. 1.

[182] The inscription has been restored as 'rivei a[quam corrump]ere non licet' (it is forbidden to pollute the water of the watercourse); Thomas and Wilson 1994: 149.

[183] Cic. *Balb.* 45.

[184] Livy, 31. 49. 3, 35. 41. 8.

[185] *ORF*[4] 42–3; cf. Livy, 39. 44. 4; Shatzman 1975: 16, 252; this suggests that he probably had estates along the Aqua Anio Vetus, as the Aqua Appia (the only other possibility) runs underground for most of its length.

[186] A. I. Wilson 2002*b*: 7; Lewis 1997: 20–36.

[187] Oleson 1984: 201–4, 242–8, 353–4.

no reason to doubt that they were present in agricultural ones as well. Lifting-wheels driven by the force of a stream or river were sufficiently familiar to a first-century audience for Lucretius to use one as an explanatory analogy for cosmic rotation.[188]

Wilson suggests that 'water-lifting devices... represented considerable capital investment undertaken with the deliberate aim of maximising returns' and this consideration also seems to lie behind the adoption of water-powered devices, 'evidently with the expectation that the greater output and lower running costs of such equipment (over animal- or man-powered techniques) would recoup the higher initial outlay'.[189] The diffusion of the watermill around the Mediterranean seems to have occurred in the centuries between its invention, probably around the middle of the third century BC (as argued by Lewis), and the first century AD.[190] The first mention of a watermill comes in a poem by Antipater of Thessalonica dating from the first century BC and the earliest dated watermill of which traces have been found is that at Chaplix (near Avenches in Switzerland), where the mill-race timbers have been dated, by dendrochronology, to AD 57/58.[191] A comment of Pliny the Elder's, from roughly the same period, suggests that the use of watermills throughout Italy could have been common.[192]

While technological development in cereal agriculture in Italy was limited to the diffusion of iron tools (not necessarily an insignificant advance), there were notable improvements in the processing of grain with the development of the 'Pompeian' donkey-mill in the late third century (on the basis of evidence from Morgantina in Sicily) or perhaps even early fourth century (on the basis of a rotary mill found on the wreck of a Greek merchant ship off Mallorca, dating possibly from 375–350).[193]

Progress was also made in the processing of olives and grapes. Cato's *De Agricultura* discusses a number of reasonably expensive items of capital equipment: the largest were the *torcularium*, or press for olives or grapes; the *trapetus*, or rotary mill for crushing olives; and the *fornax* or limekiln.[194] An example of an olive-oil press was discovered in Campania in 1779, at Casa di Miri in the area of Gragnano. The general layout (symmetric plan, concrete slabs, wine press with lever and hoist) resembled the description of an oil mill in Cato.[195] As Mattingly notes: 'It is worth stressing that mills and presses are not necessary for making oil. The involvement of a press is generally an indicator of a higher form of social or economic organisation.'[196] Improvements were gradually made to the 'Catonian' design of press between 150 BC and AD 50. Wine presses were made more efficient with a change from ropes and levers to a screw press, an innovation that Pliny the Elder, writing in the third quarter of the first century AD, dates to 'within the last hundred years', with a further technical refinement 'within the last twenty'.[197] Columella talks of the superiority of the oil mill over the *trapetus*, which is the

[188] Lucr. 5. 516. [189] A. I. Wilson 2002*b*: 6, 31. [190] Lewis 1997.

[191] *Anthologia Graeca* 9. 418; A. I. Wilson 2002*b*: 10–11.

[192] Plin. *HN* 18. 97: 'maior pars Italiae nudo utitur pilo, rotis etiam quas aqua verset obiter et mola' (the greater part of Italy uses a bare pestle, and also wheels turned by moving water, and a millstone (trans. Loeb V 251)).

[193] Williams-Thorpe and Thorpe 1990. [194] Cato, *Agr.* 18, 20–2, 38.

[195] Brun 2004: 20–1. [196] D. J. Mattingly 1988*d*: 157. [197] Plin. *HN* 18. 317.

only type of oil press mentioned by Cato.[198] By the second century AD, enormous presses, each capable of producing 9,000 to 10,000 kg of olive oil per annum, were operating in Africa, serving estates engaged in the commercial production of olive oil for overseas distribution.[199] At the other end of the supply chain, in Rome, the hill of broken oil transport amphorae behind the Tiber wharves, Monte Testaccio, represents a staggering total import, mainly dating to the second and third centuries AD, of some 53 million amphorae containing 6 billion litres of oil, initially mainly from south-western Spain and subsequently from Africa.[200]

Marine resource production is yet another manifestation of the expansion, as well as the diversification, of agriculture. From the second half of the first century impressive installations including systems of tanks, dams, and channels for use in fish farming start to appear on the Mediterranean coast. During the Imperial period, large-scale fish-salting, fish-sauce manufacturing, and murex production facilities are recorded on the Atlantic coasts of Morocco, Spain, and Brittany.[201] These developments started in the late second century, as is shown by occasional Republican remains, for example a salting vat from Pompeii dating from this period.[202]

Finally, Varro, writing in the first century BC, and Columella and Pliny the Elder, in the first century AD, show a clear understanding of the principles of ley farming, an agricultural system where the field is alternately seeded for grain and left fallow or planted with fodder crops.[203] This development was important for two reasons. First, it would have meant that some Roman farmers owned cattle, thereby acquiring large amounts of manure which they could use to fertilize arable land.[204] The Roman agronomists recommended applying more than twice as much manure as has been customary in modern Italian farming and, in turn, this would have resulted in Roman wheat yields that were higher than those typically achieved through most of medieval and modern Italy. Secondly, the provision of fodder would have allowed significant improvements in the size and fecundity of livestock. As Ward-Perkins says: 'Cattle and, to a lesser extent, other domesticated animals show a marked rise in average size in Roman times. These larger animals, like modern cattle, carried a much greater weight of meat than their pre-Roman ancestors . . . [This] could be achieved in an economic environment, like that of Roman times, that encouraged some specialisation in the use of land and its deployment of labour'. Increased meat consumption would in turn have produced a relatively high level of nutrition and biological standard of living for elements of the Roman population. If this was a widespread practice, it could further suggest that even poor Romans enjoyed a healthy level of meat consumption and received an adequate calorie intake.[205]

198 Columella, *Rust.* 12. 52. 6; Cato, *Agr.* 22.

199 D. J. Mattingly 1988*a*, 1988*b*.

200 Almeida 1984.

201 Greene 1986: 79; A. I. Wilson 1999, 2006*b*; Hitchner 2005: 216.

202 A. I. Wilson 2006*b*: 529.

203 e.g. Pliny the Elder (*HN* 18. 187, 191), pointing to procedures used in Campania, describes various rotation systems under which no more than one-third of the land was left fallow.

204 Varro, *Rust.* 2. *praef.* 6, and Cato quoted at Cic. *Off.* 2. 89.

205 Erdkamp 2005: 34–53; Kron 2002, 2008: 74–6, 80; Ward-Perkins 2005: 145. As de Ligt says (2012: 24): 'the problem is to know whether the practices that the Roman agronomists describe were

While, therefore, precise dating of the development and adoption of new technologies in the ancient world is extremely difficult, it is nevertheless probable that, by the second century or early first century BC, a variety of new or developed devices and techniques would have been available in Italy. These included the *torcularium* and the *trapetus* for the processing of food, hydraulic infrastructures for irrigation, and a number of water-lifting and water-powered devices, as well as a range of more sophisticated strategies for food production. Several of the new technological developments would have required considerable capital expenditure to implement. For example, Cato states that the cost of purchasing a mill near Suessa and transporting and assembling it is HS 629 (and HS 724 if it is obtained from Pompeii). These costs are equivalent to three or four times our estimate, in Ch. 11, of average per capita GDP in mainland Italy in 150 BC, though well within the reach of men who could afford to buy a number of slaves.[206]

As is shown by the archaeological finds and the literary references which we have discussed, members of the Roman elite, newly enriched from the wars of the second century, were in a position to make these investments to improve the efficiency and productivity of their agricultural interests.

THE AGRARIAN CRISIS OF 133 BC

The expansion of investment farming is a priori likely to have had a profound impact on Italy's rural economy. As Purcell has put it, 'the introduction, for whatever reason, into an agricultural system, which has been basically devoted to simple subsistence strategies, of large-scale production of non-staple agricultural goods should have had far-reaching consequences throughout that society'.[207] So how important a part did the development of investment farming play in the major agrarian crisis that erupted in the late 130s, and what does the crisis tell us about elite patterns of landholding during the second century?

Our main evidence for the crisis comes from the accounts of Appian and Plutarch (the former being fuller), who in turn seem to have used a common (unidentifiable) source that drew on various speeches by Ti. Gracchus as well as on a 'book' written by his brother, Gaius.[208] A common thread running through all our ancient sources is the decline of the free peasant. Diodorus and Appian state that Ti. Gracchus' supporters came from the country. According to Cicero and Plutarch, C. Gracchus in 123 sought votes in country districts near Rome for the bill against Popillius Laenas.[209] Appian and Plutarch speak of a concentration of land in the *ager publicus* in the hands of the rich, and part of the explanation for the crisis perhaps lies in the sense of exclusion felt by the poorer elements of the Roman community in the face of the increasing affluence of the elite.[210] Under

used only by a relatively small group of landowners and in certain areas or by significant sections of the free farming community across Italy'.

[206] Cato, *Agr.* 22. 3; pp. 290–2. [207] Purcell 1985: 1.

[208] Plut. *Ti. Gracch.* 8; Rich 2008: 544.

[209] Diod. Sic. 34/5. 6. 1; App. *B. Civ.* 1. 13–14; Cic. *Cat.* 4. 4; Plut. *C. Gracch.* 3. 2.

[210] App. *B. Civ.* 1. 7–8; Plut. *Ti. Gracch.* 8. 2–3.

the programme of reform that he introduced, Ti. Gracchus limited to 500 *iugera* the amount of *ager publicus* that an individual could hold (Appian describes this as a revival of an earlier law) and added the right for each son to hold an additional 250 *iugera*. P. Scipio Nasica Serapio and M. Octavius are the only senators known to us as owners of public land in excess of 500 *iugera* at the time of the crisis of 133, but we can assume that there were others, given the opposition in the senate to the proposals and the fact that Ti. Gracchus' opponents were able to hamstring the agrarian commission's activities.[211] Plutarch also reports how C. Gracchus described in his book that Ti. Gracchus, while travelling through Etruria, had been struck by the extent to which estates were cultivated by what he believed to be 'imported barbarian slaves' and by the absence of free peasants.[212] According to Appian, Ti. Gracchus claimed that the number of agricultural slaves was constantly increasing.[213] None of the sources says anything about a decline in the number of citizen smallholders (*assidui*), caused by men ceasing to satisfy the property qualification.[214] But they do describe a decline in the size of the free Italian population, caused by a failure to rear children. According to Appian, 'the Italian people were suffering from depopulation and a shortage of men, worn down as they were by poverty and taxes and military service';[215] and he specifically states that the purpose of Ti. Gracchus' measure was to procure more manpower (εὐανδρία).[216]

This evidence is open to a number of different interpretations. The traditional explanation is that after the Second Punic War, the Italian countryside saw the deracination, as Toynbee termed it, of its free peasantry, following the introduction of slave-staffed estates, while soldiers, now fighting abroad, were no longer able to return to their farms between campaigning seasons. The number of slaves in Italy increased, while the number of free peasants declined, and the tensions that this produced resulted in the agrarian crisis of 133. Brunt identified the progressive impoverishment of a growing proportion of the free population as one of the main factors behind the picture of demographic decline or stagnation that seems to emerge from the literary tradition and the Republican census figures.[217] Hopkins, on the other hand, paid almost no attention to rural poverty as a driving force. For him, the lucrative wars of the second century boosted the wealth of the Roman elite, who invested much of their gains in Italian land, especially within reach of the growing market of Rome.[218] In part, these acquisitions were made possible by the fact that so many Roman soldiers were serving abroad. Also, the crucial importance of the free rural population as a source of military recruits made it impossible to rely on wage labour. Partly for this reason, wealthy landowners preferred to use slaves, many of whom were prisoners

211 Plut. *Ti. Gracch.* 10. 5, 13. 3. 212 Plut. *C. Gracch.* 8. 7. 213 App. *B. Civ.* 1. 9.

214 Until the end of the second century, service in the legions was, except in grave emergencies, restricted to freeborn citizens possessing a certain property qualification, who were known as *assidui*.

215 App. *B. Civ.* 1. 7: τοὺς δ᾽ Ἰταλιώτας ὀλιγότης καὶ δυσανδρία κατελάμβανε, τρυχομένους πενίᾳ τε καὶ ἐσφοραῖς καὶ στρατείαις.

216 App. *B. Civ.* 1. 11. 217 Toynbee 1965: ii 87–105, 155–89; Brunt 1971*a*: 345–75.

218 'The creation of large estates in Italy commensurate with the wealth, power and ostentation of the Roman elite, "conquerors of the world", required the mass extrusion of Italian peasants from their land' (Hopkins 1978: 56).

of war.[219] When soldiers had been fighting in Italy, they had been able to return to their farms during the winter months, but after six years serving overseas, their families would have fallen into debt and had their farms taken over by wealthy creditors.[220]

There is a broad consensus in modern scholarly opinion that Ti. Gracchus' aim was the restoration of Roman manpower primarily for military reasons;[221] but recently the causes of the crisis and its impact on the social and economic development of Italy have undergone a significant reappraisal. Wim Jongman has cast doubt on the scale and extent of slave-staffed estates by suggesting that the number of slaves employed in agricultural activity by the Roman elite was considerably fewer than previously imagined. Nathan Rosenstein has questioned the conventional wisdom that military service was a major contributory factor in the supposed decline of the Roman peasant, and survey data have suggested that the Roman peasantry may in fact have been much more robust than previously thought. Saskia Roselaar has emphasized the importance of understanding the location and legal status of available *ager publicus* in Italy in the second century and the relevance of these factors both to the development of investment farming and to the issues that the Gracchi sought to address. Finally, Scheidel, de Ligt, and Lo Cascio, in particular, have re-ignited the debate over the size of the Italian population during the late Republic and highlighted the importance of demography for an understanding of the causes of the agrarian crisis.[222]

PUBLIC LAND

Ager publicus populi Romani (public land of the Roman people) consisted both of land that the Roman state had taken over from Italian communities when they were first conquered and of other territory that had come under the control of the Roman state; for example, Roman allies who sided with Hannibal during his invasion of Italy were punished by having their land confiscated. In the early Republic, the only kind of *ager publicus* was *ager occupatorius*, a term that is frequently used in the modern scholarship to denote all undistributed state-owned land.[223] This was land that the state did not require or use for the moment, since the Romans had acquired more land from their conquered Italian enemies than they actually needed. The land could be occupied by any Roman citizen who wanted to farm it and it was not administered or managed in any way by the Roman state. The occupier had no legal title and the land could be taken away at any time, so there was no security of tenure. The person who worked *ager*

[219] Hopkins 1978: 11–13. [220] Hopkins 1978: 30.

[221] Badian 1972: 682; Rich 1983: 299–305, 330; Rathbone 2003: 159; Rosenstein 2004: 156–8; Roselaar 2010: 229.

[222] Jongman 2003*b*; Rosenstein 2004; Roselaar 2010; Scheidel 2004, 2005, 2006, 2008; de Ligt 2004, 2012; Lo Cascio 1994*a*, 1994*b*, 1999*a*, 1999*b*, 2001. See Fredreiksen 1970–1 for initial scepticism about the traditional view.

[223] This term and others describing different legal categories of *ager publicus*, such as *ager quaestorius*, are probably jargon invented by the so-called '*agrimensores*', who were land surveyors writing during the Principate (Rathbone 2003: 142; Campbell 2000).

occupatorius held it as a *precarium*, a holding on sufferance, that could be taken back at any time by its real owner, the state. It is possible, as Roselaar believes, that, in many cases, the original inhabitants would have been allowed to continue working land that had been seized from them and had become *ager publicus*, and that this may have been regarded by the Romans as an ingenious stratagem for keeping their Italian allies under control.[224]

According to Appian, towns were established on some *ager publicus* or it was given to colonists, or sold, or leased; but the greater part was not allocated and anyone could occupy it on payment of a rent to the state.[225] There is in fact no evidence for rent being charged on arable *ager occupatorius*, but the Roman state did charge citizens for grazing animals on the large amounts of non-arable *ager publicus* which the state also owned. The technical term for this public pasture was *ager scripturarius*, because the fee per animal payable for its use and collected by *publicani* was called *scriptura*. The two main documented zones of *ager scripturarius* were the Sabine/Samnite highlands and the coastal plains of southern Apulia.[226]

The annexation by rich landlords of large areas of land to which Appian refers was not necessarily a new development in the second century and attempts by popular leaders to restrict this practice probably go back to the fourth century. The first such law, the *lex Licinia de modo agrorum*, is dated by Livy to the tribunes of 367, C. Licinius Stolo and L. Sextius Lateranus, and it seems to have confined individual holdings of land to a maximum of 500 *iugera*: 'quid legem Liciniam excitavit de quingentis iugeribus nisi ingens cupido agros continuandi?'[227] (what provoked the Licinian law about the five hundred *iugera* except the uncontrolled desire of joining field to field?).[228]

But the purpose and the date of the *lex Licinia* are both disputed. The orthodoxy of Barthold Niebuhr, established in the early nineteenth century, that the *lex Licinia* only concerned *ager publicus*, has recently been challenged by Kunkel, Rathbone, Rich, and Roselaar.[229] No source, apart from Appian, states that the *lex Licinia* affected *ager publicus* and it is possible that the terms of this law have been heavily corrupted by its revival by Ti. Gracchus. Livy speaks of a pre-Gracchan law being applied simply as limiting the amount of land that a man might 'occupy' (*possidere*).[230] Cato, Tiro, Varro, and numerous later authors also all present the pre-Gracchan limit just as a restriction on the amount of land that a man could 'have' (*habere*) or 'occupy' (*possidere*).[231] Even though Appian took the pre-Gracchan, like the Gracchan, limit to apply to public land, we cannot be sure that this was how it was interpreted by the common source of Appian and Plutarch.

224 Roselaar 2008: 577, 2010: 84, 89, 94.
225 App. *B. Civ.* 1. 7.
226 Rathbone 2003: 143, 167–70; Roselaar 2010: 92. Plautus (*Truc.* 141–51) refers to the leasing of public pastures.
227 Speech of Cato *ap.* Livy, 34. 4. 9 (*ORF*[4] 66); cf. Livy, 6. 35. 5. According to Appian (*B. Civ.* 1. 8) the law also confined grazing rights to 100 'larger' animals (presumably cattle) and 500 'smaller' animals (presumably sheep, goats, and pigs).
228 Trans. Loeb IX 423.
229 Niebuhr 1811–12; Kunkel 1995: ii. 493–7; Rathbone 2003; Rich 2008; Roselaar 2010.
230 Livy, 10. 13. 14 cf. Livy, 6. 35. 5–6, 7. 16. 9, 34. 4. 8.
231 Rich 2008: 543–51.

Rich revives a suggestion of two early nineteenth-century German scholars, Hüllman and Huschke, that the 500 *iugera* Licinian limit had applied to all holdings of land, both public and private, but that Ti. Gracchus revived it just as a limit on holdings of public land.[232] Rich and Roselaar both argue for a date for the law of 367. Rathbone, on the other hand, prefers to suppose, like another early nineteenth-century scholar, Puchta, that the Licinian limit applied only to private land and suggests a date of around 290. He points to the centrality of the concept of private property, including *ager privatus*, in Roman society and law since the time of the Twelve Tables (in which there is no allusion to *ager publicus*). This consideration has also led Rathbone to challenge the traditional view that wide tracts of *ager publicus* were still available at the beginning of the second century. He argues that *ager publicus* was a 'transient' category and that, by the second century, the amount of *ager publicus* was very limited because most of it had been privatized.[233]

But, in fact, there is no concrete evidence for the privatization of public land, other than in the form of colonial settlements and viritane distributions, before the end of the third century, at which point parts of the *ager publicus* (but only in central-western Italy) were indeed sold off on both a freehold and leasehold basis. In 211/10, punishment had been meted out to Capua for siding with Hannibal and, as a consequence, the entire *Ager Campanus*, with the sole exception of lands belonging to those who had remained loyal to Rome, had become *ager publicus*. In 209, leasehold assignments of land to individuals were made by the censors (*ager censorius*), when a (presumably) large chunk of the *Ager Campanus* was leased out.[234] Next, in 205 and in order to finance the invasion of Africa, the quaestors were instructed to sell (*vendere*) a small part of the *Ager Campanus*.[235] This is the only datable occurrence of the sale of land by the quaestors, although the *agrimensores* refer to land so allocated as *ager quaestorius* (the term does not appear in any Republican source), so it is perhaps possible that other land was sold in this way. Finally, at the end of the war, land in the *suburbium* of Rome was also, in effect, sold on a leasehold basis. The background to this was that, in 210, citizens had given their gold and silver to the state to finance the war effort and it was decided that the Roman state should pay the money back in three instalments. But when, in 200, the time came for the repayment of the second instalment, there was no money available. So the senate decided to let the state's creditors have use of *ager publicus* within fifty miles of Rome (in effect in the *suburbium* of Rome) on the payment of a peppercorn rent of one as per *iugerum*, so that it could be swapped back for cash at a later date.[236] Presumably the creditors generally held on to their land, which was known as *ager in trientabulis*, because it was still mentioned as a category of land in the *lex agraria* of 111.[237]

232 Hüllman 1832; Huschke 1835; Rich 2008: 545–60; Roselaar 2010: 100–4.

233 Puchta 1841; Rathbone 2003. Others such as Gabba (1989: 203) date the *lex Licinia* to the post-Hannibalic period.

234 Livy, 27. 11. 8, 27. 3. 1. The censors also appear to have sold some land near Capua in 199 and in Auximum and Calatia in 174 (Livy, 32. 7. 3, 41. 27. 10); Roselaar 2010: 128–33.

235 Livy, 28. 46. 4; Roselaar 2010: 121–7.

236 Livy, 29. 36. 11–12, 29. 16. 1–3, 31. 13. 6–9; Roselaar 2010: 127–8.

237 *lex agraria* 31–2.

It would appear that the process of the leasehold assignation of the *ager censorius* in Campania was not without practical difficulty. The Roman state certainly did not have the resources to verify, measure, and mark boundaries in dozens of locations, so that in many cases accurate surveys were probably never carried out to determine the area of land that had been leased out. By 205, it was already necessary to attempt to define the boundaries of the *Ager Campanus*, by encouraging individuals to declare what land should be public.[238] But similar problems recurred in 173. At the beginning of that year, both consuls had been assigned the Ligurians as their *provincia*. However, one of the consuls, L. Postumius Albinus, was suddenly diverted by the senate to Campania to stop landowners annexing excessive quantities of *ager publicus*.[239] He ended up spending most of the year there and the result was that 'magna pars agri Campani . . . recuperata in publicum erat' (a great part of the *Ager Campanus* . . . was recovered for the state). Rathbone links these actions with the laying out of the massive centuriation grid of 200 *iugera* blocks in the *Ager Campanus*, which he assumes was carried out by Postumius at this time.[240] In the following year, after tribunician legislation, new leases over the reclaimed land were issued by the censors.[241] But seven years later, in 165, there had to be a further exercise in land recovery. This time, the senate gave the *praetor urbanus*, P. Cornelius Lentulus, the task of buying land in the *Ager Campanus* from private individuals so that it could again become *ager publicus*. It is significant perhaps that, having completed his task, he had a large bronze map of the land in question put up in the *atrium Libertatis*.[242]

There are several points to be made here. First, sales of public land, whether on a freehold or leasehold basis, appear principally to have been emergency measures occasioned by the Second Punic War. Secondly, no concerted effort seems to have been made to collect rents from the leasehold *ager censorius* in the *Ager Campanus* before the late 170s. Thirdly, rather than being a transient category, *ager publicus* was still considered to be a valid way to hold land in the 160s, as is shown by Cornelius Lentulus' purchase of land in the *Ager Campanus*, which, in effect, was renationalization of private property. But, finally and crucially, the privatization of public land at this time only affected central-western Italy, and large swathes of *ager publicus* located on the periphery of Italy, in Cisalpine Gaul, Picenum, or southern Italy, remained *ager occupatorius*.[243]

So the real significance of this privatization process is that it altered the availability of land in central-western Italy. Even before this process began, a

[238] Livy, 27. 3. 1; 28. 46. 4–5; Gabba 1989: 197. [239] Livy, 42. 1. 6, 42. 19. 1; cf. p. 219.

[240] Rathbone 2003: 158. [241] Livy, 42. 19. 1; cf. Livy, 42. 1. 6; 42. 8. 4; 42. 9. 7.

[242] Gran. Lic. 28. 31–6; Cic. *Leg. agr.* 2. 82; Gabba 1989: 198–9; Roselaar 2010: 117. These problems in the *Ager Campanus* tie in with some of the issues of which we hear in other parts of Italy. We mentioned earlier the punishment of ranchers (*pecuarii*) who, in the 190s, had grazed too many animals on the *ager publicus* (Livy, 33. 42. 10, 35. 10. 11–12), and an inscription, probably from the late 130s which was found at Polla, 77 km south-east of Salerno, makes clear that the encroachment of ranchers was still an issue then: 'eidemque primus fecei . . . ut de agro poplico aratoribus cederent paastores' (*ILLRP* 454: I was also the first to make herdsmen give way to ploughmen on public land). Although there are differing interpretations of the circumstances to which this inscription refers (cf. Roselaar 2010: 176 n. 103), part of it mentions events in Sicily, so it is possible that this statement relates to problems on the *ager publicus* there.

[243] Roselaar 2010: 133.

number of towns in Latium and Sabinum had been granted Roman citizenship without losing any land; and the bulk of the *ager publicus* that did exist there had been assigned to Roman citizens in viritane distributions or in colonies. In Etruria, most of the public land gradually disappeared with the establishment of colonies in the early second century. Within fifty miles of Rome itself, much of the public land was turned into *ager in trientabulis*. In Campania, colonies had been founded and much of the *Ager Campanus* had been sold or leased out. Although the *Ager Campanus* was probably the largest remaining tract of *ager occupatorius* in central-western Italy, and was not fully privatized until 59, it was presumably, by the 130s, already largely held by established occupiers (*possessores*). As we have already seen, there was a high degree of regional agricultural specialization in Italy, with *pastio villatica* ('market gardening') predominantly around Rome, wine and oil in Campania and Etruria, and animal husbandry further south, which meant that there were differing pressures on land throughout Italy. An area's proximity or access to domestic or export markets would have been the principal determinant of demand for land. So it was not so much a question of the amount of land that was generally available throughout Italy as its location. Competition would have been strongest nearer to the market of Rome, in the *suburbium*, and in areas that were producing for the export markets in wine and olive oil; and, importantly, these were the areas in which, by the 130s, most land was actually held on a freehold or leasehold basis, and was, therefore, not available for distribution by the Roman state.

These considerations suggest that if, as seems likely, Appian (or his source) was describing conditions in central-western Italy (which of course would have been the region about which the Gracchi would have had the most information), he would have been correct to state that the rich had managed to gain control of most of the *ager occupatorius* in the region if, by this, he meant the purchase and leasing of public land that had taken place at the time of the Second Punic War. It remains an open question as to how much land was acquired by the rich through the purchase of smallholdings from peasants, but it should be noted that Cato never talks of the acquisition of *ager publicus*; he only mentions the purchase of land from a willing seller. The significance of large slave-staffed estates as a cause of the agrarian crisis may have been less than previously assumed, but the traditional view that the growth of commercial estates took place mainly on *ager occupatorius* is also wrong.[244]

THE 'ROBUST' ROMAN PEASANT

We know very little about the peasant population during this period, as it has left practically no literary or archaeological trace. We do not even really know where they lived. Although it is clear that some town-dwellers cultivated the adjoining fields, Foxhall is convinced by Patterson's arguments, building on Garnsey's work,

[244] Roselaar 2010: 155, 180.

that the rural poor in many regions lived in more or less nucleated settlements, in *pagi* and *vici*; but the evidence for the second century specifically is nugatory.[245]

The allotments made by the Roman state to its military veterans do provide some indication of the minimum size of peasant landholdings. The recurrent eulogy of the small farm in Latin literature was matched by the Romans' commitment to the policy of colonization and viritane land assignments as a means not only of reproducing artificially the traditional Italian structure of the small farm, but also of providing sufficient land to allow settlers to meet the minimum property qualification necessary to serve in the army. This is the only possible explanation for the 'army standard issue' parcels of land that were still being granted (regardless of the amount of labour a veteran had at his disposal) in the citizen colonies founded in northern and southern Italy soon after the Second Punic War. The large numbers of settlers and the very small plots (sometimes no larger than five *iugera*) which they apparently mostly received are, as Hopkins has emphasized, evidence in themselves of considerable impoverishment:[246] 'Peasants were unlikely to walk three hundred or more kilometres from their ancestral homes in central Italy unless they were pushed hard—especially when for many of them the prize was less than four hectares (ten acres) of land'.[247] The importance attached to smallholdings in Italy during the second century is further confirmed in the *lex agraria* of 111, encouraging, as it does, the formation of private holdings of thirty *iugera* in size.[248]

If we go back to the end of the third century, the Second Punic War had a dramatic effect on the pattern of landholding in Italy. After the battle of Trasimene, in the summer of 217, Hannibal's operations were confined largely to the south and southern-central parts of the peninsula.[249] In the aftermath of the war, major viritane distributions were carried out in these areas because large swathes of *ager publicus* had become available as a result of confiscations from cities that had sided with Hannibal. In Livy's account of the year 201, we read that *ager publicus* in Samnium and Apulia was distributed among the African veterans of Scipio Africanus.[250] We are also told that other legionaries who had seen long service in Spain, Sardinia, and Africa received allotments of *ager publicus* in 199.[251] This was followed by a programme of conquest and colonization in the Po Valley, upon which the Romans embarked at the beginning of the second century.[252]

245 Cic. *Leg. agr.* 2. 89; Garnsey 1979; J. R. Patterson 1987; Foxhall 1990: 108. Excavations of a largely first-century AD site at Forum Novum (Vescovio), which appear to reveal only an administrative centre consisting entirely of public buildings without any sign of residential housing, might be considered to be supportive of Foxhall's view (H. Patterson et al. 2000: 401–2; Gaffney, Patterson, and Roberts 2001; A. I. Wilson 2002*a*: 264–5).

246 Livy, 39. 55. 7–9 and 40. 29. 1–2 for grants of small plots of land. A plot of five *iugera* is about 25% larger than a modern football pitch.

247 Hopkins 1978: 57; Foxhall 1990: 104; Gabba 1989: 205. See now Fentress's analysis of the centuriation pattern at Saturnia in the Albegna Valley (Carandini and Cambi 2002: 124–6) with the critique of A. I. Wilson 2004: 570–3.

248 Brunt 1971*a*: 77ff.; Hopkins 1978: 64; Lintott 1994*c*: 63, 74, 87; Rathbone 2003: 166.

249 Livy, 28. 11. 9; Cornell 1996: 101–11; cf. Toynbee 1965: ii. 286–312.

250 Livy, 31. 4. 1, 31. 49. 5.

251 Livy, 32. 1. 6.

252 At least eight *coloniae maritimae* were founded between 199 and 184 and between three and six larger *coloniae civium Romanorum* between 184 and 181.

From the Roman state's point of view, the use of public land for viritane settlement during a period of high military mortality would have made perfect sense, since it would have increased the likelihood that the recipients of the allotments and their descendants would have remained *assidui* and so liable to military service.[253] But it should be emphasized again that these settlements were placed in the periphery of Italy, predominantly in the extreme south and north, not in the central-western area where investment farming was to be concentrated. In fact, during the programme of colonization organized by the Roman senate between 199 and 177, the population of central-western Italy was reduced by anything up to 100,000 men, women, and children.[254] Meanwhile, large numbers of Latin citizens appear to have migrated to the city of Rome to take advantage of the opportunities offered there by increased expenditure on construction and logistics.[255] After 177, however, once the conquest of Cisalpine Gaul and Liguria had been completed, the programme of colonization ended, as there was no longer a strategic need for military colonies, and perhaps too because of political jealousy within the elite over the office of founding commissioners.[256] It is no coincidence that in 128, probably as part of the measures to mitigate the agrarian problems, a new colony was established in Italy at Auximum, the first for fifty years; three more followed soon afterwards at the instigation of C. Gracchus at Capua, Tarentum, and Scolacium Minervum.[257] Nor is it a coincidence that almost all the surviving epigraphical traces of the work of the Gracchan commissioners, in the form of *cippi*, have been found in southern Italy, in Campania, Picenum, Samnium, Apulia, and Lucania, the regions that saw vast extensions of Roman *ager publicus* as a result of confiscations after the war against Hannibal.[258] Indeed, Roselaar calculates that the total size of all the centuriations that have been ascribed to Gracchan activity is a massive 1,307,200 *iugera* or 3,268 km^2.[259]

But what of the situation in central-western Italy? In his Preface to the *De Agricultura*, Cato seems to take for granted the continued existence of a free peasantry and its availability for military service. He gives no hint or indication that they were a threatened class, let alone that they were threatened by the very type of agriculture about which he himself was writing.[260] Consequently Cato's silence provides no evidence, even for Latium and Campania, about the extent to which peasant agriculture may or may not have been in decline. The one thing that Cato does reveal about the population pattern is that a large pool of free agricultural labourers was available for temporary hire. The cultivation of vines and olives demanded a heavy annual input of casual seasonal labour, and we must suppose that the vast majority of these labourers were recruited from families who had their own small farms, which provided them with their basic subsistence.

[253] De Ligt 2012: 153.

[254] The figure is Hopkins's (1978: 64), although he fails to take account of locals in Latin colonies in his calculation.

[255] See p. 227.

[256] Salmon 1970: 112–13; Rosenstein 2004: 222 n. 185, 278 n. 105.

[257] According to Vel. Pat. 1. 15. 2–3, a colony was founded at Auximum in 157; Salmon (1963: 10–13) prefers to assign this to 128, but North (1992) argues for Velleius' dating. C. Gracchus' colonies at Tarentum and Scolacium Minervum were in the far south of Italy, where there were still large areas of *ager publicus* available (Plin. *HN* 3. 95 places 'Scolagium' in the toe of Italy).

[258] Cornell and Matthews 1982: 57.

[259] Roselaar 2010: 251–2.

[260] Cf. Frederiksen 1970–1: 337.

Cato's advice to be nice to your neighbours implies the very local hiring of this extra labour: 'Vicinis bonus esto . . . Si te libenter vicinitas videbit . . . operarios facilius conduces'[261] (be good to your neighbours . . . If the neighbourhood views you positively . . . it will be easier to secure labourers). In other words, not only did the villa system require a large seasonal labour force, but a free peasantry was the only possible source to supply this demand.[262] The corollary is that the villa system was more economic because it carried no surplus labour, and this was not just because it utilized slave labour, but because it exploited the underemployment of the neighbouring free peasantry. Indeed, Rathbone attempts a rough calculation of the profitability of slave labour for the cultivation of 100 *iugera* of vines and 50 *iugera* of olives, and compares this with the profitability of other possible labour systems. He concludes that slave labour was not more economic than free; that when used on its own, it was considerably less profitable; and that a slave-staffed villa cultivating vines and/or olives as cash crops depended on the seasonal hiring of free peasant labour to make these crops economically viable.[263] Interestingly, Cato does not mention the use of tenant farmers by an absentee landlord and it is unclear whether tenancy existed, let alone whether it was widespread, during the second century. De Neeve argues that there was no tenancy before the end of the second century, because it is not mentioned before this in our surviving sources.[264] Rosenstein agrees with this view, pointing out that Livy, when talking of the Hannibalic War, and Appian, when talking of the period before the Gracchan reforms, mention only slaves and not tenants cultivating the land of the rich.[265] De Ligt, on the other hand, argues that provisions in the Twelve Tables concerning *pignoris captio* and *venditio filii* could have provided the legal framework for agricultural tenancy much earlier.[266] Arguably, though, tenancy would have held few attractions for wealthy landowners, if, as Appian states and the traditional explanation of the Gracchan crisis holds, free peasants were likely to be called up for military service overseas.[267]

The traditional account also holds that absent peasants were replaced by slaves, because slavery made it possible to maintain agricultural production in Italy in spite of the high levels of recruitment into the army. The median size of the army, during the period 225 to 23 BC, has been calculated to have been between 13 and 15 per cent of all adult male citizens, an average of perhaps 110,000 Italian peasants in the army at any one time. In the second century, citizens served for anything between six and sixteen years in the army.[268] The traditional view, therefore, argues that, as the second century progressed and as Rome fought more campaigns outside Italy, the number of peasants available to work on the land of the rich would have been reduced and it would have become more difficult for soldiers to return home during the winter months to take care of their own properties. Even two or three years in the legions might have been enough to ruin them.

[261] Cato, *Agr.* 4; Astin 1978: 247–8, 257.
[262] For peasant survival strategies in general, see Erdkamp 2005: 79–95.
[263] Rathbone 1981: 13–15. [264] De Neeve 1984: 119–21.
[265] Livy, 26. 35. 5; App. *B. Civ.* 1. 7; Rosenstein 2004: 181–2.
[266] De Ligt 2000, 2012: 104–5. [267] App. *B. Civ.* 1. 7. [268] See pp. 25–6.

Recently, though, Rosenstein has questioned whether the increased intensity of Roman military service in the second century really was one of the problems that led to the rural crisis that Ti. Gracchus sought to address. Using the *fasti triumphales* and the accounts of fighting in Italy during the Second Punic War and subsequently against the Gauls and Ligurians, he shows that Roman warfare had already been reliant on year-round military service since 300 BC or earlier. Secondly, the legions were principally made up of men between the ages of 17 and 30 (with only an estimated 14% being over 30) and, given that Roman men tended to marry in their late twenties, the impact of several years' overseas service on the farms and the families which these legionaries left behind would have been limited. In any case, under normal circumstances, at least half the men aged between 17 and 30 would not have been serving in the legions at any one time and most legionaries were not expected to serve in many consecutive campaigns. Finally, there was the beneficial impact on peasant family incomes from the *stipendium* and, at times, the donatives and booty that soldiers received, as well as there being one less mouth to feed back on the farm.[269]

Rosenstein's points are well made and his analysis is probably correct for the period down to the 160s when military service was highly remunerative.[270] But they probably do not account for the negative effect on family incomes and the morale of soldiers serving overseas during the unrewarding wars fought in Spain between 154 and 133, that is in the two decades immediately preceding the Gracchan crisis. There must, after all, have been some point, other than pure rhetoric, to Sallust's statement that 'the people were worn down by military service and poverty'.[271]

Recent work by archaeologists has, nevertheless, suggested that traditional peasant agriculture in central-western Italy was more resilient in the second century than had previously been supposed. However, the conclusions of these studies must be treated with care. The pitfalls involved in comparing the results of different surveys are clearly seen in the case of the *Ager Cosanus*, where two surveys covering the same region found entirely different patterns of site sizes and chronologies, because of differing approaches to data collection.[272] The first survey, carried out by the Wesleyan University, intensively 'sherded' sites that had been identified previously.[273] The second was carried out in conjunction with the excavation of the villa at Settefinestre, and covered both the *Ager Cosanus* and the Albegna Valley to the north. This survey aimed at a more systematic coverage of the region, based on a sampling strategy of surveying kilometre-wide trenches running east–west and north–south at 5-km intervals. It has tended to find a larger number of smaller sites, which has led to different reconstructions of the region's history.[274]

[269] Rosenstein 2004: 31, 85–8, 101–2, 141–2. [270] See p. 287.

[271] Sall. *Iug.* 41. 7: 'populus militia atque inopia urgebatur'; cf. App. *B. Civ.* 1. 7 quoted at Ch. 7 n. 215.

[272] Potter 1979: 95–6; Rathbone 1981: 17. The *Ager Cosanus* lies on the Etrurian coast about 140 km to the north of Rome. It was originally part of the territory of Vulci, confiscated after that city's defeat in 280; the Latin colony of Cosa was founded in 273 and the land centuriated. In 197 the senate gave permission to Cosa to enrol 1,000 additional colonists.

[273] Dyson 1978: 253–5; Morley 1996: 131.

[274] Carandini and Settis 1979; Morley 1996: 131.

Neither survey found much evidence for third-century occupation of the territory. The patterns of centuriation are clear, but the great majority of Republican sites date to the second or first century, and can plausibly be linked to the recolonization of the area in 197. Shortly afterwards, the town of Cosa was flourishing, probably as a result of its involvement in the growing wine trade, and its immediate hinterland was densely occupied with small sites.[275] At some point, however, there was a dramatic change. According to Celuzza and Regoli, 90 per cent of the small sites were abandoned by the middle of the first century, but the difficulty lies in dating this change more precisely. Gabba believes that 'around the end of the second century and the beginning of the first century, colonial allotments in the area of the Latin colony of Cosa were replaced by vast "industrialized" plantations similar to the Catonian estate; aided by ease of access to the sea, they displayed a strong trend towards producing for the market'. Such a precise timing of the change does not seem to be warranted by the archaeological evidence, but it was certainly through this area that Tiberius Gracchus had passed, probably along the coast road, the Via Aurelia Vetus, and seen the land being cultivated by what he believed to be slaves.[276]

There is a contrast between the archaeological remains of the coastal *Ager Cosanus* and those of the interior. Along the coast, villas are noticeably denser, whereas the Albegna Valley was characterized by continuity of settlement; the small, presumably colonial, sites do not appear to have suffered the same decline in the first century. It is tempting to connect this to the fact that it was less closely involved in the wine trade—amphorae are found in the area, but no kilns.[277] As Wilson points out, the presence of villas along the route of the Via Aurelia may explain Ti. Gracchus' reaction, even though the landscape was not typical of the whole of Etruria.[278] The pattern that emerges, therefore, is of a much stronger survival of smaller sites inland, whereas the spread of very large estates which absorbed their neighbours may well have been limited to the prime coastal and river valley areas, because they were better connected to the international trade routes.[279]

A similar contrast between coastal and inland areas is found in the region of northern Campania that contained the *Ager Falernus*, the Massico and the territories of Suessa, Aurunca, and Sinuessa. Strabo knew that the fertility of these districts was linked to the presence of volcanic deposits which resulted in good wine-growing soils. The names of the Campanian vintages, *falernum*, *massicum*, *gauranum*, *surrentinum*, *salernum*, *trifolinum*, are well-known from Latin literature. Besides famous wines, Campania produced notable quantities of olive oil. Venafrum, on the border with Samnium, was particularly renowned. Cato mentions it. Strabo, Varro, and Pliny the Elder put it above all other varieties. For Horace, it is the absolute benchmark in culinary matters. It was used particularly as a base for perfumes and Martial lauded it for that quality. Capua had the

275 The town of Cosa itself effectively died in the first century AD, when other provinces, especially Spain and southern Gaul, came to dominate the market for wine and fish products (Fentress 1994; A. I. Wilson 2002*a*: 263).

276 Plut. *Ti. Gracch.* 8. 7; Nagle 1976; Celuzza and Regoli 1982; Gabba 1989: 238.

277 Attolini 1991; Carandini and Cambi 2002: 135; Witcher 2006*b*:103.

278 A. I. Wilson 2004: 573.

279 Morley 1996: 132; Greene 1986: 109.

greatest concentration of perfumeries, but they were also found in many other urban centres: at Pompeii, Paestum, and Puteoli.[280] We shall discuss in the next chapter the connection between perfume and the eastern trade through Delos. Graeco-Italic amphorae appeared in the region from the early second century, and the arrival of Dressel 1 amphorae was accompanied by the development of kilns along the coast. Many sites have the remains of wine or oil presses, and Arthur's survey also found ancient vine trenches.[281] Two sites at Francolise, to the east of the *Ager Falernus*, show the frustrations of using archaeological evidence for the late Republican period.[282] Both were platform villas of modest proportions (one dating to the second century, the other to the beginning of the first) which were rebuilt on a much more impressive scale around 30 BC. The first contains no evidence for its productive activities until an olive oil separating vat was added in the remodelling; the second contains a threshing floor, along with rooms in the *pars rustica* for an overseer and family as well as other labourers. In other words, the villas themselves may have been constructed in the second century or early first, but the evidence for the processing of agricultural products comes only from later remodelling. We may compare the Villa di Posta Crusta in Apulia, where, again, its origins date back to the second century, but the evidence of oil production dates only from the total reconstruction of the villa on a larger scale during the Principate.[283]

In southern Etruria, the survey of 2,600 km^2 conducted by the British School of Rome between the 1950s and the 1970s has revealed a high density of rural settlement in both the Republican and early Imperial periods. The survey concluded that the period after 300 BC saw the decline of the Etruscan towns, further dispersal of settlements into the countryside, and the construction of major arterial roads through the area. In the northern part of the survey area (the *Ager Faliscus*), 35 per cent of the sites were interpreted to be the remains of small buildings such as shepherds' huts, whilst 43 per cent were classed as small farms, of sufficient architectural distinction to possess masonry walls, floor mosaics, and painted wall-plaster. The remaining 22 per cent comprised villas with such additional features as baths and colonnaded courtyards. The larger villas occurred more frequently in the southern part of the overall survey area, which was nearer to Rome, with an average density of around one to every 2 km^2.[284] Since 1997, a major restudy of the material from the South Etruria Survey has been conducted under the name of the Tiber Valley Project, also under the auspices of the British School at Rome. The restudy questions the validity of the earlier conclusions of steady growth during the Republican period and tentatively suggests that there was a sharp drop in settlement numbers between the mid-third and mid-second centuries, which fits with the argument for the longer-term impact of the Second Punic War and the expansion of the population of Rome discussed above. However, there is a major

[280] Strabo, 5. 3. 10, 5. 4. 8; Varro, *Rust.* 1. 2. 6; Plin. *HN* 3. 60, 15. 8, cf.18. 111; Cato, *Agr.* 146. 1; Hor. *Carm.* 2. 6. 12, Hor. *Sat.* 2. 4. 69, 2. 8. 45; Mart. 13. 101; Tchernia 1986: 60–3, 276–84; Brun 2004: 12–13; Morley 1996: 133–4.

[281] Arthur 1991: 71–8; Morley 1996: 134.

[282] Cotton 1979; Cotton and Métraux 1985; Morley 1996: 134.

[283] Brun 2004: 28.

[284] The survey reports were published in *PBSR* 26 (1958), 63–134; 30 (1962), 116–207; 31 (1963), 100–58; 33 (1965), 70–112; 36 (1968); Potter 1979: 120–37 provides a synthesis of the results, discussing rural settlement in the classical period; Greene 1986: 103–9.

methodological issue. The restudy of the black-slip pottery (about 7,050 sherds) from the original survey showed that only 20 per cent of the material was capable of providing a date that is more precise than the generic chronological span of the group as a whole (that is 350–0 BC). Of this 20 per cent, the vast majority (approximately 1,150 sherds) can be dated to the period 350–250, with only a tiny amount (about 250 sherds) capable of being dated to the period 250–150.[285]

In sum, the archaeological evidence, such as it is, is too partial and too scarce to have a conclusive bearing on the question of changing patterns of land tenure and exploitation in the second century. Archaeological surveys have demonstrated the presence of smallholdings in certain areas of central-western Italy, but, with the current state of our knowledge, they cannot determine whether, and to what extent, there was a general decline in the number of small farmers, or a shift in the pattern of agricultural holdings from small independent units to larger estates worked by slave labour and devoted to commercial production. Such indicators as there are suggest that larger estates were confined to the prime coastal and river valley areas.

THE DEMOGRAPHIC GROWTH OF THE FREE POPULATION OF ITALY

Demographic developments during the second century have also been at the centre of the recent debate over the causes of the agrarian crisis. According to Appian and Plutarch, Ti. Gracchus, when launching his programme of agrarian reform, seems to have claimed that the number of Italians had begun to decline in absolute terms.[286] But there is now a growing body of scholarly opinion that argues that there was in fact an expansion in the free population during the second half of the second century and that this contributed towards the problems described in the sources.

Although the size of the total population of mainland Italy is not known from any ancient source for any point during our period, we do have some relevant evidence in the form of the Republican censuses reported by various ancient sources, as well as a breakdown of Italian military manpower resources in 225 reported by Polybius.[287] There are some problems with the Polybius passage, but there is no reason to doubt that his account is derived from an official survey of allied manpower resources reported by Fabius Pictor, a contemporary of the Second Punic War.[288] As for the figures contained in the censuses, they appear to have largely survived the process of manuscript transmission intact and so represent one of the few sets of data for the Republican period that can be studied serially (Table 7.1). In the late nineteenth century, K. J. Beloch used these numbers to produce a model of the demographic history of Republican Italy and this model was refined and developed by Peter Brunt eighty years or so later.[289] Although there is still some debate about precisely what these censuses represent, the widely

285 Patterson, Giuseppe, and Witcher 2004: 15–16.

286 App. *B. Civ.* 1. 7, 1. 9; Plut. *Ti. Gracch.* 8. 3.

287 Polyb. 2. 24.

288 De Ligt 2012: 41, 47–9, for a refutation of the problems raised by Scheidel (2004: 3–4).

289 Beloch 1886; Brunt 1971*a*.

Table 7.1. Census Figures 265 BC–AD 14[290]

Year	Census Figure	Source
265/4 BC	292,234	Eutr. *Hist.* 2. 18
252/1 BC	297,797	Livy, *Per.* 18
247/6 BC	241,712	Livy, *Per.* 19
241/0 BC	260,000	Hieron. *Ol.* 134. 1
234/3 BC	270,713	Livy, *Per.* 20; cf. Plb. 2. 24
209/8 BC	137,108	Livy, 27. 36. 7
204/3 BC	214,000	Livy, 29. 37. 5
194/3 BC	143,704	Livy, 35. 9. 2
189/8 BC	258,318	Livy, 38. 36. 10
179/8 BC	258,794	Livy, *Per.* 41
174/3 BC	269,015	Livy, 42. 10. 2–3
169/8 BC	312,805	Livy, *Per.* 45
164/3 BC	337,022	Livy, *Per.* 46; cf. Plut. *Aem.* 38
159/8 BC	328,316	Livy, *Per.* 47
154/3 BC	324,000	Livy, *Per.* 48
147/6 BC	322,000	Euseb. Armen. Ol. 158. 3
142/1 BC	327,442	Livy, *Per.* 54
136/5 BC	317,933	Livy, *Per.* 56
131/0 BC	318,823	Livy, *Per.* 59
125/4 BC	394,736	Livy, *Per.* 60
115/14 BC	394,336	Livy, *Per.* 63
86/5 BC	463,000	Hieron. *Ol.* 173. 4
70/69 BC	910,000	Phlegon fr. 12. 6
28 BC	4,063,000	*Res Gestae* 8. 2
8 BC	4,233,000	*Res Gestae* 8 .3
AD 14	4,937,000	*Res Gestae* 8. 4

accepted view is that of Beloch and Brunt, that they counted free adult males aged 17 and over.[291] It also seems probable that the censuses were consistently prepared on the same basis until at least 69 BC, after which there was, at some point, an unreported change in recording practices.[292] If the censuses are reasonably accurate and do indeed represent the number of adult males aged 17 and over, then that would mean that the figures that they contain could give some guidance, by extrapolation, as to the rate of change in the free population. The problem, though, is to interpret these data in the light of some of the events and developments, as described by a number of ancient authors, that may have influenced demographic trends and that sometimes suggest a picture at variance with what the census numbers themselves portray.

Brunt's and Hopkins's estimates remain the best starting point for any discussion of demographic developments during this period. Brunt's conclusions were

[290] Brunt 1971*a*: 13–14.

[291] Brunt 1971*a*: 15–25 ('censa sunt capita civium tot'); this is, however, disputed by those (referenced in De Ligt 2004: 738 n. 29) who believe that the Republican censuses counted only the adult male population above the property qualification for military service.

[292] Brunt's view was that the Augustan censuses may have included all citizens and their families, with the possible exception of those aged under one, as well as widows and orphans, although this too is still debated.

that the free population of Italy, including the Roman citizenry, experienced a modest decline between the mid 220s and the early years of the Principate. In fact, he estimated that the total population of the Italian mainland rose from 5 million in 225 BC to 7 million under Augustus, but he believed that the increase mainly came from a rise in slave numbers. In turn, Hopkins used the detailed evidence collected by Brunt to estimate that the free population of Italy declined from roughly 4.5 million in 225 to approximately 4 million in 28.[293]

Lo Cascio, however, in a series of articles which builds on work by Frank and Wiseman, has proposed a different model, the so-called 'high-count'.[294] He has argued that the last two centuries BC were a period of rapid demographic growth, that the Augustan censuses still counted adult males only, and that the Italian population in 225 BC must have been of the order of 6 to 8 million and somewhere in the region of 15 million under Augustus—very significantly higher than Brunt's and Hopkins's estimates.[295] There are many objections to Lo Cascio's argument, not least the fact that his view can be maintained only by assuming that the Roman censuses of the second century and of the first half of the first century were completely wrong.[296] More generally, it is difficult to understand why the Romans would have had to resort to sizeable imports of slaves to satisfy their labour demands if the free population was as large and growing as rapidly as the high counters suggest. On the other hand, how do we explain the agrarian and social crisis that apparently lay behind the Gracchan land reforms if Italy was as under-populated as the low count, as espoused in the Beloch-Brunt model, implies?[297]

The crucial period for the determination of demographic trends during the last two centuries of the Republic is the three decades preceding the Gracchan land reforms. The census figures after 164/3 show a steady decline in the numbers of those registering until a sudden recovery in 125/4. According to Brunt, and on the low-count view, the Roman citizen body stopped growing from the mid 160s onwards and the principal reason was that a steady increase in rural and urban poverty led a growing number of Roman citizens to postpone marriage.[298] This is in line with the overall picture presented by the ancient sources that the agrarian

293 Brunt 1971*a*: 131, following Beloch 1886; Hopkins 1978: 68–9. Brunt estimated a total free population in peninsular Italy (i.e. central and southern Italy) in 225 of about 3.1 m. He added a free population for Cisalpine Gaul of 1.4 m. to make a total free population for mainland Italy of 4.5 m. Adding 500,000 slaves gave him a grand total of 5 m. free and non-free inhabitants for mainland Italy.

294 Frank 1924; Wiseman 1969: 72–5; Lo Cascio 1994*a*, 1994*b*, 1999*a*, 1999*b*, 2001. Lo Cascio's arguments are further developed by Morley 2001. Rosenstein (2004: 137, 145ff.) argues that high military mortality (he estimates that between 34% and 40% of soldiers died whilst in service during the second century), rural epidemics, and large-scale migration to Rome from the countryside initially produced opportunities for those left behind. This resulted in a very rapid increase in the birth rate and so an expansion in the size of the free rural population. This increase was, he argues, exceptionally large, from 1.3% to 1.5% p.a. growth between 200 and 168 and 0.6% to 0.8% p.a. between 168 and 124.

295 Kron (2008) argues that the introduction and spread of sophisticated strategies of agricultural production could have made it possible for Roman farmers to achieve the high grain yields required to sustain a hypothetical population of between 15 and 16 m.

296 De Ligt 2004: 728–31 and 2012: 44–7, 177–9. See Scheidel 2005 and 2008 for his persuasive rejection of the high count.

297 Scheidel 2008: 42; De Ligt 2012: 35.

298 Brunt 1971*a*: 138–40. But see now Rosenstein 2004: 85–8, discussed earlier.

law of 133 was an attempt to deal with a perceived decline in the free Italian population during the period preceding the Gracchan land reforms.[299]

But a major problem with the low-count model is that the relatively low census figure for 131/0 is followed by much higher figures for the years 125/4 and 115/14. If these figures are to be believed, the censors of 125/4 were able to register some 75,000 additional adult male citizens, 24 per cent more than their predecessors of 131/0, which seems to be an enormous increase.[300] The figures for 125/4 and 115/14 are, however, credible. Brunt was able to argue that there were some 412,000 Roman men at the time of the census of 70/69 who came from families that had held Roman citizenship before 90.[301] If we take into account the probability that some 35,000 Roman citizens were killed during the Cimbrian Wars and a further 50,000 during the Social War, it seems probable that there were more than 400,000 adult male citizens during the final decades of the second century.[302] There are, therefore, no good reasons for doubting the validity of the census figures of 125/4 and 115/14. In short, the theory that the Roman citizen body started to contract from the late 160s onwards makes it impossible to make sense not only of the census figure for 125/4 and 115/14, but also of the census of 70/69.[303] How then to reconcile the high census figures for 125/4 and 115/14 with the relatively low figures for the period 159/8 to 131/0?

De Ligt argues convincingly that the census figures for the period 159/8 to 131/0 make sense if we assume that a simultaneous expansion of the free population and of the numbers of slaves in central-western Italy pushed an increasing number of free peasants below the property threshold for military service, with their property holdings shrinking to less than 5 *iugera*. This led to fewer adult male citizens being registered.[304] On this interpretation, a low-count model that incorporates the idea that the population continued to increase during the three decades leading up to 131 makes it possible to take seriously Ti. Gracchus' claim that large numbers of rural citizens were declining into poverty and that this development was undermining Rome's military potential by reducing the number of available *assidui*. The steep rise in the census figures between 131/0 and 125/4 can then be explained by the partial implementation of the Gracchan land reforms which persuaded tens of thousands of citizens, who had fallen below the property threshold, to register themselves with the censors because they wanted to benefit from this scheme.[305]

Ti. Gracchus was, therefore, correct in assuming that the number of impoverished Roman citizens was steadily increasing. At the same time, he believed he had witnessed, during his trip through Etruria, a startling increase in the number of

[299] App. *B. Civ*. 1. 7, 1. 9; Plut. *Ti. Gracch*. 8. 3; cf. Sall. *Iug*. 41. 7.

[300] De Ligt 2004: 740.

[301] Brunt 1971*a*: 83, 97–8.

[302] Brunt 1971*a*: 82–3.

[303] De Ligt 2004: 741.

[304] De Ligt 2012: 174, 168–9, 287. Ownership of 5 *iugera* seems to have been enough to meet the property qualification for legionary service in the mid-second century. An alternative explanation offered by de Ligt in an earlier article (2004: 744) and by Rosenstein (2004: 156–8) is that a growing number of adult male citizens became reluctant to serve in the legions and sought to evade military service by avoiding registration by the censors.

[305] Brunt 1971*a*: 78–80; De Ligt 2012: 174.

rurally employed slaves. Finally, he was worried by the downward trend in census returns. On the basis of these three observations, he concluded, incorrectly, that the free population of Italy had begun to decline in absolute terms as a result of the expansion of agricultural slavery.[306] In fact, the number of Roman citizens continued to grow throughout the second century.

De Ligt's analysis represents something of a middle ground between the Brunt/ Hopkins low-count model and Lo Cascio's high-count estimate and it has the merit of making sense of most of the surviving evidence. It is also a useful check on the GDP estimates that we shall be producing (in Ch. 11), because the greater the increase in the population, the more difficult it becomes to demonstrate that there was per capita economic growth during our period.

There is one final problem with the census figures. The rise in the numbers between 204/3 and 169/8 appears to be remarkably steep (46% in thirty-five years—see Table 7.2), and there are some seemingly random fluctuations. But in fact the census figure for 169/8 is only 5 per cent higher than the equivalent figure for 252/1 (from the middle of the First Punic War), which suggests that, during the three or four decades following the end of the Second Punic War, the free population recovered to what were in effect mid-third century levels, before the devastations wrought by the First Punic War (note that the census figure for 234/3 is about 7% lower than that for 265/4) and the Second Punic War. One explanation of the seemingly random fluctuations could be under-registration, which was clearly regarded as being a problem by the censors themselves. For example, those of 169/8 took the unusual step of registering soldiers on leave from Macedonia, which suggests that they made a greater effort to arrive at a reliable registration than their predecessors.[307] Likewise, the censors of 204/3 sent out envoys to record soldiers serving overseas.[308] Another contributing factor to these fluctuations may have been the disenfranchisement of 38,000 Campanians during the Second Punic War and their subsequent re-enfranchisement.[309]

In summary, therefore, the Roman census figures can be seen to have a certain consistency and, although by no means a perfect proxy indicator, they can be used to provide some rough guidance as to the rate of change in the free population of mainland Italy. The figure for 28 BC in Table 7.3 is the one given for the census of that year. For the starting point in 225BC, we accept the arguments of de Ligt and

Table 7.2. Selected Roman censuses (% change)

	265/4	252/1	234/3	204/3	169/8 BC
Census	292,234	297,797	270,713	214,000	312,805
% change		*2%*	*-9%*	*-21%*	*46%*

[306] De Ligt 2004: 754.

[307] Livy, 43. 14. 7–8; cf. Vell. Pat. 2. 7. 7. The view of Brunt (1971*a*: 33, 79) was that all Roman census figures must be increased by *at least* 10% because the task of registering the entire adult male population must have been beyond the powers of the censors.

[308] Livy, 29. 37. 5.

[309] Hopkins 1978: 33.

Table 7.3. Italian free population (estimated)

	225	200	150	100	50	28 BC
Free population (000s)	3,900	3,002	4,533	5,110	4,645	4,063
% change		*-22%*	*51%*	*13%*	*-9%*	*-13%*

have lowered the Brunt/Hopkins estimate for the free population of Italy in 225 BC from 4.5 million to 3.9 million.[310]

SLAVES

Cato assumes, in the *De Agricultura*, that the estates he is describing will be largely staffed by chattel slaves. He recommends a permanent labour force of thirteen slaves for the 240 *iugera* olive farm and sixteen for the vineyard. At exceptionally busy times, notably at harvest, the permanent slave workforce is supplemented with temporary free labour, the availability of which Cato mentions as an important consideration in choosing a farm. Columella implies a similar combination of workforces in his discussion of the advantages and disadvantages of using slaves and tenants to work different types of land. A combination of slaves, wage labourers, and tenants seem to have cultivated Horace's Sabine property. A group of slaves worked in the estate of C. Laelius at Formiae in the second century.[311]

It is likely that the origins of the slave-based agricultural economy which we see operating in the *De Agricultura* goes back at least to the age of the Samnite Wars. It is impossible to calculate a reliable number for the total enslaved during the third century, but we have sufficient examples to give some sense of the scale. It has been computed, for example, that Roman annalists record the enslavement of over 60,000 enemies by the Romans in the brief period 297 to 293, and a high proportion of these slaves were presumably used in agriculture.[312] The mass enslavements of the First Punic War (for example the 25,000 inhabitants of Agrigentum who were enslaved when the Romans took the city in 262) continue this trend.[313] A further indication that the slave mode of production was not abnormal in the third century is that Livy says that it was difficult to renew the cultivation of farms in Italy in 206, since free farmers were far away from their lands and there was a shortage (*inopia*) of slaves.[314]

This trend towards the use of non-free labour, particularly in central-western Italy, was further intensified during the late third century and the first half of the

[310] De Ligt 2004: 732–8; 2012: 71–2, 190, table 4.3. For de Ligt, Polybius' manpower figures imply a total free population in peninsular Italy in 225 of about 2.9 m. To this must be added the free population of Cisalpine Gaul, which de Ligt estimates to be 1 m., which produces a total for mainland Italy of 3.9 m. free inhabitants.

[311] Cato, *Agr.* 1. 3, 5. 4, 136–7, 144–50; Columella, *Rust.* 1. 7; Hor. *Ep.* 1. 14. 1–3; Cic. *Rep.* 1. 61; Foxhall 1990: 102–3; Astin 1978: 245; Rathbone 1981: 19, 22; Garnsey 1979: 2.

[312] Harris 1979: 59; Rathbone 1981: 22.

[313] Diod. Sic. 23. 9. 1; cf. Polyb. 29. 7.

[314] Livy, 28. 11. 8–9.

second century, because of the number of war captives that fell into Roman hands. During the Second Punic War, 85,000 people were enslaved, while between 201 and 167 the total was more than 300,000.[315] This number includes the 150,000 Epirotes enslaved by Aemilius Paullus on the orders of the senate, in 167, at the end of the Third Macedonian War, an action that Ziolkowski believes occurred because of a shortage of agricultural slaves in Italy. He argues that the fall in their numbers had been caused by an epidemic (*pestilentia*) that had broken out in 174, and that the mass enslavement was an attempt to redress this decline.[316] Evidence that some at least of these captives were brought to Italy, to be used in agriculture, can be found in a passage from Varro's *Res Rusticae*, which, a century later, mentions their descendants approvingly: 'Itaque propter has cognationes, Epiroticae familiae sunt inlustriores ac cariores'[317] (therefore, on account of these relationships, Epirote slave families are better regarded and more expensive). But it is perhaps unlikely that the Romans would have shipped all 150,000 slaves to Italy. Presumably a large proportion of the Epirote captives never left Epirus and served there as slaves on the farms which they had previously owned themselves but which now belonged to their Roman captors.[318] Cicero's friend Atticus, for example, owned estates in Epirus by the first century.[319]

Another example of mass enslavement comes from II Maccabees, when Nicanor of Syria enslaves Jews in the 160s. The author says that Nicanor needed to raise 2,000 talents in order to secure funds for the tribute due to Rome and that he was prepared to sell slaves at the very low price of ninety to the talent.[320] But this means that in order to raise 2,000 talents at this price, he would have needed to enslave 180,000 Jews. As we have already seen, Livy states that the balance of the Syrian indemnity was paid off in 173.[321] And yet both this passage and another at II Maccabees 3: 11 contain references to the difficulties that the Seleucids were having in paying the Roman indemnity. Our passage could well reflect an attempt, perhaps during the 170s, to enslave Jews in order to raise the necessary money. That the slaves were to be exported is implied by the fact that Nicanor 'sent to the cities of the sea coast inviting them to buy Jewish slaves'. Given the timing, the slaves could have been intended either for the fields of Italy or for the Spanish mines, which were probably already becoming a large-scale user of slaves by this date.[322]

Other evidence for the growing size of the agricultural slave population in the second century is not difficult to find. In 196, the Roman army intervened to suppress a 'conspiracy of slaves' in Etruria that seems to have been widespread.[323] In 185 there was a large uprising of slave shepherds in the public pastureland of Apulia.[324] Sicily was convulsed by two slave revolts in 138–132 and 104–101, the former having been provoked by the mistreatment of slaves by the Greek owner

[315] As Ziolkowski 1986: 74–5 points out, the sources are so fragmentary that the number of slaves they mention can only be a fraction of the real total.

[316] Ziolkowski 1986; cf., too, the curious incident of the mass enslavement of Ligurians by the consul M. Popillius Laenas, in 173, and their subsequent release on the orders of the senate (Livy, 42. 8). The senate's decision to force Popillius to buy back the captives was probably made in order to secure a tranquil Italy ahead of the looming war with Perseus.

[317] Varro, *Rust.* 1. 17. 5.

[318] Professor Michael Crawford (pers. comm.).

[319] See Ch. 8.

[320] II Macc. 8: 10–11.

[321] Livy, 42. 6. 6–7; Table 2.2 note.

[322] Diod. Sic. 5. 36. 3–4.

[323] Livy, 33. 36. 1–3.

[324] Livy, 39. 29. 8–9.

of a large ranching estate at Henna.[325] Enormous numbers are ascribed to the rebels by our sources—20,000 rising to 200,000—though Posidonius merely puts Eunus' original force at 6,000 and Cleon's at 5,000. The slaves are said to have been partly herdsmen and partly agricultural slaves working in chain gangs. In 104 the pattern was repeated. After some sporadic outbreaks, a major uprising of 2,000–6,000 men occurred at Heraclea. We do not hear specifically of any Roman slave owners in the first revolt but, in the second, P. Clonius, Vettius, and the Varii brothers are mentioned. In a contemporary inscription, a Roman magistrate operating in Italy and Sicily at the end of the first revolt claims to have rounded up and returned to their masters 917 runaway slaves of Italian owners.[326] After a slave rising in 133, 500 slaves were crucified at Minturnae and 4,000 at Sinuessa;[327] and of course we have the story of Ti. Gracchus passing through Etruria in the late 130s and being shocked at the land being cultivated by what he believed to be slaves.[328] Shortly afterwards, slaves are the first category of traded goods mentioned in the Customs Law of Asia in a section that dates to the 120s: '[ὑπὲρ σωμάτων ἀνδρείων ἢ θηλείων ἐκτὸς σωμάτων] παιδαρίων κορασίων μή τι πλεῖον τέλους ἑκάστης κεφαλῆς δηναρίων πέντε διδόναι ὀφειλέτω{ι}'[329] ([For male or female slaves except] male and female child [slaves] one is not obliged to pay as *telos* more than five denarii a head).[330]

These indications of large inflows of slaves into Italy during the second century suggest both that there was net growth in the servile population and that slave imports made a meaningful contribution to overall demographic expansion. But the problem again is data shortage, as we have no ancient accounts or estimates of their total numbers.[331] Anecdotal literary references to the numbers of slaves captured in war or traded by civilians, whilst conveying a sense of the magnitude of these inflows, are ultimately useless for establishing long-term totals. Ziolkowski has calculated from literary sources that the mean annual rate of wartime enslavement between 217 and 167 was 7,600.[332] But this includes the 150,000 Epirotes enslaved in 167 (many of whom may have stayed in Epirus), without which the mean drops to 4,700, and, more importantly, it would not pick up inflows mentioned in lost sources or, indeed, inflows that have not been recorded in any source. As far as the trading of slaves by civilians is concerned, the only number that we have is one provided by Strabo, who tells us that the island of Delos was capable of handling 10,000 slaves a day, a figure which could just be an inaccurate shorthand for 'a large number'.[333] Even if we knew the numbers of slaves imported into Italy, we do not know the impact of slave fertility, manumission, and mortality on the size of the servile population.

At the same time, Jongman has estimated that only about 100,000 chattel slaves were engaged in the cultivation of grapes and olives during the early years of the

325 Posidonius *FGrH* IIA 87 F. 108 = Diod. Sic. 34/5. 2. 2ff.; cf. Flor. 2. 7. 3ff.; second revolt: Diod. Sic. 36. 3ff.; Flor. 2. 7.10ff.

326 *ILLRP* 454; Lintott 1994*b*: 26–7.

327 Oros. 5. 9. 4.

328 Plut. *Ti. Gracch.* 8. 7.

329 Customs Law of Asia 12.

330 Trans. Crawford in Cottier et al. 2008: 31.

331 Several modern attempts have been made to guess or to estimate them, e.g. Brunt 1971*a*: 12–5 (3 m. under Augustus); Hopkins 1978: 68–9 (500,000 in 225 and 2 m. in 28 BC).

332 Ziolkowski 1986: 74–5.

333 Strabo, 14. 5. 2.

Principate, the implication being that slave numbers were even smaller in the second century.[334] Even if we allow for the likelihood, as Rosenstein argues, that slave ownership was widespread across Roman society, so that large numbers of slaves were employed on family farms of modest size, Jongman's finding, if correct, must lead to a radical revision downwards in the total number of slaves assumed to be present in the population of second-century mainland Italy.[335] If, even at its height, the extent of slave-based investment farming in Italy was far more limited than previously thought, then the implication must be that in the second century there would have been many fewer slave-staffed estates, even in central-western Italy. Moreover, they would probably have been smaller in size than previously imagined, a notion that fits with the more modestly sized slave-staffed farms that Cato describes and with the literary evidence for the size of elite estates discussed at the beginning of this chapter.[336] It then becomes increasingly difficult to maintain that the spread of rural slavery was a major factor in the deracination of the Roman peasantry.

Against this unpromising background, the most intelligent attempt to provide a quantitative reconstruction of the size of the servile population of Italy during the late Republic is that of Scheidel, who suggests that slave numbers were considerably smaller than is commonly portrayed.[337] Using a bottom-up model and building on Jongman's estimates for rural slavery, he arrives at a series of estimated ranges for different categories of slave which have some degree of credibility at least, based as they are on the likely demand for slaves in urban and rural environments.[338] His conclusions are that male and female slaves of all ages numbered between 130,000 and 270,000 in 200 BC and that by 1 BC this range had risen to between 850,000 and 1,860,000.[339] These numbers imply total imports of somewhere between 1.7 million and 4.4 million slaves (depending on attrition rates) over the course of the last two centuries BC. What makes Scheidel's model convincing is that it receives a degree of endorsement from the early modern Brazilian slave system. Like Rome, Brazil not only had relatively high rates of manumission, but also encompassed unhealthy cities and malarial rural areas. From 1550 to 1850, between 3.5 and 4.5 million African slaves were shipped to Brazil; yet its total slave population never exceeded 1.5 million at any given time. Brazil's ratio of imports to population size, of two or three to one, broadly matches Scheidel's range of estimates for Roman Italy.[340]

If then, *faute de mieux*, we use a rough average of Scheidel's estimates for the slave population of Italy and assume that there was steady growth between 200 and 1 BC (with a dip in slave numbers during the Second Punic War[341]), we arrive at the estimated numbers in Table 7.4 for the servile population between 225 and 28 BC.

[334] Jongman 2003*b*: 113–14.
[335] Rosenstein 2008: 5–7; Scheidel 2005.
[336] Cf. Rosenstein 2004: 17.
[337] Scheidel 2005.
[338] Scheidel 2005: 77; Lo Cascio 2010: 25 points to a number of drawbacks with Scheidel's approach.
[339] Scheidel 2005: 77, table 2, suggests that, in both 225 and 1 BC, approximately 60% of these slaves were urban.
[340] Scheidel 2005: 78.
[341] Livy, 28. 11. 8–9 mentions a shortage of slaves in 206.

Table 7.4. Italian slave population (estimated)

	225	200	150	100	50	28 BC
Slaves (000s)	250	190	490	800	1,200	1,400
% change		*-24%*	*158%*	*63%*	*50%*	*17%*

A DEMOGRAPHIC MODEL OF LATE REPUBLICAN ITALY

If we combine these estimated numbers for slaves with those for the free Italian population, which we assumed showed moderate growth, our preferred demographic model for the total population of mainland Italy would be as shown in Table 7.5. These estimates suggest that the total combined free and servile population of Italy grew by 57 per cent between 200 and 150 and by 18 per cent between 150 and 100; it contracted by 1 per cent between 100 and 50 BC. One of the principal demographic factors that affected the Italian population after the Gracchi was the resumption of mass military mortality, with large-scale warfare against the Cimbri, Teutones, and Ambrones in the last decade of the second century and among Italians in the 80s. At this point, a period of prolonged dislocation would have affected the free population of mainland Italy, with high levels of military mobilization and mortality, continuing urbanization, and increasing numbers of Roman citizens emigrating permanently outside Italy. If Brunt's estimates are accepted, adult male citizens living overseas numbered about 215,000 by 28 BC.[342] Meanwhile, the number of slaves continued to increase.

If we dig a bit deeper into these numbers, we can see that there were several factors shaping the Italian population, the enormous growth in slave numbers being the most obvious. But the movement of population to urban environments was also significant. We assume, with Scheidel, that the population of Rome grew from 150,000 to 375,000 (+150 per cent) in the second century BC, and from 375,000 to 600,000 (+ 60 per cent) in the first half of the first century BC, and that the other Italian cities grew from 300,000 to 450,000 to 600,000 over the same period.[343] If the numbers for slaves and urban dwellers in Table 7.6 are

Table 7.5. Italian total population (estimated)

	225	200	150	100	50	28 BC
Free population (000s)	3,900	3,002	4,533	5,110	4,645	4,063
% change		*-22%*	*51%*	*13%*	*-9%*	*-13%*
Slaves (000s)	250	190	490	800	1,200	1,400
% change		*-24%*	*158%*	*63%*	*50%*	*17%*
TOTAL (000s)	4,150	3,192	5,023	5,910	5,845	5,463
% change		*-23%*	*57%*	*18%*	*-1%*	*-7%*

342 Brunt 1971*a*: 263. Crawford (2008: 640) argues that there was a much higher percentage of Roman citizens living overseas after 90 (maybe as much as 50%) than either Frank (10–20%) or Brunt (7.5%) suggests.

343 Scheidel 2007: 327; cf. De Ligt 2004: 738 and Brunt 1971*a*, who estimated about 375,000 inhabitants of Rome in 130 BC.

Table 7.6. Italian population breakdown (estimated)[344]

	200	150	100	50 BC
Slaves (000s)	190	490	800	1,200
Free population (000s)				
Urban	450	700	825	1,200
Rural	2,552	3,833	4,285	3,445
TOTAL (000s)	3,192	5,023	5,910	5,845
Slaves	6%	10%	14%	21%
Free population				
Urban	14%	14%	14%	20%
Rural	80%	76%	72%	59%
TOTAL	100%	100%	100%	100%

vaguely correct, there was a significant fall in the free rural population in the first half of the first century.

We may, then, summarize demographic developments in Italy between the Second Punic War and the Gracchi as follows. By the end of that war, the population of Italy must have fallen significantly from its pre-war levels with, in particular, the number of adult male Romans and other allies having been severely reduced by military losses. However, after 200, mobilization rates fell from their earlier record levels and military attrition would have diminished considerably, while a programme of colonization provided a 'new deal' for impoverished peasants. As a result, the free population would have rapidly returned to more normal levels, although its rate of growth would probably have been constrained by the higher rates of disease found in the urban environments to which some of the population was gradually moving, and by a succession of epidemics in 187, 182–180, 176–175, 174, and 165.[345] In central-western Italy specifically, the growth of the free population in the first decades of the second century was mitigated somewhat by the establishment of colonies in the periphery, especially in Cisalpine Gaul. We assume, with de Ligt, that the free population continued to grow after 163 (only two further epidemics are recorded over the next century in 142 and in 87), but not on the scale proposed by the high counters. The combination of this continued growth in the free population, the end of the policy of colonization (which had removed people from central Italy to the periphery), increased competition for land (which was most severe in central-western Italy), the growing importance of commercial agriculture, high levels of slave imports, and less lucrative wars all conspired to produce the issues that the Gracchi tried to address. As de Ligt neatly summarizes it: 'The Gracchan land reforms reflect a situation in which large landowners had limited access to free labour and in which free labourers had limited access to the kind of land they preferred.'[346]

[344] Cf. De Ligt 2012: 190, table 4.3.

[345] References at Wiseman 1969: 74 n. 125.

[346] De Ligt 2012: 280.

PRIVATIZATION

With the benefit of hindsight, we can see that what the Gracchi started was a process of denationalization and privatization, with the period from 133 to 111 being crucial in the transformation of arable *ager publicus* into private land. As Roselaar has noted, 'the Gracchi were the first to act on the notion that public land was not a suitable system of landholding'.[347]

Appian states that plots of *ager publicus* allocated to the poor under Ti. Gracchus' law could not be sold and Plutarch adds that the plots assigned by his brother, C. Gracchus, were liable to rent.[348] It seems likely, therefore, that the Gracchan allotments that were granted to the poor became private on condition that a rent was paid on them and that they became *ager privatus vectigalisque* as a result. This was a legal construction that allowed the state to retain some measure of control over the assigned land, while granting to the Gracchan settlers leasehold ownership of 500-*iugera* plots (with the additional amount for sons).[349] On the other hand, those who had held arable *ager occupatorius* before 133 (the *veteres possessores*) were probably granted ownership over their existing plots on a freehold basis, but again of course only up to the maximum size of 500 *iugera* (and the additional amount for children). It is also probable that sale of the plots of the *veteres possessores*, like those of the new Gracchan settlers, was forbidden, although the plots of both categories of landholders were heritable.[350]

The three post-Gracchan agrarian laws, which Appian goes on to summarize, were further steps in this gradual privatization process, although their precise chronology is much disputed.[351] According to Appian, the first law allowed occupiers of *ager publicus* (certainly the Gracchan settlers and perhaps the *veteres possessores* too) to sell the land they held. The second law, generally identified with a *lex Thoria*, mentioned scathingly by Cicero as a 'faulty and useless law', and dated by some to about 118, stopped any further distributions of public land and made occupied land the property of its current holders on payment of a rent.[352] This law presumably turned the freehold property of the *veteres possessores* into *ager privatus vectigalisque*, so effectively into leasehold land. Finally, the third law which Appian mentions (and which is probably to be identified with the *lex agraria* of 111) reversed this process and abolished this rent. The first eleven lines of the *lex agraria* suggest that all holdings of land within the 500-*iugera* limit were henceforth to be recognized as private.

So, by the end of the penultimate decade of the second century, most of what had once been arable *ager publicus* in Italy had been privatized or was controlled by some town, with the main exception being the *Ager Campanus*. *Ager*

[347] Roselaar 2010: 288. [348] App. *B. Civ.* 1.10; Plut. *C. Gracch.* 9.2.

[349] Rathbone 2003: 165; Roselaar 2010: 233–7.

[350] There is debate over the exact legal position after 133 of the holdings of the *veteres possessores*; see Roselaar 2010: 236.

[351] App. *B. Civ.* 1. 27. In addition to the problem of chronology, the question of which one of the three laws should be identified with the *lex agraria* of 111 is still in dispute —see Roselaar 2010: 260–71 for the main arguments and Rathbone 2003: 164–6 for an alternative identification and a different chronology from the ones given here. For the purposes of this chapter, it is of little importance which theory is the more likely to be correct.

[352] Cic. *Brut.* 136.

scripturarius was not subject to the privatization process. What was left of the arable *ager occupatorius* was privatized under Sulla, when land was needed for distribution to military veterans. After this period we never hear of *ager occupatorius* again. The only arable public land still available was the *ager censorius* in Campania, which was eventually privatized in 59 BC.[353]

Who were the winners and losers from this process of privatization and what was the impact on the elite? Roselaar believes that insecurity of possession limited investments in land at precisely the time when the growth of the market for agricultural products and the increase in interregional trade would have made them highly profitable.[354] This is unlikely. The lack of anything other than ad hoc administration on *ager occupatorius* before the Gracchi meant that, in general, the occupiers could hold land uninterruptedly for a number of years. In any case, Appian implies that most *possessores* had not expected to be dispossessed after such a long time and had invested anyway.[355]

The big gainers were of course the Roman peasantry. Within twenty-two years of Ti. Gracchus' reform, *veteres possessores* and Gracchan settlers had acquired full ownership of a plot of 500 *iugera*, or 1,000 *iugera* if they had two children. But it should also be remembered that this did not solve everything and that problems in the countryside continued into the next century. In fact Ti. Gracchus' land law was one of about twenty attempts made in the course of the next hundred years to solve agrarian problems by law and by the redistribution of land to the poor.[356]

To an extent, the Roman elite lost out as a result of the Gracchan reforms, as is clear from the backlash they prompted.[357] But the reforms would have directly affected only those of the wealthy who, before 133, had held large areas of *ager occupatorius* above the 500-*iugera* limit in southern Italy or elsewhere in the peripheral regions, where the large-scale redistribution by the Gracchan commissioners of the still available public land primarily occurred. After all, it was, as we have seen, the suitably located private land of small farmers in central-western Italy that the rich were principally interested in acquiring, not public land.

The main losers, therefore, were the Italian allies, since it is clear that much of the public land that was assigned after 133 lay within the boundaries of Latin and allied states. The *lex agraria* of 111 sums up the Gracchan allocations as being 'to Roman citizens by lot' and this would have meant that many non-Romans, both peasants and members of the local elites, would, under the Gracchan and subsequent legislation, have been deprived of land that they had long occupied as *possessores* before 133, albeit with no legal title or rights of ownership. This process would have had a serious impact on the relationship between the Romans and the Italians and it would have been a direct cause of the Social War a few decades later.[358]

353 Roselaar 2010: 136, 297. 354 Roselaar 2010: 119.

355 App. *B. Civ.* 1. 10. 356 Brunt 1988: 240; Hopkins 1978: 59.

357 Kron (2008: 110) states that 'the senatorial elite recognized the serious challenge which a new model of politics based on the aggressive use of tribunician legislation represented and when defeated through the normal mechanisms of government chose to use violence to reassert their control'. But economic motives must also have played a part in the elite's response.

358 Rathbone 2003: 160; Roselaar (2010: 228) is more circumspect on this point, suggesting that allies could also have profited from these regulations by being granted 500-*iugera* plots.

CONCLUSION

Most of the evidence for large-scale investment in land by the Roman elite comes from later periods and we must be wary of casual retrojections. Such literary evidence as does exist for landownership by the elite during the second century suggests that landholdings were confined to a limited area in central-western Italy and points to the existence of a greater number of small and medium-sized estates than in the first century, when they tended to be larger. There is very little sign of agricultural exploitation in the provinces by the Roman elite outside Sicily before the end of the second century, although it is possible that this lack of evidence is merely a result of the paucity of our sources, in particular the lack of a Cicero. The archaeological evidence, such as it is, is too scarce to have any conclusive bearing on the question of evolving patterns of land tenure in the second century, but the changing pattern of settlement suggests that the process of change was a gradual one, rather than a single dramatic displacement of the small farmer by elite landowners. Larger villas appeared intermittently over the course of a century. Settefinestre is a useful case in point. Located precisely in the region that has produced the most amphora evidence for the export of wine, the villa was not built before the second quarter of the first century and was only in its prime by the second half of that century. But it is likely that the building of the villa took place only several decades after the start of slave-based production, on the proceeds of successful farming. Survey evidence also suggests that the spread of very large estates that absorbed their neighbours may well have been limited to the prime coastal and river valley areas, as the pattern of inland sites shows a much stronger survival of smaller sites.

Cato's *De Agricultura* was not a revolutionary tract but it does mark the start of a period of more intensive agricultural exploitation by the Roman elite. The work stands at the beginning of a significant expansion in the export of wine, as represented by Dressel 1 amphorae. Although precise dating is difficult, the archaeological record indicates a large trade along the south coast of Gaul with about two and a half times as many cargoes of these Dressel 1 amphorae in the period between about 150 and 1 BC as cargoes of Graeco-Italic amphorae in the equivalent preceding period (about 300–150). The available evidence suggests that this change was primarily a response to the development of a particular market, a trade in wine principally to Gaul. A similar evidentiary issue prevents us from saying anything meaningful about a whole range of other commodities, because they were most probably transported overseas (if they were so transported) in containers that were themselves made of perishable materials such as wicker baskets and sacks. It could be that it was not just wine and olive oil that were being exported from Italy on a large and growing scale, but other agricultural commodities as well. It is worth emphasizing again that we would not know about the growth in the trade in wine with the western Mediterranean during the second century, were it not for the increasing number of amphora finds in the last fifty years or so. Only one ancient author, Diodorus, mentions the trade, and his account seems to refer to the late first century. Although Cato describes agricultural specialization and the growing of cash crops in his treatise, he makes no mention of the ultimate destinations of the resulting products. But it is probable that Rome and other rapidly developing urban centres also provided important markets for perishable food products.

Cato's work provides the first literary evidence for investment farming by absentee landlords. Probably modelled on Greek farms in Magna Graecia and Sicily and on Carthaginian plantation estates, the villa system must have been introduced into the Roman world in the second half of the third century and have spread during the second century to become the most rational system of agricultural exploitation. Throughout Cato's work there is an unmistakable interest in obtaining the best returns and spending as little as possible. A concern for profit predominates and this type of investment farming is viewed exclusively as a financial venture. Cato emphasizes that the absentee landowner whose property he describes must seek to sell his produce. In comparing alternative sources of income, Cato naturally thought of balancing greater security against the possibility of greater returns, preferring the former. Income from agriculture is *stabilissimus*. This is an economic consideration and there are no grounds for doubting the financial awareness of Roman proprietors. Roman agriculture in general, like other sectors of the ancient economy, is often characterized as technologically underdeveloped, especially when compared to later periods. But there were some significant advances. By the second century, capital investment in plant to maximize returns seems to lie behind the adoption of a number of these new technologies, devices, and techniques, in particular extensive hydraulic infrastructures to support intensive farming, water-lifting and water-powered machines, more sophisticated strategies for food production, and more efficient presses to process grain, wine, and oil. Levels of land productivity in second-century Roman Italy were much higher than previously thought.

Appian's and Plutarch's accounts of the agrarian crisis of 133 suggest that the issue that the Gracchi tried to address was a perceived decline in the citizen peasant population, which they and others connected with the growth of slave-staffed estates. However, as Cato makes clear, the villa system also required a large seasonal labour force and a population of free peasants was the only possible source to supply this demand. The size of the population of mainland Italy during the late Republic is still open to dispute and the trench warfare (as Crawford has termed it[359]) between the 'high counters' and 'low counters' seems set to continue. But the indications are that, rather than there being a demographic decline, there was moderate endogenous growth in the free Italian population during the three decades leading up the Gracchan crisis. There was also an increase in the number of slaves used in the countryside, although this increase is often exaggerated. At the same time, the availability of land in Latium, Etruria, and Campania (the principal areas in which the villa system seems to have operated) was reduced, during and shortly after the Second Punic War, by a process of privatization of the *ager publicus* located there. This meant that, by the 130s, what had once been public land in these areas was actually held on a freehold or leasehold basis by members of the Roman elite and was, therefore, not available for distribution by the Roman state. The lack of *ager publicus* in central-western Italy also meant, as Rathbone suggests, that 'the smallholder declined, not because

[359] s.v. 'Population—Roman' in *OCD*[4].

the rich monopolised public land but because [the smallholders] themselves tended to sell their allotments'.[360] This combination of shortage of land and growth in population may have been sufficient to cause an increasing number of Roman citizens to fall below the property census limit for military service. The solution of the Gracchi was to assign land on a freehold basis to *veteres possessores* and on a leasehold basis to the poor. The effect of this policy was that, by 125, there had been a sharp increase in the number of Roman citizens registering for the census. A series of further laws followed, which meant that by the last decade of the second century, the vast bulk of arable land in mainland Italy was in private hands. If the agrarian crisis was at heart about property rights and security of possession, the position of the Roman elite was largely unchanged at the end of the process of agrarian reform, despite the sabre-rattling and political violence. Some members of the elite may have lost out if, before 133, they had held land above the 500-*iugera* limit on *ager occupatorius* in the peripheral regions of Italy. But otherwise their ownership of land in the economically important region of central-western Italy would have been unaffected. The same was not true of the Italian allies who lost large amounts of land on the *ager occupatorius* located in their territories to the Gracchan settlers.

In summary, the indications are that, in the middle of the second century, there was an inflection point in the intensity of agricultural exploitation in central-western Italy by the Roman elite. At the same time, the peasant population appears to have suffered a fall in its standard of living, although it slowly recovered as a result of the privatization of the land assigned to it under the Gracchan reforms. It is no coincidence that the start of this increased elite activity appears to follow the vast influx of capital in the form of booty, indemnities, and revenues from the Spanish mines and that it coincides with the destruction of Carthage and of Corinth and the development of an eastern trade through Delos in slaves and luxury goods, which we shall discuss in the next chapter. Members of the Roman elite were becoming richer. They had acquired ownership of the most economically productive land in Italy, close to the expanding market of Rome and to the ports from which they could export their wine and olive oil to the western Mediterranean. They had also gained the means to invest in a more profitable system of agricultural production.

[360] Rathbone 2003: 136; Roselaar 2010: 201.

8

Trade, Capital, and Interconnected Markets

ἔμπορε, κατάπλευσον, ἐξελοῦ, πάντα πέπραται[1]

INTRODUCTION

We ended Chapter 4 with the Romans having established a method for exploiting their recently acquired province of Asia. We shall end the present chapter with the massacre by Mithradates VI of Pontus in 88, when, according to one source, eighty thousand Roman citizens, 'scattered among the cities of Asia for the sake of business', were killed.[2] Even if we allow for exaggeration, it appears that the number of Romans (seemingly many of them businessmen) who were killed in Asia was large. Who were they and what were they doing there?

Hopkins's view was that the main source of new wealth for the Roman elite during the late Republic was provincial government. Income from the empire flowed into the purses of the privileged because of the opportunity that provincial government gave for peculation and extortion.[3] Roman *equites*, on the other hand, 'collected taxes and administrative charges, amenably lent provincials money with which to pay their taxes, at a suitable rate of interest; and in case of non-payment foreclosed on the mortgages. In this way, among others, Roman citizens became the owners of large estates in the provinces and the conquering elite of the Romans gradually acquired wealth commensurate with their conquest of the Mediterranean basin.'[4]

While the activities of Verres and others tend to support the Hopkins view of senatorial enrichment, at least in the 70s, and the accounts of Plutarch and Appian support his theory of publican and equestrian enrichment, at least in the 80s, there is limited evidence for either before 88. We must look elsewhere for the activities that increased the wealth of the equestrian and senatorial classes during the final quarter of the second century. We have already mentioned that Frank's view was that the Gracchan recapture of the *ager publicus* in Italy prompted Romans to make provincial investments and that the official activities of the *publicani* opened

[1] Proverb quoted by Strabo (14. 5. 2) in connection with the slave trade of Delos: 'Merchant, sail in, unload your ship, everything has been sold'.

[2] Val. Max. 9. 2 ext. 3: 'in Asia per urbes negotiandi gratia dispersa'; Brunt 1971*a*: 224–7 discusses the probable exaggeration of the number killed.

[3] Hopkins 1978: 41. [4] Hopkins 1978: 47.

up the ways and means for doing this.[5] While this is a plausible explanation, it is not the whole story and the accounts of both Frank and Hopkins underestimate the importance of trade and the availability of a liquid stock of financial capital in the wealth creation process. Others have espoused a similar view to this. Rauh, for example, believes, first, that Roman trade expanded in the wake of Roman military imperialism and, secondly, that the volume of trade that occurred in the Mediterranean between 167 and 67 was the largest ever experienced in the ancient world.[6] However, he places no emphasis whatsoever on what we believe to have been a crucially important factor: the availability of financial capital.

Spufford, in *Money and its Use in Medieval Europe*, attributes the commercial revolution of the thirteenth century AD to 'the link between silver-mining and the development of trade and industry'.[7] In the thirteenth century, 'central European silver moved from newly developed mining areas, such as Bohemia, Meissen and Harz, through Flanders and the Champagne Fairs to Genoa, Florence, Pisa and Venice and on, via Alexandria, to the eastern Mediterranean and, via Constantinople and the Crimea, to Cathay'.[8] In the other direction came 'luxury goods, items such as clothing and furnishings from Flanders and Tuscany; pepper and spices from Asia; silks from Constantinople and China. The increase in demand for luxury goods, backed up by the ready availability of large amounts of silver specie, brought about an enormous quantitative change in the volume of international trade.'[9] This also happened in sixteenth-century AD Europe after the arrival of vast amounts of bullion from the New World. Trade with the Baltic and the Orient expanded greatly, financed largely by exports of European silver.[10]

A similar development seems to have taken place in the Mediterranean in the second century BC. The indemnities and booty taken by the Romans from the end of the Second Punic War onwards, together with the capture of the silver mines of Spain and Macedonia and their subsequent development, have been discussed in Chs. 2 and 3 as has, in Chs. 5 and 6, a probable large increase in the Roman money supply that occurred after 150. Of the near 46,000 talents of plunder (equivalent to 1,050 tonnes of silver) that arrived at Rome in the fifty years that followed the Second Punic War, most of the indemnities and much of the booty came from the enormously wealthy Hellenistic East. It is impossible to assess the size of the Hellenistic stock of bullion or the significance of the output of mines in the areas under the control of Hellenistic monarchs. Gold and silver were mined in Greece, Macedonia, Thrace, Anatolia, Medea, and Egypt, but we have no numbers for output.[11] One of the few details we have is that Alexander the Great had, by 330, captured, mainly from the Persian treasuries in Mesopotamia, a total of 180,000 talents, the equivalent of 4,169 tonnes of silver.[12] But the important point here is that this was not just a process of reshuffling the cards, as riches were redistributed from east to west. Plunder brought immobilized and sequestered wealth, such as

[5] Frank 1933: 388; see this volume p. 141.
[6] Rauh 2003: 201. [7] Spufford 1988: 134.
[8] Spufford 1988: 137, 154; the 'signature' of this sudden increase in medieval silver production is visible in the rates of lead deposition found in Sweden, Greenland, Spain, and Switzerland (see Fig. 3.1.).
[9] Spufford 1988: 251. [10] Goldstone 1984: 1126. [11] Shepherd 1993.
[12] Diod. Sic. 17. 80. 3; Strabo, 15. 3. 9; Just. *Epit.* 12. 1. 1; cf. de Callataÿ 1989: 260–4.

state reserves and temple treasures, into circulation again and put them to productive use.

Just as the commercial revolutions of the thirteenth and sixteenth centuries AD seem to have been driven by trade, so the evidence for an increase in trade in the Roman world in the second half of the second century BC is also very compelling. We discussed in the previous chapter the export of central Italian wine to western Europe. The trade that developed in the eastern Mediterranean, which we shall now examine, was equally striking. Strabo relates that, between the years 166 and 87, the island of Delos was transformed into the most important *emporium* in the eastern Mediterranean and more specifically into the centre of a trade in slaves and luxury goods.[13] We can deduce from epigraphic evidence that *negotiatores* ('merchants' or 'businessmen') and *trapezitai* ('bankers') from numerous points in the Mediterranean installed themselves on Delos and that a large cosmopolitan community developed.

CICERO

As we have repeatedly mentioned, one major problem we immediately face in attempting to trace the development of the Roman private sector during the second half of the second century and the beginning of the first century is that the vast bulk of the source evidence for wealth creation in the Roman world during the Republican period comes from the years 70 to 40, thanks to the Ciceronian corpus, in particular his letters, and that no equivalent source is available for our period. As Hatzfield commented in 1919: 'Far from being surprised by finding a quantity of [sc. epigraphic] texts in Asia relating to *Romaioi*, on the contrary one must deplore the fact that we possess so little of them and resign oneself to the fact that they give us only an insufficient idea of the number of *negotiatores* and of their activity.'[14]

This difficulty has been justifiably highlighted, for example by Kallet-Marx, who, in the context of the province of Asia, argues that the consequences of its creation as a Roman province have been largely overvalued by historians and that the real starting point of control and exploitation of the province was the re-establishment of Roman control by Sulla, followed by its extension under Lucullus and Pompey.[15] Ferrary, on the other hand, sees a reasonably steady progression from the establishment of the Asian province to the time of Cicero. He believes that the presence of a magistrate in the province was a guarantee of security and also made it possible (for Romans, but also for Latins and indeed Italians) to find, on the spot, a competent magistrate to regulate disputes.[16] Be that as it may, we possess truly precise and abundant information only for the time of Cicero and the problem is to decide what it is legitimate to infer about private wealth creation for the decades between the establishment of the province of Asia and the Mithradatic crisis.

[13] Strabo, 10. 5. 2. [14] Hatzfeld 1919: 46.
[15] Kallet-Marx 1995*a*: 125–60. [16] Ferrary 2001, 2002.

There are two distinctive features of the world of Cicero between 70 and 40 that are relevant to this issue: the presence of Roman businessmen in the provinces and the availability of financial capital.

NEGOTIATORES IN THE 60s AND 50s

Negotiatores were merchants who engaged in overseas *negotia*, a wide term covering activities integral to trade and business. Duncan-Jones has argued that unlike, say, Florentine society in the Renaissance, Roman society remained one with heavy prejudices against trade and traders. He believes that a society in which senators were forbidden to own large ships and shopkeepers were admitted to the town council only if *honesti viri* were in short supply was one that tried hard to separate involvement in trade from high social position.[17] But Cato, an upholder of traditional senatorial values, said nothing whatever in his *De Agricultura* about the disreputability of *mercatura*, talking only of its profitability and its risks.[18] Furthermore, Nepos says that it was not from indolence but from conviction (*iudicio*) that Cicero's friend T. Pomponius Atticus held aloof from the affairs of state ('fugisse rei publicae procurationem'), making clear that the reason for Atticus' choice not to pursue public office was his own preference rather than possible prejudice against him because of his position as a businessman.[19]

In the 60s and 50s Roman *negotiatores* were everywhere. Cicero was constantly asked to write letters of introduction to provincial governors in favour of businessmen operating in the provinces.[20] In Cilicia there were enough Romans to provide a respectable contingent in the army; in Cyprus enough to require a few days' special sitting of the law court.[21] Caesar speaks repeatedly of Roman merchants in Gaul and even undertakes to clear an Alpine pass for them.[22] In Spain Varro found it possible to levy a war contribution of HS 28 m. (1,167 talents) on citizens alone.[23] Sicily was of course the nearest and oldest of the provinces and many Romans were in business there.[24] In Africa, Cicero mentions C. Anicius, T. Pinarius, Q. Turius and Sex. Aufidius as having *negotia* there, as did the father of M. Caelius Rufus, an eminent *eques*.[25] In Greece there are again many references to *negotiatores*. M. Mindius was in business in Elis and T. Manlius at Thespiae.[26] Roman *publicani*, *negotiatores*, *faeneratores* and *mercatores* (publicans, businessmen, lenders, and merchants) are recorded in distant

[17] Duncan-Jones 1990: 46.

[18] Cato, *Agr. praef.* 3: 'Mercatorem autem strenuum studiosumque rei quaerendae existimo, verum et supra dixi, periculosum et calamitosum' (the merchant, however, I consider to be an energetic man and one bent on making money; but, as I said before, it is a dangerous career and one liable to disaster); cf. D'Arms 1981 *passim*.

[19] Nep. *Att.* 15. 3; Cic. *Att.* 13. 3. 1.

[20] Frank 1933: 388.

[21] Cic. *Att.* 5. 18. 2, 5. 21. 6.

[22] Caes. *B. Gall.* 3. 1, 7. 3, 7. 55.

[23] Caes. *B. Civ.* 2. 18.

[24] e.g. Cic. *II Verr.* 2. 153: 'qui Syracusis, qui Agrigenti, qui Panhormi, qui Lilybaei negotiantur'; cf. Cic. *II Verr.* 2. 31, 2. 69, 2. 71, 3. 36, 3. 55, 3. 60, 3. 61, 3. 93, 3. 97, 4. 37, 4. 42, 4. 46, 5. 161; Cic. *Fam.* 13. 33.

[25] Cic. *Fam.*12. 21, 24, 26, 27; Cic. *Cael.* 73.

[26] Cic. *Fam.* 13. 26, 13. 22.

regions such as Bithynia-Pontus and Syria.[27] C. Rabirius Curtius Postumus, the agent of Pompey who assumed control of the finances of Egypt in 58, 'was very active in the public arena, conducting a great deal of business, for he possessed considerable shares in the publican companies' (magnas partes habuit publicorum).[28] Rabirius also lent money throughout the Mediterranean, employed a freedman agent at Ephesus and Naxos, engaged in overseas commerce with his own cargo fleet (importing paper, linen, and glass from Egypt), and produced wine and oil for export on his own estates.[29]

But Asia Minor appears to have become a favourite area for elite Roman overseas investment. Specific references to Romans who are 'in business in Asia' or in given cities, such as Pergamum, Smyrna, Tralles, and Lampsacus, are numerous.[30] Caerellia, a wealthy female acquaintance of Cicero's, had *res, nomina, possessiones* in Asia.[31] C. Malleolus had lent money there while serving as a quaestor: 'praeterea pecunias occuparat apud populos et syngraphas fecerat' (he had moreover invested money locally and had entered into contracts).[32] Curtius Mithres, a freedman of Rabirius, lived at Ephesus. Laenius Flaccus of Brundisium had business interests in Bithynia as well as Cilicia. Aulus Trebonius had several agents operating in several parts of Cilicia.[33] Others with interests in Asia include Marcillus, P. Messienus, L. Nostius, L. Oppius, and Q. Selicius.[34] Verres, while quaestor of Dollabella, made investments in Asia.[35] T. Aufidius, who went on to be the governor of Asia, probably in 65, had previously had a small share in a *societas publicanorum* operating in Asia.[36] C. Falcidius, referred to in the *Pro Flacco* of 59, had bought the tithes of Tralles for HS 900,000 (38 talents).[37] In the same speech, C. Appuleius Decianus is mentioned as having had business in Asia since 85 and estates in Apollonis.[38] In a letter of 51 or 50, Cicero recommends a friend of his, L. Genucilius Curvus, who has *negotia* (businesses) in the area of the Hellespont and holds, in the territory of Parium on the Propontis, land 'quod semper obtinuit sine ulla controversia'(!)[39] In the 40s L. Egnatius Rufus has *negotia* in Asia (having been a procurator there in 58).[40]

27 Bithynia: App. *Mith.* 75; Caes. *B. Civ.* 3. 103. Syria: Cic. *Dom.* 60; Cic. *Sest.* 93; Cic. *Prov. cons.* 9–10; Cic. *Pis.* 41, 48; Cic. *Q. Fr.* 2. 11. 2; 2. 12. 1; 3. 2. 2; Dio Cass. 39. 55. 5.

28 Cic. *Rab. Post.* 4; Malmendier 2005 adduces this passage as part of her argument that Romans owned and traded shares in *societates publicanorum*.

29 Cic. *Rab. Post.*; Cic. *Fam.* 13. 69. 1. For the multiple *negotia* of Rabirius, see Wiseman 1971: 199; Shatzman 1975: 100 n. 4, 395–6; D'Arms 1980: 28. In this context it is also interesting to note Nep. *Att.* 6. 4, which states that Atticus was never involved in a *societas publicanorum* either as a *praes* or as a *manceps*. As we can see from the case of Rabirius, there were some *negotiatores* and financiers who were involved with *societates publicanorum*—a warning that we should not be too quick to overcategorize the business interests of *equites* at this time.

30 e.g. Cic. *Deiot.* 26; Cic. *Flac.* 71; Romans lending money to Greeks in Lampsacus when Verres was in Asia: 'nonnulli togati creditores Graecorum' (Cic. *II Verr.* 1. 73, 74).

31 Cic. *Fam.* 13. 72. 1: 'money, accounts, physical property'.

32 Cic. *II Verr.* 1. 91; we may note in passing that the word *syngrapha* was so well known that it could be used in a Latin speech at Rome. For the possible meanings of the word, see Hollander 2007: 44–8.

33 Curtius: Cic. *Fam.* 13. 69; Flaccus: Cic. *Fam.* 13. 63; Trebonius: Cic. *Fam.* 1. 3.

34 Cic. *Fam.* 13. 54, 13. 51, 13. 46, 13. 43, 1. 5. 4.

35 Cic. *II Verr.* 1. 91.

36 Val. Max. 6. 9. 7: 'T. Aufidius, cum Asiatici publici exiguam admodum particulam habuisset, postea totam Asiam proconsulari imperio obtinuit.'

37 Cic. *Flac.* 91.

38 Cic. *Flac.* 70, 80.

39 Cic. *Fam.* 13. 53.

40 Cic. *Fam.* 13. 45, 73–4.

AVAILABILITY OF FINANCIAL CAPITAL IN THE 60s AND 50s

In the 60s and 50s it is clear not only that there were some very wealthy individuals around, but that there was a liquid and sophisticated market for lending and borrowing money on a very significant scale.

We have a few casual statements about the sizes of individual estates that might be of some value in determining what was considered wealth. M. Licinius Crassus, generally supposed to be the wealthiest Roman of his day (after Sulla, who had built up a large fortune by confiscation), had at one time property estimated to be worth HS 200 m. (8,333 talents).[41] He valued his property in 55 at 7,100 talents.[42] Pompey's fortune was about the same. His property, when confiscated, was sold for about HS 200 m. (8,333 talents); and his son was offered back a part of it, worth HS 70 m. (2,916 talents), by the senate in 39 BC.[43] These are the largest fortunes reported for any Romans of the Republic. By comparison, the two largest fortunes in private hands in the first century AD were HS 400 m. (16,666 talents). Duncan-Jones suggests that each of these last two fortunes had a value in real terms of 0.75 m.–1.5 m. tonnes of wheat (assuming a range of wheat prices from HS 1.75 to HS 3.5 per modius); and on the same basis we can calculate the fortunes of Crassus and Pompey as being in the region of 0.38 m.–0.75 m. tonnes of wheat. By comparison, the largest private fortunes in England between the mid-sixteenth and mid-seventeenth centuries AD appear to have been equivalent to only 0.021 m.–0.042 m. tonnes of wheat.[44]

Clodius' mansion was worth HS 14.8 m. (616 talents) and the Tusculan villa of Scaurus HS 30 m. (1,250 talents).[45] Demetrius, a Syrian from Gadara, who was probably taken prisoner by Pompey but was quickly made a Roman citizen to become one of Pompey's most reliable financial agents, left property worth 4,000 talents.[46] Lucullus paid 2.5 m. drachmas (416 talents) for his estate at Baiae.[47] On the other hand, one indication of increasing wealth in the late Republic is that the finest house in the city of Rome in 78, that of Lepidus, was said, thirty-five years later, not to have been in the top one hundred.[48]

The scale of liabilities was equally impressive. The world of Cicero shows lending and borrowing of money to be an integral part of the economic activities of the elite. The wealth of Apollonius of Panhormus, Cicero's *amicus atque hospes* (friend and host) in Sicily, comprised *familia, pecus, villae, pecuniae creditae* (slaves, livestock, farms, and loans).[49] We can compare Seneca's depiction a century later of lending out money as being one of the features of 'a man of means': 'familiam formosam habet et domum pulchrum, multum serit, multum fenerat'[50] (he has a handsome collection of servants, a beautiful house, a lot of land

[41] Plin. *HN* 33. 134; Cic. *Parad.* 49. [42] Plut. *Crass.* 2. 2. [43] Dio Cass. 48. 36. 5.

[44] Duncan-Jones 1974: 4 n. 8: 'Wheat equivalents are no more than an approximate index of real wealth, since wheat prices may fluctuate substantially. But they offer a much better basis for comparisons between different societies than any monetary equations.' For a lengthier discussion of wheat prices and levels of wealth in the late Republic, see Ch. 11.

[45] Plin. *HN* 36. 103; 36. 115. [46] Plut. *Pomp.* 2. 4.

[47] Plut. *Mar.* 34; Frontin. *Aq.* 1. 5, 8, 10. [48] Plin. *HN* 36. 109; Hopkins 1978: 49.

[49] Cic. *II Verr.* 5. 20. [50] Sen. *Ep.* 41. 7.

under cultivation, and a lot of money out at interest) and Pliny the Younger's statement, in the same period, that he invests part of his funds outside landed estates in the form of loans: *aliquid tamen fenero*.[51] Indeed Shatzman lists twenty-five senators from the late Republic who are known from literary evidence to have engaged in lending money.[52] It is clear that a number of these *faeneratores* (moneylenders) commanded considerable resources.[53] At one point in the 60s, Julius Caesar was said to have had borrowings of 1,300 talents.[54] At the time of the Catilinarian Conspiracy, Q. Considius provided a loan of HS 15 m. (625 talents), possibly on behalf of a syndicate of friends, relatives, and business associates.[55] Moreover, the fact that Cicero refers in his letters to moneylending so frequently suggests that there was little or no stigma attached. Indeed the complicated nature of Cicero's finances and property is striking. Throughout his life Cicero was borrowing money and lending surplus funds and, in particular, between 46 and 43 he was the debtor and creditor of many people at the same time.[56]

But Romans did not lend only to their fellow-citizens. They also advanced money to kings. In 88, Nicomedes III of Bithynia, who agreed to pay M. Aquillius for restoring him to the throne, also borrowed money from some of Aquillius' companions.[57] By the middle of the first century, M. Brutus was lending money to Ariobarzanes, the king of Cappadocia and also to the Cypriot city of Salamis.[58] Pompey had also lent money to Ariobarzanes and the interest alone ran to 400 talents per annum.[59] King Ptolemy Auletes owed 10,000 talents to Romans on debts and recent services.[60]

Romans were also lending money to cities in the East. When, in 84, Sulla imposed an indemnity of 20,000 talents on those cities of Asia that had taken the side of Mithradates, Roman moneylenders took advantage of the situation: they lent the funds that were required to pay the indemnity, charged the cities very high interest, and forced them to mortgage much of their public property.[61] Because of the effect of compounding, this loan had grown to 120,000 talents in fourteen years and created unprecedented levels of financial distress. In the end, in the winter of 71/70, Lucullus had to bring in measures to mitigate the situation.[62] But this was not an isolated example. Even though abuses were sufficiently flagrant for a *lex Gabinia* of 67 or 58 to forbid the lending at interest to ambassadors of provincial cities or of friendly kings, a few years later we find that individual Romans are still lending to Greek cities.[63] In the mid 50s, M. Cluvius of Puteoli was lending money to a number of communities in Asia Minor: Alabanda, Mylasa, Caunus, Bargylia, and Heraclea in Caria.[64] The city of Nicaea in Bithynia owed T. Pinnius about HS 8 m. (333 talents).[65] In 60, Castricius had recently collected a debt from Tralles in Lydia and was lending money to Smyrna.[66] Atticus

[51] Plin. *Ep*. 3. 19. 8. [52] Shatzman 1975: 76.

[53] See Ch. 10 for a more detailed discussion of providers of credit in the first century.

[54] Plut. *Caes*. 5. 4. [55] Val. Max. 4. 8. 3.

[56] Shatzman 1975: 422; as Frederiksen 1966: 131 says, there is no reason to think that the complex monetary deals in Cicero's letters were at all unusual; cf. generally for this period Harris (2006) and see Ch. 10.

[57] App. *Mith*. 11. [58] Cic. *Att*. 5. 21. 10–12, 6. 1. 5–7, 6. 2. 7–9, 6. 3. 5.

[59] Cic. *Att*. 6. 1. 3. [60] Cic. *Rab. Post*. 6. [61] App. *Mith*. 62–3; Plut. *Sull*. 25. 2.

[62] Plu. *Luc*. 7. 5, 20. 4. [63] Cic. *Att*. 5. 21. 12; 6. 2. 7.

[64] Cic. *Fam*. 13. 56. 1–3. [65] Cic. *Fam*. 13. 61. [66] Cic. *Flac*. 54, 75.

had difficulty collecting debts from Sicyon and from Ephesus;[67] and as a young man Atticus acted as an intermediary between the city of Athens and some lenders.[68]

Indeed Atticus belongs to a category of financiers who lived in Italy but who had interests (for example money out on loan) in the provinces. The services he performed for Cicero and others reveal the level of financial sophistication that Rome had achieved by the 50s. The transfer of money without the movement of cash is evidenced by the way in which Cicero, by using Atticus as an intermediary, was able to send money to his son Marcus, who was studying in Athens.[69] When Cicero arrived in Asia Minor in July 51, he spent several days at Ephesus, where he met Philogenus, Atticus' *procurator* in Asia. With Philogenus he transacted a *permutatio* (that is, the transfer of funds without the physical transfer of coin) that he had agreed with Atticus. Atticus in this case was able to assist with the transfer of funds that Cicero needed in Asia because he himself had interests there. Atticus' agents in the province of Asia, usually either freedmen or Italian businessmen, could cash letters of credit for Cicero, just as others of his agents could monitor Atticus' loans in Athens and manage his estate in Epirus.[70] But these were not just services that Atticus performed for Cicero. Nepos explains that Atticus 'negotia procuraret' (looked after businesses), having been chosen as a 'fixer' not only by Cicero, but also by his brother Quintus, by M. Cato, Q. Hortensius, Aulus Torquatus, and many other *equites* besides. While Atticus maintained the pretence of being too 'well bred' to engage in 'sordid' publican activities, he clearly possessed considerable accumulated assets, investments, and property throughout the Mediterranean.

In fact, the basis of Atticus' wealth can be traced with some certainty. Q. Caecilius, Atticus' uncle, was an *eques* whom Nepos describes as *dives*. Upon his death in 58, he left Atticus HS 10 m. (416 talents), being three-quarters (*ex dodrante*) of his fortune of HS 13.3 m. (555 talents).[71] As a result of this bequest, and including the inheritance he had received from his own father, Atticus had an estate of about HS 12 m. (500 talents). Nepos describes him as 'in primis lautus eques Romanus' (presumably a reference to his wealth, i.e. 'one of the richest Roman knights'). He says that Atticus possessed no luxury villas in Italy, only farms (*rustica praedia*) at Arretium and at Nomentum, and that all his income came from his possessions in Epirus and at Rome ('omnisque eius pecuniae reditus constabat in Epiroticis et urbanis possessionibus').[72]

So we have two 'in primis lauti equites Romani' in the 50s, Caecilius and Atticus, both very well off, but not in the category of 'super-rich', both with fortunes of approximately 500 to 550 talents. To put this in context, P. Cornelius Scipio Africanus, probably one of the wealthiest Romans of his day, had, as we have seen, a fortune of only about 260 talents a century earlier.[73]

[67] Cic. *Att.* 1. 13, 1. 20. 4, 2. 13. 2, 5. 13. 2, 5. 20. 10.

[68] Nep. *Att.* 2. 2. 4; as Hatzfeld 1919: 204 says, if Atticus did this, it was perhaps because the financiers were his compatriots.

[69] Cic. *Att.* 12. 24. 1; 12. 27. 2; 12. 32. 2; 13. 37. 1; 14. 7. 2; 14. 16. 4; 14. 20. 3; 15. 15. 4; 15. 17. 1; 15. 20. 4; 16. 1. 5. For the risks surrounding the physical transfer of coin, *vecturae periculum*, see Cic. *Fam.* 2. 17. 4 and this volume p. 101.

[70] Cic. *Att.* 5. 13. 2; 5. 15. 2; Andreau 1978: 53; Shatzman 1975: 423.

[71] Nep. *Att.* 5. 1–2; the inheritance is also mentioned without numbers by Val. Max. 7. 8. 5.

[72] Nep. *Att.* 14. 3.

[73] See pp. 35–7.

A century or so later, Duncan-Jones reaches a very rough estimate for the capital value of Pliny the Younger's landholdings alone of HS 17 m. (708 talents).[74]

If we move back in time, the interesting thing for our period is not Atticus but his father, in particular the wealth that the latter created and that Atticus was later to inherit. Atticus was born in about 109. His family had been Roman *equites* and his father is described as careful and rich *for those times*: 'T. Pomponius Atticus, ab origine ultima stirpis Romanae generatus, perpetuo a maioribus acceptam equestrem obtinuit dignitatem. Patre usus est diligente et, tum erant tempora, diti'[75] (T. Pomponius Atticus, descended from the most ancient Roman stock, never abandoned the equestrian rank, which he had inherited from his ancestors. His father was attentive to business and rich for those days).

His father died early, leaving Atticus with an inheritance of HS 2 m. (83 talents) and the latter subsequently moved to Athens in 86.[76] Nepos says that Atticus was able to live comfortably ('parum se splendide gesserit') off this patrimony and also states (although the text may be corrupt at this point) that Atticus consistently limited his expenses to HS 3,000 per month, so HS 36,000 per annum or equivalent to a yield of 1.8 per cent on his patrimony.[77] Atticus' father had, therefore, built up a considerable fortune during the end of the second and beginning of the first century.

A passage from Pliny the Elder gives another index of the rapid growth in individual wealth during this period.[78] He notes that Scipio Aemilianus, who died in 129, left 32 pounds of silver, that Q. Fabius Maximus Allobrogicus (*cos.* 121) was the first person to own 1,000 pounds of the metal, and that Livius Drusus, during his tribunate in 91, had 10,000 pounds.

Sthenius of Thermae provides a further example of wealth creation.[79] By the time of the *Verrines*, Sthenius was a wealthy old man who was 'civitatis suae nobilissimus' (the noblest man of his state).[80] But he had been a young man in Asia, which makes him contemporary not only with the Delian record of a N. St(h)enius M. f., as a *magister* in about 113, but also with the Delian slave trade.[81]

DELOS IN THE SECOND CENTURY

Delos provides the earliest and most detailed remains of a Roman *emporium* to survive anywhere in the Mediterranean world. The prosperity of the island and its transformation initially into the most thriving port of the Cyclades and subsequently of the Aegean is surprising when looked at merely in geographical terms, since it was an infertile island with a mediocre anchorage. But, as Hatzfield noted,

[74] Duncan-Jones 1974: 20. [75] Nep. *Att.* 1. 1. [76] Nep. *Att.* 14. 2, 2. 1–2.

[77] Nep. *Att.* 13. 6–7. Nepos explains that he knows about Atticus' monthly expenditure because of his intimacy with him and familiarity with his domestic arrangements.

[78] Plin. *HN* 33. 141.

[79] For Sthenius, see Cic. *II Verr.* 2. 83–118, 147, 3. 41, 4. 41, 5. 109, 128; Plut. *Pomp.* 10. 6.

[80] Cic. *II Verr.* 2. 106; Rauh 1993: 57.

[81] Cic. *II Verr.* 2. 83: *cum esset in Asia adulescens*; Hatzfeld, *BCH* 36 (1912), 81; for Sthenius' wealth: Cic. *II Verr.* 2. 93, 112; for his age: Cic. *II Verr.* 2. 91.

because Delos was a shrine, it had become an international town; and because it was an international town, it became a place of commerce.[82]

It is in the middle of the third century that we see the first Italians appear in Greek territories with epigraphical references and anecdotal contacts becoming more amply attested. There is a bilingual dedication at Rhodes by a Roman called Lucius Folius,[83] which is probably to be dated to the early third century, and there is the appearance of an Italian in an Aetolian proxeny list of 263. The man's name is *ΟΛΚΑΙΟΣ* (perhaps Volcaius or Holcaius) and he is styled Ῥωμαίος.[84] There is the fortunate arrival of a a Roman ship (Ῥωμαικὴ ναῦς) to pick up Aratus in 252.[85]

From 250 onwards a trickle of Italian names begins to appear in inscriptions on Delos.[86] Italian merchant ships began to cross the Adriatic from the Latin colony of Brundisium (founded in 244) despite the incursions of Illyrian pirates that were the cause of the First Illyrian War in 229.[87] Later on they took advantage of the conflicts between Greek cities to sell Italian products to the warring parties. In 183, the Achaean League protested to the Roman senate about the dealings of some Italians who were supplying weapons and wheat to the Messenians (who were at the time in revolt against the League).[88]

Plautus gives an insight into the dynamics of trade in the early second century when he has Charinus, the son of a wealthy merchant, explain in the prologue of the *Mercator* that his father:

> agrum se vendidisse atque ea pecunia
> navem, metretas quae trecentas tolleret,
> parasse atque ea se mercis mercatum undique,
> adeo dum, quae tum haberet, peperisset bona.[89]
> (He had sold the farm and with the money bought
> a ship of 300 *metretae*
> and marketed his cargoes of merchandise everywhere
> until he had acquired the wealth which he then possessed.)

Later the father builds a ship for Charinus:

> . . . et mercis emit,
> parata navi imponit, praeterea mihi
> talentum argenti ipsus sua adnumerat manu
> . . . Rhodum venimus, ubi quas merces vexeram
> omnis ut volui vendidi ex sententia.[90]
> (. . . and he bought merchandise,
> loaded the now completed vessel, and furthermore counted
> me out a talent of silver with his own hand
> . . . we arrived at Rhodes, where I sold my whole cargo
> quite to my satisfaction.)

Before the Third Macedonian War, Rhodes had enjoyed an excellent relationship with Rome, but it soured badly following widespread rumours at Rome about

82 Hatzfeld 1919: 34, 36.
83 *ILLRP* 245.
84 *IG* IX 1^2 1. 17. 51.
85 Plut. *Arat.* 12.
86 Zalesskij 1982: 27–8.
87 Polyb. 2. 8. 3.
88 Polyb. 23. 9. 12; 23. 17. 3; cf. Polyb. 28. 2. 2 for Sicilian corn imported to Rhodes in 169.
89 Plaut. *Merc.* 75–8.
90 Plaut. *Merc.* 87–9, 93–4.

Rhodian collaboration with Perseus. In 167, the senate proceeded to punish the Rhodians. It issued a *consultum*, freeing all parts of Caria and Lycia, which had been given to Rhodes in 188 after the defeat of Antochus III of Syria.[91] In addition, the Rhodians were forced to withdraw their garrisons from the Carian towns of Caunus and Stratoniceia, which had been under Rhodian control even before Apamea;[92] and, either at this point or later, Rhodes lost its hegemony of the Rhodian Nesiotic League.[93] Finally, the senate gave control of Delos to the Athenians and granted ἀτέλεια, duty-free status, to its port. As a result, the Athenians were not allowed to levy import or export duties on any of the trade that passed through the island. The scale of the trade that was already taking place in the Aegean can be seen in the fact that Rhodes, till then the main Aegean entrepôt, saw a massive trade shrinkage reflected in an 85 per cent fall in her customs duties from 1 m. drachmas per annum to 150,000 drachmas per annum.[94] These numbers suggest that the trade passing through Rhodes was very significant. If Rhodian customs duty was 2 per cent, as is generally assumed by analogy with practice in other Greek states, and if the trade was mainly entrepôt trade, as the Rhodian complaint about Delos implies, its value would be about 4,166 talents per annum, even if duty was paid both on entry and departure, and double that if it was not.[95]

During the first few years of Athenian control of Delos, the inscribed decrees of the *boule* (council) and *ekklesia* (assembly) were typical of Athenian civic institutions. As time went on, these records became increasingly infrequent and appear to have stopped altogether after 145/144.[96] Inscriptions begin to mention new residents, most of them from the eastern Mediterranean and the Italian peninsula. As Rauh says, 'while some eastern merchants at Delos came from cities as close as western and southern Asia Minor, the majority came from places further abroad, including Antioch, Laodicea, Arados, Berytus, Tyre, Sidon, Ascalon, Samaria, Alexandria, and from more exotic points still further east, such as Gadara, Heliopolis, Arabian Nabataea, Gerra on the Persian gulf, and in one instance from as far away as Minaei in south Yemen'.[97] Merchants from the Latin west were *Romaioi*, or sometimes *Italikoi*, seemingly generic terms for *negotiatores* who came from Rome, central Italy, and, to an extent, from southern Italy and Sicily.[98] The Delian inscriptions cite more than 750 Italian names, from 184 *gentes*.[99]

Strabo refers to Delos in two passages and in both he emphasizes that the growth of the island resulted from the destruction of Corinth in 146. In the first he says that the merchants (οἱ ἔμποροι—not specifically Roman merchants) changed their place of business from Corinth to Delos following the destruction of the former in 146. They were attracted by τῆς ἀτελείας τοῦ ἱεροῦ and the good location

[91] Polyb. 30. 5. 12. [92] Polyb. 30. 21. 3–5.
[93] Fraser and Bean 1954: 154–72. [94] Polyb. 30. 31. 12 with Walbank 1979: 459–60.
[95] Duncan-Jones 1990: 37. [96] Rauh 1993: 23.
[97] Rauh 1993: 28; cf. Mavrojannis 2002: 165 n. 7; Tréheux (1992) gives 68 ethnics from Antioch, 64 from Berytos, 2 from Laodicea in Phoenicia, 47 from Alexandria, 35 from Laodicea in Syria, 32 from Hieropolis, 31 from Tyre, 23 from Sidon, 16 from Ascalon, and 12 from Salamis.
[98] Hatzfeld 1919: 238–44 believed the *Romaioi* and *Italikoi* were principally from southern Italy, but more recently Solin 1982 and Cébeillac-Gervasoni 2002 have shown that most came from futher north.
[99] Hasenohr and Müller 2002: 13.

of the harbour, 'as it is on the sea route from Italy and Greece to Asia'. Even before the destruction of Corinth, the festival of Apollo was more like a commercial affair (ἥ τε πανήγυρις ἐμπορικόν τι πρᾶγμα ἔστι) and was frequented by *Romaioi*, more than by any other people. Under their rule, the Athenians took great care of the merchants. But after the Mithradatic crisis, the island became desolate (ἐρήμη) and remained in an impoverished condition until Strabo's time.[100]

The second passage gives Strabo's reasons for the growth of the slave trade in the East. In a discussion of Cilicia, he says that pirates based there grew in power because of the profitability of the exportation of slaves (ἡ δὲ τῶν ἀνδραπόδων ἐξαγωγὴ ... ἐπικερδεστάτη γενομένη).[101] The reasons for these large gains were that the slaves were easy to catch and that the market for these slaves, Delos, 'was not very far away and was large and rich in money' (τὸ ἐμπόριον οὐ παντελῶς ἄπωθεν ἦν μέγα καὶ πολυχρήματον). It was capable of handling 10,000 slaves per day.[102] Strabo then goes on to say that the cause of this growth of the slave trade was the fact that the Romans, having become rich after the destruction of Carthage and Corinth, used many slaves. The Cilician pirates, seeing easy profits, 'bloomed forth in great numbers'. The kings of both Cyprus and Egypt and the Rhodians cooperated with the pirates in the trade in humans, as they were hostile to the Syrians, and the Romans did not yet concern themselves with peoples beyond the Taurus mountains. All they did was send Scipio Aemilianus, and then 'certain others', to inspect the tribes and the cities, but they decided to take no action.[103]

As Rauh emphasizes, by about 125, a new form of public pronouncement begins to appear made by Ἀθηναίων οἱ κατοικοῦντες ἐν Δήλωι καὶ οἱ ἔμποροι καὶ οἱ ναύκληροι καὶ Ῥωμαίων καὶ τῶν ἄλλων ξένων οἱ παρεπιδημοῦντες.[104] Within a couple of years the *Romaioi* and other foreigners are also described in these inscriptions as living there (κατοικοῦντες).[105] With the passage of the *lex Sempronia de provincia Asia* in 123, which, as we have seen, formally established the tax-collecting procedure for that province, Delos also emerged as a transit point for Roman *publicani*, merchants, bankers, and magistrates passing to and from the province.[106]

Evidence from other trading communities in both Italy and the East suggests that resident foreign merchants tended to organize themselves into commercial or religious *collegia* and this also happened on Delos.[107] Specifically commercial

[100] Strabo, 10. 5. 4. [101] Strabo, 14. 5. 2.

[102] The figure of 10,000 slaves per day ought not to be taken literally, but nor should it be totally discarded, as Harris has rightly emphasized (1979: 82); for Posidonius as the source, see Strasburger 1965: 43.

[103] A familiar Roman diplomatic approach. In the 180s similarly ineffectual embassies were sent to observe the war between Eumenes II of Pergamum and Pharnaces of Pontus, but took no action (Polyb. 23. 9. 3, 24. 1. 1). McShane 1964: 157 believes that 'becoming adept at diplomatic ambiguity the Romans sometimes promised aid to both appellants on opposite sides of a quarrel'. On the other hand, Gruen 1984: 111 believes that 'the Romans, in the overwhelming majority of instances, refrained from taking sides and advocated instead a reconciliation of the contending parties'.

[104] 'Of the Athenians, those living on Delos and the merchants and the shipowners, and, of the *Romaioi* and other foreigners, those temporarily resident': *IDélos* 1645; Rauh 1993: 23.

[105] e.g. *IDélos* 1650 (*c.*123/122 BC); 1652 (*c.*118/117).

[106] Rauh 1993: 9, table I 'Roman magistrates honoured at Delos (166–88 BC)'.

[107] Frederiksen 1959: 118; Rauh 1993: 29; Gabrielsen 2001.

associations are recorded epigraphically, for example: οἱ ἐν Δήλωι τραπεζ[ῖται] (the bankers on Delos),[108] the Italian ἐλαιοπῶλαι (olive oil merchants), and οἰνοπῶλαι (wine merchants),[109] an Italian group of πλοιζομένοι (sailors),[110] and the wonderful σύνοδος τῶν πρεσβυτέρων ἐγδοχέων ἐν Ἀλεξανδρείαι (the club of the elder forwarding-agents in Alexandria).[111] The presence of the oil and wine merchants, incidentally, seems to confirm that Italian wine and olive oil was sold through Delos. But the majority of inscriptions refer to ethnically cohesive religious associations. Thus the merchants from Tyre formed themselves into the *Herakliastai* of Tyre (i.e. the worshippers of Tyrian Melkart);[112] while those from Berytos (Beirut) comprised the *Poseidoniastai* of Berytos (worshippers of Berytian Baal).[113] The importance of the Roman-Italian *collegia* of the *Hermaistai*, *Apolloniastai*, *Poseidoniastai*, and *Compitaliastai* can be gauged by the large number of Roman-Italian families recorded in inscriptions relating to them.[114]

Given that the Romans worked through patronage, it should come as no surprise that estimates based on nomenclature indicate that the majority of the *Romaioi* recorded at Delos were themselves slaves and freedmen of Hellenistic Greek and Syro-Phoenician origin who worked at Delos for Roman-Italian patron families. Hatzfeld estimated that of 231 *Romaioi* recorded on the island, 88 were freeborn, 95 were *liberti* ('freedmen'), and 48 were slaves. Rauh's survey in 1993 of inscriptions published since 1919 contains an additional 300 *Romaioi* whose names can be split, in similar proportions to those found by Hatzfeld, between freeborn (118 or 40%) and slave-born (freedmen and slaves combined, 182 or 60%).[115] The majority of the *Romaioi* on Delos were, therefore, slaves and freedmen. Their owners and patrons also appear in the island's inscriptions and hence either lived there themselves or visited regularly and perhaps even seasonally. As Rauh has demonstrated, more than sixty contemporary Roman aristocratic family names are to be found in Delian inscriptions.[116] In these inscriptions, as D'Arms put it, 'it is typically the small men who are in the foreground; whereas in the upper-class literature from Rome, the larger men are rarely named, and when they are the language in which economic activities are described (*negotium exercere* and cognates) is . . . normally imprecise and unspecific'.[117] That the social composition of the private *societas* was normally heterogeneous, and that slaves, freedmen, and other dependants, as well as freeborn partners, were all involved might be inferred too from Cicero's revealing description of such private arrangements as 'cum

[108] *IDélos* 1715.
[109] *IDélos* 1711–14; Mancinetti Santamaria 1982: 86.
[110] *IDélos* 2041.
[111] *IDélos* 1528–9.
[112] *IDélos* 1519.
[113] *IDélos* 1520, 1772–96.
[114] Rauh 1993: 30, table II: 'Roman and Italian families producing *homines collegiorum* at Delos in the pre-Sullan era (Before 81 BC)'. The list includes Roman, Latin, Etruscan, Campanian, Apulian, and Samnite *gentilicia* as well as Greek families from towns such as Heraclea, Neapolis, and Tarentum.
[115] Rauh 1993: 33 n. 70: 'In the inscriptions slaves usually designate themselves by their slave epithet followed by their Italian *gentilicium*, and the *praenomen* of their particular patron, e.g., Zenon Gerillanus Mar.- (*EAD*.30.456). Like Zenon, most slave-born merchants at Delos fail to specify a precise relationship to their *patroni*: *f(ilius)*, *l(ibertus)*, or *s(ervus)*. Freedmen usually indicate their *praenomina*, *gentilicia*, and *patronymica*, while retaining their slave epithets as *cognomina* (e.g., L. Paconius L.1. Truphon)'.
[116] Rauh 1993: 235–6, table V: 'Roman senatorial *nomina* recorded at Delos prior to the destruction of 69 BC'.
[117] D'Arms 1980: 44–5.

servis, cum libertis, cum clientibus, societates' (societies with slaves, freedmen, and clients).[118] Similarly, the *mercatores* of Puteoli, whom we meet in the *Verrines*, complained of Verres' ill-treatment, in Sicily, of their *socii*, *liberti*, and *conliberti* (business partners, freedmen, fellow freedmen).[119]

AN INTERNATIONAL TRADE IN SLAVES AND LUXURY GOODS

Strabo connects the growth in Delos' commercial prosperity with the arrival of the *Romaioi*, because it was their presence during the annual *Delia* that converted the festival into an ἐμπορικόν τι πρᾶγμα (a commercial affair). Other sources confirm the island's growth as an *emporium*. Pausanias describes Delos at this time as the 'trading station of all Greece'.[120] Pliny reports that the 'whole world thronged the markets on Delos' (mercatus in Delo celebrante toto orbe).[121] The contemporary poet Lucilius referred to the mighty port of Puteoli as 'a lesser Delos'.[122] However, although several inscriptions from the post-Mithradatic era point to the existence of slave-trading centres (στατάρια) in a number of cities, including Acmonia, Smyrna, Magnesia on the Maeander, Thyatira, and Ephesus, no firm epigraphical or archaeological evidence has so far been discovered to confirm Strabo's emphasis on the importance of the slave trade in Delos.[123] As Harris suggests, the explanation is perhaps that most slave traders did not regard themselves as such, because they also traded in other commodities rather than exclusively in slaves.[124]

What makes the veracity of Strabo's report so likely is that it fits well with other evidence, in particular the collapse of Seleucid Syria, which resulted in pirate bands establishing themselves in western Cilicia and starting to conduct repeated slave raids.[125] At first the marauding activities of the pirates seem to have been not only tolerated by the Rhodians and the kings of Cyprus and of Egypt, but actively encouraged.[126] However, the pirates in due course probably grew increasingly indiscriminate and began to prey on non-Seleucid shipping.[127] By 102, their

[118] Cic. *Parad.* 46; D'Arms 1980: 41. [119] Cic. *II Verr.* 5. 154.

[120] Paus. 3. 23. 3–6. [121] Plin. *HN* 34. 9.

[122] Paul. *Fest.* 88. 4: '"minorem Delum" Puteolos esse dixerunt . . . unde Lucilius—inde Dicarchitum populos Delumque minorem' (= Lucil. 118).

[123] *IMagn.* 240; *OGIS* 524; *IEph.* 646, 3025; Coarelli (1982 and 2005) believes that the slave market may have been located in the 'Agora of the Italians'; but Trümper (2008) argues that this 'Agora' was not in fact a slave market, but rather a luxurious park-like building with a *propylon*, garden, double-storeyed porticoes, statue niches, and a lavish bath suite.

[124] Harris 1980*a*: 129–30; see this chapter, n. 29 and text, on Rabirius.

[125] Strabo, 14. 5. 2; Plut. *Pomp.* 27. 1; Joseph, *AJ* 13. 223; I Macc. 15: 1–25; Rauh 1993: 45; cf. Grainger 1991: 123.

[126] Mavrojannis 2002.

[127] The effects of piracy on trade are made explicit by Cic. *De imp. Cn. Pomp.* 32: 'Sociis ego nostris mare per hos annos clausum fuisse dicam, cum exercitus vestri numquam a Brundisio nisi hieme summa transmiserint? . . . Mercatoribus tutum mare non fuisse dicam, cum duodecim secures in praedonum potestatem pervenerint?' (do I need to tell you that the sea has been closed to our allies during these years, when your own armies never dared to venture upon the crossing from Brundisium except in the depths of winter? . . . Do I need to tell you that the sea was not safe for merchants, when

indiscriminate attacks finally outweighed the benefits of their illegal traffic. The praetor M. Antonius tried to deal with the pirates in Cilicia between 102 and 100, but was unsuccessful.[128] The *lex de provinciis praetoriis* of 100 again made Cilicia a praetorian province (ἐπαρχείαν στρατηγικὴν) and in the letters which the consul was mandated to send out to ensure that the decision was publicized, the explicitly stated aim was to ensure the freedom of navigation and the security of Roman citizens, of Latin allies, and of the citizens of those nations which were friends of the Roman people (οἵτινες ἐν τηῖ φιλίαι τοῦ δήμου Ῥωμαίων εἰσίν).[129] As Ferrary says, it is highly unlikely that these military steps would have been undertaken, if the pirates had not been damaging the interests of Roman and Italian *negotiatores* and the *societates publicanorum.*[130]

The pirates of course were eventually destroyed by Pompey in 67 after a further unsuccessful attempt by P. Servilius Isauricus in 75–73.[131]

The slaves themselves mainly came from the East, particularly from Syria.[132] We only rarely come across slaves originating from Egypt—indeed the Egyptians themselves appear to have used Syrian slaves.[133] Asia Minor provided another important source. Diodorus Siculus reports the complaint of King Nicomedes III of Bithynia in 105/4: when Marius asked him for reinforcements against the Cimbres, Nicomedes responded that nearly all his subjects, having become the prey of the *publicani*, had been reduced to slavery in the Roman provinces.[134]

Strabo says that the demand came from the West, implying that there was a regular trade in slaves between Syria and Italy. During the second half of the second century, the Italian agricultural economy was, as we saw in Ch. 7, using increasingly large numbers of slaves, which resulted in large servile populations in Italy and Sicily and in the first and second Sicilian slave revolts. We also hear of a number of slave uprisings elsewhere during the period 136 to 130: in Pergamum, at Athens, and on Delos itself.[135] A similarly increasing trend can be observed in the scale of domestic slave ownership. Shatzman has collected data on the number of domestic slaves which accompanied a senator on a journey.[136] He shows that during the period from 200 to 29 the number of slaves gradually increased from between three and five at the beginning of the second century to between ten and fifteen towards the end of the Republican period, which suggests that households contained more slaves at the end of the period than at the beginning. The evidence for Roman involvement in this trade in human beings is spotty but consistent. Several of the people whom Verres plundered during his governorship had been active as *negotiatores* during the period of the slave trade.[137] Moreover, there were

two Roman praetors were captured by the pirates?). For other pirate assaults on Roman shipping, see Macrob. *In Somn.* 3. 6. 11; Serv. *In Aen.* 8. 363; cf. Plut. *Cat. Mai.* 21 for evidence of Roman cargo fleets travelling in convoys.

128 Cic. *De or.* 1. 82; Livy, *Per.* 68.

129 Crawford 1996: no. 12, Cnidos Copy: II 6–11, III 28–41, Delphi Copy: Block B 8–13.

130 Ferrary 2002: 135.

131 Strabo, 14. 3. 3.

132 Strabo, 14. 5. 2; Mavrojannis (2002) 168; the leader of the slave revolt in Sicily in the 130s was a certain Eunous, a follower of the *Dea Syria.*

133 Fraser 1972: 74: 'It appears from the Zenon Papyri that most of the slaves in Ptolemaic Egypt . . . were Syrians.'

134 Diod. Sic. 36. 3. 1–2.

135 Oros. 5. 9. 6.

136 Shatzman 1975: 481–2.

137 Cic. *II Verr.* 2. 13, 4. 3–6, 15, 150, 5. 47; *IDélos* 2612; Rauh 1993: 56.

slave traders amongst the *mercatores* from the East whom Verres arrested in Syracuse.[138] In a passage from another of his speeches which he quotes in the *Orator*, Cicero compares the superior wealth of Syrian and Delian slave traders and merchants with that of aristocratic Roman families:

> Neque me divitiae movent, quibus omnis Africanos et Laelios multi venalicii mercatoresque superarunt . . . neque vestis aut caelatum aurum et argentum, quo nostros veteres Marcellos Maximosque multi eunuchi e Syria Aegyptoque vicerunt . . . neque vero ornamenta ista villarum, quibus L. Paullum et L. Mummium, qui rebus his urbem Italiamque omnem referserunt, ab aliquo video perfacile Deliaco aut Syro potuisse superari.[139]
>
> (I am not moved by wealth, in which many traders and slave dealers have surpassed all the Africani and the Laelii . . . nor by raiment nor by gold and silver plate, in which our ancient heroes, the Marcelli and the Maximi, were outdone by many eunuchs from Syria and Egypt . . . nor by those ornaments of your villas, in which Lucius Paullus and Lucius Maximus, who filled Rome and Italy with these treasures, would easily have been surpassed by any Delian or Syrian.)

The increasing levels of personal wealth in Rome to which this passage refers are also evident in a number of other ways. According to Livy and Pliny the Elder, levels of ostentatious expenditure rose considerably after Rome's defeat of Antiochus.[140] Polybius assigned the first extravagance at Rome to the period immediately after Pydna. He cited as causes both Rome's confidence in her own power after the Macedonian Wars and the transfer of Macedonian riches to Rome.[141] During this same period there are brief notices in our sources of coastal estates belonging to distinguished Romans. These indicate that the first Roman luxury villas were beginning to appear along the coast of Campania by the middle of the second century. For example, a passaged preserved by Donatus places C. Laelius Sapiens (*cos.* 140) in a villa at Puteoli in the late 160s.[142] By the 140s, we have the fragment of a speech by Scipio Aemilianus in which he makes an admiring reference to *villae expolitissimae*, the first use in this context of an adjective that, by the middle of the first century, had become a conventional epithet to designate a private villa built on a sumptuous scale. These findings are in general chronological accord with some of the excavated private construction at Pompeii, where many of the largest and finest houses are to be dated to the middle of the second century.[143] As Velleius Paterculus put it, 'a negotiis in otium conversa civitas' (the state passed from activity to idleness).[144] Sumptuary laws are also an indication of the increase in private wealth. As far back as 215 a *lex Oppia* had imposed (*inter alia*) restrictions on the ownership of gold by women, but that had been primarily an economic measure in response to a serious financial crisis. It is normally assumed that the sumptuary legislation which was introduced during the second century was enacted to control expenditure on luxuries for social reasons, but perhaps too it was a functional response by an oligarchy that was beginning to feel itself under some pressure.[145] The *lex Orchia* of 181 placed restrictions on

138 Cic. *II Verr.* 5. 146.
139 Cic. *Orat.* 232.
140 Livy, 39. 6. 7–9; Plin. *HN* 33. 138.
141 Polyb. 31. 25. 6–8, 31. 29.
142 Donat. *Vit. Ter.* 4; D'Arms 2003: 20.
143 Coarelli 1977: 19; Pesando 1997: 268–71; Torelli 1999: 8.
144 Vell. Pat. 2. 1. 1.
145 Cf. Appadurai 1986 : 25.

expenditure for banquets, while the *lex Fannia* of 161 strengthened and elaborated the provisions of the *lex Orchia*. A third law of 143, the *lex Didia*, extended sumptuary restrictions to the whole of Italy.[146] A final index of increasing wealth is provided by gladiatorial shows. Since 264 BC, prominent funerals had been accompanied by gladiatorial contests. Over the next hundred years, the numbers involved in these contests grew steadily from three pairs of gladiators performing in the Forum Boarium in 264, to 22 in 216, 25 in 200, 120 in 183, and 74 in 174. According to Polybius, by the 160s the cost of a gladiatorial show produced on a generous scale was at least thirty talents.[147]

Unsurprisingly there is evidence to suggest increasing trade in luxury items to meet the growing demands of the wealthy elite in Rome and Italy. The Mahdia shipwreck, dating from between 110 and 90 and found off the coast of Tunisia, carried a cargo of sixty-seven marble columns and capitals, together with bronze statues, four large marble craters, bronze bed fittings for twenty-two couches, five massive marble candelabra, and a number of bronze lamps and vessels.[148] By comparison, the cargoes imported into Sicily in the 70s from Asia, Syria, Tyre, and Alexandria by the 'mercatores, homines locupletes atque honesti' of Puteoli ('wealthy and respected merchants', as Cicero describes them) provide examples of luxury items that would not have survived into the archaeological record. They included Tyrian purple, incense, perfumes, linen fabrics, jewels, pearls, Greek wines, and Asiatic slaves.[149] A section of the Customs Law of Asia, probably dating from the 120s, also points to a trade in luxury goods. The 'worker of fresh purple fish from the sea' (ὁ ἰχθύι κογχυλίωι θαλασίωι νεαρῶι χρώμενος) is to pay a premium rate of 5 per cent against a normal rate of 2½ per cent.[150] Rauh suggests that the same demographic evidence of an eastern Mediterranean role in the slave trade (the appearance at Delos of merchants from Berytos, Tyre, and Ascalon) also points to a thriving trade in luxury goods through Delos.[151] Both Pliny the Elder and Cicero connect the island with luxury products, including fine bronze-ware and *vasa Deliaca*.[152] Serial numbers on the bronze bed fittings found on the Mahdia wreck indicate that perhaps as many as two thousand were produced each year, probably on Delos, since Pliny identifies the island as the major production centre for these items.[153] Pliny also reports that the most highly praised perfume 'in antiquity' had come from there, a point reinforced by the number of *unguentarii* (perfumers) who are mentioned amongst those Roman-Italian families on Delos whose professions are also recorded in epigraphic or literary evidence from Italy.[154] Archaeological evidence also points to the existence of perfume and purple dye production on the island.[155] Since the raw materials for these products

[146] References in Frank 1933: 198–9 and *MRR* I 472. De Ligt 2002: 3–12; Wallace-Hadrill 2008: 315–55.

[147] Livy, 23. 30. 15, 31. 50. 4, 39. 46. 2–3, 41. 28. 11; Polyb. 31. 28. 5–6; Millar 1984: 10.

[148] Parker 1992: 252; Hellenkemper Salies 1994; Wallace-Hadrill 2008: 361–71.

[149] Cic. *II Verr.* 5. 145–6, cf. 157. Apart from containers, jewels, and pearls, none of these items would have survived to be found in a modern survey of a wreck.

[150] Customs Law of Asia, lines 11, 20.

[151] Rauh 1993: 52.

[152] Plin. *HN* 34. 9; Cic. *Rosc. Amer.* 133.

[153] Faust 1994; Wallace-Hadrill 2008: 422–4.

[154] Plin. *HN* 13. 4; Rauh 1993: 54–5, table III: 'Professions Recorded in Italy for Roman-Italian Families at Delos'; cf. this volume pp. 171–2.

[155] Perfume: Brun 1999; purple dye: Bruneau 1969, 1978.

had to be imported from further east, Pliny's evidence confirms the importance of oriental luxuries as a component of Delian trade, as do the inscribed epigrams written in honour of Philostratos Philostratou of Ascalon which mention myrrh, incense, and nard.[156]

This trade in luxury products clearly has parallels with the one that appeared in the thirteenth century AD, to which we referred at the beginning of this chapter, not least the fact that a number of the goods being traded were coming from quite a long way east. Frankincense, for example, comes from specific areas of Arabia (in particular what is now southern Oman) and the Horn of Africa, pearls from the Persian Gulf, and jewels from India.[157] Most of the literary evidence for this trade refers to the late first century BC and the first century AD. The fleet of 120 ships that was sailing from Egypt to India the year that Strabo travelled up the Nile (25/4 BC) shows the importance of trade with the Far East at that time.[158] But as early as the first half of the second century there is evidence that sea trade was already taking place across the Indian Ocean. A fragmentary Egyptian papyrus records a maritime loan for a voyage to the 'scent-producing (Ἀρωματοφόρος) land', presumably Arabia or the Horn of Africa.[159] Most of those involved are Greek Egyptians, but the *dramatis personae* include two Massiliots, a Carthaginian, and a Spartan, as well as two men with Latin names—an extraordinary mixture of nationalities, foreshadowing the multi-ethnic population on Delos in the second half of the same century.

THE SPREAD OF ITALIAN TRADING NETWORKS

Delos therefore became an *emporium* for merchants involved in vast markets in slaves and luxury goods. The complex trading networks which these merchants established enabled the elite of Roman Italy and Sicily to gain access to the merchandise of the eastern Mediterranean, the Middle East, and beyond. Verres, for example, was exporting from Syracuse (of course without paying any customs duties!) gold, silver, ivory, purple dye, cloth from Malta, carpets, Delian ware, Corinthian vases, wheat, and honey.[160] The *mercatores* whose vessels reached Sicilian ports carried a range of Oriental commodities.[161] But it is clear that these were not new phenomena in the 70s, rather a development of processes that were

156 *IDélos* 2549 I–II; Mancinetti Santamaria 1982.

157 Incense: Plin. *HN* 12. 51–65; Singer 2007. Along the southern coast of India and even towards the interior, where quartz and beryl were available, Roman denarii from the late Republic have been found (Suresh 2004: 28–9). The analysis by Will (1991) of fragments of Coan transport amphorae found at Arikamedu near Pondicherry on the south-east coast of India suggests that the foreign trading presence could have begun as early as the end of the second century. This would be about the time of the discovery of the monsoon winds by Ptolemaic mariners, which led to the replacement of the arduous and costly overland trade routes by direct passages from the western shores of the Arabian Sea to India (Strabo, 2. 3. 4; Plin. *HN* 6. 100–1, 6. 106). It would also coincide with the invention of the bilge pump (see p. 143).

158 Strabo, 2. 5. 12; Casson 1989: 12, 25, 228–9; 1991; cf. p. 99.

159 *Sammelb.* III 7169.

160 Cic. *II Verr.* 2. 176.

161 Cic. *II Verr.* 5. 146; see this chapter p. 205.

already under way in the second half of the second century. As we have seen, information gleaned from shipwreck archaeology suggests that there was a step increase in the volume of consignment traffic in the Mediterranean at that time.[162] But it was not just wine and olive oil that was carried. The literary evidence for the conveyance of luxury goods such as bronzeware, textiles, jewels, incense, perfumes, and fine works of art, as well as slaves, demonstrates the complexity of Mediterranean trade.

As early as the third quarter of the second century, we can see its economic impact. Onomastic convergences (discussed more fully on pp. 223–4) suggest that, no doubt principally through the agency of their dependants, the slaves and freedmen whom we find in Delian inscriptions, the elites of a number of central Italian towns were profiting from the new possibilities of enrichment that were offered by participation in the lucrative eastern trade. If we combine literary and epigraphical evidence, we can trace the involvement of a number of families who appear to have participated in the trade between Italy, Delos, the East, and, in some instances, other markets in the Mediterranean. For example, the fortune of the Seius family, probably from Campania, was certainly connected with the development of trade with the East, as is evident from the presence of this *gens* in Delos from the middle of the fourth century.[163] Hatzfeld compiled thirteen attestations of the name Seius or Seios at Delos.[164] Thus a freedman, C. Seius Cn. l, in or about 113, makes with some other *magistri* a gift to Jupiter Secundanus.[165] More recently, the name 'Sehius' has been discovered on Delos amongst a group of seal imprints probably used to authenticate the private acts of *negotiatores* on the island.[166] By the 50s, M. Seius was a friend of Cicero and looked after the affairs of Atticus in Asia.[167] Other members of the *gens* appear to have been involved in the mining business in Spain: seven lead ingots have been found carrying the name 'Q. Seius P(ublii) fi(lius) Men(enia tribu) Postumus'.[168] Rauh offers similar analyses of specific families such as the Cluvii, Castricii, Titinii, Publilii, Paconii, and Lollii.[169] A common feature of them all is that they had business interests in several different locations; and indeed for our period we have evidence, less comprehensive than that for Delos, of Roman businessmen operating in a number of other parts of the Mediterranean.

The influx of *negotiatores* into Macedonia in the wake of the establishment of Roman rule in 146 is well documented, and inscriptions from Anthemous and Mygdonia testify to the early presence of Roman *negotiatores* in Chalcidice during the second century, well before the foundation of the Roman colony at Cassandreia.[170] Their presence in what appears to be the backwaters of Chalcidice is probably to be associated with the exploitation of the resources of a region rich in agricultural products and, most importantly, in timber and minerals (especially gold and silver). We also find Italians trading in other parts of Greece and the islands. Thus the Annii, Aufidii, Babullii, Caecilii, Castricii, Crepereii, Granii, Mundicii, Ofellii, Orbii, Paconii, Trebellii, and Valerii found in epigraphic documents in Delos are also found at Athens between 150 and 89. Aristakos and his

162 At Ch. 7. 163 Deniaux 2002. 164 Hatzfeld 1912: 75–6.
165 *ILLRP* 760. 166 Boussac 1988: 325, 1993: 687. 167 Cic. *Att.* 5. 13. 2, 12. 11.
168 Domergue 1990: 255. 169 Rauh 1993: 47–51, 226–30; Flambard 1982: 72–5.
170 Loukopoulou 1996; Rizakis 2001; Kremydi-Sicilianou 2005: 99–100.

brother, honoured in an Athenian proxeny decree towards the middle of the second century, seem to be identical with the two sons of the banker Heraclides of Tarentum who settles in Delos with all his family.[171] At Argos, Ephesus, and Apamea, inscriptions that mention the same Italian community employ indifferently either 'Italici qui . . . negotiantur', or 'Italici . . . qui consistunt' and their Greek equivalents.[172] Mithradates' address to the Chians indicates that there was an Italian community there: 'εὖνοι καὶ νῦν ἐστὲ Ῥωμαίοις, ὧν ἔτι πολλοὶ παρ' ἐκείνοις εἰσί, καὶ τὰ ἐγκτήματα Ῥωμαίων καρπούσθε, ἡμῖν οὐκ ἀναφέροντες.'[173] (you favour the Romans even now, and many of your citizens are still with them. You are reaping the fruits of the Roman lands on Chios, on which you pay us no tribute). In Cos, likewise, there existed at the start of the first century an Italian community which was spared at the time of the massacre of 88.[174] Occasional *negotiatores* such as M. Spedius Naso, a merchant of purple on Cos, are also found in inscriptions.[175] In Boeotia by about 100 we find values given in Roman denarii, a suggestion perhaps that Roman business was beginning to bring the denarius into Greece, although, as we have seen, it did not become common until later in the first century.[176]

The one main exception to this pattern of Roman commercial involvement in the Aegean is Rhodes. Diplomatic relations between Rome and Rhodes had been restored to a better footing following the signing of a treaty of alliance in 164. Shortly afterwards, Rhodes was permitted to take control of the Carian city of Calynda and those Rhodian citizens who owned property in Lycia and Caria were allowed to recover possession.[177] A Rhodian squadron supported the Romans in the Third Punic War; and, following Mithradates VI's invasion of the province of Asia, Rhodes became one of the few refuges for Roman citizens fleeing the massacres, welcoming the fleeing army of C. Cassius and valiantly resisting the siege of Mithradates' forces.[178] But the impact of the grant of ἀτέλεια to Delos had been great and it would appear that, in the mid 160s, Rhodes very rapidly lost the economic initiative in the western Mediterranean, Aegean, and Black Sea. The island continued to be an important commercial centre, but it appears that the direction of its trade shifted markedly. Again, amphora remains, in this case the stamped handles of Rhodian wine amphorae, provide the main evidence.[179] What they show is that, during the decades between the end of the Third Macedonian War in 167 and the outbreak of the Mithradatic War in 88, Rhodes lost its dominant maritime commercial position in several long-standing markets: the western Mediterranean, the Adriatic, the Black Sea regions, and parts of the Aegean. To a large extent, the rapidly expanding exports of wine from Italy and their eventual virtual monopoly, which we discussed in Ch. 7, seem to account for this loss of markets in the west. In the Aegean, Knidian wine amphorae, in particular, supplant the formerly dominant Rhodian ones. Instead, Rhodian merchants seem to have redirected their trade in wine to Alexandria, which

171 *IG* II 428, 437; Hatzfeld 1919: 42. 172 e.g. *CIL* III 531; Hatzfeld 1919: 194.
173 App. *Mith.* 47. 174 Tac. *Ann.* 4. 14. 175 Paton and Hicks 1881: no. 309.
176 *IG* VII 4147; see this volume pp. 96–7; cf. too the mention of denarii in a passage from the Customs Law of Asia, line 12 (quoted on p. 99), probably dating from the 120s.
177 Polyb. 30. 21. 3–5. 178 App. *Mith.* 24–7. 179 Lund 1999; Rauh 1999.

probably assured them of a large stake in the export trade in grain from Egypt. Perhaps because of these developments, there is a striking lack of literary or epigraphical evidence for the presence of Italian merchants in Rhodes from the mid-second century down to the end of the Roman Republic. One of the rare Latin inscriptions from Rhodes talks of 'c(ives) R(omani) qui in Asia negotiantur' (Roman citizens who do business in Asia);[180] but there is nothing to compare with the large *corpus* of epigraphical evidence for Italian settlement and business involvement on Delos.

Evidence for Asia is also limited, but we can see that, having become a Roman province, it not only attracted magistrates and *publicani*, but also businessmen. At Pergamum, there are the first hints of their presence soon after the death of Attalus III. When defending itself against Aristonicus, the city decided to give citizen rights to *paroikoi*, amongst whom were a certain number of Italians. In the lists of new citizens from the year 133 containing around 200 names, seven of them can be identified.[181] The Italians of Ephesus were already sufficiently numerous by around 100 to be organized like those of Delos. An inscription refers to one of their *collegia*, with a *magister* named P. Veturius P. l. Rodo, who is without doubt the freedman of P. Veturius, father of L. Veturius P. f., likewise a *magister* of a Delian college at the end of the second century. At Smyrna we find Apollonius the son of Publius from Catania.[182] But apart from these few references, most of the evidence for their presence in the province comes from the brief accounts of the events of 88. According to Valerius Maximus and Memnon of Heraclea, 80,000 died; according to Plutarch it was 150,000; or more generally some tens of thousands of victims according to Cicero. Appian mentions Romans being killed at Tralles, Ephesus, Pergamum, Adramyttium, and Caunos, in their thousands.[183] In Lydia, the *cives Romani* who were in the region at this time found they could flee to the 'unattached islands' of the marsh of Gyges, where pursuit was impossible, which prompted a note in Pliny the Elder's *Natural History*.[184] Even if the numbers furnished by the sources for those killed are very exaggerated, they, nevertheless, testify to the importance of the Italian presence in Asia at this date and the very real disaffection with Roman power.[185]

For the West, the literary evidence is also sparse, but consistent, in showing the presence of Roman traders. In Africa, Carthage had been a great trading power with large numbers of merchant ships as well as war fleets.[186] Late in the Second Punic War, as many as 100 merchantmen had been sent to Italy in an abortive attempt to help Hannibal.[187] The docks at Carthage, probably dating from the first half of the second century, had 220 ship berths, a number almost paralleled at Cyzicus in the Black Sea, but at very few other ports.[188] After 146, it is unlikely that

180 *CIL* III 12266. 181 *IPerg*. 249. 1. 14–15. 182 Hatzfeld 1919: 238; *CIG* 3142.

183 Val. Max. 9. 2 ext. 3; Memn. *FGrH* III B 434. F. 22. 9; Plut. *Sull.* 24. 4; Cic. De *imp. Cn. Pomp.* 11; App. *Mith.* 22–3; Ferrary (2002) 145.

184 Plin. *HN* 2. 209.

185 For a sceptical view of the numbers, see Brunt 1971*a*: 224–7.

186 Plin. *HN* 7. 199; Strabo, 16. 2. 23; 3. 5. 11; Dion. Hal. *Ant. Rom.* 5. 20. 1; Thuc. 6. 34. 2; Polyb. 18. 35.

187 App. *Hann.* 54; Duncan-Jones 1990: 36. 188 App. *Pun.* 96; Strabo, 12. 8. 11.

Italians gained a monopoly over the Carthaginian trading network (other big Punic cities such as Utica were potential beneficiaries from her fall), but during the Jugurthine War we hear of large numbers of Roman and Italian traders at Utica, Vaga and Cirta.[189]

In the case of Spain, direct references to the activities of *negotiatores* are virtually non-existent after the end of the Second Punic War, but the sheer numbers of slaves working in the mines by the 150s suggest the involvement of *negotiatores* in the slave trade there. At the same time, amphora finds, as we saw in Ch. 7, reveal the boom in the trafficking of wine and olive oil, not only to Spain, but also to other parts of Western Europe.

Narbonese Gaul was soon overrun by the Romans after the Via Domitia was built to Spain and a citizen colony was planted at Narbo in 118. For our period we have few facts, but two speeches of Cicero reveal what had been going on. The *Pro Quinctio* concerns a dispute which came to court in 81, but which involved events that had occurred earlier, while the *Pro Fonteio* refers to conditions in 74. The *Pro Quinctio* deals with a *societas* which had been formed many years before 81 between two Romans, Quinctius and Naevius, both apparently from the city. The men engaged on an extensive scale in farming and grazing north of Narbo: 'pecuaria res ampla et rustica sane bene culta et fructuosa'.[190] As Christol says, the people who inhabit the world represented in the *Pro Quinctio* are what we would call entrepreneurs: 'they have a spirit of adventure, want to make their fortunes and, in order to do so, are prepared to start a speculative business'.[191] In the *Pro Fonteio* the Romans in Gaul are designated in four groups: *publicani, agricolae, pecuarii, ceteri negotiatores* (publicans, farmers, herders, other businessmen);[192] and, even if we allow for exaggeration, Cicero's statements that 'referta Gallia negotiatorum est' (Gaul is stuffed full of businessmen) and that 'nummus in Gallia nullus sine civium Romanorum tabulis commovetur' (not a coin can move in Gaul without the transaction being recorded in the account books of Roman citizens) indicate that commerce in the province was advancing rapidly.[193] In the 60s, Catiline used a certain P. Umbrenus as an intermediary with the Gallic Allobroges because he had transacted business in Gaul and knew a number of their leading men.[194]

The literary, epigraphic, and archaeological evidence, then, more comprehensive for Delos but still available for Sicily, Macedonia, Greece, Asia, Africa, Spain, and Narbonese Gaul, suggests that *negotiatores* were active in many parts of the Mediterranean during our period. Add to this the boom in consignment traffic evidenced by the growth in the number of shipwrecks and ceramic finds in both terrestrial and marine contexts, and it is clear that by the end of the second century, Roman and Italian trade was expanding rapidly.

[189] Utica: Sall. *Iug.* 64. 5; Vaga: 47. 1; Cirta: 26. 3.

[190] Cic. *Quinct.* 12. [191] Christol 2002: 47.

[192] Cic. *Font.* 46; to this list we may add miners. About 60 km from Narbo, at the site of some mines at the modern Lascours, near the village of Villemagne-L'Argentière, have been found some *tesserae* carrying the name 'societas Rut[eonorum]' (Christol 2002: 50).

[193] Cic. *Font.* 11. [194] Sall. *Cat.* 40. 2.

FINANCIAL CAPITAL IN THE *EMPORIA*

We emphasized at the beginning of this chapter the importance of financial capital in promoting trade. We have already examined in Ch. 6 the credit-creation role of financial intermediaries in the Roman world, and both literary and inscriptional evidence demonstrates their presence in Delos in the late second and early first centuries. In his explanation of why Delos became the preferred location for the slave trade, Strabo mentions two factors, one geographic, the other financial: *τὸ ἐμπόριον οὐ παντελῶς ἄπωθεν ἦν μέγα καὶ πολυχρήματον* (the emporium was not very far away and was large and rich in money). Mavrojannis correctly interprets *πολυχρήματον* as 'plein de capitaux, c'est-à-dire de *trapezitai* qui finançaient sur place les *emporoi* acheteurs'.[195]

In fact, financiers from the West were already in the Aegean in the early second century. Around 200, a Syracusan, Timon the son of Nymphodoros, was awarded a proxeny by the *demos* of the island of Tenos. He had lent money to the confederation of the *Nesiotai*.[196] The earliest known banker on Delos from mainland Italy is Marcus Minatius Sexti f., who gave the large sum of 7,000 drachmas to the *Poseidoniastai* of Berytos just after 153/2 and in return had a statue and a crown dedicated to him as well as receiving other honours.[197] After him came the Gerillani; six Gerillani are attested on Delos, at least two of whom were bankers. In an inscription from about 100, the merchants of the island, in honouring Maraius Gerillanus in a dedication to Apollo, Artemis, and Leto, refer to him as a *τραπεζίτης* (banker).[198] The inscription also describes Maraius as a *Romaios* but, as we have seen, this means only that he was a member of the Italian community, since Gerillanus is a southern Italian name.[199] The Gerillanus family continued to operate its bank into the 80s, with a Maraius Gerillanus—perhaps the son of the earlier Maraius, perhaps the earlier Maraius himself—being honoured with two dedications, one set up by all the inhabitants of Delos, including the merchants and ship captains, the other by the businessmen alone: *[οἱ ἐν Δήλωι πραγματε]υόμενοι* (those doing business on Delos).[200] Our knowledge of the financial affairs of the Aufidii derives principally from an inscription erected in honour of an Aufidius Bassus on Tenos in the 70s or 60s which describes in detail the financial services of the Aufidii to the island's government.[201] Ten Aufidii are attested on Delos, two of them definitely bankers. L. Aufidius was honoured by two inscriptions erected in the 80s, one set up by his freedmen, the other by the merchants and ship captains of the island.[202] There is also other, more circumstantial, evidence. For example, according to Cicero, Q. Lucceius (perhaps the father of Cicero's friend L. Lucceius, who had property in Puteoli) owned 'the largest bank' at Rhegium in the late 70s. In the 90s the Lucceii were patrons of a freedman active on Delos.[203] Bankers from other parts of

[195] Mavrojannis 2002: 170; rather than just 'rich'. Cf. Polyb. 18. 35. 9–11 (describing Carthage).

[196] *IG* XII 5. 816; 817. 5–11; Hatzfeld 1919: 28–9, 197.

[197] *IDélos* 1520; Bogaert 1968: 187–8; the date is provided by the mention of the archon Pheidrias in line 91.

[198] *IDélos* 1725. [199] Barlow 1978: 102, 137 n. 14.

[200] *IDélos* 1726, 1727. [201] *IG* XII 5. 860. [202] *IDélos* 1728, 1729.

[203] Cic. *II Verr.* 5. 165: 'Q. Lucceius qui argentariam Regi maximam fecit'; *IDélos* 1763; Lucceius' villa at Puteoli: Cic. *Fam.* 5. 15. 2; D'Arms 1980: 64.

the Mediterranean were also active on the island. By 106/105 the banker Philostratos Philostratou of Ascalon was established on the island. He hired two poets to celebrate his piety and generosity, and then inscribed both epigrams in his own honour on his exedra in the 'Agora of the Italians'.[204] He and his sons were likewise honoured by the Ἰταλικοί, δικαιοσύνης καὶ φιλαγαθίας ἕνεκεν (by the *Italikoi* because of his justice and love of goodness).[205] Finally, just north of the round monument in the centre of the 'Agora of the Compitaliastai', a group of bankers erected a base bearing the inscription: οἱ ἐν Δήλωι τραπεζ[ῖται] (the bankers on Delos).[206]

Evidence from other Mediterranean *emporia* at this time is scarce, but the world that Naevius represents in the *Pro Quinctio* is one in which monetary liquidity is available everywhere. It is clear that Romans had the capacity to engage in business activities in both the province of Gallia and at Rome, be it property transactions or the sale of slaves.[207] It was to Narbo that P. Quinctius went in order to auction his goods: 'auctionem in Gallia P. hic Quinctius Narbone facturum esse proscribit earum rerum quae ipsius erant privatae'[208] (this P. Quinctius had a notice put up in Gaul that he would sell some private property of his own at Narbo). Narbo appears in the *Pro Quinctio* as the centre of financial life in Transalpine Gaul at this period and the place of reference for those Italians established *in Gallia*.[209]

The most plausible explanation for the bankers' presence in Delos and in other *emporia* is that they were providing trade and auction finance. As we have already described, Cato the Elder was providing trade finance by the middle of the second century.[210] Hopkins believed that the Roman coin supply was a major factor in the increase of trade in the late Republic.[211] But as we have seen, coin does not necessarily flow between regions on a scale commensurate with the volume of trade, and the evidence from Delos suggests that the role of financial intermediation was greater.[212] All these examples give us a better understanding of a passage of the *De Imperio Cn. Pompei*, where Cicero shows the damage done to business by the troubled situation in Asia. There are, he says, three categories of people interested in the restoration of peace in the East: firstly *publicani*; then the *negotiatores* and, besides them, those who 'in provincia pecunias magnas collocatas habent' (those who have large amounts of money invested in the province).[213]

Πολυχρήματον (rich in money), *pecunias magnas* (large amounts of money), chance epigraphic survivals naming a number of τραπεζῖται (bankers)—the references are few, but consistent. Financial capital was readily available in Delos and Narbo and, according to Strabo, it was available in quantity in the former.

[204] *IDélos* 2549 I–II; Mancinetti Santamaria 1982; *IDélos* 2253 is our earliest dated reference to him. By the time of Philostratos' residence on Delos, Ascalon had fallen into the Maccabean orbit (Grainger 1991: 144).

[205] *IDélos* 1722.

[206] *IDélos* 1715. For the rise of bankers at Delos in general, see *IDélos* 1520, 1715–29; cf. Crawford 1985: 125; Rauh 1993: 93; Barlow 1978: 101–9, 247–9.

[207] Cf. L. Aufidius Vinicianus Epagatinus, aedile at Fundi, who received a dedication at Narbo (*CIL* XII 4357).

[208] Cic. *Quinct.* 15. [209] Christol 2002: 49.

[210] Plut. *Cat. Mai.* 21. 5–6, quoted on pp. 145.

[211] Hopkins 1980: 106. [212] See pp. 100–1.

[213] Cic. *De imp. Cn. Pomp.* 18; Hatzfeld 1919: 204.

CONCLUSION

The emergence of a large resident alien community on Delos in the second half of the second century was directly related to the growing commercial importance of the island. It was a consequence not only of the grant of ἀτέλεια in 167, but of other equally important developments such as the Roman destruction of Carthage and Corinth, the rapid collapse of the Seleucid Empire, the growth in the number of bankers on the island, and the creation of the Roman province of Asia. Only after these later events, as the inscriptions corroborate, did the Roman and eastern Mediterranean population at Delos truly begin to surge, reaching an estimated 20,000 to 30,000 residents at its peak.[214]

The development of the *emporium* at Delos was cut off in its prime in 87 by the attack of Mithradates VI of Pontus. In the previous year the king had invaded the Roman province of Asia and had had little difficulty in persuading provincials to join in the massacre of all Romans and Italians living in their midst. This explosion of violence, directed not only by the Asian provincials but by the entire Greek world against the local Roman business establishment, offers compelling evidence of the deleterious consequences of the slave trade and Roman domination of the region. Mithradates made financiers a special target. He offered to remit half their debts to borrowers who killed their Roman or Italian creditors (thereby showing that he appreciated the importance of financiers and the popular appeal of debt cancellations).[215]

Outside Asia, the *emporium* at Delos was singled out as the most important target of this rebellion. A Pontic fleet killed some 20,000 Romans and Italians on the island and in its immediate vicinity, and enslaved the surviving women and children.[216] As the epigraphic evidence shows, the *negotiatores* of Delos were scattered throughout the eastern Mediterranean, but especially to Asia Minor.[217]

The only account of the financial effects of the invasion that we have appears in the *De Imperio Cn. Pompei*, in which Cicero emphasizes the interconnectedness of public and private finances in Rome and the *pecuniae Asiaticae*:

> haec fides atque haec ratio pecuniarum, quae Romae, quae in foro versatur, implicata est cum illis pecuniis Asiaticis et cohaeret; ruere illa non possunt, ut haec non eodem labefacta motu concidant.[218]
>
> (this credit and this system of moneys, which operates at Rome in the Forum, is bound up in, and is linked with, those Asian moneys; the loss of the one inevitably undermines the other and causes its collapse.)

It would have been impossible for Cicero to have made this kind of public statement if a substantial amount of financial capital had not been invested in Asia and Delos at the time of Mithradates' invasion.

214 Rauh 1993: 27. 215 App. *Mith.* 22: χρήσταις δ'ἐπὶ δανειστὰς ἥμισυ τοῦ χρέους.

216 App. *Mith.* 28; cf. Paus. 3. 23. 4; Posidonius *FGrH* IIA 87 F. 36.

217 Rauh 1993: 72–3, table IV: 'Relocation of Roman and Italian families from Delos to Asia Minor in the first century BC'.

218 Cic. *De imp. Cn. Pomp.* 19.

9

The Creation of 'Material Complexity'

Tantae molis erat Romanam condere gentem[1]

INTRODUCTION

In his book, *The Fall of Rome and the End of Civilisation*, Brian Ward-Perkins discusses the economic regression and the disappearance of material complexity and sophistication that occurred in the post-Roman west in the fifth century AD. He argues that what was lost when the barbarians invaded was an enormous material culture combined with a complex system of production and distribution. In this chapter we look at a key stage, perhaps the major stage, in the creation of that material culture, arguing that the main stimulus to increased construction and manufacturing activity was provided by the revenues that Rome received during the second century.[2]

Rome's use of the profits of war to expand its infrastructure was nothing new. The Aqua Anio Vetus was built with the proceeds of the booty captured from Pyrrhus.[3] But what happened in the second century was on a vastly different scale: there was a great transformation in the physical appearance of the city. Cornell saw that 'there was a shift from victory monuments, dedicated by generals and financed from the booty of one-off campaigns, towards civic buildings and public amenities constructed at public expense and eventually funded from regular taxation and the exploitation of permanent provinces'.[4] It is certainly true that during our period civic building was principally financed by the state, but the intensity of the building that is revealed by the regular contracts for the construction and repair of Rome's public buildings and infrastructure recorded in our sources for the first half of the second century (especially by Livy) still seems to correlate closely with the size of revenue inflows from booty and indemnities.

[1] 'Such time, such toil, requir'd the Roman name, | Such length of labour for so vast a frame'. Verg. *Aen.* 1. 33, trans. John Dryden (1697).

[2] Ward-Perkins (2005: 120) is nevertheless correct to emphasize that 'the complex system of production and distribution . . . was an older and more deeply rooted phenomenon than an exclusively "Roman" economy. Rather it was an "ancient" economy that in the eastern and southern Mediterranean was flourishing long before Rome became at all significant.'

[3] Frontin. *Aq.* 1. 6.

[4] Cornell 2000: 48.

On the other hand, a number of towns in central and southern Italy show a different pattern. Here, there are clear Hellenistic influences apparent in the monumental structures that they begin to erect, reflecting increasing trade contacts with the eastern Mediterranean. Indeed this construction activity appears to have been funded in large part by the euergetism of members of local elites who had made their money not only from sharing in the booty that Rome had seized during the second century but also, crucially, from participating in the lucrative new trade in slaves and luxury goods centred on Delos.

As we shall see, the economic stimuli generated by the increase in construction activity were profound, but the dynamics of manufacturing in its different aspects are sometimes more difficult to discern. In the second half of this chapter we try to determine the processes that lay behind the production of manufactured items and the extent of elite involvement in them. The term 'manufacturing', of course, covers a variety of activities. In Ch. 3, we examined the large scale of the mining industry in Spain. Refining silver was a hard and complicated business and the number of men involved in silver production there (Polybius mentions 40,000 around Carthago Nova in about 150[5]) could have exceeded those in any other productive activity except agriculture.[6] In this chapter, we also consider other types of manufacturing carried out in Italy for a range of items from ceramics, textiles, and household items to military and agricultural equipment.

ROME

The first decade following the end of the Second Punic War was clearly a difficult one, characterized by a shortage of funds. No public building or related activities are recorded for the Roman censors of 199, and the censors of 194 and 189 let very few contracts.[7] This fits with and confirms what we know of the difficulties faced by the treasury during the Second Punic War;[8] indeed the censors of 199 seem to have been more concerned with finding additional sources of revenue: they instituted *portoria venalicium* at Puteoli and Capua (and at an unidentified 'Castrum'), the first reference we have to these taxes.[9] There is a further indication that money was in short supply. Work on one of the first monuments to be built in Rome after the end of the Second Punic War, the Temple of the Magna Mater (Cybele) on the Palatine, took thirteen years to complete, 204 to 191.[10] However, immediately after the war against Antiochus III, things began to change. In 187, part of the booty from Cn. Manlius Vulso's Asian campaign was used to repay an additional tax (Livy terms it a *stipendium*) that had been imposed on the Roman

5 Polyb. 34. 9. 8–9 = Strabo, 3. 2. 10.

6 Cf. Rihll 2001 on silver extraction in Laurium.

7 Livy, 34. 44. 4–5, 35. 9. 1, 37. 58. 1, 38. 28. 3.

8 On *inopia aerarii*, see Ch. 1.

9 Livy, 32. 7. 3; *portoria venalicium* should probably be understood as tolls on goods for sale, i.e. not on personal possessions (Lintott 1993: 84 n. 83). None of our sources gives any indication as to the rate of *portorium* or indeed of the method of charging during this period (de Laet 1949: 62–3).

10 Livy, 36. 36.4: 'tredecim annis postquam locata erat, dedicavit eam M. Iunius Brutus'.

People, possibly in relation to paying the army during the Second Punic War or perhaps for the war against Antiochus.[11] According to Pliny the Elder, there was more money around and levels of ostentatious expenditure rose considerably: 'Populus Romanus stipem spargere coepit Sp. Postumio Q. Marcio cos.; tanta abundantia pecuniae erat'[12] (the Roman people began to spray their cash around in the consulship of Spurius Postumus and Quintus Marcius. So great was the abundance of money.) Shortly afterwards, Rome began to find itself able to afford public investment on a scale that would have been unimaginable in the third century. Whereas the censors who took office in 199, 194, and 189 were cautious in their building activities, their successors in 184 were a different matter; they kicked off a remarkable period of expenditure on utilitarian infrastructure.

As we discussed in Ch. 1, Rome at the beginning of the second century probably had a rather unsophisticated and haphazard physical appearance. Livy talks of 'speciem ipsius urbis nondum exornatae neque publicis neque privatis locis'[13] (the appearance of the city itself which had not yet been adorned in either its public or its private spaces).

Much of the building was probably still in wood and stone, with very few grandiose edifices with the exception of the two aqueducts, a few paved roads, and a sewer. And it was in fact with the renovation of the Cloaca Maxima that the censors of 184—Cato the Elder and L. Valerius Flaccus—initiated a period in which successive colleges of censors contracted for public works on a very large scale. Cato and Flaccus incurred enormous expense, probably 6 million denarii alone, on the renovation of the sewer;[14] and in addition they are known to have constructed a new road, a mole or causeway, two business buildings, and the Basilica Porcia.[15] Their successors, the censors of 179, had at their disposal, for use in building operations over the next five years, funds equal to the entire *vectigalia* received by the state in one year, and those of 169 had half a year's *vectigalia*, despite the cost of the Third Macedonian War then being fought.[16]

The increased importance of trade is shown by the developments undertaken during this period and one magistrate stands out in the construction of new port and commercial infrastructure: M. Aemilius Lepidus, who as aedile (193), consul (187 and 175), and censor (179) initiated major works related to trade and communications at Rome and elsewhere. As curule aedile in 193, Aemilius Lepidus, together with his colleague L. Aemilius Paullus, developed the *emporium* downstream in the area to the south-west of the Aventine and also erected two

[11] Livy, 39. 7. 1–5; Harl (1996: 44) believes that it was a *tributum* levied during the war against Antiochus.

[12] Plin. *HN* 33. 138.

[13] Livy, 40. 5. 7.

[14] Dion. Hal. *Ant. Rom.* 3. 67. 5.

[15] Livy, 39. 44. 5–7.

[16] Livy, 40. 46. 16, 44. 16. 9. It is of course impossible to know what a year's tax revenue amounted to at this period. Perhaps, as Frank (1933: 144) suggests, the *vectigalia* had grown in size between 179 and 167. They are more likely to have contracted, as is suggested by the problems at the end of the 170s discussed below. The income of the Roman state in 62 BC (the first mention of a definite sum for a year's *vectigal*) was 85 m. denarii (Plut. *Pomp.* 45), compared with an average estimated income for the first half of the second century of 14 m. denarii (Frank 1933: 145): Roman state income possibly increased sixfold over a 100-year period.

porticoes.[17] A year later a *porticus* was erected for the timber dealers.[18] As censor in 179, Aemilius Lepidus, with his colleague in that office, M. Fulvius Nobilior, provided more harbour and trading facilities. They built a dock on the Tiber, several porticoes nearby for traders and retailers, the Basilica Aemilia, a fish market and some shops, as well as the Pons Aemilius across the Tiber. They reconstructed the market (*macellum*) of Rome, on the future site of the Forum Pacis. Finally, Aemilius Lepidus also built, in the same censorship and at public expense, a pier at Terracina, reputedly to serve his own estates, although it presumably also advantaged the whole region, the products of which included Caecuban wine, lime, and firewood.[19] The next set of censors, in 174, Q. Fulvius Flaccus and A. Postumius Albinus, continued the work of Aemilius Lepidus and improved the *emporium* and the porticoes above it.[20]

With the increase in public wealth, more road building appears to have become possible. We saw in Ch. 1 that, following the construction of the Via Appia at the end of the fourth century, the Romans had, during the third, built the Viae Aurelia, Clodia, Amerina, and Flaminia, the last having been built from Rome to Ariminum probably in about 220. In 187 Aemilius Lepidus, as consul, constructed the Via Aemilia from Ariminum to Placentia, while his colleague, C. Flaminius, ran a road from Arretium to Bononia.[21] In his second consulship (175), Aemilius Lepidus seems to have laid out the long road from Bononia to the recent colony of Aquileia.[22] Road building also featured highly in the programme of the censors of 174. Livy refers to contracts for surfacing roads outside the city with gravel and kerbstones (roads inside the city were to be paved with *silex*) and for the building of bridges in a number of different locations.[23] By this stage very little of the road system would have been paved in stone and it was probably at this time that the Via Flaminia was covered in a layer of gravel.[24] Similarly, the reason for the references to bridges in the programme of the censors of 174 is presumably because fords and ferries had sufficed previously.

All this construction work was very utilitarian. In total, during the second century, at least twelve monumental porticoes were constructed in Rome and at least four basilicas, but no permanent stone theatre, no amphitheatre, and no monumental complex of public baths.[25] But clearly a culture that is putting up more buildings, however utilitarian, has a great deal of capital. So it is no surprise that the high expenditure of the colleges of censors for 189, 184, 179, and 174 coincided with the period during which the indemnity of Antiochus III was being paid to Rome and booty was still coming into the *aerarium* on a significant scale.[26]

[17] Livy, 35. 10. 12. The remains of an enormous dock warehouse with a barrel-vaulted concrete roof had been long been known as the Porticus Aemilia. However, the structure has now been identified as the *navalia* (Tucci 2006) and a recent re-evaluation proposes a later date for the building, in the Sullan era (Tuck 2000).

[18] Livy, 35. 41. 10. [19] Livy, 40. 51. 2–7; for Terracina, see DeLaine 1995: 560.

[20] Livy, 41. 27. 8; Rickman 1971: 121. [21] Livy, 39. 2. 6, 39. 2. 10.

[22] Strabo, 5. 1. 11; Harris (1971: 163–8) argues that most of the major trunk roads of Italy were constructed in the second century.

[23] Livy, 41. 27. 5–12, though it should be noted that the text of Livy is incomplete.

[24] Wiseman 1970*b*: 149 n. 214.

[25] As pointed out by Cornell (2000: 53). [26] See Table 2.2.

During the first half of the second century, booty and indemnities alone totalled nearly 46,000 talents. But this remarkable figure obscures as well as illuminates, because the money did not arrive in a regular flow. In particular, during the second half of the 170s, the Syrian indemnity came to an end. For twelve years the Romans had been receiving over 1,000 talents per annum of incremental revenue from this source, and suddenly the annual amount of indemnities that Rome received dropped to the 200 talents per annum which she received from Carthage.

By 173 there are perhaps indications that the money was beginning to run out. As we have seen, one of the consuls of that year, L. Postumius Albinus, was suddenly sent by the senate to Campania to stop landowners engrossing excessive quantities of *ager publicus*, and in the following year new leases over the reclaimed land were issued.[27] There can be little doubt that Postumius' sudden diversion to Campania was made in order to raise revenue for the Roman state. Next, part of the Syrian indemnity was paid late, at least four years behind schedule, in 173.[28] We do not know when the Syrian default occurred, as we do not know how many instalments were paid off belatedly in 173; but the final instalment had originally been due to be paid in 176. If the default had in fact happened earlier, a possible occasion would have been in 179, when the censors of that year introduced several new *vectigalia* and *portoria*, presumably at the colonies founded after 199.[29] If the Syrians had stopped paying their indemnity in that year, then the censors might have introduced the new *portoria* to make up at least part of the shortfall in funding. A further indication of possible financial difficulty is that the Aqua Marcia, which was started in 144 and completed in 140, may not have been an entirely new structure, but the completion of one that Livy mentions as having been contracted for by the censors of 179, but left unfinished.[30]

Of course, things changed again for the better, after the arrival of the booty from the Third Macedonian War (5,000 talents and 150,000 Epirote slaves). In addition, the Macedonians began to pay a tribute to Rome, albeit at half the rate that they had done previously to Perseus.[31] There are hints that this was happening elsewhere too. I Maccabees 8: 2 describes how, amongst their other achievements, the Romans brought the Gauls 'under tribute' (ὑπὸ φόρον). This is not mentioned by any of our other sources and it may be inaccurate, as certain other elements of this passage of I Maccabees undoubtedly are. Nevertheless, this report of what Judas Maccabeus had heard about Rome in the 160s perhaps contains an echo of an indemnity or tax imposed upon the Cisalpine Gauls following the actions against them undertaken by M. Popilius Laenas in the late 170s.

During the 150s we have the evidence for the reopening of the Macedonian mines in 158, the relatively low level of bullion in the *aerarium* in 157, and then the relatively high level of income from the Spanish silver mines towards the end of the decade.[32] Finally, we have the sack of Corinth and the destruction of Carthage in 146. What were Rome's expenditure patterns during this period?

[27] See p. 165.

[28] Livy, 42.6. 6–7; see Table 2.2 n. a.

[29] Livy, 40. 51. 8.

[30] Livy (40. 51. 7) says this was because the plans were blocked by an aristocrat through whose lands it had to pass, but this seems far-fetched; cf. Astin 1967: 109.

[31] Plut. *Aem.* 28. 6.

[32] See Ch. 3.

Most of the evidence we have for construction work during the second century comes from its early years. As Coarelli argues, it is impossible to suppose that the apparent decline in building activity after 167, and especially after 150, is not the consequence of the poverty of the literary tradition and in particular of the loss of the full text of Livy.[33] That spending on infrastructure did continue, to cater to a rapidly expanding population in Rome (normally in itself a sign of economic growth), is evidenced by the construction of two new aqueducts in 144 and 125, the hugely expensive Aqua Marcia and the Aqua Tepula, which together increased the water supply to the city by more than 80 per cent.[34] Indeed the construction of the Aqua Marcia (as well as the contemporaneous repairs to the Aqua Appia and the Aqua Anio Vetus) is directly attributed by Frontinus to population growth: 'quoniam incrementum urbis exigere videbatur ampliorem modum aquae'[35] (since the growth of the city was seen to demand a more substantial supply of water). As Coarelli points out, the urgency with which the building of the Aqua Marcia was undertaken can be inferred from the fact that oversight of the work was entrusted, quite exceptionally for the Republic, to the urban praetor, Q. Marcius Rex.[36] Evidence for the censorship of 142 (that of Scipio Aemilianus and Mummius) is limited, but it does not appear to have been constrained by lack of funds, despite the contemporaneous construction of the Aqua Marcia. Amongst other works, the ornamental ceiling of the Capitoline temple was gilded and arches were added to the Pons Aemilius.[37] In addition to the building of the aqueducts, expensive roads were constructed in the period 155–118: in Macedonia (Via Egnatia[38]), in Spain (Via Domitia[39]), in Italy (Via Postumia, Via Annia, Via Popillia and possibly others[40]), and in Asia. There, several milestones inscribed with the name of Manius Aquillius, the governor of Asia in the early 120s, have been found on the main roads leading from Ephesus (which was to become the seat of the Roman governor) to Tralles, Laodicea, and the valley of the Maeander, to Smyrna and Pergamum and from Adramyttium through Sardes, Laodicea, and Tacina to Side on the south coast.[41] As we noted in Ch. 4, C. Gracchus embarked on a large road-building programme and constructed the first state granaries of which we know, the *horrea Sempronia*, in order to store grain for later disbursement.[42] From later in the century, there are substantial surviving traces of the *horrea Galbana* attributed to Ser. Sulpicius Galba (*cos.* 108). The building contained 140 storage rooms on the ground floor alone, which covered more than 20,000 m^2.[43]

There are signs too that construction techniques were evolving in two ways: to satisfy the increased demand for grander buildings on the one hand and, on the other, to speed up the actual process of construction and to lower the cost of building. After the sack of Corinth, temples began to be constructed in marble, the

33 Coarelli 1977: 7.

34 Frank 1933: 226 suggests, probably correctly, that the booty from Corinth and Carthage covered the cost of the Aqua Marcia, on which see p. 24.

35 Frontin. *Aq.* 1. 7.

36 Coarelli 1977: 17.

37 Plin. *HN* 33. 57; Livy, 40. 51. 4; Coarelli (1977: 16–18) points to the volume of coinage issued in the mid 130s which he believes is to be explained at least in part by the building activities of the censors of 136.

38 Polyb. 34. 12. 2a–8.

39 Polyb. 3. 39. 8.

40 Wiseman 1970*b*.

41 Comprehensive references for the milestones in Mitchell 1999: 19, table I.

42 Festus, 370L; Plut. *C. Gracch.* 6. 3.

43 Rickman 1971: 5, 101; Mattingly and Aldrete 2000: 146.

first examples being the Temple of Jupiter Stator, vowed by Metellus Macedonicus in 146, and the Temple of Mars, vowed by D. Junius Brutus Callaicus in 132, using marble transported from Greece.[44] But it is the development of Roman concrete as a quick and economical substitute for ashlar masonry that is most notable. DeLaine has studied the economics of Roman construction in quantitative terms by analysing the labour costs of building with different materials, since these costs represent the prime expense of any type of construction.[45] She shows that Roman methods of 'concrete' construction required considerably less labour, and therefore less cost, than dressed stone per unit of walling. Indeed in rough terms she demonstrates that the relative cost of using tufa ashlar was about four times as expensive as using *opus incertum*, that is concrete faced with small irregularly shaped pieces of stone.[46] The relative cheapness of concrete is thought to be what made it feasible for everyday domestic and commercial construction. Indeed Coarelli argued that it was largely the upsurge in private building in Rome during the second century that led to the development of the technique in the first place.[47] During the course of the second century, concrete facings gradually became more regular until, probably at the time of the Gracchi, a facing known as *opus reticulatum*, consisting of a network of pyramidal-shaped pieces of stone, with their bases set diagonally and forming a diamond pattern, was introduced. The reasons for this change are not clear. Some have argued that the rapid growth of the city in the later second century led to the introduction of 'industrialized' building techniques, using regular standardized components suitable for a mass labour force, perhaps largely consisting of slaves.[48] But DeLaine has also shown that *opus reticulatum*, while still considerably cheaper than tufa ashlar, was nevertheless roughly twice as expensive as *opus incertum*.[49] According to Vitruvius, *opus reticulatum* had a tendency to fracture. He goes on to say that 'incerta caementa. . . . non speciosam sed firmiorem quam reticulata praestant structuram'[50] (the rough stone of the *opus incertum* . . . makes a structure which, though not attractive, is stronger than the *opus reticulatum*). This implies that aesthetic considerations were the main reason for the introduction of *reticulatum*.[51]

In Rome itself, therefore, the increase in the construction of civil infrastructure during the second century was principally funded by the Roman state. Moreover, the intensity of this building activity appears to correlate closely with the flows of revenue into the *aerarium*, at least during those periods for which we have evidence for both. The increased demand for new buildings, private as well as public, also led to the development of new construction techniques.

ITALIA

Civic construction by the Roman state was not limited to just the city of Rome. For example, we know from Livy that in 174 the Roman censors Q. Fulvius Flaccus and

[44] Cornell 2000: 49. [45] Delaine 2001. [46] Delaine 2001 esp. 243.

[47] Coarelli 1977: 16–17; the podium of the Temple of Castor in the Forum is probably the oldest securely datable example of concrete construction, from around 117, although an earlier dating for the *porticus Aemilia* would push this back to the 190s.

[48] e.g. Cornell 2000: 53. [49] Delaine 2001 esp. 243.

[50] Vitr. *De arch.* 2. 8. 1. [51] Torelli 1995: 214–15.

A. Postumius Albinus contracted, *cum magna gratia colonorum* (with the great thanks of the colonists), for the construction of buildings in a number of citizen colonies and *municipia* outside Rome. At Calatia (on the edge of the Ager Campanus) and at Auximum (12 km from the Adriatic coast in Picenum), walls were constructed, as well as *tabernae* (shops) around the forum of each town.[52] A temple was contracted to be built at Fundi (on the edge of the Ager Caecubus in southern Latium, which had received citizenship in 188[53]), an aqueduct at Potentia (a citizen colony founded in 184, on the Adriatic coast in Picenum), and a temple and a paved road at Pisaurum (modern Pesaro, also a citizen colony founded in 184, further north on the Adriatic coast in the Ager Gallicus). The text of Livy becomes corrupt at this point but it appears to say that each of Potentia and Pisaurum also received a forum which was surrounded by porticoes and shops, and that buildings of a type termed '*magalia*' appear to have been constructed at Sinuessa, a well-established maritime colony on the Campanian coast.

But the towns of central Italy were not just reliant on funding by the Roman state. From the extravagant euergetism of the local elite in certain cities in Latium and Campania, it can be seen not only that a significant proportion of new civil construction was financed by individuals but that these officials had considerable resources to spend.[54] For example, in the late second or early first century at Aletrium, some 70 km south-east of Rome in Latium, L. Betilienus L. f. Varus displayed almost 'pharaonic activity'.[55] He transformed the appearance of his home town by constructing various buildings, including a portico, a basilica, and a gymnasium, as well as aqueducts and pavements:

> L.Betilienus L.f. Vaarus | haec quae infera scripta | sont de senatu sententia | facienda coiravit: semitas | in oppido omnis, porticum qua | in arcem eitur, campum ubei | ludunt, horologium, macelum, | basilicam calecandam, seedes, | [l]acum balinearium; lacum ad | [p]ortam, aquam in opidum adqu. | arduom pedes CCCXXXX fornicesq. | fecit, fistulas soledas fecit. | Ob hasce res censorem fecere bis, | senatus filio stipendia mereta | esse iousit, populusque statuam | donavit Censorino.[56]
>
> (Lucius Betilienus Varus, the son of Lucius, by a vote of the senate took care of all the works which are recorded below: all the street-paths in the town; the colonnade along which people walk to the citadel; a gymnasium; a sundial; a meat market; a basilica covered with stucco; seats; a bathing pool; he constructed a reservoir by the gate; an aqueduct about three hundred and forty feet long, leading into the city and to the hill of the citadel; also the arches and sound water pipes. In reward for these works, the senate made him a censor twice and ordered that his son be exempt from military service; and the people bestowed the gift of a statue on him over the title of Censorinus.[57])

This type of euergetism was not demonstrated by locals alone. When the Roman commander L. Mummius destroyed Corinth in 146, the statues and paintings he

[52] Livy, 41. 27. 10–13. [53] Livy, 8. 36. 9.

[54] Latium: Aletrium, Formiae, Praeneste, and Signia; Campania: Caiatia, Capua, Heculaneum, Minturnae, Nola, Pompeii, Puteoli, and Sinuessa; Cébeillac-Gervasoni 1998: 118–25, 2002: 22.

[55] As Torelli (1995: 218) terms it. [56] *ILLRP* 528 (= *CIL* I^2 1529).

[57] Trans. Loeb, 'Remains of Old Latin' IV p. 147, slightly revised.

brought back from there and other Achaean cities were displayed in towns across Italy.[58]

But it is the building of monumental sanctuaries with a Hellenistic appearance that seems to have been particularly characteristic of this period in central Italy. In the late second century and in the first decades of the first century, a number of cities appear to have carried out costly renovations of their urban environments, inspired by eastern models such as Pergamum, Cos, Lindos, and Delos. Before the beginning of the first century, the sanctuaries of Fortuna Primigenia at Praeneste and of Hercules Victor at Tibur had been reconstructed on a mammoth scale, an indication of the levels of wealth being achieved in those parts of Italy that had commercial links with the eastern Mediterranean.[59] Grandiose examples have also been identified at Fregellae, Cora, Signia, Pietravairano, and Gabii. Even the Samnite sanctuaries of the central Appenines, Pietrabbondante, S. Giovanni in Galdo, Vastogirardi, and others, were rebuilt in Hellenistic style in the same period, with colonnades and, in the case of the late second-century phase at Pietrabbondante (and unlike at Rome), a theatre.[60] At Pompeii, there is a major period of urban renewal and improvement in civic amenities which starts around the middle of the second century.[61]

The spectacular increases in the fortunes of these cities no doubt derived from a variety of sources, including their share of the booty gained from assisting in Rome's conquest of the Mediterranean littoral and, in particular, in the third quarter of the second century, from the sacking of Corinth and Carthage. As Patterson points out, individual soldiers in the allied armies received the same quantities of booty as their Roman counterparts.[62] Perhaps too, improvements in the management of agricultural land enabled increased exploitation and returns (see Ch. 7). But an additional factor was the rapid development of Delos and the significant profits brought in by the eastern trade in slaves and luxury goods, which led to the enrichment of their local elites.

Onomastic convergences can give, especially in some unusual and less widespread names exclusive to certain cities, precise indications of the geographic origin of the holders: for example, Magulnius, Mantius, Orcevius, and Saufeius at Praeneste. Nine of the twenty-two *gentilicia* (family names) of the thirty-eight magistrates known from Praeneste in the second half of the second century are found amongst the names of traders on inscriptions from the eastern Mediterranean, including four from Delos. Indeed there is a significant overlap, of between 40 and 60 per cent, between the *gentilicia* of the municipal leaders of a number of Latin and northern Campanian cities and those of individuals present in eastern cities connected to commerce.[63] This type of onomastic overlap suggests therefore

[58] Frontin. *Str.* 4. 3. 14; Plin. *HN* 34. 36, 34. 12; Parma colonia: *CIL* I^2 630; Rome: *CIL* I^2 629; Pompeii: R. S. Conway, *The Italian Dialects* (1897) no. 86 (in Oscan); Nursia: *CIL* I^2 628; Cures: *CIL* I^2 631; Trebula Mutuesca: *CIL* I^2 627; Fregellae: Bizzari, *Epigraphica* 1973 xxxv: 140–2.

[59] Bodei Giggliono 1977: 72–3; D'Arms 1980: 65–6; Wallace-Hadrill 2008: 106–43.

[60] Wallace-Hadrill 2003.

[61] Wallace-Hadrill 2008: 129–37.

[62] J. R. Patterson 2006: 611. When in 177, exceptionally, the allied troops were granted half the booty that the Roman soldiers received, it led to great ill-feeling and a silent protest at the general's triumph (Livy, 41. 13. 8).

[63] Cébeillac-Gervasoni 1998: 178–91, 2002: 23–4, 28.

that, no doubt principally through the agency of their dependants, the slaves and freedmen whom we find in Delian inscriptions, these local aristocrats were profiting from the new possibilities of enrichment that were offered by participation in the trade in slaves and luxury goods through Delos. The wealth of Betilienus Varus' family may in part have been derived from the export of olive oil from the region of Brundisium, by again exploiting the commercial openings made possible by the Roman conquest of the Aegean.[64]

As early as the third quarter of the second century, therefore, we can see the economic impact of the Delian trade in central Italy both through the euergetism of the local elites and the construction of monumental sanctuaries based on Hellenistic models.

CONSTRUCTION

The construction projects of the second century required a great deal of financial capital to execute, but the consequent economic benefits and stimuli that they provided would also have been profound. This is because expenditure on buildings and infrastructure can have a multiplier effect (sometimes termed a 'trickle-down' effect) on an economy as a whole. The payments made to (free) contractors, architects, and labourers increase the recipients' incomes, part of which may in turn be spent on other goods and services, to create a theoretically endless (though diminishing) chain of expenditure. In this way the net effect on overall income and, particularly in the case of construction projects, on employment would have been several times larger than the initial sums expended.[65]

A well-known text of Polybius conveys precisely this chain of events and suggests that it was occurring on a significant scale:

> *πολλῶν γὰρ ἔργων ὄντων τῶν ἐκδιδομένων ὑπὸ τῶν τιμητῶν διὰ πάσης Ἰταλιας εἰς τὰς ἐπισκευὰς καὶ κατασκευὰς τῶν δημοσίων, ἅ τις οὐκ ἂν ἐξαριθμήσαιτο ῥᾳδίως, πολλῶν δὲ ποταμῶν, λιμένων, κηπίων, μετάλλων, χώρας, συλλήβδην ὅσα πέπτωκεν ὑπὸ τὴν Ῥωμαίων δυναστείαν, πάντα χειρίζεσθαι συμβαίνει τὰ προειρημένα διὰ τοῦ πλήθους, καὶ σχεδὸν ὡς ἔπος εἰπείν πάντας ἐνδεδέσθαι ταῖς ὠναῖς καὶ ταῖς ἐργασίαις ταῖς ἐκ τούτων· οἱ μὲν γὰρ ἀγοράζουσι παρὰ τῶν τιμητῶν αὐτοὶ τὰς ἐκδόσεις, οἱ δὲ κοινωνοῦσι τούτοις, οἱ δ' ἐγγυῶνται τοὺς ἠγορακότας, οἱ δὲ τὰς οὐσίας διδόασι περὶ τούτων εἰς τὸ δημοσίον.*[66]

[64] Desy 1989: 166; Manacorda 1994: 30; J. R. Patterson 2006: 610–11.

[65] Millett 2001: 25; Keynes (1936: 131 and 220) recommended (ironically) the building of cathedrals as a remedy for unemployment. More recently, in the 1990s, the Japanese government helped to maintain an unemployment rate below 5% (at a time when Western economies were experiencing double-digit rates) by embarking on a number of massive infrastructure projects.

[66] Polyb. 6. 17. 2–4; Walbank (1957: 692) is correct to suggest: (1) that Polybius identifies the πλῆθος (people), with the *publicani*; cf. Livy, 24. 18. 13, where the phrase 'haec inclinatio animorum *plebis* ad sustinendam inopiam aerarii' refers to an offer of contractors to do work on credit; and (2) that this picture of a large-scale system of public contracts in which 'everyone' is involved is only true of the period just before 150, with Polybius retrojecting these conditions into his account of the Roman state at the time of Cannae.

(Many projects are given out by the censors through the whole of Italy. These include the repair and construction of public buildings (and it would not be easy to number them), as well as many rivers, harbours, gardens, mines, and land; in fact everything that falls under Roman dominion. All these projects are handled by the people, and almost, so to speak, everyone is involved either in the sale of these contracts or in the kinds of business to which they give rise. For some are the actual purchasers of the contracts from the censors, some are the partners of these purchasers, some act as guarantors for the purchasers, while yet others pay over their own savings to the state as surety.)

There is no mention in this passage, or in any of our other sources for the Republic, of the civil servants, such as the *curatores aquarum* (curators of the aqueducts) and other officials concerned with public buildings who existed under the Principate. Rather, this passage makes clear that public building works (τὰς ἐπισκευὰς καὶ κατασκευὰς τῶν δημοσίων) during the second century were let out on contract by the censors.[67] Polybius emphasizes the scale on which this was taking place by stating that 'almost, so to speak, everyone is involved either in the sale of these contracts or in the kinds of business (ἐργασία) to which they give rise'.

Less clear is the evidence for the organization of labour and the roles and responsibilities of the different individuals within the construction industry. A couple of notices suggest that this industry had already developed an institutional framework by the early part of the second century. In Cato's *De Agricultura*, the calculation of the cost of building a villa is expressed as a fixed price per roof tile, clearly a measure of area;[68] and the foundation of the *collegium* of the builders (the *fabri tignarii*) was thought in Plutarch's time to go back to Numa.[69] The mythical element in this foundation story suggests that the *collegium* was an ancient institution, probably in existence by the second century, as it certainly was by the middle of the first. As DeLaine says, the *collegium* could have facilitated the gathering together of workers to fulfil a contract;[70] for the second-century construction boom must have employed an immense number of skilled technicians and labourers.

Some indication of the size of the labour force required can at least be inferred from DeLaine's study of the construction industry during the Principate. She has conducted detailed quantitative studies of specific examples of building in order to analyse the scale of materials and manpower required in their construction. For example, by her calculations, the Baths of Caracalla required, on average, about 6,000 men working on site for twelve hours each day for 300 days over four years,

[67] We can compare the contract for the maintenance of a temple at Rome described in Cic. *II Verr.* 1. 130, or the letting of contracts for the paving of the Via Caecilia (*ILLRP* 465) The formula of magistrates, 'locaverunt . . . probaverunt', often occurs in inscriptions (e.g. *ILS* 5892). The practice is also attested in the municipalities: *ILLRP* 518 (the *lex Puteolana de parieti faciundo* of 105—see this volume, p. 80); Brunt 1980: 85. Occasionally, contracts could be let out by other Roman magistrates. Thus C. Gracchus who, as tribune, enacted laws for constructing roads and granaries, was, according to Plut. *C. Gracch.* 6. 3, surrounded by a large group of contractors and artisans (πλῆθος ἐργολάβων, τεχνιτῶν); App. *B. Civ.* 1. 23 says that he laid a large group of contractors and craftsmen (πλῆθος ἐργολάβων καὶ χειροτεχνῶν) under an obligation to him.

[68] Cato, *Agr.* 14. 4–5; DeLaine 2000: 127.

[69] Plut. *Num.* 17.

[70] DeLaine 2000: 132.

with almost 10,000 at peak periods of construction. Half of these would have been unskilled or partly skilled.[71] Of course no single complex of this size was constructed during the second century, but the Aqua Marcia, constructed between 144 and 140 with a length of 91 km, was a massive civil engineering project that could bear comparison.

An additional factor boosting employment was that all the building materials had to be transported to the construction sites. Most of the basic stone building materials of Rome could be supplied reasonably locally and many of the quarries that produced stone for ashlar construction were located within easy access of rivers.[72] But there were no suitable waterways serving the tufa and basalt quarries to the south of Rome. As many as 2,500 to 3,500 ox carts on average were probably needed to keep the builders of the Baths of Caracalla at work.[73] Obviously the construction of these baths is an extreme case dating from nearly four centuries after the period we are discussing, and no quantitative work has yet been carried out on buildings of the second century BC. But DeLaine herself believes, extrapolating from figures based on the building industry of Severan Rome, that it is possible that, during much of the last two centuries BC and the first two centuries AD, when public building was flourishing, as much as 4–6 per cent of the total population of Rome, perhaps 15 per cent of the adult males, could have been employed in construction work.[74]

But this industry was not the only large urban employer. A vast transport and logistics service sector would also have developed to support the expanded port and warehouse facilities that were constructed in the second century reflecting the general increase in trade that we noted in Chs. 7 and 8. Great numbers must have been employed in unloading cargo and transporting it from the docks to the warehouses and ultimately the shops of Rome. There was no good natural harbour at the mouth of the Tiber. In Republican times, ships tied up at riverside wharfs or had their cargoes offloaded onto lighters while riding at anchor offshore of Ostia.[75] Mattingly and Aldrete, in their analysis of the mechanics of Rome's food supply system, calculate that, by the first century AD, this process would have involved many thousands of people. By then, the porters, dockworkers, and boatmen had been institutionalized into various *collegia* and an official bureaucracy had developed to administer the supply system.[76] That said, a seventy-tonne ship was capable of making the twenty-two mile journey up the Tiber to Rome.[77] So it is possible that seagoing vessels in the second century were able to make this journey without trans-shipment of goods, although with the construction of larger ships, from the final quarter of that century onwards, such trans-shipment would have been necessary. But even the smaller seagoing boats of the second century would still have had to be towed up the river. Once at Rome, human labour would

71 DeLaine 2000: 131.

72 Strabo, 5. 3. 7; DeLaine 1995: 559, 2000: 133 fig. 6.10.

73 DeLaine 2000: 135; for the second century BC, Cato (*Agr.* 22. 3) provides specific information about land transport costs by ox-drawn cart.

74 Delaine 2001: 231.

75 Dion. Hal. *Ant. Rom.* 3. 44. 3; Strabo, 5. 3. 5; Mattingly and Aldrete 2000: 145.

76 Mattingly and Aldrete 2000: 148–57.

77 Dion. Hal. *Ant. Rom.* 3. 44. 3; Mattingly and Aldrete 2000: 148.

have been required for porterage. As Rickman stresses, the narrow entrances and multiple levels of Roman warehouses were designed for men who carried the loads, without the use of carts or draught animals. Such a system would have required large numbers of labourers employed solely as porters.[78]

To a greater or lesser extent, slave labour was no doubt employed in the logistics sector of the economy as it was in the construction industry.[79] But it is unlikely that slaves on their own provided the entire labour force for both these industries in the second century. Once again we have only fragments of information to piece together, but it does appear that there was significant immigration of free labour into Rome. In 187, the Latin allies complained to the senate that large numbers of their citizens had migrated to the city and had been assessed there. The senate sympathized with their appeal, according to Livy, because 'already then a multitude of foreigners was burdening the city' (iam tum multitudine alienigenarum urbem onerante).[80]

In the end, 12,000 Latins returned home. But the problem appears to have recurred at various points during the second century. In 177, a *senatus consultum* ordered Latin allies resident at Rome to return to their own cities;[81] and in 126, the tribune M. Junius Pennus expelled foreigners (*peregrini*) from the city.[82] The attempts made to increase Rome's water supply are, of course, yet another indication of the growth of its population during this period and are specifically attributed by Frontinus to urban growth (*incrementum urbis*).[83] There might, of course, be a variety of explanations for this trend towards immigration, but the obvious one is that Rome, with its ambitious building programme and expanding transportation requirements, was seen by rural populations as providing easier and more profitable opportunities for employment than did agriculture.

MANUFACTURING

Buildings are one obvious aspect of the creation of a more complex material culture, but there are also signs of a booming market for consumer goods in Italy starting in the second century. Initially the demand came from the Italian elite and was satisfied by imports from the Hellenistic East, as we saw in the previous chapter; but, by the middle of the first century, production of a whole range of consumer items was shifting to Italy, with demand coming from wider sections of the Italian population.[84] As Wallace-Hadrill says, there is 'clear documentation in Pompeii and Herculaneum of the enthusiasm with which sub-elite levels embraced if not luxury then at least sub-luxury'.[85] The problem is to map examples of this trend and, in particular, to determine how the production of manufactured items was organized during the late Republic, since the literary and

[78] Rickman 1971: 8, 11, 79, 86.

[79] e.g. in the first century Crassus is said by Plutarch (*Crass.* 2. 4) to have owned 500 slave architects and builders whom he employed to redevelop buildings bought up at a very low cost.

[80] Livy, 39. 3. 4–6.

[81] Livy, 41. 8. 6–12, 41. 9. 9–10.

[82] Cic. *Off.* 3. 47.

[83] Frontin. *Aq.* 1. 7.

[84] Wallace-Hadrill 2008: 356–440.

[85] Wallace-Hadrill 2008: 371.

epigraphic sources tell us virtually nothing about the scale of their production and the processes involved. Even the term for a business overseer, *institor*, does not occur before its appearance in a text of Cicero written in 44.[86] Some clues can, however, be found in later periods. For example, from the late first century BC onwards, bricks, tiles, terracotta lamps, and Arretine red-glaze pottery (*terra sigillata*) carry stamps applied during the production process, and lease contracts for potteries survive from third-century AD Egypt. These kinds of evidence can allow us to trace some of the steps in the organization of production across a variety of industries in a way impossible to do for the Republic because of poor survival rates. They also provide a potential model that can be compared with the limited evidence we have from the second century BC.[87]

In mid-third century AD Oxyrhynchus, for example, the production of amphorae was carried out by artisans who were independent of the estate producing the olive oil or wine. The exact mechanism for this production is revealed by a series of three leases for potteries on vineyards.[88] The potter himself leased a pottery belonging to the owner of the land on which they were situated. The lessor provided the pottery, including the necessary tools and raw materials such as clay, water, pitch, and fuel. The lessee provided the manpower. In these labour contracts, the lessees received wages, as well as allowances of wine, in exchange for delivering large numbers of vessels.[89]

More sketchy is our knowledge of the mass production of *terra sigillata* at Arretium which began in the late first century BC. But, again, stamps on the *terra sigillata* referring to people involved in its production provide some indication of the organization of the fine ceramic industry there. Such evidence as exists suggests that it too was legally based on *locatio-conductio* lease contracts with independent artisans who leased the workshops from the landowners. There is no cogent evidence at Arretium for large, single-unit production involving a high degree of subdivision of labour. Rather, the organizational framework for the industry was a series of small, independent, but nucleated workshops, partly sharing such facilities as kilns.[90]

The same phenomenon is also apparent in the terracotta lamp industry, the organization of which can be traced to some extent from the signatures, first appearing in the 20s BC, on the bases of common lamps or 'Firmalampen' which were a common household item throughout the Roman world.[91] Brick production too appears to have been organized in the same way. Steinby interprets the brick stamps (which appear to have been used from the first century AD onwards) to be the documentation of a legal, *locatio-conductio* contract between the landowner, as owner of the raw materials, and the brick makers, as producers working under contract.[92]

86 Cic. *Phil.* 2. 97; Aubert 1994: 28.

87 Professor Michael Crawford points out that large numbers of second-century BC Oscan tile stamps survive, which might provide a fruitful line of enquiry.

88 *POxy.* L 3595–7; Cockle 1981.

89 Ruffing 1999: 104–6; Kehoe 2007*a*: 562.

90 Fülle 1997: 127, 135, 145.

91 Harris 1980*b*: 128.

92 Steinby 1993*b*; the evidence for this comes from the study by Helen (1975) of a sample of 9,000 stamped bricks from excavations at Ostia dating from the first two centuries AD.

Finally, the textile industry reveals, as Kehoe says: 'a similar separation of the ownership and production of raw materials and the organisation of manufacturing characteristic of other industries'.[93] Again, production tended to be organized on a modest scale with independent producers working in relatively small workshops, for example in the six dyeworks and eleven fulling establishments that have been identified at Pompeii and the twenty-two fulleries or dyeworks found at Timgad.[94]

These examples suggest that, under the Principate and across a variety of manufacturing industries, the ownership of natural resources and the organization of the productive processes were separate. The landowner provided the raw materials while another party, economically independent of the landowner, organized the production, providing the management and taking on the risk associated with it. In modern parlance, manufacturing was 'vertically unintegrated'. In the next section we shall see how this model can add to our understanding of the way in which elite Romans of the second century BC responded to economic opportunities.

ELITE INVOLVEMENT

Some idea of the breadth and vibrancy of manufacturing activities in the early second century can be gleaned from the plays of Plautus, who employs Latin words for a large number of specialized workers, ranging from the expected, such as *figularii* (potters) and *fabri* (carpenters), through *fullones* (fullers) and *textores* (weavers), to the less obvious, such as *restiones* (rope makers) and *ampullarii* (makers of leather bottles).[95] As Frank rightly emphasizes, the manufacturing of arms for Roman soldiers during this period must also have been extensive, when the average number of legions in the field between 200 and 168 was 8.75 and, between 167 and 91, 6.48.[96] Cato's *De Agricultura* lists at various points an enormous range of household items and a large variety of agricultural equipment, from basic utensils such as rakes, hoes, and spades to a number of reasonably expensive items of capital equipment, the largest being the *torcularium*, or press for olives or grapes, and the *trapetus*, or rotary mill for crushing olives.[97]

But evidence of direct elite involvement in manufacturing in the second century is not easy to find. There is no mention by Cato of manufacturing as a potentially lucrative occupation in the *praefatio* to the *De Agricultura*. Only farming, moneylending, and trading warrant a mention. A glance at the list of the business interests of senatorial families during this period collected by Wiseman does not reveal any obvious connections.[98] Apart from Cato, whom we discuss shortly, the closest we come to any senatorial interests outside agriculture and finance are C. Terentius Varro (*cos.* 216), described by Valerius Maximus as being the son of

[93] Kehoe 2007*a*: 564. [94] Jongman 1988: 155–86; A. I. Wilson 2001: 272, 285.

[95] Frank 1933: 177. [96] Frank 1933: 179; Brunt 1971*a*: 422–34.

[97] Cato, *Agr.* 10, 18, 20–2, 38, 135; see pp. 158–9 for the archaeological evidence.

[98] Wiseman 1971: 197–202, appendix iv: 'Business Interests of Senatorial Families'.

a retail butcher and, by Livy, as an *institor mercis* in his father's meat business;[99] and M. Aemilius Scaurus, the father of the consul of 115, who was said to have been involved in the charcoal trade.[100] There are, however, a number of indications that elite landowners had an underlying role in the exploitation of natural resources and the provision of raw materials such as stone, lime, and clay, in accordance with the 'vertically unintegrated' model discussed earlier.

Most of the basic stone building materials of Rome could be supplied reasonably locally: from the volcanic deposits thrown up by the Sabatini volcanoes to the north and the Latial volcanoes to the south (the Alban Hills), and from the travertine quarries below Tibur. There were clay deposits for bricks and ceramics on the Tiber around Rome itself, but especially to the north of the city as far as Orte. Lime for the mortar used in *opus incertum* and *reticulatum* was produced from the limestone of the Apennine range, to the north in the Monti Sabini, to the east near Tibur, or around Terracina, where ready access to the sea made transport easier.[101] Writing in the 30s BC, Varro excludes stone quarries, sandpits, and claypits from agriculture proper, but adds: 'which is not to say that they are not to be worked on land where it is suitable and profitable'.[102] In the same passage, he says that the Sasernae (probably writing in the second decade of the first century) had included the working of claypits in their agricultural treatise; and Cato's *De Agricultura* provides what is in fact our only ancient description of lime production as a natural part of an estate with access to raw materials.[103] In addition to its use for construction, lime was principally employed as a fertilizer in agriculture and the inclusion in the *De Agricultura* of a description of a *fornax calcaria*, or limekiln, is probably to be associated with the latter.[104] But its mention illustrates how elite involvement in the production of raw materials could have developed from agricultural to wider uses.

Cato is the only senator from the second century for whose economic interests we have anything other than patchy evidence. Later in life, according to Plutarch, Cato became more interested in making money, having come to the conclusion that agriculture was more entertaining than profitable. He turned to more secure ways of generating income which, as he himself said, could not be 'ruined by Jupiter':

> *ἁπτόμενος δὲ συντονώτερον πορισμοῦ τὴν μὲν γεωργίαν ἡγεῖτο μᾶλλον διαγωγὴν ἢ πρόσοδον, εἰς δ' ἀσφαλῆ πράγματα καὶ βέβαια κατατιθέμενος τὰς ἀφορμὰς ἐκτᾶτο λίμνας, ὕδατα θερμά, τόπους κναφεῦσιν ἀνειμένους, ἔργα πίσσια, χώραν ἔχουσαν αὐτοφυεῖς νομὰς καὶ ὕλας, ἀφ' ὧν αὐτῷ χρήματα προσῄει πολλὰ μηδ' ὑπὸ τοῦ Διός, ὥς φησιν αὐτός, βλαβῆναι δυναμένων.*[105]

> (However, as he applied himself more strenuously to money-getting, he came to regard agriculture as more entertaining than profitable, and invested his capital in business that was safe and sure. He bought pools, hot springs, places given over to fullers, pitch-works, and land with natural pasturage and forests, all of which brought him in much money, and 'could not', as he himself said, 'be ruined by Jupiter'.[106])

[99] Val. Max. 3. 4. 4; Livy, 22. 25. 19. [100] *De vir. ill.* 72. 1–2.

[101] DeLaine 1995: 556–8, fig.1, 2000: 133 fig. 6.10, 134; cf. this volume p. 17.

[102] Varro, *Rust.* 1. 2. 22–3: 'neque ideo non in quo agro idoneae possunt esse non exercendae, atque ex iis capiendi fructus'.

[103] Cato, *Agr.* 38. [104] Dix 1982: 341.

[105] Plut. *Cat. Mai.* 21. 5. [106] Trans. Loeb II 367, revised.

The combination of 'pools, hot springs, places given over to fullers' mentioned in this passage may seem unlikely. But, in the fulling process, wool has to be soaked in hot water to rinse off the grease. In southern Etruria and in other parts of Italy, the hot springs that form themselves into standing pools provide exactly the conditions needed by fullers. Together with the mention of 'pitch-works' (although the phrase ἔργα πίσσια may be corrupt) and 'land with natural pasturage and forests', Plutarch is informing us that Cato turned from farming to the highly profitable exploitation of natural resources which could be used to provide the raw materials for a number of industries.[107]

So was there a pickup in manufacturing production during the second century? Because of the poor survival rates of most manufactured items, the answer to this question can most easily be traced in the ceramic industries that supported agriculture. The enormous numbers of amphorae found in terrestrial and marine contexts show that, during the second century, ceramic production increased substantially in the areas where wine and olive oil were produced. For Dressel 1 transport amphorae, it has been estimated that there were at least one hundred kiln sites along the western coast of Italy. At present only a minority of Dressel 1A amphorae can be assigned to specific production sites, but studies have shown that the Etrurian kilns of Albinia and Cosa were the two most important suppliers of amphorae to Gaul.[108] For the Dressel 1B amphorae, a number of kiln sites are known, principally in Campania, Latium, and Etruria. Occasionally some amphorae do carry stamps. Thus, most of the amphorae found in the upper Grand Congloué wreck bore stamps marked SES, together with production marks, and in a few cases still retained stoppers with the name *L. Titi. C. f.*;[109] but there is no way of telling whether the names Ses(tius) and Titus refer to the producers of the amphorae or their contents.[110] The SES stamps probably indicate that the amphorae were manufactured at or near Cosa, presumably on or near the estates of the prominent Etrurian Sestius family known to have lived there.[111] The Cosa area accounts for 70 per cent of all Sestius stamps found so far on land and Cosa is the only place where almost all known varieties of Sestius stamps occur. The same stamp occurs on amphorae found on sites and in shipwrecks in an area stretching from Cosa around the coast of Gaul.

Ceramic production, therefore, provides evidence for an expansion of manufacturing activity in the countryside in the second century. But it is important to emphasize that ceramic production itself can only have been a very small part of the Roman manufacturing economy as a whole. Pots are low-value, high-bulk items. They are useful to us in assessing levels of manufacturing output, because they are one of the few artefacts to have survived in the archaeological record unlike, say, cloth, wood, leather, and basketwork. There is no reason to suppose

[107] e.g. pitch was used not only in shipbuilding but also in the wine industry; Plin. *HN* 14. 127; Cockle 1981: 94.

[108] A third important production centre, in the Ager Cosanus at Feniglia, has now been identified (Loughton 2003: 182).

[109] Benoit 1952: 249–55; Manacorda 1978; Greene 1986: 92; Parker 1992: 201.

[110] Cf. too the stamps of C. Rabirius Postumus (Shatzman 1975: 395–6; Wiseman 1971: 199).

[111] Cic. *Att.* 15. 29. 1; D'Arms 1980: 55–62 gives a full description of the business activities of the Sestii.

that the production and distribution of clothing, footwear, and tools were less extensive than those of pottery.[112]

The survival of amphorae remains has also led to the widespread but probably erroneous assumption that the production of the majority of manufactured items took place in the countryside. As Wilson wrote, as recently as 2001: 'the prevailing opinion still gives only a minimal role to urban manufacturing'.[113] For the second century, we again only have nods and winks, but Cato's *De Agricultura* does give advice on the central Italian towns in which it is best to buy a whole range of items from clothing to household utensils and agricultural equipment. Cato mentions Rome, Cales, Minturnae, Venafrum, Suessa, Pompeii, Nola, Capua, and Casinum.[114] Clearly, some of the products he describes will have been produced in the countryside and retailed in the towns, but the language Cato uses suggests an urban context for the manufacture of a number of them. Thus, the best ropes for olive and wine presses are made at Casinum by L. Tunnius, and at Venafrum by C. Mennius, the son of L. Mennius: 'Funem torculum siquis faciet, Casini L. Tunnius, Venafri C.Mennius L.f.'. The best rotary mills are made at Pompeii and at 'Rufrius' yard at Nola': 'Nolae ad Rufri maceriam'. Bronzeware was produced at Capua. Later in the second century, the growth of the Delian trade in oriental luxuries produced more specialist manufactures aimed at a wealthy group of elite consumers. According to Pliny the Elder, Naples, Capua, and Praeneste became production centres for the perfume trade and he also reports that Delos itself produced the most highly praised perfume in antiquity.[115] The names of a number of *unguentarii* (perfumers) whose professions are recorded in epigraphic or literary evidence from Italy are also recorded amongst Roman-Italian families on Delos.[116] For example, an *unguentarius* named L. Novius Dionysi(us) L. l. is recorded at Capua and a *Διονύσιος Νούιος Λευκίου* (Dionysius Novius, the son of Lucius) appears on Delos.[117] There is one final intriguing point relating to urban manufacturing. Rome's fourth aqueduct, the Aqua Tepula, was constructed in 125. The springs that fed it were located on the northern slopes of the Alban Hills at the foot of Monte Cimino and the water that came from them was warm (60 °F), giving the aqueduct its name. As a result, the water was probably not suitable for drinking and Dodge suggests that the aqueduct may well have been introduced originally for industrial uses in order to free up the Aqua Marcia for drinking.[118]

CONCLUSION

In the 190s there are hints in our sources (notably the lack of significant expenditure by the censors of that decade) that, despite the Carthaginian and Macedonian indemnities, Rome's financial difficulties persisted. But the booty that Manlius

[112] Ward-Perkins 2005: 94. [113] A. I. Wilson 2001: 271.

[114] Cato, *Agr.* 135. 1–3. [115] Plin. *HN* 13. 4.

[116] Rauh 1993: 54–5, table III: 'Professions Recorded in Italy for Roman-Italian Families at Delos'; cf. this volume pp. 171–2 and 205–6.

[117] *CIL* X 3975; *IDélos* 1764.

[118] Dodge 2000: 174–5; or possibly for agricultural irrigation (cf. Purcell 2007: 363).

Vulso brought back from Asia and, in particular, the indemnity of Antiochus III were transforming events. They ushered in a remarkable period of expenditure on infrastructure (especially by the censors of 184, 179, and 174). As Coarelli noted, however, the loss of the full text of Livy, especially after 150, probably disguises the fact that building activity continued at a high level. That it did continue in this way is in any case suggested by our other, more limited sources, as it is too by the development of new construction techniques, especially concrete as a lower cost alternative to tufa ashlar. The Roman state itself funded most of the construction of civic infrastructure that took place during the second century and the state's expenditure patterns seem to correlate well with what we know about the inflows of revenue into the *aerarium*. Outside Rome, the trade with the East in slaves and luxury goods appears to have generated sufficient wealth, at the level of the individual, to allow great displays of euergetism. The monumental sanctuaries built in a number of central Italian towns reflect these trading contacts with the Hellenistic world in their style of construction.

But the building boom of the second century had a wider impact. The economic multiplier effect of increased expenditure on buildings and infrastructure would most readily have been seen in the levels of employment in the construction industry; and for this we find echoes in our sources. The need to transport large volumes of building materials to Rome (and indeed to other central Italian towns), combined with the increase in trade, probably also resulted in increased employment in the logistics sector of the economy. All this suggests that increased construction and trade produced a large inflection point in Roman economic activity.

Evidence for manufacturing is extremely limited, but it does appear that in the second century BC, as was to be the case under the Principate, elite involvement in manufacturing was limited primarily to the provision, from rural estates, of raw materials to be used in construction and manufacturing. It is artisans such as the ones we mentioned earlier, Tunnius of Casinum, Mennius of Venafrum, and Novius Dionysius of Capua, who undertake the actual production of manufactured goods.

Why did the elite not become involved directly in the manufacturing process? It is a reasonable inference that there were only limited returns to be generated in manufacturing basic items such as amphorae. The profit margin was in the commodity that the amphorae contained and in raw materials such as clay, pitch, and stone. As Kehoe says: 'The economic opportunities created by the production of raw materials for manufacturing were therefore more attractive for the elite than the actual production and marketing of the manufactured goods themselves.'[119]

In terms of the manufacturing processes themselves, one might have imagined that the huge expansion that occurred in the production of, for example, clay artefacts required an organization different from normal small-scale workshop production.[120] But there does not appear to be any sign of this. What we find under the Principate are examples of workshops clustering in a particular area. As Fülle puts it: 'The formation of this kind of nucleated workshop industry seems

[119] Kehoe 2007*a*: 563. [120] Fülle 1997: 145.

to be a more spontaneous, evolutionary process of economic development, as against the establishment of a highly organised manufactory, which needs the deliberate decisions of an investor to come to life.'[121] That said, although the vast majority of manufacturing activity was undoubtedly organized in small workshops, the aggregate production of such units may well have been significant.[122]

So was there an *increase* in manufacturing activity during our period? In certain sectors there clearly was. The archaeological evidence proves that amphorae production soared and, if one can interpret the shift in Cato's economic interests from agriculture to the provision of raw materials as something more than an idiosyncratic quirk, then the same was probably true of the textile industry, as it was too of the provision of basic materials for the construction industry and for other forms of manufacturing.

[121] Fülle 1997: 145. [122] Cf. Mattingly and Salmon 2001*b*: 10.

10

After the Credit Crunch

'Roman history can be profitably studied from several viewpoints which complement each other.'[1]

INTRODUCTION

In Ch. 6, we discussed the importance of deposit banks and functionally similar institutions for a healthy economy, and we found considerable evidence for the presence of such institutions in the Roman world of the second and early first centuries BC. This chapter aims to provide a somewhat speculative answer to the question of why deposit banks seem to be sufficiently numerous in the second century to crop up without comment in contemporary literary works and yet, by the time we get to the more extensive works of Cicero, they barely receive a mention. It also seeks to explain why we do not hear of a really large Roman bank evolving during the last century of the Republic.

General opinion would now probably be that there were two broad categories of providers of credit in the last century of the Republic and the first two centuries of the Principate. First, there were institutions that we would recognize as deposit-taking banks. They were termed *argentariae* or *mensae* and were operated by individuals called *argentarii*. These were professional bankers (professionals, in that banking was their main occupation) who accepted deposits, normally interest-bearing, from their clients, made payments for these clients, and lent out the pooled money at interest. This is the kind of bank that Demosthenes defined in one of his speeches in the fourth century BC as 'a business operation producing risk-laden revenues from other people's money' (ἐργασία προσόδους ἔχουσ' ἐπικινδύνους ἀπὸ χρημάτων ἀλλοτρίων).[2]

The second group were individuals, whom Andreau has termed *les financiers de l'aristocratie*, or 'aristocratic financiers'.[3] These were people who came from the political and social elite who were lending out their own surplus funds, sometimes large amounts of money, either directly or through intermediaries, to other members of the same social elite, as well as to foreign kings and cities. Although functionally similar to deposit banking, their activity was not a profession; rather the 'aristocratic financiers' were investors deploying their surplus funds in order to

[1] Hopkins 1978: 1. [2] Dem. 36. 11. [3] Andreau 1978: 48–50, 1999: 13–15.

achieve a good return on their capital or, occasionally, making loans to help friends or to curry favour with politicians. We shall use the term 'aristocratic financiers', in this precise sense of non-professional portfolio investors, throughout this chapter.

The conventional explanation for the apparent scarcity of references to *argentarii* in the historical record after 88 BC is that it is just a result of bias in our main source, Cicero, who, like other members of the Roman elite, preferred to use the 'aristocratic financiers' to borrow money. After all (so the argument goes), the vast bulk of the available evidence on financial practice during this period is to be found in Cicero's letters and speeches. Therefore, this evidence accurately portrays Roman banking practice only to the extent that Cicero's writings reflect normal financial operations. However, we shall argue that the apparent disappearance of the *argentarii* is not merely a result of literary genre dictating evidence and so providing a distorted picture of financial institutions at this time. Rather, their disappearance is due to a serious impairment of deposit banks caused by the credit crisis of the 80s BC.

To begin with, though, we should explain in more detail why the distinction between professional deposit-taking bankers and 'aristocratic financiers' (i.e. non-professional portfolio investors) is so important. As we saw in Ch. 6, the problem of funding economic activity is that savers are not necessarily entrepreneurs. How do you get one group to lend to the other? When a borrower is a member of his family or a friend, the lender is in a position to evaluate whether or not the borrower is likely to repay the loan. If he is not, it becomes significantly more difficult for the lender to assess his ability to repay. One way round this problem, which is in effect a problem of lack of information ('asymmetric knowledge' in the jargon), is to use a financial intermediary, such as a deposit bank. As Temin puts it: 'The bank solves the problem of finding borrowers and lenders because they each know to go to the bank to place their excess purchasing power or to borrow.'[4] In theory, therefore, a financial system in which deposit banks are operating extensively and successfully will be more economically efficient than a less sophisticated one in which most lending is between individuals and so the problem of asymmetric knowledge impairs the lending process.

BANKS IN THE FIRST CENTURIES AD AND BC

We have already seen, in Ch. 6, how deposit banks appear to have been ubiquitous in the Roman world of the second and early first centuries BC. If we skip forward to the first and second centuries AD, there is, again, considerable epigraphical, archival, and literary evidence for the existence of deposit banks. Inscriptions from this period attest forty-seven *argentarii* and *coactores* and twelve *nummularii* in Rome, and seventeen *argentarii* and *coactores* and ten *nummularii* in the towns of Italy.[5] Borrowing from banks reached down to the level of 'the small

[4] Temin 2004: 710–11.

[5] Andreau 1987: 315; Rathbone and Temin 2008: 404–5 and 406–7 suggest that all the 400 or so towns of Italy had at least one bank, and many (a hundred or more?) had several. They believe that it is unlikely that there were fewer than a thousand banks in first-century AD Rome and Italy.

shippers and petty businessmen who appear in the tablets of the Sulpicii'.[6] Both these and the Iucundus tablets are best interpreted as small parts of the records of banking firms.[7] Much of the Sulpicius archive, for example, is to do with lending and borrowing. Thus the Sulpicii borrowed the not insubstantial sum of HS 94,000 (about 4 talents) for just over a month to finance smaller short-term loans.[8] There are also a number of references to bankers in literary texts. For example, Tacitus recounts that, when Tiberius decided to rescue the credit market in AD 33, he did so by providing HS 100 million of loans through the *mensae*, 'the banks'.[9] There are several passages from the *Digest* that mention banks or bankers.[10]

But in the middle of the first century BC the picture is very different. Despite numerous references to financial matters, the voluminous Ciceronian corpus contains only a handful of references to *argentarii*, and these are mostly in Cicero's earlier speeches, which refer back to the 70s and 80s. Thus in the 70s, Verres executed a banker named Herrenius, who lived in Leptis in north Africa. More than one hundred Roman citizens appealed to Verres on Herrenius' behalf:

> Interrogetur Flavius, si voles, quinam fuerit T. Herennius, is quem ille argentariam Lepti fecisse dicit; qui cum amplius centum cives Romanos haberet ex conventu Syracusano qui eum non solum cognoscerent sed etiam lacrimantes ac te implorantes defenderent, tamen inspectantibus omnibus Syracusis securi percussus est.[11]
>
> (Let Flavius be asked, if you like, who T. Herennius was, the man who, he says, had a bank at Leptis; who, though he had more than a hundred Roman citizens from the community of Syracuse, who not only identified him, but even defended him with their tears and their entreaties to you, was still struck with an axe in the sight of all the Syracusans.)

In the same speech Cicero mentions another banker, Lucceius, who was operating in Rhegium:

> Quid enim dicit aliud C. Numitorius, quid M. et P. Cottii, nobilissimi homines ex agro Tauromenitano, quid Q. Lucceius, qui argentariam Regi maximam fecit, quid ceteri?[12]
>
> (For what else does C. Numitorius say? What else do M. and P. Cottius say, most noble men of the district of Tauromenium? What else does Q. Lucceius say, who operated the largest bank in Rhegium? What else do all the others say?)

Pythius, who ran a bank at Syracuse, was the central figure in an anecdote in Cicero's *De Officiis*: 'Pythius, qui esset ut argentarius apud omnes ordines gratiosus'[13] (Pythius who, as a banker, found favour with all levels of society). Cicero mentions two bankers in his *Pro Caecina*, written in 69, but again referring back to earlier events. The first is M. Fulcinius, one of the leading men of Tarquinii, who ran a 'not ignoble' bank in Rome (and who will be discussed in more detail later);[14] and Sextus Clodius Phormio, a hostile witness for the plaintiff and, therefore, a

[6] Rathbone and Temin 2008: 384. [7] Andreau 1999: 35; Rathbone and Temin 2008: 399.

[8] *TPSulp.* 69; Rathbone and Temin 2008: 398.

[9] Tac. *Ann.* 6. 17. 3: 'tulit opem Caesar disposito per mensas milies sestertio'; other references at Andreau 1987: 65 n. 17.

[10] References at Andreau 1987: 66 n. 18. [11] Cic. *II Verr.* 5. 155.

[12] Cic. *II Verr.* 5. 165. [13] Cic. *Off.* 3. 58.

[14] Cic. *Caecin.* 10–11: 'Romae argentariam non ignobilem fecit'.

disreputable character.[15] Clodius participated in auctions at Rome during the 80s.[16] Finally, and in the context of the same decade, Cicero mentions two financiers in the *Pro Quinctio*: C. Quinctius owed money to a P. Scapula, who may perhaps have been a banker, but is not explicitly called one (he may just have been an individual who had lent money to Quinctius).[17] The second is a certain Sextius, who, though again not explicitly called a banker by Cicero, looks as if he might well have been one, because Cicero refers to a meeting taking place 'at the counter of Sextius'.[18]

That is the sum total of references to *argentarii* in Cicero's speeches and philosophical works. Even more surprisingly, however, there is not a single explicit allusion to an *argentarius* in any of Cicero's correspondence, despite the fact that he was heavily in debt for much of the period that his letters cover. Instead, there are numerous references to credit being provided by members of the Roman elite, or, to use Andreau's term, by 'aristocratic financiers'. For example, in 62, Cicero was desperately in need of money to pay for a house on the Palatine. He had tried to borrow from Gaius Antonius, the governor of Macedonia;[19] but, at the beginning of 61, he wrote to his friend Atticus to say that things were moving much too slowly and that it was imperative that he borrowed. He goes on: 'Opinor ad Considium, Axium, Selicium confugiendum est. Nam a Caecilio propinqui minore centesimis nummum movere non possunt'[20] (I think that I shall have to throw myself on the mercy of Considius, Axius, and Selicius. For from Caecilius not even his associates can extract money at less than 1 per cent [per month]). Andreau has shown that all these individuals were members of the Roman social and political elite.[21] Indeed, Shatzman is able to list twenty-five senators from the late Republic who are known from literary evidence to have engaged in lending money.[22] By AD 33, according to Tacitus, the whole senate was involved in this activity.[23] As we saw in Ch. 8, individual members of the Roman elite also lent money to kings and cities in the Greek East. In 88, we can detect the first sign of this new development: Nicomedes III of Bithynia, who agreed to pay Marcus Aquillius for restoring him to the throne, also borrowed money from some of Aquillius' companions.[24] Appian's language and the tone of his story suggest that these companions were Aquillius' legates. By the middle of the first century, Marcus Brutus was lending money to Ariobarzanes, the king of Cappadocia, and also to the Cypriot city of Salamis.[25] Pompey had also lent money to Ariobarzanes and the interest alone ran to 400 talents per annum.[26]

15 Cic. *Caecin.* 27: 'argentarius Sex. Clodius cui cognomen est Phormio, nec minus niger nec minus confidens quam ille Terentianus est Phormio' (Sextus Clodius, a banker, whose surname is Phormio, a man no less black and no less confident than that Phormio in Terence).

16 Cic. *Caecin.* 6, 27.

17 Cic. *Quinct.* 17: 'cum pecuniam C. Quinctius P. Scapulae debuisset'.

18 Cic. *Quinct.* 25: 'ad tabulam Sextiam'.

19 Cic. *Fam.* 5. 5.

20 Cic. *Att.* 1. 12. 1.

21 Andreau 2002: 124–7.

22 Shatzman 1975: 76.

23 Tac. *Ann.* 6. 16. 3: 'neque enim quisquam [sc. senator] tali culpa vacuus' (not one [senator] was free from similar guilt).

24 App. *Mith.* 11: παρὰ τῶν ἑπομένων Ῥωμαίων.

25 Cic. *Att.* 5. 21. 10–12, 6. 1. 5–7, 6. 2. 7–9, 6. 3. 5.

26 Cic. *Att.* 6. 1. 3.

King Ptolemy Auletes owed large amounts of money to various Romans, including C. Rabirius Postumus.[27]

As we touched on in Ch. 6, Heichelheim, Barlow and, most recently, Harris have argued that this system of aristocratic lending was made more efficient by a legal procedure known as *delegatio debitoris*, under which a *nomen*, in the sense of 'an outstanding loan', could be used as a way of paying for an item.[28] Harris believes, for example, that a common method of paying for large property purchases in the late Republic was by delivering *nomina*, which he interprets to be debts owed to the purchaser of the property by a third party. In addition there is some limited evidence, from the 40s BC, that there was a secondary market in such *nomina*. Thus Cicero considered selling a debt, when he was anxious to buy a property:

> Si enim Faberianum [sc. nomen] venderem, explicare vel repraesentatione non dubitarem de Silianis, si modo adduceretur ut venderet. Si venalis non haberet, transirem ad Drusum vel tanti quanti Egnatius illum velle tibi dixit.[29]
>
> (For if I sold the Faberius debt, I wouldn't hesitate to settle for Silius' place, even on a cash basis, if only he could be induced to sell. If he was not going to sell, I'd turn to Drusus, even at the price which Egnatius told you he is asking.)[30]

Vettienus was willing to buy a debt of Cicero's, although for only half its nominal value:

> Sed tamen ne nihil de re, nomen illud, quod a Caesare, tris habet condiciones, aut emptionem ab hasta (perdere malo, etsi praeter ipsam turpitudinem hoc ipsum puto esse perdere) aut delegationem a mancipe annua die (quis erit cui credam, aut quando iste Metonis annus veniet?) aut Vettieni condicione semissem.[31]
>
> (However, not to omit business altogether, that debt, assigned to me by Caesar, can be handled in three ways: either a purchase at an auction (I would prefer to lose the money, although, apart from the discredit involved, I think that's what this would amount to), or a transfer by the principal a year hence (whom could I trust and when will that 'Meton's year' arrive?), or a half-payment on Vettienus' terms.)[32]

From passages such as these, in which casual references are made to *nomina*, it appears that transactions of this kind were not considered to be unusual. The creditor examined each *nomen* which was offered to him to determine whether it was likely to be repaid.[33] This suggests that *nomina* were functionally similar to what we would term 'negotiable notes' or 'securitized debt'.

Despite the absence of any explicit references in Cicero's correspondence, it has been argued by some scholars that a handful of passages do in fact refer to *argentarii*. Thus Frank labels an individual called Egnatius as a 'banker', although Cicero does not use the term *argentarius* to describe him.[34] Cicero merely tells

[27] Cic. *Rab. Post.* 6, 21.

[28] Heichelheim 1938: 554–7; Barlow 1978: 155–68; Harris 2006: 8–9, 15.

[29] Cic. *Att.* 12. 31. 2.

[30] Trans. Loeb XXIV 263, slightly revised.

[31] Cic. *Att.* 12. 3. 2. For a discussion of this problematic passage, see Shackleton Bailey 1966: 398–9.

[32] Trans. Loeb XXIV 263, slightly revised.

[33] Note Atticus' concern over some *nomina* that Faberius offered to transfer to Cicero in the year 46: Cic. *Att.* 12. 2a. 1, 13. 32. 1, 12. 5a; 13. 3. 1, 13. 4. 2, 13. 33. 1–2, 13. 4. 2; see p. 265.

[34] Frank 1933: 350.

Atticus that 'the money is with Egnatius'.[35] Similarly, and for no obvious reason, Frank describes Vestorius as a banker.[36] Andreau believes that there is only one individual mentioned in Cicero's correspondence who may have been an *argentarius*, although again he is not so termed by Cicero. This is Vettienus, who appears in eight letters during the period 49 to 44.[37] Andreau's argument is principally based on the fact that Cicero jokingly calls Vettienus a *monetalis*, in response to the latter, in similar vein, having referred to Cicero as *proconsul*.[38] But this reference to the *tresviri monetales*, 'moneyers', who were responsible for producing the Roman coinage, need not imply that Vettienus was any more an *argentarius* than he was an 'aristocratic financier'. Cicero presumably calls Vettienus a *monetalis*, because the latter is a source of money.

There is a similar ambiguity in a letter written in 60. Cicero has to find a loan to fit out his villas in Tusculum and Pompeii, and he complains that he is 'overwhelmed' by debts which he has taken on 'around the Forum': 'Tusculanum et Pompeianum valde me delectant, nisi quod me, illum ipsum vindicem aeris alieni, aere non Corinthio sed hoc circumforaneo obruerunt'[39] (my properties at Tusculum and Pompeii really please me, except that they have overwhelmed me, the champion of debt, with the bronze of others—not a Corinthian bronze but the kind you get around the Forum). The expression 'around the Forum' (*circumforaneo*) may be an allusion to *argentarii*, but it is just as likely to be to 'aristocratic financiers'. There are references in a number of texts to individuals involved in the world of finance meeting at the Janus medius and the Puteal Libonis, both of which were situated in the Forum.[40] For example in the *De Officiis*, Cicero says:

> Sed toto hoc de genere, de quaerenda, de collocanda pecunia, (vellem etiam de utenda), commodius a quibusdam optimis viris ad Ianum medium sedentibus quam ab ullis philosophis ulla in schola disputatur.[41]
>
> (But this whole subject of acquiring money, of investing money (I wish I could also include spending money) is more profitably discussed by certain excellent men sitting by the middle Janus, than by any philosophers of any school.[42])

The 'excellent men sitting by the middle Janus' to whom Cicero refers in this passage are also said by him to have erected a statue to L. Antonius, calling him the patron of the Janus medius.[43] Both these texts speak of the lending of money and of the placing out of loans, but again it is impossible to determine whether the individuals involved in these activities were *argentarii* or 'aristocratic financiers'. Scholiasts commenting on two passages from Horace which mention the Janus medius consistently speak of *creditores* (creditors) and *faeneratores* (moneylenders).[44] According to Cicero,

[35] Cic. *Att.* 11. 3. 3: 'pecunia apud Egnatium est'. [36] Frank 1933: 351.

[37] Andreau 1987: 690–3; Cic. *Att.* 10. 5. 3; 10. 11. 5; 10. 13. 2; 10. 15. 4; 12. 3. 2; 15. 13a. 1; 15. 20. 1; 15. 13. 3.

[38] Cic. *Att.* 10. 11. 5. [39] Cic. *Att.* 2. 1. 11.

[40] The expression 'Janus medius' or 'Janus' appears in two inscriptions and eight texts (references at Andreau 1987: 707 nn. 32 and 34); for possible locations of the Janus medius, see Andreau 1987: 707–9.

[41] Cic. *Off.* 2. 87. [42] Trans. Loeb XXI 265, slightly revised.

[43] Cic. *Phil.* 6. 15; cf. 7. 16.

[44] Ps-Acr. *ad* Hor. *Epist.* 1. 1. 52–9: 'Duo iani ante basilicam Pauli steterunt, ubi erant loca faeneratorum'; Ps-Acr. *ad* Hor. *Sat.* 2. 3. 18: 'Iani statuae tres erant; ad unam illarum solebant convenire

faeneratores also gathered at the Puteal Libonis: in the *Pro Sestio*, Cicero ridiculed his enemy Gabinius, saying that he was 'puffed up with rage against the *Puteal* and the flocks of *faeneratores*'.[45]

This raises the question of whether we should equate the 'aristocratic financiers' (in Andreau's limited sense of those from the political and social elite who were lending out their own surplus funds) with these *faeneratores*.[46] But the word *faenerator* appears to have had a wider meaning than this narrow sense and to be used as a generic term for anyone involved in providing credit.[47] Thus Cicero, in discussing the attitude of various groups towards Caesar in December 50, says that the *faeneratores*, the *publicani* (tax collectors), and the *agricolae* (farmers) are neutral.[48] M. Caelius Rufus, in 48, says that the *faeneratores* approve of Caesar.[49] The modern assumption is that the term *faenerator* carries negative overtones;[50] and the verb *fenerari*, as used by Cato in the second century BC, certainly seemed to do so.[51] Hence, the word *faenerator* is often translated as 'usurer'. But by the middle of the first century BC, this no longer appears to hold true. Indeed Considius, one of the lenders upon whose mercy Cicero thought he might throw himself, appears to have referred to himself as a *faenerator*:

> In Q. quoque Considio saluberrimi exempli nec sine parvo ipsius fructu liberalitas adnotata est. Qui Catilinae furore ita consternata re publica, ut ne a locupletibus quidem debitae pecuniae propter tumultum pretiis possessionum deminutis solvi creditoribus possent, cum centies atque quinquagies sestertii summam in faenore haberet, neque de sorte quemquam debitorum suorum neque de usura appellari a suis passus est, quantumque in ipso fuit, amaritudinem publicae confusionis privata tranquillitate mitigavit, opportune mirificeque testatus se nummorum suorum, non civilis sanguinis esse faeneratorem: nam qui nunc praecipue negotiatione delectantur, cum pecuniam domum cruentam retulerunt, quam inprobando gaudio exultent cognoscent, si diligenter senatus consultum, quo Considio gratiae actae sunt, legere non fastidierint.[52]

> (In Q. Considius too was noted an act of liberality, setting a most wholesome example and with no small profit for himself. When the Republic was thrown into shock by Catiline's madness, so that in the upheaval even the rich could not pay their creditors the money they owed, because property values had fallen and, although he had HS 15 million out on loan, he would not let his agents call upon any of his debtors either for principal or for interest. As far as he could, he softened the bitterness of public turmoil

creditores et feneratores'; Porph. *ad* Hor. *Epist.* 1. 1. 52–9: 'Ad ianos eos qui sunt in regione basilicae Pauli, feneratores consistunt'; Porph. *ad* Hor. *Sat.* 2. 3. 18: 'Quia omnes ad Ianum in basilica consistabant feneratores.'

45 Cic. *Sest.* 18: 'puteali et faeneratorum gregibus inflatus'.

46 Andreau 1999: 11 says that 'even though the word *faenerator* could, in all periods, be applied to anyone who advanced interest-bearing loans, very early on it came to designate particular men who specialised in lending money, or usurers'; cf. too Verboven 2008: 211–18.

47 The same is true of the Greek equivalent: δανειστής. Thus Caesar, as governor of Spain in 61, dealt with δανεισταί (moneylenders) in his province, allowing them two-thirds of their debtors' income (Plut. *Caes.* 12. 1–2).

48 Cic. *Att.* 7. 7. 5.

49 Cic. *Fam.* 8. 17. 2; Syme 1939: 72–3 calls them 'bankers'.

50 e.g. Verboven 2008: 214: 'the word *faenerator* carries very negative connotations and is avoided as much as possible'.

51 Cic. *Off.* 2. 89 (quoted on p. 259).

52 Val. Max. 4. 8. 3.

by his private composure in opportune and wonderful attestation that he was a *faenerator* of his own money, not of citizens' blood. For people who nowadays especially delight in business, when they have brought bloodstained money home, will see how reprehensible is the joy in which they exult, provided they do not disdain to read carefully the senatorial decree which thanks Considius.[53])

Cicero does not himself use the term *faenerator* to describe Considius, or for that matter Caecilius, Selicius, or Axius.[54] Cicero also borrowed money through Cluvius of Puteoli and Atticus borrowed through Vestorius, but again he does not call them *faeneratores*.[55] In fact, Cicero applies the term *faenerator* to only three named individuals: to Scaptius and Mantinius, the agents of Brutus in his 200-talent loan to Salamis;[56] and to Verres.[57] This, however, is hardly surprising. Atticus advised Cicero on his financial affairs, sometimes managing them directly, and Cicero's correspondence is full of orders and directions to Atticus. It is precisely because Atticus and Cicero both already knew the individuals to whom they were referring that it was unnecessary to use an economic identifier, such as *faenerator*, to describe them.

Various explanations have been offered as to why the *argentarii* largely disappear from the record, only to reappear in the first century AD. As we said at the beginning of this chapter, the conventional one is that deposit banks did not disappear and that this impression is just a result of bias in our main source, Cicero, who, like other members of the Roman elite, preferred to use the 'aristocratic financiers' to borrow money. In other words, the picture that we have of financial institutions is skewed because we do not have a first-century BC Plautus or Terence; nor, for that matter, do we have a second-century BC Cicero. As far as we can tell, however, the role of these 'aristocratic financiers' in providing credit appears to have been a new phenomenon. Only one example of elite borrowing and lending before the first century has survived: L. Aurelius Cotta (*tr. pl.* 154), who tried to use the sacrosanctity of his office to evade his *creditores*, but was prevented from doing so by his fellow tribunes.[58] As we have seen, Polybius mentions senators using a bank in the 160s and we hear that Aemilius Scaurus considered becoming a banker later in the same century.[59]

Jongman produces a different argument, suggesting that it was precisely because they were so rich that the Roman elite borrowed from each other, the argument being that there was nobody else to turn to but their own kind.[60] But this begs the question of why there is no record of a really large Roman bank in the second or first centuries BC, comparable (*mutatis mutandis*) to that, say, of Pasion at Athens in the fourth century BC, to which they could have turned.[61]

53 Trans. Loeb I 431, slightly revised.
54 Cic. *Att.* 1. 12. 1.
55 Cic. *Att.* 6. 2. 3.
56 Cic. *Att.* 5. 21. 12, 6. 1. 5; the elite probably used intermediaries or brokers (*intercessores, proxenitae*) such as Scaptius and Mantinius to disguise their involvement in loans. Rathbone and Temin 2008: 389 believe that these specialist brokers formed 'the core of the group whom the Romans called *faeneratores* ("usurers"). Broking was probably the main function of the elusive men of the middle Janus.'
57 Cic. *II Verr.* 2. 170, 186–91.
58 Val. Max. 6. 5. 4; Lucil. 440–2.
59 Polyb. 31. 27. 6–7; *De vir. ill.* 72. 2.
60 Jongman 2003*a*: 196.
61 e.g. Dem. 36. 5–6. It also begs the question of why there is no record of a large Roman bank under the Principate, but that is beyond the scope of this book.

Howgego turns the question round and suggests that one of the reasons why banks failed to develop into major financial institutions, facilitating and stimulating economic growth, is that they tended not to be used by the elite.[62]

Harris, on the other hand, has suggested that the spread of the system of easily transferred debts, in other words the system of *delegatio debitoris*, meant that professional bankers actually lost some of their importance.[63]

There may be elements of truth in some or all of these views. However, we still have to explain the apparent ubiquity of banks in the second century BC, as well as the fact that during this period members of the elite, the senators whom Polybius mentions at 31. 27. 6–7, clearly used a bank and had fifty talents on deposit with it. Again, we should remind ourselves that a financial system that operates principally with deposit banks will, in theory, be more economically efficient than one in which most lending is between individuals. Why did the system of credit provision change and why did banks apparently fail to develop into large financial institutions?

THE PROBLEMS OF THE 80s BC

In fact the economic, legal, and regulatory environment of the second century BC and the early first century BC was one in which we would have expected Roman banks to prosper and to have grown in size.

As we have seen in earlier chapters, in second-century BC Rome, increased inflows of bullion from warfare, from mining and, eventually, from provincial taxation, combined with a probable expansion in the availability of credit to produce a massive increase in Rome's money supply. Or to put it another way, in second-century BC Rome, there was a boom in monetary liquidity. This growth in the supply and availability of money in turn resulted not only in more funding being available for the Roman military, but also in increased economic activity. On top of all this there was the added bonus that there does not appear to have been any concept of taxing the profits of a banking business. This is exactly the economic environment in which Roman banks should have prospered.

The legal and regulatory environment in which Roman banks operated was also extremely liberal and liberating. Roman banks operated under private law, which meant that they could benefit from a legal system that recognized private property, contracts, and enforcement.[64] But they were not themselves constrained by mountains of legislation specific to their industry. As Rathbone and Temin have pointed out, there are several rulings in the *Digest* that mention bankers or banking, but no separate chapter on the industry.[65] Important though they were, there appear to have been only a handful of legal rules specific to banking that had developed by the late second or early first century BC. For example, the author of the *Rhetorica ad Herrenium*, probably writing in the 80s, states:

[62] Howgego 1992: 29; cf. Rauh 1989: 70.

[63] Harris 2006: 12.

[64] Cf. Hitchner 2005: 221: 'as anyone who has participated in a business venture in the high risk rough and tumble of a developing country knows, only the absence of secure rights of property and the rule of law will truly stop investment and participation'.

[65] Rathbone and Temin 2008: 392.

> Consuetudine ius est id quod sine lege aeque ac si legitimum sit usitatum est; quod genus, id quod argentario tuleris expensum ab socio eius recte petere possis.[66]
>
> (Legal custom is that which, in the absence of any statute, is by usage endowed with the force of statute law; for example, the money you have deposited with a banker you may rightly seek from his partner.[67])

This passage suggests that, in the case of a *societas* between bankers, partners were legally obliged to return a deposit placed with another partner. Other rules dating back to this period of which we know (there may have been others) included provisions that bankers had to make their records available in legal cases, that compensation for reciprocal debts between a banker and his client was automatic, and that the informal promise by a banker to pay his client's debts (*receptum argentarii*) was legally enforceable.[68]

The legal framework surrounding the activities of bankers may have been expanding, but, most importantly, banks were not licensed or regulated by the state; nor was there any self-regulation. There was no central bank. The officials in charge of the *aerarium* were annually elected magistrates, a pair of quaestors (increased to twenty by Sulla), but, as Williams has emphasized, they had no executive authority to form policies or to take decisions.[69] The quaestors' primary responsibilities were to act as curators of the bullion, cash, and documents stored in the *aerarium*, and to make payments when required to do so by law or by *senatus consultum*. Decisions on levels of coin production were taken by the senate, but there does not appear to have been any day-to-day regulation or oversight of the banks. Ad hoc decisions might be taken, for example, to cap usurious rates of interest, but these were few and far between; and, in any case, they tended, eventually, to be honoured more in the breach than in the observance.[70] Even today, nobody thinks about the banking system until there is a problem.

Banks were, therefore, pretty well unrestricted in their activities. As Rathbone and Temin say: 'A banker was what a banker did, and a Roman chose to deal with a bank, as one legal opinion puts it "going on its public reputation" (*fidem publicam secuti*).'[71] This was fine when things were going well, but would have been disastrous when they went wrong. The lack of regulation meant that there was, in the jargon, a very high level of systemic risk. There was no safety net if a bank went bust. There was no lender of last resort, because the Roman state did not lend.

By contrast, during the 2008 credit crisis, for example, emergency policy responses were consciously arrived at by governments, regulators, and central banks. They included measures such as the full or partial nationalization of certain banks, the encouragement of the mergers of others, and the decision to let banks such as Lehmans fail. Government funding was provided, followed by quantitative easing in order to stabilize the money supply, and to try to restimulate battered economies. However imperfectly, our modern system works because there are

66 *Rhet. Her.* 2. 13. 19.
67 Trans. Loeb I 93.
68 Andreau 1987: 597–602, 615–31; Petrucci 2002.
69 Williams 1998: 174.
70 e.g. Livy, 35. 7. 2–5; cf. Tac. *Ann.* 6. 16.
71 Rathbone and Temin 2008: 394; *Dig.* 42. 5. 24. 2 (Ulpian).

central banks, regulatory bodies, and finance ministries which are charged with the task of overseeing the financial system.

In Republican Rome none of this existed, and the shortcomings of the system were highlighted in 88. In that year, a major financial crisis occurred because of the joint effects of the Social and Mithradatic Wars. It deepened when Sulla marched on Rome and a civil war began.

The first tangible evidence for problems comes in 89, when the Social War had hurt the economy and made debts hard to repay.[72] Livy's epitomator says that the citizen body was burdened by debt; and Appian says that debtors delayed payments 'on the plea of war and civil commotion'. Sempronius Asellio, the urban praetor, began to allow actions to be taken by debtors against their creditors, according to an obsolete law forbidding interest-bearing loans. He was lynched by a mob of angry creditors and killed.[73]

In the following year, further problems were added to the dislocations caused by the Social War. In 88, Mithradates VI of Pontus invaded the province of Asia. In the *De Imperio Cnaei Pompeii*, Cicero describes how this resulted, first, in the loss of the *pecuniae Asiaticae* (moneys invested in and lent into Asia); secondly, in the collapse of *fides* (credit) at Rome; and, thirdly, in the interruption of repayments of loans at Rome, '*solutione impedita*':

> Nam tum, cum in Asia res magnas permulti amiserant, scimus Romae, solutione impedita, fidem concidisse. Non enim possunt una in civitate multi rem ac fortunas amittere, ut non plures secum in eandem trahant calamitatem. A quo periculo prohibete rem publicam, et mihi credite, id quod ipsi videtis: haec fides atque haec ratio pecuniarum, quae Romae, quae in foro versatur, implicata est cum illis pecuniis Asiaticis et cohaeret; ruere illa non possunt, ut haec non eodem labefacta motu concidant.[74]
>
> (For then, when very many people lost large fortunes in Asia, we know that there was a collapse of credit (*fides*) at Rome, because repayments were interrupted (*solutione impedita*). It is indeed impossible for many individuals in a single state to lose their property and fortunes without involving still greater numbers in their ruin. Defend the Republic from this danger; and believe me when I tell you—what you see for yourselves—that this credit and this system of monies, which operates at Rome in the Forum, is bound up in, and is linked with, those Asian monies (*pecuniae Asiaticae*); the loss of the one inevitably undermines the other and causes its collapse.)[75]

This passage of Cicero is remarkable in its contemporary tone. Substitute 'US subprime' for 'the Asian monies' and the 'UK banking system' for 'the system of monies which operates at Rome in the Forum' and it could have been written

[72] Williams 1998: 177 correctly emphasizes the intimate connection between 'the public *inopia* of the 80s and the profound crisis in private credit', which have 'generally been treated as discrete phemonena'.

[73] Livy, *Per.* 74: 'Cum aere alieno pressa esset ciuitas, A. Sempronius Asellio praetor, quoniam secundum debitores ius dicebat, ab his qui faenerabant in foro occisus est' (when the state was crushed by debt, the praetor, A. Sempronius Asellio, was killed in the Forum by those who lent money, because he was allowing actions by debtors); cf. App. *B. Civ.* 1. 54, who says that the δανεισταί (moneylenders) killed him and Val. Max. 9. 7. 4, who says that it was the *creditores.*

[74] Cic. *De imp. Cn. Pomp.* 19. [75] Trans. Loeb IX 31, slightly revised.

about the credit crisis of 2008, which was caused by the increasing default rates on high-risk US mortgage loans provided to people on low or no salaries; mortgage loans that had been repackaged and sold on to banks and investors around the world. Indeed, what is so striking about Cicero's text is that it clearly talks about linked financial markets around the Roman world. The financial capital represented by the *pecuniae Asiaticae* is linked explicitly to the Forum in Rome. In the paragraphs immediately preceding the passage just quoted, Cicero talks of the destruction of the financial capital which had been directly invested in the province of Asia by *publicani* and by Roman businessmen. So our text does not seem to refer to them. At the beginning of our passage, Cicero says that 'there was a collapse of credit (*fides*) at Rome, because repayments were interrupted', and so the implication must be that what Cicero is referring to here is the monetary resources of affluent Romans that have also been channelled into Asia in the form of loans. It is no coincidence that the historian Appian says that during the massacres of Italians and Romans in Asia in 88, Mithradates made δανεισταί (moneylenders) a special target.[76]

The response of officials of the Roman state to this growing crisis was poor. Instead of providing assistance to support the banks and to encourage them to lend at a time of extreme financial distress, they successively took several measures which made the situation worse.

In 88, the tribune, Sulpicius Rufus carried a *plebiscitum* limiting each senator's debts to a mere 2,000 denarii.[77] The content and the aim of the law are uncertain and in any case it was declared invalid upon the death of Sulpicius in the same year. But, given its timing during a period of financial crisis, it is likely to have been an attempt to prevent senators engaging in finance by restricting the amount of money that they could borrow. Later in the same year, 88 BC, a further law concerning debt was introduced by the consuls, Sulla and Pompeius Rufus. The only source for the *lex Cornelia Pompeia* is a fragment of Festus which suggests that the law perhaps allowed some kind of partial repayment of loans by debtors, as well as capping the rate of interest that could be charged by creditors: 'Unciaria lex appellari coepta est, quam L. Sulla et Q. Pom(peius Rufus) tulerunt, qua sanctum est ut debitores <duo>decimam partem . . . '[78] (the law, passed by L. Sulla and Q. Pompeius Rufus, began to be called 'the unciarial law', by which it was permitted that debtors . . . <twelfth> part . . .). Two years later, the suffect consul of 86, Valerius Flaccus, carried an even more radical law, the *lex Valeria de aere alieno*, which cut debts by three-quarters: ' . . . suffectus Valerius Flaccus, turpissimae legis auctor, qua creditoribus quadrantem solvi iusserat . . . '[79] (. . . the suffect consul Valerius Flaccus, the author of a very shameful law, in which he had decreed that one quarter of a debt should be paid to creditors . . .). Shortly afterwards we

[76] App. *Mith.* 22. [77] Plut. *Sull.* 8.

[78] Festus 516L; Barlow 1978: 122 suggests that *faenus unciarium* probably means that $8\frac{1}{3}$% p.a. was set as the maximum rate of interest in Rome, but 12% p.a. is more commonly assumed to have been the maximum rate.

[79] Vell. Pat. 2. 23. 2; cf. Sall. *Cat.* 33. 2: 'ac novissume memoria nostra propter magnitudinem aeris alieni volentibus omnibus bonis argentum aere solutum est' (and not long ago, within our memory, because of the scale of outstanding debt, silver was paid in bronze, with the consent of all good men').

find the quaestor Fonteius repaying some old debts at one-quarter of their value;[80] and the *lex Valeria* seems to have been behind Cicero's elusive statement in the *Pro Quinctio* that it was not enough to examine the books of account, when settling a debt:

> Cum pecuniam C. Quinctius P. Scapulae debuisset, per te, C. Aquili, decidit P. Quinctius quid liberis eius dissolveret. Hoc eo per te agebatur quod propter aerariam rationem non satis erat in tabulis inspexisse quantum deberetur, nisi ad Castoris quaesisses quantum solveretur.[81]
>
> (Since C. Quinctius owed money to P. Scapula, P. Quinctius [his brother], according to your decision, C. Aquilius, settled how much he had to pay to Scapula's children. The question had to be handled by you, because, owing to financial procedure, it was not enough to have examined the account books for the amount of the debt, unless you made enquiries at the temple of Castor as to how much had to be paid.[82])

All these laws must of course have benefited debtors enormously, but equally clearly all of them, and in particular the *lex Valeria*, would have significantly worsened the position of the deposit banks.

If things were not already bad enough for the deposit bankers, the Sullan proscriptions of the late 80s put another nail in the coffin. Sulla declared certain Roman citizens who were his political enemies to be outlaws and confiscated their property:

> [Sulla] proscriptorum liberis ius petendorum honorum eripuit et bona eorum vendidit, ex quibus plurima primo rapuit. Redactum est sestertium ter milies quingenties.[83]
>
> ([Sulla] deprived the sons of the proscribed of the right to stand for office, and sold off their property, a very large amount of which he seized for his own use. The proceeds were HS 350 million.[84])

The proscriptions affected bankers in two ways. First, they caused the price of land to fall, which in turn meant that the security available to bankers declined.[85] Secondly, according to Appian, guilt by association could put an individual on the proscription lists, and a loan constituted an association.[86]

Compounding the problem for the banks in the 80s was a lack of monetary liquidity in Italy. Although, as we have seen, the Roman money supply at this time consisted of bank deposits and coinage in circulation, and not just of coinage alone, the efficient working of Rome's banking system would still have depended on a sufficient supply of denarii in order to function properly. In a hard-money economy, one in which little or no token money circulates, the availability of deposits in the form of coin directly influences the ability of banks to operate and to make loans.

Although coin issuance at Rome in the 90s was not large, and although there had been a slight drop in the silver standard of the coinage in the years immediately preceding the Social War, it does not look as though these developments reflected any problems at the *aerarium*.[87] Pliny reported the reserve in the

80 Cic. *Font.* 1–2.
81 Cic. *Quinct.* 17 (81 BC referring to 83 BC).
82 Trans. Loeb VI 25, slightly revised.
83 Livy, *Per.* 89.
84 Trans. Loeb XIV 113, slightly revised.
85 Plut. *Crass.* 6. 6.
86 App. *B. Civ.* 1. 96.
87 Williams 1998: 181; Walker 1980: 62–3.

aerarium for the year 91, as he did for 157 and for 49; but in the case of 91, our manuscripts have lost an important line, and as a result we do not know the amount of the gold and silver bullion, but only of the coined silver. This amounts to just over HS 1.6 m. or 67 talents, which is not an enormous sum.[88] But, as Williams comments, the subsequent sharp increase in coin production from 90 onwards does not suggest a lack of bullion in the treasury at that time.[89]

Certainly there was some minor tinkering with the coinage, but none of it had far-reaching significance. In the years immediately preceding the Social War, the quinarius had been revived in a debased form, and seems to have taken over from the old victoriatus, to which it was made equivalent.[90] The *lex Papiria* (probably of 91) lowered the standard of the as from uncial to semuncial and authorized new issues of the silver sestertius.[91] Livius Drusus (probably the tribune of 91) apparently proposed to debase the silver coinage by mixing it with an eighth part of bronze. There is, however, no evidence to suggest that such coins were ever issued by the Roman state, although the law did foreshadow the debasement that was to follow.[92]

The Social War in particular led to a significant increase in the level of coin issuance at Rome, probably because of the large number of troops that had to be paid.[93] The Roman monetary response was to produce more coinage in the year 90 than in any other single year in the history of the Republic.[94] This trend continued in the 80s. Verboven calculates that issues of denarii from 91–80 make up, on average, 36 per cent of all the denarii minted between 157 and 50, compared to only 32 per cent for all issues of denarii minted between 79 and 50. Even after thirty years of shrinkage, the output of the 80s still made up more than a third of the coinage in circulation in 50 BC.[95] Indeed the cost of the war was so large that the Roman state had to resort to a limited debasement of the silver coinage. As Howgego says: 'The debasement of the coinage is arguably as good an indicator as we have of the fiscal inadequacy of the Roman empire.'[96] Between 89 and 87, the silver fineness of the denarius was reduced to a level no higher than 94 per cent.[97] We can compare an earlier crisis-driven debasement which occurred at the height of the Second Punic War and which reduced the silver fineness down to about 89 per cent.[98]

[88] Plin. *HN* 33. 55; Frank 1933: 265–71 argues that the *aerarium* was poor in the 90s.

[89] Williams 1998: 174; Crawford 1974: 650–1 for some idea of the small size of the issues of the 90s.

[90] Plin. *HN* 33. 46; Williams 1998: 181.

[91] Plin. *HN* 33. 46; Crawford 1985: 183–5.

[92] Plin. *HN* 33. 46: 'Livius Drusus in tribunatu plebei octavam partem aeris argento miscuit' (Livius Drusus in his tribunate of the plebs mixed an eighth part of bronze into the silver); Crawford 1985: 190: 'Pliny perhaps misplaced the undoubted debasement of 89–87 or recorded a measure never put into effect.'

[93] Brunt (1971*a*: 438) estimates that there were about 150,000 citizens in service at its height, which would have cost about HS 70 m. p.a. or approximately 3,000 talents p.a.

[94] Crawford 1974: 650–1. [95] Verboven 2003: 59. [96] Howgego 2009: 292

[97] The degree of fineness might have been lower: 'in the last few years it has become clear that the sampling technique used by Walker 1980 meant that his samples contained too much of the enriched part of the coin's surface; other coins for which he found this sort of fineness have turned out to be much less fine, around 80%' (Burnett 1998: 171 n. 29).

[98] Howgego 1995: 112. In a hoard found at Tarentum, the fineness of the quadrigati had been reduced to 30%.

But the steep rise in public expenditure because of increased military spending was not the only fiscal feature of the early 80s; state revenues were shrinking simultaneously. We have already described how the taxes from Asia were lost after Mithradates' invasion in 88; in addition, various taxes within Italy also disappeared because of the Social War: 'an obliti estis, Italico bello amissis ceteris vectigalibus, quantos agri Campani fructibus exercitus alueritis?'[99] (have you forgotten, when all your other taxes were lost in the Italian war, how many armies you fed with the produce of the Ager Campanus?) Anecdotal literary evidence confirms this picture of financial strain during the decade and suggests that the Roman state had to adopt emergency measures.[100] For example, public land was sold off at Rome in 89 and again in 81 in order to raise cash.[101] Extra taxes were imposed both within Italy and abroad.[102] In 88, unspecified items of public property, perhaps temple treasures or land, were also sold, producing 9,000 pounds of gold to pay for the army that Sulla was about to lead against Mithradates.[103]

The end of the Social War, far from bringing relief, only produced different problems, which meant that the underlying cash flow problems continued. For, with the enfranchisement of Italy in 88, men who had previously been allied soldiers now had to be paid directly by Rome;[104] although, to some extent, the demonetization and (presumed) melting down of the substantial allied coinage by the Romans, after the end of the Social War, would have helped to increase monetary liquidity at Rome.[105] In 84–80, Sulla even briefly introduced a gold coinage, although it was only from 46 onwards that gold was minted on a large and regular basis. But, despite this, the general fiscal problem at Rome persisted and, in 82, the senate decided to melt down gold and silver sacred treasures to make coin:

> C. autem Mario Cn. Carbone consulibus civili bello cum L. Sulla dissidentibus, quo tempore non rei publicae victoria quaerebatur, sed praemium victoriae res erat publica, senatus consulto aurea atque argentea templorum ornamenta, ne militibus stipendia deessent, conflata sunt: digna enim causa erat, hine an illi crudelitatem suam proscriptione civium satiarent, ut di immortales spoliarentur! Non ergo patrum conscriptorum uoluntas, sed taeterrimae necessitatis truculenta manus illi consulto stilum suum inpressit.[106]
>
> (When the consuls, C. Marius and Cn. Carbo, were contending with L. Sulla in civil war, a war not fought at that time for the victory of the Republic but with the Republic as victory's reward, gold and silver temple ornaments were melted down by decree of the senate to provide pay for the troops. To be sure, it was a worthy cause to despoil the immortal gods: for one side or the other to glut their cruelty by proscription of their fellow countrymen! It was not the will of the conscript fathers therefore that pressed its pen on that decree but the savage hand of an appalling necessity.[107])

There are other signs of financial stress at a more micro level, even if they are difficult to interpret. According to Cicero, the value of money was 'tossed about'

---

[99] Cic. *Leg. agr.* 2. 80. [100] The best account is Crawford 1974: 637–8.

[101] 89 BC: Oros. 5. 18. 26–7; Plut. *Pomp.* 4. 1; 81 BC: Cic. *Leg. agr.* 2. 35.

[102] App. *B. Civ.* 1. 102.

[103] App. *Mith.* 22; Williams 1998: 175–6.

[104] Previously allied communities had raised *tributum* locally in order to pay the soldiers whom they sent to fight for Rome (Nicolet 1978; Crawford 1985: 187).

[105] Burnett 1998: 166. [106] Val. Max. 7. 6. 4. [107] Trans. Loeb II 167, slightly revised.

so much that no one knew what they had. In 86 or 85, the praetors and the tribunes of the plebs tried to resolve the problem by issuing an edict. Marius Gratidianus, who stole all the credit for the edict from his colleagues, received many honours from a grateful people:

> Ne noster quidem Gratidianus officio viri boni functus est tum, cum praetor esset, collegiumque praetorium tribuni plebi adhibuissent, ut res nummaria de communi sententia constitueretur; iactabatur enim temporibus illis nummus sic, ut nemo posset scire, quid haberet. Conscripserunt communiter edictum cum poena atque iudicio constitueruntque ut omnes simul in rostra post meridiem escenderent. Et ceteri quidem alius alio, Marius ab subselliis in rostra recta idque, quod communiter compositum fuerat, solus edixit. Et ea res, si quaeris, ei magno honori fuit; omnibus vicis statuae, ad eas tus, cerei. Quid multa? Nemo umquam multitudini fuit carior.[108]
>
> (Even our Gratidianus did not perform the duty of a good man. When he was a praetor, the tribunes of the plebs summoned the college of praetors in order to decide a monetary matter by joint resolution; for at that time money was being tossed about so much that no one could tell what they had. Together they wrote an edict with the penalty and the judgement and decided that they should all mount the rostra at the same time in the afternoon. But while all the others dispersed, Marius went straight from the benches to the rostra and, on his own, formally announced what had been drafted by all the praetors together. And that matter, if you ask, brought him great honour; in all the neighbourhoods, there were statues of him and, beside them, incense and candles. Why go on? No one was ever dearer to the masses.)

Precisely what Cicero was referring to in this elusive statement is not clear, although the incident and the edict must have been sufficiently familiar to his contemporary audience in the 40s (more than forty years after the event) to require no further explanation. Furthermore, whatever Gratidianus actually did, the result appears to have been the re-establishment of trust in the coinage.[109]

Pliny comments that the edict instituted a new way of testing denarii: 'Igitur ars facta denarios probare, tam iucunda plebei lege, ut Mario Gratidiano vicatim tota statuas dicaverat'[110] (therefore, a procedure was developed for testing denarii, by a law that was so pleasing to the plebs that all the neighbourhoods consecrated statues to Marius Gratidianus). This statement led Frank to believe that Gratidianus introduced a new means of testing for officially produced plated denarii, authorized by Livius Drusus' law of 91.[111] Crawford, however, argues that all plated Roman coins are forgeries and that none were ever produced by the Roman state;[112] and some support for this view comes from Sulla's reorganization of the courts in 81. Under the *lex Cornelia de falsis*, a permanent court was established for cases involving forgeries of all kinds, including counterfeit coins.[113]

It is perhaps easier, therefore, to provide a context for the edict of Gratidianus and its popularity (Cicero's 'no one was ever dearer to the masses') in widespread concern at the debasement of the silver coinage between 89 and 87. Crawford believes that the unofficial exchange rate between bronze and silver coins was

[108] Cic. *Off.* 3. 80. [109] Cf. Williams 1998: 181. [110] Plin. *HN* 33. 132; cf. 34. 27.
[111] Frank 1933: 265–71. [112] Crawford 1974: 560–2.
[113] Paulus *Sent.* 5. 25. 1, 1A = *Dig.* 48. 10. 19; *Dig.* 48. 10. 8–9; Cic. *II Verr.* 1. 108.

fluctuating and that Gratidianus' edict enforced the official 16:1 exchange rate;[114] and it is entirely credible that lack of confidence over the value of the silver coinage would have manifested itself in concern at the rate of exchange between silver and bronze coins that was offered by shopkeepers and money changers. In fact, the sensitivity of a population to any form of tampering with the exchange rate between silver and bronze coins is shown by a Pergamene inscription of the second century AD.[115] This preserves an imperial letter (thought to be Hadrianic) concerning alleged profiteering by local money changers who were responsible for exchanging silver denarii for local bronze coins at official exchange rates. In the Pergamene example, one additional bronze as of profit taken, only occasionally, by the local money changers was sufficient to instigate an appeal by the local populace to the Roman emperor.

Thus far, in considering the problems with coinage in the 80s and their impact on the banks, we have focused on the supply of denarii minted in Rome for use in Italy. As we mentioned earlier, a sufficient supply of denarii was crucial for the proper functioning of banks operating in Italy. But matters were rather more complicated for Italian banks operating in other territories controlled by the Romans. For, at this period, the Roman denarius was the dominant coinage only in Italy, Sicily, Gallia Narbonensis, and probably Africa, where the Carthaginian coinage is presumed to have disappeared after 146, to be replaced by Roman denarii.[116] Elsewhere in Rome's empire, as we saw in Ch. 5, local coinages continued to circulate. In Spain, the Roman denarius only began to become common during the late second century. Before that, the so-called 'Iberian denarius' constituted a substantial element of the coinage.[117] In Greece, local coinages continued to be struck by individual Greek *poleis*.[118] Of these, the 'New Style' Athenian tetradrachm was by far the largest, becoming a regional coinage in southern Greece and beyond, and continuing to be struck in substantial quantities down to the time of Sulla.[119] Likewise, the denarius played little, if any, role in Asia Minor before 50 BC and there is no hoard evidence of any significance before the 40s.[120] In the province of Asia, the cistophoric coinage continued to be struck after Attalus III had bequeathed his kingdom to Rome in 133. None of these civic coinages, with the exception of the Athenian tetradrachm, appear to have travelled to any noticeable extent outside the states to which they belonged, and none of them, including the Athenian tetradrachm, ever circulated in Italy. In particular, they were not, in the jargon, fungible with the denarius.

At this time the Romans appear neither to have had a policy of replacing these local coinages nor to have attempted to control the volume of their emission. So, although several different currencies circulated within Rome's empire, Rome's 'monetary policy' was in effect restricted to minting sufficient denarii for the

[114] Crawford 1985: 189–93; he further argues that *aeraria ratio*, mentioned at Cic. *Quinct.* 17, should be taken to refer to the exchange rate between bronze and silver. This is wrong. It must refer to the measures for debt relief introduced under the *lex Valeria* (see pp. 246–7).

[115] *OGIS* 484; Macro 1976; I am grateful to Professor Howgego for pointing out the relevance of this inscription.

[116] The hoard evidence for Africa is very thin; only eleven hoards known to contain Republican denarii have been found (Crawford 1985: app. 42 and Burnett 1987*b*: 175, 180–1).

[117] Ripollès 2005: 82–4.

[118] Warren 1999; Crawford 1985: 197.

[119] Crawford 1985: 125.

[120] Kinns 1987.

Roman state's immediate needs in those areas where the denarius circulated.[121] In fact there were few mechanisms by which the Roman state could have utilized these local coinages to expand its supply of denarii. It could melt down and re-coin the currency of a defeated enemy, as it probably did with the Carthaginian coinage at the end of the Third Punic War. Similarly, the retrieval, in 86 BC, of the cash from the legacy of King Ptolemy Apion of Cyrene (which had been bequeathed to the Roman people in 96) probably contributed to an improvement in the silver fineness of the denarius and allowed relatively large-scale issues inscribed with the legend EX A(RGENTO) P(UBLICO).[122] Sulla even confiscated supplies of precious metal, perhaps including coin, from the temples of Epidaurus, Olympia, and Delphi, when he brought his expeditionary force against Mithradates to Greece.[123] But these were exceptional events. Probably the only regular influence that these local coinages might have had on the supply of denarii was if the Roman mint melted down and re-coined local civic currency received as payment of *stipendium* (tax) by a tributary state. Otherwise, local coinages were allowed to circulate without interference from the Roman state.

This lack of interference opened up a profitable sideline for banks operating in areas such as the Greek East, because the lack of fungibility between the denarius and local coinages would have necessitated the provision of currency exchange facilities.[124] But an Italian bank operating, say, on Delos faced the same problem as it did in Italy. For just as the efficient working of Rome's banking system depended on a sufficient supply of denarii in order to function properly, banks operating on Delos could only transact currency exchange and lend money to local traders and businessmen if a sufficient supply of the relevant local civic coinages was available. All would have been well before 88, but the activities of Mithradates on the mainland of Asia Minor and in the Aegean put a stop to that.

BANKS IN TROUBLE

The laws of the 80s concerning debt, the effects of the Social and Mithradatic Wars, especially the loss of the *pecuniae Asiaticae*, and the problems with the various coinages combined to create an environment in which it was increasingly difficult for banks to operate. It is worth pausing to consider a simple model of how in practice a Roman deposit bank might have found itself trouble.

Let us imagine a small bank operating in Rome in the late 90s BC.

The owner of the bank has put up capital of HS 35,000 of his own money; and, being prudent, he keeps this HS 35,000 in cash as a reserve in case something goes wrong. This is the silver coinage on the asset side of Balance Sheet 1 (Table 10.1). The banker then accepts a deposit of HS 50,000 from a senator and another of HS 15,000 from an *eques*, which means that he has total deposits of HS 65,000. Next, he lends HS 10,000 to a farmer who wants to buy a new olive press and HS 55,000

[121] Cf. Harris 2006: 22. [122] Crawford 1974: 605, 650–3. [123] Plut. *Sull.* 12, 19.

[124] e.g. forty years later Cicero had HS 2.2 m.-worth of cistophori in Asia that he wanted to exchange (Cic. *Att.* 11. 1. 2); Hollander 2007: 42.

Table 10.1. Bank balance sheet 1

Assets	HS	Liabilities	HS
Silver coinage	35,000	Deposit (senator) of silver coinage	50,000
Loan (to farmer)	10,000	Deposit (*eques*) of silver coinage	15,000
Loan (to trader)	55,000	Capital	35,000
TOTAL ASSETS	100,000	TOTAL LIABILITIES AND CAPITAL	100,000

Table 10.2. Bank balance sheet 2

Assets	HS	Liabilities	HS
Silver coinage	35,000	Deposit (senator) of silver coinage	50,000
Loan (to farmer)	10,000	Deposit (*eques*) of silver coinage	15,000
Loan (to trader)	0	Capital	35,000
TOTAL ASSETS	45,000	TOTAL LIABILITIES AND CAPITAL	100,000

to a trader who wants to buy a cargo of wine for export to Asia. The cash reserve of HS 35,000, expressed as a percentage of the bank's total assets, is now 35 per cent and this percentage is what would be termed, in modern banking parlance, a 'reserve ratio'. Most modern banks operate with reserve ratios of less than 10 per cent, but medieval bankers typically maintained reserve ratios as high as 29–30 per cent.[125] We do not know whether Roman deposit bankers maintained reserve ratios, but it may be considered highly likely that they were prudent enough to have done so.

But in 88, the disastrous news arrives that the trader has been killed in Asia and the banker cannot recover the HS 55,000 that he has lent to him. The result, if we look at Balance Sheet 2 (Table 10.2), is that the loan is no longer an asset but a headache. It has disappeared.

The banker can use the reserve of silver coinage (HS 35,000) to repay the deposit to the *eques* (HS 15,000). But while the HS 10,000 loan to the farmer and the HS 20,000 that remains of the reserve of silver coinage can be applied towards repayment of the deposit that has been accepted from the senator, these amounts cover only part (HS 30,000) of the HS 50,000 that is owed. The banker is unable to repay the senator the final HS 20,000 of his deposit. As can be seen, from Balance Sheet 3 (Table 10.3), the bank is bust, because its liabilities exceed its assets; and the banker has lost his own original capital of HS 35,000.

So did banks become bankrupt during the 80s BC? That is what is implied by Cicero's statement in the *De Imperio*, quoted earlier, that *fides* collapsed at Rome

[125] See Ch. 6 n. 22 for an explanation of the reserve ratio and De Roover 1948: 318 for medieval banks' reserve ratios. Harris (2006: 5, 11, 20) implies that the money multiplier effect of a deposit bank can only happen in a 'partial reserve' or 'fractional reserve' banking system: 'For every dollar of reserves, there are several dollars of extra money'. But in fact a system of this kind, though prudent, is not a necessity for the money multiplier to operate. For a fuller account, see Fischer, Dornbusch, and Schmalensee 1988: 173–5.

Table 10.3. Bank balance sheet 3

Assets	HS	Liabilities	HS
Silver coinage	20,000	Deposit (senator) of silver coinage	50,000
Loan (to farmer)	10,000	Deposit (*eques*) of silver coinage	0
Loan (to trader)	0	Capital	0
TOTAL ASSETS	30,000	TOTAL LIABILITIES AND CAPITAL	50,000

and that *solutio* was *impedita*; and there is other evidence too to suggest that banks were very stressed at this time.

During his invasion of Asia, Mithradates made financiers a special target. He offered to remit half their debts to borrowers who killed their Roman or Italian creditors.[126] Also in the East, and in the wake of the crisis, an inscription from Ephesus dating from about 85, which contains a law about debt, allows bankers ten years to pay back their depositors;[127] a rescheduling of debt that our mythical banker would have been extremely pleased to have been granted. Most interestingly, Cicero tells us in a passage from the *Pro Caecina*, written in 69, that a banker by the name of Marcus Fulcinius, who operated 'a not ignoble bank at Rome', sold a farm to his wife during what Cicero terms 'those times when it was very difficult to make repayments' (temporibus illis difficillimis solutionis). Cicero must here be referring to the payment crisis of 88, which he describes using similar terminology ('solutione impedita') in the passage we quoted earlier from the *De Imperio*.[128] Despite Cicero's suggestion in the *Pro Caecina* that Fulcinius' sale of the property to his wife was entirely altruistic, a cynic might suggest that it was arranged so that Fulcinius could get his hands on some cash. The passage goes on to say that the bank was wound up some time after:

> M. Fulcinius fuit, recuperatores, e municipio Tarquiniensi; qui et domi suae cum primis honestus existimatus est et Romae argentariam non ignobilem fecit. Is habuit in matrimonio Caesenniam, eodem e municipio summo loco natam et probatissimam feminam, sicut et vivus ipse multis rebus ostendit et in morte sua testamento declaravit. Huic Caesenniae fundum in agro Tarquiniensi vendidit temporibus illis difficillimis solutionis; cum uteretur uxoris dote numerata, quo mulieri res esset cautior, curavit ut in eo fundo dos conlocaretur. Aliquanto post iam argentaria dissoluta Fulcinius huic fundo uxoris continentia quaedam praedia atque adiuncta mercatur.[129]
>
> (M. Fulcinius, judges, was from the municipality of Tarquinii. He was considered to be one of the most honourable men in his home town and he operated a not ignoble bank at Rome. He was married to Caesennia, a lady from the same municipality, born in the highest rank and held in the highest esteem, as he showed in many ways while he was alive, and also declared by his will at his death. To this Caesennia he sold a farm in the Ager Tarquiniensis, during those times when it was very difficult to make repayments. As he was using his wife's dowry that comprised minted coin, he took care to invest her dowry in that farm so that the woman would have a more prudent investment. Some time afterwards, the bank now having been wound up, Fulcinius bought some land that was contiguous and adjacent to this farm of his wife's.)

126 App. *Mith.* 22: χρήσταις δ' ἐπὶ δανειστὰς ἥμισυ τοῦ χρέους.
127 *Syll.*^{3} 742. 58–62.
128 Cic. *De imp. Cn. Pomp.* 9.
129 Cic. *Caecin.* 10–11.

It is unlikely that all banks were affected in the same way. No doubt some banks, like that of Fulcinius, disappeared, but it is probable that the capital base of many of those that did survive was seriously impaired, to the extent that they were inhibited from growing in size.

DEPOSITORS' REACTIONS

With banks collapsing and doubts about the viability of those that remained, it is scarcely surprising that people did not want to leave their money on deposit with financial institutions that they regarded as seriously impaired. The risks of doing so had increased significantly.

At times of increased financial risk, people tend to become very conservative about what they do with their money, and they may react in any of three ways.

The first is that they may decide to hold what they consider to be the safest financial asset, cash; and, in a hard-money economy such as Rome's, that meant coin. This is exactly what seems to have happened in the years following the credit crisis of the 80s. As Crawford has shown, hoarding of coin in Italy increased to exceptional levels during the 80s and early 70s (and it happened again in 49 BC as a result of the insecurity generated by Julius Caesar's invasion of Italy).[130]

The second thing that happens is that people become more discriminating about credit risk and counterparty risk. In a Roman context, that would have meant that if a potential lender wished to generate a return on his surplus cash, he would probably have chosen to lend money directly to an acquaintance or a family member. This is because he, as the lender, would have been in a better position to evaluate whether or not the borrower was likely to repay the loan. If, however, the potential borrower did not fall into either of these categories, it would have become significantly more difficult for the lender to assess his creditworthiness (that is, the risk of lending to him), especially as the lender would have been operating in a pre-print culture in which financial information was scarce and unreliable. This very much describes the picture of 'aristocratic financiers' that emerges from Cicero's correspondence. What is so striking about the form of credit provision that his letters describe is that there are often personal ties between borrower and lender. In the example quoted earlier, Quintus Caecilius, the man from whom Cicero did not want to borrow because he charged too much, was Atticus' uncle.[131] The man from whom he had tried to borrow in the first place, Gaius Antonius, had been his fellow consul in 63 and, in the end, it was in fact Antonius who came up with the money.[132]

The third typical reaction to increased financial risk is a widening of risk 'spreads'; that is a widening in the size of the premium demanded for taking on extra risk. If the lender is prepared to lend outside his group of family or acquaintances, the lender wants to be rewarded for taking on that additional risk. For a

[130] Crawford 1969*b*, 1985: 193; Caesar banned anyone from holding more than 15,000 denarii (Dio Cass. 41. 38. 1): see this chapter p. 261.

[131] Cic. *Att.* 1. 12. 1.

[132] Cic. *Att.* 1. 14. 7.

Roman lending within Italy at this time, there was the immediate problem that the interest rate that he could charge was probably capped by the *lex Cornelia Pompeia* of 88 at 12 per cent per annum. The only way that a lender could charge a higher interest rate was to lend to an overseas borrower and, again, there is evidence that this happened. When in 84 Sulla imposed an indemnity of 20,000 talents on those cities of Asia that had taken the side of Mithradates, Appian says that the Roman δανεισταί (moneylenders), took advantage of the situation: they lent the funds that were required to pay the indemnity, charged the cities very high interest, and forced them to mortgage much of their public property.[133] Because of the effect of compounding, this loan had grown to 120,000 talents in fourteen years, which suggests that the interest rates that were being charged were of the order of 30 per cent per annum. In the end, in the winter of 71/70, Lucullus had to bring in measures to mitigate the situation.[134] But this was not an isolated example. Similarly and from the same period, a well-known inscription from Gytheion in the Peloponnese shows two Romans, Numerius and Marcus Cloatius, lending money to that city at the eye-poppingly high rate of 48 per cent per annum.[135] Even though abuses were sufficiently flagrant for a *lex Gabinia* of 67 or 58 to forbid the lending at interest to ambassadors of provincial cities or of friendly kings, a few years later we find that individual Romans are still lending to Greek cities.[136] In the mid-50s, M. Cluvius of Puteoli was lending money (on behalf of Pompey) to a number of communities in Asia Minor: Alabanda, Mylasa, Caunus, Bargylia, and Heraclea in Caria.[137] The city of Nicaea in Bithynia owed T. Pinnius about HS 8 m. (333 talents).[138] In 60, Castricius had recently collected a debt from Tralles in Lydia and was lending money to Smyrna.[139] Atticus had difficulty collecting debts from Sicyon;[140] and, as a young man, he had acted as an intermediary between the city of Athens and a group of demanding financiers.[141] Cicero talks of the rich men who would 'send out their freedmen for lending and pillaging in the provinces' (dimissiones libertorum ad fenerandas diripiendasque provincias).[142] There were variations on this theme of lending overseas in order to generate higher returns, which, if nothing else, show that definitions of financial activity cannot always be kept within neat boundaries. For example, P. Sittius, according to Cicero, was not just lending out his own surplus funds: he was borrowing in Rome to lend out in the provinces: 'Ita Romae debuit ut in provinciis et in regnis ei maximae pecuniae deberentur'[143] (so he borrowed money at Rome in order that very large sums could

[133] App. *Mith.* 62–3; Plut. *Sull.* 25. 2.

[134] Plut. *Luc.* 7. 5, 20. 4; Lucullus reduced the interest rate to 12% p.a., cancelled all interest above this level, and allocated one quarter of each debtor's income to his creditor. Within four years the province cleared off its debt. Subsequently, 12% p.a. seems to have become the usual legal maximum in the provinces. Certainly this rate was enforced by Cicero in Cilicia (Cic. *Att.* 5. 21. 10–13, 6. 1. 5–6, 6. 1. 16, 6. 2. 1, 6. 2. 9, 6. 3. 5). In spite of this limit, Brutus' agent, Scaptius, tried to extort 48% p.a. from the citizens of Salamis (Cic. *Att.* 5. 21. 10–13, 6. 1. 5–6, 6. 2. 7, 6. 2. 9).

[135] *Syll.*^{3} 748; later reduced to 24% p.a.

[136] Cic. *Att.* 5. 21. 12; 6. 2. 7; Asc. *Corn.* 58c.

[137] Cic. *Fam.* 13. 56. 1–3.

[138] Cic. *Fam.* 13. 61.

[139] Cic. *Flac.* 54, 75.

[140] Cic. *Att.* 1. 13. 1, 1. 20. 4, 2. 13. 2.

[141] Nep. *Att.* 2. 2. 4; as Hatzfeld 1919: 204 says, if Atticus did this, it was perhaps because the financiers were his compatriots.

[142] Cic. *Parad. St.* 46.

[143] Cic. *Sull.* 58.

be lent out by him in the provinces and kingdoms). Cicero tells us that one of the people to whom Sittius was lending money was the king of Mauretania.[144]

Similarly Rabirius Postumus was lending out both his own money and that of his friends: 'nec suam solum pecuniam credidit, sed etiam amicorum'[145] (nor did he lend only his own money, but even that of friends). In borrowing money in Rome in order to lend it out in the provinces, both Sittius and Rabirius were, functionally at least, acting as bankers.[146] Sittius, for example, had worked out that, if he could borrow at Rome at, say, 12 per cent per annum, and lend to the king of Mauretania at, say, 17 per cent per annum, then he could make a margin, that is a profit, of 5 per cent per annum on the amount he lent. In the jargon, he was 'gearing up', and banks and hedge funds still do that today.

BANKING FOR THE MASSES

Catiline's conspiracy in 63 BC produced the second great debt crisis of the late Republic. Looking back in the following year, Cicero said that he had 'raised the siege of the *faeneratores*'.[147] Indeed Cicero often spoke of the Catilinarian conspiracy as aimed at defrauding creditors, and he styled himself as the 'champion of debt' (*vindex aeris alieni*).[148] According to Sallust, Catiline promised the abolition of debts (*tabulae novae*) and proscriptions of the rich.[149] A reduced level of monetary liquidity was again the underlying problem, as it had been in the 80s, and it led to the squeeze on debtors that underlay the Catilinarian crisis. One of Catiline's generals, C. Manlius, is made by Sallust to speak of the violence, cruelty, and savagery of the *faeneratores*.[150]

As we saw earlier, the massive issues of denarii in the 80s seem not to have solved a continued shortage of money in Italy, which led the senate in 82 to order the melting down of temple treasures.[151] Furthermore, as Crawford has argued, the loss of liquidity resulting from the substantial numbers of large denarius hoards that were buried and not recovered in the 80s and the 70s was not made good in the 70s or the 60s, which were periods of small issues of denarii.[152] Indeed the aggregate stock of denarii apparently starts to decrease after the early 70s, after rising steadily for generations.[153] Proof positive of the continuing problem of the insufficiency of the coinage is that, in 63, Cicero tried to stop the export of gold

144 Cic. *Sull.* 56. 145 Cic. *Rab. Post.* 5.

146 Note that, within Andreau's definition, which we have adopted, Sittius was not an *argentarius*; it is clear from Cicero's comments in the *Pro Sulla* that banking was not Sittius' 'profession'. As we have already seen, there were no regulatory structures or tax legislation to prevent Sittius from acting as a 'quasi-bank'.

147 Cic. *Fam.* 5. 6. 2. 148 Cic. *Att.* 2. 1. 11.

149 Sall. *Cat.* 21. 2; cf. Dio Cass. 37. 25. 4: χρεῶν ἀποκοπαί. 150 Sall. *Cat.* 33. 1.

151 Val. Max. 7. 6. 4. 152 Crawford 1985: 193. 153 Hopkins 1980: 109.

and silver from Puteoli, no doubt in order to prevent a further reduction in the level of monetary liquidity.[154]

Our elite sources suggest that, at the time of the Catilinarian conspiracy, there was widespread indebtedness among the more humble members of Roman society. Cicero lists, at *In Catilinam* 2. 17–23, the groups of people who constituted Catiline's supporters. Among them are failed Sullan colonists and others at the lower end of the economic scale who had fallen into debt and were hoping for some release through civil unrest:

> Quartum genus est sane varium et mixtum et turbulentum; qui iam pridem premuntur, qui numquam emergunt, qui partim inertia, partim male gerendo negotio, partim etiam sumptibus in vetere aere alieno vacillant.[155]
>
> (The fourth group is a motley assortment of trouble-makers; those who have been in financial straits for years, who never get their heads above water, who are staggering under age-old debts, which result partly from laziness, partly from failure in business, partly too from extravagance.[156])

Similarly, Sallust states that amongst the other supposedly disreputable types whom Catiline was able to gather around himself were people who were in debt:

> Nam quicumque impudicus, adulter, ganeo, manu, ventre, pene bona patria laceraverat quique alienum aes grande conflaverat, quo flagitium aut facinus redimeret... ei Catilinae proximi familiaresque erant.[157]
>
> (For whatever wanton, adulterer, or glutton had wasted his patrimony in play, feasting or debauchery, anyone who had contracted an immense debt so that he might buy immunity from disgrace or crime... all these were nearest and dearest to Catiline.[158])

Who advanced these loans to the poorer elements of Roman society, to the Sullan colonists, and to the disreputable types of whom Cicero speaks? Our sources give no indication other than Sallust's and Cicero's use of the catch-all term *faeneratores*, and it is impossible to say whether the providers of credit were *argentarii* or 'aristocratic financiers'. It is perfectly possible that small deposit banks (or at least deposit banks that had shrunk in size during the *tempora difficillima* of the 80s) owned by professional *argentarii* continued to operate in various parts of Rome's empire and to provide credit to the small-scale merchant and farmer.[159] Perhaps smaller banks (like that of the Sulpicii in the first century AD) continued to provide credit to those involved in running a business, 'gerendo negotio'.[160] Relatives of

[154] Cic. *Vat.* 12, *Flac.* 67; the mid-50s show a short recovery, after which the stock again decreased towards the end of the decade, back to the level of the early 50s (Verboven 2003: 57).

[155] Cic. *Cat.* 2. 21.

[156] Trans. Loeb X 91.

[157] Sall. *Cat.* 14. 2; cf. 20. 13, 24. 3; even the Gallic tribe, the Allobroges, whom Catiline tried to draw into his conspiracy, was indebted (Sall. *Cat.* 41. 1).

[158] Trans. Loeb 25.

[159] As Von Reden 2002: 146 puts it: 'Clear distinctions must be made between different purposes of credit and their institutional background, in particular between the needs of the general population and those members of a very small elite whose activities, despite being fewer in number, may have been economically more significant than the aggregate number of activities of the rest of the population.'

[160] Cic. *Cat.* 2. 21; but even this may be a mistaken impression. Although, at first sight, the sums in the Campanian tablets may appear small, the 77 tablets of the Sulpicius archive dating between AD 35 and AD 55 record, as Rathbone and Temin 2008: 405 have shown, transactions worth HS 1.28 m. (53 talents), equivalent to an average transaction size of HS 16,623 (0.69 of a talent). This average figure is by no means nugatory.

the Aufidii, who had operated a banking business on Delos at the end of the second century, were still active on Tenos in the 70s or 60s.[161] The bankers mentioned in the *Verrines* were active at Leptis and Rhegium in the 70s.[162] Also it is perfectly possible that short-term auction finance of the type mentioned by Cicero in the *Pro Caecina* continued to exist.[163] We cannot, therefore, be certain who the lenders were in the 60s, but our model for the impairment of the deposit banks in the 80s should not be taken to imply the total disappearance of such institutions. We should view deposit banking in the first century not as an absolute that was either present or absent, but as an industry which, over time, varied in size and scale. It is perfectly possible that some deposit banks did continue to function in the 70s and 60s, albeit operating with smaller balance sheets and accepting deposits from, and lending to, smaller clients.

THE ATTITUDE OF THE STATE

Where is the Roman state in all this? The conventional Roman attitude to moneymaking, as put forward by Tacitus in Book 6 of the *Annales*, was negative:

> Sane vetus urbi faenebre malum et seditionum discordiarumque creberrima causa eoque cohibebatur antiquis quoque et minus corruptis moribus. Nam primo duodecim tabulis sanctum ne quis unciario faenore amplius exerceret, cum antea ex libidine locupletium agitaretur; dein rogatione tribunicia ad semuncias redactum, postremo vetita versura. Multisque plebi scitis obviam itum fraudibus quae toties repressae miras per artes rursum oriebantur.[164]
>
> (The evil of interest on loans was indeed of old standing in Rome and a very frequent cause of sedition and discord, and it was therefore constrained by an ancient and less corrupt morality. For, in the first place, the Twelve Tables prohibited anyone from exacting more than the unciarial rate of interest,[165] when, previously, the rate had been determined by the whim of the rich. Then, by a tribunician bill, interest was reduced to half that amount, and, finally, compound interest was forbidden. But, as often as the many plebiscites were introduced to repress fraudulent behaviour, it reappeared through ingenious schemes.)

This negative attitude towards credit was based on *mos maiorum*, that is, the idealized memory of men such as Cincinnatus, who worked their own small farms and had no need of money. The survival of that ideal, of the 'horny-handed man of the soil', which became obsolete in practice as soon as Rome progressed beyond what was essentially a subsistence economy, was largely due to the opinions and influence of Cato the Elder, whom Cicero admiringly quotes as comparing lending to murder: 'Cum ille, qui quaesierat, dixisset "quid fenerari?", tum Cato "quid hominem", inquit, "occidere?"[166] (When the man who was questioning him said, 'What about lending?', then Cato replied: 'What about killing a man?')

The laws of the 80s, in particular the *lex Cornelia Pompeia* and *the lex Valeria*, also suggest that contemporary Roman legislators did not care about the operation

161 *IG* XII 5. 860; for the Aufidii on Delos see p. 125. 162 See p. 237.
163 Cic. *Caecin.* 16; Andreau 1984: 105; 1987: 47, 155–61; Rauh 1989: 59.
164 Tac. *Ann.* 6. 16.
165 For *faenus unciarium* (the unciarial rate of interest), see n. 78. 166 Cic. *Off.* 2. 89.

of what we would call the capital markets. They display no understanding of the importance of banks, nor of the role of credit creation in producing economic growth. As our discussion of the coinages of this period has shown, the main concern of officials of the Roman state was bullion supplies and minted denarii, and there was no comprehension that encouraging banks to lend *more* would actually increase the amount of money in circulation.

The same pattern emerges from later credit crises. In addition to those of 88 and 63, we know of financial crises in 49 BC and AD 33, both of which were also aggravated by a lack of monetary liquidity and both of which show little understanding of the importance of credit institutions for a healthy economy.

The cause of the crisis in 49 was the insecurity generated by Julius Caesar's imminent invasion of Italy.[167] But even before this, there had been problems. Late in 51 or early in 50, a maximum interest rate of 12 per cent per annum had been decreed by both the senate and the tribunes.[168] By 49, there was a rush for cash. Dio Cassius tells us that, because of the uncertainty, nervous creditors began to seek repayment of the principal of their loans in 'silver', that is in coin.[169] It became increasingly hard for borrowers to find the money with which to pay off their debts, and Cicero's letters of 49 and 48 frequently mention *nummorum caritas*.[170] Even if debtors were willing to sell land to raise cash (and many were not willing to do so for social and for legal reasons[171]), they were selling into a falling market. This meant that, if a property on which a loan had been secured was offered in settlement of that debt, it did not necessarily cover the full amount. Thus, by the time Caesar arrived in Italy in 49, he found that credit had tightened. As he himself put it: 'Cum fides tota Italia esset angustior neque creditae pecuniae solverentur'[172] (since credit in the whole of Italy was tighter and loans were not being repaid).

Compounding the problem were two other factors. First, the civil war of 49 took money out of circulation through hoarding in the same way as it had done in the 80s.[173] Secondly Caesar himself increased the feeling of insecurity by his seizure of the *aerarium* and the coinage it contained in order to pay his troops.[174] As Frederiksen puts it, 'in 49, even more than in the similar crises of 86 or 63, soldiers had to be paid and paid immediately, for legion did not fight legion without powerful inducement'.[175] Caesar, therefore, used all means to raise coin and, in addition to stealing state funds, sold off Gallic gold for silver.[176]

[167] Frederiksen 1966 remains fundamental.

[168] *senatus consultum*: Cic. *Att.* 5. 21; tribunes: Dio Cass. 41. 37. 2.

[169] Dio Cass. 41. 37. 3.

[170] Cic. *Att.* 7. 18. 4 (Feb. 49 BC), 9. 9. 4. (Mar. 49), 10. 11. 2 (May 49), 10. 15. 4 (May 49); Frederiksen 1966: 132; Williams 1998: 177; Verboven 2003: 52 points out that *nummorum caritas* means literally not 'lack of money', but 'expensiveness of money', and refers to the high interest rates charged on loans.

[171] Frederiksen 1966: 128–30. [172] Caes. *B. Civ.* 3. 1. 2. [173] Dio Cass. 41. 38. 1.

[174] Cic. *Att.* 7. 21. 2, 10. 4. 8, 10. 8. 6; Plin. *HN* 33. 56; Dio Cass. 41. 17. 1–2; Plut. *Caes.* 35; App. *B. Civ.* 2. 41; Oros. 6. 15. 5; Caes. *B. Civ.* 1. 33. 3 does not mention it (!). Ironically, this action probably improved the liquidity situation ultimately, by releasing into the economy huge sums of money that would otherwise have lain idle in the *aerarium*.

[175] Frederiksen 1966: 132.

[176] Suet. *Iul.* 54. 2 claims that the gold was sold off cheaply, but this might be an exaggeration.

In order to try to remedy the crisis, Caesar ordained a number of measures soon after his arrival in Rome.[177] The first stipulated that, in settlement of a debt, creditors should accept property at a valuation (*aestimatio*) at pre-war prices:

> Constituit, ut arbitri darentur; per eos fierent aestimationes possessionum et rerum, quanti quaeque earum ante bellum fuisset, atque eae creditoribus traderentur. Hoc et ad timorem novarum tabularum tollendum minuendumve, qui fere bella et civiles dissensiones sequi consuevit, et ad debitorum tuendam existimationem esse aptissimum existimavit.[178]
>
> (He decided that arbitrators should be appointed, who would make valuations of real estate and movable property at pre-war levels, and that these valuations would be given to creditors. He considered that this was the most suitable method of removing or diminishing the fear of debt cancellations (which tends to follow war and civil strife) and of maintaining the good favour of debtors.[179])

Secondly, he revived an older law forbidding anyone to hold more than 15,000 drachmas (HS 60,000, or 2.5 talents) in silver or gold.[180] In the following year further measures followed indicating that the problems persisted. Dio Cassius reports that, in late 48, Caesar cancelled all interest accrued on loans since the war began (as well as one year's rent up to a maximum of HS 2,000); he also raised the valuations of property to their value at the time the loan was taken out.[181] Suetonius adds that Caesar also decreed that any interest paid, or recorded formally as having been paid, should be deducted from the amount of the original loan.[182] If we assume interest had been paid for two years at 12 per cent per annum, this was effectively a cancellation of one-quarter of the amount of the original loan.

It is clear from the writings of Cicero that, despite Caesar's measures, the tightness of credit continued into 46 and 45.[183] Tacitus mentions a 'lex Caesaris de modo credendi possidendique intra Italiam' in his discussion of the economic crisis under the emperor Tiberius in AD 33.[184] In view of the fact that, according to Suetonius, the senate acted in that year 'ut faeneratores duas patrimonii partes in solo collocarent, debitores totidem aeris alieni statim solverent', it is usually inferred that Julius Caesar's law too must have prescribed investment of a proportion of capital in Italian land, hence 'possidendi intra Italiam' in the passage quoted next.[185] This provision must presumably have been intended by Caesar to increase the circulation of money.[186] Frederiksen dates the law to late 46 or 45 and he also places a *lex Julia de bonis cedendis* in the same period.[187] This latter law allowed

[177] Caes. *B. Civ.* 3. 1; Dio Cass. 41. 37–8; App. *B. Civ.* 2. 48; Plut. *Caes.* 37. 1; Frederiksen 1966: 133–4.

[178] Caes. *B. Civ.* 3. 1. 2; cf. Dio Cass. 41. 37. 3.

[179] Trans. Loeb II 197, slightly revised.

[180] Dio Cass. 41. 38. 1.

[181] Dio Cass. 42. 51. 1; Frederiksen 1966: 133–4 for dating.

[182] Suet. *Iul.* 42: 'deducto summae aeris alieni si quid usurae nomine numeratum aut perscriptum fuissent'.

[183] Frederiksen 1966: 134 n. 49 for the ancient evidence of the continued tightness of credit.

[184] Tac. *Ann.* 6. 16–17: see p. 262.

[185] Suet. *Tib.* 48; cf. Plin. *Ep.* 6.19.

[186] Frederiksen 1966: 134; Williams 1998: 178.

[187] 'When Caesar, in the capacity of *praefectus morum*, brought forth a flourish of reformatory legislation' (Frederiksen 1966: 134, 138).

insolvent debtors to cede their property to their creditors while retaining enough to sustain themselves. One other relevant action of Caesar's was the minting of a large gold coinage in 46. This came after a few smaller emissions in 48–47, and he no doubt minted the gold because there was not enough silver available to keep his promises to his soldiers (the output of gold coins in 45 and 44 was considerably lower).[188] But whether intentional or not, the effect would have been to increase monetary liquidity.

Before we analyse the credit crisis of the 40s further, it is worth looking first at the financial collapse of AD 33, which is described in detail by Tacitus:

> Interea magna vis accusatorum in eos inrupit qui pecunias faenore auctitabant adversum legem dictatoris Caesaris qua de modo credendi possidendique intra Italiam caventur, omissam olim, quia privato usui bonum publicum postponitur... Sed tum Gracchus praetor, cui ea quaestio evenerat, multitudine periclitantium subactus rettulit ad senatum, trepidique patres (neque enim quisquam tali culpa vacuus) veniam a principe petivere; et concedente annus in posterum sexque menses dati quis secundum iussa legis rationes familiares quisque componerent. Hinc inopia rei nummariae, commoto simul omnium aere alieno, et quia tot damnatis bonisque eorum divenditis signatum argentum fisco vel aerario attinebatur. Ad hoc senatus praescripserat, duas quisque faenoris partes in agris per Italiam conlocaret. Sed creditores in solidum appellabant nec decorum appellatis minuere fidem. Ita primo concursatio et preces, dein strepere praetoris tribunal, eaque quae remedio quaesita, venditio et emptio, in contrarium mutari quia faeneratores omnem pecuniam mercandis agris condiderant. Copiam vendendi secuta vilitate, quanto quis obaeratior, aegrius distrahebant, multique fortunis provolvebantur; eversio rei familiaris dignitatem ac famam praeceps dabat.[189]
>
> (Meanwhile a great force of accusers fell on those who were increasing their money by lending at interest in defiance of a law passed by Caesar, the dictator, about the procedure for lending money and for holding land in Italy, a law long obsolete because the public good takes second place to private interest... But then, Gracchus, the praetor, who had responsibility for the inquiry, was compelled by the number of people at risk to refer the matter to the senate. The nervous senators, not one of whom was free from similar guilt, sought indulgence from the emperor. He yielded and a year and six months were granted, within which everyone had to arrange their private finances in accordance with the law. Hence there was a scarcity of money, since, at the same time, a great shock had been given to the whole credit market, and minted coin was ending up in the imperial treasury or the state treasury, because so many people had been convicted and their property sold piecemeal. To address this, the senate had directed that every creditor should invest two-thirds of their capital in Italian land. But creditors were demanding payment in full and it was not seemly to break faith if one faced such a demand. So, at first, there were disorderly meetings and entreaties; then there was a din in the praetor's court and the very scheme that had been intended as a remedy, the sale and purchase of land, proved the contrary, because the *faeneratores* had hoarded all their money for buying land. Large-scale selling was followed by reduced prices, and the more debt a man had, the more disastrous it was for him to sell, and many were ruined. The loss of an estate destroyed dignity and reputation.)

Tacitus portrays the crisis as having been prompted by a series of unprovoked accusations against individuals for lending money at interest in contravention of the law of Julius Caesar 'de modo credendi possidendique intra Italiam', which, as

[188] Woytek 2003. [189] Tac. *Ann.* 6. 16–17; see the discussion of Williams 1998: 178.

we have just seen, ordained that a proportion of a man's wealth must be invested in Italian land. Tacitus' account suggests that most senators were in breach of the law. He says that, when creditors were forced to invest a proportion of their capital in land, they had to call in their loans. The availability of credit declined and money once again became scarce. As a consequence, many debtors could not repay their loans and creditors foreclosed on their property. This threw many properties onto the market with the result that land prices fell rapidly, which in turn led to more foreclosures. Sales of the goods of the condemned drew large amounts of coin into the treasury and out of private hands.

At last Tiberius came to the rescue:

> donec tulit opem Caesar disposito per mensas milies sestertio factaque mutuandi copia sine usuris per triennium, si debitor populo in duplum praediis cavisset. Sic refecta fides et paulatim privati quoque creditores reperti. Neque emptio agrorum exercita ad formam senatus consulti, acribus, ut ferme talia, initiis, incurioso fine.[190]
>
> (Until Caesar brought help by distributing through the banks one hundred million sesterces, and allowing borrowing on a large scale without interest for three years, provided the borrower gave to the people security in land equivalent to double the amount of the loan. Credit was thus restored, and gradually private lenders were found. But the purchase of land was not carried out according to the provisions of the senate's decree, rigour at the outset, as generally happens, ending in negligence.)

Tiberius, then, provided three-year interest-free loans totalling HS 100 m. (4,166 talents), through the banks, to hard-pressed debtors. This increased the flow of money, eased the problems of liquidity, and stopped the foreclosures. Debts could be paid, money lent, and land prices allowed to rise to their former levels. In simple terms, Tiberius restored stability by putting more money into circulation and quickly forgot about the injunction on creditors to invest in land. Although it is not mentioned by any literary source, it also appears from numismatic evidence that, as an additional measure to ease the crisis, more coin was minted. The relative amount of precious-metal coinage in circulation increased significantly after these events, with the average output of denarii growing by eight times and that of aurei by three times in the last six years of Tiberius' reign.[191]

There are, of course, differences between all these credit crises. In the 80s the crisis was provoked by the Social and Mithradatic Wars and especially by the loss of the *pecuniae Asiaticae*, in the 60s by a conspiracy to overthrow the Roman government, in the 40s by a civil war, and in AD 33 by a series of gratuitous accusations against leading creditors. There are, however, a number of similarities that help to illuminate the options available to the Roman state in handling monetary crises.

The first option, which we can observe operating in the 80s and 40s BC and in the 30s AD, was to mint more coin. In the 80s, there were large issues of silver denarii, followed, under Sulla, by some small issues of gold coin. In the 40s too, gold coins were minted, eventually in great quantities; but the issuance of denarii was not an option for Julius Caesar since, as is shown by his seizure of the *aerarium*, he was desperate to get his hands on as much silver as possible to pay his troops. And there was the rub. The problem with attempting to improve monetary liquidity by issuing more coin was that it was crucially dependent, at

[190] Tac. *Ann.* 6. 17. [191] Duncan-Jones 1994: 25, 251.

least before the introduction of the gold coinage in the 40s, on having adequate supplies of silver. As is shown by the limited debasement of the denarius at the beginning of the 80s, sufficient supplies of silver were not always available and this could lead to manipulation of the bullion content of the coinage by the state.

The second option was to limit hoarding, as Caesar did in 49, in order to keep coinage in circulation. But it was impossible for the Caesarian regime to police compliance with this law, unless informants were allowed to operate, which Dio Cassius specifically says they were not.[192] An attempt, with the same objective of maintaining the supply of coin, was made by Cicero in 63, when he restricted the export of gold and silver.

The third option, which was to assist debtors by forcing creditors to invest in land and which was tried in the 40s BC and in AD 33, was ill-conceived and doomed to failure. The only result, as Tiberius discovered, was that creditors called in their loans, forcing debtors to sell property, which in turn caused a collapse in land prices. Similarly ill-conceived was Caesar's insistence that creditors should accept unrealistic (i.e. non-market) pre-war valuations on land offered in settlement of a debt. The only result of this was to punish lenders and to discourage them from further lending.[193] Other measures of Caesar's were even more overtly hostile to lenders, namely his cancellation of all interest accrued on loans since the war began, and the deduction of any interest already paid from the amount of the original loan. In all but name, this last measure was a partial cancellation of debt, similar in effect, if not in scale, to the *lex Valeria* of 86. It is little surprise that *nummorum caritas* appears to have dragged on into the 40s.

In fact, apart from the minting of new coin, the only government measure helpful to lenders during any of these crises was the provision of liquidity through interest-free loans by Tiberius in AD 33—functionally the same as what we would call quantitative easing. That worked because it stimulated more lending, since the funding of loans cost nothing, provided that sufficient collateral was posted. Most of the other measures during the previous century add up to a sad litany of economic mismanagement. One other approach that might have helped was for the Roman state to borrow from the private sector; but, after the Second Punic War, this was, for whatever reason, never seen as a viable approach and no issue of Roman government bonds ever took place.

ECONOMIC IMPACT

We said in Ch. 6 that a deposit bank produces a 'money multiplier' effect, which will expand the money supply; and that such expansion will normally influence the level of economic activity. On these grounds alone the impairment of the deposit banks by the crisis of the 80s BC should theoretically have damaged the economy, because it restricted the supply of money. Nor do we believe that a system of *delegatio debitoris*, securitized debt, would have been sufficient to take

[192] Dio Cass. 41. 38.3.

[193] Cf. Cicero's joke to Papirius Paetus at Cic. *Fam.* 9. 16. 7, discussed by Frederiksen 1966: 135.

up the slack. It seems inherently unlikely that the secondary market in loans made by and to members of the Roman elite was sufficiently active, extensive, and liquid to achieve this. This is because, even in the relatively small world of the Roman elite, the potential acquirer of a loan would be taking on the credit risk of a debtor who might not be known to him and, even more importantly, whose ability to repay the loan might be totally unclear. So, for example, when faced with the *nomina* that Faberius wanted to transfer to him in the year 46, Cicero anxiously tells Atticus that he knows nothing about a certain Caelius, a debtor for one of these *nomina*: 'De Caelio tu quaeres, ut scribis; ego nihil novi. Noscenda autem est natura, non facultas modo'[194] (please make enquiries about Caelius, as you suggested in your letter; I know nothing about him. We need to know about his character, not just his means).

The evidence we have been examining, a large part of which comes from Cicero, suggests that there was a significant change in the institutional structure of the capital markets of first-century BC Rome. It portrays a financial world in which most lending is between individuals and in which the problem of asymmetric knowledge impairs the lending process. It is not a world in which deposit banks appear to have an extensive role. Of course, this evidence could be biased, since it principally reflects the financial activities of the circles in which Cicero moved. Inevitably, therefore, the black-and-white picture of financial change that we have presented conceals a number of areas that are very grey. For example, it is perfectly possible that banks, like that of, say, the Sulpicii, which dealt with the small shippers and petty businessmen of Puteoli in the first century AD, continued to operate: it might just be that the evidence is lacking. We are not, therefore, saying that Roman deposit banks disappeared completely by the middle of the first century BC; nor are we saying that a system of transferable *nomina*, operated by 'aristocratic financiers', did not exist in the second century BC. What we are saying is that it is likely that, by the mid-first century BC, there were fewer banks in existence, with smaller balance sheets, that the main providers of credit had become the 'aristocratic financiers', instead of the *argentarii*, and that this development could have had a negative impact on the wider Roman economy, or, at least, could have prevented it from reaching its full potential. The crisis of 88 and the legislation of the 80s were the principal causes of this change. They are also the reason why we do not hear of any large Roman banks evolving in the first century BC.

194 Cic. *Att.* 12. 5a.

Part IV

Quantification

11

Forecasting the Past

'All right,' said Deep Thought. 'The Answer to the Great Question . . .'
'Yes . . . !'
'Of Life, the Universe and Everything . . .' said Deep Thought.
'Yes . . . !'
'Is . . .' said Deep Thought, and paused.
'Yes . . . !'
'Is . . .'
'Yes . . . !!! . . . ?'
'Forty-two,' said Deep Thought, with infinite majesty and calm.[1]

INTRODUCTION

The above passage comes from Douglas Adams's satirical sci-fi adventure, *The Hitchhiker's Guide to the Galaxy*. Deep Thought is a computer that has been created by a pan-dimensional, hyper-intelligent race of beings to come up with 'the Answer to The Ultimate Question of Life, the Universe, and Everything'. When, after seven and a half million years of calculation, the answer finally turns out to be 42, Deep Thought admonishes Loonquawl and Phouchg (the dismayed receivers of the Ultimate Answer) that '[I] checked it very thoroughly, and that quite definitely is the answer. I think the problem, to be quite honest with you, is that you've never actually known what the question was.'

So if we wish to quantify the Roman economy in the second century and early first century BC, what is the question? Are we attempting to measure the size of Rome's economy at a particular point in time, or are we seeking to measure the rate of growth of its economy over a period of time? These are two different, if interrelated, issues. The former seeks to provide an answer to the question of when levels of activity in the Roman Republican economy were high or low relative to other periods, and indeed to other economies, and the latter to the question of the degree to which economic activity increased over a period of time, in our case during the late Republic.[2] If we seek to measure economic growth, which is what we shall be attempting to do in this chapter, there are then further questions: did this growth simply mirror an increase in population or was there any real per capita growth and,

[1] Douglas Adams, *The Hitchhiker's Guide to the Galaxy*. [2] Cf. Scheidel 2009*a*: 52.

if so, what drove it? These questions are not easy to answer and this chapter serves as much to highlight how little we know as to provide the 'Ultimate Answer'.

During the last thirty years or so, a number of ancient historians and econometricians have produced experimental reconstructions of the Roman economy for various dates during the Principate. Some scholars have expressed a high degree of scepticism at these attempts, criticizing them for their lack of a sound evidentiary base and for the likelihood, given the shortage of reliable underlying data, that they contain wide margins of error. Unsurprisingly, such reconstructions can differ from each other by significant orders of magnitude;[3] and this has led these same scholars to question whether estimates derived from sometimes dubious assumptions are in any way helpful in this kind of investigation. As the directors of the Oxford Roman Economy Project, Alan Bowman and Andrew Wilson, put it: 'We are not enthusiastic about simply constructing alternative scenarios on more or less flimsy premises and testing them by the relative strength or weakness of the consequences which flow from them.'[4] An alternative approach (which Bowman and Wilson have espoused) is to focus on the more robust micro-data and to use proxies of economic performance in order to build up a picture of economic behaviour, based on more detailed and perhaps more reliable evidence. And indeed quantification of the Roman economy, using micro-data and proxy variables, would be our preferred approach. But, as we shall see, the work that has been produced so far on this type of data is, as yet, so limited in its range that it is impossible to say anything meaningful about per capita real growth in second- and first-century BC Rome without enlisting the aid of estimates for the majority of the important variables. Such estimates are often conjectural and inevitably fragile. We are convinced, however, that this problem goes, as they say, with the territory. There are simply not enough quantifiable data sets available at present on which to build a concrete, synoptic, numerically based quantification of the Roman economy for the late Republican period. Undoubtedly, more research and study will gradually produce more data series, real or proxy. Who would have believed fifty years ago that samples taken from the ice cap of Greenland or mounds investigated on the Mediterranean seabed would have allowed us to produce data series that shed light on mineral extraction and trade?[5] But this process of research will take time and, meanwhile, we can only use the tools we have and draw conclusions that are justified by and fit our limited evidence.

Our methodology in this chapter will be to attempt to measure the size of the Roman Republican economy at three different dates, 150 BC, 100 BC, and 50 BC, so that, by comparing the conjectured size of that economy at each of these dates, we can see whether real per capita economic growth occurred. For each of these dates, we shall try to reconstruct Roman GDP by producing estimates from the income side. We shall then see whether, on the basis of such limited data as are available, plausible estimates of GDP from the expenditure side can be produced that fit satisfactorily with these income estimates. Finally, we shall construct hypothetical numbers for the Italian money supply and its velocity of circulation to see whether these too can theoretically fit with our estimates from the income side of GDP. These

[3] e.g. Temin 2006: HS 9.15 bn. and Goldsmith 1984: HS 20.9 bn. for AD 14.

[4] Bowman and Wilson 2009*b*: 55; cf. 12 and 54.

[5] Friedman (forthcoming) gives a less optimistic view of the credibility of the data for atmospheric pollution.

three different approaches are unlikely to be even remotely accurate taken individually, but together they may give some degree of probabilistic plausibility.[6] Our approach is, in fact, not so dissimilar to current techniques used by investment banking analysts to forecast the future performance of a modern economy. Indeed, for someone who has spent years reading the musings of modern business economists, there is a strong feeling of *déjà vu* when one attempts to produce what is in effect a 'forecast' of the historical Roman Republican economy.

One immediate problem with which we are faced is how to define the geographical area that encompassed the Roman economy in the second and first centuries BC. For this was a period when Rome was expanding her *imperium* through the Mediterranean, sometimes annexing territory (such as Sicily and parts of Spain), sometimes seeking to control territory through quisling kings (for example in western Asia Minor through the Attalids), sometimes just exerting a more or less nebulous form of 'control' (as in Greece). What areas do we include? Are we measuring the whole of this embryonic empire or the impact of the acquisition of that empire on a smaller geographical area or on a narrower group of people, for example on mainland Italy, on the *civitas romana*, or just on the Roman elite? We believe that it makes sense to confine our analysis to mainland Italy, not least because the focus of this study has been on the Roman and Italian elite and, during the second century, the bulk of that elite was domiciled in this area. Another consideration is that, as part of our analysis, we shall be relating economic growth within this area to the size of the Roman money supply, and mainland Italy was also the principal area of circulation of the denarius. This currency also, of course, circulated in Sicily from the end of the third century, probably in Africa after 146, and in Spain and Gaul from the final quarter of the second century, but it is clear that none of the other bullion currencies that existed within Rome's expanding empire ever circulated within Italy itself.

This chapter is, then, highly theoretical and, in many parts, conjectural. But my hope is that the tentative conclusions that it reaches can be improved upon over time as more evidence is discovered and that, at the very least, the methodology will prove interesting and provoke further debate on how the impasse created by the pervasive scarcity of ancient economic data can be overcome.

MEASURING ECONOMIC GROWTH

Economic growth is the increase in the output of an economy over time. It is a process of change over time and its significance lies in its contribution to the prosperity of a community or groups within a community.

In the official terminology of modern national accounts, growth is usually measured in terms of an increase over time in real, that is inflation-adjusted, gross domestic product (GDP) or gross national product (GNP). Gross domestic

[6] Even in the contemporary national accounts of the United Kingdom, there are 'statistical discrepancies' (£214 million in 2003—though admittedly only 0.2% of the total) and GDP announcements by all modern nations are frequently subject to revision.

product can be considered in three different ways: as the domestic output, defined as the value added in production of all final goods and services within a particular territory or country (termed the value-added approach to GDP); as the total domestic income of residents of the particular territory or country (the income approach to GDP); and as the total domestic expenditure by residents of a particular territory or country on consumption and investment goods (the expenditure approach to GDP). To find GDP under the expenditure approach, it is necessary to deduct imports and to add exports, since some domestic expenditure will be channelled to imported goods (e.g. to buy slaves from Delos), while expenditure by non-residents on goods produced by domestic residents (e.g. Italian wine exported to Gaul) will add to the incomes of these residents. The resulting GDP numbers from each of these three approaches should exactly match each other, although in practice there are often statistical discrepancies.

GNP under the income approach is GDP plus or minus net receipts from transfers of property (interest, rent, dividends, and profits) or labour income from the rest of the world. This would include, for example, the profits of an Italian merchant operating in Delos that are remitted back to Italy. There is also a further measure with which it is useful to think in the context of second-century BC Rome: national disposable income (NDI) is GNP plus or minus net current transfers received in money or in kind from the rest of the world (these would include booty, indemnities, and taxes in money or in kind).[7] One final important consideration is that changes in price levels over time can affect comparisons between GDP (or GNP) numbers for different years. In order to highlight the difference in the monetary value of national income and the 'real' value of national income, GDP and GNP numbers are adjusted to take account of inflationary effects. This is done by using a broad-based price index called the GDP-deflator (or GNP-deflator). It can then be determined whether economic growth has occurred over a period of time in real terms. We shall discuss this further below.

The question of economic growth is also closely tied to the question of demographic change. This is because an increase in total GDP could just be due to a simple increase in population and it is, therefore, important to distinguish between this type of 'aggregate' or 'extensive' growth on the one hand and, on the other, 'per capita' or 'intensive' growth, represented by an increase over time in income per head ('per capita GDP'), in which greater efficiencies in production mean that, on average, each economic agent is producing more.[8] Thus, for example, if total GDP rises only slightly faster than the increase in population, there will be a small improvement in per capita GDP, that is in living standards.[9] So even if we can identify that economic growth did occur, we cannot say whether it was per capita growth without some idea of what happened to the size of the population over the

[7] Maddison 2007: 45. [8] Bowman and Wilson 2009*b*: 28.

[9] Per capita GDP is used by many developmental economists as an approximation of general national well-being. It is only right to point out, however, that it is criticized as not measuring economic growth well enough, especially in countries where there is a significant portion of economic activity that is not part of measured financial transactions. More recent theories of human development have begun to see beyond purely financial measures of development, for example with measures such as the availability of medical care, education, equality, and political freedom. One measure used is the Genuine Progress Indicator, which relates strongly to theories of distributive justice.

same period. Equally importantly, we cannot estimate the growth rate of some of the elements of GDP without having an estimate for the underlying population. In this chapter we shall use the population estimates for mainland Italy that we developed in Ch. 7 (summarized in Table 7.5), where we followed de Ligt in assuming that the free population grew moderately during the second century, before experiencing a modest decline in the first half of the first century, and Scheidel for the size of the slave population. These estimates suggested that the total combined free and servile population of Italy grew by 57 per cent between 200 and 150, and by 18 per cent between 150 and 100, and then proceeded to contract by 1 per cent between 100 and 50 BC.

Neoclassical economic theory suggests that an increase in the *growth potential* ('supply side') of an economy can come about in five highly interrelated ways:

1. a greater quantity of natural resources (land, raw materials, etc.);
2. a greater quantity of labour;
3. a greater quantity of capital;
4. increased productivity (conventionally measured in terms of 'output per worker'); and
5. technological progress.

All five inputs contribute to the growth process, but modern growth theory emphasizes the critical role played by capital. This is because increasing capital relative to labour should allow people to be more productive. Moreover, poor countries with less capital per person will grow faster because each investment in capital will produce a higher return than rich countries with ample capital.[10] That said, because of diminishing returns on capital, economies will eventually reach a point (called a 'steady state') at which no new increase in capital will create economic growth. An increase in the money supply or a reduction in the rate of interest or taxation can further stimulate the growth process by increasing current spending in the economy.

The 'demand side' of an economy is also important. Advantage can only be taken of an increase in an economy's potential growth rate (that is, the potential can only be turned into actual growth) if the economy is being operated at a high and expanding level of aggregate demand. Aggregate demand is the total amount of expenditure on domestic goods and services (composed of consumption expenditure, investment expenditure, and state expenditure) and net exports (exports less imports). Again, increasing capital has a significant role in stimulating aggregate demand, via multiplier effects. Expenditure on buildings and infrastructure, for example, can, as Keynes identified, have a multiplier effect (sometimes termed a 'trickle-down' effect) on the wider economy. In an ancient context, the payments made to (free) contractors, masons, architects, labourers, and other manufacturers and suppliers, increased the recipients' incomes, part of which may in turn have been spent on other goods and services, to create a theoretically endless (though

10 As an example, over the period 1973–2001, the average per annum growth rate in real per capita GDP for China was 5.32% and for the USA was 1.86%; in 1973 real per capita GDP was US$ 839 in China and US$ 16,689 in the USA (Silver 2007: 199 n. 5).

diminishing) chain of expenditure. In this way the net effect on employment and income would have been several times larger than the initial sums expended.[11]

The institutional framework in which an economy operates can also be of significance. This dimension of economic growth has been emphasized by Douglass North, an exponent of what has been termed 'new institutional economics' (NIE).[12] New institutional economics builds on neoclassical economics by taking into account the constraints affecting economic activity and decision making and the stimuli provided by the type and configuration of an economy's institutions. North argues that the impact of institutional frameworks and structures on economic activity is key and that some societies have frameworks that do more to encourage productive innovation and to reduce the difficulties and the costs of economic activity than others. Economic history teaches us that massive increases in total factor productivity (TFP)—i.e. increases in GDP that cannot be explained by increases in measured inputs—can result from changes in institutional quality or improved economic or political organization. This is the case even if technology remains constant. In a recent empirical study, Hall and Jones found that 'differences in social infrastructure [i.e. differences in institutions and government policies] across countries cause large differences in capital accumulation, educational attainment and productivity; and therefore large differences in income across countries'.[13] As Silver has pointed out, in 1988, ten years after the market-oriented reforms in China, real GDP per capita was 85.5 per cent greater than in 1978. By way of comparison, in 1978 real GDP per capita was only 44.4 per cent higher than in 1968.[14]

THE DIAGNOSTIC FEATURES OF A GROWING ECONOMY

Whatever we are seeking to measure during the late Republic, the immediate problem is the lack of quantifiable documentary and archaeological data. We have very few numbers and even fewer reliable ones.[15] Such data as we do have shine only narrow beams of light on some of the key areas of economic activity. So why bother? Maddison, the high priest of historical macro-economic estimation, summarizes his manifesto thus: 'Quantification clarifies issues which qualitative analysis leaves fuzzy. It is more readily contestable and likely to be contested. It sharpens scholarly discussion, sparks off rival hypotheses, and contributes to the dynamics of the research process.'[16]

Although macro-economic quantification was in fact first attempted in the seventeenth century, it fell out of fashion until the 1950s, when it became a major tool for macro-economic policy analysis. The first set of standardized national accounts (for the sixteen countries that were then members of the Organization for

[11] Millett 2001: 25; Keynes 1936: 131, 220 recommended (sarcastically) the building of cathedrals as a remedy for unemployment. More recently, in the 1990s, the Japanese government helped to maintain an unemployment rate below 5% (at a time when Western economies were experiencing double-digit rates) by embarking on a number of massive infrastructure projects.

[12] D. C. North 1990, 2005.

[13] Hall and Jones 1999: 114, cited by Silver 2007: 221.

[14] Silver 2007: 221.

[15] Scheidel 1996.

[16] Maddison 2007: 1.

European Economic Co-operation) were not published until 1954 and, even in the first decade of the twenty-first century, implementation of the system of standardized national accounts in the former communist Eastern bloc was not complete.[17] It is scarcely surprising, therefore, that the history of macro-economic estimates for Rome has a short academic pedigree. It is only since the late 1970s that some ancient historians and econometricians have tried to reconstruct Roman GDP and per capita incomes, building on the work of economic historians of the early modern period.[18] Most of these attempts have aimed to provide an estimate of the size of the Roman economy in a particular year, in other words a static snapshot of the scale of the Roman economy at a particular moment in time (generally AD 14), rather than to provide an estimate of the rate of growth (or contraction) of the Roman economy over a period of time.

Thus, in his 1980 'Taxes and Trade' article, Keith Hopkins included a rough estimate of the per capita subsistence level in the Roman Empire in terms of food, clothing, heat, and housing, and suggested that the output of the Empire would average out at less than twice the minimum subsistence level. The quantitative economic historian, Raymond Goldsmith, estimated national income in AD 14, on a per capita basis, from the expenditure side and presented a reconciliation from the income side.[19] Subsequent GDP estimates have been produced by Peter Temin and by Angus Maddison, who adjusted and commented at length on Goldsmith's numbers.[20]

Most of the reconstructions that have been produced in the last thirty or so years have started with the income side of Roman GDP and an estimate of an individual's annual subsistence consumption multiplied by an estimated population.[21] The resulting number is then tweaked by adding estimates for various components of GDP such as elite income. Thus, Maddison accepted Goldsmith's estimate of total GDP for the whole empire in AD 14, but he raised Goldsmith's estimate of elite income (which he regarded as being 'much too low' at 17% of GDP) to 26 per cent of GDP. Similarly, Goldsmith assumed that there were 40,000 *equites* in the empire in AD 14, with an average fortune of HS 500,000 and an average income of HS 30,000, and, further, that 60 per cent of them were Italian residents. He further estimated that there were 360,000 *decuriones* (Maddison reduced this estimate to 240,000) residing in 3,000 cities of the Empire.[22]

Recently, Walter Scheidel and Steven Friesen have attempted to establish 'a convergent range of estimates of the size of the GDP of the Roman Empire at the time of its putative demographic peak in the mid-second century AD'; and, by developing a model of income distribution and inequality, have asked who enjoyed the fruits of that economy. Their conclusion is that the total income of the Roman Empire was HS 20 bn. per annum; that the state and local government captured a small share of total income, of not much more than 5 per cent; that the top 1.5 per cent of households controlled around 20 per cent of total income; that economically 'middling' non-elite groups accounted for a modest share of the

[17] Maddison 2007: 1, 295–6. [18] e.g. Bairoch 1977. [19] Goldsmith 1984.

[20] Temin 2006; Maddison 2007: 33–62.

[21] There is an assumption shared by several scholars that the typical Roman lived at subsistence level (e.g. Jongman 2000: 271).

[22] Maddison 2007: 48.

population (around 10%) but perhaps another 20 per cent of total income; and that the vast majority of the population lived close to subsistence but cumulatively generated more than half overall output. They assume that, in terms of average per capita performance, the Roman economy did not dramatically differ from most other pre-industrial systems, and fell short of the achievements of the most advanced economies of the early modern world, those of the Netherlands and the United Kingdom.[23]

Does this type of experimental reconstruction of the size of the Roman economy in a particular year help us, and are the right questions being asked? Or does an estimate of this kind merely produce a tangled web of conjecture? Some scholars have expressed a high degree of scepticism. This is because, at the most basic level, we simply do not have enough reliable numbers to aggregate into a completely accurate estimate of Roman GDP at any period of its history.

Problems with the kind of macro-estimation adopted by historical econometricians, such as Goldsmith and Maddison, have led some scholars interested in the performance of the Roman economy over time to take a different, less numerically precise approach by trying to identify possible drivers of economic growth. Saller, for example, seeks to demonstrate that the conditions existed that would have made growth possible, by identifying possible causes of growth. In his article *Framing the Debate over Growth in the Ancient Economy*, he points to factors such as trade (which in turn allows for agricultural and manufacturing specialization), intensification of capital investment (e.g. state investment in infrastructure and private residential construction), improved technology, and the institutional framework for economic activities.[24] To Saller's list we might add other factors such as fiscal drivers (rates of taxation), warfare (as a driver of state expenditure and so manufacturing), and the cost of labour. A second approach is to identify symptoms that might suggest growth did indeed occur. This means looking for phenomena that are likely to be reflections of (rather than criteria for) growth, such as urbanization, increased consumption, improved standards of living, increases in elite wealth, and increased information dissemination.[25] In line with this, Bowman and Wilson focus on the more robust micro-data that might be made to address the larger issues and patterns of economic behaviour: 'The way to proceed is to accumulate large general data sets, analyse them, test them for biases, isolate the biases by probing more detailed case studies, and then see how those studies affect out understanding of the total data set again.'[26] By analysing and using proxies of economic performance such as the number of shipwrecks as an indicator of levels of trade, attempts can be made to build up a picture of economic behaviour based on more detailed and perhaps more reliable evidence.

This is not to say that these proxies do not sometimes turn out to be themselves problematic. For example, the shipwrecks about which we know hold mostly amphorae cargoes and loads of architectural marble, as these survive on the seabed as a protective mound in a way that other, perishable cargoes, and sometimes their containers, do not. As Wilson asks: 'Does the decline in the number of known wrecks from the second to the seventh centuries AD therefore

[23] Scheidel and Friesen 2009: 62–4.
[24] Saller 2002: 261–6.
[25] Bowman and Wilson 2009*b*: 13, 30.
[26] A. I. Wilson 2009*a*: 245.

reflect an absolute decline in the number of trading voyages, or is it at least partly explicable by a move from amphorae to wooden barrels as the preferred containers for trading liquids?'[27] There are similar issues surrounding the use as proxies of the rates of lead deposition found in the ice of Greenland, the peat bogs of Spain, and the lakes of Sweden. Indeed more work needs to be done on atmospheric transports and on lead isotope analysis before we can identify the relative importance of the most probable polluters: Roman Spain and Han China.[28]

There are sometimes also problems with the way these kinds of data have been used. First, increases in given proxy variables are commonly interpreted as signs of economic growth. However, they need not always indicate this.[29] For example, the massive infrastructure projects undertaken by the Japanese government in the 1990s might conceivably be interpreted as a sign of economic growth by archaeologists of the future, if independent reports or statistical data fail to survive. But in fact these projects were initiated in order to provide a Keynesian stimulus to a contracting economy (and were only partly successful in their aim).[30] Secondly, representations of proxy data generally portray this material in absolute terms by focusing on quantity per period rather than the rate of change between periods. So if we are interested in examining the rate of change in economic activity over time, these data sets need to be reconfigured accordingly. For example, the bell curve in the proxy data for shipwrecks translates to substantial annual rates of increase in the third, second, and early first centuries BC and to stagnation and eventual net contraction thereafter. As Scheidel says, 'this perspective strongly privileges the late Republican period'.[31] Problems such as these do not invalidate the exercise, but they do mean that proxy data cannot just be assumed to indicate economic growth. We need, on the one hand, to analyse and interpret the data and, on the other, to combine and compare them with other indicators if we want to gain a better understanding of what the evidence actually does show.

Finally, the NIE approach has recently been adopted by a number of economic historians of the Roman world who have begun to analyse the institutional environment surrounding the Roman economy, most notably in *The Cambridge Economic History of the Greco-Roman World*. As Kehoe has emphasized, this environment can encompass both formal and informal institutions. The formal institutions include, for example, the laws that the Roman state established to define property rights, legal rules relating to farm tenancy and other aspects of land tenure, and the courts. In addition, the institutional environment embraces the informal institutions that help to determine how formal institutions work, that is the social values and practices that help to establish the 'rules of the game', for example education.[32] There are problems, though, in producing a numerical quantification of the economic impact of such institutions. In the modern world, the results of institutional change can be observed in, for example, the

[27] A. I. Wilson 2009*a*: 219–21.

[28] A. I. Wilson 2009*b*: 78; and see Friedman (forthcoming) for a very cautious review of the data for atmospheric pollution.

[29] Scheidel 2009*a*: 46.

[30] Cf. Scheidel 2009*a*: 64.

[31] Scheidel 2009*a*: 52; A. I. Wilson 2009*b*: 77.

[32] Kehoe 2007*b*: 29–30.

statistically derived GDP numbers that result. In an ancient context, results are much more difficult to evaluate.

If, then, we are sceptical of reconstructions of the size of the Roman economy in a particular year and if we generally lack reliable numerical and proxy data series, how can we measure or even demonstrate per capita economic growth in the Roman world? In what follows, we shall attempt to model a probabilistic quantification of the Roman economy during the second and early first centuries by analysing it from several different angles. The aim is to produce a matrix of variables that might collectively and through comparison give some indication of whether real per capita economic growth did occur during this period. By way of background, we shall begin by looking at the supply side of the economy, that is, the economy's growth potential, and how it was particularly influenced by warfare and trade. We shall then consider two variables that are crucial for any discussion of real per capita economic growth: inflation and population. Next we shall present a series of snapshots of the Italian economy from the income side of GDP at fifty year intervals (150 BC, 100 BC, and 50 BC). Our procedure uses individual elite wealth (for which we have sporadic notices) as a starting point and we extrapolate income pyramids from these data. This procedure is highly conjectural, but it does produce some interesting and historically credible results, into which can be fitted, quite reasonably, both some general trends in living standards that we can derive from ancient accounts and the very small number of reports of non-elite individual income. We then attempt to quantify Italian GDP from the expenditure side by examining state investment and consumption (about which we know something) and private investment and consumption (about which we know very little). Finally we examine how changes in the Roman money supply might have reflected or influenced Italian economic growth during this period, by combining what we know of the money supply with hypothetical numbers for levels of monetization and the velocity of circulation of money to produce a series of estimates of Italian nominal GDP. We shall not try to quantify Italian GDP by output (the value-added approach to GDP), since we have no information that would be remotely helpful in such an exercise. However, the implication of an increase in real GDP, as calculated using the income and expenditure approaches, is that the value-added approach to GDP, if it was possible to calculate that, would show the same increase, since the resulting numbers from all three approaches should exactly match each other. Again, because of lack of data, we shall not attempt to estimate Italian GNP, although we shall make some remarks, at the end of this chapter, on Italian national disposable income (NDI). In effect, what we are doing here is adapting the technique that Hopkins called the 'wigwam argument', in which there are several pieces of evidence, each insufficient or untrustworthy in itself, that seem collectively to confirm a proposition: 'each pole would fall down by itself, but together the poles stand up, by leaning on each other; they point roughly in the same direction, and circumscribe "truth"'.[33]

[33] Hopkins 1978: 19–20.

WAR, TRADE, AND THE SUPPLY SIDE OF THE REPUBLICAN ECONOMY

As we saw in Ch. 2, the core competence of the Roman state in the second century BC was warfare, but it should not be assumed that it had a negative influence on the Roman economy. It is well understood from later European history how warfare promoted economic development in the long term.[34] As we said in the Introduction, the establishment of Rome's empire produced an extraordinary return on investment, as the accumulated surpluses of the Mediterranean and adjacent lands were appropriated by the conquerors. But war had other more profound economic effects. We mentioned earlier that an increase in the growth potential, or the supply side, of an economy can be stimulated by greater quantities of natural resources, labour, and capital, as well as through increased productivity and technological progress. Increases in all of these inputs are apparent in the Roman economy of the second century and the principal catalysts were trade and, in particular, warfare. Indeed in the first half of the second century, warfare was in many ways a much more forceful mechanism than the market in mobilizing the economic resources of the Mediterranean in Rome's favour. This mechanism may also explain why the biggest expansion in commercial activity appears to have pre-dated the peaceful conditions of the early Empire.[35]

In bald economic terms, Rome's military expansion produced a greater quantity of natural resources, both in terms of raw materials, through its capture of the Spanish mines, and in terms of land: its conquests resulted in the acquisition of more *ager publicus*, the foundation of more colonies, and, eventually, the establishment of more provinces. Many of these provinces already had well-established agricultural economies and developed networks of trade and communication. War also brought in a greater quantity of cheap labour in the form of slaves. The inflow of slaves, who presumably were living at or close to subsistence, meant that labour input per head of population in mainland Italy would have grown, with increased productivity as a result. This was for the simple reason that enslavement forced victims to work harder at below-market rates of wage labour. Labour productivity in mainland Italy was probably also helped by the construction of better infrastructure, and again warfare was a stimulus in at least part of this process. The creation, for example, of a road network, by the military for the military, had the economically beneficial side effect of allowing commercial traffic to move more efficiently.

The wars of the second century also, of course, resulted in the Roman state accumulating unprecedented quantities of capital. The massive amounts of booty and indemnities that she extracted from defeated enemies have been described in detail in Ch. 2, as have the proceeds of the Spanish and Macedonian silver mines in Ch. 3 and the increasing amounts of capital from provincial taxation in Ch. 4. Much of this haul was melted down and issued in the form of silver denarii to soldiers and to workmen on state infrastructure projects. In the wider context of the Mediterranean, this process was not just a case of reshuffling the cards, as riches were redistributed from east to west. Plunder brought immobilized and

[34] e.g. McNeill 1982. [35] A point emphasized by Bang 2009: 204–5.

sequestered wealth, such as state reserves and temple treasures, into circulation again and put them to productive use.

There can be little doubt that the other important engine of growth for the Italian economy, during the last two centuries BC, was trade, as it has been for many other countries at different stages of development. This is because increased trade contributes to economic growth in a number of ways. By producing a more efficient allocation of resources within a country, it enables economies of scale and division of labour. It compensates for the unfavourable location of natural resources. It encourages more complex manufacturing, so that a wide range of goods can be produced at a given place, using a mixture of local and imported materials or components. It increases the effective size of markets reached by producers and transmits growth from one part of the world to another. It can also contribute directly to state revenues, if it is taxed, as it was by the Romans through *portoria*. In less-developed countries, trade also facilitates urbanization and the growth of cities beyond the capacity of their immediate hinterlands to supply them. In sum, its effects can be far-reaching. To illustrate, in the world economy since 1950 there has been a massive liberalization of world trade, first under the auspices of the General Agreement on Tariffs and Trade (GATT) established in 1947, and now under the auspices of the World Trade Organization, which replaced GATT in 1993. This liberalization of trade has led to a massive expansion in the growth of world trade and acted as an important driver of world economic output. The volume of world trade has grown sixteen times (at an average compound rate of just over 7% p.a.) and world GDP has expanded fivefold. In some individual countries, notably China and in South-East Asia, the growth of exports has exceeded 10 per cent per annum. Exports have tended to grow fastest in countries with more liberal trade regimes and these countries have experienced the fastest growth of GDP.[36] Indeed some have pointed out that because of the success of certain Asian countries, especially Japan, Taiwan, and South Korea, which have wholeheartedly embraced it, export-led growth should be considered the best strategy for promoting development.

As we saw in Ch. 8, the expansion in Italian long-distance commerce in the second and first centuries was driven by an import demand for slaves and luxury goods (the trade in slaves confimed by literary evidence and that in luxuries by both archaeological and textual evidence) and by an export demand for wine and olive oil (evidenced by finds of enormous numbers of transport amphorae in both maritime and terrestrial contexts) which continued until the end of the period we are discussing.[37] Trends in the commercial exchange of other soft and perishable commodities are invisible because of the failure of both the commodities themselves and their transport containers to survive in the archaeological record. However, the distribution of dated shipwrecks in the Mediterranean provides a powerful index of commercial development and of the volume of goods traded. Despite the difficulties involved in interpreting the data from the time of the Principate onwards, which we touched on earlier, the rise in the number of wrecks

[36] Thirlwall 2000: 5.

[37] See Chs. 7 and 8. The import demand for wine and olive oil only seems to have become in any way meaningful in the second half of the first century BC (Meijer 2002: 140–1).

Table 11.1. Mediterranean seaborne trade by volume (estimated)

	249–200	199–150	149–100	99–50 BC
No. of shipwrecks	21	60	97	108
% change		*186%*	*62%*	*11%*
Increase in average ship size				20%
Total volume of trade (index)	100	286	462	617
% change		*186%*	*62%*	*34%*

in the second and first centuries, before the usage of the barrel became widespread, must reflect a genuine increase in maritime trading activity.[38] The fifty-year probability graph for shipwrecks that Wilson has constructed (reproduced in Fig. 7.1) shows that the number of wrecks surged by 186 per cent in the first half of the second century, by 62 per cent between 150 and 100, and by a further 11 per cent increase in the first half of the first century. However, this last figure, for the first half of the first century, presumably understates the actual increase in trade, since it does not account for what appears to have been a growth in ship size. As we discussed in Ch. 7, bigger ships begin to appear in the early first century,[39] with the increase in size probably driven by the invention of the bilge pump at the end of the second century. We assume, in Table 11.1, that this added a further 20 per cent to trade volumes in the first half of the first century.

The diffusion of improved technologies, which was facilitated by increased trade, was also conducive to economic development. Waterwheels and water-lifting devices increased the efficiency of farming, as did the dissemination of new types of intensive farming described in the agricultural treatises. Water-extraction devices for drainage allowed the mining of enriched deposits below the natural water table. More sophisticated construction techniques were evolved to satisfy the increased demand for grander buildings, to speed up the actual process of construction, and to lower its cost. Roads and the bridges that carried them over water were of a uniformly high technical quality, capable of carrying wheeled vehicles with heavy loads. In fact Roman roads represented a development that was unparalleled in the world, with the exception of China, down to the development of the English canal system in the eighteenth century and the arrival of the railways in the nineteenth century AD. Roads promoted economic connectivity and integration because they helped the movement not only of goods and products but also of people, money, information, technology, and ideas. In turn they encouraged urbanization by making money and markets more accessible. They would have overcome many of the transport constraints that affected most other ancient, medieval, and early modern societies for which, by comparison with ancient Rome, market integration would have remained comparatively thin and fragmented.

There is one major *caveat*, however. For modern industrialized societies, technological progress based on fossil fuels has been a key driving force behind sustained, intensive economic growth. For Italy of the second century BC, it is less easy to find evidence to show how long the generation and dissemination of technological innovations and improvements supported economic growth on a

[38] Cf. A. I. Wilson 2009*a*: 219–21. [39] Meijer 2002: 139–40.

sustained basis. That is not to deny the potential importance of technology for Rome at this period, but merely to question whether, for example, the invention of the bilge pump at the end of the second century, which was one of the factors enabling larger seagoing ships to be built, generated sustained growth in trade over several centuries or merely produced, in economic terms, a one-off increase during the late Republican period.[40]

One further aspect of supply side economics should be mentioned. As we said earlier, a government can stimulate the growth process by increasing current spending in the economy through tax cuts. The suspension of *tributum* in 167 was in effect a tax cut. Thereafter, Roman citizens paid no income tax. Private wealth was not subject to progressive taxation—indeed private property in Italy remained exempt from tax until the end of the third century AD. Moreover, indirect rates of tax under the Republic were not especially heavy. As we have seen, the main income of the Roman state came from *vectigalia*. These included all kinds of revenues from public and private properties: *scriptura* (pasture tax) and tithes (*decuma*, only collected in the provinces, at a rate of 10%); revenues from state monopolies (taxes on salt, minium, silphium, and perhaps pitch); customs dues (*portoria*, normally at a rate of 2% or 2½%); and the tax on manumission (*vicesima libertatis*, established in 357).[41]

Certain institutions and configurations of institutions would also have been conducive to economic growth. The gradual diffusion through mainland Italy of Latin as a common language, the use of the denarius as a common currency, the spread of common systems of measurement, the legal facilitation of commerce under Roman law, and the development of the *societas* as the preferred organizational model for business can all reasonably be expected to have reduced transactional costs and, in general, to have promoted economic development. Of course, not all institutional procedures were efficient and considered. There were no state monetary institutions charged with the task of overseeing the financial system. There was no overarching, formally planned, economic policy for Rome's embryonic empire—just a series of measures to meet current needs.[42] But certain of these measures would have resulted in improved economic efficiencies. For example, C. Gracchus' introduction in the late 120s of the system of *censoria locatio*, under his *lex Sempronia de provincia Asia*, allowed the Romans to budget for large projects for at least five years ahead and reduced their dependency on less certain forms of income, such as booty and mining revenues.

At the same time, we should remember that the Roman state never borrowed, apart from as a crisis measure during the Second Punic War. The level of state expenditure was never greater than the amount that could be funded by the actual holdings of bullion in the *aerarium*. This one factor had a major impact on the shape and balance of the Roman economy. On the one hand, it meant that the

[40] Scheidel 2009*a*: 69, for example, presents a picture of one-off unsustainable growth followed by Malthusian pressure.

[41] Polyb. 6. 17; Aubert 1994: 330–1; Duncan-Jones 1974: 5. At *Att.* 2. 16. 1 (59 BC), Cicero probably exaggerates to make a point when he says that the only domestic tax remaining in Italy after the abolition of customs dues and the privatization of the Ager Campanus is the manumission tax. He conveniently omits, for example, *scriptura*.

[42] See Kay (2013).

Roman public sector never carried any debt which had to be serviced by interest payments. On the other, the Roman state's unwillingness to take on liabilities (and so to gear up the public sector's balance sheet by borrowing from an increasingly wealthy elite) meant that the level of state spending was considerably less than it theoretically could have been. In fact, wealthy individuals themselves undertook much of the expenditure that we might, in a modern society, regard as being the state's responsibility, euergetistically financing the construction of temples and other public buildings, paying for state entertainment, such as games, and using their own *familiae* (household establishments) to staff provincial administrations. Furthermore, in the absence of Roman government bonds, the Roman elite's demand for financial assets could only be satisfied by depositing money with banks, by lending directly to other members of the Roman elite, or by advancing credit to foreign states, cities, and kings. The absence of public-sector debt thus had the consequence of channelling resources into, and stimulating growth in, the private sector of the economy.

It need hardly be said that the impact of institutional developments and configurations such as these is not numerically quantifiable and, as Scheidel rightly warns, an NIE approach 'cannot help us address the problem of how to choose between different models of change' (i.e. intensive or extensive growth).[43]

THE GDP DEFLATOR

It is vital to understand and, if possible, to quantify the rate of inflation during this period, if we are going to search for evidence of *real* (that is, inflation-adjusted) economic growth. But the problem is, as we saw in Ch. 5, that we have no price series for our period; in fact, the only prices we have for soft commodities are a handful of data points for wheat. To make matters worse, two of these data points, which are for wheat prices mentioned by Polybius from mid-second-century Cisalpine Gaul (HS 0.44 per modius) and Spain (HS 1 per modius), are mentioned by that author precisely because they were notably low; and so it becomes highly questionable whether they can be used as valid comparators with the only wheat prices we have that do not appear to be the result of special circumstances, those provided by Cicero in the *Verrines* for Sicily in the late 70s BC. So we really have very little idea what a 'normal' price for wheat would have been in Rome in the 150s. Even in the *Verrines*, the wheat prices mentioned range from HS 20 at Rome in 74 BC, during a pre-harvest shortage, to HS 2 or HS 3 a couple of years later in Sicily. And, over time, the price of wheat did not necessarily just go up: the median price of wheat in 70s BC Sicily was 42 per cent higher than the median in Egypt at the end of the first century AD.[44] If we are to use any of these data points, probably the least extreme approach is to compare Polybius' price of HS 1 in Spain in the late 150s with Cicero's price of HS 2 in the late 70s, which suggests an average inflation rate of 0.87 per cent per annum over the intervening period. On its own,

[43] Scheidel 2009*a*: 58. [44] Rathbone 2009: 306.

Table 11.2. Inflation and the GDP deflator (estimated)

	200	150	100	50 BC
Price change (index)	100	120	180	234
GDP Deflator		-20%	-50%	-30%
Compound annual rate		-0.37%	-0.81%	-0.53%
Wheat: HS per modius	1.5	1.8	2.7	3.5

however, this number does not inspire much confidence. But the numismatic history of small denomination Roman bronze coins possibly provides an indication of the rate of retail food price inflation. In the last years of the Second Punic War, the sextans was minted in large quantities, but a century later the coin had in effect ceased to be a functional coin and was only occasionally struck. Eventually it was no longer minted, which left the quadrans as the smallest bronze coin (Crawford dates this change to 91/90).[45] This development suggests that, between the middle of the second century and about 90 BC, prices of low-value goods had risen at a rate sufficient to make the sextans unusable in the marketplace. Crudely, if an item, which in 150 was priced at a sextans (one-sixth or 16.66% of an as), could only be purchased in 90 for a quadrans (one-quarter or 25% of an as), the implication is that the price of that item had risen by 50 per cent during the intervening period. This development can probably be connected with the retariffing of the silver denarius from 10 bronze asses to 16, which sharply reduced the purchasing power of the bronze coinage relative to silver.

One area of the economy in which the rate of inflation was undoubtedly increasing more rapidly than this, during the second half of the second century and the first half of the first century, was in the prices paid by the elite for 'luxury' goods, residential houses, and estates, as we can see from anecdotal references.[46] Again, though, we have no data series that would enable us to quantify these increases with any degree of accuracy.

In sum, we have no precise idea about what the rate of inflation was during the second and first centuries, and it is difficult to see how we ever could have, given the paucity of data. As a working hypothesis, therefore, we have adopted what we believe represents the 'medium case' for inflation, and we suggest that prices increased by 20 per cent during the first half of the second century (a compound rate of 0.37% p.a.), by 50 per cent between 150 and 100 BC (0.81% p.a.), and by 30 per cent between 100 and 50 BC (0.53% p.a.). This would mean that over the period at which we shall be looking in most detail, 150 to 50 BC, prices increased by 95 per cent, a compound rate of 0.67 per cent per annum.[47] On the basis of these estimated rates of inflation, we shall apply the GDP deflators and the prices of wheat set out in Table 11.2 to the nominal GDP estimates that we develop in the rest of this chapter. The reader is free to experiment with other values.

[45] Crawford 1985: 177. [46] See p. 104.

[47] Burnett (1982: 133–4, 1987*a*: 108) argues that it took a century for wheat prices to double.

GDP FROM THE INCOME SIDE

If we try to quantify GDP by income for mainland Italy, we are faced with a seemingly insurmountable problem, as we have no ancient reports on general levels of income, let alone aggregate income. We have only a very small number of notices of individual wealth and a few scattered references to rates of pay. We can also perhaps infer, with a greater or lesser degree of plausibility, some general trends in living standards from ancient accounts. For example, at the end of the Second Punic War, there must have been considerable destitution amongst Italian peasants whose livelihood had been disrupted by the war. One of the objectives of the programme of colonization in the Po Valley upon which the Roman government embarked at the beginning of the second century was probably to compensate this category of the population for the loss of their original landholdings, and it resulted in the resettlement of up to 30,000 families between 200 and 177. The large numbers of settlers and the very small plots that apparently they mostly received are, as Hopkins said, evidence in themselves of considerable impoverishment.[48] So the assumption must be that, at the beginning of the second century, a not insignificant section of the Roman population, probably well in excess of those that were resettled, were living at or near the level of subsistence.

In defining subsistence we follow Scheidel and Friesen, both in using Robert Allen's concept of a 'bare bones basket' and in calculating it and other measures of income in terms of wheat equivalent (since this allows cross-temporal and cross-cultural comparisons).[49] The 'bare bones basket' represents the lowest-cost configuration of goods that ensures both base-level calorie intake and the rudimentary provision of clothing, fuel (e.g. for heating and cooking), and shelter for an adult man. Using papyrological evidence from mid-first to mid-second-century AD Egypt, Scheidel and Friesen calculate this to be 390 kg of wheat equivalent on a gross basis (i.e. including tax and investment).[50] Allen has also introduced the concept of a 'respectability basket', which is a consumption basket that would have provided a much more adequate, if still far from luxurious, existence. This is set at 940 kg of wheat equivalent on a gross basis and is at a level that was normally above the average income of an unskilled worker in a pre-modern society and that, in some cases, was barely exceeded by the incomes of higher-earning skilled craftsmen. We follow Maddison in assuming an employment rate (or 'participation rate') of 36 per cent of the total free population, that is, one worker for every 1.78 non-workers.[51]

By the second quarter of the second century, increased demand for immigrant slave labour suggests either that the price of slaves was falling, because of an increasing supply of captives, or that the average income of Roman peasants was rising in real terms. In both cases, slaves could only have been of interest to their purchasers, if they were a cheaper form of human labour than free men and

[48] Hopkins 1978: 57. The size of allotments varied enormously from 5 *iugera* (slightly larger than a football pitch) to parcels of ten times that size at 51½ *iugera* (Toynbee 1965: 654–5).

[49] Allen 2009; Scheidel and Friesen 2009: 68–9.

[50] While direct taxation ceased to be collected from Roman citizens in 167 BC and from her allies after 88 BC, we have for simplicity's sake used this figure to represent subsistence for free people and for slaves in the following discussion.

[51] Maddison 2007: 47.

women.[52] As we saw in Ch. 7, it looks as though the overwhelming majority of these captives were brought to Italy to be used in agriculture. With the passage of time, however, there was presumably a negative impact of slave income levels on the real income of the free population.[53] We can see a reflection of this in the statements in our sources, which suggest that a growing number of country-dwelling citizens were reduced to poverty during the decades preceding the Gracchan land reforms and which attribute this in part to the use of slave labour by rich landowners.[54]

The negative demographic impact of slaves working in the agricultural sector was also reflected in the drift of free population towards the cities. The attempts made to increase Rome's water supply, which resulted in the building of the Aqua Marcia, are just one indication of the growth of the urban population during the period between the 180s and the 140s and are specifically attributed by Frontinus to the growth of the city (*incrementum urbis*).[55] This kind of urban population growth was driven by opportunity. The construction projects that started in the 180s would have increased demand for labour and produced a Keynesian multiplier effect, making urban wages attractive relative to rural incomes. As early as 187, the Latin allies complained to the senate that large numbers of their citizens had migrated to the city and had been assessed there. In the end, 12,000 Latins returned home.[56] Ten years later, the problem appears to have recurred, with the result that a *senatus consultum* ordered Latin allies resident at Rome to return to their own cities.[57] Livy remarks that, in the 180s, 'iam tum multitudine alienigenarum urbem onerante';[58] and a passage from Polybius gives a vivid impression of the scale on which public building was taking place by the middle of the second century: '*πολλῶν γὰρ ἔργων ὄντων τῶν ἐκδιδομένων ὑπὸ τῶν τιμητῶν διὰ πάσης Ἰταλίας εἰς τὰς ἐπισκευὰς καὶ κατασκευὰς τῶν δημοσίων, ἅ τις οὐκ ἂν ἐξαριθμήσαιτο ῥᾳδίως*'[59] (many projects are given out by the censors through the whole of Italy for the repair and construction of public buildings and it would not be easy to number them).

Similarly, a vast transport and logistics service sector was required to carry large volumes of building materials to Rome (and indeed to other central Italian towns), to support the expanded port and warehouse facilities that were constructed in the second century, and to service the general increase in trade which we described in Chs. 7 and 8. The creation of this service industry would have resulted in increased employment and real income growth. Inevitably, though, not all urban immigrants fared well economically. C. Gracchus' introduction of a corn dole in the late 120s and its expansion during the first half of the first century suggest that elements of the urban plebs were suffering extreme poverty.

Wage levels are generally irrecoverable, but we do have some snippets from the first half of the second century. According to Cato, a craftsman (*faber*) will assemble a mill for 'at least' HS 8.[60] If we assume that this is HS 8 for two days' work (although Cato gives no guidance on this) and that the craftsman can work

[52] Cf. Lo Cascio 2010: 27–30; Scheidel 2007: 341 believes that this increased demand for slaves probably also reflected the fact that free population growth was constrained by a combination of attrition factors. But we take a more optimistic view of population growth.

[53] Scheidel 2007: 339 n. 73.

[54] App. *B. Civ.* 1. 7.

[55] Frontin. *Aq.* 1. 7.

[56] Livy, 39. 3. 4–6.

[57] Livy, 41. 8. 6–12, 41. 9. 9–10.

[58] Livy, 39.3.4-6.

[59] Polyb. 6. 17. 2.

[60] Cato, *Agr.* 21. 5.

at this rate for 250 days per annum, his annual income would be HS 1,000. If we assume a participation rate of 36 per cent, this income translates into wheat equivalent numbers for each family member of 1,316 kg or 3.4 times subsistence, at a wheat price of HS 1.8 per modius, and is just above the 'respectability' level.[61] An annual income of HS 1,000 would also place this individual at a level just below half of what some have argued was probably the then equestrian threshold of HS 2,400 of income (calculated as a 6% return on HS 40,000, or 100,000 asses[62]). If correct, this presumably indicates that a skilled technician, capable of assembling the mill, for its time a technologically advanced piece of equipment, could command a premium level of remuneration of HS 4 per day.

Cato also says that it will cost HS 72 for six men and their oxen to transport a mill, a job taking six days.[63] If we ignore the capital cost of the oxen, this suggests that a drover could earn roughly HS 2 per day. Again, if we assume that he can find 250 days' work at this rate per annum, his annual income would be HS 500, which translates into wheat equivalent numbers for each family member of 658 kg, 69 per cent above subsistence but 30 per cent below 'respectability'. Finally Cicero gives us another stray reference in the 70s when he happens to mention that a casual labourer at Rome can earn HS 3 per day.[64] Again, if we assume that he can get 250 days' work at this rate per annum, his annual income would be HS 750. At a wheat price of HS 3.5 per modius, this translates into wheat equivalent numbers for each family member of 508 kg, 30 per cent above subsistence but 46 per cent below 'respectability'.

The stipend for an ordinary soldier in the second century was 120 denarii (HS 480) per annum.[65] In addition, individual Roman and allied soldiers at this time gained from the seizure of plunder. The main beneficiaries of this were undoubtedly the generals and their immediate entourages, but donatives to those further down the social scale were not insignificant. It is estimated that, between 201 and 167, a total of 13,271,000 denarii was distributed to 362,900 recipients.[66] On average this represents a donative of 36 denarii (HS 144) per legionary, and so an increase in remuneration of 30 per cent. The multiplier effect would have been enormous, with these male recipients schematically translating into a total, including wives and children, of perhaps one million beneficiaries and the money percolating into the wider population. The importance of these donatives is confirmed by the fact that military service became increasingly unpopular during the unrewarding wars fought in Spain between 154 and 133.[67] This absence of donatives would have meant a reduction in per capita income for many families and perhaps

[61] HS 1,000/HS1. 8 per modius = 556 modii/0.152 = 3,658 kg × 0.36 = 1,316 kg.

[62] Crawford 1985: 149–50 for a discussion of census thresholds in the context of the shift to reckoning in sestertii. It is not known what the property qualification for equestrian status was during the second century. Wiseman 1971: 66 speculates that it was about 40,000 or 50,000 HS. By the late first century, the qualification was HS 400,000 and, although it is not known for certain when this change was introduced, it was probably under the *lex Roscia* of 67 (Brunt 1988: 146). Cf. Brunt 1971*a*: 700, who was rightly sceptical of the argument of Nicolet 1966: 46–68 that HS 400,000 was already the equestrian census qualification during the Second Punic War.

[63] Cato, *Agr.* 22.3. [64] Cic. *Q. Rosc.* 28.

[65] See p. 22; Brunt 1950: 51, using Polyb. 6. 39. 12; Brunt 1971*a*: 411, 1988: 262 n. 94.

[66] Harl 1996: 43, table 3.2, based on Brunt 1971*a*: 393–4, 644–7.

[67] Rosenstein 2004: 53; references at Roselaar 2010: 217 n. 253.

prompted Sallust's comment that, during this period, 'populus militia atque inopia urgebatur'.[68] Perhaps too it explains the timing of the Gracchan *lex militaris*, which stopped deductions for clothing and equipment from the *stipendium*, and which was in effect a one-off salary increase for soldiers, presumably designed to make military service more appealing.[69] Suetonius states that Julius Caesar doubled the *stipendium* for legionaries and we know that the rate stood at 225 denarii per annum under Augustus.[70] This suggests that the rate of *stipendium* remained at approximately the same level from the second century until the middle of the first century, in which case its value in real terms must have been gradually reduced by inflation.[71] Having been worth the equivalent of 1,754 kg of wheat in 150 BC (equivalent to a per capita income of 632 kg, at a 36% participation rate and at a wheat price per modius of HS 1.8[72]), the *stipendium* had, on our assumed inflation figures, reduced in value to 1,170 kg by 100 BC (equivalent to a per capita income of 421 kg, at a 36% participation rate and at a wheat price per modius of HS 2.7), and to only 902 kg by 50 BC. This last figure is equivalent to a per capita income of 325 kg, at a 36 per cent participation rate and at a wheat price per modius of HS 3.5, and so is actually just below the subsistence level of 390 kg. This must partly explain the high level of donatives paid out by military commanders during the first century BC: in compensation for the fall in the real value of the army stipend, booty had to be redistributed to ordinary soldiers on an even larger scale than previously. In the 60s, between 86 m. and 91 m. denarii were paid out in the form of military bonuses and in total, between 69 and 29 BC, a staggering 1 bn. denarii were disbursed in this way.[73]

At the same time, there are various anecdotal pieces of evidence for the growing wealth of the Italian elite during our period, which suggests that inequality in the

[68] Sall. *Iug.* 41. 7: 'the people were oppressed by military service and poverty'; cf. App. *B. Civ.* 1. 7; see pp. 160–1 and 170.

[69] Frank 1933: 192 conjectures that 36 denarii were deducted from a soldier's annual stipend of 120 denarii to cover the cost of food and 9 denarii to cover the cost of clothing.

[70] Suet. *Iul.* 26. 3: 'stipendium in perpetuum duplicavit'; Speidel 1992.

[71] If Julius Caesar doubled the stipend and the rate was 225 denarii p.a. under Augustus, one implication is that the rate had been 112½ denarii p.a. before Julius Caesar. So how to reconcile this number with the figure of 120 denarii p.a. mentioned earlier? J. B. Campbell (*OCD*[3] s.v. stipendium) suggests that, if the pay of 2 obols per day mentioned by Polybius represented 5 asses, the *stipendium* in the mid-second century would actually have been 180 denarii p.a. With the revaluation of the denarius from 10 asses to 16 asses (in about 140), the stipend would have fallen from 180 denarii p.a. to 112½ p.a. This suggestion is ingenious, but unlikely to be correct. Why would the Romans have cut army pay at a time when income from their expanding empire was increasing? Much more plausible is the explanation of Brunt 1950: 51–2 that 2 obols per day, which Polyb. 6. 39. 12 says that a legionary received, were equivalent to 3⅓ asses, before the denarius was retariffed from 10 to 16 asses. According to Plin. *HN* 33. 45, the retariffing did not affect military pay, implying that soldiers continued to receive 120 denarii p.a. By the time of Augustus, however, this artificial practice had ceased (Tac. *Ann.* 1. 17. 6 talks of legionaries receiving 10 asses per day, which is equivalent to 225 denarii p.a.). Brunt conjectures that it was Julius Caesar who brought the practice to an end, when he 'doubled' the *stipendium*. He goes on: 'The legionary was credited with only 3⅓ *asses* per day, yet these had been worth 5⅓: if Caesar nominally tripled the *stipendium* by raising it to 10 *asses*, but at the same time ended the artificial relation of *as* to *denarius*, it was a change which could reasonably be described as a doubling of the *stipendium*.'

[72] HS 480/HS 1.8 per modius = 267 modii/0.152 = 1,754 kg × 0.36 = 632 kg.

[73] Scheidel 2007: 330–1; cf. Maddison 2007: 56.

overall distribution of assets and in levels of income increased dramatically. We saw in Ch. 1 that relatively high levels of private wealth already existed amongst some, at least, of the senators and the *equites* at Rome at the end of the third century, despite the disruption of the Second Punic War. Thus the capital value of a contract to supply clothing to the legions in Spain, totalling at least 800,000 denarii (133 talents) and split between a syndicate of nineteen *publicani*, suggests that the capital contribution of each of them was just under 40,000 denarii.[74] During the second century there are a number of indications of growing elite wealth. We hear of increasing levels of ostentatious expenditure and of the introduction of sumptuary laws to deal with this perceived problem.[75] There is steady growth in the numbers of gladiators fighting at the funerals of prominent Romans and the associated costs increase dramatically.[76] The number of domestic slaves that accompany a senator on a journey grows;[77] and indeed the huge inflows of slaves and net growth of the servile population during this time imply massive accumulation of wealth by the slave-purchasing elite. By the second half of the second century at least, equestrian entrepreneurs were benefiting as contractors for the exploitation of the Spanish mines and, shortly afterwards, as tax farmers in Asia. They also gained from the remittance home of the profits of successful trading activities in *emporia* such as Delos, as is demonstrated by the monumentalization and infrastructure initiatives that took place in parts of Latium and Campania. Pliny the Elder notes that Scipio Aemilianus, who died in 129, left 32 pounds of silver, that Q. Fabius Maximus Allobrogicus (*cos.* 121) was the first person to own 1,000 pounds of the metal, and that M. Livius Drusus, whom Diodorus describes as being the richest man in Rome, had 10,000 pounds during his tribunate in 91.[78] We can also point to the increase in the size of the fortunes of individual elite Romans, both senators and *equites*; and notices in our sources of the growing cost of elite housing and real estate.[79] Most famously, the finest house in the city of Rome in 78, that of Lepidus, was said, thirty-five years later, not to have been in the top one hundred.[80] In 53, P. Clodius Pulcher bought the house of M. Aemilius Scaurus for HS 14.8 million, equivalent to 617 talents.[81] To put this in context, P. Cornelius Scipio Africanus, probably one of the wealthiest Romans of his day, had, as we have seen, a fortune of only about 260 talents a century earlier, equivalent, using our GDP deflator, to 520 talents at 50 BC prices.[82]

It is then possible to identify certain trends in income and wealth, but this falls a long way short of a synoptic GDP analysis. Scheidel and Friesen have cleverly attempted to circumvent the lack of ancient evidence for income levels in their analysis of the imperial elite in the mid-second century AD by using Vilfredo Pareto's finding that a larger portion of the wealth and income of any society is

[74] See p. 12.

[75] References in Frank (1933) 198–9 and *MRR*.I 472; De Ligt 2002: 3–12 interprets the sumptuary laws as symbolic legislation 'to affirm simplicity and restraint as central Roman values, while defining *luxuria* as foreign intrusion'; cf. Wallace-Hadrill 2008: 315–55.

[76] Livy, 23. 30. 15, 31. 50. 4, 39. 46. 2–3, 41. 28. 11; Polyb. 31. 28. 5–6; Millar 1984: 10.

[77] Shatzman 1975: 481–2.

[78] Plin. *HN* 33. 141; Diod. Sic. 37. 10. 1; cf. Shatzman 1975: 276.

[79] See pp. 196–7 and 104.

[80] Plin. *HN* 36. 109.

[81] Plin. *HN* 36. 103. We do not, however, know whether Clodius Pulcher used any leverage to buy the house.

[82] See pp. 35–7.

owned by a smaller percentage of the people in that society and that the distribution of that wealth and income tends to fall into a predictable pattern, governed by power laws.[83] They have demonstrated that, if the number of elite households in AD 150 had dropped by two-thirds every time the level of wealth doubled, the resulting figures for elite income would have been within historically plausible bounds and consistent with a range of comparative evidence from other societies at other periods. This approach is not as far-fetched as it may at first sight appear. Even the Romans thought in terms of pyramids of wealth. For example, according to Livy, in 214 BC wealthy citizens were told to contribute to the cost of supplying rowers for the fleet in proportion to their census ratings made just before the outbreak of war. Those who had property worth between 50,000 and 100,000 asses had to supply one sailor and six months' stipend, those with between 100,000 and 300,000 had to provide three sailors and a year's stipend, and so on, with senators at the top of the tree obliged to furnish eight sailors and one year's stipend.[84]

We have adapted Scheidel and Friesen's approach and applied it to the free population of late Republican Italy. Our procedure uses the sporadic notices of individual elite wealth as a starting point and we extrapolate income pyramids from these data. We follow the conventional practice (also used by Scheidel and Friesen[85]) of putting mean annual net income at 6 per cent of wealth.[86] An individual slave's income is separately calculated as being equivalent to an annual consumption of 390 kg of wheat, at the then assumed prevailing price of wheat.[87] This is on the presumption that the majority of slaves would have fared no better than surviving at this 'bare-bones' level of subsistence, although there would, of course, have been exceptions. The income numbers for slaves are then aggregated with the cohort income figures for the free population to produce a series of snapshots of the Italian economy from the income side of GDP at fifty-year intervals (150 BC, 100 BC, and 50 BC). This procedure produces some interesting and historically credible results, into which can be fitted, quite reasonably, both the general trends in living standards that we discussed earlier and the very small number of reports of individual wealth or income that can be derived from ancient texts.

Given that Scipio Africanus, presumably one of the wealthiest Romans of his day, had a fortune in the 160s of about 260 talents,[88] our starting assumption is that, by 150, the largest fortune in Italy was double that figure at 520 talents (HS

[83] Scheidel and Friesen 2009: 79–82. Pareto's finding is also known as the Pareto Principle or the '80:20 rule'. At the end of the nineteenth century, Pareto (1848–1923) discovered that 80% of Italy's land was owned by 20% of the population. He then carried out surveys on a variety of other countries and found that a similar distribution applied, although the proportions could vary. Thus Pareto's data on British income taxes, in his *Cours d'économie politique* (1896–7), indicated that about 30% of the British population received about 70% of the income. As a more recent example, the *1992 United Nations Development Program Report* showed that, in 1989, the richest 20% of the world's population controlled 82.7% of the world's GDP by income.

[84] Livy, 24. 11. 6–9. [85] Scheidel and Friesen 2009: 75.

[86] One can debate *ad nauseam* whether it is realistic to use a single number for mean interest rates of return over a period of a century. There is scant evidence. We have no doubt that rates varied over time and that this is a blunt instrument. Nevertheless, it does enable comparisons to be made, however crude.

[87] Which we assume was HS 1.8 in 150, HS 2.7 in 100, and HS 3.5 in 50 BC.

[88] See pp. 35–7.

Table 11.3. Power-law distribution of households by income: 150 BC

	No. of households	Nominal household income (HS)	Nominal category income (HS m.)	Nominal per capita income (HS)	Real per capita income (HS)
	(A)	(B)	(A × B)		
	1	749,000	0.7		
	4	374,400	1.5		
	12	187,200	2.2		
	42	93,600	3.9		
	150	46,800	7		
	525	23,400	12.3		
	1,838	11,700	21.5		
	6,433	5,650	37.6		
	22,516	2,925	65.9		
Elite households	*31,521*		*153*	1,747	**1,747**
	78,806	1,463	115		
	275,821	731	202		
	965,374	366	354		
	280,358	337	95		
Non-elite households	*1,600,359*		*766*	172	**172**
TOTAL FREE HOUSEHOLDS	*1,631,880*		**919**		
Free population	4,533,000				
Slaves (individuals)	*490,000*	107	**52**	107	**107**
TOTAL POPULATION	5,023,000				
Income GDP			**971**	193	**193**

Note: Nos. of households are rounded.

12.5 million), generating a 6 per cent annual return equivalent to HS 750,000. Using this income figure as a starting point, we have calculated, in Table 11.3, the power-law distribution of households by income, by assuming that the number of households increased by a factor of 3.5 every time wealth halved.[89] This is a steeper pyramid than would have been produced if we had used a factor of 3, as Scheidel and Friesen did in their calculation of elite wealth in the second century AD. But if we did not use a higher factor, we would have half the free Italian population trying to survive at a level of income that was below subsistence, which of course seems highly implausible. A possible explanation for the greater steepness of the pyramid in 150 BC compared with the second century is the concentration of more limited wealth amongst a numerically smaller elite.

[89] An alternative approach could of course be to use a polynomial function rather than a simple power-law factor.

Several conclusions follow from this procedure. In the first place, it may help us to identify the size and income of what might be termed the Italian elite. Both these variables are unknown, although attempts have been made on more or less flimsy evidence to estimate them for later periods.[90] We can be reasonably confident that there were about 300 senators in office before Sulla and around 600 after his reform of the senate,[91] but the number of Roman *equites* for any period is unknown. The range of assumptions for the number of *equites* resident in Italy during the late Republican and early Imperial periods is from 5,000 (Jongman) to 24,000 (Goldsmith).[92] Our procedure produces about 30,000 Italian households in 150 BC with annual incomes in excess of HS 2,400, which represents a 6 per cent return on capital of HS 40,000—the presumed minimum Roman equestrian census threshold. This number for elite Italian households has a degree of plausibility, because it ties in with Plutarch's account of 20,000 Roman *equites* supporting Cicero in the 60s BC and Polybius' mention of 23,000 Roman and Campanian *equites* in 225 BC.[93] But it is important to emphasize that, in our calculations, the number of individuals above the equestrian level of wealth should not be interpreted to be the same as the number of individuals holding Roman equestrian status. We are considering the whole of Italy, so the pyramids of household wealth include non-Roman citizens in the years 150 and 100 BC. They would include, for example, both Italian provincials with business interests in the eastern Mediterranean and increasing numbers of wealthy freedmen. One indication that we are in the correct general area for equestrian-level wealth is that, according to our calculations, average elite household income in 150 is HS 4,853, which is equivalent to a 6 per cent return on a capital sum of 20,000 denarii, which in turn is half the value of each individual contribution of the nineteen *publicani* who successfully bid for the contract to supply the Spanish army during the Second Punic War.

As for the rest of the free population, 1.6 million non-elite households have an average income of HS 479 (HS 172 per capita), which at a wheat price of HS 1.8 per modius is equivalent to 629 kg of wheat per person.[94] Of these 1.6 million households, the 280,000 poorest (i.e. 778,000 individuals) have a maximum annual per capita income of HS 122, which would buy 446 kg of wheat at HS 1.8 and which is, therefore, 14 per cent above subsistence. Slave income (at subsistence) is HS 107 per capita.

Estimated GDP from the income side in 150 BC is, therefore, HS 971 million; GDP per capita is HS 193 and is equivalent, at a wheat price of HS 1.8 per modius, to 705 kg, 81 per cent above subsistence and 25 per cent below 'respectability' of 940 kg (or HS 257, at a wheat price of HS 1.8 per modius). In fact, if we use Scheidel and Friesen's analysis of where this ranks in terms of sustainability, the 'average'

[90] e.g. Goldsmith 1984: 277–8 estimates that elite income represented 17% of total income in AD 14. Maddison 2007: 48 puts the figure at 26%. Scheidel and Friesen 2009: 77 have independently calculated a range of 16–29% in the mid-second century AD.

[91] Dio Cass. 54. 14. 1.

[92] Goldsmith 1984: 277–8 guesses that there were 40,000 *equites* in AD 14, of whom 60% resided in Italy; Jongman 1988: 193 (followed by Scheidel 2005: 66 'for want of evidence'). For *decuriones*, the estimated numbers are 20,000 (Jongman) and 52,000 (Goldsmith).

[93] Plut. *Cic.* 31. 1; Polyb. 2. 24. 14.

[94] HS 479/HS 1. 8 per modius = 266 modii/0.152 = 1,751 kg × 0.36 = 630 kg.

inhabitant of Italy in 150 BC had a standard of living equivalent to a peasant with a few goats.[95]

M. Livius Drusus, whom Diodorus describes as being the richest man in Rome, owned 10,000 pounds of silver during his tribunate in 91 BC.[96] But we have no way of calculating his total wealth from this one piece of information. So, as a starting point for our calculation of wealth in 100 BC, we have used Atticus' father, who died in about 90 BC and who bequeathed to his son an inheritance of HS 2 m. (equivalent to 83 talents).[97] He is described by Nepos as being 'rich for those times'. We assume that Nepos' description places him in roughly the same category of wealth as Q. Caecilius, whom the same author also describes as *dives*, and who seems to be in the top eighty wealthiest Italians in the 50s BC (see p. 296). A return of 6 per cent on HS 2 m. is HS 120,000, and we assume that this places Atticus' father in the top eighty Italians in terms of wealth at this time. As in Table 11.3, we use in Table 11.4 a figure of 3.5 for the factor by which cohort size increases every time wealth halves.

There are now perhaps 100,000 Italian households above the old minimum Roman equestrian property qualification of HS 40,000 (an income of HS 2,400) and maybe 3,000 or so above the first-century late Republican threshold of HS 400,000 (an income of HS 24,000), so we are at a crossroads and this perhaps explains why the Romans raised the threshold for equestrian status to 100,000 denarii at some point in the first century. It also suggests that this increase was driven by the combination of a massive 70 per cent growth in mean elite income

[95] Scheidel and Friesen 2009: 83.

[96] Cicero, in his *De republica* (3. 17), has one of his interlocutors, L. Furius Philus, say: 'Cur autem, si pecuniae modus statuendus fuit feminis, P. Crassi filia posset habere, si unica patri esset, aeris milliens salva lege, mea triciens posset . . . ' (Why, on the other hand, if a limit had to be set on the amount of money that women could own, should the daughter of P. Crassus, if she were his only child, be able to have *aeris milliens* without breaking the law, while my daughter is not able to have *triciens*?) The reference is to P. Licinius Crassus Dives Mucianus (*cos.* 131) and it raises the question of whether this passage can be used as a guide to the level of wealth enjoyed by an elite Roman in 129 BC (the date at which the dialogue is set). This passage is part of Philus' argument that the *lex Voconia* of 169 BC unfairly restricted the rights of women to inherit. The terms of the law are imperfectly understood, because its contents and provisions are only known from casual references such as this. However, it is commonly interpreted as prohibiting wealthy men from naming women as heirs but allowing them to leave legacies to women up to a certain proportion of their estates. The difference, therefore, between what the daughters of Crassus and Philus can receive is a function of the values of the estates of their respective fathers. In this context, how should we translate the numbers that Cicero uses? If one follows Pliny the Elder, who says (*HN* 33. 133) that multiples of 100,000 were used to express large numbers, the term *aeris milliens* could indicate 'one hundred million sesterces' (i.e. *milliens centena milia sestertium*, literally 'one thousand times one hundred thousand', or the equivalent of 4,167 talents) and the term *triciens* could indicate 3 m. sesterces. This is how these terms are understood by the editors of the *Oxford Latin Dictionary* (although the use of the word *milliens* by Cicero at *Div. Caec.* 19, to which they refer, is similarly ambiguous). It is also so understood by Frank (1933: 299), and by C. W. Keyes in his Loeb translation (XVI p. 199). Alternatively, the term *aeris milliens* could mean 'one million sesterces' (i.e. one thousand times one thousand), and the term *triciens* could indicate 'thirty thousand sesterces'. This is how these terms were translated by Francis Barham in the early nineteenth century, and more recently by Zetzel (1999: 65). Either way, the passage is highly rhetorical and set in an imaginary dialogue taking place some seventy-five years before its date of composition. Therefore, it probably cannot be taken to be a reliable guide to the actual level of Publius Crassus' wealth.

[97] Nep. *Att.* 1. 1.

Table 11.4. Power-law distribution of households by income: 100 BC

	No. of households	Nominal household income (HS)	Nominal category income (HS m.)	Nominal per capita income (HS)	Real per capita income (HS)	Real per capita income (% change) 100/150 BC
	(A)	(B)	(A × B)			
	1	1,920,000	1.9			
	4	960,000	3.8			
	12	480,000	5.8			
	42	240,000	10.1			
	150	120,000	18			
	525	60,000	31.5			
	1,838	30,000	55.1			
	6,433	15,000	97			
	22,516	7,500	169			
Elite households	*31,521*		*392*	4,477	**2,984**	71%
	78,806	3,750	296			
	275,821	1,875	517			
	965,374	938	906			
	488,478	469	229			
Non-elite households	*1,808,479*		*1,948*	388	**259**	51%
TOTAL FREE HOUSEHOLDS	*1,840,000*		**2,340**			
Free population	5,110,000					
Slaves (individuals)	*800,000*	160	**128**	160	**107**	0%
TOTAL POPULATION	5,910,000					
Income GDP			**2,468**	418	**279**	45%

Note: Nos. of households are rounded.

and of inflation, which had gradually reduced the value of the second-century wealth qualification.

On this analysis, 1.8 million non-elite households have an average income of HS 1,077, which, at a wheat price of HS 2.7 per modius, is 945 kg of wheat per person, more or less at the 'respectability' level of 940 kg of wheat and a 50 per cent increase in real terms between 150 and 100 BC.[98] Despite this, the number of free Italians living just above subsistence (at 412 kg per capita) has actually grown by 74 per cent to 1.3 million individuals, which suggests that 25 per cent of the free population was now surviving at this level, compared with 17 per cent a half-century earlier. These numbers, if they are correct, therefore suggest that the rich were getting richer and that those at the bottom of the pile were becoming progressively poorer, in

[98] HS 1,077/HS2.7 per modius = 399 modii/0.152 = 2,624 kg × 0.36 = 945 kg.

Table 11.5. Power-law distribution of households by income: 50 BC

	No. of households	Nominal household income (HS)	Nominal category income (HS m.)	Nominal per capita income (HS)	Real per capita income (HS)	Real per capita income (% change) 50/100 BC
	(A)	(B)	(A × B)			
	1	12,000,000	12			
	3	6,000,000	18			
	8	3,000,000	24			
	22	1,500,000	33			
	61	750,000	46			
	168	375,000	63			
	462	187,500	87			
	1,271	93,750	119			
	3,495	46,875	164			
	9,611	23,438	225			
Elite households	*15,102*		*791*	18,856	**9,697**	225%
	26,430	11,720	310			
	72,683	5,860	426			
	199,878	2,930	586			
	549,665	1,465	805			
	808,242	733	592			
Non-elite households	*1,656,898*		*2,719*	591	**304**	7%
TOTAL FREE HOUSEHOLDS	*1,672,000*		**3,510**			
Free population	4,645,000					
Slaves (individuals)	*1,200,000*	207	**248**	207	**107**	0%
TOTAL POPULATION	5,845,000					
Income GDP			**3,758**	643	**331**	19%

Note: Nos. of households are rounded.

a reflection of the problems that led to the Gracchan land reforms and to the introduction of the corn dole.

Estimated GDP from the income side in 100 BC is, therefore, HS 2,468 m., an increase in real terms of 69 per cent on 150 BC, although the increase in population reduces the real per capita increase to 45 per cent. GDP per capita is now HS 279 in real terms and is equivalent to 1,020 kg of wheat. The increase in GDP per capita is actually less than the rate of income growth for the free population, because, by 100 BC, there are 63 per cent more slaves living at subsistence, which serves to reduce the mean level of national income.

Levels of elite wealth in the world of Cicero (Table 11.5) are much higher than those that preceded them. According to Pliny the Elder, M. Licinius Crassus, generally supposed to be the wealthiest Roman of his day (after Sulla, who had built up a large fortune by confiscation), had property estimated to be worth HS 200 m. (8,333 talents), although we do not know whether this was net or gross of borrowings.[99] Pompey's fortune was about the same and his property, when confiscated, was sold for about HS 200 million.[100] We have assumed that the wealthiest Roman in Italy in 50 BC had a fortune of this size. A return of 6 per cent on HS 200 m. is HS 12 million. We also know that Demetrius, a Syrian from Gadara, who was probably taken prisoner by Pompey but was quickly made a Roman citizen to become one of Pompey's most reliable financial agents, left property worth HS 96 m. (4,000 talents), which suggests that he had (at a 6% yield) an income of HS 5.76 million.[101] This would put him in the top ten of wealthy Italian residents. Q. Caecilius, an *eques*, whom Nepos describes as *dives* (rich), had a fortune of HS 13.3m. (555 talents), and so an assumed income of HS 799,000 per annum placing him in the top eighty or so wealthy Italians at the time.[102] According to Cicero, a wealthy man would have an income of HS 600,000 per annum.[103]

Sulla confiscated the property of over 1,600 wealthy Romans and this would have distorted the income profiles of the Italian population and, in particular, the elite. We reflect this by assuming that the number of households increased by a factor of 2.75 every time wealth halved. One consequence of this is that the total number of elite Italian households with wealth above the minimum Roman equestrian census threshold of HS 400,000, at about 15,000 in 50 BC, was considerably fewer than in 150 and 100, although we should not forget that, by the middle of the first century BC, many Roman citizens with equestrian levels of wealth were probably domiciled outside mainland Italy. For example, the Utican 'Three Hundred' in North Africa had to pay Julius Caesar a fine of HS 200 m. in 47 BC.[104] That averaged out at HS 670,000 per household, which, at a return of 6 per cent, suggests that these households had an income of at least HS 40,200 per annum, or two-thirds higher than the equestrian wealth threshold. Within Italy, it is clear that elite wealth has grown dramatically, with mean per capita incomes for this section of the population standing at HS 18,856 in nominal terms and HS 9,697 in real terms—more than three times the level in 100 BC in real terms. As we saw in Ch. 8, the wealthy but parsimonious Atticus limited his expenditure to HS 36,000 per annum, a figure roughly double the level that we have calculated for nominal mean per capita elite income in 50 BC.[105] As far as non-elite incomes are concerned, 1.6 million households have an average income of HS 1,641, which, at a wheat price of HS 3.5 per modius, is equivalent to 1,111 kg of wheat per person, an 18 per cent increase in real terms since 100 BC.[106] One factor contributing to this increase in the average for non-elite incomes was no doubt the emigration of poorer citizens to the provinces, although of course there was still a substantial number of urban poor who received the corn dole. On this analysis, the negative impact on Italian income GDP of the great increase in the slave population was in effect offset by increases in the incomes of the free population and, in particular, by the large increase in elite income.

[99] Plin. *HN* 33. 134; cf. Plut. *Crass.* 2. 2, where his fortune is put at 7,500 talents.

[100] Dio Cass. 48. 36. 5.

[101] Plut. *Pomp.* 2. 4.

[102] Nep. *Att.* 5. 1–2. If one is looking for other examples of wealthy equestrians, the city of Nicaea in Bithynia owed T. Pinnius about HS 8m. (333 talents): Cic. *Fam.* 13. 61.

[103] Cic. *Parad.* 49.

[104] Caes. *B. Afr.* 90.

[105] Nep. *Att.* 13. 6–7.

[106] HS 1,641/HS 3.5 per modius = 469 modii/0.152 = 3,086 kg × 0.36 = 1,111 kg.

Estimated GDP from the income side in 50 BC is therefore HS 3,758 m., an increase in real terms of 17 per cent on 100 BC. GDP per capita is now HS 331 in real terms and is equivalent to 1,209 kg of wheat, an increase of 19 per cent in real terms over the figure for 100 BC.

In sum, these results suggest that real GDP per capita in mainland Italy increased by 72 per cent between 150 and 50 BC, an average annual compound growth rate of 0.54 per cent. By way of comparison, Madison has estimated that the rate of average annual compound growth in real per capita GDP in Western Europe between AD 1500 and 1820 was 0.14 per cent per annum, and that growth in the same area, between AD 1820 and 1870, was 0.98 per cent per annum.[107] So, on this analysis, an average annual compound rate of 0.54 per cent places growth in mainland Italy in the late Republic significantly above the rate of growth achieved in Western Europe before the Industrial Revolution, but significantly below that achieved by that area after the Industrial Revolution.

Within the figure of 72 per cent growth for mainland Italy between 150 and 50 BC, elite income per capita increased in real terms more than fivefold and the income per capita of the free non-elite population grew by 77 per cent. It is worth pointing out too that, if there had in fact been no inflation during this period (we have assumed that prices increased by 95% over the century), non-elite per capita incomes would have more than tripled and elite per capita incomes would have increased more than tenfold between 150 and 50 BC. We also emphasize again that our estimates are crude, back-of-the-envelope efforts, although we have tried to anchor them as far as is possible in the snippets of ancient evidence that we have for wealth and incomes. Our estimate for the nominal GDP of mainland Italy in 50 BC of HS 3,758 m. can be compared with Maddison's estimate for the same geographical area in AD 14 of HS 3,738 million.[108] This purely fortuitous equivalence (in nominal terms) could suggest that our estimates are too optimistic, or that Maddison's are too pessimistic, or that the disruption caused by the death of the Republic had a deleterious effect on the Italian economy.

GDP FROM THE EXPENDITURE SIDE

In the sections that follow we shall examine the components of the expenditure side of the Italian economy and consider how they are likely to have changed during the second century and the first half of the first century. We shall begin by looking at the expenditure patterns of the Roman state for which, unlike for the private sector, we do have some reasonably reliable data from ancient sources that can assist us in producing an approximate numerical quantification.

[107] Maddison 2007: 383, table A.8.

[108] Maddison 2007: 50; Scheidel and Friesen 2009 only produce an estimate for the whole Empire.

1. The Roman state

Because the Roman state did not borrow during the period we are considering, its expenditure could never have been greater than the income it received, be it in money or in kind. So one way forward is to estimate the income that the Roman state received (a procedure that still, of course, involves a fair amount of conjecture) and then compare it with those components of state expenditure for which we have reasonably credible data or can, at least, construct plausible estimates, such as military costs. This will then allow us to attach approximate values to those elements of state expenditure for which we have no numerical data, such as construction financed by the state.

The figures for indemnities, which are based on literary sources, are reasonably certain down to 150 BC, but are patchy thereafter. The numbers for booty are estimated, but for the first half of the second century there is at least some evidentiary basis in the sums reported by Livy. Mining revenue is derived from Polybius' figure for the Roman state's income from silver production around Carthago Nova in about 150. Provincial taxes are estimates based on Plutarch's account of Pompey's statements of the Roman state's income before and after his eastern conquests. All other numbers in Table 11.6 are completely conjectural and there is no numerical evidence of which I am aware that can offer any help. The totals, therefore, represent estimates, with some basis at least in figures reported by ancient sources, of the resources available to the Roman state for expenditure on its consumption and investment. One can, of course, argue with virtually every single component in this table (with the possible exception of the indemnities between 199 and 150), but in aggregate they give a reasonably credible idea of the scale of Roman state income.

Given that the Roman state only spent what it earned, the totals in Table 11.6 for state income in each fifty-year period must also represent the maximum amount of state investment and state consumption during those periods. We shall look at state consumption first and then move on to consider state investment in buildings and infrastructure.

Table 11.6. State income in millions of denarii (estimated)

	199–150	149–100	99–50 BC
Indemnities	164	30	120
Booty	115	100	220
Mines	104	450	450
Tributum till 167	60	0	0
Provincial taxes	0	123	630
Land rents[a]	70	70	70
Tithes[b]	130	130	130
Portoria and other *vectigalia*	50	100	150
TOTAL STATE INCOME	**693**	**1,003**	**1,770**

[a] The numbers could well be too high: e.g. Rathbone (2003: 175) estimates revenues from the Ager Campanus at only HS 3 m. p.a. (750,000 denarii). On the other hand, *scriptura* (pasture tax) would presumably have been a major item of income.

[b] The number for 199–150 BC may be too high. Erdkamp (2005: 212) has demonstrated that, while most of the grain carried to Republican Italy appears to have been tax grain, during the first half of the second century at least, tax grain from overseas was mainly shipped to Roman armies fighting outside Italy.

There are two principal items that comprise state consumption in the second and first centuries: military expenditure and the grain subsidy, of which the former was by far the more significant. Expenditure on state administration was not a meaningful factor during the Republic. As most non-military state functions were delegated to the *publicani*, there was virtually no state bureaucracy, apart from the tiny staffs supporting the senior magistrates, the law courts, and the treasury. Nor was there any provision of social services by the state before the introduction of the grain subsidy by C. Gracchus, although the operation of the Gracchan agrarian commissions and of the grain subsidy would have entailed a small amount of additional cost.

It is possible to make an approximate estimate of the total cost of Rome's military commitment. If we follow Frank's calculation that, at the end of the third century, roughly 600,000 denarii paid for the stipend of one Roman legion for a year,[109] and use Brunt's figures for the number of legions each year,[110] we can calculate that between 200 and 151 the Roman state spent 228 m. denarii on army pay alone.

But at some point between the mid-second century and the 60s BC, it appears that the annual cost of a legion rose from roughly 600,000 denarii to approximately 1.5 million denarii.[111] We do not know what that date was. Crawford hypothesized in *Roman Republican Coinage* that this increase could have taken place under C. Gracchus in 123, but there is no concrete evidence at all for this being the date of the change. If we were to follow Crawford and assume that 123 BC was the date of the increase, then the cost of the army stipend, between 150 and 101, would have been 362.1 m. denarii and 1,456.5 m. denarii between 100 and 51. If, however, we assume that the increase to 1.5 m. denarii occurred instead at some point during the first half of the first century, then the cost of the army stipend between 150 and 101 would be reduced to 213.6 m. denarii; and, if we assume that that increase occurred in, say, 69 BC, the cost between 100 and 51 would have been 968.2 m. denarii. Given that, as we saw, the Roman state's total income between 100 and 51 BC was probably only of the order of 1.8 bn. denarii, it seems almost inconceivable that 1.5 bn. denarii of this could have been spent on army stipends alone and so, in our estimates in Table 11.7, we assume that the increase in the annual cost of a legion to 1.5 m. did not occur before the 60s BC.

In addition to being paid, Roman troops needed to be supplied. Continuous warfare required the manufacture of vast amounts of weapons and equipment. Weapons were supplied by the state, but, strictly speaking, some of the other

Table 11.7. Cost of army stipends in millions of denarii (estimated)

	199–150	149–100	99–50 BC
Assuming increase to 1.5 m. den. in 123 BC	228	362	1,457
% change		*59%*	*302%*
Assuming increase to 1.5 m den. in 69 BC	228	214	968
% change		*–6%*	*452%*
Aggregate no. of legions	383	345	971

[109] Frank 1933: 76, discussed in Ch. 2.
[110] Brunt 1971*a*: 424, 432.
[111] Crawford 1974: 696–707.

Table 11.8. Total military costs in millions of denarii (estimated)

	199–150	149–100	99–50 BC
Army stipend	228	214	968
Food for allies	73	80	16
Arms, tents, transport, etc.	57	80	120
Navy	66	30	50
TOTAL	**424**	**404**	**1,154**

expenditure should be counted under the heading of private consumption, since it appears from Polybius that deductions were made for food, clothing and replacement arms.[112] It was not until C. Gracchus' *lex militaris* that terms of military service were altered so that clothing was supplied at the expense of the state.[113] There were other elements of military expenditure too, with fleets of up to 150 ships being commissioned.[114] Making some adjustments to Frank's estimates for the additional cost of military expenditure and, contra Crawford, assuming that the cost of a legion did not increase until the 60s BC and that the Romans did pay the cost of their allies' corn, we have estimated the figures set out in Table 11.8 for military costs.[115]

The other significant element of state consumption expenditure was the corn dole. Under the *lex frumentaria*, which C. Gracchus promulgated in the late 120s, grain was provided to the plebs at a fixed, subsidized price: 'Leges tulit, inter quas frumentariam, ut senis et triente frumentum plebi daretur'[116] (he carried laws, amongst which was the one relating to grain, which provided that grain should be given to the *plebs* for six and one-third asses). We do not know how far this price of six and one-third asses (HS 1.6) for one modius of corn stood below the market price. Frank conjectures that the grain was sold off at half price and HS 3.2 may well have been the price in 123 BC; but it would of course subsequently have varied considerably, as we can see from the range of prices quoted in Cicero's *Verrines*.[117] Numbers of recipients are also unknown. Sulla abolished the corn dole, but, following its reintroduction in 73 under the *lex Terentia Cassia*, there were perhaps 40,000 citizens receiving 5 modii per month (so a total of 2.4 m. modii p.a.). This may also have represented the scale of distribution from its inception under Gracchus. To allow for fluctuations in the price of wheat, we have assumed in our calculations that the cost to the state was 1.5 m. denarii per annum until 62 BC (with an eleven-year gap between 84 and 73, following Sulla's abolition of the corn dole and before its reintroduction). By the time of Caesar, the number

112 Polyb. 6. 21. 6–7, 39. 15; Brunt 1971*a*: 405.

113 Plut. *C. Gracch.* 5; Diod. Sic. 35. 25. By Augustus' time the cost of clothing was again deducted from pay, so the law must have been repealed after Gracchus' death (Brunt 1971*b*: 85).

114 For the war against Perseus, a fleet of 100 ships had to be built and 50 old quinqueremes recommissioned (Livy, 42. 27. 1; 43. 12 .9).

115 Frank 1933: 142–4.

116 Livy, *Per.* 60.

117 Rathbone 2009: 304 summarizes the evidence.

Table 11.9. Expenditure: state consumption in millions of denarii (estimated)

	199–150	149–100	99–50 BC
Military costs	424	404	1,154
Corn doles	0	34	185
Supertaxes repaid	23	0	0
Other expenses	40	100	150
aerarium balance	18	0	0
TOTAL STATE CONSUMPTION	**505**	**538**	**1,489**

Table 11.10. Expenditure: state investment in millions of denarii (estimated)

	199–150	149–100	99–50 BC
State income	693	1,003	1,770
less state consumption	505	538	1,489
STATE INVESTMENT EXPENDITURE	**188**	**465**	**281**

of recipients had risen to 320,000 and so we further assume that, following the *lex Porcia* of 62, the cost may have been as high as 12 m. denarii per annum.[118]

The addition of these estimated numbers for the corn dole to the estimated figures for military costs combined with a very generous allowance for 'other' expenses results in the model at Table 11.9 for state consumption. The *aerarium* balance in that table is derived from Pliny's numbers for the holdings in the *aerarium* in 157, and a balance of comparable proportions is assumed to have remained for the next century, when we have only incomplete numbers from Pliny the Elder. The figure for repayment of supertaxes is a guess of Frank's, but I can see no way of improving upon it.[119]

Now that we have arrived at figures for state consumption, the level of state investment (Table 11.10) can be derived for each fifty-year period by subtracting these figures from the numbers for state income that we estimated earlier (Table 11.6).

The next question is therefore whether these resulting estimates for state investment expenditure are credible.[120] Capital expenditure by the Roman state appears, throughout our period, to have been focused on utilitarian construction, with major components being roads and the water supply. Although many urban remains from the Republican period lie uninvestigated beneath their imperial successors, we know from Livy that there was a remarkable period of expenditure by the Roman state on civic buildings, public amenities, and roads in the first half of the second century, especially by the censors of 184, 179, and 174. This appears to have begun the transformation of the city of Rome (and indeed of a number of

118 Brunt 1971*a*: 378, 381; Crawford 1974: 705–7; Plut. *Cat. Min.* 26. 1; Plut. *Caes.* 8. 4. Hopkins 1978: 39 n. 52 puts the corn dole in 60 BC at HS 58 m. p.a. (= 14.5 m. denarii p.a.).

119 Frank 1933: 145.

120 Frank 1933: 145, 228 made what he himself terms 'decidedly conjectural' estimates of total state spending on construction during the period from 200–157 BC of 20 m. denarii and of 225 m. denarii for the period between 150 and 90; Scheidel 2007: 9.

citizen colonies and *municipia* outside Rome) from an urban space built largely in wood and stone, which Livy describes as 'nondum exornata neque publicis neque privatis locis' (not yet adorned in either its public or private spaces), into the sophisticated city, clad in marble, with its aqueducts and statues, that we know from its imperial remains.[121]

Money was the principal driver. As we saw in Ch. 9, the major catalyst was the arrival at Rome of the indemnity of Antiochus III and the booty that Manlius Vulso brought back from Asia in 187. More generally, the Roman state's capital expenditure patterns during the twenty years that followed, in particular the intensity of building activity, appear to correlate closely with what we know about the inflows of revenue into the *aerarium* and the state's financial position. The development of new construction techniques, especially concrete as a lower-cost alternative to tufa ashlar, helped in this process. But we have only a limited knowledge, mainly from literary sources, of the construction work undertaken by the state.[122] At Rome, in the late 190s, a new port and commercial infrastructure were constructed. Rome's sewers were overhauled at a cost of 6 m. denarii, and large structures were built. These included the Basilica Porcia (184), the Pons Aemilius (179), the Basilica Fulvia-Aemilia (179), the Macellum (179), the Basilica Sempronia (169), and the Porticus Octavia (168). New roads were built within Italy and, in all probability, many of the existing roads which had been laid down in the previous century were upgraded with paving. Some of these projects would have been very expensive. The earliest evidence we have for the cost of road construction comes from the early second century AD, when it appears to have been HS 21 per foot.[123] If we are conservative and assume that prices tripled between the first half of the second century BC and AD 100, so that the cost of constructing one foot of road was HS 7 per foot in the 180s BC, the cost of building one mile of road at that time would have been HS 37,000 per mile, or roughly one million denarii for every 100 miles. Actual costs may well have been higher. Other significant projects included the partial draining of the Pomptine marshes by the consul M. Cornelius Cethegus in 160.[124]

Although the full text of Livy is lost for the second half of the century, it is clear that major construction projects continued. No doubt in some censorships there was little or no capital investment by the state.[125] But we learn from a variety of sources of the construction of what are presumably some of the most notable undertakings. Marble-clad temples began to appear after the sack of Corinth in 146. The Aqua Marcia, costing 7,500 talents, was built in the 140s, and the Aqua Tepula in the 120s. Some of the roads that were built during this period were enormous undertakings, for example those connecting Italy with Spain and Greece. The Via Domitia, which ran between Italy and Spain, had to cross the Ligurian Alps, and so required significant feats of engineering. At Rome, substantial public building works included the Porticus Metelli (146), and the arches that were added

[121] Livy, 40. 5. 7.

[122] A list of building activity at Rome between 200 and 78 BC (with ancient references) is provided by Coarelli 1977: 20–2; see too L. Richardson 1992: 448–50.

[123] Duncan-Jones 1974: 157–9. [124] Livy, *Per.* 46.

[125] Crawford 1974: 699 believes that this was true of the censors of 154 (who were prevented from building a theatre) and of those of 147, 102, and 89 (who held office in time of war).

to the Pons Aemilius in 142. From the last decades of the century, we have a further large road-building programme under C. Gracchus, the construction of the Horrea Sempronia (123), which were public granaries for storing the grain provided to the plebs under Gracchus' *lex frumentaria*, the Basilica Opimia (121), the restored temple of Magna Mater (110), the Porticus Minucia Vetus (*c.*110), the Via Aemilia and a rebuilt Pons Milvius (109), the substantial Horrea Galbana (108), as well as the construction of canals by M. Aemilius Scaurus (*cos.* 115) to drain the marshes beside the River Po.[126] These are the major state building projects from the second century of which we happen to know and they can represent only a selection of the ones that were actually undertaken.

In the first half of the first century, major projects included the enormous dock warehouse with a barrel-vaulted concrete roof, conventionally identified as the Porticus Aemilia and recently re-evaluated as having been built in the Sullan era, the construction of the *tabularium*, finished in 78, the temple of Iuppiter Optimus Maximus, which was dedicated in 69, and a stone embankment for the Tiber in 54.[127] But the most notable feature of this period is that there are comparatively fewer state projects mentioned in our sources and this probably reflects reality, since this was a half century during which there were periods of civil war at home and interruptions in the flow of taxation from abroad. It is not surprising, therefore, that our independent estimates of state expenditure suggest a slow down in public capital investment between 100 and 50 BC.

In Table 11.11, we have simply divided the half-century figures for state consumption and investment in Table 11.10 by 50 to produce annualized figures and converted them to sesterces in order to provide a rough approximation for state expenditure in 150, 100, and 50 BC.

A number of conclusions follow from these calculations. The first is that, while it is clear that a growing share of growing state resources was funnelled into Rome's urban environment and into major communication and infrastructure projects during the second century, state investment in the first half of the first century actually fell, as resources were diverted to the military. The rebuilding of the temple of Iuppiter Optimus Maximus, for example, took fourteen years to complete. Secondly, although expenditure on the military accounted for the largest proportion of state expenditure, it does not follow that it always contributed to economic *growth*. In fact, on our calculations, total military expenditure actually fell in the

Table 11.11. State expenditure in HS m. (estimated)

	199–150	149–100	99–50 BC
State consumption p.a.	40	43	119
State investment p.a.	15	37	22
TOTAL STATE EXPENDITURE P.A.	55	80	141
GDP	971	2,468	3,758
State expenditure as % of GDP	*5.7%*	*3.2%*	*3.8%*

126 Strabo, 5. 1. 11. 127 Coarelli 2007.

second half of the second century from the level achieved between 199 and 150, before sharply increasing from the Social War onwards.[128] This suggests that military expenditure was a detractor from economic growth during the second half of the second century, before again becoming a major driver from the late 90s onwards. Finally these numbers show how small state expenditure was as a percentage of GDP. Unless we have severely underestimated the numbers for state expenditure, it represents a smaller percentage of the pie in nominal terms in 50 BC (3.8%) than it did a century earlier (5.7%).

2. Expenditure: Personal Consumption

In the second century, the Roman state was a rapidly urbanizing society but agriculture still represented by far the largest sector of the economy in terms of output, and food accounted for the largest proportion of private sector consumption demand.[129] There are, however, no data time series that can enable us to discover whether levels of food consumption changed in any material way during our period, enabling the transformation of a largely subsistence economy which had previously produced only a small surplus into a market economy that produced and consumed a large surplus. There are occasional references to famine and to crisis measures intended to deal with a sudden scarcity, such as the inscription from Thessaly dated to 129 which shows the aedile, Q. Metellus, requesting the shipment of a large amount of grain to Rome.[130] On the other hand, the high level of agricultural capital investment that has been identified in the region immediately around Rome suggests increased demand and consumption of food products in the metropolis; while the benefits of increased agricultural production using slave labour are also evident from the growth in the export trade in wine and olive oil.[131] Changing patterns of food consumption may be capable of approach through new avenues. For example, recent work by King and MacKinnon has focused on the changing Roman diet and the increasing consumption of meat as a sign of growing economic prosperity;[132] as have studies of bone size and mean height, using skeletal anthropometric data, by Kron and by Klein Goldewijk and Jongman.[133] Because these factors are in some ways measurable, this is perhaps a fruitful approach, although there are inevitable problems in interpreting the biological data and in trying to identify meaningful changes in standards of living over relatively short time periods.[134] In the same vein, one way of assessing the level of living standards amongst the poor might be to study whether, over time, there was an increase in the use of quality manufactured goods by these elements of Roman society.

In the meantime, there is little we can do except to fall back on estimates for food expenditure. We have done this by setting out three categories of personal

128 Table 11.8; Brunt 1971*a*: 424, 432, 435–45, 449.

129 Cf. Hopkins 1978: 15.

130 Garnsey, Gallant, and Rathbone 1984; Garnsey and Rathbone 1985.

131 Ch. 7.

132 King 1999; MacKinnon 2004; summarized in Jongman 2007: 613–14.

133 Kron 2005; Klein Goldewijk and Jongman (forthcoming); cf. Scheidel 2007 339–41.

134 Allen 2009: 328; A. I. Wilson 2009*b*: 74.

Table 11.12. Expenditure GDP in HS m. (estimated)

	150	100	50 BC
State expenditure:			
State consumption	40	43	119
State investment	15	37	22
Personal consumption (food/clothing/fuel):			
Basic subsistence consumption	537	946	1,210
Additional 'respectability' consumption	239	731	935
Additional 'discretionary' consumption	47	121	291
Other private consumption and investment	*93*	*590*	*1,181*
TOTAL GDP	**971**	**2,468**	**3,758**
State expenditure as % of GDP	*5.7%*	*3.2%*	*3.8%*
Food/clothing/fuel consumption as % of GDP	85%	73%	65%
Real per capita growth in consumption of food/clothing/fuel as % of GDP		46%	5%

consumption (we define personal consumption as comprising food, clothing, and fuel). In the first category, we make the not unreasonable supposition that the entire Italian population, both free and servile, was consuming at least at the level of subsistence (wheat equivalent of 390 kg per capita). In Table 11.12 this is termed 'basic subsistence consumption'. We then assume in the second category that, in addition, those elements of the free population who had, according to our earlier estimates, incomes between subsistence and the 'respectability' level of income (wheat equivalent of 940 kg per capita) would spend the vast bulk of any such additional income on more food, clothing, and fuel. This is termed 'additional "respectability" consumption' in the table. The third and final category is 'additional "discretionary" consumption' and here the working assumption is that anyone with an income over and above 'respectability' would spend 10 per cent of that income on further items of food, clothing, and fuel. It thus principally reflects increased personal consumption by the elite. For example, spending on wine, as a luxury good, possibly increased as a percentage of total consumption expenditure and, in general, increasing elite consumption is reflected in the sumptuary laws that were passed in the second century.[135] All this suggests that per capita consumption of food, clothing, and fuel grew in real terms by 46 per cent between 150 and 100, and by 5 per cent between 100 and 50 BC. However, because GDP was itself growing at a faster rate in real terms, the proportion of GDP accounted for by these items falls over the period. In Table 11.12 we use the numbers derived earlier for GDP from the income side; the numbers for state expenditure and personal consumption are expressed as percentages of these numbers.

3. Expenditure: Other private consumption and investment

But there are still significant elements of economic expenditure that remain unaccounted for and that appear in Table 11.12 as a balancing item, termed

[135] Morley 1996: 113, discussed in Ch. 7.

Table 11.13. Other private consumption and investment in HS m. (estimated)

	150	100	50 BC
Other private consumption and investment:			
nominal	93	590	1,181
% change		*534%*	*100%*
real	93	393	607
% change		*323%*	*54%*

'other private consumption and investment'. In Table 11.13 we show our estimated figures, in both nominal and real terms, for this catch-all category and we shall now attempt to identify and quantify its components.

The growth of the construction and transport industries would, as we discussed above, have had a positive effect on urban incomes and thus on private consumption in general, both at Rome and at other central Italian cities, as too would the recycling of the profits remitted home by traders in the eastern Mediterranean. But the element of private consumption that is most visible in the archaeological record, as well as in stray references in literary sources, is expenditure on luxury goods, a consequence initially of the increasing spending power of the elite. As Wallace-Hadrill emphasizes, this elite was not limited to the Roman political class; it also included the political and mercantile elites of Italian cities:

> When we encounter the material evidence of the high living of the late Republic, spreading villas with their painted walls evoking fantastical architecture, mosaic pavements in the tiny tesserae of *opus vermiculatum*, marble statues and table legs, magnificent bronze mixing vessels and self-heating boilers, or beds with decoration in inlaid bronze of Dionysiac figures, nymphs and donkeys' heads, it is only too easy to attribute them instinctively to the 'Roman nobility'. The archaeological record firmly contradicts that assumption. They are found spread across Italy, and not just in the villas of Roman holiday-makers, but in the burials of the local elites. Luxury became not merely a possible way of indicating status, but perhaps the most important and indispensable.[136]

Spending on luxury consumable and domestic durable goods was, as we have seen, made possible not only by the one-off predatory reallocation of assets from Rome's defeated enemies to Roman citizens, but also by rising real incomes for this section of the population, as they used their new-found wealth to generate additional investment returns from agriculture, manufacturing, trade, participation in the *societates publicanorum*, and bank deposits. Increasing elite consumption is reflected in the textual and archaeological evidence for a growing demand for luxury goods (discussed in detail in Ch. 8), which were supplied both domestically and through imports. The Mahdia wreck, for example, dating from between 110 and 90 BC and found off the coast of Tunisia, is totemic evidence for the increasing wealth of, and consumption by, the Italian elite. The sunken vessel carried a cargo that included marble columns, bronze statues, vases, and candelabra.[137] To quote Wallace-Hadrill again: 'The sheer frequency with which parallels for the fine objects on the wreck are found in Pompeii . . . is surely not because

[136] Wallace-Hadrill 2008: 450.

[137] Parker 1992: 252; Hellenkemper Salies 1994.

Pompeii was exceptional in anything but the mode of its preservation . . . It reflects accurately the culture diffused across the Bay of Naples of which Puteoli was a major point of distribution, and Baiae and the other luxury resorts major points of consumption'.[138] The 'soft' cargoes, imported into Sicily in the 70s from Asia, Syria, Tyre, and Alexandria by the 'mercatores, homines locupletes atque honesti' of Puteoli (merchants, rich and honourable men, as Cicero describes them), provide a corresponding example. They included Tyrian purple, incense, perfumes, linen fabrics, jewels, pearls, Greek wines, and Asiatic slaves.[139] One effect of the growth of the Delian trade in oriental luxuries in the second half of the second century was to produce more specialist manufactures aimed at a wealthy group of elite consumers. Naples, Capua, and Praeneste became production centres for the perfume trade and a number of *unguentarii* (perfumers) whose professions are recorded in epigraphic or literary evidence from Italy are also recorded amongst Roman-Italian *familiae* on Delos.[140] During the first century BC, production of a range of other luxury items gradually shifted to Italy, this import substitution being stimulated by the spread of the 'consumer boom' from the elite to a broad sub-elite. By the middle of the first century AD, as studies of Pompeii show, bronze, terracotta, and glass, with the occasional piece of silverware, provided the needs of the ordinary household.[141] It is worth reminding ourselves too that, at a more mundane level, important pottery products such as bricks, tiles, and amphorae were produced in Italy for domestic use.

In Table 11.14 below, we assume that spending on luxury consumable and domestic durable goods represented the equivalent of 5 per cent of income over and above the level of 'respectability' in 150, and 20 per cent in 100 and in 50 BC.

As we have seen, it was principally the Roman state that funded the civil construction that took place at Rome during the second century. Outside Rome, however, and in particular in certain cities in Latium and Campania, where monumental sanctuaries with a Hellenistic appearance were built, a significant proportion of new civil construction was financed by individual citizens, such as Betilienus Varus at Aletrium.[142] It seems to be generally agreed, however, that most Italian cities did not expand rapidly during the second century and that the fast expansion of urban populations throughout Italy started only after the conclusion of the Social War.[143] There are some notable exceptions to this general pattern. At Pompeii, for example, a major episode of urban renewal and development seems to have started around the middle of the second century.[144] Some of the largest and finest houses there, such as the House of the Faun, are to be dated to this time, as is the appearance of the first Roman luxury villas along the coast of Campania.[145] We assume that private construction investment in Italy outside Rome in 150 was equivalent to our estimate of state investment in the same year and that spending on private construction grew by one and a half times in real terms over a period of one hundred years.

[138] Wallace-Hadrill 2008: 366–70. [139] Cic. *II Verr.* 5. 145–6, cf. 157.

[140] Plin. *HN* 13. 4; Rauh 1993: 54–5, table III: 'Professions Recorded in Italy for Roman-Italian Families at Delos'.

[141] Wallace-Hadrill 2008: 421. [142] Ch. 9.

[143] Gabba 1972; Gros 1990. [144] Wallace-Hadrill 2008: 129–37.

[145] Coarelli 1977: 19; Pesando 1997: 268–71; Torelli 1999: 8; D'Arms 2003: 20.

Another economically significant development may have been the construction of residential housing at Rome itself.[146] Its public building projects and expanding transportation requirements provided employment on a grand scale and there is, as we have seen, evidence for the large-scale movement of free labour into the city. This growth in population would have required the construction of significant amounts of additional accommodation, although virtually no trace of non-aristocratic residential housing survives in the archaeological record.[147] Remains of purpose-built *insulae* (residential blocks) have been found in Rome, but they mainly date from the Principate. However, we know that such apartment blocks were being built by the first century at least, because Cicero owned *insulae* in the Argiletum near the Forum and on the Aventine (from which he received an income of HS 80,000 p.a.).[148] Furthermore, Livy recounts a prodigy in 218, in which a cow climbs up to the third floor of a building in the *Forum Boarium*, and this may indicate that *insulae* existed in some form considerably earlier.[149] In Pompeii and Herculaneum, *cenacula* (upstairs apartments) have been identified adjacent to wealthy residences and this kind of popular housing is sometimes also assumed to have been present in Rome, although few examples have been preserved archaeologically.[150] Given, therefore, the impossibility of estimating a rate of growth for Rome's residential housing from archaeological remains, another option is to use changes in the volume of water supplied to the city. These can be roughly calculated by extrapolating from Frontinus' figures for the flows of the aqueducts and they suggest that, in 144, the Aqua Marcia increased the supply of water within the city by 66 per cent and that the Aqua Tepula increased it by a further 10 per cent in 125.[151] There are problems, though, with simply using these percentages as a proxy index for residential housing. In the first place, water was obviously used for purposes other than purely domestic ones (fountains, industry, and baths come to mind).[152] Secondly, no new aqueducts were built after the Aqua Tepula until the Aqua Julia was constructed in 33 BC. This suggests either that the population of Rome did not significantly increase in size over the next ninety years, which is unlikely, or, more probably, that the Marcia and the Tepula provided more water than was required by the second-century Roman population. These considerations lead us to speculate that private construction investment at Rome in 150 BC represented the equivalent of two-thirds of estimated state investment in that same year and that private construction investment grew by 60 per cent in real terms over the succeeding century.

Rural environments also provide evidence of significant growth in the private sector's capital stock. As we saw in Ch. 7, rural settlement appears to have been intensive in the region immediately around Rome. It is clear from Quilici's survey of the Tor Sapienza quadrangle that, in addition to villas, numerous cisterns and water-supply systems were built to meet the water requirements of the area and

146 Cf. Coarelli 1977.

147 J. R. Patterson 2010: 222.

148 Cic. *Att.* 12. 32. 2; 16. 1. 5. Note that this sum alone would put him in the top 2,000 or so richest Italians by income in Table 11.5.

149 Livy, 21. 62. 3.

150 J. R. Patterson 2000: 273–5.

151 Frontin. *Aq.* 2.81–2 Brunt 1971*a*: 384; Dodge 2000: 177, 184–5. As we saw in Ch. 9, the water of the Tepula was probably not suitable for drinking and may well have been introduced originally for industrial or bathing purposes in order to free up the Marcia for drinking.

152 Duncan-Jones 1974: 261.

there is considerable evidence for the construction of presses for olives or grapes. By the mid-first century, we find sophisticated agro-villas, such as the villa of Settefinestre near Cosa, presumably built on the proceeds of decades of successful viticulture.[153] Cato's advice in his *De Agricultura* on the suppliers from which it was best to buy agricultural equipment in central Italy, be it the best ropes for olive and wine presses from Casinum and Venafrum or rotary mills from Pompeii and Nola, reflects the demand that led to this investment. Owners of villas invested in the building of roads to link their farms with existing roads (*diverticula*).[154] Cato gives us the costs of a few pieces of farm equipment (e.g. the cost of a mill is stated to be just under HS 1,000[155]), but this does not help us much in constructing a synoptic estimate of rural capital investment. We can only make assumptions, therefore, and we suggest that, in 150 BC, rural capital investment was the most significant component of the 'other private consumption and investment' category in Table 11.14, on the basis that the vast bulk of the population lived in the countryside, that food represented the bulk of expenditure within the Italian economy, and that there is considerable evidence of fixed capital formation in rural areas to support agricultural production. For want of any more concrete evidence, we have used crude conjectural estimates of the relative sizes of Italy's urban and rural populations and assumed that rural capital investment was the equivalent of four times estimated state investment in 150 and that it grew by four and a half times in real terms over the following one hundred years.

Private sector capital investment was not just limited to the construction of buildings or agriculture. We have seen that silver mining in Spain in the second century was probably in the hands of private individuals (we have argued in Ch. 3 that it was chiefly handled by the *societates publicanorum*). It is clear that there was significant private sector investment in the equipment required to extract ore from the ground, since we hear of technological applications that entailed major capital expenditure. Both Diodorus and Strabo mention the use of the Archimedes screw for pumping out water;[156] and Polybius describes the use of water for the

Table 11.14. Breakdown of other private consumption and investment in real terms (HS m., estimated)

	150	100	50 BC
Luxury consumable and domestic durable goods	23	162	299
Private urban investment: Rome	10	15	16
Private urban investment: rest of Italy	15	20	23
Rural capital investment	60	200	268
Mining, quarrying, shipping, etc. investment	5	8	11
Exports	*80*	*150*	*210*
less Imports	*100*	*162*	*220*
Net exports	−20	−12	−10
OTHER PRIVATE CONSUMPTION AND INVESTMENT IN REAL TERMS	93	393	607

[153] Ch. 7. [154] Laurence 1998: 140–3.
[155] Cato, *Agr.* 22. 3. [156] Diod. Sic. 5. 37. 3–4; Strabo, 3. 2. 9.

crushing of ore, which suggests that businessmen were investing in the construction of aqueducts to bring water to the area of the mines.[157] The rates of extraction implied by the increasing levels of lead found in the Greenland ice cores provide an index of sorts for the scale of this capital investment. In Italy itself, the quarrying of stone and the production of cement for buildings, ports, and roads was hugely significant. Similarly, the evidence of shipwrecks provides an index for the rate of private sector investment in merchant vessels. Again, we should note that larger ships, which would of course have cost more to construct, were built from the early first century onwards. Mining, quarrying, the production of building materials and shipbuilding are assumed to be HS 5 million in 150 and to grow in line with the index of trade in Table 11.1, that is by 2.2 times in real terms, over a period of one hundred years.

Finally, trade is the category of evidence that has been most heavily exploited in order to demonstrate growth and decline in the Roman economy and this partly reflects the extent of the evidence relating to trade in the archaeological record.[158] Ironically, though, there is a major problem in quantifying the impact of trade on the Italian economy in national accounting terms, for the simple reason that it is difficult to identify the relative sizes of imports and exports. As we saw in Ch. 7, Tchernia tried to quantify Italian wine exports to Gaul by using the number of shipwrecks known in the early 1980s to produce an estimate of the average number of voyages per annum over the century in which Dressel 1 amphorae were in use.[159] Tchernia discovered, from the Royal Navy's records of the early nineteenth century AD, that only one-third of their wrecked brigs could generally be found, and that this was normally because they had sunk in relatively shallow water (like the Dressel 1 wrecks). He used this proportion (i.e. 3) to gross up the number of forty-four shipwrecks that were known from the southern coast of France in the early 1980s and that had carried Dressel 1 amphorae. This produced a hypothetical total of 132 Dressel 1 shipwrecks off the south of France. Next he doubled this number to include possible wrecks around the island of Corsica (grand total therefore 264). Finally he used the loss rate (2%) of ships on voyages during the eighteenth century AD from Europe to the Antilles and America to gross up the 264 Dressel 1 wrecks into a total, over a century, of 13,200 voyages or 132 per annum. If 2,000 amphorae, each containing 20 or 25 litres of wine, had, been carried on each voyage, there would have been a total annual export of 6 m. litres, worth 263,000 denarii or over HS 1 m. at, say, 3 denarii per amphora.[160] The actual amount and value exported is highly likely to have been significantly more than this, because it is undoubtedly much more difficult for us to find a wreck after two millennia, even using twenty-first century technology, than it would have been to find a recently sunk wreck in the nineteenth century.[161] In sum, while Tchernia's cunning attempt at quantification is to be applauded, it does not get us very far.

On the other hand, and as far as imports are concerned, what might have been the single most important innovation in the sphere of labour organization, a

[157] Strabo, 3. 2. 10 = Polyb. 34. 9. 10–11.

[158] Bowman and Wilson 2009*b*: 24.

[159] Tchernia (1986) 85–7; see p. 144.

[160] For the cost of wine at 3 denarii per amphora at Pompeii, see Duncan-Jones 1974: 46 n. 3, 364.

[161] Morley 1996: 113 estimates between 12 m. and 15 m. litres p.a., implying a value of between HS 2 m. and HS 2.5 m.

major expansion in the use of chattel slavery, began, as we have seen, in the second century and continued into the first. The import of perhaps between 3 million and 4 million slaves over the course of two centuries, combined with the demand implied by the scale of the workforce in the mines of Spain (40,000 in the 150s according to Polybius), suggests that this was a major area of investment and, consequently, import demand by the private sector. Again, though, we do not know the price of these slaves, nor their precise numbers, so quantification continues to be problematic.

For the purpose, therefore, of calculating GDP by expenditure, and in the absence of reliable synoptic statistics, we assume that the value of exports of soft commodities, in particular wine and olive oil, was consistently lower than the value of imports of slaves and luxury goods, and that, as a result, Rome's trade balance was negative throughout this period. Having said that, we are the first to admit that the available data are insufficient to test this assumption in anything remotely approaching a rigorous fashion. We have made a guess at levels of imports and exports and assumed that imports grew by 2.2 times over one hundred years, in line with the index for the total volume of trade in Table 11.1. Exports are assumed to grow by 2.6 times over the same period, in line with the growth in Dressel 1A amphorae.

Of course, none of these calculations prove that mainland Italian GDP from the expenditure side equals the figures that we obtained for GDP from the income side. But they do show that it is possible to match those numbers with plausible and coherent estimates of the individual components of GDP from the expenditure side.

MONEY

Any attempt to come up with a meaningful and realistic quantitative analysis of economic growth in the last two centuries BC is, as we have stated repeatedly, bedevilled by a lack of hard data. Michael Crawford realized this in the 1960s and it led him to produce his three great works on the Roman coinage of the late Republic, *Roman Republican Coin Hoards*, *Roman Republican Coinage*, and *Coinage and Money under the Roman Republic*. What he believed was that an analysis of the Roman coinage, of which copious examples have survived, was a way of cutting through the Gordian knot of data shortage which bedevils the Roman economy of this period. His quantitative work on the size of coin issues in *Roman Republican Coinage* was developed by Hopkins in his 'Taxes and Trade' article, as we saw in Ch. 5.

The reason for attempting to quantify the Roman coinage is that it represents part of the M element in Irving Fisher's equation of exchange: $MV=Py$. Let us remind ourselves that, in this equation, M is the Roman money supply and V is its velocity of circulation. In other words V is the number of times a unit of money is spent in a year, which makes it equivalent in practice to the ratio of GDP to M. MV is equal to the price level (P) multiplied by real output (y). Or, to put it another way, MV is equivalent to nominal GDP, and it would of course be very useful to discover this. However, inevitably, there are problems.

In the first place, we need to decide what counts as M. Despite the criticisms laid against them, Crawford and Hopkins appear to have shown that the minting of silver denarii expanded significantly between 157 and 50.[162] Our only quibble is that Hopkins's figure for the amount of silver coinage in circulation at the start of the period is far too low at 35 million in 157 and 50 million in 150 BC and is in serious need of upward revision. It is true that the amount of silver denarii in circulation between 200 and 150 is difficult to estimate, because there are only eighteen hoards known from this period and they do not provide a representative sample of total coinage over this half century.[163] It is also theoretically possible (though unattested) that some payments were made by weight of unminted silver, rather than in coin. But, in crude terms, the indemnities, booty, and mined silver received between 200 and 150 probably totalled somewhere in the region of 300 m. denarii; if we assume that only a minor portion of this was minted as denarii, the amount of silver coinage in circulation in 150 BC could easily have reached 75 million. Of course not all of this silver coinage would have circulated in mainland Italy and we assume that varying proportions of the coinage supply circulated in Sicily, in Africa after 146, in Spain after 120, and in Gallia Narbonensis after 118.[164] It should be noted in Table 11.15 that, although the estimated number of denarii in circulation in 50 BC is one-third higher than in 100 BC, this disguises considerable variation in the intervening fifty years. Hopkins's estimate of the evolution of the denarii in circulation during this period, based on Crawford's output estimates, shows a considerable growth in the second half of the second century, stopping in the 90s, but reappearing stronger than ever in the 80s. In fact, Hopkins estimated that, between 80 and 60 BC, the stock of denarii probably declined.

But what else should be included in the *M* of mainland Italy? Bronze coins were of course ubiquitous, but we have little idea as to what their total outstanding value at any one time might have been. In what follows we assume that they represent an additional 3 per cent by value of the coinage element of the money supply of mainland Italy. On the other hand, it is clear that local civic coinages, which continued to be minted in several conquered territories, should not be included, since none of them appear ever to have circulated in Italy. Furthermore, although several scholars have suggested the possibility that large payments were made with gold bullion, the evidence for this is very sketchy and we see no convincing reason to incorporate gold as a meaningful element of *M*.[165] As we discussed in Ch. 2, gold may well have been principally used as a store of value

Table 11.15. Denarii (m.) in circulation (estimated)

	150	100	50 BC
Denarii in circulation	75	**300**	**400**
% change		*200%*	*33%*
% of total denarii in Italy	90%	70%	60%
Denarii in Italy	**68**	**210**	**240**

162 See Ch. 5; Lockyear 2007. 163 Harl 1996: 40 n. 7.

164 Of course, by and large, the eastern provinces continued to use their own local civic coinages down to the 40s BC.

165 Howgego 1992: 9–10; Hollander 2007: 140; Verboven 1997: 67.

before the 40s BC.[166] But this would not mean that gold was any more part of Roman *M* than, say, a mound of grain in a warehouse—both could function as a store of wealth and both could be used, for example, to guarantee debts. What it does imply is that gold would to an extent have relieved silver coin from having to act as the principal instrument for wealth storage and the logical result of this would have been a higher velocity of circulation for silver coins than might otherwise have been the case if they had been the only instrument of this kind.

More significant is the presence of banks and the spread of relatively sophisticated financial intermediation arrangements, because Roman *M* was composed not only of coin in circulation but also of bank deposits.[167] The problem, though, is that we have no obvious way of quantifying the total size of Roman bank deposits. We do not know how many banks were operating in Italy during our period, let alone the amount of credit they extended, or the percentage of the Roman money supply their deposits represented. In any case, the amount of bank deposits would have changed over time. As we have seen, there is a strong likelihood that the number of banks and their balance sheets expanded during the second century, only to contract in the aftermath of the financial crisis of 88. Intriguing evidence from medieval England may shed some light on the Roman situation. From the thirteenth century AD onwards, a system was introduced in England for registering loans in the courts of major towns, and a number of the rolls on which these loans were originally recorded have survived.[168] These can be compared with the size of the gold and silver coinage element of the English money supply, which can be estimated to some degree from mint records. What this comparison suggests is that the use of credit tended to move in step with the supply of coinage, rather than, for example, acting to make up for a shortfall of money. When the coinage element of the money supply contracted, so too did credit.[169] Nightingale calculates that, in England in the second half of the fourteenth century AD, the amount of outstanding credit was roughly equivalent to half the value of the coinage in circulation.[170] Of course, the institutional structure of medieval England for the provision of credit was different from that of Rome. In medieval England there were no domestic banks apart from the facilities provided by Italian merchant companies in London. They received some deposits, made loans, and transferred funds, chiefly overseas. While all merchants, however modest, gave extensive trade credit, most loans of cash were made by the more prosperous members of urban and village society, including the clergy, to people known to them.[171] Rome, on the other hand, appears to have had deposit banks, although after 88 BC they may have been fewer in number and those that survived the crisis of that year may well have been smaller in size, which would have led to more credit provision by wealthy individuals in the manner of medieval England (as we argued in Ch. 10). Nevertheless, this comparison does provide an indication for a pre-modern economy of the relationship between coin and credit and, by extension (at least for an economy with healthy banking institutions), between coin and deposits.

166 See pp. 23–4. 167 Discussed in Ch. 6. 168 Nightingale 2004: 63.
169 Nightingale 1990, 1997, 2004. 170 Nightingale 2004: 65.
171 I am grateful to Pamela Nightingale for clarifying this point.

Table 11.16. Total bank deposits in mainland Italy in millions of denarii (estimated)

	150	100	50 BC
Denarii in circulation	**75**	**300**	**400**
% change		*200%*	*33%*
% of total denarii in Italy	90%	70%	60%
Denarii in Italy	**68**	**210**	**240**
Value of bronze coin in Italy	**2**	**6**	**7**
Bank deposits as % of Italian denarii	8%	12%	5%
Bank deposits in Italy	**5**	**25**	**12**
Coin + bank deposits (*M*)	**75**	**241**	**259**
% change		*221%*	*7%*

In Table 11.16, we have assumed conservatively that bank deposits in 150 were equivalent to 8 per cent of the coin in circulation and that this proportion rose to 12 per cent in 100, before falling back to 5 per cent in 50 BC in the aftermath of the credit crisis of the 80s. The only bank deposit whose size we know during the Roman Republic is that of Scipio Aemilianus who had 300,000 denarii on deposit with one banker in the late 160s. Total conjectured bank deposits of 5 m. denarii in 150 do not seem excessive in view of this.

Our second problem is that the Fisher equation captures only the monetized economy, since the equivalence it contains is between nominal output and the monetary measure, *MV*, and so does not include any production that was not purchased with money. Howgego believes that 'it is entirely likely that levels of monetization changed over time, so that an increase in the quantity of money might well have been taken up by an increase in the proportion of transactions which were monetized'.[172] And indeed it is difficult to say how monetized late Republican Italy actually was. Coin hoards are of little help in solving this problem. The finds themselves represent only the burial and non-recovery of coins hidden in the ground and so cannot act as a guide for levels of monetization. Even if one believes that hoards could be used as such a guide, the evidence is limited during our period, because peninsular Italy witnessed merely twelve years of significant and, at least in part, narrowly localized combat in the last two centuries BC.[173]

The current consensus would probably be that, by 150, urban monetization, at least, was very advanced.[174] Cicero, of course, thinks and talks in monetary terms, but so does Polybius a century earlier. The plays of Plautus and Terence, which portray a broader cross-section of society and were produced for a wider audience, also represent a world that is highly monetized. Furthermore, the structure of the denarius coinage introduced in 212 included denominations small enough to cope

172 Howgego 2009: 288.

173 Crawford 1985: 178, map 27 with appendix 45. The German incursions into the Po Valley in 102/1, the Social War in 91–89, Sulla's invasion of Italy in 83/2, and the Spartacus slave uprising of 73–71. Otherwise civil war operations in Italy were confined to generally brief campaigns in 77, 63, 49, 43, and 41/40 (Scheidel 2007: 333).

174 Crawford 1970; Burnett 1987*a*; Howgego 1992.

Table 11.17. Level of monetization in mainland Italy: non-agrarian expenditure and urban personal consumption (HS m., estimated)

	150	100	50 BC
State consumption (Table 11.12)	40	43	119
State investment (Table 11.12)	15	37	22
Luxury consumable and domestic durable goods (Table 11.14)	23	243	581
Private urban investment: Rome (Table 11.14)	10	23	31
Private urban investment: rest of Italy (Table 11.14)	15	30	45
Mining, quarrying, shipping, etc. investment (Table 11.14)	5	12	21
Net imports (Table 11.14)	20	18	19
Urban basic subsistence consumption (Table 11.12)	75	132	242
Urban additional 'respectability' consumption (Table 11.12)	33	102	187
Urban additional 'discretionary' consumption (Table 11.12)	7	17	58
TOTAL NON-AGRARIAN EXPENDITURE AND URBAN PERSONAL CONSUMPTION	243	657	1,325
% monetized	*50%*	*90%*	*95%*
Nominal value of monetized non-agrarian expenditure and urban personal consumption	**122**	**591**	**1,259**

with everyday purchases, which suggests that monetization of the retail trade, in the cities at least, was largely under way.

In order to give a more nuanced picture of monetization in mainland Italy, we have developed separate conjectural estimates for levels of monetization in urban and rural environments. We begin, in Table 11.17, by estimating the scale of non-agrarian expenditure and urban personal consumption within mainland Italy in 150, 100, and 50 BC. To produce these conjectural estimates, we have used the numbers we developed in the table referenced for each item. Under this heading, we have included all state expenditure; private sector expenditure on luxury consumable and domestic durable goods; private sector urban investment; mining, quarrying, and shipping investment; and net imports. We have further assumed that 14 per cent of the population in 150 and 100, and 20 per cent in 50 BC were responsible for 'urban' personal consumption. We have then proceeded to estimate that, by 150, somewhere approaching half of this non-agrarian/urban section of the Italian economy was monetized and that this figure increased to 90 per cent by 100 and to 95 per cent by 50 BC. This allows us to give hypothetical numbers for the nominal value of monetized non-agrarian expenditure and urban personal consumption at each of these dates.

The picture in the countryside is more mixed. As we saw in Ch. 5, Polybius refers to the use of coin in country inns in Cisalpine Gaul and coins have been found on a number of rural sites throughout Italy. Indeed, it would be surprising if monetization was not developing in the countryside by this time. This is because of the settlement on Italian land of veterans, who had become accustomed to the regular use of coin.[175] Something of the order of one half of all citizens served in the army, each probably for an average period of just under seven years, and all of them were paid in coin. Cato the Elder certainly reveals the countryside to be at least partly monetized: in his *De Agricultura*, for example, the *paterfamilias* is advised to

[175] Hollander 2007: 150.

review the cash accounts on his arrival at his farm.[176] The wages of the *faber* (craftsman) who assembles a mill are expressed in sesterces, as are those of the men who transport it.[177] This suggests that urban supply networks were already significantly monetized by this time and were gradually integrating rural production centres and markets. But there are a number of instances in this same work that show that barter was still being used as the preferred form of exchange in certain transactions. The leasing of land and the cost of milling are expressed in kind.[178] The price of a *trapetus* (mill) bought at Suessa is given as HS 400 plus fifty pounds of olive oil, which suggests a combination of part payment in coin and the vestigial remains of a barter system. More generally, the levels of production for direct consumption and non-monetized exchange must always have been very significant in a predominantly agrarian economy. Taxes, rents, some types of wage, and even loans in kind were still common under the Principate.[179] That said, the larger, more commercially oriented estates, on the 'investment farming' model described in Ch. 7, were producing a considerable surplus with the express intention of selling it to domestic urban populations and overseas. We have, therefore, divided the agrarian economy into two categories—small independent farms and large estates—and assumed different levels of monetization for each.

We have assumed, in Table 11.18, that:

1. small independent farms (peasants, colonists, military veterans, etc.) accounted for 69 per cent of total Italian basic subsistence consumption in 150, 60 per cent in 100, and 52 per cent in 50 BC;
2. they accounted for 43 per cent of additional 'respectability' and 'discretionary' consumption in 150 and 100, and 40 per cent in 50 BC;
3. 50 per cent of rural capital investment was made by small independent farms; and
4. small independent farms directly consumed or bartered the majority of their own production and purchased for cash only a small part of what they consumed (25 per cent in 150, 30 per cent in 100, and 35 per cent in 50 BC).

Table 11.18. Level of monetization in mainland Italy: agrarian expenditure: small independent farms (HS m., estimated)

	150	100	50 BC
Basic subsistence consumption (Table 11.12)	370	570	633
Additional 'respectability' consumption (Table 11.12)	103	315	374
Additional 'discretionary' consumption (Table 11.12)	20	52	116
Rural capital investment (Table 11.14)	30	150	260
TOTAL AGRARIAN EXPENDITURE: SMALL INDEPENDENT FARMS	523	1,087	1,383
% monetized	*25%*	*30%*	*35%*
Nominal value of monetized agrarian (small farm) Expenditure	**131**	**326**	**484**

[176] Cato, *Agr.* 2. 5. [177] Cato, *Agr.* 21. 5, 22. 3–5.
[178] Cato, *Agr.* 136, 144–50. [179] Howgego 1992: 22–8.

As far as large estates owned by wealthy members of the elite are concerned, we have estimated in Table 11.19 that:

1. they accounted for 17 per cent of total Italian basic subsistence consumption in 150, but that this proportion subsequently grew, as more slaves were used on the estates, to 26 per cent in 100, and to 28 per cent in 50 BC;
2. they accounted for 43 per cent of additional 'respectability' and 'discretionary' consumption in 150 and 100, and 40 per cent in 50 BC;
3. 50 per cent of rural capital investment was made by large estates;
4. in 150 BC, 50 per cent of this part of the economy was monetized, 60 per cent in 100, and 75 per cent in 50 BC.

These suggested levels of monetization for large estates reflect their more specialized production activities and hence their presumed greater integration into more monetized urban and international trade networks.[180] We assume that large estates directly consumed or bartered the rest of their own production.

On this analysis, summarized in Table 11.20, the level of monetization in the Italian economy grew from 39 per cent in 150 to 68 per cent in 50 BC and the key

Table 11.19. Level of monetization in mainland Italy: agrarian expenditure: large estates (HS m., estimated)

	150	100	50 BC
Basic subsistence consumption (Table 11.12)	92	244	335
Additional 'respectability' consumption (Table 11.12)	103	315	374
Additional 'discretionary' consumption (Table 11.12)	20	52	117
Rural capital investment (Table 11.14)	30	150	261
TOTAL AGRARIAN EXPENDITURE: LARGE ESTATES	245	761	1,087
% monetized	*50%*	*60%*	*75%*
Nominal value of monetized agrarian (large estate) expenditure	**123**	**457**	**815**

Table 11.20. Level of monetization in mainland Italy: total nominal value of monetized expenditure in HS m. as percentage of nominal income GDP (estimated)

	150	100	50 BC
(A) Nominal value of monetized non-agrarian expenditure and urban personal consumption	122	591	1,259
(B) Nominal value of monetized agrarian (small farm) expenditure	131	326	484
(C) Nominal value of monetized agrarian (large estate) expenditure	123	457	815
TOTAL NOMINAL VALUE OF MONETIZED EXPENDITURE (A+B+C)	**376**	**1,374**	**2,558**
Nominal income GDP	971	2,468	3,758
TOTAL NOMINAL VALUE OF MONETIZED EXPENDITURE AS % OF NOMINAL INCOME GDP	**39%**	**56%**	**68%**

180 Cf. Rathbone 1991: 318–30 for the monetized nature of the Appianus estate in third-century AD Egypt and see Cato's mention of cash accounts (*Agr.* 2.5).

drivers of this change were the increasing commercialization of the non-agrarian economy, the growth in the proportion of the non-agrarian economy (from 13% in 150 to 34% a century later), and, within the agrarian economy, the growth of larger, more commercially oriented estates which were selling products to urban populations and exporting them overseas.

The third problem that we face is how to measure the other function on the monetary side of the Fisher equation, V, about which, as Hopkins noted, 'we know virtually nothing', since it is so difficult to measure.[181] As we have seen, in his 'Taxes and Trade' article, Hopkins suggested that Roman M increased greatly between 157 and 50, but that prices (P) remained steady. The Fisher equation tells us that under these circumstances something must have happened to either V or y (or both) in order for equilibrium to be restored. That is, either the velocity of circulation dropped or the quantity of goods produced increased, and Hopkins's conclusion was that both occurred.[182] Velocity, as an unknown variable within the equation, could theoretically be calculated if the other functions (M, P, and y) were known, but of course they are not; rather, we are trying to use V and M to shed light on Py.

An attempt has been made to measure velocity of circulation empirically, from coin wear.[183] But, as Howgego has pointed out, this approach has a fundamental problem: 'If coin is carried around but not used for exchange then it does not circulate; by contrast coin kept in a bank but transferred from one party to another does circulate.'[184] Against this unpromising background, it becomes tempting either to say that Roman V was a constant, or to avoid the issue of V altogether. Hollander, for example, tries to use demand theory to circumvent the problem (and fails).[185] So how can we approach Roman V? It is, again, monetary historians of the medieval and early modern periods who can provide some assistance. They have been able to make more progress in analysing V than their ancient counterparts, because more quantitative data exist in the form of mint records, prices, and population.[186] Even then, as Mayhew remarks, 'these estimates cannot hope to be more than best guesses and the variables calculated from these estimates, including velocity and growth, can only be approximations and are highly speculative'. Mayhew's research suggests that, in England, between AD 1300 and 1700, a period during which the country was largely monetized, V

[181] Hopkins 2002. [182] Hopkins 1980: 109.

[183] Duncan-Jones 1987. [184] Howgego 1992: 12.

[185] Hollander 2007: 141–55, esp. p. 141 and n. 27—'Soon after Fisher developed his exchange equation, A. C. Pigou adapted it to create a new equation ($M^d = kPy$) defining the demand for money. (Note that the exponent in this equation should be understood to mean "the demand for" M rather than "to the d power.") He replaced the idea of money's velocity of circulation with the variable k which represents "the proportion of resources" kept in the form of money. Instead of talking about how many transactions are made within an economy, he looked at how much money people want to hold. [. . .] Demand theory posits that money is just one of many forms in which wealth can be held and that an individual's demand for money will depend on the utility and potential returns offered by a range of assets.' But what Hollander does is to start by using the money demand equation, $M^d = kPy$ (instead of $MV = Py$), only to change the demand function, M^d, into the simple function M (so transforming the equation into $M = kPY$), on the erroneous assumption that demand for money always equals supply. This is manifestly wrong in principle (otherwise V would not fluctuate, which it does in fact do), and is wrong for the Roman Republic in particular, as is shown by the periodic laments about *caritas nummorum* in the middle years of the first century BC.

[186] Mayhew 1995*a*, 1995*b*.

had a median value of 3.9. During periods when money was plentiful, *V* was around 3.5, but when monetary conditions were stressed, it could rise to 6.3 (AD 1600) or even 9.3 (AD 1561).[187] What the detail in this analysis suggests is that *V* changed over time. It tended to fall during periods when money, in all its forms, became more plentiful and to rise when monetary conditions were stressed. In a largely monetized economy, therefore, a particularly high velocity of circulation is more likely to be a symptom of monetary distress than a healthy economy. Mayhew's approach was to value all output/income as if it were purchased with coin, although he did of course realize that much was not actually transacted in coin. This generated *V* numbers which were very high, because they actually included all sorts of ways of doing without coin, such as barter, credit, labour/service rents, rents in kind, etc. He then used falling *V* as an index of increasing monetization. A slightly different approach is taken by Bordo and Jonung, who have argued that *V* in a monetizing economy will normally follow a U-shaped path over time. As in Mayhew's approach, declining velocity is explained by monetization, because the growth of the monetary economy, at the expense of barter and production for own use, initially increases the demand for holding money.[188] Rising velocity, on the other hand, is explained by the emergence of financial assets that substitute for money and lower the demand for holding money.[189] For example, if a sum of money is lent by one individual to another or by a bank to a borrower, it is *V* that is increased (rather than *M*). Similarly, if a payment is made by means of a ledger transfer (on the liability side of a bank's balance sheet) from one depositor to another, in lieu of coin, then this would also increase *V* rather than *M*, since such a transfer would not serve to increase the total amount of deposits at the bank.[190] Bordo and Jonung are dealing with the early modern and modern periods, and so it may be wondered how applicable their analysis is to Rome. But if we are correct in suggesting the development, during the second century BC, of more financial assets that substituted for money, such as loans and bank deposits, and, in the middle of the first century BC, increased lending between individual members of the elite, it is likely that *V* would have been higher at the end of the period than at the beginning.

In Table 11.21, we assume that Velocity in 150 is low, because the Italian economy is in the process of monetizing. We have, therefore, opted for a *V* of 1.26×, since the lowest *V* identified in the modern period was 1.15 in Denmark in AD 1906. As Silver says: 'It is difficult to think of a lower *V* unless the average coin went directly from mint to hoard without first "passing Go"!'[191] We have then

Table 11.21. Velocity of circulation of money in mainland Italy (estimated)

	150	100	50 BC
Velocity (*V*)	1.26×	1.43×	2.47×

[187] Mayhew 1995*a*: 239–40.

[188] Another factor reducing velocity would, of course, be hoarding in time of war.

[189] Silver 2007: 205; Bordo and Jonung 1987, 1990.

[190] In fact, *M* would only increase if a new deposit was made at the bank.

[191] Silver 2007: 205.

Table 11.22. 'Mayhew' *V*

	150	100	50 BC
(A) Nominal GDP from the income side	HS 971 m.	HS 2,468 m.	HS 3,758 m.
(B) Silver and bronze coin in circulation	HS 280 m.	HS 864 m.	HS 988 m.
A / B (= 'Mayhew' *V*)	3.47×	2.86×	3.80×

gone on to assume that *V* increases to 1.43× in 100 BC, by which time the level of monetization in the economy might have reached 56 per cent, and to 2.47× by 50 BC, nearly double the level in 150 BC.

At first sight, these figures are well below the level that Mayhew suggests is the average for England between AD 1300 and 1700. But if we had used Mayhew's approach of valuing all GDP as if it was purchased with coin (Table 11.22), so dividing 'nominal GDP from the income side' by 'coin in circulation', we would have obtained numbers of 3.47×, 2.86×, and 3.80× for velocity in Italy in 150, 100, and 50 BC. These would have been much closer to Mayhew's median value of 3.9 in England between AD 1300 and 1700. In effect, all we have done in arriving at our numbers for *V* is to speculate on the value of bank deposits and the proportion of the economy that was monetized.

Before we continue, it is worth pausing to consider briefly the only attempt, other than Hopkins's, to measure an ancient economy using coinage as a key factor. Makis Aperghis's model of the Seleucid royal economy in the third and second centuries BC endeavours 'to determine, independently from the sources, plausible relationships between the four factors of the economy of Seleucid Mesopotamia: population, production, taxation and coinage'.[192] 'More population should generally mean more production,[193] which in turn should lead to greater taxation and, in a monetary economy, to an increased amount of coinage in circulation to pay the taxes'.[194] Aperghis's starting assumption is that the Seleucid kingdom monetized its economy because it paid its soldiers and administrators in cash, and so needed to extract taxation in coin from the peasantry. These peasants obtained the coin by selling produce to the cities where the soldiers and the administrators spent their wages. In this 'tax collection—administrative payments' cycle, coin flows from state coffers to soldiers, to cities, to peasants, and back to state coffers; the Seleucids mint tetradrachms to 'top up' the money supply and keep the cycle going.[195]

192 Aperghis 2001: 72.

193 Malthus would be spinning in his grave!

194 Aperghis 2001: 69.

195 Aperghis concludes that, with a population of between 5 and 6 million, and with taxation being levied at a rate of roughly 1,000 talents per million of population, the royal revenues from Mesopotamia were of the order of 6,000 talents p.a. The amount of Seleucid tetradrachm coinage in circulation in Mesopotamia is estimated by Aperghis to have been between 1,000 and 2,000 talents per million inhabitants (large enough to enable the payment of 1,000 talents of taxation per million inhabitants), and so totalling somewhere between 5,000 and 12,000 talents. In his subsequent book, Aperghis lowers his estimate of Mesopotamia's population to between 4 m. and 5 m., and raises taxation revenue per million of population to 1,250 talents (Aperghis 2004: 247–62). Silver 2007: 205 calculates the value of *V* implied by this model to be 2.1.

Aperghis's approach has attracted much criticism for what one reviewer termed his 'acrobatic speculation'. Some of the assumptions and estimates he used in calculating, for example, population size, and his assertion that all taxation payments were made in silver rather than in kind have drawn particular criticism.[196] Aperghis also omits any consideration of the effect of trade on the coinage, merely stating that Mesopotamia was a 'closed system' and that 'the value of inter-regional trade was probably small'.[197] This is debatable, to say the least. What is also clear is that, whether or not Aperghis's approach works for Mesopotamia, his model does not fit late Republican Rome. In the second and first centuries BC, Rome had a more complicated economy than the one that Aperghis depicts for Mesopotamia, not least because Roman citizens were not directly taxed after 167.

Nevertheless, what is interesting about Aperghis's approach is that it provokes consideration of how money in an ancient economy might have worked. In his model of Seleucid Mesopotamia, Aperghis outlines a system in which money was used to top up a simple cycle; money certainly oiled the wheels of the Mesopotamian economy, but, as portrayed by Aperghis, it is a reflection of economic activity, rather than a stimulant. At Rome, on the other hand, money appears to have been a driver of economic growth. The increased inflows of bullion into second century Rome led to the increased minting of coin, which was issued to pay soldiers and state suppliers, as well as workmen on state-sponsored infrastructure projects. Once these coins were issued, they did not automatically come back into the state's coffers, as they are conjectured by Aperghis to have done in Seleucid Mesopotamia, because of the absence of direct taxation on Roman citizens after 167. The only mechanism by which denarii circulating within Italy could re-enter the *aerarium* was through indirect taxation such as *portoria*, the payment of rent on *ager publicus*, the tax on the manumission of slaves, and revenues from state monopolies. Otherwise, they continued to circulate within the private sector of the Roman economy and so promoted monetization of private sector transactions. In fact the most significant indicator of money driving Roman economic activity is to be found in cases where diminished liquidity caused chaos. The financial crises of 88 BC, 63 BC, 49 BC, and AD 33 were all either caused or aggravated by a lack of monetary liquidity, as we saw in Ch. 10.

So is it possible to fit the monetary variables we have been discussing into any kind of meaningful picture of the Roman economy so that we can use *MV* as a possible way of measuring growth in nominal GDP? To calculate *MV*, and using the column headed 100 BC in Table 11.23 as an example, we can summarize our procedure thus:

1. The outstanding supply of denarii in 100 BC (300 m.) is taken from the graph (reproduced in Fig. 5.1) that Hopkins presented, using Crawford's estimates, in his 'Taxes and Trade' article (the figure for 150 BC having been increased to 75 m. denarii for the reasons discussed earlier).
2. Seventy per cent of these denarii, or 210 m., is assumed to have circulated in mainland Italy (and 30% in Africa, Sicily, Gallia Narbonensis, and Spain).

[196] De Callataÿ 2004; Ma 2007.
[197] Aperghis 2001: 86.

Table 11.23. Mainland Italian *MV* and GDP (estimated)

	150	100	50 BC
Denarii in circulation (m.)	**75**	**300**	**400**
% change		*200%*	*33%*
% of total denarii in Italy	90%	70%	60%
Denarii in Italy (m.)	**68**	**210**	**240**
Value of bronze coin in Italy (den. m.)	**2**	**6**	**7**
Bank deposits as % of Italian denarii	8%	12%	5%
Bank deposits in Italy (den. m.)	**5**	**25**	**12**
Coin + bank deposits (*M*) (den. m.)	**75**	**241**	**259**
% change		*221%*	*7%*
Velocity (*V*)	**1.26×**	**1.43×**	**2.47×**
***MV* (den. m.)**	**95**	**345**	**639**
Italy: % monetized	39%	56%	68%
MV grossed up by	*0.39*	*0.56*	*0.68*
Italian nominal GDP (*Py*) (den. m.)	**244**	**616**	**940**
= (HS m.)	**976**	**2,464**	**3,760**

3. Bronze coins are assumed to represent an additional 3 per cent by value of the coinage element of the money supply of mainland Italy, so the equivalent of 6 m. denarii.
4. Total bank deposits are conservatively assumed to represent an additional 12 per cent of the outstanding silver coinage, or 25 m. denarii (much lower, of course, than the ratio in which Nightingale believes outstanding credit stood to the supply of coinage in the fourteenth century AD).
5. Coinage and bank deposits are added together to produce a figure for the total money supply, *M*.
6. The resulting figure of 241 m. denarii for Italian *M* is multiplied by *V* of 1.43 to produce *MV* of 345 m. denarii, which is equivalent to the nominal GDP of 'monetized' mainland Italy. (The crucial importance of *V* is clearly illustrated here, as a doubling of *V* results in a doubling of nominal GDP); and
7. Fifty-six per cent of the economy of mainland Italy is assumed to have been monetized in 100 BC and so the figure for *MV* is grossed up by a factor of 0.56 to produce a figure of 616 m. denarii or HS 2,464 m. for the size of total nominal GDP (i.e. *Py*) in mainland Italy in 100 BC.

It is, of course, no coincidence that these numbers for *Py* are virtually the same as the nominal GDP numbers from the income side produced earlier. This may just be regarded as juggling with figures and I do not pretend that no alternative reconstruction is possible. But the aim here is to show that it is possible to arrive at a coherent figure for nominal GDP by combining estimates for coinage in circulation with controlled conjectures about other monetary variables derived from studies of the medieval and early modern periods.

NATIONAL DISPOSABLE INCOME

To remind ourselves, GNP under the income approach is GDP plus or minus net receipts from transfers of property (interest, rent, dividends, and profits) or labour income from the rest of the world. NDI is GNP plus or minus net current transfers received in money or in kind from the rest of the world (these would include booty, indemnities, and taxes in money or in kind).

We have absolutely no information that would allow us to hazard even a remote guess as to the size of Italian net receipts from transfers of property or labour income, so we have not attempted to reconstruct Italian GNP. However, in a period in which numerical data are scarce, references in our sources allow us to construct some estimates of net current transfers into mainland Italy. During the second century, the Romans received money and bullion from war booty, war indemnities, mining revenues, and provincial taxation on a scale that dwarfed anything they had received previously. From booty and indemnities alone it was the equivalent of 1,050 tonnes of silver between 200 and 150, or an average of 21 tonnes per annum. The Spanish mines by the 150s were generating 35 tonnes of silver per annum (mirrored in the dramatic upswing in the volume of lead deposits in the Greenland ice cores) and the provinces (of which Asia was the most important) were perhaps producing the equivalent of about 190 tonnes of silver per annum by the early first century. Income transfers of this kind into mainland Italy from Rome's embryonic empire and defeated enemies would have meant that the NDI of mainland Italy was higher than its GDP. In Table 11.24 we have annualized these capital inflows and expressed them in sesterces so that we can show their relationship to our estimates for income GDP.

What this shows is that mainland Italian NDI is between 2 and 3 per cent higher than its GDP throughout the period, although, as we have stated, these numbers take no account of rent from overseas property, interest on overseas loans, net receipts from transfers of property to or from overseas, or overseas labour income. By way of comparison, Maddison made a rough quantification of tax and transfers from the rest of the Roman Empire and estimated 'peninsular Italy's NDI to be about 7 per cent above its GDP in AD 14'.[198]

Table 11.24. National disposable income, in HS m., of mainland Italy (estimated)

	199–150	149–100	99–50 BC
Indemnities	656	120	480
Booty	460	400	880
Mines	416	1,800	1,800
Provincial taxes	0	692	2,920
TOTAL	1,532	3,012	6,080
Annualized overseas income	31	60	122
plus GDP	971	2,468	3,758
NATIONAL DISPOSABLE INCOME	**1,002**	**2,528**	**3,880**
Premium of NDI to GDP	3%	2%	3%

[198] Maddison 2007: 44–5, 51.

CONCLUSION

There can be little doubt that successful warfare produced a major increase in the growth potential of the Roman Republican economy of the second and first centuries BC, and there is abundant evidence for aggregate growth occurring in the volume of output and exchange. The distribution of dated shipwrecks in the Mediterranean provides a powerful index of commercial development, and the increase in the volume of silver denarii in circulation suggests that the economy as a whole was expanding. Indeed it is possible to identify a specific configuration of variables that facilitated real economic growth. Massive capital inflows, commercial expansion, the availability of cheap immigrant labour, a redistribution of population in favour of urban environments, the gradual diffusion of improved production technology, and the spread of more sophisticated financial intermediation arrangements were all strongly conducive to economic growth.

The question, though, that we have tried to answer in this chapter is whether this was quantifiable *real per capita* economic growth. To recapitulate, our approach has been to present a series of snapshots of the economy of mainland Italy from the income side of GDP at fifty year intervals (150 BC, 100 BC, and 50 BC). We used sporadic notices of individual elite wealth as a starting point and extrapolated income pyramids from these data. This procedure produced some historically credible results, into which can be fitted, quite reasonably, both the general trends in living standards that we can derive from ancient accounts and the very small number of reports of non-elite individual income that can be gleaned from ancient texts. Next, we attempted to quantify Italian GDP from the expenditure side, by examining state and private investment and consumption as well as the balance of trade. Large parts of this last exercise involved a high degree of guesswork, but again it was possible to construct a probabilistic quantification that fitted with our estimates of GDP from the income side. Finally, as a check on our numbers for income GDP, we went on to construct a further series of estimates of Italian nominal GDP, by combining what we know or can infer about the Roman money supply with hypothetical numbers for the velocity of circulation of money, in order to produce an estimate of Roman *MV*. Of course this 'wigwam' approach is highly conjectural, but at present there are simply not enough quantifiable data sets available on which to build a concrete, synoptic, numerically based quantification of the Roman economy for the late Republican period. Regardless of the inherent fragility of our estimates, we have been able to reconstruct general contextual conditions and to clarify the logical implications of our different GDP estimates. One can, therefore, dispute the final numbers at which we arrived for Italian GDP in 150, 100, and 50 BC, but the aim here has not been to achieve precision in our estimates for the size of that economy at any of these dates, which is clearly impossible, given the notoriously meagre data available and the paucity of our knowledge; rather it has been to seek to demonstrate that real per capita economic growth is likely to have occurred and to try and attach some tentative numbers to that growth.

There are two significant variables that have a crucial bearing on whether this attempt can be considered to have been successful: the size of the Italian population and the rate of inflation during the period concerned. For inflation, there is precious little data from which to derive anything more than a crude GDP deflator. However, one clear conclusion is that, even if one assumes, as we have done, that prices rose by 95 per cent between 150 and 50 BC, real GDP growth is likely to have occurred. As far as demographic considerations are concerned, we opted, in arriving at our free population assumptions in Chapter 7, to follow de Ligt's arguments that this section of the population grew moderately during the second century, before experiencing a modest decline in the first half of the first century. We also followed Scheidel's estimates for the size of the slave population. The combination of these assumptions with our GDP estimates suggested that real per capita GDP grew by 72 per cent between 150 and 50 BC, an average annual compound growth rate of 0.54 per cent. However, if the 'high counters' are ever proved to be correct, this rate of increase would probably have to be significantly reduced. On the other hand, the corollary of accepting the high count is that the size of the Italian economy during this period would have been vastly larger.

In the meantime, there are several more granular conclusions which can be stated with varying degrees of confidence. The first is that the wealth of the elite and their incomes grew significantly, perhaps as much as fivefold, between 150 and 50 BC and that the per capita income of the free non-elite population also grew (by 77% on our estimates), which suggests that income disparities increased significantly during this period. In that context, we estimated that in 100 BC a quarter of the free population was surviving at a level just above subsistence, which perhaps reflected the problems that led to the Gracchan land reforms and to the introduction of the corn dole. The second conclusion is that, while the expansion in the supply of silver denarii in the second half of the second century and the first half of the first century (a consequence of the huge inflows of bullion into the Roman *aerarium*) was undoubtedly a significant contributory factor to the growth of the economy, the velocity at which money circulated around that economy was an equally important determinant of economic growth. Studies of the medieval and early modern periods can help us to arrive at plausible rates for this variable. But the fact remains that we have no ancient evidence that can be of any assistance in determining what the actual rates of *V* were. As far as expenditure is concerned, a striking feature of the Republican economy is the tiny proportion accounted for by the state: 5.7 per cent in 150, 3.2 per cent in 100, before increasing slightly to 3.8 per cent in 50 BC. Constrained by its unwillingness to borrow, the Roman state's expenditure was limited to the army, the corn dole, and investment in urban infrastructure and roads. In this light, while military expenditure was a major catalyst of economic growth, it was not, perhaps surprisingly, a significant constituent of the economy in itself. Similarly, the increasing levels of private expenditure on luxury consumables and domestic consumables, though highly visible in those ancient texts that moralize on the subject of *luxuria* as well as in the archaeological record, were dwarfed economically by expenditure on food, clothing, and fuel.

We have given repeated 'health warnings' throughout this chapter and I shall end with a final one. Despite the use of numbers, the estimates we have produced are assumptions, not facts. As we suggested at the beginning, this chapter should serve as much to highlight how little we know about the late Republican economy as to provide the 'Ultimate Answer'.

Summary and Conclusions

We have endeavoured to explain the dynamics of the Roman economy in the second and early first centuries BC and to identify the important points of economic change and why they occurred. Our argument has been that, during the second century, increased inflows of bullion combined with the contemporaneous expansion of the availability of credit to produce a large increase in monetary liquidity. This in turn resulted in a major upward inflection in Roman economic activity and the creation both of a more complex system of production and distribution and of an enormous material culture that was to reach its height under the Principate.

We have seen that the city of Rome had grown rapidly at the end of the fourth and beginning of the third century, as is shown by the building of the first two aqueducts into Rome: the Aqua Appia in 312 and the Aqua Anio Vetus in 272. The *plebiscitum Claudianum* of 218 and archaeological finds of fine pottery and Graeco-Italic amphorae in the Mediterranean and central France attest to the expansion of Roman trade during the third century. It also seems that some of the economic developments which we see in the second century represent the continuation of processes that had begun earlier, under the influence of contact with the Hellenistic world. By the time of the Second Punic War, Rome was probably already one of the most significant cities in the Mediterranean, with a population of perhaps 200,000. She controlled peninsular Italy, Corsica, Sardinia, and part of Sicily and was already beginning to establish a network of roads. Physically, the city of Rome itself was, by the early second century, still 'a city which had not yet been adorned' (urbs nondum exornata[1]), probably with an unsophisticated, haphazard appearance. The executive machinery of Rome, with the exception of the army, was tiny; there was no tradition of employing men of high status on a salary for a long term, either in the public or the private sphere, and as a result there was a reliance on the *publicani* as suppliers of goods and services to the Roman state. However, despite the seizure of booty and some 5,000 talents of war indemnities during the third century, the demands of the Second Punic War revealed that Rome's resources were not enormous. By 214, the treasury was empty, a development mirrored in a dramatic fall in the weight of the bronze coinage and the debasement of silver from about 97 per cent fine down to about 89 per cent, probably in 213. It was only with the financial help of its own elite that Rome was able to survive—in itself an indication of the level of wealth already attained by certain individuals of senatorial and equestrian rank.

[1] Livy, 40. 5. 7.

During the second century, however, vast quantities of bullion came to Rome in the form of war booty and indemnities from most of its defeated enemies, notably Carthage, Macedonia, and Syria. These sources of precious metal were supplemented by, and in time mainly replaced by, silver bullion from the Spanish and Macedonian mines and provincial tax revenues from Rome's expanding empire.

We have relatively precise figures from literary sources for war indemnities totalling 27,280 talents between 200 and 150—five times the amount that Rome received in the whole of the third century. Booty is more difficult to quantify, as the record is incomplete. Frank provided a 'highly hypothetical' valuation of the booty that came in during the period from 200 to 157 of about 18,000 talents, which gives some indication of the scale of income from this source. If we add these two amounts together, we can see that, from warfare alone, Rome received more than 45,000 talents over a fifty-year period.

At the same time, both Polybius and the archaeological record suggest that, by the mid-second century, significant quantities of silver bullion were being mined in Spain. For the region around Carthago Nova in south-east Spain, which probably saw the initial focus of Roman mining activity, Polybius provides the only surviving contemporary description of mining operations. He visited the area in person and he tells us that 40,000 miners were producing, for the Roman *demos*, 25,000 drachmas per day. That is about 1,500 talents per annum, equivalent to approximately 35 tonnes of silver per annum. Polybius' evidence is supported by the rates of lead deposition in the second century found in the lakes of Sweden and Russia, in the ice cap of Greenland, and in the peat bogs of Spain and Switzerland. These suggest that, during this period, smelting activities from silver and lead mining in Spain created high levels of atmospheric pollution.

In the last quarter of the century, provincial taxation began to represent a larger slice of the pie. By 120 at the latest, the Romans were taxing their new province of Asia. Some idea of the scale of the revenues that Rome was eventually extracting from the province comes from Cicero. Before Pompey's conquests, the regular public revenues were said to have been over 8,000 talents per annum from up to twelve provinces. In 66, in the *De Imperio Cn. Pompeii*, Cicero stressed the fact that Asia provided a large part of that sum. Sixty years earlier, with about half the number of provinces, the relative importance of Asia must have been much greater.

During the second century, therefore, the Romans received money and bullion from war booty, war indemnities, mining revenues, and provincial taxation on a scale that dwarfed anything they had received previously. From booty and indemnities alone there was the equivalent of 1,050 tonnes of silver over a fifty-year period, or an average of 21 tonnes per annum. The Spanish mines, by the 150s, were generating 35 tonnes of silver per annum; and the provinces, the most important of which was Asia, were producing perhaps the equivalent of 190 tonnes of silver per annum by the early first century (although, of course, the actual bullion component of provincial taxation is unknown, since this source included payment in kind).

The numismatic corollary of these vast inflows of bullion, which effectively turbocharged the Roman monetary economy, was that the coinage element of Rome's money supply started to expand rapidly from the middle of the second century onwards. Indeed, the supply of Roman silver coins increased significantly, perhaps as much as tenfold, between 157 and 50. Of course, not all of this silver coinage would have circulated in mainland Italy, and we have assumed that varying proportions of the coinage supply circulated in Sicily, in Africa after 146, in Spain after 120, and in Gallia Narbonensis after 118. But, in the East, no significant quantities of denarii are found in Greek hoards until the time of Sulla, only local coinages; and the denarius does not seem to have become a major currency in the Greek world until the 30s BC. Similarly, there is no evidence for denarii being used to any significant extent in Asia Minor until the 40s at the earliest. The evidence for the countryside of Italy, Sicily, and Cisalpine Gaul is very limited, but our model suggests that the level of monetization in the Italian economy could have grown from 39 per cent in 150 BC to 68 per cent in 50 BC, with the key drivers of this change being the increasing commercialization of the non-agrarian economy, the growth in the proportion of the non-agrarian economy, and, within the agrarian economy, the growth of larger, more commercially oriented estates, which were selling products to urban populations and exporting them overseas. If we assume, therefore, that the bulk of the increased supply of denarii was used in mainland Italy, the monetary impact of such an increase would normally be either to cause prices to rise or to increase the level of economic activity. But there is nothing to suggest anything other than a relatively modest level of retail price inflation, although there is evidence for more extreme price movements in luxury goods. Overall, we have suggested that prices increased by 80 per cent during the first half of the second century (a compound rate of 0.37% p.a.), and by 95 per cent between 150 and 50 BC (a compound rate of 0.67% p.a.).

The general lack of major inflationary pressures is all the more remarkable given that there is also considerable evidence that the activities of early Roman financial intermediaries provided a mechanism for the creation of money beyond the available supply of precious metals, thereby serving to expand Rome's total money supply. Passages from contemporary second-century authors prove that Rome's *argentarii* functioned like modern bankers in a number of ways. In the first place, Plautus reveals that they fulfilled both a deposit and a credit function, since they lent out deposits which they accepted (and these deposits were sometimes of a large size, as Polybius' story about Scipio Aemilianus demonstrates). Such a mechanism would have served to expand Rome's money supply and, thereby, to encourage an increase in effective demand. In other words, a growth in bank lending would have led to an expansion in the volume of commercial transactions and activity. Secondly, passages from both Plautus and Polybius suggest that money could be transferred by a written entry in the banker's records, without the movement of cash, a feature which would have had significant and positive implications for the financing of, for example, trade.

These inflows of capital and the money-multiplier effect of deposit banking transformed Rome and eventually Italy in a number of ways.

The physical manifestation of this monetary expansion was in building and construction. Our sources suggest that, in the 190s, the financial difficulties that Rome had faced during the Second Punic War continued. But the booty that Manlius Vulso brought back from Asia in 188 after the defeat of Antiochus III of Syria and, in particular, the 15,000 talent indemnity that Antiochus was forced to pay led to a remarkable period of expenditure on infrastructure by the censors of 189, 184, 179, and 174. In the second half of the century, new expensive roads were constructed in Italy, Macedonia, Spain, and Asia. The building of two new aqueducts, the Aqua Marcia and the Aqua Tepula, more than doubled Rome's water supply. A culture that is constructing more numerous and more substantial buildings, roads, and aqueducts clearly has a great deal of money.

But in fact the most significant, immediate, and direct beneficiaries of these inflows of capital were Rome's military forces themselves, as is indicated by the high proportion of revenue that was spent on this area. Governments reveal their policies by their spending decisions and the Roman senate, in the first half of the second century, made the choice to spend considerably less of Rome's revenues on infrastructure than it did on warfare. The simple fact is that Rome's involvement in warfare in the second century would not have occurred to the same extent, if the money had not been available to pay for its armed forces; and the high rate of expenditure on Rome's military was financed by the proceeds of warfare itself: by plunder and by the imposition of indemnities on defeated enemies. In this sense, warfare became economically self-perpetuating.

At the same time there was a strong link between income from warfare and the increased wealth of certain members of the elite, in particular of military commanders. The indications can be found in our source material, although quantification is difficult. P. Cornelius Scipio Africanus provides a unique example of aristocratic enrichment through his share of the spoils of war (*manubiae*), but even the relatively precise numbers we appear to have for him probably do not tell the whole story.

During the first half of the second century, there is an emerging awareness of basic financial management at a state level on the part of the senate. The terms of the indemnity charged to Antiochus III indicate that the Romans were becoming more aggressive in raising funds for the state, which suggests in turn that the Romans realized that they could raise significant state finance through the imposition of indemnities. As the century progresses, we can observe the Roman senate beginning to match receipts of cash with public expenditure, most obviously on infrastructure. A demonstration of this development came when the Antiochus indemnity was finally paid off in the second half of the 170s. For twelve years the Romans had been receiving over 1,000 talents per annum of incremental revenue from indemnities and suddenly the annual amount dropped to 200 talents (Table 2.2). This must have had an impact, and indeed there are signs that the senate did notice the loss. We have noted how the unusual events of 173 (such as the activities of the consul L. Postumius in Campania) perhaps become more understandable in this context; and it also helps to explain why the Romans seized Perseus' treasure and enslaved 150,000 Epirotes at the end of the Third Macedonian War. In turn, these seizures probably explain the closure of the Macedonian mines in 167. Flush with cash, the Romans did not need to exploit this source of revenue; but, by 158, with no further booty or indemnities arriving in the treasury, there was a requirement for new sources of revenue. From this time onwards output from the silver mines of Macedonia, and especially from those of Spain, grew in importance. By the end of the 150s, the Spanish mines alone were contributing 1,500 talents per annum of revenue and Rome's income from external sources was at least back to the level achieved in the 180s. It is no coincidence that the construction of the Aqua Marcia, the single most expensive building project undertaken during the Republic, begins shortly after the sacking of Carthage and Corinth.

How did Roman thinking about state funding develop? Hopkins believed that 'the Romans made their way rather jerkily from a tradition of plunder to a stable system of taxation'.[2] But the legislation of C. Gracchus marks a very clear change. It stands at the beginning of a more controlled and thoroughgoing exploitation of the resources of the Mediterranean by the Romans. We have argued that Appian was correct in his representation that no revenues were collected by the Romans in Asia until C. Gracchus introduced his *lex Sempronia de provincia Asia* in the late 120s. The latter's introduction of the system of *censoria locatio* under this law was a forward-looking measure for ensuring that the revenues of Asia would be maximized and available to finance his economic programme. As such, it was the first clearly identifiable attempt by an individual Roman magistrate to produce a systematic state budget in support of a massive programme of public expenditure. It produced a stable system of taxation that enabled the Romans to budget for large projects at least five years ahead and reduced their dependency on more variable and less certain forms of income such as plunder and mining revenues.

But the increase in monetary liquidity also had a much wider and more profound impact upon the private sector. If we look at other periods of history, we can see a direct link between expanding supplies of money and economic activity. The impact of New World bullion on the economy of sixteenth-century AD Europe is one example; another is the commercial revolution of the thirteenth century AD, when the increase in demand for luxury goods, backed up by the ready availability of large amounts of silver coin, brought about an enormous quantitative change in the volume of international trade. During the second half of the second century BC, there appears to have been a similarly significant inflection point in both the geographic spread and intensity of commercial and trading networks. We can observe, on the one hand, a huge increase in the export from Italy of more specialized agricultural products such as wine and olive oil and, on the other, the large-scale importation to Italy and the Western Mediterranean of slaves and luxury goods.

Ward-Perkins gives two closely related answers to the question of how a complex economy can produce more commodities than a very basic one, and thereby feed more mouths: 'First, if agricultural products could be readily exported and sold (whether in a regional or an international market), then farmers could specialise in producing those crops for which local conditions were particularly suited. Secondly, specialisation, and the ability to turn crops into cash, allowed farmers to invest in improvements that, in turn, increased productivity yet further.'[3] As the second century progresses, there appears to have been a notable shift in the direction of agricultural exploitation by the Roman elite towards this kind of specialization. We can trace the development of new agricultural techniques and increasing capital investment in newly developed technologies; and we can observe this increased specialization through the introduction of the cash crop, the growth in the use of slavery in the countryside, and the financial logic underlying the kind of farming that Cato's *De Agricultura* and the works of other agrarian writers represent. The evidence from amphorae finds, in both marine and terrestrial contexts, as well as survey evidence, suggests that this intensification of agricultural production was in part a response to the formation of a particular market, a trade in wine to the western Mediterranean, in particular to Gaul. We can date the 'take-off' in this trade to a shift in the shape of amphorae used to transport the wine from

[2] Hopkins 1978: 16. [3] Ward-Perkins 2005: 144.

Graeco-Italic to Dressel 1A, a shift that probably took place between about 150 and 130 BC. This type of intensive investment farming by absentee landlords appears mainly to have occurred in central-western Italy, but it was not, of itself, directly responsible for the tensions that resulted in the agrarian crisis of 133, as some previous commentators have assumed. It was the process of privatization of *ager publicus* in Latium, Etruria, and Campania which took place in the late third and early second centuries that led to the crowding out of smallholders as the Roman elite acquired the most suitably located land to supply the growing metropolis of Rome and to satisfy demand from export markets.

At the same time, a sharp increase in the availability of financial capital in the areas controlled by Rome drove the growth of a high-volume trade in slaves and luxury goods between Italy and the East. In 167, at the end of the Third Macedonian War, the senate guaranteed duty-free status to the port of Delos. Within twenty years or so of this grant, epigraphic evidence shows the beginnings of new communities on the island, principally from the eastern Mediterranean and the Italian peninsula. Strabo's account provides the only surviving testimony to Delos' emergence as a centre of an enormous trade in slaves to the Roman West after the destruction of Corinth in 146, although other sources too mention Delos' status as a major *emporium*. The same demographic evidence of an eastern Mediterranean role in the slave trade also points to a thriving trade in luxury goods, which is further confirmed by inscriptional, literary, and archaeological evidence. Strabo explains that Delos became the preferred location for the slave trade in part for financial reasons, implying the presence of financial intermedaries who provided on-the-spot trade finance to merchants. There is, in fact, considerable epigraphic evidence for the presence of Italian bankers on Delos at this time. Similar developments can be tracked elsewhere in the Mediterranean.

Thus, during the second half of the second century and the beginning of the first, a sharp increase in the availability of financial capital in the areas controlled by Rome drove the growth of a high-volume trade in slaves and luxury goods between Italy and the East. This trade, in turn, contributed to a significant increase in the level of municipal and personal wealth in a number of central Italian cities where members of the local elites appear to have had trading contacts with Delos and the East. This development can be observed most clearly in the euergetism of local magistrates and in the construction of monumental sanctuaries in a number of cities.

The liquidity boom had other effects too. First, the economic stimuli that resulted from the combination of increased trade and large-scale building programmes would have been profound, because of the multiplier effects of these developments on the wider economy. Indeed we can trace the growth of a manufacturing sector in support of such activities, although elite involvement seems to have been limited to the provision of raw materials to nucleated workshops, each operated by an individual proprietor, rather than the ownership of large-scale manufactories themselves. The lack of a second-century equivalent to Cicero who might provide more detail is particularly frustrating, but the example of Cato the Elder shows that the modern portrayal of agriculture as being of overwhelming importance for elite investment during the second century obscures a more complex range of other interests, such as finance and the exploitation of natural resources. Secondly, there was a significant increase in the level of individual wealth. Men such as the eminent

Sicilian, Sthenius of Thermae, who had made his money in Asia in the late second century, and Atticus' father, an *eques*, who left his son an inheritance equivalent to 83 talents, are examples of this trend. The dominance of the *publicani* in construction projects, mining, tax-farming, and the other activities that Polybius describes suggests that groups of wealthy men either had, or could raise, huge sums of money more easily than the state and could better afford to spread their risks over several years.[4] The prosperity of the *publicani* would have increased even further when they gained control of the Spanish mines and probably of the Macedonian mines by the mid-150s and when they acquired responsibility for revenue collection in Asia in the 120s.

But there were other, less welcome side-effects. We know from Cicero's *De Imperio Cn. Pompeii* that there was a credit crisis at Rome in 88, as a result of Mithradates VI's invasion of the province of Asia. At the same time, there are other indications of economic and monetary problems in the 80s. By the 60s BC, there is the virtual disappearance from our sources of any mention of *argentarii* and of the form of financial intermediation that they had provided during the second century. Instead we mainly hear of wealthy individuals ('aristocratic financiers', as Andreau terms them) providing credit to fellow members of the elite, as well as to kings and cities in the Hellenistic East. We have argued that this was a reflection of a real change in the way the market for credit operated at Rome rather than merely of the existing financial practices of an elite of which our principal source, Cicero, was a member. By the mid-first century BC there were probably fewer banks in existence, with smaller balance sheets; the main providers of credit had become 'aristocratic financiers', instead of the *argentarii*; and this development could, at the very least, have prevented the wider Roman economy from reaching its full potential.

Nevertheless, there can be little doubt that successful warfare did produce a major increase in the growth potential of the Republican economy of the second and first centuries BC and there is considerable evidence for aggregate growth occurring in the volume of output and trade. But it is less clear whether this resulted in *real per capita* economic growth. In the previous chapter we attempted to produce probabilistic quantifications of the size of the Italian economy at three different dates, 150, 100, and 50 BC, so that, by comparing the conjectured size of the economy at each of these dates, we could see whether real per capita economic growth occurred. For each date, we tried to reconstruct Italian GDP by producing estimates from the income side. The sporadic notices in ancient sources of individual elite wealth were used as a starting point and income pyramids were extrapolated from these data. Next, an attempt was made to quantify Italian GDP from the expenditure side for the same dates, by examining state and private investment and consumption, as well as the balance of trade. Large parts of this exercise involved a high degree of guesswork, but again it was possible to construct a probabilistic quantification that fitted with the estimates of GDP from the income side. Finally, hypothetical numbers for the Italian money supply and its velocity of circulation were constructed for the same dates to see whether these too could theoretically fit with the estimates of GDP from the income side. These three different approaches

[4] Polyb. 6. 17. 2.

are unlikely to be even remotely accurate taken individually, but together they give some degree of probabilistic plausibility. Our conclusion was that it is very likely that real per capita economic growth did occur in mainland Italy between 150 and 50 BC and our model suggests that real GDP per capita in mainland Italy increased by 72 per cent between 150 and 50 BC, an average annual compound growth rate of 0.54 per cent.

Bibliography

Alföldy, C. (1974). *Noricum*. London.

Allen, R.C. (2009). 'How Prosperous were the Romans?: Evidence from Diocletian's Price Edict', in Bowman and Wilson (2009*a*), 327–45.

Almeida, E. R. (1984). *Il Monte Testaccio: ambiente, storia, materiali*. Rome.

Amandry, M., Hurter, S., and Bérend, D. (eds.) (1999). *Travaux de numismatique grecque offerts à George Le Rider*. London.

Anderloni, L., Llewellyn, D. T., and Schmidt, R.H. (eds.) (2009). *Financial Innovation*. London.

Andreau, J. (1968). 'Banque grecque et banque romaine dans le théâtre de Plaute et de Térence', *MEFR* 80: 461–526.

—— (1978). 'Financiers de l'aristocratie à la fin de la république', in Frézouls (1978), 47–62.

—— (1984). 'Histoire des métiers bancaires et évolution économique', *Opus* 3: 99–114.

—— (1987). *La Vie financière dans le monde romain: Les métiers de manieurs d'argent (IVe siècle av. J.-C.-IIIe siècle ap. J.-C.)*. Rome.

—— (1999). *Banking and Business in the Roman World*. Cambridge.

—— (2002). 'Markets, Fairs and Monetary Loans', in Cartledge, Cohen, and Foxhall (2002), 113–29.

Aperghis, G. G. (2001). 'Population—Production—Taxation—Coinage: A Model for the Seleukid Economy', in Archibald et al., 69–102.

—— (2004). *The Seleukid Royal Economy: The Finances and Financial Administration of the Seleukid Empire*. Cambridge.

Appadurai, A. (1986). *The Social Life of Things: Commodities in Cultural Perspective*. Cambridge.

Archi, G. G., David, M., Levy, E., Marichal, R., and Nelson, H. L. W. (1956). *Pauli Sententiarum Fragmentum Leidense (Cod. Leid. B.P.L. 2589)*. Leiden.

Archibald, Z. H., Davies, J., Gabrielsen, V., and Oliver, G. J. (eds.) (2001). *Hellenistic Economies*. London.

Arthur, P. (1991). *The Romans in Northern Campania: Settlement and Land Use around the Massico and the Garigliano Basin*. Archaeological Monographs of the British School at Rome 1. London.

Ashby, T. (1935). *The Aqueducts of Ancient Rome*. Oxford.

Ashton, R. (2013). 'The Use of the Cistophoric Weight Standard outside the Pergamene Kingdom', in Thonemann (2013*a*), 245–64.

Astin, A. E. (1967). *Scipio Aemilianus*. Oxford.

—— (1978). *Cato the Censor*. Oxford.

Attolini, I. (1991). 'Political Geography and Productive Geography between the Valleys of the Albegna and the Flora in Northern Etruria', in Barker and Lloyd, 142–52.

Aubert, J.-J. (1994). *Business Managers in Ancient Rome: A Social and Economic Study of* Institores: *200 bc–ad 250*. Leiden.

—— (ed.) (2003). *Tâches publiques et enterprise privée dans le monde romain: Actes du Diplôme d'Études Avancées, Universités de Neuchâtel et de Lausanne 2000–2002*. Geneva.

—— (2004). 'The Republican Economy and Roman Law: Regulation, Promotion, or Reflection?', in Flower, 160–78.

Backendorf, D. (1998). *Römische Münzschätze des zweiten und ersten Jahrhunderts v. Chr. vom italienischen Festland*. Berlin.

Badian, E. (1968). *Roman Imperialism in the Late Republic*. 2nd edn. Oxford.

—— (1972). *Publicans and Sinners: Private Enterprise in the Service of the Roman Republic*. Ithaca, NY.

Bairoch, P. (1977). 'Estimations du revenu national dans les sociétés occidentales pré-industrielles et au dix-neuvième siècle: Propositions d'approches indirectes', *Revue économique* 28.2: 177–208.

Bang, P. F. (2009). 'The Ancient Economy and New Institutional Economics', *JRS* 99: 194–206.

Barker, G. (1995). *A Mediterranean Valley: Landscape Archaeology and Annales History in the Biferno Valley*. London.

—— and Lloyd, J. (eds.) (1991). *Roman Landscapes: Archaeological Survey in the Mediterranean Region*. Archaeological Monographs of the British School at Rome 2. London.

Barlow, C. T. (1978). 'Bankers, Moneylenders and Interest Rates in the Roman Republic', Ph.D. Thesis, University of North Carolina, Chapel Hill.

Beard, M. (2007). *The Roman Triumph*. Cambridge, Mass.

Bechtold, B. (2007). 'Alcune osservazioni sui rapporti commerciali fra Cartagine, la Sicilia occidentale e la Campania (IV-metà del II sec. a.C.): nuovi dati basati sulla distribuzione di ceramiche campane e nordafricane/cartaginesi', *BABesch* 82.1: 51–76.

Begley, V. and De Puma, R. (eds.) (1991). *Rome and India: The Ancient Sea Trade*. Madison, Wis.

Bell, M. (2007). 'An Archaeologist's Perspective on the *Lex Hieronica*', in Dubouloz and Pittia, 187–203.

—— and Holloway, R. R. (1988). 'Excavations at Morgantina, 1980–1985: Preliminary Report XII', *AJA* 92.3: 313–42.

Beloch, K. J. (1886). *Die Bevölkerung der griechisch-römischen Welt* Leipzig.

Benoit, F. (1952). 'L'Archéologie sous-marine en Provence', *Rivista di Studi Liguri* 18: 249–55.

Berger, A. (1953). 'Encyclopedic Dictionary of Roman Law', *TAPS* 43.2: 335–807.

Berry, C. (1994). *The Idea of Luxury: A Conceptual and Historical Investigation*. Cambridge.

Bilde, P., Engberg-Pedersen, T., Hannestad, L., Zahle, J., and Randsborg, K. (1993). *Centre and Periphery in the Hellenistic World*. Studies in Hellenistic Civilization, 4. Aarhus.

Bintliff, J. and Sbonias, K. (eds.) (1999). *Reconstructing Past Population Trends in Mediterranean Europe (3000 bc–ad 1800)*. Oxford.

Black, A., Wright, P., Bachman, J. E., and Davies, J. (1998). *In Search of Shareholder Value: Managing the Drivers of Performance*. London.

Bodei Giglioni, G. (1977). 'Pecunia fanatica: l'incidenza economica dei templi laziali', *Rivista Storica Italiana* 89: 33–76.

Bogaert, R. (1968). *Banques et banquiers dans les cités grecques*. Leiden.

—— (1976). *Epigraphica III: Texts on Bankers, Banking and Credit in the Greek World*. Leiden.

—— (1994). *Trapezitica Aegyptiaca: Recueil de recherches sur la banque en Égypte gréco-romaine*. Florence.

Bon, S. E. and Jones, R. (eds.) (1997). *Sequence and Space in Pompeii*. Oxford.

Bongenaar, A. C. V. M. (ed.) (2000). *Interdependency of Institutions and Private Entrepreneurs*. MOS Studies 2. Leiden.

Bordo, M. D. and Jonung, L. (1987). *The Long-run Behaviour of the Velocity of Circulation: The International Evidence*. Cambridge.

—— —— (1990). 'The Long-run Behaviour of Velocity: The Institutional Approach Revisited', *Journal of Poly Modeling* 12: 165–97.

Boussac, M.-Fr. (1988). 'Sceaux déliens', *RA* 1988: 307–40.

—— (1993). 'Archives personnelles à Délos', *CRAI* 1993: 677–93.

Bowman, A. K. (forthcoming). 'Taxation and Fiscal Controls', in Bowman and Wilson (forthcoming *a*).

—— and Wilson, A. (eds.) (2009*a*). *Quantifying the Roman Economy: Methods and Problems*. Oxford Studies on the Roman Economy 1. Oxford.

—— —— (2009*b*). 'Quantifying the Roman Economy: Integration, Growth and Decline?', in Bowman and Wilson (2009*a*), 3–84.

——— (eds.) (2011). *Settlement, Urbanisation and Population.* Oxford Studies on the Roman Economy 2. Oxford.

——— (eds.) (forthcoming *a*). *Trade, Commerce and the State in the Roman World.* Oxford Studies on the Roman Economy 4. Oxford.

——— (eds.) (forthcoming *b*). *Mining, Metal Supply, and Coinage in the Roman World.* Oxford Studies on the Roman Economy 5. Oxford.

Brännvall, M.-L., Bindler, R., Emteryd, O., Nilsson, M., and Renberg, I. (1997). 'Stable Isotope and Concentration Records of Atmospheric Lead Pollution in Peat and Lake Sediments in Sweden', *Water, Air, and Soil Pollution* 100: 243–52.

——— Renberg, I., Emteryd, O., Bartnicki, J., and Billström, K. (1999). 'The Mediaeval Metal Industry was the Cradle of Modern Large-scale Atmospheric Lead Pollution in Northern Europe', *Environmental Science and Technology* 33: 4391–5.

Braudel, F. (1985). *Civilisation and Capitalism 15th–18th Century*, iii. *The Perspective of the World.* London.

Brehaut, E. (1933). *Cato the Censor on Farming.* New York.

Bresson, A. (2002). 'Italiens et Romains à Rhodes et à Caunos', in Müller and Hasenohr, 147–62.

—— and Descat, R. (eds.) (2001). *Les Cités d'Asie Mineure occidentale au IIe siècle a.C.* Bordeaux.

Britnell, R. H. and Campbell, B. M. S. (eds.) (1995). *A Commercialising Economy: England, 1086 to c. 1300.* Manchester.

Broughton, T. R. S. (1938). 'Roman Asia', in Frank (1938), 499–916.

Brun, J.-P. (1999). 'Laudatissimum fuit antiquitus in Delo insula: La Maison 1B du Quartier du Stade et la production des parfums à Délos', *BCH* 123: 87–155.

—— (2004). *Archéologie du vin et de l'huile dans l'Empire romain.* Paris.

Bruneau, P. (1969). 'Documents sur l'industrie délienne de la pourpre', *BCH* 93: 759–91.

—— (1978). 'La Fabrication de la pourpre à Delos', *BCH* 102: 110–14.

Bruno, V. J. and Scott, R. T. (1993). *Cosa IV: The Houses.* Memoirs of the American Academy in Rome 38. Pennsylvania.

Brunt, P. A. (1950). 'Pay and Superannuation in the Roman Army', *PBSR* 18: 50–71.

—— (1971*a*). *Italian Manpower 225 B.C.–A.D. 14.* Oxford.

—— (1971*b*). *Social Conflicts in the Roman Republic.* London.

—— (1980). 'Free Labour and Public Works at Rome', *JRS* 70: 81–100.

—— (1988). *The Fall of the Roman Republic.* Oxford.

Buck, C. H. (1940). *A Chronology of the Plays of Plautus.* Baltimore.

Burn, A. R. (1962). *Persia and the Greeks.* London.

Burnett, A.M. (1982). 'The Currency of Italy from the Hannibalic War to the Reign of Augustus', *Annali dell'Istituto Italiano di Numismatica* 29: 125–37.

—— (1987*a*). *Coinage in the Roman World.* London.

—— (1987*b*). 'Africa', in Burnett and Crawford, 175–85.

—— (1989). 'The Beginnings of Roman Coinage', *Annali dell'Istituto Italiano di Numismatica* 36: 33–64.

—— (1991). *Interpreting the Past: Coins.* London.

—— (1998). 'The Coinage of the Social War', in Burnett, Wartenberg, and Witschonke, 165–72.

—— and Crawford, M. H. (eds.) (1987). *The Coinage of the Roman World in the Late Republic: Proceedings of a Colloquium Held at the British Museum.* BAR International Series 326. Oxford.

—— Amandry, M., and Ripollès, P. P. (1992). *Roman Provincial Coinage*, i. London.

—— Wartenberg, U., and Witschonke, R. (eds.) (1998). *Coins of Macedonia and Rome: Essays in Honour of Charles Hersh.* London.

Bury, J. B., Barber, E. A., Bevan, E., and Tarn, W. W. (eds.) (1923). *The Hellenistic Age: Aspects of Hellenistic Civilisation.* Cambridge.
Buttrey, T. V. (1989). 'Review of Crawford (1985)', *CP* 84: 69–76.
——(1993). 'Calculating Ancient Coin Production: Facts and Fantasies', *NC* 153: 335–52.
——(1994). 'Calculating Ancient Coin Production II: Why It Cannot Be Done', *NC* 154: 341–52.
——Erim, K. T., Groves, T. D., and Holloway, R. R. (1989). *The Coins: Morgantina Studies*, ii. Princeton, NJ.
Callender, M. H. (1965). *Roman Amphorae with Index of Stamps.* London.
Camodeca, G. (1999). *Tabulae Pompeianae Sulpiciorum. TPSulp: edizione critica dell'archivio puteolano dei Sulpicii.* Rome.
Campbell, B. (2000). *The Writings of the Roman Land Surveyors. Introduction, Text, Translation, and Commentary.* London.
Campo, M. (ed.) (1995). *Tresors del món antic, VII Cicle de Conferències, Barcelona, del 14 al 30 de novembre de 1994.* Barcelona.
Canali de Rossi, F. (2002). *Iscrizioni storiche ellenistiche: decreti per ambasciatori greci al senato. Testo critico, traduzioni e commento.* Rome.
Carafa, P. (1997). 'What was Pompeii before 200 bc? Excavations at the House of Josephus II, in the Triangular Forum and in the House of the Wedding of Hercules', in Bon and Jones, 13–31.
Carandini, A. (1983). 'Columella's Vineyard and the Rationality of the Roman Economy', *Opus* 2: 177–203.
——(1989). 'Italian Wine and African Oil: Commerce in a World Empire', in Randsborg, 15–24.
——and Cambi, F. (eds.), with M. G. Celuzza and E. Fentress (2002). *Paesaggi d'Etruria: Valle dell'Albegna, Valle d'Oro, Valle del Chiarone, Valle del Tafone.* Rome.
——and Ricci, A. (eds.) (1985). *Settefinestre: una villa schiavistica nell'Etruria romana.* Modena.
——and Settis, S. (1979). *Schiavi e padroni nell' Etruria romana: la villa di Settefinestre dallo scavo alla mostra.* Bari.
Carlsen, J. (2003). 'Public Land in the Western Provinces of the Roman Empire', in Aubert (2003), 179–92.
——and Lo Cascio, E. (eds.) (2009). *Agricoltura e scambi nell'Italia tardo-repubblicana.* Bari.
Carradice, I. (1983). *Coinage and Finances in the Reign of Domitian, ad 81–96.* BAR International Series 178. Oxford.
Carter, H. and Partington, I. (1981). *Applied Economics in Banking and Finance,* 2nd edn. Oxford.
Cartledge, P. A. and Harvey, F. D. (1985). *Crux: Essays in Greek History Presented to G. E. M. de Ste. Croix on his 75th Birthday.* London.
——Cohen, E. E., and Foxhall, L. (eds.) (2002). *Money, Labour and Land: Approaches to the Economies of Ancient Greece.* London.
Casson, L. (ed.) (1989). *The Periplus Maris Erythraei.* Princeton, NJ.
——(1991). 'Ancient Naval Technology and the Route to India', in Begley and De Puma, 8–11.
Cébeillac-Gervasoni, C. (1998). *Les Magistrats des cités italiennes de la seconde guerre punique à Auguste.* Rome.
——(2002). 'Note relative aux élites du Latium et de la Campanie et à leurs rapports avec la Méditerranée orientale', in Müller and Hasenohr, 21–8.
Celuzza, M. G. and Regoli, E. (1982). 'La Valle d'Oro nel territorio di Cosa', *DArch* ns 4: 31–62.
Chandarvarkar, A. G. (1977). 'Monetization of Developing Economies', *International Monetary Fund Staff Papers* 24.3: 665–715.

Chankowski, V. and Duyrat, F. (eds.) (2004). *Le Roi et l'économie: autonomies locales et structures royales dans l'économie de l'empire séleucide. Actes des rencontres de Lille (23 juin 2003) et d'Orléans (29–30 janvier 2004).* Topoi: Orient-Occident, Suppl. 6. Lyons.
Chevallier, R. (1958). 'Essai de chronologie des centuriations romaines de Tunisie', *MEFRA* 70: 61–128.
——(1976). *Roman Roads.* London.
——(1983). *La Romanisation de la Celtique du Pô: Essai d'histoire provinciale.* Rome.
Chorley, R. J. and Haggett, P. (1968). *Socio-economic Models in Geography.* London.
Christie, N. (ed.) (1995). *Settlement and Economy in Italy, 1500 BC–AD 1500: Papers of the Fifth Conference of Italian Archaeology.* Oxford.
Christol, M. (2002). 'Narbonne: Un autre *emporion* à la fin de l'époque républicaine et à l'époque augustéenne', in Müller and Hasenohr, 41–54.
Churchill, J. B. (1999). '*Ex qua quod vellent facerent*: Roman Magistrates' Authority over *Praeda* and *Manubiae*', *TAPA* 129: 85–116.
Clavel-Lévêque, M. and Hermon, E. (eds.) (2004). *Espaces intégrés et ressources naturelles dans l'Empire romain.* Franche-Comté.
Clayton, G. (1971). *British Insurance.* London.
Clemente, G. (1974). *I romani nella Gallia meridionale, II–I sec. a.C.: politica ed economia nell'età dell' imperialismo.* Bologna.
——Coarelli, F., and Gabba, E. (eds.) (1990). *Storia di Roma II : L'impero mediterraneo, i. La repubblica imperiale.* Turin.
Coarelli, F. (1977). 'Public Building in Rome between the Second Punic War and Sulla', *PBSR* 32: 1–23.
——(1982). 'L' "Agora des italiens" a Delo: il mercato degli schiavi?', in Coarelli, Musti, and Solin, 119–45.
——(2005). 'L' "Agora des italiens". Lo statarion di Delo?', *JRA* 18: 196–212.
——(2007). *Rome and Environs : An Archaeological Guide.* Berkeley and Los Angeles.
—— and Patterson, H. (eds.) (2008). *Mercator Placidissimus: The Tiber Valley in Antiquity: New Research in the Upper and Middle River Valley. Rome, 27-28 February 2004.* Rome.
——Musti, D., and Solin, H. (1982). *Delo e l'Italia.* Opuscula Instituti Romani Finlandiae 2. Rome.
Cockle, H. (1981). 'Pottery Manufacture in Roman Egypt: A New Papyrus', *JRS* 71: 87–97.
Cohen, E. E. (1992). *Athenian Economy and Society: A Banking Perspective.* Princeton, NJ.
——(2005). 'Commercial Law', in Gagarin and Cohen, 290–302.
Cooley, A. (2003). *Pompeii.* London.
Cornell, T. J. (1989*a*). 'The Recovery of Rome', in *CAH* VII.2^2, 309–50.
——(1989*b*). 'The Conquest of Italy', in *CAH* VII.2^2, 351–419.
——(1995). *The Beginnings of Rome: Italy and Rome from the Bronze Age to the Punic Wars (c.1000–264 BC).* London.
——(1996). 'Hannibal's Legacy: The Effects of the Hannibalic War on Italy', in Cornell, Rankov, and Sabin, 97–113.
——(2000). 'The City of Rome in the Middle Republic (400–100 BC)', in Coulston and Dodge, 42–60.
——and Matthews, J. F. (1982). *Atlas of the Roman World.* Oxford.
——Rankov, B., and Sabin, P. (eds.) (1996). *The Second Punic War: A Reappraisal.* London.
Cottier, M., Crawford, M. H., Crowther C. V., Ferrary, J. L., Levick, B. M., Salomies, O., and Wörrle, M. (2008). *The Customs Law of Asia.* Oxford.
Cotton, M. A. (1979). *The Late Republican Villa at Posto, Francolise.* London.
——and Métraux, G. P. R. (1985). *The San Rocca Villa at Francolise.* Rome.
Coulston, J. and Dodge, H. (eds.) (2000). *Ancient Rome: The Archaeology of the Eternal City.* Oxford.

Crawford, M. H. (1964). 'War and Finance', *JRS* 54: 29–32.
—— (1969*a*). *Roman Republican Coin Hoards*. London.
—— (1969*b*). 'Coin Hoards and the Pattern of Violence in the Late Republic', *PBSR* 37: 76–81.
—— (1970). 'Money and Exchange in the Roman World', *JRS* 60: 40–8.
—— (1974). *Roman Republican Coinage*. London.
—— (1985). *Coinage and Money under the Roman Republic: Italy and the Mediterranean Economy*. London.
—— (ed.) (1996). *Roman Statutes*. BICS Suppl. 64. London.
—— (2008). 'States Waiting in the Wings', in De Ligt and Northwood, 631–43.
—— (forthcoming). 'Metal and Coinage', in Bowman and Wilson (forthcoming *b*).
Crawley Quinn, J. (2004). 'The Role of the 146 Settlement in the Provincialization of Africa', in Khanoussi, Ruggeri, and Vismara, 1593–601.
Crook, J. (1976). 'Classical Roman Law and the Sale of Land', in Finley (1976), 71–83.
Cruickshank, W. W. (1992). *Apodosis: Essays Presented to Dr W. W. Cruickshank to Mark his Eightieth Birthday*. London.
Cunliffe, B. (ed.) (1988). *The Temple of Sulis Minerva at Bath*, ii. *The Finds from the Sacred Spring*. Oxford.
Dalby, A. (1998). *Cato: On Farming*. Totnes.
Dancy, J. C. (1954). *A Commentary on I Maccabees*. Oxford.
D'Arms, J. H. (1981). *Commerce and Social Standing in Ancient Rome*. Cambridge, Mass.
—— (2003). *Romans on the Bay of Naples*. Bari. First published 1970, Cambridge.
—— and Kopff, E. C. (eds.) (1980). *The Seaborne Commerce of Ancient Rome: Studies in Archaeology and History*. MemAmAc 36. Rome.
David, J.-M. (1996). *The Roman Conquest of Italy*. Oxford.
Davies, O. (1935). *Roman Mines in Europe*. Oxford.
De Callataÿ, F. (1987). 'La Politique monétaire de Mithridate VI Eupator, roi du Pont (120–63 av. J.-C.)', in Depeyrot, Hackens, and Moucharte, 55–66.
—— (1989). 'Les Trésors achéménides et les monnayages d'Alexandre: espèces immobilisées et espèces circulantes?', *REA* 91: 259–74.
—— (1995). 'Calculating Ancient Coin Production: Seeking a Balance', *NC* 155: 289–311.
—— (1997). 'Le Volume des émissions monétaires dans l'antiquité', *Annali dell'Istituto Italiano di Numismatica* 44: 53–62.
—— (1998). 'The Coins in the Name of Sura', in Burnett, Wartenberg, and Witschonke, 113–17.
—— (2004). 'La Richesse des rois séleucides et le problème de la taxation en nature', in Chankowski and Duyrat, 23–47.
—— (2005). 'The Graeco-Roman Economy in the Super Long-run: Lead, Copper, and Shipwrecks', *JRA* 18: 361–72.
—— (2013). 'The Coinages of the Attalids and their Neighbours: A Panoramic View', in Thonemann (2013*a*), 207–44.
—— Depeyrot, G., and Villaronga, L. (eds.) (1993). *L'Argent monnayé d'Alexandre le Grand à Auguste*. Brussels.
De Jesus, P. (1978). 'Metal Resources in Ancient Anatolia', *AS* 28: 97–102.
De Laet, S. J. (1949). *Portorium*. Bruges.
DeLaine, J. (1995). 'The Supply of Building Materials to the City of Rome: Some Economic Implications', in Christie, 555–62.
—— (2000). 'Building the Eternal City: the Construction Industry in Imperial Rome', in Coulston and Dodge, 119–41.
—— (2001). 'Bricks and Mortar: Exploring the Economics of Building Techniques at Rome and Ostia', in Mattingly and Salmon (2001*a*), 230–68.
De Ligt, L. (1991). 'Review of Andreau (1987)', *Mnemosyne* 44: 490–7.

——(2000). 'Studies in Legal and Agrarian History II: Tenancy under the Republic', *Athenaeum* 88: 377–91.

——(2002). 'Restraining the Rich, Protecting the Poor: Symbolic Aspects of Roman Legislation', in Jongman and Kleijwegt, 1–45.

——(2004). 'Poverty and Demography: The Case of the Gracchan Land Reforms', *Mnemosyne* 57: 725–57.

——(2007). 'Roman Law and the Roman Economy: Three Case Studies', *Latomus* 66: 10–25.

——(2012). *Peasants, Citizens and Soldiers: Studies in the Demographic History of Roman Italy 225 BC–AD 100*. Cambridge.

——and Northwood, S. (eds.) (2008). *People, Land and Politics: Demographic Developments and the Transformation of Italy, 300 BC–AD 14*. Leiden.

Demougin, S., et al. (1994). *L'Italie d'Auguste à Dioclétien: Actes du colloque international (Rome, 25–28 mars 1992)*. Rome.

De Neeve, P. W. (1984). *Colonus: Private Farm-Tenancy in Roman Italy during the Republic and the Early Principate*. Amsterdam.

——(1985). 'The Price of Agricultural Land in Roman Italy and the Problem of Economic Rationalism', *Opus* 4: 77–109.

Deniaux, E. (2002). 'Les *gentes* de Délos et la mobilité sociale à Rome au Ier siècle av. J.-C.: l'exemple de Marcus Seius et des Seii', in Müller and Hasenohr, 29–39.

Depeyrot, G. (1993). 'La République romaine', in De Callataÿ, Depeyrot, and Villaronga, 77–110.

——Hackens, T., and Moucharte, G. (eds.) (1987). *Rhythmes de la production monétaire de l'antiquité à nos jours: actes du colloque international organisé à Paris du 10 au 12 janvier 1986*. Louvain-la-Neuve.

De Roover, R. (1948). *Money, Banking, and Credit in Mediaeval Bruges*. Cambridge, Mass.

Derow, P. S. (1979). 'Polybius, Rome, and the East', *JRS* 69: 1–15.

——(1988). 'Rome, the Fall of Macedon and the Sack of Corinth', in *CAH* VIII^2, 290–323.

——(2003). 'The Arrival of Rome: from the Illyrian Wars to the Fall of Macedon', in Erskine, 51–70.

De Ste. Croix, G. E. M. (1956). 'Greek and Roman Accounting', in Littleton and Yamey, 14–74.

De Sanctis, G. (1916). *Storia dei Romani III*. 7 pts. in 4 vols. Turin.

Desy, P. (1989). *Les Timbres amphoriques de l'Apulie républicaine*. Oxford.

De Vries, J. and van der Woude, A. (1997). *The First Modern Economy: Success, Failure, and Perseverance of the Dutch Economy, 1500–1815*. Cambridge.

Di Giuseppe, H. (1994). 'La Villa romana di S. Pietro di Tolve: rapporto preliminare di scavo 1988–1992', *BollStBas* 10: 91–120.

Dix, B. (1982). 'The Manufacture of Lime and its Uses in the Western Roman Provinces', *Oxford Journal of Archaeology* 1: 331–45.

Dodge, H. (2000). '"Greater than the Pyramids": The Water Supply of Ancient Rome', in Coulston and Dodge, 166–209.

Domergue, C. (1990). *Les Mines de la péninsule ibérique dans l'antiquité romaine*. Rome.

Dubouloz, J. and Pittia, S. (eds.) (2007). *La Sicile de Cicéron: Lectures de Verrines. Actes du colloque de Paris, 19–20 mai 2006, organisé par l'UMR 8585, Centre Gustave Glotz*. Besançon.

Duncan-Jones, R. P. (1974). *The Economy of the Roman Empire: Quantitative Studies*. Cambridge.

——(1976). 'The Price of Wheat in Roman Egypt under the Principate', *Chiron* 6: 241–62.

——(1987). 'Weight-loss as an Index of Coin Wear in Currency of the Roman Principate' in Depeyrot, Hackens, and Moucharte, 237–56.

——(1990). *Structure and Scale in the Roman Economy*. Cambridge.

DUNCAN-JONES, R. P. (1994). *Money and Government in the Roman Empire*. Cambridge.
—— (2006). 'Roman Customs Dues: A Comparative View', *Latomus* 65: 3–16.
DYSON, S. L. (1978). 'Settlement Patterns in the *Ager Cosanus*: The Wesleyan University Survey 1974–76', *JFA* 5: 251–68.
ECK, W. and MÜLLER-LUCKNER, E. (eds.) (1999). *Lokale Autonomie und römische Ordnungsmacht in den kaiserzeitlichen Provinzen vom 1. bis 3. Jahrhundert*. Munich.
ECKSTEIN, A. M. (2008). *Rome Enters the Greek East*. Oxford.
EDWARDS, C. and WOOLF, G. (eds.) (2003). *Rome the Cosmopolis*. Cambridge.
ENGELMANN, H. and KNIBBE, D. (1986). 'Das *Monumentum Ephesenum*. Ein Vorbericht', *EA* 8: 19–32.
—— —— (1989). 'Das Zollgesetz der Provinz Asia. Eine neue Inschrift aus Ephesos', *EA* 14: 1–206.
ERDKAMP, P. (1998). *Hunger and the Sword: Warfare and Food Supply in Roman Republican Wars (264–30 BC)*. Amsterdam.
—— (2005). *The Grain Market in the Roman Empire: A Social, Political and Economic Study*. Cambridge.
ERSKINE, A. (ed.) (2003). *A Companion to the Hellenistic World*. Oxford.
ÉTIENNE, R. (1958). *Le Culte impérial dans la Péninsule Ibérique, d'Auguste à Dioclétien*. Paris.
FABBRICOTTI, E. and MENOZZI, G. (2006). *Cirenaica: studi, scavi e scoperte. Atti del X Convegno di Archeologia Cirenaica. Chieti 24–26 Novembre 2003. Nuovi dati da città e territorio*. BAR International Series. Oxford.
FALLU, E. (1973). 'Les *rationes* du proconsul Cicéron. Un exemple de style administratif et d'interprétation historique dans la correspondance de Cicéron', *ANRW* 1.3: 208–38.
FAUST, S. (1994). 'Die Klinen', in Hellenkemper Salies, i. 573–606.
FENTRESS, E. (1994). 'Cosa in the Empire: The Unmaking of a Roman Town', *JRA* 7: 208–22.
—— (2001). 'Villas, Wine and Kilns: The Landscape of Jerba in the Late Hellenistic Period', *JRA* 14.1: 249–86.
—— and PERKINS, P. (1988). 'Counting African Red Slip Ware', *L'Africa Romana* 5: 205–21.
FERRARY, J.-L. (2001). 'Rome et les cités grecques d'Asie Mineure au IIe siècle', in Bresson and Descat, 93–106.
—— (2002). 'La Création de la province d'Asie et la présence italienne en Asie Mineure', in Müller and Hasenohr, 133–46.
FINLEY, M. I. (ed.) (1976). *Studies in Roman Property*. Cambridge.
—— (1985*a*). *Ancient History: Evidence and Models*. London.
—— (1985*b*). *The Ancient Economy*, 2nd edn. London.
FISCHER, S., DORNBUSCH, R., and SCHMALENSEE, R. (1988). *Introduction to Macroeconomics*, 2nd edn. New York.
FISHER, D. (1989). 'The Price Revolution: A Monetary Interpretation', *Journal of Economic History* 49.4: 883–902.
FISHER, I. (1911). *The Purchasing Power of Money*. London.
FLAMBARD, J.-M. (1982). 'Observations sur la nature des *magistri* italiens de Délos', in Coarelli, Musti, and Solin, 67–77.
FLOWER, H. I. (ed.) (2004). *The Cambridge Companion to The Roman Republic*. Cambridge.
FOXHALL, L. (1990). 'The Dependant Tenant: Land Leasing and Labour in Italy and Greece', *JRS* 80: 97–114.
FRANK, T. (1924). 'Roman Census Statistics from 225 to 28 BC', *CP* 19: 329–41.
—— (1933). *An Economic Survey of Ancient Rome*, i. *Rome and Italy of the Republic*. Baltimore.
—— (ed.) (1937). *An Economic Survey of Ancient Rome*, iii. *Britain, Spain, Sicily, Gaul*. Baltimore.

——(ed.) (1938). *An Economic Survey of Ancient Rome*, iv. *Africa, Syria, Greece, Asia Minor*. Baltimore.

Fraser, P. M. (1972). *Ptolemaic Alexandria*, i. Oxford.

——and Bean, G. E. (1954). *The Rhodian Peraea and Islands*. London.

Frederiksen, M. W. (1959). 'Republican Capua: A Social and Economic Study', *PBSR* 27: 80–130.

——(1966). 'Caesar, Cicero and the Problem of Debt', *JRS* 56: 128–41.

——(1970–1). 'The Contribution of Archaeology to the Agrarian Problem in the Gracchan Period', *Dialoghi di archeologia* 4–5: 330–57.

Frézouls, E. (ed.) (1978). *Le Dernier Siècle de la république romaine et l'époque augustéene*. Strasbourg.

Friedman, H. (forthcoming). 'Atmospheric Pollution Proxies for Roman Metal Production', in Bowman and Wilson (forthcoming *b*).

Frier, B. W. (1976). 'Review of M. H. Crawford's *Roman Republican Coinage*', *Phoenix* 30: 375–82.

——(1981). 'Roman Coinage and Army Pay: Techniques for Evaluating Statistics', *QT* 10: 28–95.

Fry, M. J. (1995). *Money, Interest, and Banking in Economic Development*, 2nd edn. Baltimore.

Fulford, M. and Wallace-Hadrill, A. (1999). 'Towards a History of Pre-Roman Pompeii: Excavations beneath the House of Amarantus (I.9.11-12), 1995–8', *PBSR* 67: 37–144.

Fülle, G. (1997). 'The International Organization of the Arretine *Terra Sigllata* Industry: Problems of Evidence and Interpretation', *JRS* 87: 111–55.

Gabba, E. (1972). 'Urbanizzazione e rinnovamenti urbanistichi nell' Italia centro-meridionale del 1 secolo a.C.', *SCO* 21: 73–112.

——(1988*a*). *Del buon uso della ricchezza*. Milan.

——(1988*b*). 'Riflessioni antiche e moderne sulle attività commerciali a Roma nei secoli II e I a.C.', in Gabba (1988*a*), 89–105.

——(1988*c*). 'Ricchezza e classe dirigente romana fra III e I sec. a.C.', in Gabba (1988*a*), 27–44.

——(1989). 'Rome and Italy in the Second Century BC', in *CAH* VIII^2, 197–243.

Gabrielli, C. (2003). 'Lucius Postumius Megellus at Gabii: A new fragment of Livy', *CQ* 53: 247–59.

Gabrielsen, V. (1993). 'Rhodes and Rome after the Third Macedonian War', in Bilde et al., 132–61.

——(1997). *The Naval Aristocracy of Hellenistic Rhodes*. Studies in Hellenistic Civilization 6. Aarhus.

——(2001). 'The Rhodian Associations and Economic Activity', in Archibald et al., 215–44.

——Bilde, P., Engberg-Pedersen, T., Hannestad, L., and Zahle, J. (1999). *Hellenistic Rhodes: Politics, Culture, and Society*. Studies in Hellenistic Civilization 9. Aarhus.

Gaffney, V., Patterson, H., and Roberts, P. (2001). 'Forum Novum—Vescovio: Studying Urbanism in the Tiber Valley', *JRA* 14.1: 59–79.

Gagarin, M. and Cohen, D. (eds.) (2005). *The Cambridge Companion to Ancient Greek Law*. Cambridge.

Garnsey, P. (1979). 'Where Did Italian Peasants Live?', *PCPhSoc* 25: 1–25.

——(1988). *Famine and Food Supply in the Graeco-Roman World. Responses to Risk and Crisis*. Cambridge.

——and Hopkins, K. (eds.) (1983). *Trade in the Ancient Economy*. London.

——and Rathbone, D. (1985). 'The Background to the Grain Law of Gaius Gracchus', *JRS* 75: 20–5.

——Gallant, T., and Rathbone, D. (1984). 'Thessaly and the Grain Supply of Rome during the Second Century BC', *JRS* 74: 30–44.

Gazzetti, G. (1995). 'La villa romana in località Selvicciolo (Ischia di Castro - Vt.)', in Christie, 297–302.

Goetzmann, W. and Rouwenhorst, G. (eds.) (2005). *The Origins of Value: The Financial Innovations that Created Modern Capital Markets.* Oxford.

Goldberg, S. M. (1998). 'Plautus on the Palatine', *JRS* 88: 1–20.

Goldsmith, R. W. (1984). 'An Estimate of the Size and Structure of the National Product of the Early Roman Empire', *Review of Income and Wealth* 30: 263–88.

Goldstein, J. A. (1983). *II Maccabees: A New Translation with Introduction and Commentary.* Garden City, NY.

Goldstone, J. A. (1984). 'Urbanization and Inflation: Lessons from the English Price Revolution of the Sixteenth and Seventeenth Centuries', *American Journal of Sociology* 89.5: 1122–60.

Gordon, W. M. and Robinson, O. F. (1988). *The Institutes of Gaius: Translated with an Introduction by W. M. Gordon and O. F. Robinson.* London.

Grainger, J. D. (1990). *The Cities of Seleukid Syria.* Oxford.

—— (1991). *Hellenistic Phoenicia.* Oxford.

Greene, K. (1986). *The Archaeology of the Roman Economy.* London.

—— (2000). 'Technological Innovation and Economic Progress in the Ancient World: M. I. Finley Re-Considered', *Economic History Review* ns 53.1: 29–59.

Gros, P. (1990). 'L'urbanizzazione dopo la Guerra Sociale', in Clemente, Coarelli, and Gabba, 831–55.

Gruen, E .S. (1984). *The Hellenistic World and the Coming of Rome.* Berkeley, Calif.

—— (1990). *Studies in Greek Culture and Roman Policy.* Leiden.

Habicht, C. (1975). 'New Evidence on the Province of Asia', *JRS* 65: 64–91.

—— (1979). *2. Makkabäerbuch.* Jüdische Schriften aus hellenistisch-römischer Zeit 3. Gütersloh.

Hall, R. E. and Jones, C. L. (1999). 'Why Do Some Countries Produce So Much More Output per Worker than Others?', *Quarterly Journal of Economics* 114: 83–116.

Hamilton, E. (1934). *American Treasure and the Price Revolution in Spain.* Cambridge, Mass.

Hansen, E. V. (1971). *The Attalids of Pergamon.* Ithaca, NY.

Häpke, N. (1915). *C. Semproni Gracchi oratoris Romani fragmenta collecta et illustrata.* Munich.

Harl, K. W. (1996). *Coinage in the Roman Economy, 300 BC to AD 700.* Baltimore.

Harris, W. V. (1971). *Rome in Etruria and Umbria.* Oxford.

—— (1979). *War and Imperialism in Republican Rome 327–70 BC.* Oxford.

—— (1980*a*). 'Towards a Study of the Roman Slave Trade', in D'Arms and Kopff, 117–40.

—— (1980*b*). 'Roman Terracotta Lamps: The Organization of an Industry', *JRS* 70: 126–45.

—— (1989). 'Roman Expansion in the West', in *CAH* VIII², 107–62.

—— (ed.) (1993*a*). *The Inscribed Economy: Production and Distribution in the Roman Empire in the Light of* instrumentum domesticum. JRA Suppl. Ser. 6. Ann Arbor, Mich.

—— (1993*b*). 'Between Archaic and Modern: Problems in Roman Economic History', in Harris (1993*a*), 11–29.

—— (ed.) (2005). *Rethinking the Mediterranean.* Oxford.

—— (2006). 'A Revisionist View of Roman Money', *JRS* 96: 1–24.

Hasenohr, C. and Müller, C. (2002). 'Gentilices et circulation des Italiens: quelques réflexions méthodologiques', in Müller and Hasenohr, 11–20.

Hassall, M., Crawford, M., and Reynolds, J. (1974). 'Rome and the Eastern Provinces at the End of the Second Century BC: The So-called "Piracy Law" and a New Inscription from Cnidos, *Fouilles de Delphes* III, 4, no. 37; *AJA* 1972, 64–5', *JRS* 64: 195–220.

Hatzfeld, J. (1912). 'Les Italiens résidant à Délos mentionnés dans les inscriptions de l'île', *BCH* 36: 5–218.

—— (1919). *Les Trafiquants italiens dans l'orient hellénique.* Paris.

Havrilesky, T. M. and Boorman, J. T. (1982). *Money Supply, Money Demand and Macroeconomic Models.* Arlington Heights, Ill.

Healy, J. F. (1978). *Mining and Metallurgy in the Greek and Roman World.* London.

Heather, P. (2005). *The Fall of the Roman Empire: A New History*. London.
Heichelheim, P. (1938). *Wirtschaftsgeschichte des Altertums vom Paläolithikum bis zur Völkerwanderung des Germanen, Slaven und Araber*. Leiden.
Heil, M. (1991). 'Einige Bemerkungen zum Zollgesetz aus Ephesos', *EA* 17: 9–18.
Heinen, H., Stroheker, K., and Walser, G. (eds.) (1983). *Althistorische Studien Hermann Bengtson zum 70. Geburgtstag dargebracht von Kollegen und Schülern*. Historia Einzelshriften 40. Wiesbaden.
Hekster, O., de Kleijn, G., and Slootjes, D. (eds.) (2007). *Crises and the Roman Empire. Proceedings of the Seventh Workshop of the International Network Impact of Empire (Nijmegen, June 20–24, 2006)*. Leiden.
Helen, T. (1975). *Organization of Roman Brick Production: An Interpretation of Roman Brick Stamps*. Helsinki.
Hellenkemper Salies, G. (1994). *Das Wrack. Der antike Schiffsfund von Mahdia*. 2 vols. Cologne.
Herrmann, P. and Malay, H. (2007). *New Inscriptions from Lydia*. Vienna.
Herzog, R. (1919). *Aus der Geschichte des Bankwesens im Altertum: Tesserae Nummulariae*. Giessen.
Heurgon, J. (1976). *L'Italie préromaine et la Rome républicaine: Mélanges offerts à Jacques Heurgon*. Rome.
Hirt, A. M. (2010). *Imperial Mines and Quarries in the Roman World: Organizational Aspects 27 BC–AD 235*. Oxford.
Hitchner, R. B. (2002). 'Olive Production and the Roman Economy: The Case for Intensive Growth in the Roman Empire', in Scheidel and Von Reden, 71–83.
—— (2005). '"The Advantages of Wealth and Luxury": The Case for Economic Growth in the Roman Empire', in Manning and Morris, 207–22.
Hodge, A. T. (1992). *Roman Aqueducts and Water Supply*. London.
Hollander, D. B. (2007). *Money in the Late Roman Republic*. Leiden.
Holleaux, M. (1938). *Études d'épigraphie et d'histoire grecques*, ii. Paris.
Hong, S., Candelone, J.-P., Patterson, C. C., and Boutron, C. F. (1994). 'Greenland Ice Evidence of Hemispheric Pollution Two Millenia Ago by Greek and Roman Civilizations', *Science* 265.5180 (23 Sept.): 1841–3.
Hopkins, K. (1978). *Conquerors and Slaves*. Cambridge.
—— (1980). 'Taxes and Trade in the Roman Empire (200 BC–AD 400)', *JRS* 70: 101–25.
—— (2002). 'Rome, Taxes, Rents and Trade', in Scheidel and Von Reden, 190–230.
Horden, P. and Purcell, N. (2000). *The Corrupting Sea: A Study of Mediterranean History*. Oxford.
Houghton, A. (2004). 'Seleucid Coinage and Monetary Policy of the 2nd Century BC: Reflections on the Monetization of the Seleucid Economy', in Chankowski and Duyrat, 49–75.
Howgego, C. (1992). 'The Supply and the Use of Money in the Roman World 200 BC to AD 300', *JRS* 82: 1–31.
—— (1994). 'Coin Circulation and the Integration of the Roman Economy', *JRA* 7: 5–21.
—— (1995). *Ancient History from Coins*. London.
—— (2009). 'Some Numismatic Approaches to Quantifying the Roman Economy', in Bowman and Wilson (2009*a*), 287–95.
—— Heuchert, V., and Burnett, A. (2005). *Coinage and Identity in the Roman Provinces*. Oxford.
Hüllman, K. D. (1832). *Römische Grundverfassung*. Bonn.
Huschke, P. E. (1835). *Über die Stelle des Varros von den Liciniern (de re rust. 1.2.9), nebst einer Zugabe über Fest. v. Possessiones und Possessio: Zwei Abhandlungen aus dem Gebiete der Alterthumswissenschaft und Rechtsgeschichte*. Heidelberg.
Innes, D. C., Hine, H., and Pelling, C. (1995). *Ethics and Rhetoric: Classical Essays for Donald Russell on his Seventy-Fifth Birthday*. Oxford.

JACZYNOWSKA, M. (1962). 'The Economic Differentiation of the Roman Nobility at the End of the Republic', *Historia* 11: 486–99.

JEHNE, M. and PFEILSCHIFTER, R. (eds.) (2006). *Herrschaft ohne Integration? Rom und Italien in republikanischer Zeit*. Frankfurt.

JOLOWICZ, H. F. and NICHOLAS, B. (1972). *Historical Introduction to the Study of Roman Law*. 3rd edn. Cambridge.

JONES, A. H. M. (1960). *Studies in Roman Government and Law*. Oxford.

JONES, C. P. (2004). 'Events Surrounding the Bequest of Pergamon to Rome and the Revolt of Aristonicos: New Inscriptions from Metropolis', *JRA* 17: 469–85.

JONES, D. (2006). *The Bankers of Puteoli: Finance, Trade and Industry in the Roman World*. Stroud.

JONES, E. L. (2000). *Growth Recurring: Economic Change in World History*. Oxford.

JONES, G. D. B. (1980). 'The Roman Mines at Rio Tinto', *JRS* 70: 146–65.

JONGMAN, W. M. (1988). *The Economy and Society of Pompeii*. Amsterdam.

—— (2000). 'Hunger and Power: Theories, Models and Methods in Roman Economic History', in Bongenaar, 259–84.

—— (2003*a*). 'A Golden Age: Death, Money Supply and Social Succession in the Roman Empire', in Lo Cascio (2003), 181–96.

—— (2003*b*). 'Slavery and the Growth of Rome: The Transformation of Italy in the Second and First Centuries BCE', in Edwards and Woolf, 100–22.

—— (2007). 'The Early Roman Empire: Consumption', in Scheidel, Morris, and Saller, 592–618.

—— (ed.) (forthcoming). *Economic Growth in Classical Antiquity*.

—— and KLEIJWEGT, M. (eds.) (2002). *After the Past: Essays in Ancient History in Honour of H. W. Pleket*. Mnemosyne Suppl. 233. Leiden.

KALLET-MARX, R. M. (1995*a*). *Hegemony to Empire. The Development of the Roman Imperium in the East from 148 to 62 BC*. Oxford.

—— (1995*b*). 'Quintus Fabius Maximus and the Dyme affair (*Syll*^{3} 684)', *CQ* 45: 129–53.

KAY, P. B. (2013). 'What Did the Attalids Ever Do for Us? A View from the *Aerarium*', in Thonemann (2013*a*), 121–48.

KEAY, S. (2003). 'Recent Archaeological Work in Roman Iberia (1990–2002)', *JRS* 93: 146–211.

KEHOE, D. P. (1988). *The Economics of Agriculture on Roman Imperial Estates in North Africa*. Göttingen.

—— (1992). *Management and Investment on Estates in Roman Egypt during the Early Empire*. Bonn.

—— (1993). 'Economic Rationalism in Roman Agriculture', *JRA* 6: 476–84.

—— (1997). *Investment, Profit and Tenancy: The Jurists and the Roman Agrarian Economy*. Ann Arbor, Mich.

—— (2007*a*). 'The Early Roman Empire: Production', in Scheidel, Morris, and Saller, 543–69.

—— (2007*b*). *Law and Rural Economy in the Roman Empire*. Ann Arbor, Mich.

KENNEY, E. J. (1982). *The Cambridge History of Classical Literature. The Early Republic*. Cambridge.

KEYNES, J. M. (1936). *The General Theory of Employment, Interest and Money*. London.

KHANOUSSI, M., RUGGERI, P., and VISMARA, C. (eds.) (2004). *L'Africa romana: ai confini dell' Impero: contatti, scambi, conflitti. Atti del XV convegno di studio Tozeur, 11–15 dicembre 2002*. Rome.

KING, A. (1999). 'Diet in the Roman World: A Regional Inter-site Comparison of the Mammal Bones', *JRA* 12: 168–202.

KINNS, P. (1987). 'Asia Minor', in Burnett and Crawford, 105–19.

KLEIN GOLDEWIJK, G. and JONGMAN, W. M. (forthcoming). 'They Never Had It So Good: Roman Stature and the Biological Standard of Living'.

KLEINER, F. S. and NOE, S. P. (1976). *The Early Cistophoric Coinage: The American Numismatic Society*, Numismatic Studies 14. New York.

KNAPP, R. C. (1977). 'The Date and Purpose of the Iberian Denarii', *NC* 137: 1–18.
——(1987). 'Spain', in Burnett and Crawford, 19–42.
KREMYDI-SICILIANOU, S. (2005). '"Belonging" to Rome, "Remaining" Greek: Coinage and Identity in Roman Macedonia', in Howgego, Heuchert, and Burnett, 95–106.
KRON, J. G. (2002). 'Archaeozoological Evidence for the Productivity of Roman Livestock Farming', *Münstersche Beiträge zur antiken Handelsgeschichte* 21.2: 53–73.
——(2005). 'Anthropometry, Physical Anthropology, and the Reconstruction of Ancient Health, Nutrition, and Living Standards', *Historia* 54: 68–83.
——(2008). 'The Much Maligned Peasant: Comparative Perspectives on the Productivity of the Small Farmer in Classical Antiquity', in De Ligt and Northwood, 17–70.
KUNKEL, W. (1995). *Staatsordnung und Staatspraxis der Römischen Republik.* Munich.
LAFON, X. (2001). *Villa Maritima: Recherches sur les villas littorales de l'Italie romaine (IIIe siècle av. J.-C./IIIe siècle ap. J.-C.).* Rome.
LARSEN, J. A. O. (1938). 'Roman Greece' in Frank (1938), 259–498.
LAURENCE, R (1998). 'Land and Transport in Roman Italy: Costs, Practice and the Economy', in Parkins and Smith, 129–48.
LAWRENCE, R. (1999). *The Roads of Roman Italy.* London.
LEIGH, M. (2004). *Comedy and the Rise of Rome.* Oxford.
LEONE, A., PALOMBI, D., and WALKER, S. (eds.) (2007). *Res Bene Gestae: Ricerche di storia urbana su Roma antica in onore di Eva Margareta Steinby.* Lexicon Topographicum Urbis Romanae, Suppl. IV. Rome.
LEU NUMISMATICS (2005). *Auction Leu 93, 10 May 2005.* Zurich.
LEVINE, R. (1997). 'Financial Development and Economic Growth: Views and Agenda', *Journal of Economic Literature* 35 (June): 688–726.
LEWIS, M. J. T. (1997). *Millstone and Hammer: The Origins of Water Power.* Hull.
LINTOTT, A. W. (1993). *Imperium Romanum.* London.
——(1994*a*). 'The Crisis of the Republic: Sources and Source-problems', in *CAH* IX^2, 1–15.
——(1994*b*). 'The Roman Empire and its Problems in the Late Second Century', in *CAH* IX^2, 16–39.
——(1994*c*). 'Political History 146–95 BC' in *CAH* IX^2, 40–103.
——(1999). *The Constitution of the Roman Republic.* Oxford.
LIOU, B. and POMEY, P. (1986). 'Directions des recherches archéologiques sous-marines', *Gallia* 43: 547–76.
LITTLETON, A. C. and YAMEY, B. S. (eds.) (1956). *Studies in the History of Accounting.* London.
LIVERANI, P. (1984). 'L'Ager Veientanus in età repubblicana', *PBSR* 52: 36–48.
LLEWELLYN, D. T. (2009). 'Financial Innovation and the Economics of Banking and the Financial System', in Anderloni, Llewellyn, and Schmidt, 1–41.
LO CASCIO, E. (1994*a*). 'The Size of the Roman Population: Beloch and the Meaning of the Augustan Census Figures', *JRS* 84: 23–40.
——(1994*b*). 'La dinamica della popolazione in Italia da Augusto al III secolo', in Demougin et al., 91–125.
——(1999*a*). 'Popolazione e risorse agricole nell'Italia del II secolo a.C.', in Vera, 217–45.
——(1999b). 'The Population of Roman Italy in Town and Country', in Bintliff and Sbonias, 161–71.
——(2001). 'Recruitment and the Size of the Roman Population from the Third to the First Century BCE', in Scheidel (2001), 111–37.
——(ed.) (2003). *Credito e moneta nel mondo romano.* Bari.
——(2004). 'Peuplement et surpeuplement: leur rapport avec les ressources naturelles', in Clavel-Lévêque and Hermon, 135–52.
——(ed.) (2006). *Innovazione tecnica e progresso economico nel mondo romano: Atti degli incontri capresi di storia dell'economia antica (Capri 13–16 aprile 2003).* Bari.

Lo Cascio, E. (2008). 'Roman Census Figures in the Second Century BC and the Property Qualification of the Fifth Class', in De Ligt and Northwood, 239–56.

—— (2009). 'Urbanisation as a Proxy of Demographic and Economic Growth', in Bowman and Wilson (2009*a*), 87–106.

—— (2010). 'Thinking Slave and Free in Coordinates', in Roth, 21–30.

—— and Malanima, P. (2005). 'Cycles and Stability: Italian Population before the Demographic Transition (225 BC–AD 1900)', *Rivista di storia economica* 21: 5–40.

Lockyear, K. (1999). 'Hoard Structure and Coin Production in Antiquity: An Empirical Investigation', *NC* 159: 215–43.

—— (2007). *Patterns and Process in Late Roman Republican Coin Hoards, 157–2 BC*. Oxford.

López-Sánchez, F. (2005). 'Moneda ibérica y *hospitium*', *XIII International Congress of Numismatics, Madrid, September 2003*. Madrid, i. 511–15.

Loughton, M. E. (2003). 'The Distribution of Republican Amphorae in France', *Oxford Journal of Archaeology* 22: 177–207.

Loukopoulou, L. D. (1996). 'The Fortunes of the Roman Conventus of Chacidice', in Rizakis (1996), 143–8.

Lowe, B. (2009). *Roman Iberia: Economy, Society and Culture*. London.

Lund, J. (1999). 'Rhodian Amphorae in Rhodes and Alexandria as Evidence of Trade', in Gabrielsen et al., 187–204.

Ma, J. (2000). *Antiochos III and the Cities of Western Asia Minor*. Oxford.

—— (2007). 'Review of Aperghis (2004)', *Hermathena* 182: 182–8.

MacKinnon, M. (2004). *Production and Consumption of Animals in Roman Italy: Integrating the Zooarchaeological and Textual Evidence*, JRA Suppl. 54. Portsmouth, RI.

McKnight, B. E. (1971). *Village and Bureaucracy in Southern Sung China*. Chicago.

McNeill, W. H. (1982). *The Pursuit of Power: Technology, Armed Force, and Society since AD 1000*. Chicago.

Macro, A. D. (1976). 'Imperial Provisions for Pergamum: *OGIS* 484', *GRBS* 17: 169–79.

McShane, R. B. (1964). *The Foreign Policy of the Attalids of Pergamum*. Urbana, Ill.

Macve, R. H. (1985). 'Some Glosses on "Greek and Roman Accounting"', in Cartledge and Harvey, 233–61.

Maddison, A. (2007). *Contours of the World Economy 1–2030 AD: Essays in Macroeconomic History*. Oxford.

Magie, D. (1950). *Roman Rule in Asia Minor*. Princeton, NJ.

Malcovati, H. (1976). *Oratorum Romanorum Fragmenta Liberae Rei Publicae*. 4th edn. Turin.

Malmendier, U. (2005). 'Roman Shares', in Goetzmann and Rouwenhorst, 31–42.

Manacorda, D. (1978). 'The Ager Cosanus and the Production of the Amphorae of Sestius: New Evidence and a Reassessment', *JRS* 68: 122–31.

—— (1994). 'Produzione agricola, produzione ceramica e proprietà delle terre nella Calabria romana tra repubblica e imperio', in *Epigrafia della produzione e della distribuzione. Actes de la VIIe Rencontre franco-italienne sur l'épigraphie du monde romain (Rome, 5 à 6 juin 1992)*. Collection de l'École française de Rome 193, 3–59.

Mancinetti Santamaria, G. (1982). 'Filostrato di Ascalona, banchiere in Delo', in Coarelli, Musti, and Solin, 79–89.

Mandelbrot, B. B. and Hudson, R. L. (2004). *The (Mis)Behaviour of Markets*. London.

Manning, J. G. and Morris, I. (eds.) (2005). *The Ancient Economy: Evidence and Models*. Stanford, Calif.

Marchetti, P. (1978). *Histoire économique et monétaire de la deuxième guerre punique*. Brussels.

Marquardt, J. (1888–92). *Organisation de l'empire romain*, ii, trans. P. Louis-Lucas and A. Weiss. Paris.

Martínez-Cortizas, A., Pontevedra-Pombal, X., Nóvoa-Muñoz, J. C., and García-Rodeja, E. (1997). 'Four Thousand Years of Atmospheric Pb, Cd and Zn Deposition Recorded by the Ombrotrophic Peat Bog of Penido Vello (Northwestern Spain). *Water, Air and Soil Pollution* 100: 387–403.

—— García-Rodeja, E., Pontevedra-Pombal, X., Nóvoa-Muñoz, J. C., Weiss, D., Cheburkin, A., and Shotyk, W. (2000). 'Atmospheric Pb Deposition During the Last 4,000 years Recorded by Two Ombrotrophic Peat Bogs in NW Spain', *Proceedings of the 11th International Heavy Metals Conference, Ann Arbor, MI, USA*. Ann Arbor, Mich.

Marzano, A. (2007). *Roman Villas in Central Italy: A Social and Economic History*. Leiden.

Maselli, G. (1986). *Argentaria: Banche e banchieri nella Roma repubblicana: organizzazione, prosopografia, terminologia*. Bari.

Mattingly, D. J. (1988*a*). 'Megalithic Madness and Measurement: Or How Many Olives Could an Olive Press Press?', *Oxford Journal of Archaeology* 7.2: 177–95.

—— (1988*b*). 'The Olive Boom: Oil Surpluses, Wealth and Power in Roman Tripolitania', *Libyan Studies* 19: 21–41.

—— (1988*c*). 'Oil for Export? A Comparison of Libyan, Spanish and Tunisian Olive Oil Production in the Roman Empire', *JRA* 1: 33–56.

—— (1988*d*). 'Olea Mediterranea?', *JRA* 1: 153–61.

—— and Aldrete, G. S. (2000). 'The Feeding of Imperial Rome: The Mechanics of the Food Supply System', in Coulston and Dodge, 142–65.

—— and Salmon, T. (eds.) (2001*a*). *Economies Beyond Agriculture in the Classical World*. London.

—— —— (2001*b*). 'The Productive Past', in Mattingly and Salmon (2001*a*), 3–14.

Mattingly, H. B. (1972). 'The Date of the *Senatus Consultum de Agro Pergameno*', *AJPh* 93: 412–23.

—— (1977). 'Coinage and the Roman State', *NC* 137: 199–215.

Mavrojannis, T. (2002). 'Italiens et Orientaux à Délos: considérations sur l'"absence" des *negotiatores* romains dans la Méditerranée orientale', in Müller and Hasenohr, 163–79.

Mayhew, N. J. (1995*a*). 'Population, Money Supply, and the Velocity of Circulation in England, 1300–1700', *Economic History Review* ns 48.2: 238–57.

—— (1995*b*). 'Modelling Medieval Monetization', in Britnell and Campbell, 55–77.

Mazzarino, A. (1952). *Introduzione al De Agri Cultura di Catone*. Rome.

—— (1962). *M. Porci Catonis: De Agri Cultura*. Leipzig: Teubner.

Meadows, A. (1998). 'The Mars/Eagle and Thunderbolt Gold and Ptolemaic Involvement in the Second Punic War', in Burnett, Wartenberg, and Witschonke, 125–34.

—— (2001). 'Money, Freedom, and Empire in the Hellenistic World', in Meadows and Shipton, 53–64.

—— (2013). 'The Closed Currency System of the Attalid Kingdom', in Thonemann (2013*a*), 149–205.

—— and Shipton, K. (2001). *Money and its Uses in the Ancient Greek World*. Oxford.

Meijer, F. (2002). 'Wrecks in the Mediterranean as Evidence of Economic Activity in the Roman Empire', in Jongman and Kleijwegt, 135–55.

Metcalf, D. M. and Oddy, W. A. (eds.) (1980). *Metallurgy in Numismatics*, i. London.

Meyer, E. A. (2004). *Legitimacy and Law in the Roman World: Tabulae in Roman Belief and Practice*. Cambridge.

Mickwitz, G. (1937). 'Economic Rationalism in Graeco-Roman Agriculture', *English Historical Review* 52: 577–89.

Migeotte, L. (1984). *L'Emprunt public dans les cités grecques*. Quebec.

—— (1992). *Les Souscriptions publiques dans les cités grecques*. Geneva.

Millar, F. (1964). 'The *Aerarium* and its Officials under the Empire', *JRS* 54: 33–40.

—— (1984). 'The Political Character of the Classical Roman Republic, 200–151 bc', *JRS* 74: 1–19.

MILLAR, F. (1986). 'Politics, Persuasion and the People before the Social War (150–90 BC)', *JRS* 76: 1–11.
MILLER, M. H. (1986). 'Financial Innovation: The Last Twenty Years and the Next', *Journal of Financial and Quantitative Analysis* 21.4: 459–71.
MILLETT, P. (1991). *Lending and Borrowing in Ancient Athens*. Cambridge.
—— (2001). 'Productive to Some Purpose? The Problem of Ancient Economic Growth', in Mattingly and Salmon (2001*a*), 17–48.
MITCHELL, S. (1999). 'The Administration of Roman Asia, 133 BC to AD 250', in Eck and Müller-Luckner, 17–46.
—— (2008). 'Geography, Politics and Imperialism in the Asian Customs Law', in Cottier et al., 165–201.
MOMMSEN, TH. (1861). 'Die Chronik des Cassiodorus Senator vom J. 519 n. Chr. nach den Handshriften herausgegeben', *Abhandlungen der königlich sächsischen Gesellschaft der Wissenschaften* 8: 547–696.
—— (1879). *Römische Forschungen*, ii. Berlin.
—— (1894). *The History of Rome*, iv, trans. W. P. Dickson. London.
—— (1920). *Römische Geschichte*. 12th edn. Berlin.
MOORE, B. J. (1988). *Horizontalists and Verticalists: The Macroeconomics of Credit Money*. Cambridge.
MOORE, T. J. (1991). '*Palliata Togata*: Plautus *Curculio* 462–86', *AJPh* 112: 343–62.
—— (1998). *The Theater of Plautus: Playing to the Audience*. Austin, Tex.
MOREL, J.-P. (1989). 'The Transformation of Italy, 300–133 BC: The Evidence of Archaeology', in *CAH* VIII^2, 477–516.
MØRKHOLM, O. (1966). *Antiochus IV of Syria*. Copenhagen.
—— (1980). 'The Chronology and Meaning of the Wreath Coinages of the Early 2nd Cent. BC', *OT* 9: 145–58.
—— (1984). 'The Chronology of the New Style Coinage of Athens', *ANSMN* 29: 29–42.
MORLEY, N. D. G. (1996). *Metropolis and Hinterland: The City of Rome and the Italian Economy, 200 BC–AD 200*. Cambridge.
—— (2001). 'The Transformation of Italy, 225–28 BC', *JRS* 91: 50–62.
—— (2007). 'The Early Roman Empire: Distribution', in Scheidel, Morris, and Saller, 570–91.
—— (2010). *The Roman Empire: Roots of Imperialism*. London.
MROZEK, S. (1985). 'Zum Kreditgeld in der frühen römischen Kaiserzeit', *Historia* 34: 310–23.
MÜLLER, C. (1996). 'Les *nomina romana* à Thespies du IIe s. a.C. à l'édit de Caracalla', in Rizakis (1996), 157–66.
—— and HASENOHR, C. (eds.) (2002). *Les Italiens dans le monde grec IIe siècle av. J.-C.–Ier siècle ap. J.-C.: Circulation, activités, intégration*. BCH Suppl. 41. Athens.
MÜLLER, H. (2009). 'Reparationszahlungen an Rom zur Zeit der römischen Republik', *Tyche* 24: 77–95.
ÑACO, T. (2006). 'Rearguard Strategies of Roman Republican Warfare in the Far West', in Ñaco and Arrayás, 149–67.
—— (2007). 'The Late Republican West: Imperial Taxation in the Making?', in Hekster, de Kleijn, and Slootjes, 218–31.
—— and ARRAYÁS, I. (eds.) (2006). *War and Territory in the Roman World / Guerra y territorio en el mundo romano*. BAR International Series 1530. Oxford.
NAGLE, D. B. (1976). 'The Etruscan Journey of Tiberius Gracchus', *Historia* 25: 487–9.
NICOLET, C. (1966). *L'ordre équestre à l'époque républicaine (312–43 av. J.-C.)*. Paris.
—— (1976). 'Le Cens senatorial sous la République et sous Auguste', *JRS* 46: 20–38.
—— (1978). 'Le Stipendium des alliés italiens', *PBSR* 46: 1–11.
—— (2000*a*). *Censeurs et publicains: Économie et fiscalité dans la Rome Antique*. Paris.

——(2000*b*). 'Économie, societé et institutions au IIe siècle av. J.-C.: de la *lex Claudia* à l'*ager exceptus*', in Nicolet (2000*a*), 19–43.

NIEBUHR, B. G. (1811–12). *Römische Geschichte*. Berlin.

NIGHTINGALE, P. (1990). 'Monetary Contraction and Mercantile Credit in Later Medieval England', *Economic History Review* ns 43: 560–75.

——(1997). 'England and the European Depression of the Mid-Fifteenth Century', *Journal of European Economic History* 26: 631–56.

——(2004). 'Money and Credit in the Economy of Late Medieval England', in Wood, 51–71.

NORTH, D. C. (1990). *Institutions, Institutional Change and Economic Performance*. Cambridge.

——(2005). *Understanding the Process of Economic Change*. Princeton, NJ.

NORTH, J. A. (1992). 'Deconstructing Stone Theatres', in Cruickshank, 75–83.

OLESON, J. P. (1984). *Greek and Roman Mechanical Water-Lifting Devices: The History of a Technology*. Toronto.

——(ed.) (2008). *The Oxford Handbook of Engineering and Technology in the Classical World*. Oxford.

ORIGO, I. (1957). *The Merchant of Prato: Francesco di Marco Datini, 1335–1410*. New York.

PARETO, V. (1964). *Cours d'économie politique: Nouvelle édition par G.-H. Bousquet et G. Busino*. Geneva.

PARKER, A. J. (1992). *Ancient Shipwrecks of the Mediterranean and the Roman Provinces*. London.

PARKINS, H. and SMITH, C. (eds.) (1998). *Trade, Traders and the Ancient City*. London.

PASS, C., LOWES, B., and DAVIES, C. (1998). *Collins Dictionary of Economics*. Glasgow.

PATON, W. R. and HICKS, E. L. (1881). *The Inscriptions of Cos*. Oxford.

PATTERSON, H., DI GIUSEPPE, H., and WITCHER, R. (2004). 'Three South Etrurian "Crises": First Results of the Tiber Valley Project', *PBSR* 72: 1–36.

——DI GENNARO, F., DI GIUSEPPE, H., FONTANA, S., GAFFNEY, V., HARRISON, A., KEAY, S. J., MILLETT, M., RENDELI, M., ROBERTS, P., STODDART, S., and WITCHER, R. (2000). 'The Tiber Valley Project: The Tiber and Rome through Two Millenia', *Antiquity* 74.284 (June): 395–403.

PATTERSON, J. R. (1987). 'Crisis: What Crisis? Rural Change and Urban Development in Imperial Appenine Italy', *PBSR* 55: 134–46.

——(2000). 'Living and Dying in the City of Rome: Houses and Tombs', in Coulston and Dodge, 259–89.

——(2006). 'Rome and Italy', in Rosenstein and Morstein-Marx, 606–24.

——(2010). 'The City of Rome Revisited: From Mid-Republic to Mid-Empire', *JRS* 100: 210–32.

PEACOCK, D. P. S. and WILLIAMS, D. F. (1986). *Amphorae and the Roman Economy: An Introductory Guide*. London.

————(eds.) (2007). *Food for the Gods: New Light on the Ancient Incense Trade*. Oxford.

PECK, L. L. (2005). *Consuming Splendor: Society and Culture in Seventeenth-Century England*. Cambridge.

PERELLI, L. (1975). 'La chiusura delle miniere macedoni dopo Pidna', *Riv. Filol.* 103: 403–12.

PÉREZ JIMÉNEZ, A. (2006). *Hijos de Mercurio: banqueros, prestamistas, usureros y transacciones comerciales en el mundo Mediterráneo*. Madrid.

PESANDO, F. (1997). *Domus: edilizia privata e società pompeiana fra III e I secolo a.C.* Rome.

PETRUCCI, A. (1991). *Mensam exercere: studi sull' impresa finanziaria romana, II secolo a.C.–metà del III secolo d.C.* Naples.

——(2002). *Profili giuridici delle attività e dell' organizzazione delle banche romane*. Turin.

PETZL, G. (1987). *Die Inschriften von Smyrna II.1*. Bonn.

PIGANIOL, A. (ed.) (1954). *Atlas des centuriations romaines de Tunisie*. Paris.

PIGOU, A. C. (1917). 'The Value of Money', *Quarterly Journal of Economics* 32: 38–65.
PLEKET, H. W. (1983). 'Urban Elites and Business in the Greek Part of the Roman Empire', in Garnsey and Hopkins, 131–44.
—— (1993). 'Agriculture in the Roman Empire in Comparative Perspective', in Sancisi-Weerdenburg et al., 317–42.
POTTER, T. W. (1979). *The Changing Landscape of South Etruria*. London.
PRESTON, H. S. (1983). 'Roman Republican Coin Hoards: An Age Correction and Other Comments', *Annali dell'Istituto Italiano di Numismatica* 30: 83–93.
PRICE, M. (1987). 'Southern Greece', in Burnett and Crawford, 95–103.
PUCHTA, G. F. (1841). *Cursus der Institutionen*. Leipzig.
PURCELL, N. (1985). 'Wine and Wealth in Ancient Italy', *JRS* 75: 1–19.
—— (1988). 'Review of Tchernia (1986) and Carandini and Ricci (1985)', *JRS* 78: 194–8.
—— (1995). 'On the Sacking of Carthage and Corinth', in Innes, Hine and Pelling, 133–48.
—— (2005*a*). 'The Archaeology of Agrarian Change in Roman Italy', Ancient History and Classical Archaeology Seminar, 10 May 2005, Oxford University. Unpublished.
—— (2005*b*). 'The Ancient Mediterranean: The View from the Customs House', in Harris, 200–32.
—— (2007). 'The *Horti* of Rome and the Landscape of Property', in Leone, Palombi, and Walker, 361–78.
QUILICI, L. (1974). *Collatia: Forma Italiae, Regio I 10*. Rome.
—— and QUILICI GIGLI, S. (1986). *Fidenae*. Rome.
QUILICI GIGLI, S. (1987). 'Su alcuni segni dell'antico paesaggio agrario presso Roma', *ArchLaz* 8: 152–8.
—— (1989*a*). 'L'acquedotto di Ponte del Ponte nell'antico paesaggio agrario della zona di Corchiano', *Xenia* 17: 55–64.
—— (1989*b*). 'Paesaggi storici dell'agro falisco: i prata di Corchiano', *O.Rom.* 17: 123–35.
RADNOTI-ALFÖLDI, M. (1984). 'Der Stater des T. Quinctius Flamininus', *NZ* 98: 19–26.
RANDSBORG, K. (ed.) (1989). *The Birth of Europe: Archaeology and Social Development in the First Millenium AD*. Analecta Romana Instituti Danici Suppl. XVI. Rome.
RATHBONE, D. W. (1981). 'The Development of Agriculture in the "Ager Cosanus" during the Roman Republic: Problems of Evidence and Interpretation', *JRS* 71: 10–23.
—— (1991). *Economic Rationalism and Rural Society in Third-Century AD Egypt: The Heroninos Archive and the Appianus Estate*. Cambridge.
—— (2003). 'The Control and Exploitation of *Ager Publicus* in Italy under the Roman Republic', in Aubert (2003), 135–78.
—— (2009). 'Earnings and Costs: Living Standards and the Roman Economy (First to Third Centuries AD)', in Bowman and Wilson (2009*a*), 299–326.
—— and TEMIN, P. (2008). 'Financial Intermediation in First Century AD Rome and Eighteenth Century England', in Verboven, Vandorpe, and Chankowski, 371–419.
RAUH, N. K. (1989). 'Finance and Estate Sales in Republican Rome', *Aevum* 63: 45–76.
—— (1993). *The Sacred Bonds of Commerce: Religion, Economy and Trade Society at Hellenistic Roman Delos 166–87 BC*. Amsterdam.
—— (1997). 'Who Were the Cilician Pirates?', in Swiny, Hohlfelder, and Wylde-Swiny, 263–83.
—— (1999). 'Rhodes, Rome, and the Eastern Mediterranean Wine Trade, 166–88 BC', in Gabrielsen et al., 162–86.
—— (2003). *Merchants, Sailors and Pirates in the Roman World*. Stroud.
RAWSON, E. (1976). 'The Ciceronian Aristocracy and its Properties', in Finley (1976), 85–102.
—— (1985). *Intellectual Life in the Late Roman Republic*. London.
REGER, G. (1994). *Regionalism and Change in the Economy of Independent Delos*. Berkeley, Calif.
RENBERG, I., PERSSON, M. W., and EMTERYD, O. (1994). 'Pre-industrial Atmospheric Lead Contamination Detected in Swedish Lake Sediments', *Nature* 368: 323–26.

—— Brännvall, M.-L., Bindler, R., and Emteryd, O. (2000). 'Atmospheric Lead Pollution History during Four Millenia (2000 bc to 2000 ad) in Sweden', *Ambio* 29.3: 150–6.

—— Bindler, R., and Brännvall, M.-L. (2001). 'Using the Historic Atmospheric Lead-Deposition Record as a Chronological Marker in Sediment Deposits in Europe', *The Holocene* 11: 511–16.

—— Brännvall, M.-L., Bindler, R., and Emteryd, O. (2002). 'Stable Lead Isotopes and Lake Sediments: A Useful Combination for the Study of Atmospheric Lead Pollution History', *Science of the Total Environment* 292.1–2: 45–54.

Ribbeck, O. (1898). *Comicorum Romanorum Fragmenta*. Leipzig.

Rich, J. W. (1983). 'The Supposed Roman Manpower Shortage of the Later Second Century bc', *Historia* 32: 287–331.

—— (1993). 'Fear, Greed and Glory: The Causes of Roman War-making in the Middle Republic', in Rich and Shipley, 38–68.

—— (2008). 'Lex Licinia, Lex Sempronia: B. G. Niebuhr and the Limitation of Landholding in the Roman Republic', in De Ligt and Northwood, 519–72.

—— and Shipley, G. (eds.) (1993). *War and Society in the Roman World*. London.

Richardson, J. S. (1976). 'The Spanish Mines and the Development of Provincial Taxation in the Second Century bc', *JRS* 66: 140–52.

—— (1987). 'The Purpose of the *Lex Calpurnia de Repetundis*', *JRS* 77: 1–12.

—— (1996). *The Romans in Spain*. Oxford.

Richardson Jr., L. (1992). *A New Topographical Dictionary of Ancient Rome*. Baltimore.

Rickman, G. (1971). *Roman Granaries and Store Buildings*. Cambridge.

Rihll, T. E. (2001). 'Making Money in Classical Athens', in Mattingly and Salmon (2001*a*), 115–42.

Ripollès, P. P. (1987). 'Estimación del número de cuños originales utilizados en la ceca de Valentia', in Depeyrot, Hackens, and Moucharte, 133–9.

—— (2005). 'Coinage and Identity in the Roman Provinces: Spain', in Howgego, Heuchert, and Burnett, 79–94.

Rizakis, A. D. (ed.) (1996). *Roman Onomastics in the Greek East: Social and Political Aspects. ΜΕΛΕΤΗΜΑΤΑ* 21. Athens.

—— (2001). 'L'Émigration romaine en Macédoine et la communauté marchande de Thessalonique: Perspectives économiques et sociales', *BCH Suppl.* 41: 109–32.

Rollinger, C. (2009). *Solvendi sunt nummi: Die Schuldenkultur der späten römischen Republik im Spiegel der Schriften Ciceros*. Berlin.

Roselaar, S. T. (2008). 'Regional Variations in the Use of the *Ager Publicus*', in De Ligt and Northwood, 573–602.

—— (2010). *Public Land in the Roman Republic: A Social and Economic History of Ager Publicus in Italy 369–89 bc*. Oxford.

Rosenstein, N. (2004). *Rome at War: Farms, Families, and Death in the Middle Republic*. Chapel Hill, NC.

—— (2008). 'Aristocrats and Agriculture in the Middle and Late Republic', *JRS* 98: 1–26.

—— and Morstein-Marx, R. (eds.) (2006). *A Companion to the Roman Republic*. Oxford.

Rosman, K. J. R., Chisolm, W., Hong, S., Candelone, J.-P., and Boutron, C. F. (1997). 'Lead from Carthaginian and Roman Spanish Mines Isotopically Identified in Greenland Ice Dated from 600 bc to 300 ad', *Environment, Science and Technology* 31: 3413–16.

Rostovtzeff, M. (1941). *The Social and Economic History of the Hellenistic World*. Oxford.

—— (1957). *Social and Economic History of the Roman Empire*. Oxford.

Roth, U. (ed.) (2010). *By the Sweat of Your Brow: Roman Slavery in its Socio-Economic Setting*. London.

Rotondi, G. (1912). *Leges publicae populi Romani*. Milan.

Ruffing, K. (1999). *Weinbau im römischen Ägypten*. St Katherinen.

SALLER, R. P. (2002). 'Framing the Debate over Growth in the Ancient Economy', in Scheidel and Von Reden, 251–69.
SALMON, E. T. (1963). 'The *Coloniae Maritimae*', *Athenaeum* 41: 3–38.
—— (1970). *Roman Colonization under the Republic*. Ithaca, NY.
SANCISI-WEERDENBURG, H., VAN DER SPEK, R. J., TEITLER, H. C., and WALLINGS, H. T. (eds.) (1993). *De Agricultura: In Memoriam Pieter Willem de Neeve*. Amsterdam.
SCHEIDEL, W. (1996). 'Finances, Figures and Fiction', *CQ* 96: 222–38.
—— (ed.) (2001). *Debating Roman Demography*. Leiden.
—— (2004). 'Human Mobility in Roman Italy, I: The Free Population', *JRS* 94: 1–26.
—— (2005). 'Human Mobility in Roman Italy, II: The Slave Population', *JRS* 95: 64–79.
—— (2006). 'The Demography of Roman State Formation in Italy', in Jehne and Pfeilschifter, 207–26.
—— (2007). 'A Model of Real Income Growth in Roman Italy', *Historia* 56: 322–46.
—— (2008). 'Roman Population Size: The Logic of the Debate', in De Ligt and Northwood, 17–70.
—— (2009*a*). 'In Search of Roman Economic Growth', *JRA* 22: 46–70.
—— (2009*b*). 'New Ways of Studying Incomes in the Roman Economy', in Bowman and Wilson (2009*a*), 346–52.
—— and FRIESEN, S. J. (2009). 'The Size of the Economy and the Distribution of Income in the Roman Empire', *JRS* 99: 61–91.
—— and VON REDEN, S. (eds.) (2002). *The Ancient Economy*. Edinburgh.
—— MORRIS, I., and SALLER, R. P. (eds.) (2007). *The Cambridge Economic History of the Greco-Roman World*. Cambridge.
SCHUTTER, K. H. E (1952). *Quibus annis comoediae Plautinae primum actae sint quaeritur*. Groningen.
SCRAMUZZA, V. M. (1937). 'Roman Sicily', in Frank (1937), 225–377.
SEGRE, M. (1938). 'Iscrizioni di Licia', *Clara Rhodos* 9: 179–208.
SETTLE, D. M. and PATTERSON, C. C. (1980). 'Lead in Albacore: Guide to Lead Pollution in Americans', *Science* 207: 1167–76.
SHACKLETON BAILEY, D. R. (ed.) (1966). *Cicero's Letters to Atticus*, iv. Cambridge.
SHATZMAN, I. (1972). 'The Roman General's Authority over Booty', *Historia* 21: 177–205.
—— (1975). *Senatorial Wealth and Roman Politics*. Brussels.
SHEPHERD, R. (1993). *Ancient Mining*. London.
SHERK, R. K. (1969). *Roman Documents from the Greek East: Senatus Consulta and Epistulae to the Age of Augustus*. Baltimore.
SHERWIN-WHITE, A. N. (1982). 'The *Lex Repetundarum* and the Political Ideas of Gaius Gracchus', *JRS* 72: 18–31.
SHOTYK, W., WEISS, D., APPLEBY, P. G., CHEBURKIN, A. K., FREI, R., GLOOR, M., KRAMERS, J. D., REESE, S., and VAN DER KNAAP, W. O. (1998). 'History of Atmospheric Lead Deposition since 12,370 ^{14}C yr bp from a Peat Bog, Jura Mountains, Switzerland', *Science* 281: 1635–40.
—— —— KRAMERS, J. D., FREI, R., CHEBURKIN, A. K., GLOOR, M., and REESE, S. (2001). 'Geochemistry of the Peat Bog at Étang de la Gruère, Jura Mountains, Switzerland, and its Record of Atmospheric Pb and Lithogenic Trace Metals (Sc, Ti, Y, Zr, and REE) since 12,370 ^{14}C yr bp', *Geochimica et Cosmochimica Acta* 65.14: 2337–60.
SILVER, M. (2007). 'Roman Economic Growth and Living Standards: Perceptions Versus Evidence', *Ancient Society* 37: 191–252.
SINGER, C. (2007). 'The Incense Kingdoms of Yemen: An Outline History of the South Arabian Incense Trade', in Peacock and Williams (2007), 4–27.
SMALL, A. M. (1974). 'Excavations at Monte Irsi, Italy, 1971–1973', *Échos du Monde Classique / Classical Views* 18: 20–2.

——Moncton, S. G., Buck, R. J., and Simpson, C. J. (1992). 'Excavations at Gravina di Puglia, 1991: Interim Report', *Échos du Monde Classique / Classical Views* 36: 189–99.

Solin, H. (1982). 'Appunti sull'onomastica romana a Delo', in Coarelli, Musti, and Solin, 101–7.

——(1996). 'Ancient Onomastics: Perspectives and Problems', in Rizakis (1996), 1–10.

Speidel, M. A. (1992). 'Roman Army Pay Scales', *JRS* 82: 87–106.

Spufford, P. (1988). *Money and its Use in Medieval Europe*. Cambridge.

——(2002). *Power and Profit: The Merchant in Medieval Europe*. London.

Starr, C. G. (1980). *The Beginnings of Imperial Rome: Rome in the Mid-Republic*. Ann Arbor, Mich.

Steinby, E. M. (ed.) (1993*a*). *Lexicon Topographicum Urbis Romae*, i. *A–C*. Rome.

——(1993*b*). 'L'organizzazione produttiva dei laterizi: un modello interpretativo per l'*instrumentum* in genere?', in Harris (1993), 139–44.

——(ed.) (1995). *Lexicon Topographicum Urbis Romae*, ii. *D–G*. Rome.

Stewart, N. S. (2002). 'The Technology and Control of Mining in Roman Britain', D.Phil Thesis, Oxford.

Stockton, D. (1979). *The Gracchi*. Oxford.

Strasburger, H. (1965). 'Poseidonios on Problems of the Roman Empire', *JRS* 55: 40–53.

Strauss, J. (2006). 'Roman Trade in the Eastern Mediterranean', Ph.D. Thesis, London.

Suresh, S. (2004). *Symbols of Trade: Roman and Pseudo-Roman Objects Found in India*. Delhi.

Swain, S. (2013). *Economy, Family, and Society from Rome to Islam. A Critical Edition, English Translation, and Study of Bryson's 'Management of the Estate'*. Cambridge.

Swiny, S., Hohlfelder, R. L., and Wylde-Swiny, H. (eds.) (1997). *Res Maritimae: Cyprus and the Eastern Mediterranean from Prehistory to Late Antiquity*. Atlanta.

Syme, R. (1939). *The Roman Revolution*. Oxford.

Tarn, W. W. (1923). 'The Social Question in the Third Century', in Bury et al., 108–40.

Tchernia, A. (1986). *Le Vin de l'Italie romaine: Essai d'histoire économique d'après les amphores*. BEFAR 261. Rome.

——(2009). 'L'Exportation du vin: Interprétations actuelles de l'exception gauloise', in Carlsen and Lo Cascio, 91–113.

Temin, P. (2004). 'Financial Intermediation in the Early Roman Empire', *Journal of Economic History* 64.3: 705–33.

——(2006). 'Estimating the GDP of the Early Roman Empire', in Lo Cascio (2006), 31–54.

——(forthcoming). 'Growth Theory for Ancient Economies', in Jongman (forthcoming).

Terrenato, N. (2001). 'The Auditorium Site and the Origins of the Roman Villa', *JRA* 14: 5–32.

Teuffel, W. S. (1889). *Studien und Charakteristiken zur griechischen und römischen Literaturgeschichte*. Leipzig.

Thirlwall, A. P. (2000). 'Trade, Trade Liberalisation and Economic Growth: Theory and Evidence', *African Development Bank. Economic Research Papers* 63. Abidjan.

Thomas, R. and Wilson, A. (1994). 'Water Supply for Roman Farms in Latium and South Etruria', *PBSR* 62: 139–96.

Thomsen, R. (1957). *Early Roman Coinage: A Study of the Chronology*. Copenhagen.

Thonemann, P. (2011). 'Eumenes II and Apollonioucharax', *Gephyra* 8: 1–12.

——(ed.) (2013*a*). *Attalid Asia Minor: Money, International Relations and the State*. Oxford.

——(2013*b*). 'The Attalid State, 188–133 BC', in Thonemann (2013*a*), 1–47.

Tomber, R. (2008). *Indo-Roman Trade: From Pots to Pepper*. London.

Torelli, M. R. (1982). 'La *De Imperio Cn. Pompeii*: Una politica per l'economia dell'impero', *Athenaeum* 60: 3–49.

——(1995). *Studies in the Romanization of Italy*. Edmonton.

——(1999). *Tota Italia: Essays in the Cultural Formation of Roman Italy*. Oxford.

Touratsoglou, I. (1987). 'Macedonia', in Burnett and Crawford, 53–78.

Toynbee, A. J. (1965). *Hannibal's Legacy: The Hannibalic War's Effects on Roman Life*. London.
Treggiari, S. (1969). *Roman Freedmen during the Late Republic*. Oxford.
Tréheux, J. (1992). *Inscriptions de Délos, Index I : Les étrangers, à l'exclusion des Athéniens de la clérouchie et des Romains*. Paris.
Trümper, M. (2004). 'The Oldest Original Synagogue Building in the Diaspora: The Delos Synagogue Reconsidered', *Hesperia* 73: 51–98.
—— (2008). *Die 'Agora des Italiens' in Delos: Baugeschichte, Architektur, Ausstattung und Funktion einer späthellenistischen Porticus-Anlage*. Internationale Archäologie 104. Rahden/Westfalen.
Tucci, P. L. (2006). 'Navalia', *Archeologia Classica* 57: 175–202.
Tuck, S. L. (2000). 'A New Identification for the "Porticus Aemilia"', *JRA* 13: 175–82.
Tunnicliffe, J. N. (1990). 'The Italian Involvement in Greece from the Third Century bc to 167 bc', D.Phil Thesis, Oxford.
United Nations Development Program (1992). *1992 Human Development Report*. New York.
Van Norstrand, J. J. (1937). 'Roman Spain', in Frank (1937), 119–224.
Vera, D. (ed.) (1999). *Demografia, sistemi agrari, regimi alimentari nel mondo antico: atti del convegno internazionale di studi (Parma, 17–19 ottobre 1997)*. Bari.
Verboven, K. (2002). *The Economy of Friends: Economic Aspects of Amicitia and Patronage in the Late Republic*. Brussels.
—— (2003). '54–44 bce: Financial or Monetary Crisis?', in Lo Cascio (2003), 49–68.
—— (2008). '*Faeneratores, Negotiatores* and Financial Intermediation in the Roman World (Late Republic and Early Empire)', in Verboven, Vandorpe, and Chankowski, 211–29.
—— Vandorpe, K., and Chankowski V. (eds.) (2008). *Pistoi Dia Tèn Technèn; Bankers, Loans and Archives in the Ancient World: Studies in Honour of Raymond Bogaert*. Leuven.
Visonà, P. and Frey-Kupper, S. (1996). 'The Romanization of the *Ager Bruttius* and the Evidence of Coin Finds. Part I', *SNR* 75: 77–100.
Volk, T. R. (1987). 'Mint Output and Coin Hoards', in Depeyrot, Hackens, and Moucharte, 141–221.
—— (1995). 'The Hoard as a Diagnostic Tool: The Different Patterns of Roman Silver Currency in Hispania and Italy at the End of the 2nd Century bc', in Campo, 41–62.
Von Reden, S. (2002). 'Money in the Ancient Economy: A Survey of Recent Research', *Klio* 84: 141–74.
Waggoner, N. M. (1979). 'The Propontis Hoard (*IGCH* 888)', *RN*[6] 21: 7–29.
Walbank, F. W. (1957). *A Historical Commentary on Polybius*, i. Oxford.
—— (1979). *A Historical Commentary on Polybius*, iii. Oxford.
—— (1983). '*Via illa nostra militaris*: Some Thoughts on the Via Egnatia', in Heinen, Stroheker, and Walser, 131–47.
Walker, D. R., (1978). *The Metrology of the Roman Silver Coinage, Part 3*. BAR Suppl. Ser. 40. Oxford.
—— (1980). 'The Silver Contents of the Roman Republican Coinage', in Metcalf and Oddy, 55–72.
—— (1988). 'The Roman Coins', in Cunliffe, 279–358.
Wallace-Hadrill, A. (2003). 'The Cities of Central Italy in the Second Century bc: Hellenization, Romanization and Local Identity'. Ancient History Seminar, 4 November 2003, Oxford University. Unpublished.
—— (2008). *Rome's Cultural Revolution*. Cambridge.
Ward-Perkins, B. (2005). *The Fall of Rome and the End of Civilisation*. Oxford.
—— Mills, N., Gadd, D., and Delano Smith, C. (1986). 'Luni and the *Ager Lunensis*: The Rise and Fall of a Roman Town and its Territory', *PBSR* 54: 81–146.
Warmington, E. H. (1938). *Remains of Old Latin*, iii. Cambridge, Mass.
Warren, J. A. W. (1999). 'More on the "New Landscape" in the Late Hellenistic Coinage in the Peloponnese', in Amandry, Hurter, and Bérend, 375–93.

Wassink, A. (1991). 'Inflation and Financial Policy under the Roman Empire to the Price Edict of 301 AD', *Historia* 40: 465–93.

Welles, C. B. (1934). *Royal Correspondence in the Hellenistic Period: A Study in Greek Epigraphy*. New Haven, Conn.

White, D. (1963). 'A Survey of Millstones from Morgantina', *AJA* 67.2: 199–206.

White, K. D. (1967). 'Latifundia. A Critical Review of the Evidence on Large Estates in Italy and Sicily up to the End of the First Century AD', *BICS* 14: 62–79.

Will, E. L. (1991). 'The Roman Shipping Amphorae from Arikamedu', in Begley and De Puma, 151–6.

Williams, J. H. C. (1998). 'Coinage, Credit and the *Aerarium* in the 80s BC', in Burnett, Wartenberg, and Witschonke, 173–83.

Williams-Thorpe, O., and Thorpe, R. S. (1990). 'Millstone Provenancing Used in Tracing the Route of a Fourth-Century BC Greek Merchant Ship', *Archaeometry* 32.2: 115–37.

Wilson, A. I. (1999). 'Commerce and Industry in Roman Sabratha', *Libyan Studies* 30: 29–52.

—— (2001). 'Timgad and Textile Production', in Mattingly and Salmon (2001*a*), 271–96.

—— (2002*a*). 'Urban Production in the Roman World', *PBSR* 70: 231–73.

—— (2002*b*). 'Machines, Power and the Ancient Economy', *JRS* 92: 1–32.

—— (2004). 'Tuscan Landscapes: Surveying the Albegna Valley. Review of Carandini and Cambi (2002)', *JRA* 17.2: 569–76.

—— (2006*a*). 'New Light on a Greek City: Archaeology and History at Euesperides', in Fabbricotti and Menozzi, 141–52.

—— (2006*b*) 'Fishy Business: Roman Exploitation of Marine Resources', *JRA* 19.2: 525–37.

—— (2008). 'Villas, Horticulture and Irrigation Infrastructure in the Tiber Valley', in Coarelli and Patterson, 731–68.

—— (2009*a*). 'Approaches to Quantifying Roman Trade', in Bowman and Wilson (2009*a*), 213–49.

—— (2009*b*). 'Indicators for Roman Economic Growth: A Response to W. Scheidel', *JRA* 22: 71–82.

—— Bennett, P., Buzaian, A. M., Buttrey, T., Göransson, K., Hall, C., Kattenberg, A., Scott, R., Swift, K., and Zimi, E. (2002). 'Euesperides (Benghazi): Preliminary Report on the Spring 2002 Season', *Libyan Studies* 33: 85–123.

—— —— —— —— Fell, V., Found, B., Göransson, K., Guinness, A., Hardy, J., Harris, K., Helm, R., Kattenberg, A., Morley, G., Swift, K., Wootton, W., and Zimi, E. (2003). 'Euesperides (Benghazi): Preliminary Report on the Spring 2003 Season', *Libyan Studies* 34: 191–228.

—— —— —— Fell, V., Found, B., Göransson, K., Guinness, A., Hardy, J., Harris, K., Helm, R., Kattenberg, A., Tébar Megias, E., Morley, G., Murphy, A., Swift, K., Twyman, J., Wootton, W., and Zimi, E. (2004). 'Euesperides (Benghazi): Preliminary Report on the Spring 2004 Season', *Libyan Studies* 35: 149–90.

—— —— —— Found, B., Göransson, K., Guinness, A., Hardy, J., Holman, J., Kattenberg, A., Morley, G., al-Mugasbi, M., Swift, K., Vaughan-Williams, A., Wootton, W., and Zimi, E. (2005). 'Euesperides 2005: Preliminary Report on the Spring 2005 Season', *Libyan Studies* 36: 135–82.

—— —— —— Cherstich, L., Found, B., Göransson, K., Holman, J., Lane, R., Morley, G., Russell, B., Swift, K., Vaughan-Williams, A., and Zimi, E. (2006). 'Euesperides 2006: Preliminary Report on the Spring 2006 Season', *Libyan Studies* 37: 117–57.

Wilson, A. J. N. (1966). *Emigration from Italy in the Republican Age of Rome*. Manchester.

Wiseman, T. P. (1969). 'The Census in the First Century BC', *JRS* 59: 59–75.

—— (1970*a*). 'The Definition of "Eques Romanus" in the Late Republic and Early Empire', *Historia* 19: 67–83.

—— (1970*b*). 'Roman Republican Road-Building', *PBSR* 38: 122–52.

—— (1971). *New Men in the Roman Senate, 139 BC–AD 14*. Oxford.

WITCHER, R. (2005). 'The Extended Metropolis: *Urbs*, *Suburbium* and Population', *JRA* 18.1: 120–38.

——(2006*a*). 'Broken Pots and Meaningless Dots? Surveying the Rural Landscapes of Roman Italy', *PBSR* 64: 39–72.

——(2006*b*). 'Settlement and Society in Early Imperial Etruria', *JRS* 96: 88–123.

WOOD, D. (ed.) (2004). *Medieval Money Matters*. Oxford.

WOOLF, G. (1992). 'Imperialism, Empire and the Integration of the Roman Economy', *World Archaeology* 23: 283–93.

——(2000). 'Peasant Economics'. Roman Economy Semester Two, St Andrews University. Unpublished.

WÖRRLE, M. (2000). 'Pergamon um 133 v. Chr.', *Chiron* 30: 543–76.

WOYTEK, B. (2003). *Arma et nummi: Forschungen zur römischen Finanzgeschichte und Münzprägung der Jahre 49 bis 42 v. Chr.* Vienna.

YOUNG, G. K. (2001). *Rome's Eastern Trade*. London.

ZALESSKIJ, N. N. (1982). 'Les Romains à Délos (de l'histoire du capital commercial et du capital usuraire romain)', in Coarelli, Musti and Solin, 21–49.

ZANKER, P. (ed.) (1976). *Hellenismus in Mittelitalien*. Göttingen.

ZETZEL, J. E. G. (1999). *Cicero: On the Commonwealth and on the Laws*. Cambridge.

ZEVI, F. (1976). 'L'identificazione del tempio di Marte "in Circo" e altre osservazioni', in Heurgon, ii. 1047–66.

ZIOLKOWSKI, A. (1986). 'The Plundering of Epirus in 167 BC: Economic Considerations', *PBSR* 54: 69–80.

——(1993). '*Urbs Direpta*, or How the Romans Sacked Cities', in Rich and Shipley, 69–91.

Index of Sources

[Anonymous]
Bellum Hispaniense
27. 1–3: 139

[Anonymous]
De Viris Illustribus
65: 69, 137
72. 1–2: 230
72. 2: 122, 242
73. 1: 138

[Anonymous]
Rhetorica ad Herennium
2. 13. 19: 243–4

Ampelius
33. 3: 61

Anthologia Graeca
9. 418: 158

Appian
Bella Civilia
1. 7: 161, 163, 169, 170, 173, 176, 286, 288
1. 7–8: 160
1. 8: 163
1. 9: 161, 173, 176
1. 10: 125, 141, 184, 185
1. 11: 161
1. 13–14: 160
1. 21: 69
1. 22: 77, 78–9
1. 23: 70, 225
1. 24: 70
1. 27: 184
1. 96: 247
1. 102: 249
2. 41: 260
2. 48: 261
5. 4: 60, 76, 81, 82
Hannibalica
54: 209
Hispanica
19: 44
43: 56
43–4: 70–1
44: 56
51–2: 28
59: 78
60: 31
78: 25 n. 36
Macedonica
9. 3: 38
Mithridatica
11: 195, 238
12. 57: 64
22: 213, 246, 249, 254
22–3: 209
24–7: 208
28: 213
47: 208
62: 61
62–3: 195, 256
75: 193
Punica
96: 209
135: 137
136: 138
Syriaca
38: 39

Asconius
In Cornelianam
58C: 256
In Orationem in Toga Candida
93C: 14 n. 39

Athenaeus
4. 152: 145
6. 274c: 104

Caesar
Bellum Africum
90: 296
97. 3: 137
Bellum Civile
1. 33. 3: 260
2. 18: 192
3. 1: 261
3. 1. 2: 127, 260, 261
3. 103: 101, 193
Bellum Gallicum
3. 1: 192
7. 3: 192
7. 55: 192

Cassiodorus
Chronicon
sub anno 158 BC: 56–7, 98

Cato
De Agricultura
praef. 1: 114
praef. 3: 192
praef. 4: 152
1. 3: 152, 178
1. 6: 152
1. 7: 148, 149
2. 5: 29, 93, 315–16, 317
2. 7: 152
3. 2: 152
3. 5: 149
4: 152, 169

Cato (*cont.*)
5. 1–5: 149
5. 4: 178
7. 8: 149
10: 229
10. 1: 149
10–11: 149
11: 144
11. 1: 149
14. 4–5: 225
18: 158, 229
20–2: 158, 229
21. 5: 286, 316
22: 136, 158–9
22. 3: 29, 160, 226, 287, 309
22. 3–5: 316
38: 158, 229, 230
39. 2: 152
39ff: 149
43: 156
54. 5: 148
135: 229
135. 1–3: 232
135–6: 136
136: 316
136–7: 178
142–3: 149
144–50: 178, 316
145: 93
146: 136
146. 1: 172
149: 93
149. 2: 115
150: 93

CGL
5. 32. 1: 32

Cicero
Brutus
27: 78
136: 184
De Amicitia
6: 136
De Domo Sua
60: 193
De Imperio Cnaei Pompeii
9: 254
11: 209
14: 73
15: 72, 76
17: 73
18: 212
19: 1 n. 2, 213, 245
32: 202
De Lege Agraria
1. 5: 53, 54
1. 21: 69, 137
2. 35: 249
2. 50: 54
2. 51: 53
2. 55: 78
2. 78: 134
2. 80: 74, 249
2. 82: 165
2. 89: 167
De Natura Deorum
2. 11: 136
De Officiis
1. 150–1: 134
1. 151: 133
2. 72: 69
2. 75: 78
2. 76: 55
2. 87: 240
2. 89: 148, 159, 241, 259
3. 47: 227
3. 58: 237
3. 59: 109
3. 80: 250
De Oratore
1. 82: 203
2. 22: 136
2. 154: 103
De Provinciis Consularibus
9–10: 193
De Republica
1. 1: 17, 136
1. 14: 136
1. 61: 178
3. 16: 28
3. 17: 293
3. 40: 17, 136
Divinatio in Q. Caecilium
19: 293
Epistulae ad Atticum
1. 12. 1: 238, 242, 255
1. 13: 196
1. 13. 1: 256
1. 14. 7: 255
1. 17. 9: 81
1. 20. 4: 196, 256
2. 1. 11: 240, 257
2. 6. 2: 99
2. 13. 2: 196, 256
2. 16. 1: 282
2. 16. 4: 99
5. 13. 1: 76
5. 13. 2: 196, 207
5. 15. 2: 196
5. 18. 2: 192
5. 20. 10: 196
5. 21: 260
5. 21. 6: 192
5. 21. 10–12: 195, 238
5. 21. 10–13: 256
5. 21. 12: 195, 242, 256
6. 1. 3: 195, 238
6. 1. 5: 242
6. 1. 5–6: 256
6. 1. 5–7: 195, 238
6. 1. 16: 256
6. 1. 19: 140

6. 2. 1: 256
6. 2. 3: 242
6. 2. 7–9: 195, 238, 256
6. 2. 9: 256
6. 3. 5: 195, 238, 256
6. 5. 2: 140
7. 7. 5: 241
7. 18. 4: 127, 260
7. 21. 2: 260
9. 9. 4: 127, 260
10. 4. 8: 260
10. 5. 3: 240
10. 8. 6: 260
10. 11. 2: 127, 260
10. 11. 5: 240
10. 13. 2: 240
10. 15. 4: 127, 240, 260
11. 1. 2: 99, 252
11. 1–2: 99
11. 3. 3: 240
11. 11. 2: 127
12. 2a. 1: 239
12. 3. 2: 115, 239, 240
12. 5a: 239, 265
12. 6. 1: 99
12. 11: 207
12. 24. 1: 196
12. 27. 2: 196
12. 31. 2: 239
12. 32. 2: 151, 196, 308
12. 47. 1: 115
13. 3. 1: 192, 239
13. 4. 2: 239
13. 32. 1: 239
13. 33. 1–2: 239
13. 37. 1: 196
14. 7. 2: 196
14. 9. 1: 151
14. 11. 2: 151
14. 16. 4: 196
14. 20. 3: 196
15. 13. 3: 240
15. 13a. 1: 240
15. 15. 4: 196
15. 17. 1: 151, 196
15. 20. 1: 240
15. 20. 4: 196
15. 29. 1: 231
16. 1. 1: 151
16. 1. 5: 196, 308
16. 6. 3: 109
Epistulae ad Familiares
1. 3: 193
1. 3. 1: 140
1. 5. 4: 193
2. 16. 5: 127
2. 17. 4: 101
5. 5: 238
5. 6. 2: 257
5. 15. 2: 211
5. 20: 99
7. 17. 2: 241
9. 16. 7: 264
12. 21: 192
12. 24: 192
12. 26: 192
12. 27: 192
12. 29: 192
13. 6. 3–4: 138
13. 7. 2: 140
13. 22: 192
13. 26: 192
13. 33: 192
13. 43: 193
13. 45: 193
13. 46: 193
13. 51: 193
13. 53: 193
13. 54: 193
13. 56. 1–3: 195
13. 61: 195, 256, 296
13. 63: 193
13. 69: 193
13. 72: 193
13. 73–4: 193
Epistulae ad Quintum Fratrem
1. 2. 10: 140
2. 11. 2: 193
2. 12. 1: 193
3. 2. 2: 193
In Catilinam
2. 21: 258
4. 4: 160
In Pisonem
41: 193
48: 193
In Vatinium
12: 23, 101, 258
In Verrem (Actio II)
1. 28: 109
1. 57: 27
1. 77: 41
1. 91: 193
1. 100: 109
1. 108: 250
1. 130: 225
2. 5–7: 140
2. 13: 203
2. 31: 192
2. 69: 192
2. 71: 192
2. 83–118: 197
2. 91: 197
2. 93: 197
2. 106: 197
2. 112: 197
2. 147: 197
2. 153: 192
2. 170: 242
2. 176: 206
2. 186–91: 242
3. 12: 76, 137

Cicero (*cont.*)
3. 12: 21–2, 56, 60
3. 13: 76
3. 14: 76
3. 36: 192
3. 41: 197
3. 55: 192
3. 60: 192
3. 61: 192
3. 69: 140
3. 75: 80
3. 84: 78, 102
3. 84ff: 80
3. 90: 102
3. 93: 140, 192
3. 97: 140, 192
3. 113: 80
3. 116: 80, 81
3. 120: 82
3. 130: 80
3. 151: 76
3. 163: 102
3. 167: 74
3. 173: 102
3. 174: 102
3. 175: 102
3. 188: 102
3. 189: 102
3. 194: 102
3. 195: 78
3. 216: 103
3. 218: 79
3. 227: 103
4. 3–6: 203
4. 15: 203
4. 25: 78
4. 37: 192
4. 41: 197
4. 42: 192
4. 46: 192
4. 121: 16
4. 150: 203
5. 17: 109
5. 20: 194
5. 45: 14, 141
5. 47: 203
5. 109: 197
5. 128: 197
5. 145–6: 205, 307
5. 146: 204, 206
5. 149: 13
5. 154: 202
5. 155: 237
5. 157: 205, 307
5. 161: 192
5. 165: 211, 237
Orator ad M. Brutum
232: 204
Paradoxa Stoicorum
46: 202, 256
49: 151, 194, 296
Philippicae
2. 97: 228
6. 15: 240
7. 16: 240
Pro Caecina
6: 238
10–11: 237, 254
16: 259
18: 79
27: 238
65: 79
Pro Caelio
62: 103
73: 138, 192
Pro Flacco
46: 140
54: 195, 256
67: 23, 101, 258
70: 193
71: 193
75: 195, 256
80: 193
88: 140
91: 193
Pro Fonteio
1–2: 247
11: 126, 145, 210
12: 140
46: 140, 210
Pro Quinctio
12: 140, 210
15: 212
17: 238, 247
25: 238
Pro Rabirio Postumo
4: 193
5: 257
6: 195, 239
21: 239
30: 81
Pro Rege Deiotaro
26: 193
Pro Roscio Amerino
20: 135
21: 135
133: 205
Pro Roscio Comoedo
4: 109
28: 287
Pro Sestio
18: 241
48: 141
93: 193
Pro Sulla
56: 257
58: 256
Tusculanae Disputationes
1. 13: 17
3. 48: 69

Cichorius
ad Ulpianum
14–22: 140
CIG
3142: 209
CIL
I² 592: 87
I² 627: 223
I² 628: 223
I² 629: 223
I² 630: 223
I² 631: 223
I² 1529: 222
I² 2663a: 126
III 531: 208
III 12266: 209
X 3975: 232
XII 4357: 212
Columella
De Re Rustica
1. 7: 178
3. 3. 8–10: 153
3. 3. 9: 109
3. 12. 5: 147
12. 39. 1–2: 147
12. 52. 6: 158–9
Customs Law of Asia
11: 205
12: 99, 180, 208
20: 205
61–2: 100
72: 76
99–101: 80
144–7: 80
Demosthenes
36. 5–6: 121, 242
36. 11: 127, 235
52. 4: 109
Digesta
26. 7: 135
39. 4. 1: 43
45. 1. 122. 1: 100
46. 2. 11ff.: 115
48. 10. 8–9: 250
48. 10. 19: 250
50. 5. 3: 14 n. 39
50. 16. 27: 22
50. 16. 178: 108
50. 16. 222: 108
Dio Cassius
37. 25. 4: 257
39. 55. 5: 193
41. 17. 1–2: 260
41. 37. 2: 260
41. 37. 3: 260, 261
41. 37–8: 261
41. 38. 1: 255, 260, 261
41. 38. 1–2: 113
41. 38. 3: 264
42. 51. 1: 261
48. 36. 5: 194, 296
54. 14. 1: 292
55. 10. 5: 14 n. 39
Diodorus Siculus
5. 13: 43
5. 26. 3: 145
5. 35. 1: 44
5. 36. 2: 52
5. 36. 3–4: 52, 179
5. 36. 4–37: 49
5. 37. 3–4: 46, 309
5. 38. 2: 44
11. 25. 5: 150
13. 81. 4–5: 150
13. 83. 3: 150
17. 80. 3: 190
20. 8. 3: 150
23. 4. 1: 37
23. 9. 1: 178
29. 10: 39
29. 21: 41
31. 8. 7: 54
31. 8. 11: 30
31. 24. 1: 104
34/5. 2. 2ff: 180
34/5. 6. 1: 160
34/5. 25. 1: 60
35. 25: 26, 70, 300
36. 2. 2: 104
36. 2a. 1: 104
36. 3. 1–2: 203
36. 3ff: 180
37. 3: 104
37. 3. 5: 104
37. 10. 1: 289
Dionysius of Halicarnassus
Antiquitates Romanae
3. 44. 3: 226
3. 67. 5: 11, 24, 217
5. 20. 1: 209
7. 63. 2: 33
17. 4. 3: 155
Donatus
Vita Vergilii
4: 204
Eusebius
Chronica
2. 130–1: 61
Eutropius
2. 19. 1: 37
4. 18: 61
4. 20: 62, 63
4. 21: 70
Festus
350L: 17
370L: 69, 220
379L: 22
516L: 246

Florus
1. 35: 62
2. 3: 61
2. 7. 3: 140
2. 7. 3ff: 180
2. 7. 10ff: 180

Frontinus
De Aquae Ductu Urbis Romae
1. 5: 194
1. 6: 34, 215
1. 7: 24, 220, 227, 286
8: 194
10: 194
Strategemata
4. 1. 45: 31
4. 3. 14: 223

Fronto
Epistulae
ad Verum Imp. 2. 1. 13: 60

Gaius
Institutiones
2. 69: 21
3. 128–30: 115–16
4. 16: 21

Gellius
Noctes Atticae
2. 22. 29: 50
2. 24. 2: 37
2. 24. 2–7: 104
4. 18: 40
4. 18. 7–12: 41
6. 3. 7: 28
6. 19: 40
10. 3. 3: 79
11. 10: 64
11. 10. 3: 70
11. 10. 3–4: 77
13. 25. 26–7: 33
15. 12. 4: 77, 79

Granius Licinianus
28. 31–6: 165

Herodotus
3. 90. 1–2: 72
3. 90–6: 38 n. 137
6. 42. 2: 72

Horace
Ars Poetica
421: 131
Carmina
1. 1. 11–14: 71
2. 6. 12: 172
2. 18. 1–6: 71
Epistulae
1. 14. 1–3: 178
1. 129–30: 134
Satirae
1. 3. 137: 103
2. 4. 69: 172
2. 8. 45: 172

IDélos
35: 139
353. 29–30: 139
353. 33–4: 139
354. 29–30: 139
356bis. 22: 139
359. A. 3: 139
368. 42: 139
395. 12: 139
396. 2: 139
399. 88: 139
399. 90–1: 139
442. 154: 139
1416. 5–8: 139
1519: 201
1520: 125, 201, 211, 212
1528–9: 201
1645: 200
1650: 200
1652: 200
1711–14: 201
1715: 201, 212
1715–29: 212
1722: 212
1725: 125, 211
1726: 125, 211
1727: 125, 211
1728: 125, 211
1729: 125, 211
1763: 211
1764: 232
1772–96: 201
2041: 201
2253: 212
2549 I–II: 206, 212
2612: 203

IEph.
646: 202
3025: 202

IG
II 428: 208
II 437: 208
IV 1. 2: 64
VII 4147: 208
IX 1^2 1. 17. 51: 198
IX 1^2 2. 241. 9: 29
XII 5. 816: 211
XII 5. 817. 5–11: 211
XII 5. 860: 125, 211, 259

IGCH
233: 96
271: 96
346: 96

IGRom.
4. 134: 62
4. 292: 66

ILLRP
100: 31
211: 31
245: 198

309–17: 17
319: 29
333: 62
454: 165, 180
458: 70
465: 225
518: 80, 225
528: 222
747: 126
760: 207
1025: 126

ILS
5771: 136
5892: 225

IMagn.
240: 202

IPerg.
249. 1. 14–15: 209

IPriene
108. 223–4: 63

Isidorus
Etymologiae
16. 18. 8: 22

Josephus
Antiquitates Judaicae
13. 223: 202

Justinus
Epitome of Trogus
12. 1. 1: 190
36. 4. 5: 61
36. 4. 9: 63, 101
37. 1. 1: 65
37. 1. 2: 64
38. 5. 3: 64

Lex agr.
6: 69, 137
22: 70
31–2: 164
59: 70
66: 138
70–2: 138
82–3: 138
85–9: 138
86: 137
96ff: 139

Lex rep.
1: 79
2–3: 79
12–13: 79
16–17: 79
22: 70
22–3: 79

Livy
6. 32. 1: 10
6. 35. 5: 163
6. 35. 5–6: 163
7. 16. 9: 163
7. 20. 9: 10
8. 36. 9: 222
9. 40. 16: 14 n. 42, 113
10. 13. 14: 163
10. 27: 9
10. 46. 12: 37
21. 62. 3: 10, 308
21. 63. 3: 14
22. 15: 150
22. 25. 19: 230
22. 33. 5: 38
23. 21. 4–5: 15
23. 30. 15: 205, 289
23. 31. 1–2: 15
23. 38. 12–13: 15
23. 48. 9–49. 4: 15
23. 49. 1: 50
24. 11. 6–9: 290
24. 11. 7–9: 15
24. 18. 2: 1 n. 2, 15
24. 18. 10–15: 15, 17
24. 18. 13: 224
25. 2. 6–8: 16
26. 35. 5: 15, 169
26. 36: 15, 26
26. 36. 11–12: 17
26. 47. 7–8: 49
26. 48. 14: 31
27. 3. 1: 164, 165
27. 10. 11: 16, 23
27. 11. 8: 164
27. 36. 12: 17, 24
28. 11. 8–9: 178, 181
28. 11. 9: 15, 167
28. 38. 14: 35
28. 45. 12: 35
28. 46. 4–5: 17, 164, 165
28. 46. 4–6: 17
29. 16. 1–3: 164
29. 36. 11–12: 164
29. 37. 5: 177
30. 37. 5: 38
30. 45. 3: 30, 36
31. 4. 1: 167
31. 4. 7: 16
31. 13. 6–9: 164
31. 20. 7: 30
31. 49. 2: 30
31. 49. 5: 167
31. 50. 4: 205, 289
32. 1. 6: 167
32. 7. 3: 164, 216
32. 7. 4: 30
32. 7. 13–14: 16
32. 27. 3–4: 114
33. 10. 7: 30
33. 11. 2: 30
33. 13. 14–15: 38
33. 23. 7–9: 31
33. 29. 12: 38
33. 30. 7: 38
33. 30. 8: 38

Livy (*cont.*)
33. 36. 1–3: 179
33. 42. 10: 148, 165
34. 4. 4: 11
34. 4. 8: 163
34. 4. 9: 163
34. 10. 4: 30, 95
34. 10. 7: 30, 95
34. 21. 7: 49–50
34. 35. 11: 38
34. 44. 4–5: 216
34. 45. 1: 74
34. 46. 2–3: 30, 95
34. 52. 4–11: 30
35. 7. 2–5: 115, 119, 244
35. 9. 1: 216
35. 10. 11–12: 148, 165
35. 10. 12: 23, 218
35. 20. 12: 26
35. 21. 1: 26
35. 24. 8: 26
35. 41. 9–10: 115
35. 41. 10: 218
36. 2. 13: 76
36. 2. 15: 26
36. 4. 5–9: 40
36. 36. 2: 33
36. 36. 4: 216
37. 2. 12: 76
37. 3. 7: 35
37. 5. 3: 34
37. 45. 14: 39
37. 46. 3–4: 34
37. 50. 10: 76
37. 55. 5–6: 71
37. 56. 1–4: 71
37. 57. 11: 34
37. 57. 12: 31
37. 58. 1: 216
38. 9. 9: 38
38. 9. 13: 38
38. 28. 3: 216
38. 37. 9: 39
38. 38. 13: 39
38. 39. 6: 42
38. 50–60: 40
38. 55. 10–12: 41
39. 2. 6: 218
39. 2. 10: 218
39. 3. 4–6: 227, 286
39. 6. 4–5: 41
39. 6. 7–9: 204
39. 7. 1–5: 217
39. 24. 2: 55
39. 29. 6–7: 51
39. 29. 8–9: 179
39. 44. 5–7: 217
39. 44. 7: 76, 81
39. 44. 7–8: 82
39. 44. 7–9: 51
39. 44. 8: 51
39. 46. 2–3: 205, 289
39. 55. 7–9: 167
40. 5. 7: 10, 217, 302, 327
40. 18. 7–8: 26
40. 29. 1–2: 167
40. 34. 5: 34
40. 43. 6: 30, 95
40. 46. 16: 217
40. 51. 2: 17, 141
40. 51. 2–7: 218
40. 51. 4: 220
40. 51. 7: 219
40. 51. 8: 51, 74, 219
40. 52. 4: 35
40. 59. 1–2: 31
41. 8. 6–12: 227, 286
41. 9. 9–10: 227, 286
41. 11. 8: 30
41. 13. 8: 223
41. 27. 5–12: 218
41. 27. 8: 218
41. 27. 10: 164
41. 27. 10–13: 222
41. 28. 8–9: 28, 71
41. 28. 11: 205, 289
42. 1. 6: 165
42. 6. 6–7: 39, 98, 179, 219
42. 8. 4: 165
42. 9. 7: 165
42. 19. 1: 165
42. 27. 1: 26
42. 31. 8: 76
42. 32. 6: 29
43. 2: 78
43. 2. 12: 78
43. 4. 6–7: 32
43. 12. 9: 26
43. 14. 7–8: 177
44. 16. 9: 217
45. 4. 1: 51
45. 10. 1: 30
45. 18. 3–5: 54, 98
45. 18. 4: 50, 57
45. 18. 8: 50
45. 29. 11: 50, 54, 98
45. 34. 1–6: 30
45. 36. 6: 31
45. 40. 2: 55
45. 40. 5: 31
45. 43. 4: 57
Periochae
11: 155
46: 302
49: 78
58: 62
59: 61, 136
60: 69, 70, 137, 300
68: 203
74: 245
89: 247

Lucilius
287–8: 140
440–2: 242
456–7: 23
650–1: 66
655: 140

Lucretius
5. 516: 158

I Maccabees
8. 3: 23, 49
15. 1–25: 202

II Maccabees
3. 11: 98
8. 10: *39*, 98
8: 10–11: 30, 179

Macrobius
Commentarius in Somnium Scipionis
3. 6. 11: 203
Saturnalia
3. 16. 3: 136

Martial
13. 101: 172

Memnon
Fragmenta (FGrH)
III B 434. F. 22. 9: 209

Nepos
Atticus
1. 1: 197, 293
2. 1–2: 197
2. 2: 256
2. 2. 4: 196
5. 1–2: 196, 296
6. 4: 193
12. 4: 138
13. 6–7: 197, 296
14. 2: 197
14. 3: 196
15. 3: 192
Cato
1. 1: 17

Nonius Marcellus
728: 125

OGIS
338: 61
339: 62
484: 251
524: 202
751: 72

ORF[4]
26: 115
51: 136
66: 163
82: 34
182: 34, 77, 79
187: 70
187–8: 77
190–2: 79

Orosius
4. 7. 3: 37
5. 8. 4: 61
5. 9. 4: 180
5. 9. 6: 203
5. 10: 63
5. 10. 1–3: 62
5. 10. 1–4: 62
5. 12: 69, 70
5. 18. 26–7: 249
6. 15. 5: 260

Paulus Diaconus
Epitome of Festus
88. 4: 202

Paulus, Julius
Sententiae
5. 25. 1-1A: 250

Pausanias
3. 23. 3–6: 202
3. 23. 4: 213
7. 11. 4–8: 96
7. 16. 9–10: 139

Plautus
Asinaria
440: 121
Aulularia
317: 117
530: 124
Bacchides
1075: 31
Captivi
192–3: 120
449: 120
505: 117
Casina
23–8: 123
25–8: 119
Curculio
269: 118
371–9: 123
466–9: 118
470: 118
471: 118
476: 118
477: 118
479: 118
481: 118
482: 118
483: 118
502: 118
506–11: 119
507: 118
508: 122
618: 120
682: 123
Epidicus
25–8: 117
141–5: 122
182: 117

Plautus (*cont.*)
188: 117
343: 117
620–47: 119
Mercator
75–8: 198
87–9: 198
93–4: 198
664: 117
Mostellaria
532–54: 119
Persa
433–6: 119, 120
442–3: 119
Poenulus
727: 117
Pseudolus
296–8: 119, 123
1229–30: 120
Truculentus
66–73: 124
141–51: 163

Pliny (the Elder)
Historia Naturalis
2. 209: 209
3. 95: 168
3. 60: 9, 150, 172
3. 138: 44, 56
6. 100–1: 206
6. 106: 206
7. 140: 14
7. 199: 209
8. 196: 63
12. 51–65: 206
12. 84: 99
13. 4: 205, 232, 307
14. 47–9: 17, 136
14. 48–52: 152
14. 56: 104
14. 95: 104
14. 127: 231
15. 8: 137, 172
18. 22: 147
18. 35: 134–5, 138
18. 41–3: 152
18. 97: 158
18. 107: 2 n. 5
18. 111: 172
18. 187: 159
18. 191: 159
18. 317: 158
33. 5: 23
33. 43: 22
33. 45: 288
33. 46: 248
33. 48: 23
33. 51: 23, 38
33. 55: 22, 248
33. 55–6: 57
33. 56: 30, 55, 260
33. 57: 220
33. 72–7: 45
33. 78: 23, 44, 45, 50, 56
33. 95: 52
33. 97: 44, 45
33. 132: 250
33. 133: 293
33. 134: 194, 296
33. 135: 134
33. 138: 204, 217
33. 141: 197, 289
33. 147: 104
33. 148–9: 63
33. 149: 71
34. 9: 202, 205
34. 12: 223
34. 27: 250
34. 36: 223
34. 173: 52
36. 103: 104, 194, 289
36. 109: 194, 289
36. 115: 104, 194
37. 202: 44, 56

Pliny (the Younger)
Epistulae
3. 19. 8: 134, 195

Plutarch
Aemilius Paullus
5. 4: 136
28. 6: 54, 219
28. 11: 31, 36
29. 4: 30
29. 5: 31
32. 4–9: 30
38: 55
Aratus
12: 198
Brutus
24: 101
25: 101
Caesar
5. 4: 195
8. 4: 301
12. 1–2: 241
12. 2: 29
35: 260
37. 1: 261
55: 137
Cato Maior
1. 1: 17, 136
2. 2: 17
3. 2: 17
4. 4: 136
19: 51
21: 203
21. 5: 230–1
21. 5–6: 14 n. 40, 114, 134, 145–6, 212
27. 1: 147

Cato Minor
16: 11
18. 5: 27
26. 1: 301
38. 1: 101
59. 2: 139
61. 2: 139
Cicero
31. 1: 292
Crassus
2. 2: 194, 296
2. 4: 227
5: 53
6. 6: 247
Flamininus
9. 5: 38
Gaius Gracchus
2. 5: 77
3. 2: 160
5: 26, 69, 70, 137, 300
6: 70, 101
6. 3: 69, 220, 225
8: 70
8. 7: 161
9. 2: 184
10: 70
19. 1: 136
Lucullus
7. 5: 195, 256
20. 4: 195, 256
Marcellus
34: 194
Numa
17: 225
Pompeius
2. 4: 194, 296
4. 1: 249
10. 6: 197
11: 94
27. 1: 202
45: 72, 217
Sulla
8: 246
12: 252
19: 252
24. 4: 209
25. 2: 195, 256
Tiberius Gracchus
8: 160
8. 2–3: 160
8. 3: 173, 176
8. 7: 171, 180
10. 5: 161
13. 3: 161
14: 61, 62, 71
21: 62

Polybius
1. 3. 9: 21
1. 11. 2: 29
1. 16. 9: 37
1. 29. 7: 28
1. 39. 1–2: 28
1. 62. 8–9: 37
1. 63. 3: 37
1. 83. 7–8: 13
1. 88. 12: 37
2. 8. 3: 13, 198
2. 12. 3: 38
2. 15: 93
2. 15. 6: 102
2. 24: 173
2. 24. 14: 292
2. 24. 16: 9
3. 27. 5: 37
3. 27. 8: 37
3. 39. 8: 101, 220
3. 59. 7: 102
3. 91. 2–3: 150
6. 13: 11
6. 17: 134, 282
6. 17. 2: 43–4, 50, 286, 333
6. 17. 2–4: 224–5
6.17. 3: 52
6. 19. 2: 25
6. 19. 5: 25
6. 21. 6–7: 26, 300
6. 39. 12: 22, 26, 288
6. 39. 15: 26, 300
9. 10. 11: 27
9. 11a: 16
10. 16. 2–9: 31
10. 17. 9–10: 50
10. 19. 2: 17, 24, 26
15. 18. 7–8: 38
16. 23. 7: 35
18. 35. 4: 30, 209
18. 35. 4–12: 34
18. 35. 9–10: 136
18. 35. 9–11: 211
18. 39. 5–6: 38
18. 44. 7: 38
21. 3. 3: 38
21. 11. 9: 38
21. 14. 7: 40
21. 17. 4–5: 39
21. 17. 5: 41
21. 22. 15: 71
21. 24. 6–8: 71
21. 26. 9–14: 36
21. 30. 2: 38
21. 30. 10: 38
21. 32. 8: 41
21. 32. 8–9: 38
21. 40. 8: 41
21. 42. 14: 101
21. 42. 19: 39
21. 45. 2–3: 71
23. 9. 3: 200
23. 9. 12: 198
23. 14: 40
23. 14. 7: 40

Polybius (*cont.*)
23. 14. 7–11: 41
23. 17. 3: 198
24. 1. 1: 200
28. 2. 2: 198
29. 7: 178
30. 5. 12: 199
30. 15: 30
30. 21. 3–5: 199, 208
30. 31. 2: 24
30. 31. 12: 29, 199
31. 5. 5: 104
31. 25. 6–8: 204
31. 27: 36
31. 27. 6–7: 121, 242, 243
31. 28. 3: 35
31. 28. 5–6: 205, 289
31. 29: 204
31. 32. 8: 22, 23
32. 8. 3: 71, 72
34. 8. 7–8: 102
34. 8. 8: 139
34. 9. 8–9: 44–5, 73, 216
34. 9. 10–11: 46, 310
34. 10. 10–15: 23, 57
34. 12. 2a–8: 220
39. 5: 64

Porphyrio
ad Hor. *Epist.* 1. 1. 52–9: 240–1
ad Hor. *Sat.* 2. 3. 18: 240–1

Posidonius
Fragmenta (FGrH)
IIA 87 F. 36: 213
IIA 87 F. 47: 52, 53
IIA 87 F. 51: 56
IIA 87 F. 108: 180

POxy.
L 3595–7: 228

Propertius
2. 32. 12: 63

Pseudo-Acro
ad Hor. *Epist.* 1. 1. 52–9: 240
ad Hor. *Sat.* 2. 3. 18: 240

Pseudo-Asconius
schol. ad Cic. *II Verr.* 1. 157: 32

RC
54. 7–8: 72

RDGE
11: 61, 62
12: 67
13: 77
16: 68
43: 64
65: 67

RRC
473/4: 126

RRCH
228: 96
242: 96
465: 96
467: 96
473: 96

Sallust
Bellum Catilinae
14. 2: 258
20. 13: 258
21. 2: 257
24. 3: 258
33. 1: 257
33. 2: 246
40. 2: 210
41. 1: 258
Bellum Iugurthinum
17. 5: 137
26. 3: 138, 210
27. 5: 94
36. 1: 94
41. 7: 34, 170, 176, 288
44. 5: 138
47. 1: 138, 210
64. 5: 138, 210
Historiae
2. 43: 65

Sammelb.
III. 7169: 206

Scholia Bobiensia
135 St: 69
157 St: 81

SEG
2. 580: 72
50. 1211: 63
50. 1211. 11: 61
50. 1212: 62

Seneca (the Elder)
Controversiae
2: 62

Seneca (the Younger)
Epistulae
41. 7: 194–5
86: 17
86. 14: 136
86. 17–20: 136

Servius
In Aen. 8. 363: 203

Siculus Flaccus
Gr. P. 116 Th.: 135

Strabo
2. 3. 4: 206
2. 5. 12: 206
2. 98–9: 99
3. 2. 8: 44, 47

3. 2. 9: 46, 52, 53, 309
3. 2. 10: 44–5, 46, 53, 216, 310
3. 3. 1: 139
3. 4. 13: 56
3. 5. 11: 209
4. 2. 3: 145
4. 5. 3: 73
4. 6. 7: 23, 50
4. 6. 12: 57
5. 1. 11: 218, 303
5. 3. 5: 226
5. 3. 7: 226
5. 3. 10: 172
5. 4. 8: 172
10. 5. 2: 191
10. 5. 4: 199–200
12. 1. 4: 64
12. 3. 7: 64
12. 4. 1: 64
12. 7. 2: 72
12. 8. 1: 64
12. 8. 11: 209
13. 4. 1: 71
13. 4. 2: 61
14. 1. 38: 62, 63
14. 3. 2–4: 64
14. 3. 3: 203
14. 5. 2: 180, 189, 200, 202, 203
15. 3. 9: 190
16. 2. 23: 209

Suetonius
De Vita Caesarum
Divus Augustus
2. 3: 122
3. 1: 122
4. 2: 122
Divus Julius
26. 3: 288
42: 261
54. 2: 260
Tiberius
48: 261
Vita Terentii
1: 136

Syll.[3]
588. 102: 35
609: 34
610: 34
617. 6: 35
729: 97
742. 58–62: 254
748: 256
1007. 20–1: 72

Tacitus
Annales
1.17. 6: 288
4. 14: 208
6. 16: 244, 259
6. 16. 3: 238
6. 16–17: 261, 262
6. 17: 122, 263
6. 17. 3: 237
Historiae
3. 8: 59
3. 19: 32

Terence
Phormio
923–4: 123

Thucydides
6. 34. 2: 209

TPSulp.
69: 237

Valerius Maximus
2. 5. 1: 34
2. 10. 2: 17
3. 2. 12: 62
3. 4. 4: 229–30
3. 7. 1: 41
4. 4. 1: 31
4. 4. 8: 136
4. 8. 3: 195, 241
5. 2: 61
5. 3. 2e: 62
6. 5. 4: 242
6. 9. 7: 193
7. 6. 4: 249, 257
7. 8. 5: 196
9. 2 ext 3: 189, 209

Varro
De Lingua Latina
5. 182: 22
De Re Rustica
1. 1. 10: 147
1. 2. 6: 150, 172
1. 2. 7–8: 152
1. 2. 22: 147
1. 2. 22–3: 230
1. 16. 6: 135
1. 17. 5: 179
2. *praef* 6: 148, 159
3. 2. 7: 156
3. 2. 14: 156
3. 2. 17: 156
3. 4. 3: 156
3. 5. 9: 156
3. 16. 10–11: 148
3. 17. 5: 156
3. 17. 9: 156
Fragmenta
fr. 68: 63, 71

Velleius Paterculus
1. 15: 70
1. 15. 2–3: 168
1. 15. 4: 69, 137

Velleius Paterculus (*cont.*)
2. 1. 1: 204
2. 4. 1: 61
2. 6: 70
2. 6. 3: 69, 74, 137
2. 6. 5: 23
2. 7: 70
2. 7. 7: 177
2. 23. 2: 246
2. 38. 5: 66

Vergil
Aeneid
1. 33: 215

Vitruvius
De Architectura
2. 8. 1: 221

Zonaras
8. 16: 28, 37
8. 18: 28
9. 19: 34

General Index

account books/accounting 40, 102, 121, 124, 126, 210
  amortization 152
  depreciation 152, 153
  double-entry bookkeeping 152, 154
  see also *nomina*
Achaean League 96, 139, 198
Acilius Glabrio, M'. 31, 34
Aelius Tubero, Q. 136
Aemilius Lepidus, M. (*cos.* 187 BC) 17, 51, 141, 217–18
Aemilius Lepidus, M. (*cos.* 78 BC) 194, 289
Aemilius Paullus, L. 30, 31, 35, 36, 54, 55, 179, 217–18
Aemilius Regillus, L. 34–5
Aemilius Scaurus, M. (*cos.* 115 BC) 122, 230, 242, 303
Aemilius Scaurus, M. (*pr.* 56 BC) 194
aerarium sanctius 16, 23
aerarium Saturni 16, 17, 18, 26, 83
  booty 27, 30, 35, 41, 218
  holdings 3, 22–3, 57, 219
  and opening/closure of mines 58
  records 27, 42, 74
  reserves 247–8
  and state expenditure 25–9, 221, 233
  staff 11, 26, 244
aes alienum, *see* debt
aes grave 37, *38*
Aetolia 22 n. 7, 23 n. 15, 29, 38, *39*, 41
  Roman-Aetolian treaty 29
Afranius, L. 125
Africa
  centuriation 137, 138
  colonies in 69–70, 138
  olive oil production 137
  Roman coinage 94–5, 312
  taxation 137
Ager Caecubus 222
Ager Campanus 164, 165, 166, 184, 222, *298*
ager censorius 164, 165, 185
Ager Cosanus 170, 231 n. 108
Ager Falernus 150
Ager Faliscus 148, 172
Ager Gallicus 9, 222
ager in trientabulis 164, 166
ager occupatorius 162–3, 165, 166, 184, 185, 188
Ager Praenestinus 134
ager privatus vectigalisque 184
ager publicus (public land) 53, 160–8, 187–8
  agri Attalici 62 n. 13
  animal husbandry 148, 159, 163, 165 n. 242, 166
  colonies and 166, 167–8
  Corinth 139
  location/legal status 162
  privatization of 94–5, 164–6, 184–5
  viritane land distribution 167–8
ager quaestorius 164
ager scripturarius 163, 184–5
Ager Tarquiniensis 254
agrarian commission 69, 141, 161, 299
agrarian crises 160–2, 170, 173–8
agrarian reforms 176–7, 183, 185, 188, 189–90
agricolae, see farmers
agricultural equipment 216, 229, 232, 309
  torcularia (presses) 156, 158–9, 172, 229, 232, 309
  trapeti (rotary mills) 158–9, 229, 232, 316
  see also lime kilns; water management; water mills
agricultural exploitation 131–2, 137, 139–41, 151, 154, 186–7, 331
agricultural profitability 151–4, 155, 169
agricultural techniques 132, 331
agricultural treatises 137, 146, 147, 154, 281
agriculture, 131–88, 331–2
  absentee landowners 135, 136, 152, 187
  agrarian crises 160–2, 170, 173–8
  animal husbandry 148, 159, 163, 165 n. 242, 166
  exports 141–7
  farm management 152
  growth of free population 173–8
  investment farming 147–55
  investment in land 133–41
  investment in technology 155–60
  ley farming 159
  market gardening (*pastio villatica*) 148, 156–7, 166
  monetization, level of 316–17, *317*
  peasants and 166–73
  risk management 135
  slaves in 149, 155, 161–2, 286
  villa system 15, 132, 147, 168–9, 187
  water management 156
  woodland clearance 155
agrimensores (land surveyors) 162 n. 223, 164
Alexander III ('the Great') of Macedon 190
allies 9, 25, 54–5, 56 n. 90, 66, 79, 114–6, 138, 162–3, 183, 185, 185 n. 358, 188, 203, 227, 285 n. 50, 286, 300, *300*
Ambracia 38, *39*
amphorae (transport) 12, 141–6, 159, 172, 186, 228, 231
animal husbandry, *see* agriculture

Antiochus III of Syria 42, 65, 71, 72 n. 81, 329
indemnities 28–9, 38–41, 216–17
Antipater of Thessalonica 158
Antonius, C. 238
Antonius, L. 240
Antonius, M., ('Mark Antony') 59–60, 72, 81, 82, 122 n. 83
Antonius, M. (*cos.* 99 BC) 203
Apamea, treaty of 71, 97, 101
Aperghis monetary model of Seleucid Mesopotamia 4–5, 320–1
Apollonius of Panhormus 194
Appuleius Decianus, C. 193
Aqua Anio Vetus 10, 34, 215, 220
Aqua Appia 10, 220
Aqua Marcia 24, 219, 220, 226, 232, 286, 302, 308, 330
Aqua Tepula 220, 232, 302, 308
aqueducts 11, 24, 136 n. 30, 220, 222, 308, 329; *see also individual aqueducts*
Aquillius, M'. 63, 64–5, 78–9, 220
Aquillius, M. 195, 238
Archimedes screw 46, 309
argentariae 119, 235, *see also* banks; *mensae*
argentarii 14, 110, 113–14, 127, 236, 239–40, 242, 258, 265, 329, 333
in Cicero 237–8
in Plautus 118–20
see also bankers; *trapezitae*
Ariarathes IV of Cappadocia 42
Ariarathes V of Cappadocia 62, 64
Ariobarzanes of Cappadocia 195, 238
aristocratic financiers 109, 235, 236, 238–42, 255, *see also* daneistai
Aristonicus, revolt of 62, 63
armed forces
see army; navy
arms, *see* weapons
army 229
and agrarian crisis 169–70
and coin usage 11, 315
donatives 287–8
expenditure on 11, 25, 26, 248 n. 93, 298–300
financial difficulties 15
generals 29–30, 31–4, 41, 51, 287
military service 25, 26 n. 43, 70, 162, 168, 169, 170, 176, 287–8
rates of pay 22, 287, 288 nn. 69 & 71, 299, *299*
size of 25, 169
see also military expenditure; viritane land distribution
artefact scatters, interpretation of 133
Asia, province of
Roman businessmen in 209
Roman coinage in 98–9
Roman land ownership in 139–40
see also *lex Sempronia de provincia Asia*
assidui 161, 168, 176
meaning of 161 n. 214
associations, see *collegia*
ateleia 208, 213, *see also* duty-free status
Attalid dynasty
annual income 72 n. 82
closed monetary system 97–8
Attalus III Philometor of Pergamum 61–2
Atticus, *see* Pomponius Atticus, T.
auctions 30, 62, 63, 71, 76, 79–80, 81, 125, 212, 238, 239, 259
Aufidius, T. 193
Aufidii 125, 211, 258–9
Aurelius Cotta, L. 78–9, 242
Aurelius Orestes, L. 77

bankers 113–27, 236–44, 252–5, 264–5
on Delos 101, 124–5, 211–12, 258–9
see also *argentarii*; *coactores argentarii*; *trapezitae*
banks and banking 26, 107–28, 235–65, 313
1st century BC 237–42
1st/2nd centuries AD 236–7, 238
2nd century BC 107–25
asymmetric knowledge 236, 265
balance sheets 111, *111*, 123, 252–3, *253*, *254*, 283, 313, 319, 333
banking models 110–13, *111*, 252–3, *253*
banking crises, *see* credit crises
currency conversion 99
financial intermediation, evidence for 113–24
growth of profession 124–7
legal rules 243–4, 246
margins 110, 257
mensae 122–3, 235, 237, 263
reserve ratios 112 n. 22, 253
scale of deposits 313, *314*
see also *argentariae*; *argentarii*; bankers; money-multiplier effect; *trapezitae*
bankruptcy 16, 253
barter system 145, 316
Basilica Fulvia-Aemilia 302
Basilica Opimia 303
Basilica Porcia 11, 217, 302
Basilica Sempronia 302
Baths of Caracalla 225, 226
Betilienus L. f. Varus, L. 222
bilge pumps 143, 281, 282
Boeotia 38, *39*, 208
bonds, *see* government bonds
booty (*praeda*) 21, 27, 29–35, 41, 51, 190, 218, 219, 323, 328
distribution of 30–3
figures for 298, *298*
manubiae 32–4, 37, 330
brick production 228, 230
British School of Rome survey 172
brokers (*intercessores*, *proxenitae*) 110, 242 n. 56
bronze coins 44, 89, 94, 95, 312, 322
as 15, 16, 284
fall in weight of 15

minted coins, increase in use of 11
quadrans 103–4, 284
sextans 103–4, 284
see also *aes grave*
bronzeware 232
Bryson 152 n. 144
budgets 59, 83
bullion 190
closure of bullion mines 54, 56, 58, 98
importance to Roman state 27
as indemnities 55, 56
and price rises 87–8
see also gold; silver
bureaucracy, *see under* Roman state
businessmen, see *negotiatores*

Caecilius, Q. (Atticus' uncle) 196, 293, 296
Caecilius Isidorus, C. 134
Caecilius Metellus, L. 14
Caecilius Metellus, Q. 69, 304
Caecilius Metellus Macedonicus, Q. 220–1
Caelius Rufus, M. 138, 241
Caerellia 193
Calpurnius Piso Frugi, L. 78
Campania 9–10, 14, 17, 114, 139, 149, 168, 289, 307
ager censorius 185
ager publicus, privatization of 187, 219, 332
euergetism 222
kilns 12, 142, 231
land ownership 135–6, 150, 165
luxury villas 204, 307
olive oil production 158, 166, 171
wine trade 142, 150, 166, 171
see also Ager Campanus
capital 273, 274, 276, 279, 289, 292
availability of 194–7
in *emporia* 211–12
capital investment 45–6, 155–60, 302, 303, 304, 308–10, *309*, 316, *316*, 317, *317*
Cappadocia *39*
cargoes 100–1, 142–3, 186, 198, 205, 226, 276, 306–7
Carthage 69–70
coinage 94–5
indemnities 37–40, *38*, *39*
silver mines 44
trade networks 209–10
Carthago Nova 36, 44–5, 46–9, 50, 52, 53, 95
Carvilius Maximus, Sp. 37
Castricius, M. 195, 256
Catiline conspiracy 257–8
Cato the Elder, *see* Porcius Cato, M.
censoria locatio 76–82, 282, 331
see also *publicani*
census figures 173–4, *174*, 175–8, *177*, *178*
centuriation 137, 138, 167, 168, 171: *see also* viritane land distributions
Cicero, *see* Tullius Cicero, M.
Circus Flaminius 11
cistophori, *see* civic coinages
civic coinages 98–9, 251–2, 312
cistophori 71–2, 97, 98, 99
Greek 96–7, 98, 101, 251
Iberian denarii 95–6, 100, 251
Claudius, Q. 13–14
Claudius Marcellus, M. (*cos.* 196 BC) 16
Claudius Marcellus, M. (*cos.* 166, 155, 152 BC) 56
Cloaca Maxima 217, *see also* sewers
Cloatii 256
Clodius Pulcher, P. 194, 289
Clodius Phormio, Sex. 237–8
closed monetary systems
Attalids 71–2, 97–8
Egypt 71, 94, 99–100
Cluvius, M. 195, 242, 256
coactores argentarii 125, 236
coinage
Athenian tetradrachms 96–7, 98, 101, 251, 320
Carthage 94–5
exchange rates between silver and bronze coin 250–1
fall in Macedonian and Seleucid weight standards 98
hoards 23, 90–3, 94–6, 97, 99, 100, 248 n. 98, 251 n. 116, 257, 312, 314, 329
hoarding 92, 107, 112–13, 255, 260, 262, 264, 319 n. 188
quantification of Seleucid coinage 320–1
re-coinage 94, 252
in shipwrecks 101
see also bronze coins; civic coinages; *denarii*; Roman coinage; silver coins
collegia (associations) 125, 200–1, 209, 225, 226
colonies 10, 171, 183, 285
in Africa 69–70, 138
and *ager publicus* 163, 164, 166, 167–8
Junonia 69–70, 94, 137–8
see also viritane land distribution
Columella 147, 152, 153–4
commercial networks, *see* trade
commercium, right of 116
Considius, Q. 195, 241–2
construction materials 9–11, 230, 310
bricks 228, 230
concrete 2, 221, 302
lime 230
marble 10, 220–1, 303
tufa 10, 11, 221
construction projects 65, 217–20, 233, 301–3
basilicas 11, 217, 218, 222, 302, 303
bridges 218, 220, 302–3
business buildings 217
city walls 10
collegium of builders 225
construction industry 224–7
costs 24
and economic growth 279, 286
in Italy 221–4
porticoes 217–18, 222

construction projects (*cont.*)
  residential housing, Rome 308
  Rome 216–21
  sewers 11, 24, 217, 302
  see also aqueducts; construction materials; roads; temples
construction techniques
  opus incertum 221, 230
  opus reticulatum 221, 230
  opus vermiculatum 306
consumer goods 227: *see also* luxury goods
contracts 14 n. 39, 15, 17, 23, 228
  building/repairing contracts 24, 134
  for clothing for legions in Spain 12, 289
  publicani and 12, 15, 289
  with *societates publicanorum* 80–1
corn dole, *see* grain subsidies
Cornelius Cethegus, C. 16
Cornelius Cethegus, M. 302
Cornelius Lentulus, P. 165
Cornelius Rufinus, P. 37
  wealth of 289
Cornelius Scipio Africanus, P. 16, 17, 40–1, 136, 330
  and silver mines at Carthago Nova 50
  triumph 30
  wealth of 16, 35–7, 196, 289, 290
Cornelius Scipio Africanus Aemilianus, P. 35–6, 121, 136, 197, 200
  annexation of Punic territory 137
  bank deposits 121, 314
  villae expolitissimae 204
Cornelius Scipio Asiaticus, L. 40–1
Cornelius Scipio Nasica, P. (*cos.* 191 BC) 33
Cornelius Scipio Nasica Corculum, P. 121, 122
Cornelius Scipio Nasica Serapio, P. 62, 63, 161
Cornelius Sulla Felix, L. 195, 246
  abolition of corn dole 300
  and gold coinage 249
  proscriptions 247
  wealth of 295, 296
corruption 78–9
counterparty risk 255
court of justice (*quaestio perpetua*) 78
credit 107–28, 235–65, 313
credit crises 243–64, 333
  80s BC 243–57, 263–4
  60s BC 257–9
  40s BC 260–4
  33 AD 262–3, 264
  2008 AD 244–6
  economic impact 264–5
credit risk 110, 146, 255, 265
credit-worthiness 110
creditores 240, 242, 245 n. 73, 262, 263, see also *faeneratores*
customs duties 24, 29, 97, 199, 206: see also *portoria*
Customs Law of Asia 4, 74–5, 76, 80, 82–3, 98–9, 100, 180, 205
Cyrene: bequeathed to Rome 65

daneistai (moneylenders) 125
De Agricultura (Cato the Elder) 15, 132, 133, 136, 147, 148, 149–50, 151–2, 154, 168–9, 225, 229, 230, 232, 309, 315
debt
  aes alienum 127, 246–7, 259–60, 264
  defaults 219, 245–6
  delegatio debitoris 115–16, 239, 243, 264–5
  nomina 109, 115–16, 239
  receptum argentarii 244
  reciprocal, compensation for 244
  see also public sector debt
decumae (agricultural tithes) 55–6, 72, 75, 76, 81, 282, *298*
delegatio debitoris 115–16, 239, 243, 264–5
Delos
  2nd century BC 197–202, 213, 223, 332
  banking profession 101, 124–5, 211–12, 258–9
  importance as *emporium* 191
  perfume trade 205–6, 307
  purple dye 205–6
  slaves 180, 202–6
Demetrius of Gadara 194, 296
demographics, *see* population
denarii 2, 16, 22–3, 89–93, 251–2, 311–12
  numbers in circulation 89–93, *90*, 311–13, 321–2
  retariffing against the *as* 103–4, 284, 288 n. 71
  silver fineness 248, 252
  testing of 250
  typology 89
  see also coinage; Iberian *denarii*; Roman coinage; silver coins
deposit banks, *see* banks and banking
Didius, T. 66
didrachm coinage system 15–16, 44
diet, *see* food
Digest 108, 237, 243
Diodorus Pasparus 66
Domitius Ahenobarbus, Cn. 68
donatives 36, 170, 287–8
Duillius, C. 29, 44
duty-free status 199, 332, see also *ateleia*
dyes/dyeing, *see* purple dye production

economic growth 269–78, 297, 324–5
  construction projects and 279, 286
  and demographic change 272–3
  institutions and 282–3
  technology improvements and 281–2
  trade and 280
  warfare and 279
Egnatius Rufus, L. 193
Egypt
  bequeathed to Rome 65
  closed monetary system 94, 99–100
  gift of bullion to Rome 16

emigration of Roman citizens 182, 296
emporia 197, 202, 213, 217–18, 289
  financial capital in 211–12
  see also Delos
epidemics 175 n. 294, 179, 183
equites 15, 51, 135
  equestrian status, qualification for 12, 293–4
  financial dealings 31, 127, 189
  income 292–6
  income threshold 287
  land ownership in provinces 140
  numbers of 292
Eudemus of Pergamum 62
euergetism 216, 222–3, 224, 233, 283, 332
Euesperides 13
Eumenes II Soter of Pergamum 71–2, 97–8
Europe
  early modern 6, 87, 275, 276, 281, 318, 323, 325
  medieval 6, 47, 91, 127, 154, 159, 190, 253, 281, 313, 318, 323, 325
expenditure, *see under* GDP
export trade, *see* trade
extortion, see *repetundae*

Fabius Maximus, Paullus 67 n. 48
Fabius Maximus Aemilianus, Q. 35
Fabius Maximus Allobrogicus, Q. 197, 289
Fabius Pictor 173
faeneratores (lenders) 192–3, 195, 240–1, 257, 258
  see also *creditores*
faenus (lending) 134, 135
  see also credit
faenus unciarium (unciarial rate of interest) 246 n. 78, 259
Falcidius, C. 193
Faliscan indemnities 37, *38*
Fannius, C. 68
farmers (*agricolae*) 132, 140, 154, 159, 173, 175 n. 294, 210, 241, 258, 331
farming, *see* agriculture
field surveys 139, 156–7, 165, 170–3, 186
financial crises, *see* credit crises
financial intermediation, evidence for 113–24
financial risk 110, 255, 265
Fisher equation 88, 311, 314, 318
Flaminius, C. (*cos.* 223, 217 BC) 11, 13–14
Flaminius, C. (*cos.* 187 BC) 218
fleets
  merchant 193, 202 n. 127, 206, 209
  naval, *see* navy
Fonteius 246–7
food 131, 147
  bread-making 2
  cheese 147
  consumption patterns 304
  diet 2, 159, 304
  figs 147
  fish-farming/fish products 159
  food supply system, Rome 226
  grain supplies 69
  market gardening 148, 156–7, 166
  wheat 102–3, 139, 283, *284*
fornaces see lime kilns
fossil fuels 281
freedmen 122 n. 82, 196, 201–2, 207, 224, 256, 292
Fulcinius, M. 237, 254
fulling 229, 231
Fulvius Flaccus, Q. 30 n. 75, 31, 218, 221–2
Fulvius Nobilior, M. 51, 218
Furius, M. 31
Furius Purpurio, L. 157

Gabinius, A. 241
Gallia Cisalpina 45, 50, 93, 94, 100, 165, 183, 219, 315, 329
  population of 175 n. 293, 178 n. 310
  wheat prices 102, 103, 283
Gallia Narbonensis 137, 145, 210, 219, 312
games 16, 33, 35, 37, 123, 283
GATT (General Agreement on Tariff and Trade) 280
GDP (Gross Domestic Product) 3, 271–2, 333–4
  estimates 275–6, 285–323
  from expenditure side 297–311
    Italian private consumption expenditure and investment 304–11, *305*, *306*, *309*
    Roman state expenditure 25–9, 69–70, *298*, 298–304, *299*, *300*, *303*, *305*
  from income side 285–97
  from monetary variables 311–23
  institutions and 277–8
  per capita 272–3, 291–7, 334
  see also income
GDP deflator 272, 283–4, *284*
General Agreement on Tariff and Trade, *see* GATT
Genucilius Curvus, L. 193
Genuine Progress Indicator 272 n. 9
Gerillani 125, 211
gladiators 205, 289
GNP (Gross National Product) 271, 272, 278, 323
gold 23–4, 312–13
  Aquileia mine 57
  as booty 30
  bullion 23
  gold mines 45–6, 47, 50, 51
  price fluctuations 57
  see also Roman coinage - gold coins; shipwrecks – gold bars
government bonds 26, 264
  substitutes for 109, 283
Gracchan land reforms 176–7, 183, 185, 188, 189–90
Gracchus, C. *see* Sempronius Gracchus, C.
Gracchus, Ti. *see* Sempronius Gracchus, Ti.

grain
  production 144, 148,149, 157, 158, 159, 175 n. 295, 187
  subsidies 25, 286, 299, 300–1
  supplies 15–16, 69, 198
  see also wheat
granaries 69, 126, 220, 225 n. 67, 303
Greece
  agriculture, Roman involvement in 139
  centuriation 137
  civic coinage 96–7, 98, 100, 251
  Italians in 14–15, 124–5, 139–40, 192–3, 198–202, 207–9, 211–12
  olive oil production 139
  Roman coinage in 96–7, 100
  wheat production 139
Greenland ice core data *see under* pollution
Gross Domestic Product, *see* GDP
Gross National Product, *see* GNP
guardians: legal obligations of 135

Hannibal 44
Helvius, M. 30 n. 75
Herculaneum 227, 308
herdsmen (*pecuarii*) 132, 148: *see also* agriculture-animal husbandry
Heroninos archive 151, 154
Herrenius (banker) 237
Hieron II of Syracuse 15, 37, *38*
Hispania Ulterior 139
hoarding *see under* coinage
hoards *see under* coinage
Horrea Galbana 220, 303
Horrea Lolliana 126
Horrea Sempronia 69, 220, 303
House of the Faun, Pompeii 307
housing 11, 194, 204, 284, 307, 308
  farmhouses 151
  property values 104, 105, 289
  see also villas

Iberian *denarii* 95–6, 100, 251
Illyria 37–8, *38*
immigration to Rome 227, 286
incense 205, 206, 207, 250, 307
income
  Attalid 72 n. 82
  Italian levels of 285–97
  Italian respectability income levels 285, 287, 294, 305, *305*, *315*, 316, *316*, 317, *317*
  Italian subsistence income levels 275, 285, 305, *305*, *315*, 316, *316*, 317, *317*
  power-law distribution of Italian households by income 289–97, *291*, *294*, *295*
  Roman state 298
  soldiers' pay 22, 287–8, 299, *299*
  see also booty (*praeda*); indemnities; poverty
indemnities 21–3, 27, 37–42, 190, 298, *298*, 323, 328
  Aetolia 22 n. 7, 23 n. 15, 38, *39*, 41
  Ambracia 38, *39*
  Boeotians 38, *39*
  Cappadocia *39*
  Carthage 37–40, *38*, *39*
  Faliscans 37, *38*
  Hieron of Syracuse 37, *38*
  Illyria 37–8, *38*
  Macedonia 38, *39*, 55
  Sparta 38, *39*
  Syria 28–9, 38–9, *39*, 40, 41, 98, 101, 179, 216–17, 219
India 99, 206
inflation 87–8, 102–4, 283–4, 329
inheritance 135, 153
  Asia 61–2, 71
  Atticus 196–7, 293, 333
  Cato the Elder 16–17, 136
  Cyrene 65
  Egypt 65
  Eumenes II Soter 71–2
  Scipio Aemilianus 35–6
  women and 293 n. 96
insulae: *see* residential blocks
intercessors: *see* brokers
interest rates 114, 255–6, 260, 290 n. 86
Italian towns, monumentalization of 221–4
Iucundus tablets 237

Janus medius 240, 242 n. 56
jewellery 16, 205, 206, 207, 307
Julius Caesar, C. 60, 195, 241, 260–4
Julius Calidus, L. 138
Junius Brutus, M. 195, 238
Junius Brutus Callaicus, D. 220–1
Junius Pennus, M. 227
Junonia 69–70, 94, 137–8

Keynes, J. M. 224 n. 65, 273
kilns
  lime 158, 172, 230
  pottery 12, 228, 231

Laelius, C. 178, 204
land rents *298*
land surveyors, see *agrimensores*
lead ingots 52, 101 n. 83, 207
lead pollution 46–7, *48*, 58, 277, 328
  see also pollution
leasing 75, 138, 139, 151, 163, 184, 188, 219, 316
  ager censorius 164–6
  locatio-conductio 228
  mines 50, 52, 54
  potteries 228
lending, *see* credit; *faenus*
lex agraria (133 BC) 175–6
lex agraria (123 BC) 69
lex agraria (111 BC) 76 n. 109, 95, 137–8, 139, 164, 167, 184, 185
lex Caesaris de modo credendi possidendique intra Italiam 261, 262–3

lex Calpurnia de rebus repetundis 78, 79–80
lex Claudia, see *plebiscitum Claudianum*
lex Cnidia de piratis, see *lex de provinciis praetoriis*
lex Cornelia de falsis 250
lex Cornelia Pompeia 246, 256, 259–60
lex de piratis persequendis, see *lex de provinciis praetoriis*
lex de provinciis praetoriis 66, 203
lex Didia 205
lex Fannia 205
lex Gabinia 195, 256
lex Hieronica 74 n. 94, 75, 79
lex Iulia de bonis cedendis 261–2
lex Iulia repetundarum 14
lex Iunia 78
lex Iunia de feneratione 115
lex Licinia de modo agrorum 163–4
lex Livia 137
lex Oppia 204
lex Orchia 204–5
lex Papiria 248, 250
lex Porcia 301
lex portorii Asiae, *see* Customs Law of Asia
lex Puteolana de parieti faciundo 225 n. 67
lex Roscia 287 n. 62
lex Rubria 137, 138
lex Sempronia de provincia Asia 56 n. 85, 59–83, 200, 282, 331
lex Sempronia frumentaria 69, 70, 300, 303
lex Sempronia militaris 26 n. 43, 70, 288, 300
lex Sempronia repetundarum 76–80, 83
lex Terentia Cassia 300
lex Thoria 184
lex Valeria de aere alieno 246–7, 259–60, 264
lex Voconia 293 n. 96
Licinius Crassus, M. 194, 295–6
Licinius Crassus Dives Mucianus, P. 62, 293 n. 96
Licinius Lucullus, L. (*cos.* 151 BC) 28
Licinius Lucullus, L. (*cos.* 74 BC) 194, 195, 256
Licinius Stolo, C. 163
lime kilns (*fornaces*) 158, 172, 230
living standards 272–3, 278, 285, 304
  see also income
Livius Drusus, M. 197, 248, 250, 289, 293
Livius Salinator, M. 31
loans, *see* credit; *faenus*
local coinages, *see* civic coinages
logistics service sector 226–7, 286
Lollius Q.f. Men., M. 126
Lollius, Q. Lollius 140 n. 66
Lollius Palicanus, M. 126
Lucceii 211
Lucceius (banker) 237
Lucilius, C. 202
Lucretius Gallus, C. 32
luxury goods 99, 104, 204–6, 232, 306–7, 332
  perfume 171–2, 205–6, 232, 307
luxury villas 204–6, 307
Lycian League 64

Macedonia 54–8
  bullion mines, closure/re-opening of 54, 56–7, 98
  copper mines 54
  fall in weight of coinage 98
  indemnities *39*, 55
  iron mines 54
  tribute 219
Macellum 302
macro-economic quantification 270, 274–5, 278
magistrates 56 n. 90, 74, 180, 200, 225 n. 67, 244
  and *aerarium* 11–12, 299
  and disputes 61, 67, 191
  and corruption 78, 83
  responsibilities 76, 77
Mago the Carthaginian 137, 147, 154
  translation of treatise 147–8
Malleolus, C. 193
Manlius Acidinus, L. 51
Manlius Vulso, C n. 41
Mantinius, P. 242
manubiae 32–4, 37, 330
manufacturing 227–32
manumission 180, 321
  Brazil 181
  manumission tax 16 n. 59, 282
marble 10, 220–1, 303
Marcius Rex, Q. 220
Marius, C. 203, 249
Marius Gratidianus, M.: edict of 250–1
marriage 170, 175
Menodoros 63
mensae 122–3, 235, 237, 263, see also *argentariae*; banks
mercatores (merchants) 13, 134, 192–3, 202, 203–4
mercatura 134, 192
military expenditure 25, 26–7, *299*, 298–300, *300*, 303–4, 330
military service 25, 26 n. 43, 70, 162, 168, 169, 170, 176, 287–8
mills, *see under* agricultural equipment
Minatius Sexti f., M. 125, 211
mines/mining 43–58, 190
  closure/re-opening of mines 44, 54, 55, 56–7, 98
  copper mines 54
  Gaul 210 n. 192
  iron mines 43, 54
  publicani and 43–4, 45, 49–55, 57
  revenues 21, 43–58, 298, *298*, 323
  see also Archimedes screw; gold; silver; technology; water supply systems
mints/minting
  average output per die 91

mints/minting (*cont.*)
coin attrition rates 92
coin issuance and credit crises 263–4
Lohe deposit 92
records of 88, 92
see also Roman coinage
Minucius Rufus, Q. 16
Minucius Thermus, Q. 30
Mithradates V: 62, 64, 77
Mithradates VI: 189, 213, 245, 246, 254
monetary liquidity 112 n. 22, 127
2nd century BC 243
and 60s BC credit crisis 257–8
Caesar and 262
and coin issues 263–4
monetization 93–101, 329
levels of 314–18, *316*, *317*
rural 93, 315–17
urban 93, 314–15
money, see *pecunia*
money-multiplier effect 107, 110–12, 253 n. 125, 264
money supply 107, 121, 311–23
hoarding and 112–13, 255, 260, 264
and economic growth 88
theories concerning the Roman money supply 108–10
moneyers (*tresviri monetales*) 126, 240
moneylending, *see* aristocratic financiers; bankers; banks and banking; credit; *daneistai*; *faenus*; *faeneratores*
multiplier effects of economic inputs 224–5, 273–4, 286, 332
see also money-multiplier effect
Mummius, L. 139, 222–3

Nabis of Sparta 38
Naevius 211
national accounts 271, 274–5
national disposable income, *see* NDI
navy 50, 290, 300
expenditure 11, 15, 26
First Punic War 28
size of 26
NDI (national disposable income) 272, 278, *322*, 323
negotiable notes 109, 239; see also *nomina*
negotiatores (businessmen) 126, 140, 191, 192–3, 203, 207
new institutional economics, *see* NIE
New World 87–8, 190
Nicanor of Syria 30 n. 79, 179
Nicomedes II of Bithynia 62, 64
Nicomedes III of Bithynia 195, 203, 238
NIE 274, 277
nomina 109–10, 115–16, 239, 265, see also *delegatio debitoris*
nomina transscripticia 115–16
nummorum caritas 127, 260, 264
nummularii 126, 236

Octavius, M. 161
olive oil
oleiculture 139, 146, 148, 150
production 137, 139, 144, 146, 158–9, 166, 171
presses, *see under* agricultural equipment
trade 145, 159, 201, 224, 304
onomastics 207–8, 223–4
Oscan silver, *see under* silver coins

Pandusinus, C. 139
Pareto's law 289–90
partnerships, see *societates*
Pasion 121 n. 80, 242
pasture taxes (*scripturae*) 72, 282, *298*
patronage 201, 211, 240
peasantry 160, 161, 162, 166–73, 176, 182–3, 185, 285–6, 292–3, 320
definition of 'peasant' 132 n. 3
seasonal labour 168–9
small-holdings 167
see also income
pecuarii, *see* herdsmen
pecunia (money) 108–9, 127
pecuniae Asiaticae 245, 246
Perperna, M. 62, 63
perfume 171–2
production 205–6, 232
trade 307
perfumers 205, 232, 307
Pergamum 70–3
bequeathed to Rome 61–4
Perseus of Macedon 30 n. 79, 55
Philetaerus 71
Philip V of Macedon 38
Philogenus 196
Philostratos Philostratou of Ascalon 206, 212
Pigou money demand equation 318 n. 185
Pinnius, T. 195, 256
Piracy Law, see *lex de provinciis praetoriis*
pirates 198, 200, 202–3
pitch 148, 228, 230–1, 233, 282
Plautus 29, 116–17, 229, 314
plebiscitum Claudianum 13–14, 28–9, 134, 135, 150
plunder, *see* booty
pollution
acid rain 46
atmospheric pollution 46–7
Greenland ice core data 46–7, *48*, 277, 310, 323, 328
lead deposition in peat bogs 46, 47, *48*, 58, 277, 328
see also lead pollution
Pompeii 11, 204, 223, 227, 229, 306–7, 308
Pompeius Rufus, Q. 246
Pompeius Magnus, Cn. ('Pompey the Great') 72 n. 87, 194, 195, 203, 238, 295–6
Pomponius Atticus, T. 179, 192, 193 n. 29, 195–6, 197, 242, 256, 293, 333
wealth of 293, 296

Pons Aemilius 218, 220, 302–3
Pons Milvius 303
Popillius Laenas, M. (*cos.* 173 BC) 179 n. 316
Popillius Laenas, P. (*cos.* 132 BC) 160
population
  census figures 173–4, *174*, 175–8, *177*, *178*
  change in, and economic growth 272–3
  demographic models 174–7, *182*, 182–3, *183*
  free, growth of 162, 173–8, 224–7
  slave 162, 178–82
  urban, growth of 286
  see also immigration to Rome
Porcius Cato, M. (Cato the Elder) 11, 16–17, 28, 134, 212, 217, 241, 259, 315
  booty from Hither Spain 30
  De Agricultura 15, 132, 133, 136, 147, 148, 149–50, 151–2, 154, 168–9, 225, 229, 230, 232, 309, 315
  estates 136, 140, 153
  exploitation of natural resources 230–1
  farm management 152
  and *publicani* 51, 80–1
  risk management 145–6
  taxation of Spanish mines 49–50
Porcius Cato Uticensis, M. (Cato the Younger) 101, 196
porticoes 217–18, 222, 302–3
Porticus Aemilia 303
Porticus Metelli 302–3
Porticus Minucia Vetus 303
Porticus Octavia 302
portoria 51, 56 n. 90, 61, 72, 73 n. 89, 74, 81, 216, 219
  and economic growth 280, 282
  exemptions 75
  and trade 74, 75
  see also customs duties
Postumius Albinus, A. 218, 221–2
Postumius Albinus, L. 165, 219
Postumius Magellus, L. 155
Potosí, Peru 45 n. 18
pottery 231–2
black-slip ware 12, 132–3, 173
  coarseware for cooking 13
  kilns 12, 228, 231
  terra sigillata (red-glaze) 228
  see also amphorae (transport)
poverty 175, 176, 286; *see also* income
praeda, *see* booty
Praeneste 223
presses (*torcularia*) *see under* agricultural equipment
prices 102–4, 283–4, 329
  fluctuations in 57
  of grain 300,
  and inflation 102–4, 284
  of Italian land 141
  price rises 87–8, *see also* inflation
  of slaves 30, 104
  of soft commodities 283
  of wheat 102–3, 283, 284
  see also housing – property values
proscriptions 138, 247, 249, 257
proxenitae, *see* brokers
Ptolemy Apion of Cyrene 65
Ptolemy IV Philopator of Egypt 16
Ptolemy X Alexander I of Egypt 65
Ptolemy XII Auletes of Egypt 195, 238–9
public land, see *ager publicus*
public records 27, 42, 74
public sector debt 282–3
  see also government bonds
publicani (state contractors) 1, 12, 192–3, 241, 292, 333
  in Asia 63, 66
  contracts with 12, 15, 289
  disputes with Cato 80–1
  disputes with Pergamenes 61, 67–8
  distrust of 54–5
  and mining 45, 49–54, 57
  right to collect revenue 60, 61
  role of 1 n. 3
  and state building contracts 15
  and tax collection 75, 76, 80–2
  wealth of 292
  see also *censoria locatio*; contracts; *lex Puteolana de parieti faciundo*; *societates publicanorum*
purple dye production 13, 139, 159, 205–6
Puteal Libonis 240–1
Pylaemenes of Paphlagonia 62, 64
Pythius (banker) 237

Quinctius, P. 212
Quinctius Flamininus, T. 28, 30, 41 n. 146

Rabirius Curtius Postumus, C. 193, 238–9, 257
real estate agents 134 n. 15
receptum argentarii 244
repetundae 77, 78–80
  extortion courts 68
  see also *lex Calpurnia de rebus repetundis*; *lex Iulia repetundarum*; *lex Sempronia repetundarum*
residential blocks (*insulae*) 308; *see also* housing
Rhodes 198–9, 208
risk management 135, 145–6
  see also credit risk
roads 11, 70, 217, 222, 281, 302, 309, 310, 329
  cost of construction 302
  see also individual roads (Viae)
Romaioi 191, 199–202
Roman coinage 87–101, 105
  coin issuance 11, 14, 44, 65, 88, 89–93, 247–8, 312, 328–9
  debasement of 15–16, 247–8, 250–1, 264, 327
  didrachms 15–16, 44
  geographic range 94–101

Roman coinage (*cont.*)
gold coins 15–16, 22, 23, 249, 262, 263–4
imperial coins, iconography of 2–3
increase in use 11
outside Roman Empire 99–100
quantification of Roman coinage 89–93, *90*, 311–13, 321–2
quinarii 248
see also bronze coins; coinage; *denarii*; silver coins
Roman state
borrowing from citizens 15, 17–18, 26
bureaucracy 11–12, 26, 225, 244, 299
coinage, *see* Roman coinage
construction projects 216–21, 302–3
consumption 299–301, *301*, *303*
expenditure, *see under* GDP
income 298
investment *301*, 301–2, *303*
Rome
city of 10
construction projects 216–21
food supply system 226
residential housing 308
suburbium 148, 156, 164, 166
water supply systems 24, 227, 286, 308
see also aqueducts; sewers
rope production 229, 232
Roscius of Ameria 135
rotary mills (*trapeti*), *see under* agricultural equipment

Samnites 9
Sasernae 147, 230
Saturninus 138
Scaptius, M. 242, 256 n. 134
Scipio Aemilianus, *see* Cornelius Scipio Africanus Aemilianus, P.
Scipio Africanus, *see* Cornelius Scipio Africanus, P.
Scribonius Libo, L. 78
scripturae (pasture taxes) 72, 282, *298*
securitized debt, see *nomina*
Seii 207
Seleucid kingdom *39*, 101, 219
collapse of 219
indemnities, *see* indemnities - Syria
monetary system 320
silver bullion supplies 98
Sempronius Asellio, A. 245
Sempronius Gracchus, C. 25, 125, 160, 220, 225 n. 67, 331
corn dole 286, 300
economic thinking 76–82
lex Sempronia frumentaria 69, 70, 300, 303
lex Sempronia militaris 26 n. 43, 70, 288, 300
see also *lex Sempronia de provincia Asia*
Sempronius Gracchus, Ti. (*cos.* 177, 163 BC) 56, 70–1, 121, 122
Sempronius Gracchus, Ti. (*tr. pl.* 133 BC) 62, 70–1, 125, 160–1, 162
land commission 69, 141,161, 299
land reforms 176–7, 183, 185, 188, 189–90
senators 13–14, 18, 29, 34, 40, 290, 292
and banking 122, 127, 262–3
and corruption 77
decrees 64, 68, see also *senatus consulta*
and *equites* 12 n. 23, 68
financial interests 4, 28, 134–6, 161, 229–30, 246
landholdings 135–6, 140–1, 150, 151, 161
restrictions on 13–14, 141, 192, 246
slave ownership 203, 289
and trade 134
wealth of 4, 16, 37, 133 n. 8, 151, 289
senatus consulta 41, 71, 227, 286
closure of mines 44, 56
Senatus Consultum de Agro Pergameno 60–1, 66–9
Senatus Consultum et Foedus cum Astypalaeensibus 68
Senatus Consultum Popillianum de Pergamenis 61 n. 11, 62, 63
Sergius Orata, C. 134 n. 15
Servilius Isauricus, P. 203
Sestius stamps (on amphorae) 231
Settefinestre villa 144, 170, 186, 309
sewers 11, 24, 217, 302
Sextius Lateranus, L. 163
ships 192, 198, 209, 226
size of 143, 281, 310
shipwrecks 158, 310
Albenga 143
Antikythera 'A' 23 n. 22
coins in 101
data *144*
finds as indication of trade 12, 131, 142, 143, 276–7, 280–1, *281*, 310
gold bars 23 n. 22
Grand Congloué 142, 231
lead/copper ingots 101 n. 83
La Madrague de Giens 101 n. 82, 143
Mahdia 205, 306
probability graph for 281, *281*
Sicily 94, 140, 150, 312
Silanus, D. 147
silphium 13
silver 22–4, 27, 28, 30, 31, 35, 36, 37, *39*, 98, 312
cupeling 46
silver mines 44–5, 46–54, 56, 87, 323, 328
silver coins
Oscan silver 30, 95–6
weight of 22
see also coinage; *denarii*; Roman coinage
Sittius P. 256–7
slave-owners 140
slaves 27, 178–82, 310–11
in agriculture 149, 155, 161–2, 286
bartered for goods 145
as booty 30

in Brazil 181
Delos and 180, 202–6
income 290
increased demand for 285–6, 289
mass enslavement 28, 30, 178–80, 213, 330
negative demographic impact of 286
pirates and 200, 202–3
price of 30, 104
shortage of 15, 181 n. 341
slave imports 180
slave labour, economics/profitability of 169
slave numbers 140, 180–1, *182*, 203, 279
slave revolts 140, 179–80, 203
trade in 145, 202–6, 332
war captives 178–9, 180, 279
Social War 245, 248, 249
societates (partnerships) 145–6, 201–2
societates publicanorum 52, 80, 81, 193, 193 n. 28, 193 n. 29, 306
South Etruria Study 172
Spain 55–6
centuriation 137
coinage supply 312, *see also* Iberian *denarii*
gold mines 45–6
Roman coinage in 95–6
silver mines 44–5, 46–9, 53, 56
taxation 55–6
trade networks 210
villas 139
viticulture 139
Sparta 38, *39*
statues 35, 37, 250, 302, 306
as booty 27, 222–3
found in shipwreck 205
Sthenius of Thermae 197
stipendium, see under taxation
stock-rearing, *see* agriculture – animal husbandry
subscription lists 24
subsistence, *see under* income
Sulla, *see* Cornelius Sulla Felix, L
Sulpicius Galba, Ser. (*cos.* 144 BC) 31, 78
Sulpicius Galba, Ser. (*cos.* 108 BC) 220
Sulpicius Rufus, P. 246
Sulpicius tablets 237, 258 n. 160
sumptuary laws 204–5, 289, 305
supply side economics 279–83
Syria, *see* Seleucid kingdom

Tabula Bembina 77 n. 109
tax collectors, see *publicani*
taxation
Attalid 72
cuts in 282
decumae (agricultural tithes) 55–6, 72, 75, 76, 81, 282, *298*
in eastern Thrace 66
land/poll taxes in Africa 137
mines 49–50
phoros 37, 72, 101
provincial 1, 72–6, 298, *298*, 323, 328
publicani and 75, 76, 80–2
scripturae (pasture taxes) 72, 282, *298*
Social War and fall in 249
stipendium 21–2, 37, *38*, 55–6, 60, 76
supertaxes, repayment of 301, *301*
tax grain 56 n. 90, *298*
tributum 15 & n. 48, 38, 54, 282, *298*
vectigalia 50, 54, 55–6, 74, 217, 282
vicesima libertatis 282
vicensimae 56 n. 90
see also Customs Law of Asia; *lex Hieronica; lex Sempronia de provincia Asia; portoria*
technology
improvements in, and economic growth 281–2
investment in 155–60
mechanical water-lifting devices 15, 46, 157–8, 281, 309
mining equipment 45–6, 309
Temple of Castor 221 n. 47
Temple of Jupiter Optimus Maximus 303
Temple of Jupiter Stator 220–1
Temple of Magna Mater 216, 303
Temple of Mars 220–1
temples 11, 34–5, 222
gilding 23
in marble 220–1, 302
see also individual temples
tenancy 151, 169, 178, 277
Terence 116, 119, 314
Terentius Varro, C. 229–30
terra sigillata (red-glaze pottery) industry 228
terracotta lamp industry 228
tesserae nummulariae 125–6
Teuta of Illyria 37–8, *38*
textile industry 229
Tiber embankment 303
Tiber Valley Project 132–3, 172–3
Tiberius Julius Caesar Augustus, emperor, 262–3
Timon son of Nymphodoros 211
tithes, see *decumae*
Tor Sapienza quadrangle 156–7, 308–9
torcularia (presses), *see under* agricultural equipment
trade 141–7, 189–213, 280–1, 305–7
2nd century BC Delos 197–202
in cheese 147
commercial associations 200–1
and economic growth 280
financial capital, availability of 194–7
financial capital, in *emporia* 211–12
in luxury goods 204–6, 307
money-flows and 100–1
networks 2, 12–14, 206–10
in olive oil 145, 159, 201, 224, 304
in perfume 307
and *portoria* 74, 75

trade (*cont.*)
shipwrecks as indication of 12, 131, 142, 143, 276–7, 280–1, *281*, 310
in slaves 145, 202–6, 332
in soft commodities 147, 311
see also wine trade
transactional costs 282
trapeti (rotary mills), *see under* agricultural equipment
trapezitae (bankers) 14, 114, 119–20, 191, 211–12: see also *argentarii*; bankers
treasury, see *aerarium sanctius*; *aerarium Saturni*
tresviri monetales, *see* moneyers
triumphs 30 & n. 79, 51, 65
Tugio, M. 157
Tullius Cicero, M. 314
as absentee landlord 135
bankers 237–8
and debt 195, 238, 239–42
insulae in Rome 308
on state revenues 328
on trade 191–2
wheat prices 283
Tullius Cicero, Q. 157

unciarial rate of interest, see *faenus unciarium*
unguentarii, see perfumers
United Nations Development Program Report 290 n. 83
urbanization 182, 227, 276, 280, 281
Utica 95, 138–9

Valerius Antias 30 n. 79
Valerius Flaccus, L. (*cos.* 195 BC) 16, 217
Valerius Flaccus, L. (*cos. suff.* 86 BC) 246
Varro 152
vectigalia, see under taxation
velocity of circulation of money 105, 318–23, *319*, *322*
Vergil 152
Verres, C. 80, 242
Vestorius 240, 242
Vettienus 239, 240
Via Aemilia 218, 303
Via Amerina 10
Via Annia 220
Via Appia 9–10
Via Aurelia 10
Via Clodia 10
Via Domitia 101 n. 83, 220, 302
Via Egnatia 220
Via Flaminia 10, 218
Via Gabina 151
Via Popillia 220
Via Postumia 220
villa system 15, 132, 147, 168–9, 187
villas 150–1
agro-villas 170, 186, 309
courtyard villas 150
House of the Faun, Pompeii 307
platform villas 172
Pompeii 307
Spain 139
Villa di Posta Crusta, Apulia 172
Villa Sambuco 151
villae expolitissimae 204
see also luxury villas; Settefinestre villa; villa system
viritane land distribution 164, 166, 167–8
viticulture 139, 144, 147, 148, 150, 153, *see also* wine

wage labour 161, 168–9, 178, 225–7, 228, 286–8
wages 228, 286, 316, 320
war captives, *see under* slaves
water-lifting devices 15, 46, 156, 157–8, 281, 309–10
see also Archimedes screw
water management 156–7
drainage systems 156, 281, 302, 303
irrigation systems 156–7
see also aqueducts; water-lifting devices; water-supply systems
water mills 158
water supply systems 156–7, 301, 308–10
in mining 45–6, 281, 309–10
Rome 24, 227, 286, 308
see also aqueducts
wealth
elite wealth 133–4, 138–9, 151–2, 203–5, 232, 288–97
individual wealth 194–7, 332–3
inequality in 289–90
senatorial families 15, 16–18
see also income
weapons 26, 198, 229, 299–300, *300*
see also *lex Sempronia militaris*
Wesleyan University survey 170
wheat
price of 102–3, 283, 284, *284*
production, in Africa 137
production, in Greece 139
see also grain
wine 72, 146
amphorae, *see* amphorae (transport)
use in feasting 145
wine production 144, 166, 171
wine presses 158, 309
see also agricultural equipment; viticulture
wine trade 12, 141–3, 150, 186, 304, 310
changing networks 208–9
Delos and 201
exports from Acragas to Carthage 150
exports from Italy to Gaul 99, 141–2, 143, 144–5
World Trade Organization (WTO) 280
workshops 228, 229, 233–4, 332

The manufacturer's authorised representative in the EU for product safety is Oxford University Press España S.A. of El Parque Empresarial San Fernando de Henares, Avenida de Castilla, 2 – 28830 Madrid (www.oup.es/en or product.safety@oup.com). OUP España S.A. also acts as importer into Spain of products made by the manufacturer.

Printed in the USA/Agawam, MA
September 10, 2026

910308.187